SHAKTI AND SHAKTA

SHAKTI AND SHAKTA

ESSAYS ON ADDRESSES AND
THE SHAKTA TANTRASHASTRA

BY

JOHN WOODROFFE

GYAN

Published by

GYAN

Gyan Publishing House
5, Ansari Road
Daryaganj, New Delhi-110002
Phone: 011-47034999, 9811692060
E-mail: books@gyanbooks.com

Distribution Network
gyanbooks.com
India, USA, Canada, UK, Australia

ISBN: 978-93-6280-335-1 (PB)
First Published, 1918

2nd Impression 2024

Printed at: Gyan Press, Delhi.

SHAKTI AND SHAKTA
Author: JOHN WOODROFFE

SHAKTI AND SHĀKTA

SHRI YANTRA

SHAKTI AND SHĀKTA

ESSAYS AND ADDRESSES ON THE SHĀKTA TANTRASHĀSTRA

BY

SIR JOHN WOODROFFE

THIRD EDITION

PUBLISHERS:

GANESH & Co., (MADRAS) LTD., MADRAS—17

1927

ŚRĪ YANTRA [illegible]

PREFACE

To Third Edition

This edition has been revised and corrected throughout, and additions have been made to some of the original Chapters. Appendix I of the last edition has been made a new Chapter (VII) in the book, and the former Appendix II has now been attached to Chapter IV. The book has moreover been very considerably enlarged by the addition of eleven new Chapters. New also are the Appendices.[1] The first contains two lectures given by me, in French, in 1917, before the Societé Artistique et Litéraire Francaise de Calcutta, of which Society Lady Woodroffe was one of the Founders and President. The second represents the substance (published in the French Journal "*Le Lotus bleu*") of two lectures I gave in Paris, in the year 1921, before the French Theosophical Society (October 8) and at the Musée Guimet (October 6) at the instance of L'Association Francaise des Amis de L'Orient. At this last meeting Professor Dr. Sylvain Lévi was present and M. Masson Oursel, also of the Collège de France, in an introductory speech said that "as one increasingly explored the Tāntrik literature, hitherto almost unknown, discovery is made not of more and more dissimilarities, but of a closer and closer connection between these Scriptures and the other Religions". The Tāntrik cult was not, he said, "a mere superstitious imposition" (Simagrée superstitieuse). "Its belief that man can realize the divine in him and outside him is the postulate also of all those who have divinised the ritual word as Brahman and of all who seek in Yoga a theurgic equivalent." The Press Notices[1] (to which I might have added various-addresses and letters of approval) are reprinted not merely to serve their usual purpose as recommendations to a possible reader, but also as showing, firstly, the state of Indian opinion on the Shāstra, aṣ an integral part of Hinduism and not merely a pathological excrescence on it and secondly, the effect produced on Western minds to which the Scripture was presented for the first time. Thus, Professor Evola ("*Il Nuovo Paese*") has recently very truly remarked that the Tāntrik system here described "offers many suggestions to the West in virtue of its accentuation of Will and Power". (Offrono grande suggestione per gli Occidentali in virtù del loro accentuare essenzialmente la parte della volontà e della potenza). To him ("*Bilychnis*", October 1924) this Shākta system is one of the most important of Eastern systems (ora uno dei sistemi Orientali piu importante) raising on a grand foundation a vast ensemble of metaphysic, magic and devotion (Su questo sfondo grandioso i Tantra svolgono un vasto insieme metafisico, magico, e devozionale). Noteworthy too are the observations of Professor Dr. Winternitz in the "*Ostasiatische Zeitschrift*" (1916 Heft 3. See Chapter V of this book) that (as I have all along contended) the Tantra Shāstras deserve a study which they have previously not received, and that they have been judged without knowledge. (Aus dem gesagtem erhellt dass Avalon recht hat wenn er erklärt dass man bisher über diese literatur allzu oft geurteilt und noch mehr Abgeurteilt hat ohne sie zu kennen und dass die Tantras es verdienen, besser bekannt zu werden, als es bisher der fall gewesen ist). This statement is the more weighty, as this critic is not attracted by the Scriptures which he takes to be predominantly magical. As to this see what I have said in Chapter V *post*.

The philosopher Herman Keyserling in his now celebrated work "*Das Reise Tagebuch Einer Philosophen*", recently translated into English ("*The Travel Diary of a Philosopher*"), writes (pp. 223-224) of the Tantras that "however extravagant some of its sayings may sound, their meaning is clear and their fundamental ideas are in accordance with reason". And again (p. 231), "I personally am convinced that the teachings of the Tantras are correct on the whole, but that it is nevertheless in the order of things that they meet with less and less observance for the development of humanity tends away from ritualism." I have my doubts as regards this last point. A strong ritualistic revival is in force to-day and there is likely to be always the reciprocal reaction of Puritanism and Ritualism.

I cannot do better than conclude these foreign criticisms with a note of the recent observations of a French writer in the Journal "*L'Humanite*" in which, referring to the French edition (Bossard, Paris) of A. and E. Avalon's "Hymns to the Goddess", and other works on the Shâstra, he has nothing to say about its "puerility" or "worthlessness" but, on the contrary, writes: "These conceptions display an astonishing philosophic subtlety (Une étonnante subtilité philosophique). This volume and others of the collection show the interest which Oriental research has for all those who are interested in the evolution of humanity, the future cohesion of which may be expected because of the community of origin. We have still to learn much of Asia. Some Russian revolutionaries have called their country Eurasia, as being the junction of the two Continents. There is truth in this. If we persist in our Western decadence, it may be that the seat of civilization will pass to the East, the great primitive source of generations of men. Some poets have already said: Europe is no more and that Asia alone contains the future in its secret valleys." With such poets and their prophecies of Western decadence I disagree. Nevertheless, it is rightly said that we, Occidentals, can complete our own culture and render our thoughts more complete and humane by observation of the Orientals and establishing contact with the conscience of modern Asia; that between these extreme points of time, past and present, we shall discover fecund traditions, and our desire for a spiritual universality will find its satisfaction. It is to such minds that the great concepts of India will make appeal. I am glad to report that years of work have borne some fruit in the shape of a more discriminating judgment. For myself it is enough, as it has always been, to say here in the words of the French writer Dunoyer, "I do not oppose. Nor do I propose. I merely expose." But for this last we must both know the facts and understand them. "Get knowledge, and with getting get understanding." This process on my own part has led to the revision of some of the matter reprinted so as to bring it into accordance with my present knowledge and opinions.

BYGDIN, VALDRES,
8th August 1927

J. W.

PREFACE

To Second Edition

This present edition is practically a new work, for I have revised and added to all the original Chapters and written six new ones (1, 5, 6, 10, 14 and 15). Seven of the original Chapters embodied a set of Lectures delivered before, and at the request of, the Vivekānanda Society in Calcutta, a circumstance which will explain both the manner of them as also the "Conclusions" with which the volume closes.

These Lectures and other collected papers traverse new ground in the Literature of Indian Religion, for they are the first attempt to give an authenticated and understanding general account, from the Indian standpoint, of the chief features of the Doctrine and Practice of that class of Indian worshippers who are called Shāktas, that is, those who adore the Divine Power (Mahāshakti), as Mahādevi, the Great Mother (Magna Mater) of the universe. As this religious community shares in common with others certain principles and practices, the work is also necessarily an account of the worship and spiritual disciplines called Sādhanā which, in varying forms, are adopted by all communities of Indian worshippers (Sādhakas) governed by the Āgama and its numerous scriptures called Tantras. These Shāktas are to be found all over India, but are largely predominant in Bengal and Assam, in which former Province I have lived for about the last thirty years, and with the belief of whose people therefore I am more closely acquainted than with any other. And this, in part, accounts for the fact that I deal with their faith. Their doctrine and practice have not hitherto been understood and have been ill-spoken of, due to abuses which have occurred among the members of some sections of the community. If, then, I have succeeded in giving in this and other works a just account of the Scripture, and in reducing such evil as has been charged against some of its adherents to its right proportions, I shall be glad to have been in a position to make some small return to a Land which, more than any other, has been my home, and to which I am, in manifold ways, indebted.

Though, as I said in the last edition, I rate highly Shākta doctrine and (with some exceptions) Shākta rituals, I do not commit myself to the acceptance of everything which any Shākta may have held or done. And though I have furnished argument in favour of this much-abused faith and practice, I am not here concerned to establish the truth and rightness of either. It is sufficient for my present purpose to show that it is reasonable, and that neither it nor "the Tantra" is the absurd and altogether immoral thing which some have supposed it to be. My attitude is an objective one. I have endeavoured to explain my subject as simply and lucidly as the recondite matters treated of allow, from an entirely detached and unprejudiced standpoint.

In giving an account of Indian beliefs and practices, we, who are foreigners, must place ourselves in the skin of the Hindu, and must look at their doctrine and ritual through their eyes and not our own. It is difficult, I know, for most to do this: but until they can, their work lacks real value. And this is why, despite their industry and learning, the accounts given by Western authors of Eastern beliefs so generally fail to give their true meaning. Many,

I think, do not even make the attempt. They look at the matter from the point of view of their own creed, or, (what is much worse), racial prejudice may stand in the way of the admission of any excellence or superiority in a coloured people. The method I follow is that of the Indian commentator, who, for the nonce, adapts himself to the standpoint of the doctrine which he explains. I mention this because two of my critics seem to think that my object is to establish the superiority of this particular form of Vedāntik teaching over others. One may, of course, have one's personal preferences, but it is not my object here to establish the superiority of any school of Indian thought. This is a matter which each will decide for himself. One of these critics has said, "The Tantras are claimed to be the specific Shāstra for the Kaliyuga by the Tāntriks. Mr. Avalon seems to have taken these latter at their own valuation; and this has considerably influenced his whole estimate of these books as Shāstras or authorities on the Hindu system. In doing so, he has fallen into a series of curious errors in regard to other and particularly the Vaishnavic denominations." This criticism which was passed on one of my earlier books has been repeated as regards this. What these errors are my critics have not told me. I did not intend to deal, nor am I aware of having dealt, with the Vaishnava system beyond pointing out in the most general way that there is a Vaishnava and Shaiva as well as a Shākta Āgama. I have criticized neither this nor the Shaiva Āgama, both of which schools are also of high value. Though the instructed Western reader is aware that there are other interpretations of Vedānta besides that of Shankara, many write as if the Vedānta meant his Māyāvāda. This is not so. Vedānta is Upanishad of which there are varying interpretations. Each has certain merits and certain defects, as must necessarily be the case when we apply logic to that which is alogical.

Indeed the point which I took, and which I had hoped I had made plain was this. Tantra Shāstra does not simply mean the Shākta Tantra. The latter is only one division of Āgama which has to-day three main schools, Shākta, Shaiva, and Vaishnava. There are certain things common to all. There are certain matters wherein they differ. When it is said that the Tantra Shāstra is the scripture of the Kali age, what is meant is that the Āgama in *all* its schools is that. There are some ancient schools of Vaishnava Āgama such as the Pancharātra, and there are comparatively modern developments of Vaishnava teaching and practice such as that of the great Chaitanya. "Tāntrik" does not mean only "Shākta". This is the main error of these critics and others. Naturally, I have taken the Shāktas "at their own valuation", for my object is not to show that they are right and others wrong, or the contrary, but to state what they, the Shāktas, hold. They alone can say this. A quarrelsome attitude as regards other creeds is the mark of a lower mind and of what the Shāktas call a Pashu. I believe a different position is assumed by all higher Sadhakas to whatever denomination they belong. Certainly a wide and liberal view is taken by the Shākta. The *Sammohana Tantra* (Ch. IX) says that "it is only a fool who sees any difference between Rāma and Shiva." Each has his path which, if sincerely pursued, will procure for him the fruit of it. Whether some paths in the Indian or other Religions are better and surer than others, and gain for their followers greater fruit, I do not here discuss.

J. W.

PREFACE

To First Edition

THE present work deals with its subject only in a very general and, as far as the matter permits, popular way. I refer those who wish to pursue it further to the other works on Tantra Shâstra which are published under the name "Arthur Avalon" to denote that they have been written with the direct co-operation of others and in particular with the assistance of one of my friends who will not permit me to mention his name. I do not desire sole credit for what is as much their work as mine. I, in particular, refer my reader to the series of Articles on the Mantra Shâstra which I wrote for the "*Vedânta Kesarî*" now reprinting (since published as "*Garland of Letters*" and to the "*Serpent Power*" shortly to be published (published in 1918, 2nd (present) Edition, 1925). In this last there is given, for the first time, the rationale of Yoga through the Kundalini Shakti, the outlines of which are indicated in Chapter XVI of this volume.

The Shâkta Tantra is a Sâdhanâ Shâstra of Monistic (Advaitavâda) Vedânta. It is to me a profound and powerful system, and its doctrine of Shakti or Divine Power is one of the greatest evolved, through spiritual intuition, by the human mind which, according to its teaching, is a manifestation of the Divine Consciousness Itself (Shiva).

The Doctrine is laid on grand lines and what is not, in this Vast Land of great distances?

I write this on a high plateau in Palamow, and look across a wide stretch of tall grass with tips of waving silver, the home, until about nine years ago (when the place was first opened), of the wild bison. The green and silver of the Prairie is splashed here and there with patches of orange flower, which the blazing sun jewels with its points of light. The near distance shows the water of a mountain tarn and two clumps of trees—the groves of worship of the ancient Kolarian peoples. Here a sparse remnant adore to-day, as did their ancestors thousands of years ago. Of Brāhmanism or other Aryan faith, there is no sign. Beyond, the grassland rises to meet the great length of a mounting hill-forest, dark green against the blue of distance, in which other Hill tops beckon forward the curious mind with their lure of mystery. And this lure is all around, for the upland is girdled some fifteen hundred feet below with wooded valleys, valleys on the East black with great Sal forests, which, as those of the upland, are the haunt of bear, tiger and sambur,—wild forests, lit only here and there by rare open spaces, and the glinting stream and white sands of the Koel River. Beyond the valleys, and all around the upland are a circle of Hls rising on the East, wave upon wave. Here man, who has not known himself and his greatness seems nought, and Nature all, a feeling which deepens as night falls on the earth with quick assault, the dark dome of heaven sparkling with the light of countless rising stars, fading again at Dawn as the Visible Devatā, the resplendent joyous Sun, the Eye of Vishnu, arises from out the "Eastern Mountain".

Such a vast scene is but one of many in this, itself vast, secular, and awe-inspiring land. Such a view, we may imagine, was displayed before the eyes of the incoming Aryān peoples. Upon them the influence of the *Soil* fell, filling them with awe. The Spirit, manifesting in this

Sacred Earth, at length revealed Itself in their minds. Within them arose the Inner Sun, which is the Light of all, unveiling to the eye of mind truths hidden in its subtle garb of thought. These tenuous veils again fell away, when, by the intuition of the forest-sages, was realized the Spiritual Ether of Consciousness, whose Mother-Power (Shakti) as Will, Thought and Action ever personalizes as the life of this magnetic stretch of earth which is India, as the world of which it is an head-ornament, and as (in the words of the Indian Scripture) the countless other universes, which are but the dust of Her Sovereign Feet.

NETURHAT,
11th October, 1918.

J. W.

CONTENTS

Section 1—Introductory

Section 2—Doctrinal

Section 3—Ritual

ILLUSTRATIONS

SHAKTI AND SHAKTA

CHAPTER I

INDIAN RELIGION AS BHĀRATA DHARMA

A FRIEND of mine who read the first edition of this book suggested that I should add to it an opening Chapter, stating the most general and fundamental principles of the subject as a guide to the understanding of what follows, together with an outline of the latter in which the relation of the several parts should be shown. I have not at present the time, nor in the present book the space, to give effect to my friend's wishes in the way I would have desired, but will not altogether neglect them.

To the Western, Indian Religion generally seems a "jungle" of contradictory beliefs amidst which he is lost. Only those who have understood its main principles can show them the path.

It has been asserted that there is no such thing as Indian Religion, though there are many Religions in India. This is not so. As I have already pointed out ("Is India Civilized?") there is a common Indian religion which I have called Bhārata Dharma, which is an Āryan religion (Āryadharma) held by all Āryas whether Brahmanic, Buddhist or Jaina. These are the three main divisions of the Bhārata Dharma. I exclude other religions in India, namely, the Semitic religions, Judaism, Christianity and Islam. Not that all these are purely Semitic. Christianity became in part Āryanized when it was adopted by the Western Āryans, as also happened with Islam when accepted by such Eastern Āryans as the Persians and the Āryanized peoples of India.

Thus Sufiism is either a form of Vedānta or indebted to it.

The general Indian Religion or Bhārata Dharma holds t. . the world is an Order or Cosmos. It is not a Chaos of things and beings thrown haphazard together, in which there is no binding relation or rule. The world-order is Dharma, which is that by which the universe is upheld (Dhāryate). Without Dharma it would fall to pieces and dissolve into nothingness. But this is not possible, for though there is Disorder (Adharma), it exists, and can exist only locally, for a time, and in particular parts of the whole. Order however will and, from the nature of things, *must* ultimately assert itself. And this is the meaning of the saying that Righteousness or Dharma prevails. This is in the nature of things, for Dharma is not a law imposed from without by the Ukase of some Celestial Czar. It is the nature of things; that which constitutes them what they are (Svalakshaṇadhāraṇāt Dharma). It is the expression of their true being and can only cease to be, when they themselves cease to be. Belief in righteousness is then in something not arbitrarily imposed from without by a Lawgiver, but belief in a Principle of Reason which all men can recognize for themselves if they will. Again Dharma is not only the law of each being but necessarily also of the whole, and expresses the right relations of each part to the whole. This whole is again harmonious, otherwise it would dissolve. The principle which holds it together as one mighty organism is Dharma. The particular Dharma calls for such recognition and action in accordance therewith. Religion, therefore, which etymologically means that which obliges or *binds* together, is in its most fundamental sense the *recognition* that the world is an Order, of which each man, being, and thing, is a part, and to which each man stands in a definite, established relation; together with *action* based on, and consistent with, such recognition, and *in harmony* with the whole cosmic activity. Whilst therefore the religious man is he who feels that he is *bound* in varying ways to all being, the irreligious man is he who egoistically considers everything from the standpoint of his limited self and its interests, without regard for his fellows, or the world at large. The essentially irreligious character of such an attitude is shown by the fact that, if it were adopted by all, it would lead to the negation of Cosmos, that is Chaos. Therefore all Religions are agreed in the essentials of morality and hold that selfishness, in its widest sense, is the root of all sin (Adharma). Morality is thus the true nature of man. The general Dharma (Sāmānya Dharma) is the universal law governing all, just as the particular Dharma (Vishesha Dharma) varies with, and is peculiar to, each class of being. It follows from what is above stated that disharmony is suffering. This is an obvious fact. Wrong conduct is productive of ill, as right conduct is productive of good. As a man sows, so he will reap. There is an Immanent Justice. But these results, though they may appear at once, do not always do so. The fruit of no action is lost. It must, according to the law of causality, which is a law of reason, bear effect. If its author does not suffer for it here and now in the present life, he will do so in some future one. Birth and death mean the creation and destruction of bodies. The spirits so embodied are infinite in number and eternal. The material universe comes and goes. This in Brahmanism has been said (see Sanātana Vaidika Dharma by Bhagavān Das) to be "the Systole and Diastole of the one Universal Heart,

Itself at rest—the moveless play of Consciousness". The appearance and disappearance of the Universe is the nature or Svabhāva of That which it ultimately is. Its immediate cause is Desire, which Buddhism calls Trishṇā—or Thirst, that is desire or thirst for world-enjoyment in the universe of form. Action (Karma) is prompted by desire and breeds again desire. This action may be good (Dharma) or bad (Adharma) leading to enjoyment or suffering. Each embodied soul (Jīvātmā) will be reborn and reborn into the world until it is freed from all desire. This involves the doctrine of Re-incarnation. These multiple births and deaths in the transmigratory worlds are called Saṁsāra or Wandering. The world is a Dvandva, that is a composite of happiness and suffering. Happiness of a transitory kind may be had therein by adherence to Dharma in following Kāma (Desire) and Artha (the means) by which lawful desires may be given effect. These constitute what Brahmanism calls the Trivarga of the Purushārtha, or three aims of sentient being. But just as desire leads to manifestation in form, so desirelessness leads away from it. Those who reach this state seek Moksha or Nirvāṇa (the fourth Purushārtha), which is a state of Bliss beyond the worlds of changing forms. For there is a rest from suffering which Desire (together with a natural tendency to pass its right limits) brings upon men. They must, therefore, either live with desire in harmony with the universal order, or if desireless, they may (for each is master of his future) pass beyond the manifest and become That which is Moksha or Nirvāṇa. Religion, and therefore true civilization, consists in the upholding of Dharma as the individual and general good, and the fostering of spiritual progress, so that, with justice to all beings, true happiness, which is the immediate and ultimate end of all Humanity, and indeed of all being, may be attained.

Anyone who holds these beliefs follows the Bhārata Dharma or common principles of all Āryan beliefs. Thus as regards God we may either deny His existence (Atheism) or affirm it (Theism) or say we have no sufficient proof one way or another (Agnosticism). It is possible to accept the concept of an eternal Law (Dharma) and its sanctions in a self-governed universe without belief in a personal Lord (Īshvara). So Sāṅkhya, which proceeds on intellectual proof only, does not deny God but holds that the being of a Lord is "not proved".

There are then based on this common foundation three main religions, Brahmanism, Buddhism and Jainism. Of the second, a great and universal faith, it has been said that, with each fresh acquirement of knowledge, it seems more difficult to separate it from the Hinduism out of which it emerged and into which (in Northern Buddhism) it relapsed. This is of course not to say that there are no differences between the two, but that they share in certain general and common principles as their base. Brahmanism, of which the Shākta doctrine and practice is a particular form, accepts Veda as its ultimate authority. By this, in its form as the four Vedas, is revealed the doctrine of the Brahman, the "All-pervader," the infinite Substance which is in Itself (Svarūpa) Consciousness (Chaitanya or Chit) from Which comes creation maintenance and withdrawal, commonly called destruction (though man, not God, destroys), and Which in Its relation to the universe which the Brahman controls is known as Īshvara, the Ruling Lord or Personal God. Veda both as spiritual experience and the word "which is heard" (Shruti) is the warrant for this. But Shruti, as the ultimate authority, has received various interpretations and so we find in Brahmanism, as in Christianity, differing schools and sets adopting various interpretations of the Revealed Word.

Veda says "All this (that is, the Universe) is Brahman." All are agreed that Brahman or Spirit is relatively to us, Being (Sat), Consciousness (Chit) and Bliss (Ānanda). It is Sachchidānanda. But in what sense is "This" (Idam) Brahman? The Monistic interpretation (Advaitavāda), as given for instance by the great scholastic Shaṅkarāchārya, is that there is a complete identity in essence of both. There is one Spirit (Ātmā) with two aspects; as transcendent supreme (Paramātmā), and as immanent and embodied (Jīvātmā). The two are at base one when we eliminate Avidyā in the form of mind and body. According to the qualified Monism (Vishishṭādvaita) of the great scholastic Rāmānuja, "This" is Brahman in the sense that it is the body of the Brahman, just as we distinguish our body from our inner self. According to the Dualists (Dvaitavāda) the saying is interpreted in terms of nearness (Sāmīpya) and likeness (Sādṛishya) for, though God and man are distinct, the former so pervades and is so unextricably involved in the universe as creator and maintainer, that the latter, in this sense, seems to be Brahman through proximity.

Then again there is the Shuddhādvaita of that branch of the Āgamas which is called Shaivasiddhānta, the Vaishṇava Pancharātra doctrine, the Advaita of the Kashmirian Shaivāgama (Trika), the followers of which, though Advaitins, have very subtly criticized Shaṅkara's doctrine on several points. Difference of views upon this question and that of the nature of Māyā, which the world is said to be, necessarily implies difference upon other matters of doctrine. Then there are, with many resemblances, some differences in ritual practice. Thus it comes about that Brahmanism includes many divisions of worshippers calling themselves by different names. There are Smārtas who are the present-day representatives of the old Vaidik doctrine and ritual practice, and on the other hand a number of divisions of worshippers calling themselves Shāktas, Shaivas, Vaishṇavas and so forth with sub-divisions of these. It is not possible to make hard and fast distinctions between the sects which share much in common and have been influenced the one by the other. Indeed the universality of much of religious doctrine and practice is an established fact. What exists in India as elsewhere to-day has in other times and places been in varying degrees anticipated. "In Religion" it has been said ("Gnostics and their Remains" viii) "there is no new thing. The same ideas are worked up over and over again." In India as elsewhere, but particularly in India where religious activity has been syncretistic rather than by way of supersession, there is much which is common to all sects and more again which is common between particular groups of sects. These latter are governed in general, that is, in their older forms, by the Āgamas or Tantra-Shāstras, which, at any rate to-day and for centuries past (whatever may have been their origin), admit the authority of the Vedas and recognize other Scriptures. (As to these, see the Introduction to the Kaulāchārya Sadānanda's Commentary on the Īsha Upanishad which I have published.)

The meaning of Veda is not commonly rightly understood. But this is a vast subject which underlies all others, touching as it does the seat of all authority and knowledge into which I have not the space to enter here. There are four main classes of Brahmanical Scripture, namely, Veda or Shruti, Smṛiti, Purāṇa, and Āgama. There are also four ages or Yuga the latter being a fraction of a Kalpa or Day of Brahmā of 4,320,000 years. This period is the life of an universe, on the expiration of which all re-enters Brahman and thereafter issues from it. A Mahāyuga is composed of the Four Ages called Satya,

Tretā, Dvāpara, Kali, the first being the golden age of righteousness since when all has gradually declined physically, morally, and spiritually. For each of the ages a suitable Shāstra is given, for Satya or Kṛita the Vedas, for Tretā the Smṛitishāstra, for Dvāpara the Purāṇas, and for Kaliyuga the Āgama or Tantra Shāstra. So the Kulārṇava Tantra says:

Krite shrutyukta āchārastretāyām smriti-sambhavah
Dvāpare tu purānoktah, kalāvāgamasammatah

(see also Mahānirvāṇa Tantra I—28 *et seq.*) and the Tārāpradīpa says that in the Kaliyuga (the supposed present age) the Tāntrika and not the Vaidika Dharma, in the sense of mode of life and ritual, is to be followed (see "Principles of Tantra," Ed. A. Avalon). When it is said that the Āgama is the peculiar Scripture of the Kali age, this does not mean (at any rate to any particular division of its followers) that something is presented which is opposed to Veda. It is true however that, as between these followers, there is sometimes a conflict on the question whether a particular form of the Āgama is unvedic (Avaidika) or not. The Āgama, however, as a whole, purports to be a presentment of the teaching of Veda, just as the Purāṇas and Smṛitis are. It is that presentment of Vaidik truth which is suitable for the Kali age. Indeed the Shākta followers of the Āgama claim that its Tantras contain the very core of the Veda to which it is described to bear the same relation as the Supreme Spirit (Paramātmā) to the embodied spirit (Jīvātmā). In a similar way, in the seven Tantrik Āchāras (see Ch. *IV post*), Kaulāchāra is the controlling, informing life of the gross body called Vedāchāra, each of the Āchāras, which follow the latter up to Kaulāchāra, being more and more subtle sheaths. The Tantra Shāstra is thus that presentment of Vedantic truth which is modelled, as regards mode of life and ritual, to meet the characteristics and infirmities of the Kaliyuga. As men have no longer the capacity, longevity and moral strength required to carry out the Vaidika Karmakāṇḍa (ritual section), the Tantra Shāstra prescribes a Sādhanā of its own for the attainment of the common end of all Shāstra, that is, a happy life on earth, Heaven thereafter, and at length Liberation. Religion is in fact the true pursuit of happiness.

As explained in the next and following Chapters, this Āgama, which governs according to its followers the Kaliyuga, is itself divided into several schools or communities of worshippers. One of these divisions is the Shākta. It is with Shākta doctrine and worship, one of the forms of Brahmanism, which is again a form of the general Bhārata Dharma, that this book deals.

The Shākta is so called because he is a worshipper of Shakti (Power), that is, God in Mother-form as the Supreme Power which creates, sustains and withdraws the universe. His rule of life is Shāktadharma, his doctrine of Shakti is Shaktivāda or Shākta Darshana. God is worshipped as the Great Mother because, in this aspect, God is active, and produces, nourishes, and maintains all. Theological Godhead is no more female than male or neuter. God is Mother to the Sādhaka who worships Her Lotus Feet, the dust on which are millions of universes. The Power, or active aspect of the immanent God, is thus called Shakti. In Her static transcendent aspect the Mother or Shakti or Shivā is of the same nature as Shiva or "the Good". That is, philosophically speaking, Shiva is the unchanging Consciousness, and Shakti is its changing Power appearing as mind and matter. Shiva-Shakti is therefore Consciousness and Its Power. This then is the doctrine of dual aspects of the one Brahman acting through Its Trinity of Powers

(Ichchhā, Will; Jñāna, Knowledge; Kriyā, Action). In the static transcendent aspect (Shiva) the one Brahman does not change, and in the kinetic immanent aspect (Shivā or Shakti) It does. There is thus changelessness in change. The individual or embodied Spirit (Jīvātmā) is one with the transcendent spirit (Paramātmā). The former is a part (Aṁsha) of the latter, and the enveloping mind and body are manifestations of Supreme Power. Shākta Darshana is therefore a form of Monism (Advaitavāda). In creation an effect is produced without change in the Producer. In creation the Power (Shakti) "goes forth" (Prasarati) in a series of emanations or transformations, which are called, in the Shaiva and Shākta Tantras, the 36 Tattvas. These mark the various stages through which Shiva, the Supreme Consciousness, as Shakti, presents Itself as object to Itself as subject, the latter at first experiencing the former as part of the Self, and then through the operation of Māyā Shakti as different from the Self. This is the final stage in which every Self (Purusha) is mutually exclusive of every other. Māyā, which achieves this, is one of the Powers of the Mother or Devī. The Will-to-become-many (Bahu syām prajāyeya) is the creative impulse which not only creates but reproduces an eternal order. The Lord remembers the diversities latent in His own Māyā Shakti due to the previous Karmas of Jīvas and allows them to unfold themselves by His volition. It is that Power by which infinite formless Consciousness veils Itself to Itself and negates and limits Itself in order that it may experience Itself as Form.

This Māyā Shakti assumes the form of Prakṛiti Tattva, which is composed of three Guṇas or Factors called Sattva, Rajas, Tamas. The function of Prakṛiti is to veil, limit, or *finitise* pure infinite formless Consciousness, so as to produce form, for without such limitation there cannot be the appearance of form. These Guṇas work by mutual suppression. The function of Tamas is to veil Consciousness, of Sattva to reveal it, and of Rajas the active principle to make either Tamas suppress Sattva or Sattva suppress Tamas. These Guṇas are present in all particular existence, as in the general cause or Prakṛiti Shakti. Evolution means the increased operation of Sattva Guṇa. Thus the mineral world is more subject to Tamas than the rest. There is less Tamas and more Sattva in the vegetable world. In the animal world Sattva is increased, and still more so in man, who may rise through the cultivation of the Sattva Guṇa to Pure Consciousness (Moksha) Itself. To use Western parlance Consciousness more and more appears as forms evolve and rise to man. Consciousness does not in itself change, but its mental and material envelopes do, thus releasing and giving Consciousness more play. As Pure Consciousness is Spirit, the release of It from the bonds of matter means that Forms which issue from the Power of Spirit (Shakti) become more and more Sāttvik. A truly Sāttvik man is therefore a spiritual man. The aim of Sādhanā is therefore the cultivation of the Sattva Guṇa. Nature (Prakṛiti) is thus the Veil of Spirit as Tamas Guṇa, the Revealer of Spirit as Sattva Guṇa, and the Activity (Rajas Guṇa) which makes either work. Thus the upward or revealing movement from the predominance of Tamas to that of Sattva represents the spiritual progress of the embodied Spirit or Jīvātmā.

It is the desire for the life of form which produces the universe. This desire exists in the collective Vāsanā, held like all else, in inchoate state in the Mother-Power, which passing from its own (Svarūpa) formless state gives effect to them. Upon the expiration of the vast length of time which constitutes a day of Brahmā the whole universe is withdrawn into the great Causal Womb (Yoni) which produced it. The limited selves are withdrawn into it, and again, when the creative throes are felt, are put forth from it, each appearing in that form and state which its previous Karma had made for it. Those who do good Karma but with desire and self-regard (Sakāma) go, on death, to Heaven and thereafter reap their reward in good future birth on earth—for Heaven is also a transitory state. The bad are punished by evil births on earth and suffering in the Hells which are also transitory. Those however who have rid themselves of all self-regarding desire and work selflessly (Nishkāma Karma) realize the Brahman nature which is Sachchidānanda. Such are liberated, that is never appear again in the world of Form, which is the world of suffering, and enter into the infinite ocean of Bliss Itself. This is Moksha or Mukti or Liberation. As it is freedom from the universe of form, it can only be attained through detachment from the world and desirelessness. For those who desire the world of form cannot be freed of it. Life, therefore, is a field in which man, who has gradually ascended through lower forms of mineral, vegetable and animal life, is given the opportunity of heaven-life and Liberation. The universe has a moral purpose, namely the affording to all existence of a field wherein it may reap the fruit of its actions. The forms of life are therefore the stairs (Sopāna) on which man mounts to the state of infinite, eternal, and formless Bliss. This then is the origin and the end of man. He has made for himself his own past and present condition and will make his future one. His essential nature is free. If wise, he adopts the means (Sādhanā) which lead to lasting happiness, for that of the world is not to be had by all, and even when attained is perishable and mixed with suffering. This Sādhanā consists of various means and disciplines employed to produce purity of mind (Chittashuddhi), and devotion to, and worship of, the Magna Mater of all. It is with these means that the religious Tantra Shāstras are mainly concerned. The Shākta Tantra Shāstra contains a most elaborate and wonderful ritual, partly its own, partly of Vaidik origin. To a ritualist it is of absorbing interest.

Ritual is an art, the art of religion. Art is the outward material expression of ideas intellectually held and emotionally felt. Ritual art is concerned with the expression of those ideas and feelings which are specifically called religious. It is a mode by which religious truth is presented, and made intelligible in material forms and symbols to the mind. It appeals to all natures passionately sensible of that Beauty in which, to some, God most manifests Himself. But it is more than this. For it is the means by which the mind is transformed and purified. In particular according to Indian principles it is the instrument whereby the consciousness of the worshipper (Sādhaka) is *shaped in actual fact* into forms of experience which embody the truths which Scripture teaches. The Shākta is thus taught that he is one with Shiva and His Power or Shakti. This is not a matter of mere argument. It is a matter for experience. It is ritual and Yoga-practice which secure that experience for him. How profound Indian ritual is, will be admitted by those who have understood the general principles of all ritual and symbolism, and have studied it in its Indian form, with a knowledge of the principles of which it is an expression. Those who speak of "mummery," "gibberish" and "superstition" betray both their incapacity and ignorance.

The Āgamas are not themselves treatises on Philosophy, though they impliedly contain a particular theory of life. They are what is called Sādhanā Shāstras, that is, practical Scriptures prescribing the *means* by which happiness, the quest of all mankind, may be attained. And as lasting happiness is God, they teach how man by worship and by practice of the disciplines prescribed, may attain a divine experience. From incidental statements and the practices described the philosophy is extracted.

The speaker of the Tantras and the revealer of the Shākta Tantra is Shiva Himself or Shivā the Devī Herself. Now it is the first who teaches and the second who listens (Āgama). Now again the latter assumes the role of Guru and answers the questions of Shiva (Nigama). For the two are one. Sometimes there are other interlocutors. Thus one of the Tantras is called Īshvarakārtikeya-saṁvāda, for there the Lord addresses his son Kārtikeya. The Tantra Shāstra therefore claims to be a Revelation, and of the same essential truths as those contained in the Eternal Veda which is an authority to itself (Svataḥsiddha). Those who have had experience of the truths recorded in Shāstra, have also proclaimed the *practical means* whereby their experience was gained. "Adopt those means" they say, "and you will also have for yourself our experience." This is the importance of Sādhanā and all Sādhanā Shāstras. The Guru says: "Do as I tell you. Follow the method prescribed by Scripture. Curb your desires. Attain a pure disposition, and then and thus only will you obtain that certainty, that experience which will render any questionings unnecessary." The practical importance of the Āgama lies in its assumption of these principles and in the methods which it enjoins for the attainment of that state in which the truth is realized. The following Chapters shortly explain some of the main features of both the philosophy and practice of the Shākta division of the Āgama. For their full development many volumes are necessary. What is here said is a mere sketch in a popular form of a vast subject.

I will conclude this Chapter with extracts from a Bengali letter written to me shortly before his death, now many years ago, by Pandit Shiva-chandra Vidyārṇava, the Shākta author of the "Tantratattva" which I have published under the title "Principles of Tantra". The words in brackets are my own.

"At the present time the general public are ignorant of the principles of the Tantra Shāstra. The cause of this ignorance is the fact that the Tantra Shāstra is a Sādhanā Shāstra, *the greater part of which becomes intelligible only by Sādhanā.* For this reason the Shāstra and its Teachers prohibit their general promulgation. So long as the Shāstra was learnt from Gurus only, this golden rule was of immense good. In course of time the old Sādhanā has become almost extinct, and along with it, the knowledge of the deep and mighty principles of the Shāstra is almost lost. Nevertheless some faint shadowings of these principles (which can be thoroughly known by Sādhanā only) have been put before the public partly with the view to preserve Shāstric knowledge from destruction, and partly for commercial reasons. When I commenced to write Tantratattva some 25 years ago (some 37 years from date) Bengali society was in a perilous state owing to the influx of other religions, want of faith and a spirit of disputation. Shortly before this a number of English books had appeared on the Tantra Shāstra which, whilst ignorant of Dharma, Sādhanā and Siddhi, contained some hideous and outrageous pictures drawn by the Bengali historians and novelists ignorant of, and unfaithful to, Shāstric principles. The English books by English writers contained merely a reflection of what English-educated Bengalis of those days had written. Both are even to-day equally ignorant of the Tantra Shāstra. For this reason in writing Tantratattva I could not go deeply into the subject as my heart wished. I had to spend my time in removing thorns (objections and charges) from the path by reasoning and argument. I could not therefore deal in my book with most of the subjects which, when I brought out the first volume, I promised to discuss. The Tantra Shāstra is broadly divided into three parts, namely Sādhanā, Siddhi (that which is gained by Sādhanā) and Philosophy (Darshana). Unlike other systems it is not narrow nor does it generate doubt by setting forth conflicting views. For its speaker is One and not many and He is omniscient. The philosophy is however scattered throughout the Tantrik treatises and is dealt with, as occasion arises, in connection with Sādhanā and Siddhi. Could (as I had suggested to him) such parts be collected and arranged, according to the principles of the subject-matter, they would form a vast system of philosophy wonderful, divine, lasting, true, and carrying conviction to men. As a Philosophy it is at the head of all others. You have prayed to Parameshvara (God) for my long life, and my desire to carry out my project makes me also pray for it. But the state of my body makes me doubt whether the prayer will be granted. By the grace therefore of the Mother the sooner the work is done the better. You say 'that those who worship Parameshvara, He makes of one family. Let therefore all distinctions be put aside for all Sādhakas are, as such, one.' This noble principle is the final word of all Shāstras, all communities, and all religions. All distinctions which arise from differences in the physical body are distinctions for the human world only. They have no place in the world of worship of Parameshvara. The more therefore that we shall approach Him the more will the differences between you and me vanish. It is because both of us pray for the removal of all such differences, that I am led to rely on your encouragement and help and am bold to take up this difficult and daring work. If by your grace the gate of this Tantrik philosophy is opened in the third part of Tantratattva

I dare to say that the learned in all countries will gaze and be astonished for it is pure truth, and for this reason I shall be able to place it before them with perfect clearness."

Unfortunately this project of a third part of the Tantratattva could not be carried out owing to the lamented death of its author, which followed not long after the receipt of this letter. Naturally, like all believers throughout the whole world, he claimed for his Scripture the possession in all its details of what was true or good. Whilst others may not concede this, I think that those with knowledge and understanding and free from prejudice will allow that it contains a profoundly conceived doctrine, wonderfully worked out in practice. Some of its ideas and principles are shared (though it be under other names and forms) by all religious men, and others either by all or some Indian communities, who are not Shāktas. Leaving therefore for the moment aside what may be said to be peculiar to itself it cannot be that wholly absurd, repulsive, and infamous system ("lust, mummery and magic" as Brian Hodgson called it) which it has been said to be. An impartial criticism may be summed up in the few words that together with what has value, it contains some practices which are not generally approved and which have led to abuse. As to these the reader is referred to the Chapter on the Panchatattva or Secret Ritual.

I conclude with a translation of an article in Bengali by a well-known writer, (P. Bandyopādhyāya, in the "Sāhitya", Shrabun 1320, Calcutta, July-August 1913). It was evoked by the publication of Arthur Avalon's Translation of, and Introduction to, the Mahānirvāṇa Tantra. It is an interesting statement as regards the Shākta Tantra and Bengali views thereon. Omitting here some commendatory statements touching A. Avalon's work and the writer's "thanks a hundred times" for the English version, the article continues as follows:

"At one time the Mahānirvāṇa Tantra had some popularity in Bengal. It was printed and published under the editorship of Pandit Ānanda-chandra Vedanta-vāgīsha and issued from the Ādi-Brahma-Samāj Press. Rājā Rām Mohan Roy himself was a follower of the Tantras, married after the Shaiva form and used to practise the Tantrik worship. His spiritual preceptor, Svāmī Hariharānanda, was well known to be a saint who had attained to perfection (Siddha-purusha). He endeavoured to establish the Mahānirvāṇa Tantra as the Scripture of the Brahma-Samāj. The formula and the forms of the Brahma Church are borrowed from the initiation in Brahman worship, (Brahma-dīkshā) in this Tantra. The later Brahmas somewhat losing their selves in their spirit of imitation of Christian rituals were led to abandon the path shown to them by Rājā Rām Mohan; but yet even now many among them recite the Hymn to the Brahman which occurs in the Mahānirvāṇa Tantra. In the first era of the excessive dissemination of English culture and training Bengal resounded with opprobrious criticisms of the Tantras. No one among the educated in Bengal could praise them. Even those who called themselves Hindus were unable outwardly to support the Tantrik doctrines. But even then there were very great Tantrik Sādhakas and men learned in the Tantras with whose help the principles of the Tantras might have been explained to the public. But the educated Bengali of the age was bewitched by the Christian culture, and no one cared to enquire what did or did not exist in their paternal heritage; the more especially that any who attempted to study the Tantras ran the risk of exposing themselves to contumely from the "educated community". Mahārājā Sir Jatindra Mohan

Tagore of sacred name alone published two or three works with the help of the venerable Pandit Jaganmohan Tarkālaṅkāra. The Hara-tattva-dīdhiti associated with the name of his father is even now acknowledged to be a marvellously glorious production of the genius of the Pandits of Bengal. The venerable (Bṛiddha) Pandit Jaganmohan also published a commentary on the Mahānirvāṇa Tantra. Even at that epoch such study of the Tantras was confined to a certain section of the educated in Bengal. Mahārājā Sir Jatindra Mohan alone endeavoured to understand and appreciate men like Bāmā Khepā (mad Bāmā), the Naked Father (Nengtā Bābā) of Kaḍḍa and Svāmī Sadānanda. The educated community of Bengal had only neglect and contempt for Sādhakas like Bishe Pāglā (the mad Bishe) and Binu the Chaṇḍāla woman. Bengal is even now governed by the Tantra; even now the Hindus of Bengal receive Tantrik initiation. But the glory and the honour which the Tantra had and received in the time of Mahārājās Kṛishṇa-chandra and Shiva-chandra no longer exist. This is the reason why the Tantrik Sādhakas of Bengal are not so well-known at present. It seems as if the World-Mother has again willed it, has again desired to manifest Her power, so that Arthur Avalon is studying the Tantras and has published so beautiful a version of the Mahānirvāṇa. The English educated Bengali will now, we may hope, turn his attention to the Tantra.

"The special virtue of the Tantra lies in its mode of Sādhanā. It is neither mere worship (Upāsanā) nor prayer. It is not lamenting or contrition or repentance before the Deity. It is the Sādhanā which is the union of Purusha and Prakṛiti; the Sādhanā which joins the Male Principle and the Mother Element within the body, and strives to make the attributed attributeless. That which is in me and that for which I am (this consciousness is ever present in me) is spread, like butter in milk, throughout the created world of moving and unmoving things, through the gross and the subtle, the conscious and unconscious, through all. It is the object of Tantrik Sādhanā to merge that self-principle (Svarāṭ) into the Universal (Virāṭ). This Sādhanā is to be performed through the awakening of the forces within the body. A man is *Siddha* in this Sādhanā when he is able to awaken Kuṇḍalinī and pierce the six Chakras. This is not mere "philosophy" a mere attempt to ponder upon husks of words, but something which is to be done in a thoroughly practical manner. The Tantras say—"Begin practising under the guidance of a good Guru; if you do not obtain favourable results immediately, you can freely give it up." No other religion dares to give so bold a challenge. We believe that the Sādhanā of the Moslems, and the "esoteric religion" or secret Sādhanā (and rituals) of the Christians of the Roman Catholic and Greek Churches is based on this groundwork of the Tantras."

"Wherever there is Sādhanā we believe that there is the system of the Tantra. While treating of the Tantras some time back in the *Sāhitya*, I hinted at this conclusion and I cannot say that the author, Arthur Avalon, has not noticed it too. For he has expressed his surprise at the similarity which exists between the Roman Catholic and the Tantrik mode of Sādhanā. The Tantra has made the Yoga-system of Patanjali easily practicable and has combined with it the Tantrik rituals and the ceremonial observances (Karma-kāṇḍa); that is the reason why the Tantrik system of Sādhanā has been adopted by all the religious sects of India. If this theory of the antiquarians, that the Tantra was brought into India from Chaldea or Shākadvīpa be correct, then it may also be inferred that the Tantra passed from Chaldea to Europe. The Tantra is to be found in all the strata of Buddhism; the Tantrik

Sādhanā is manifest in Confucianism; and Shintoism is but another name of the Tantrik cult. Many historians acknowledge that the worship of Shakti or Tantrik Sādhanā which was prevalent in Egypt from ancient times spread into Phœnicia and Greece. Consequently we may suppose that the influence of the Tantras was felt in primitive Christianity."

"The Tantra contains nothing like idolatry or 'worship of the doll' which we, taking the cue from the Christian missionaries, nowadays call it. This truth, the author, Arthur Avalon, has made very clear in the Introduction to his translation. The Tantra repeatedly says that one is to adore the Deity by becoming a Deity (Devatā) himself. The Ishṭa-devatā is the very self of Ātman, and not separate from It; He is the receptacle of all, yet He is not contained in anything, for He is the great witness, the eternal Purusha. The true Tantrik worship is the worship in and by the mind. The less subtle form of Tantric worship is that of the Yantra. Form is born of the Yantra. The form is made manifest by Japa, and awakened by Mantra-shakti. Tens of millions of beautiful forms of the Mother bloom forth in the heavens of the heart of the Siddhapurusha. Devotees or aspirants of a lower order of competency (Nimna-adhikārī) under the directions of the Guru adore the great Māyā by making manifest (to themselves) one of Her various forms which can be only seen by Dhyāna (meditation). That is not mere worship of the idol! if it were so the image would not be thrown into the water; no one in that case would be so irreverent as to sink the earthen image of the Goddess in the water. The Primordial Shakti is to be awakened by Bhāva, by Dhyanā, by Japa and by the piercing of the six Chakras. She is all will. No one can say when and how She shows Herself and to what Sādhaka. We only know that She is, and there are

Her names and forms. Wonderfully transcending is Her form—far beyond the reach of word or thought. This has made the Bengali Bhakta sing this plaintive song—

"Hard indeed is it to approach the sea of forms, and to bathe in it.

Ah me, this my coming is perhaps in vain?"

"The Tantra deals with another special subject—Mantra-Shakti. It is no exaggeration to say that we have never heard even from any Bengali Pandit such a clear exposition of Mantra-Shakti as that which the author, Arthur Avalon, has given in his Introduction to the Mahānirvāṇa Tantra. We had thought that Mantra-Shakti was a thing to be felt and not to be explained to others. But the author with the force of his genius has in his simple exposition given us such explanation of it as is possible in the English language. The Tantras say that the soul in the body is the very self of the letters—of the Dhvani (sound). The Mother, the embodiment of the fifty letters (Varṇa), is present in the various letters in the different Chakras. Like the melody which issues when the chords of a lute are struck, the Mother who moves in the six Chakras and who is the very self of the letters awakens with a burst of harmony when the chords of the letters (Varṇas) are struck in their order: and Siddhi becomes as easy of attainment to the Sādhaka as the Āmalaka fruit in one's hand when She is roused. That is why the great Sādhaka Rāmaprasād awakened the Mother by the invocation—'Arise O Mother Jāgṛihi, janani)'. That is the reason why the Bhakta sang—

'How long wilt thou sleep in the Mūlādhāra, O Mother Kulakuṇḍalinī?'

"The Bodhana (awakening) ceremony in the Durgā Pūjā is nothing but the awakening of the Shakti of the Mother, the mere rousing of the consciousness of the Kuṇḍalinī. This awakening is performed by Mantra-Shakti.

The Mantra is nothing but the harmonious sound of the lute of the body. When the symphony is perfect, She who embodies the Worlds (Jaganmayī) rouses Herself. When She is awake it does not take long before the union of Shiva and Shakti takes place. Do Japa once; do Japa according to rule looking up to the Guru, and the effects of Japa of which we hear in the Tantra will prove to be true at every step. Then you will understand that the Tantra is not mere trickery, or a false weaving out of words. What is wanted is the good Guru; Mantra capable of granting Siddhi, and application (Sādhanā). Arthur Avalon has grasped the meaning of the principles of Mantra which are so difficult to understand. We may certainly say that he could only make this impossible thing possible through inherent tendencies (Saṁskāra) acquired in his previous life."

"The Tantra accepts the doctrine of rebirth. It does not however acknowledge it as a mere matter of argument or reasoning but like a geographical map it makes clear the unending chain of existences of the Sādhaka. The Tantra has two divisions, the Dharma of Society (Samāja) and the Dharma of Spiritual Culture (Sādhanā). According to the regulation of Samāja-Dharma it acknowledges birth and caste. But in Sādhana-Dharma there is no caste distinction, no Brāhmaṇa or Shūdra, no man or woman; distinction between high and low follows success in Sādhanā and Siddhi. We only find the question of fitness or worthiness (Adhikāra-tattva) in the Tantra. This fitness (Adhikāra) is discovered with reference to the Saṁskāras of past existences; that is why the Chaṇḍāla Pūrṇānanda is a Brāhmaṇa, and Kṛipāsiddha the Sādhaka is equal to Sarvānanda; that is why Rāmaprasāda of the Vaidya caste is fit to be honoured even by Brāhmaṇas. The Tantra is to be studied with the aid of the teachings of the Guru; for its language is extraordinary, and its exposition impossible with a mere grammatical knowledge of roots and inflections. The Tantra is only a system of Shakti-Sādhana. There are rules in it whereby we may draw Shakti from all created things. There is nothing to be accepted or rejected in it. Whatever is helpful for Sādhanā is acceptable. This Sādhanā is decided according to the fitness of the particular person (Adhikārīanusāre). He must follow that for which he is fit or worthy. Shakti pervades all and embraces all beings and all things—the inanimate and the moving, beasts and birds, men and women. The unfolding of the Power (Shakti) enclosed within the body of the animal (Jīva) as well as the man is brought about only with the help of the tendencies within the body. The mode of Sādhanā is ascertained with regard to these tendencies. The very meaning of Sādhanā is unfolding, rousing up or awakening of Power (Shakti). Thus the Shākta obtains power from all actions in the world. The Sādhanā of the Tantra is not to be measured by the little measuring-yard of the well-being or ill-being of your community or mine.

'Let you understand and I understand, O my mind—
Whether any one else understands it or not.'

The author, Arthur Avalon, is fully conscious of this. In spite of it, he has tried to explain almost all points making them easy to comprehend for the intellect of the materialistic civilized society of to-day. For this attempt on his part we are grateful to him."

"The Tantra has no notion of some separate far-seeing God. It preaches no such doctrine in it as that God the Creator rules the Universe from heaven. In the eye of the Tantra the body of the Sādhaka is the Universe, the *autokratos* (Ātma-shakti) within the body is the desired (Iṣhṭa) and the "to be sought for" (Sādhya) Deity (Devatā) of the Sādhaka. The unfolding of this self-power is to be brought about by self-realization (Ātma-darshana) which is to be achieved through Sādhanā. Whoever realizes his self attains to Liberation (Mukti). The author, Arthur Avalon, has treated of these matters (Siddhānta) in his work, the Tantratattva. Many of the topics dealt within the Mahānirvāṇa Tantra will not be fully understood without a thorough perusal of the book. The Principles of the Tantra must be lectured on to the Bengali afresh. If the Mahānirvāṇa Tantra as translated by Arthur Avalon is spread abroad, if the Bengali is once more desirous to hear, that attempt might well be undertaken."

"Our land of Bengal used to be ruled by Tantrik works such as the Sāradātilaka, Shāktānandataraṅgiṇī, Prāṇatoṣhiṇī, Tantrasāra, etc. Then the Mahānirvāṇa Tantra did not have so great an influence. It seems to us that, considering the form into which, as a result of English education and culture, the mind of the Bengali has been shaped, the Mahānirvāṇa is a proper Tantra for the time. Rājā Rām Mohan Roy endeavoured to encourage regard for the Mahānirvāṇa Tantra because he understood this. If the English translation of the Mahānirvāṇa Tantra by Arthur Avalon is well received by the thoughtful public in Bengal, the study of the original Sanskrit work may gradually come into vogue. This much hope we may entertain. In fact, the English-educated Bengali community is without religion (Dharma) or action (Karma), and is devoid of the sense of nationality (Jātīya Dharma) and caste. The Mahānirvāṇa Tantra alone is fit for the country and the race at the present time. We believe that probably because such an impossibility is going to be possible, a cultured, influential, rich Englishman like Arthur Avalon, honoured of the rulers, has translated and published the Mahānirvāṇa Tantra. When his Tantratattva is published we shall be able to speak out much more. For the present we ask the educated people of Bengal to read this most unprecedented

Mahānirvāṇa Tantra. Arthur Avalon has not spoken a single word to satisfy himself nor tried to explain things according to his own imagination. He has only given what are true inferences according to the principles of Shāstric reasoning. An auspicious opportunity for the English-knowing public to understand the Tantra has arrived. It is a counsel of the Tantra itself, that if you desire to renounce anything, renounce it only after a thorough acquaintance with it; if you desire to embrace anything new, accept it only after a searching enquiry. The Tantra embodies the old religion (Dharma) of Bengal; even if it is to be cast away for good, that ought only to be done after it has been fully known. In the present case a thoughtful and educated Englishman of high position has taken it upon himself to give us a full introduction to the Tantra. We can frankly say that in this Introduction he has not tried a jot to shirk or to gloss over the conclusions of the Shāstra, with the vanity of explanation born of his imagination. He has endeavoured to bring before the mind of his readers whatever actually is in the Tantra, be it regarded as either good or evil. Will not the Bengali receive with welcome such a full offering (Arghya) made by a Bhakta from a foreign land?"

CHAPTER II

SHAKTI: THE WORLD AS POWER

THERE is no word of wider content in any language than this Sanskrit term meaning 'Power'. For Shakti in the highest causal sense is God as Mother, and in another sense it is the universe which issues from Her Womb. And what is there which is neither one nor the other? Therefore the *Yoginīhṛidaya Tantra* thus salutes Her who conceives, bears, produces and thereafter nourishes all worlds: "Obeisance be to Her who is pure Being-Consciousness-Bliss, as Power, who exists in the form of Time and Space and all that is therein, and who is the radiant Illuminatrix in all beings."

It is therefore possible only to outline here in a very general way a few of the more important principles of the Shakti-doctrine, omitting its deeply interesting practice (Sādhanā) in its forms as ritual worship and Yoga.

To-day Western science speaks of Energy as the physical ultimate of all forms of Matter. So has it been for ages to the Shāktas, as the worshippers of Shakti are called. But they add that such Energy is only a limited manifestation (as Mind and Matter) of the almighty infinite Supreme Power (Mahā-Shakti) of Becoming in 'That' (Tat), which is unitary Being (Sat) Itself.

Their doctrine is to be found in the traditions, oral and written, which are contained in the Āgamas, which (with Purāṇa, Smṛiti and Veda) constitute one of the four great classes of Scripture of the Hindus. The Tantras are Scriptures of the Āgama. The notion that they are some queer bye-product of Hinduism and not an integral part of it, is erroneous. The three chief divisions of the Āgama are locally named Bengal (Gauḍa), Kashmira and Kerala. That Bengal is a home of Tantrashāstra is well known. It is, however, little known that Kashmir was in the past a land where Tāntrik doctrine and practice were widely followed.

The communities of so-called 'Tāntrik' worshippers are five-fold according as the cult is of the Sun, Gaṇesha, Viṣhṇu, Shiva or Shakti. To the Knower, however, the five named are not distinct Divinities, but different aspects of the one Power or Shakti. An instructed Shakti-worshipper is one of the least sectarian of men. He can worship in all temples, as the saying is. Thus the *Sammohana Tantra* says that "he is a fool who sees any difference between Rāma [an Avatāra of Viṣhṇu] and Shiva". "What matters the name," says the Commentator of the *Shaṭchakranirūpaṇa*, after running through the gamut of them.

The Shākta is so called because the chosen Deity of his worship (Iṣhṭadevatā) is Shakti. In his cult, both in doctrine and practice, emphasis is laid on that aspect of the One in which It is the Source of Change and, in the form of Time and Space and all objects therein, Change itself. The word Shakti is grammatically feminine. For this reason an American Orientalist critic of the doctrine has described it as a worthless system, a mere feminization of orthodox (whatever that be) Vedānta—a doctrine teaching the primacy of the Female and thus fit only for "suffragette monists". It is absurd criticism of this kind which makes the Hindu sometimes wonder whether the European has even the capacity to understand his beliefs. It is said of the Mother (in the Hymn to Her in the *Mahākāla-Saṁhitā*): "Thou art neither girl, nor maid, nor old. Indeed Thou art neither female nor male, nor neuter. Thou art inconceivable, immeasurable Power, the Being of all which exists, void of all duality, the Supreme Brahman, attainable in Illumination alone." Those who cannot understand lofty ideas when presented in ritual and symbolic garb will serve their reputation best by not speaking of them.

The Shaiva is so called because his chosen Divinity is Shiva, the name for the changeless aspect of the One whose Power of action and activity is Shakti. But as the two are necessarily associated, all communities acknowledge Shakti. It is, for the above reason, a mistake to suppose that a 'Tāntrik,' or follower of the Āgama, is necessarily a Shākta, and that the 'Tantra' is a Shākta Scripture only. Not at all. The Shākta is only one branch of the Āgamik school. And so we find the Scriptures of Shaivaism, whether of North or South, called Tantras, as also those of that ancient form of Vaishnavism which is called the Pañcharātra. The doctrine of these communities, which share certain common ideas, varies from the monism of the Shāktas and Northern Shaivas to the more or less dualistic systems of others. The ritual is to a large extent common in all communities, though there are necessarily variations, due both to the nature of the divine aspect worshipped and to the particular form of theology taught. Shākta doctrine and practice are contained primarily in the Shākta Tantras and the oral traditions, some of which are secret. As the Tantras are mainly Scriptures of Worship such doctrine is contained by implication in the ritual. For reasons above stated recourse may be had to other Scriptures in so far as they share with those of the Shākta, certain common doctrines and practices. The Tantras proper are the Word of Shiva and Shakti. But there are also valuable Tāntrik works in the nature of compendia and commentaries which are not of divine authorship.

The concept 'Shakti' is not however peculiar to the Shāktas. Every Hindu believes in Shakti as God's Power, though he may differ as to the nature of the universe created by it. Shākta doctrine is a special presentment of so-called monism (Advaita: lit. 'not-two') and Shākta ritual, even in those condemned forms which have given rise to the abuses by which this Scripture is most generally known, is a practical application of it. Whatever may have been the case at the origin of these Āgamic cults, all, now and for ages past, recognize and claim to base themselves on the Vedas. With these are coupled the Word of Shiva-Shakti as revealed in the Tantras. Shākta-doctrine is (like the Vedānta in general) what in Western parlance would be called a theology based on revelation that is, so-called 'spiritual' or supersensual experience, in its primary or secondary sense. For Veda is that.

This leads to a consideration of the measure of man's knowing and of the basis of Vedāntik knowledge. It is a fundamental error to regard the Vedānta as simply a speculative metaphysic in the modern Western sense. It is not so: if it were, it would have no greater right to acceptance than any other of the many systems which jostle one another for our custom in the Philosophical Fair. It claims that its supersensual teachings can be established with certainty by the *practice* of its methods. Theorising alone is insufficient. The Shākta, above all, is a practical and active man, worshipping the Divine Activity; his watchward is Kriyā or Action. Taught that he is Power, he desires fully to realize himself in fact as such. A Tāntrik poem (*Ānanda-stotra*) speaks with amused disdain of the learned chatterers who pass their time in futile debate around the shores of the 'Lake of Doubt'.

The basis of knowing, whether in super-sense or sense-knowledge, is actual experience. Experience is of two kinds: the whole or full experience; and incomplete experience—that is, of parts, not of, but in, the whole. In the first experience, Consciousness is said to be 'upward-looking' (Unmukhī)—that is, 'not looking to another'. In the second experience it is 'outward-looking' (Vahirmukhī). The first is not an experience of the whole, but the Experience-whole. The second is an experience not of parts of the whole, for the latter is partless, but of parts in the whole, and issuing from its infinite Power to know itself in and as the finite centres, as the many. The works of an Indian philosopher, my friend Professor Pramatha Nātha Mukhyopādhyāya, aptly call the first the Fact, and the second the Fact-section. The *Isha Upaniṣhad* calls the Supreme Experience—Pūrṇa, the Full or Whole.

It is not, be it noted, a residue of the abstracting intellect, which is itself only a limited stress in Consciousness, but a Plenum, in which the Existent All is as one Whole. Theologically this full experience is Shiva, with Shakti at rest or as Potency. The second experience is that of the finite centres, the numerous Puruṣhas or Jīvas, which are also Shiva-Shakti as Potency actualized. Both experiences are real. In fact there is nothing unreal anywhere. All is the Mother and She is reality itself. "Sā' ham" ("She I am"), the Shākta says, and all that he senses is She in the form in which he perceives Her. It is She who in, and as, him drinks the consecrated wine, and She is the wine. All is manifested Power, which has the reality of Being from which it is put forth. But the reality of the manifestation is of something which appears and disappears, whilst that of Causal Power to appear is enduring. But this disappearance is only the ceasing to be for a limited consciousness. The seed of Power, which appears as a thing for such consciousness, remains as the potency in infinite Being itself. The infinite Experience is real as the Full (Pūrṇa); that is, its reality is fullness. The finite experience is real, as such. There is, perhaps, no subject in Vedānta, which is more misunderstood than that of the so-called 'Unreality' of the World. Every School admits the reality of all finite experience (even of 'illusive' experience strictly so-called) while such experience lasts. But Shaṅkarāchārya defines the truly Real as that which is changeless. In this sense, the World as a changing thing has relative reality only. Shaṅkara so defines Reality because he sets forth his doctrine from the standpoint of transcendent Being. The Shākta Shāstra, on the other hand, is a practical Scripture of Worship, delivered from the world-standpoint, according to which the world is necessarily real. According to this view a thing may be real and yet be the subject of change. But its reality as a thing ceases with the passing of the finite experiencer to whom it is real. The supreme Shiva-Shakti is, on the other hand, a real, full Experience which ever endures. A worshipper must, as such, believe in the reality of himself, of the world as his field of action and instrument, in its causation by God, and in God Himself as the object of worship. Moreover to him the world is real because Shiva-Shakti, which is its material cause, is real. That cause, without ceasing to be what it is, becomes the effect. Further the World is the Lord's Experience. He as Lord (Pati) is the whole Experience, and as creature (Pashu) he is the experiencer of parts in it. The Experience of the Lord is never unreal. The reality, however, which changelessly endures may (if we so choose) be said to be Reality in its fullest sense.

Real however as all experience is, the knowing differs according as the experience is infinite or finite, and in the latter case according to various grades of knowing. Full experience, as its name implies, is full in every way.

Assume that there is at any 'time' no universe at all, that there is then a complete dissolution of all universes, and not of any particular universe,—even then the Power which produced past, and will produce future universes, is one with the Supreme Consciousness whose Shakti it is. When again this Power actualizes as a universe, the Lord-Consciousness from and in Whom it issues is the All-knower. As Sarvajña he knows all generals, and as Sarvavit, all particulars. But all is known by Him as the Supreme Self, and not, as in the case of the finite centre, as objects other than the limited self.

Finite experience is by its definition a limited thing. As the experience is of a sectional character, it is obvious that the knowing can only be of parts, and not of the whole, as the part cannot know the whole of which it is a part. But the finite is not always so. It may expand into the infinite by processes which bridge the one to the other. The essential of Partial Experience is knowing in Time and Space; the Supreme Experience, being changeless, is beyond both Time and Space as aspects of change. The latter is the alteration of parts relative to one another in the changeless Whole. Full experience is not sense-knowledge. The latter is worldly knowledge (Laukika Jñāna), by a limited knowing centre, of material objects, whether gross or subtle. Full Experience is the Supreme Knowing Self which is not an object at all. This is unworldly knowledge (Alaukika Jñāna) or Veda. Sense-knowledge varies according to the capacity and attainments of the experiencer. But the normal experience may be enhanced in two ways: either physically by scientific instruments such as the telescope and microscope which enhance the natural capacity to see; or psychically by the attainment of what are called psychic powers. Everything is Shakti; but psychic power denotes that enhancement of normal capacity which gives knowledge of matter in its subtle form, whilst the normal man can perceive it only in the gross form as a compound of sensible matter (the Bhūtas). Psychic power is thus an extension of natural faculty. There is nothing 'super-natural' about it. All is natural, all is real. It is simply a power above the normal. Thus the clairvoyant can see what the normal sense-experiencer cannot. He does so by the mind. The gross sense-organs are not, according to Vedānta, the senses (Indriya). The sense is the mind, which normally works through the appropriate physical organs, but which, as the real factor in sensation, may do without them, as is seen both in hypnotic and yogic states. The area of knowledge is thus very widely increased. Knowledge may be gained of subtle chemistry, subtle physiology (as of the Chakras or subtle bodily centres), of various powers, of the 'world of Spirits,' and so forth. But though we are here dealing with subtle things, they are still things and thus part of the sense-world of objects,—that is, of the world of Māyā. Māyā, as later explained, is, not 'illusion,' but Experience in time and space of Self and Not-Self. This is by no means necessarily illusion. The Whole therefore cannot be known by sense-knowledge. In short, sense or worldly knowledge cannot establish, that is, prove, what is supersensual, such as the Whole, its nature and the 'other side' of its processes taken as a collectivity. Reasoning, whether working in metaphysic or science, is based on the data of sense and governed by those forms of understanding which constitute the nature of finite mind. It may establish a conclusion of probability, but not of certainty. Grounds of probability may be made out for Idealism, Realism, Pluralism and Monism, or any other philosophical system. In fact, from what we see, the balance of probability perhaps favours Realism and Pluralism. Reason may thus establish that an effect must have a cause, but not that the cause is one.

For all that we can say, there may be as many causes as effects. Therefore it is said in Vedānta that "nothing [in these matters] is established by argument". All Western systems which do not possess actual spiritual experience as their basis, are systems which can claim no certainty as regards any matter not verifiable by sense-knowledge and reasoning thereon

Shākta, and indeed all Vedāntik teaching, holds that the only source and authority (Pramāṇa) as regards supersensual matters, such as the nature of Being in itself, and the like, is Veda. Veda, which comes from the root *vid*, to know, is knowledge *par excellence*, that is supersensual experience, which according to the Monist (to use the nearest English term) is the Experience-Whole. It may be primary or secondary. As the first it is actual experience (Sākṣhātkāra) which in English is called 'spiritual' experience.

The Shākta, as a 'monist,' says that Veda is full experience as the One. This is not an object of knowledge. This knowing is Being. "To know Brahman is to *be* Brahman." He is a 'monist,' not because of rational argument only (though he can adduce reasoning in his support), but because he, or those whom he follows, have had *in fact* such 'monistic' experience, and therefore (in the light of such experience) interpret the Vedāntik texts.

But 'spiritual' experience (to use that English term) may be incomplete both as to duration and nature. Thus from the imperfect ecstasy (Savikalpa-Samādhi), even when of a 'monistic' character, there is a return to world-experience. Again it may not be completely 'monistic' in form, or may be even of a distinctly dualistic character. This only means that the realization has stopped short of the final goal. This being the case, that goal is still perceived through the forms of duality which linger as part of the constitution of the experiencer. Thus there are Vedántik and other schools which are not 'monistic'. The spiritual experiences of all are real experiences, whatever be their character, and they are true according to the truth of the stage in which the experience is had. Do they contradict one another? The experience which a man has of a mountain at fifty miles distance, is not false because it is at variance with that of the man who has climbed it. What he sees is the thing from where he sees it. The first question then is: Is there a 'monistic' experience *in fact?* Not whether 'monism' is rational or not, and shown to be probable to the intellect. But how can we know this? With certainty only by having the experience oneself. The validity of the experience for the experiencer cannot be assailed otherwise than by alleging fraud or self-deception. But how can this be proved? To the experiencer his experience is real, and nothing else is of any account. But the spiritual experience of one is no proof to another who refuses to accept it. A man may, however accept what another says, having faith in the latter's alleged experience. Here we have the secondary meaning of Veda, that is secondary knowledge of super-sensual truth, not based on actual experience of the believer, but on the experience of some other which the former accepts. In this sense Veda is recorded for Brahmanism in the Scriptures called Vedas, which contain the *standard* experience of those whom Brahmanism recognizes as its Rishis or Seers. But the interpretation of the Vaidik record is in question, just as that of the Bible is. Why accept one interpretation rather than another? This is a lengthy matter. Suffice to say here that each chooses the spiritual food which his spiritual body needs, and which it is capable of eating and assimilating. This is the doctrine of Adhikāra. Here, as elsewhere, what is one man's meat is another man's poison. Nature works in all who are not altogether beyond her workings. What is called the 'will to believe' involves the affirmation that the form of a man's faith is the expression of his nature; the faith is the man. It is not man's reason only which leads to the adoption of a particular religious belief. It is the whole man as evolved at that particular time which does so. His affirmation of faith is an affirmation of his self in terms of it. The Shākta is therefore a 'monist', either because he has had himself spiritual experiences of this character, or because he accepts the teaching of those who claim to have had such experience. This is Āpta knowledge, that is received from a source of authority, just as knowledge of the scientific or other expert is received. It is true that the latter may be verified. But so in its own way can the former be. Revelation to the Hindu is not something stated 'from above', incapable of verification 'below'. He who accepts revelation as teaching the unity of the many in the One, may himself verify it in his own experience. How? If the disciple is what is called not fit to receive truth in this 'monistic' form, he will probably declare it to be untrue and, adhering to what he thinks is true, will not further trouble himself in the matter. If he is disposed to accept the teachings of 'monistic' religion-philosophy, it is because his own spiritual and psychical nature is at a stage which leads directly (though in a longer or shorter time as may be the case) to actual 'monistic' experience. A particular form of 'spiritual' knowledge like a particular psychic power can be developed only in him who has the capacity for it. To such an one asking, with desire for the fruit, how he may gather it, the Guru says: Follow the path of those who have achieved (Siddha) and you will gain what they gained. This is the 'Path of the Great' who are those whom we esteem to be such. We esteem them because they have achieved that which we believe to be both worthy and possible. If a would-be disciple refuses to follow the method (Sādhanā) he cannot complain that he has not had its result. Though reason by itself cannot establish more than a probability, yet when the supersensual truth has been learnt by Veda, it may be shown to be conformable to reason. And this must be so, for all realities are of one piece. Reason is a limited manifestation of the same Shakti, who is fully known in ecstasy (Samādhi) which transcends all reasoning. What, therefore, is irrational, can never be spiritually true. With the aid of the light of Revelation the path is made clear, and all that is seen tells of the Unseen. Facts of daily life give auxiliary proof. So many miss the truth which lies under their eyes, because to find it they look away or upwards to some fancied 'Heaven'. The sophisticated mind fears the obvious. "It is here; it is here," the Shākta and others say. For he and every other being is a microcosm, and so the *Vishvasāra Tantra* says: "What is here, is elsewhere. What is not here, is nowhere." The unseen is the seen, which is not some alien disguise behind which it lurks. Experience of the seen is the experience of the unseen in time and space. The life of the individual is an expression of the same laws which govern the universe. Thus the Hindu knows, from his own daily rest, that the Power which projects the universe rests. His dreamless slumber when only Bliss is known, tells him, in some fashion, of the causal state of universal rest. From the mode of his awakening and other psychological processes he divines the nature of creative thinking. To the Shākta the thrill of union with his Shakti is a faint reflection of the infinite Shiva-Shakti Bliss in and with which all universes are born. All matter is a relatively stable form of Energy. It lasts awhile and disappears into Energy. The universe is maintained awhile. This is Shakti as Vaiṣhṇavī, the Maintainer. At every moment creation, as rejuvenescent molecular activity, is going on as the Shakti Brahmāṇī. At every moment there is molecular death and loosening of the forms, the work of Rudrāṇī Shakti. Creation did not take place only at some past time, nor is dissolution only in the future. At every moment of time there is both. As it is now and before us here, so it was 'in the beginning'.

In short the world is real. It is a true experience. Observation and reason are here the guide. Even Veda is no authority in matters falling within sense-knowledge. If Veda were to contradict such knowledge, it would, as Shaṅkara says, be in this respect no Veda at all. The Hindu is not troubled by 'biblical science'. Here and now the existence of the many is established for the sense-experiencer. But there is another and Full Experience which also may be had here and now and is in any case also a fact,—that is, when the Self 'stands out' (*ekstasis*) from mind and body and sense-experience. This Full Experience is attained in ecstasy (Samādhi). Both experiences may be had by the same experiencer. It is thus the same One who became many. "He said: May I be many," as Veda tells. The 'will to be many' is Power or Shakti which operates as Māyā.

In the preceding portion of this paper it was pointed out that the Power whereby the One gives effect to Its Will to be Many is Māyā Shakti.

What are called the 36 Tattvas (accepted by both Shāktas and Shaivas) are the stages of evolution of the One into the Many as mind and matter.

Again with what warrant is this affirmed? The secondary proof is the Word of Shiva and Shakti, Revealers of the Tantra-shāstra, as such Word is expounded in the teachings of the Masters (Āchārya) in the Āgama.

Corroboration of their teaching may be had by observation of psychological stages in normal life and reasoning thereon. These psychological states again are the individual representation of the collective cosmic processes. "As here, so elsewhere." Primary evidence is actual experience of the surrounding and supreme states. Man does not leap at one bound from ordinary finite sense-experience to the Full Experience. By stages he advances thereto, and by stages he retraces his steps to the world, unless the fulness of experience has been such as to burn up in the fire of Self-knowledge the seed of desire which is the germ of the world. Man's consciousness has no fixed boundary. On the contrary, it is at root the Infinite Consciousness, which appears in the form of a contraction (Saṅkocha), due to limitation as Shakti in the form of mind and matter. This contraction may be greater or less. As it is gradually loosened, consciousness expands by degrees until, all bonds being gone, it becomes one with the Full Consciousness or Pūrṇa. Thus there are, according to common teaching, seven ascending light planes of experience, called Lokas, that is 'what are seen' (*lokyante*) or experienced; and seven dark descending planes, or Talas, that is 'places'. It will be observed that one name is given from the subjective and the other from the objective standpoint. The centre of these planes is the 'Earth-plane' (Bhūrloka). This is not the same as experience on earth, for every experience, including the highest and lowest, can be had here. The planes are not like geological strata, though necessity may picture them thus. The Earth-plane is the normal experience. The ascending planes are states of supernormal, and the descending planes of sub-normal experience. The highest of the planes is the Truth-plane (Satya-loka). Beyond this is the Supreme Experience, which is above all planes, which is Light itself, and the love of Shiva and Shakti, the 'Heart of the Supreme Lord' (*Hṛidayam parameshituḥ*). The lowest Tala on the dark side is described in the Purāṇas with wonderful symbolic imagery as a Place of Darkness where monster serpents, crowned with dim light, live in perpetual anger. Below this is the Shakti of the Lord called Tamomayī Shakti—that is, the Veiling Power of Being in all its infinite intensity.

What then is the Reality—Whole or Pūrṇa? It is certainly not a bare abstraction of intellect, for the intellect is only a fractional Power or Shakti in it. Such an abstraction has no worth for man. In the Supreme Reality, which is the Whole, there is everything which is of worth to men, and which proceeds from it. In fact, as a Kashmir Scripture says: "The 'without' appears without only *because* it is within." Unworth also proceeds from it, not in the sense that it is there *as* unworth, but because the experience of duality, to which evil is attached, arises in the Blissful Whole. The Full is not merely the collectivity (Samaṣhti) of all which exists, for it is both immanent in and transcends the universe. It is a commonplace that it is unknowable except to Itself. Shiva, in the *Yoginīhṛidaya Tantra*, says: "Who knows the heart of a woman? Only Shiva knows the Heart of Yoginī (the Supreme Shakti)." For this reason the Buddhist Tāntrik schools call it Shūnya or the Void. This is not 'nothing', but nothing known to mind and senses. Both Shāktas and some Vaiṣhṇavas use the term Shūnya, and no one suspects them of being 'Nihilists'.

Relatively, however, the One is said to be Being (Sat), Bliss (Ānanda) and Chit—an untranslatable term which has been most accurately defined as the Changeless Principle of all changing experience, a Principle of which sensation, perception, conception, self-consciousness, feeling, memory, will and all other psychic states are limited *modes*. It is not therefore Consciousness or Feeling as we understand these words, for these are directed and limited. It is the infinite root of which they are the finite flower. But consciousness and possibly (according to the more ancient views) Feeling approach the most nearly to a definition, provided that we do not understand thereby Consciousness and Feeling in man's sense. We may thus (to distinguish it) call Chit, Pure Consciousness or Pure Feeling as Bliss (Ānanda) knowing and enjoying its own full Reality. This, as such Pure Consciousness or Feeling, endures even when finite centres of Consciousness or Feeling arise in It. If (as this system assumes) there is a real causal nexus between the two, then Being, as Shiva, is also a Power, or Shakti, which is the source of all Becoming. The fully Real, therefore, has two aspects: one called Shiva, the static aspect of Consciousness, and the other called Shakti, the kinetic aspect of the same. For this reason Kālī Shakti, dark as a thundercloud, is represented standing and moving on the white inert body of Shiva. He is white as Illumination (Prakāsha). He is inert, for Pure Consciousness is without action and at rest. It is She, His Power, who moves. Dark is. She here because, as Kālī, She dissolves all in darkness, that is vacuity of existence, which is the Light of Being Itself. Again She is Creatrix. Five corpse-like Shivas form the support of Her throne, set in the wish-granting groves of the Isle of Gems (Maṇidvīpa), the golden sands of which are laved by the still waters of the Ocean of Nectar (Amṛita), which is Immortality. In both cases we have a pictorial presentment in theological form of the scientific doctrine that to every form of activity there is a static background.

But until there is in fact Change, Shakti is merely the Potency of Becoming in Being and, as such, is wholly one with it. The Power (Shakti) and the possessor of Power (Shaktimān) are one. As therefore He is Being-Bliss-Consciousness, so is She. She also is the Full (Pūrṇa), which is no mere abstraction from its evolved manifestations. On the contrary, of Her the *Mahākālī Stotra* says: "Though without feet, Thou movest more quickly than air. Though without ears, Thou dost hear. Though without nostrils, Thou dost smell. Though without eyes, Thou dost see. Though without tongue, Thou dost taste all tastes." Those who talk of the 'bloodless abstractions' of Vedānta, have not understood it. The ground of Man's Being is the Supreme 'I' (Pūrṇōham) which, though in Itself beyond finite personality, is yet ever finitely personalizing as the beings of the universe. "Sāham,"—"She I am."

This is the Supreme Shakti, the ultimate object of the Shāktas' adoration, though worshipped in several forms, some gentle, some formidable.

But Potency is actualized as the universe, and this also is Shakti, for the effect is the cause modified. Monistic Vedānta teaches that God is the material cause of the world. The statement that the Supreme Shakti also exists as the Forms evolved from It, may seem to conflict with the doctrine that Power is ultimately one with Shiva who is changeless Being. Shaṅkara answers that the existence of a causal nexus is Māyā, and that there is (from the transcendental standpoint) only a seeming cause and seeming modification or effect. The Shākta, who from his world-standpoint posits the reality of God as the Cause of the universe, replies that, while it is true that the effect (as effect) is the cause modified, the cause (as cause) remains what it was and is and will be. Creative evolution of the universe thus differs from the evolution in it. In the latter case the material cause when producing an effect ceases to be what it was. Thus milk turned into curd ceases to be milk. But the simile given of the other evolutionary process is that of 'Light from Light'. There is a similarity between the 'conventional' standpoint of Shaṅkara and the explanation of the Shākta; the difference being that, whilst to the former the effect is (from the transcendental standpoint) 'unreal', it is (from the Shākta's immanent standpoint) 'real'.

It will have been observed that cosmic evolution is in the nature of a polarization in Being into static and kinetic aspects. This is symbolized in the Shākta Tantras by their comparison of Shiva-Shakti to a grain of gram (Chanaka). This has two seeds which are so close together as to seem one, and which are surrounded by a single sheath. The seeds are Shiva and Shakti and the sheath is Māyā. When the sheath is unpeeled, that is when Māyā Shakti operates, the two seeds come apart. The sheath unrolls when the seeds are ready to germinate, that is when in the dreamless slumber (Sushupti) of the World-Consciousness the remembrance of past enjoyment in Form gives rise to that divine creative 'thinking' or 'imagining' (Sṛishṭikalpanā) which is 'creation'. As the universe in dissolution sinks into a Memory which is lost, so it is born again from the germ of recalled Memory or Shakti. Why? Such a question may be answered when we are dealing with facts in the whole; but the latter itself is uncaused, and what is caused is not the whole. Manifestation is of the nature of Being-Power, just as it is Its nature to return to Itself after the actualization of Power. To the devotee who speaks in theological language, "It is His Will." As the *Yoginīhṛidaya* says: "He painted the World-picture on Himself with the Brush which is His Will and was pleased therewith."

Again the World is called a Prapañcha, that is an *extension* of the five forms of sensible matter (Bhūta). Where does it go at dissolution? It collapses into a Point (Bindu). We may regard it as a metaphysical point which is the complete 'subjectification' of the divine or full 'I' (Pūrṇāhantā), or objectively as a mathematical point without magnitude. Round that Point is coiled a mathematical Line which, being in touch with every part of the surface of the Point, makes one Point with it. What then is meant by these symbols of the Point and Line? It is said that the Supreme Shiva sees Himself in and as His own Power or Shakti. He is the 'White Point' or 'Moon' (Chandra), which is Illumination and in the completed process, the 'I' (Aham) side of experience, She is the 'Red Point'. Both colours are seen in the microcosmic generation of the child. Red too is the colour of Desire. She is 'Fire' which is the object of experience or 'This' (Idam), the objective side of experience. The 'This' here is nothing but a mass of Shiva's own illuminating rays. These are reflected in Himself as Shakti, who, in the *Kāmakalāvilāsa*, is called the 'Pure Mirror' of Shiva. The Self sees the Self, the rays being thrown back on their source. The 'This' is the germ of what we call 'Otherness,' but here the 'Other' is and is known as the Self. The relation and fusion of these two Points, White and Red, is called the Mixed Point or 'Sun'. These are the three Supreme Lights. A = Shiva, Ha = Shakti, which united spell 'Aham' or 'I'. This 'Sun' is thus the state of full 'I-ness' (Pūrṇāham-bhāva). This is the Point into which the World at dissolution lapses, and from which in due time it comes forth again. In the latter case it is the Lord-Consciousness as the Supreme 'I' and Power about to create. For this reason Bindu is called a condensed or massive form of Shakti. It is the tense state of Power immediately prior to its first actualization. That form of Shakti, again, by which the actualization takes place is Māyā; and this is the Line round the Point. As coiled round the Point, it is the Supreme Serpent-Power

(Mahākuṇḍalinī) encircling the Shiva-Liṅga. From out this Power comes the whisper to enjoy, in worlds of form, as the memory of past universes arises therein. Shakti then 'sees'. Shakti opens Her eyes as She reawakes from the Cosmic Sleep (Nimeṣha), which is dissolution. The Line is at first coiled and one with the Point, for Power is then at rest. Creation is movement, an uncoiling of Māyā-Shakti. Hence is the world called Jagat, which means 'what moves'. The nature of this Power is circular or spiraline; hence the roundness and 'curvature' of things of which we now hear. Nothing moves in a really straight line. Hence again the universe is also called a spheroid (Brahmāṇḍa). The gross worlds are circular universal movements in space, in which, is the Ether (Ākāsha), Consciousness, as the Full (Pūrṇa), is never dichotomized, but the finite centres which arise *in* it, are so. The Point, or Bindu, then divides into three, in various ways, the chief of which is Knower, Knowing and Known, which constitute the duality of the world-experience by Mind of Matter.

Unsurpassed for its profound analysis is the account of the thirty-six Tattvas or stages of Cosmic Evolution (accepted by both Shaivas and Shāktas) given by the Northern Shaiva School of the Āgama, which flourished after the date which Western Orientalists assign to Shaṅkarāchārya, and which was therefore in a position to criticize him. According to this account (which I greatly condense) Subject and Object in Pure Being are in undistinguishable union as the Supreme Shiva-Shakti. We have then to see how this unity is broken up into Subject and object. This does not take place all at once. There is an intermediate stage of transition, in which there is a Subject *and* Object, but both are part of the Self, which knows its Object to be Itself. In man's experience they are wholly separate, the Object then being perceived as outside the Self, the plurality of Selves being mutually exclusive centres. The process and the result are the work of Shakti, whose special function is to negate, that is to negate Her own fullness, so that it becomes the finite centre contracted as a limited Subject perceiving a limited Object, both being aspects of the one Divine Self.

The first stage after the Supreme is that in which Shakti withdraws Herself and leaves, as it were, standing by itself the 'I' side (Aham) of what, when completed, is the 'I-This' (Aham-Idam) experience. But simultaneously (for the 'I' must have its content) She presents Herself as a 'This' (Idam), at first faintly and then clearly; the emphasis being at first laid on the 'I' and then on the 'This'. This last is the stage of Īshvara Tattva or Bindu, as the Mantra Shāstra, dealing with the causal state of 'Sound' (Shabda), calls it. In the second and third stage, as also in the fourth which follows, though there is an 'I' *and* a 'This' and therefore not the undistinguishable 'I-This' of the Supreme Experience, yet both the 'I' and the 'This' are experienced as aspects of and in the Self. Then as a preliminary to the division which follows, the emphasis is laid equally on the 'I' and the 'This'. At this point Māyā-Shakti intervenes and completely separates the two. For that Power is the Sense of Difference (Bheda-Buddhi). We have now the finite centres mutually exclusive one of the other, each seeing, to the extent of its power, finite centres as objects outside of and different from the self. Consciousness thus becomes *contracted.* In lieu of being All-knowing, it is a 'Little Knower', and in lieu of being Almighty Power, it is a 'Little Doer'.

Māyā is not rightly rendered 'Illusion'. In the first place it is conceived as a real Power of Being and as such is one with the Full Reality. The Full, free of all illusion, experiences the engendering of the finite centres and the centres themselves in and as Its own changeless partless Self. It is these individual centres produced from out of Power as Māyā-Shakti which are 'Ignorance' or Avidyā Shakti. They are so called because they are not a full experience but an experience of parts in the Whole. In another sense this 'Ignorance' is a knowing, namely, that which a finite centre alone has. Even God cannot have man's mode of knowledge and enjoyment without becoming man. He by and as His Power does become man and yet remains Himself. Man is Power in limited form as Avidyā. The Lord is unlimited Power as Māyā. In whom then is the 'Illusion'? Not (all will admit) in the Lord. Nor is it in fact (whatever be the talk of it) in man whose nature it is to regard his limitations as real. For these limitations are he. His experience as man provides no standard whereby it may be adjudged 'Illusion'. The latter is non-conformity with normal experience, and here it is the normal experience which is said to be Illusion. If there were no Avidyā Shakti, there would be no man. In short the knowing which is Full Experience is one thing and the knowing of the limited experience is another. The latter is Avidyā and the Power to produce it is Māyā. Both are eternal aspects of Reality, though the forms which are Avidyā Shakti come and go. If we seek to relate the one to the other, where and by whom is the comparison made? Not in and by the Full Experience beyond all relations, where no questions are asked or answers given, but on the standing ground of present finite experience where all subjectivity and objectivity are real and where therefore, *ipso facto*, Illusion is negatived. The two aspects are never present at one and the same time for comparsion. The universe is real as a limited thing to the limited experiencer who is himself a part of it.

But the experience of the Supreme Person (Parāhantā) is necessarily different, otherwise it would not be the Supreme Experience at all. A God who experiences just as man does is no God but man. There is, therefore, no experiencer to whom the World is Illusion. He who sees the world in the normal waking state, loses it in that form in ecstasy (Samādhi). It may, however, (with the Shākta) be said that the Supreme Experience is entire and unchanging and thus the fully Real; and that, though the limited experience is also real in its own way, it is yet an experience of change in its twin aspects of Time and Space. Māyā, therefore, is the Power which engenders in Itself finite centres in Time and Space, and Avidyā is such experience in fact of the finite experiencer in Time and Space. So much is this so, that the Time-theorists (Kālavādins) give the name 'Supreme Time' (Parakāla) to the Creator, who is also called by the Shākta 'Great Time' (Mahākāla). So in the *Bhairavayāmala* it is said that Mahādeva (Shiva) distributes His Rays of Power in the form of the Year. That is, Timeless Experience appears in the finite centres as broken up into periods of time. This is the 'Lesser Time' which comes in with the Sun, Moon, Six Seasons and so forth, which are all Shaktis of the Lord, the existence and movements of which give rise in the limited observer, to the notion of Time and Space.

That observer is essentially the Self or 'Spirit' vehicled by Its own Shakti in the form of Mind and Matter. These two are Its Body, the first subtle, the second gross. Both have a common origin, namely the Supreme Power. Each is a real mode of It. One therefore does not produce the other. Both are produced by, and exist as modes of, the same Cause. There is a necessary parallelism between the Perceived and the Perceiver and, because Mind and Matter are at base one as modes of the same Power, one can act on the other, Mind is the subjective and Matter the objective aspect of the one polarized Consciousness.

With the unimportant exception of the Lokāyatas, the Hindus have never shared what Sir William Jones called 'the vulgar notions of matter,' according to which it is regarded as some gross, lasting and independently existing outside thing.

Modern Western Science now also dematerializes the ponderable matter of the universe into Energy. This and the forms in which it is displayed is the Power of the Self to appear as the object of a limited centre of knowing. Mind again is the Self as 'Consciousness', limited by Its Power into such a centre. By such contraction there is in lieu of an 'All-knower' a 'Little Knower,' and in lieu of an 'All-doer' a 'Little Doer'. Those, however, to whom this way of looking at things is naturally difficult, may regard the Supreme Shakti from the objective aspect as holding within Itself the germ of all Matter which develops in It.

Both Mind and Matter exist in every particle of the universe though not explicitly displayed in the same way in all. There is no corner of the universe which contains anything either potential or actual, which is not to be found elsewhere. Some aspect of Matter or Mind, however, may be more or less explicit or implicit. So in the Mantra Scripture it is said that each letter of the alphabet contains all sound. The sound of a particular letter is explicit and the other sounds are implicit. The sound of a particular letter is a particular physical audible mode of the Shabdabrahman (Brahman as the cause of Shabda or 'Sound'), in Whom is all sound, actual and potential. Pure Consciousness is fully involved in the densest forms of gross or organic matter, which is not 'inert' but full of movement (Spanda), for there is naught but the Supreme Consciousness which does not move. Immanent in Mind and Matter is

Consciousness (Chit Shakti). Inorganic matter is thus Consciousness in full subjection to the Power of Ignorance. It is thus Consciousness identifying Itself with such inorganic matter. Matter in all its five forms of density is present in everything. Mind too is there, though owing to its imprisonment in Matter, undeveloped. "The Brahman sleeps in the stone." Life too which displays itself with the organization of matter is potentially contained in Being, of which such inorganic matter is, to some, a 'lifeless' form. From this deeply involved state Shakti enters into higher and higher organized forms. Prāṇa or vitality is a Shakti—the Mantra form of which is 'Hangsaḥ'. With the Mantra 'Hang' the breath goes forth, with 'Saḥ' it is indrawn, a fact which anyone can verify for himself if he will attempt to inspire after putting the mouth in the way it is placed in order to pronounce the letter 'H'. The Rhythm of Creative Power as of breathing (a microcosmic form of it) is two-fold—an outgoing (Pravṛitti) or involution as universe, and an evolution or return (Nivṛitti) of Supreme Power to Itself. Shakti as the Great Heart of the universe pulses forth and back in cosmic systole and diastole. So much for the nature of the Power as an Evolutionary process. It is displayed in the Forms evolved as an increasing exhibition of Consciousness from apparently, though not truly, unconscious matter, through the slight consciousness of the plant and the greater consciousness of the animal, to the more highly developed consciousness of man, who in the completeness of his own individual evolution becomes freed of Mind and Matter which constitute the Form, and thus is one with the Supreme Consciousness Itself. There are no gaps in the process. In existence there are no rigid partitions. The vital phenomena, to which we give the name of 'Life,' appear it is true with organized Matter. But Life is not then something entirely new which had no sort of being before. For such Life is only a limited mode of Being, which itself is no dead thing but the Infinite Life of all lives. To the Hindu the difference between plant and animal, and between the latter and man, has always been one rather of degree than of kind. There is one Consciousness and one Mind and Matter throughout, though the Matter is organized and the Mind is exhibited in various ways. The one Shakti is the Self as the 'String' (Sūtrātmā) on which all the Beads of Form are strung, and these Beads again are limited modes of Herself as the 'String'. Evolution is thus the loosening of the bonds in which Consciousness (itself unchanging) is held, such loosening being increased and Consciousness more fully exhibited as the process is carried forward. At length is gained that human state which the Scripture calls so 'hard to get'. For it has been won by much striving and through suffering. Therefore the Scripture warns man not to neglect the opportunities of a stage which is the necessary preliminary to the attainment of the Full Experience. Man by his striving must seek to become fully humane, and then to pass yet further into the Divine Fulness which is beyond all Forms with their good and evil. This is the work of Sādhanā (a word which comes from the root '*sādh*' 'to exert'), which is discipline, ritual worship and Yoga. It is that by which any result (Siddhi) is attained. The Tāntrik Shāstra is a Sādhanā Scripture. As Powers are many, so may be Sādhanā, which is of various kinds and degrees. Man may seek to realize the Mother-Power in Her limited forms as health, strength, long life, wealth, magic powers and so forth. The so-called 'New Thought' and kindred literature which bids men to think Power and thus to become power, is very ancient, going back at least to the Upaniṣhad which says: "What a man thinks, that he becomes."

Those who have need for the Infinite Mother as She is not in any Form but in Herself, seek directly the Adorable One in whom is the essence of all which is of finite worth. The gist of a high form of Kūlasādhanā is given in the following verse from the Hymn of Mahākālarudra Himself to Mahākālī:

"*I torture not my body with penances.*" (Is not his body Hers? If man be God in human guise why torment him?) "*I lame not my feet in pilgrimage to Holy Places.*" (The body is the Devālaya or Temple of Divinity. Therein are all the spiritual Tīrthas or Holy Places. Why then trouble to go elsewhere?) "*I spend not my time in reading the Vedas.*" (The Vedas, which he has already studied, are the record of the standard spiritual experience of others. He seeks now to have that experience himself directly. What is the use of merely reading about it? The *Kulārṇava Tantra* enjoins the mastering of the essence of all Scriptures which should then be put aside, just as he who has threshed out the grain throws away the husks and straw.) "*But I strive to attain Thy two sacred Feet.*"

CHAPTER III

WHAT ARE THE TANTRAS AND THEIR SIGNIFICANCE?

A VERY common expression in English writings is "The Tantra"; but its use is often due to a misconception and leads to others. For what does Tantra mean? The word denotes injunction (Vidhi), regulation (Niyama), Shāstra generally or treatise. Thus Shaṅkara calls the Sāṅkhya a Tantra. A secular writing may be called Tantra. For the following note I am indebted to Professor Surendranath Das Gupta. "The word 'Tantra' has been derived in the Kāshikā-Vṛitti (7-2-9) from the root 'Tan' 'to Spread' by the Auṇādika rule Sarvadhātubhyaḥ tran, with the addition of the suffix 'tran'. Vāchaspati, Ānandagiri, and Govindānanda, however, derive the word from the root 'Tatri' or 'Tantri' in the sense of Vyutpādana, origination or knowledge. In Gaṇapātha, however, 'Tantri' has the same meaning as 'Tan' 'to Spread' and it is probable that the former root is a modification of the latter. The meaning Vyutpādana is also probably derived by narrowing the general sense of Vistāra which is the meaning of the root 'Tan'."

According to the derivation of 'Tantra' from *Tan* to spread, Tantra is that (Scripture) by which knowledge (Jñāna) is spread (Tanyate, vistāryate jñānam anena, iti Tantram). The suffix *Tra* is from the root "to save". That knowledge is spread which saves. What is that but religious knowledge? Therefore, as here and generally used, Tantra means a particular kind of religious scripture. The Kāmika Āgama of the Shaiva Siddhānta (Tantrāntara Paṭala) says:

Tanoti vipulān arthān tattvamantra-samanvitān
Trānancha kurute yasmāt tantram ityabhidhīyate.

(It is called Tantra because it promulgates great knowledge concerning Tattva and Mantra and because it saves).

It is a common misconception that Tantra is the name only of the Scripture of the Shāktas or worshippers of Shakti. This is not so. There are Tantras of other sects of the Āgama, Tantras of Shaivas, Vaiṣhṇavas and so forth. We cannot speak of "The Treatise" nor of "The Tantra" any more than we can or do speak of the Purāṇa, the Saṁhitā. We can speak of "the Tantras" as we do of "the Purāṇas". These Tantras are Shāstras of what is called the Āgama. In a review of one of my works it was suggested that the Āgama is a class of Scriptures dealing with the worship of Saguṇa Īshvara which was revealed at the close of the age of the Upaniṣhads, and introduced partly because of the falling into desuetude of the Vaidika Āchāra, and partly because of the increasing numbers of persons entering the Hindu fold who were not competent (Adhikārī) for that Āchāra. I will not however deal with this historical question beyond noting the fact that the Āgama is open to all persons of all castes and both sexes, and is not subject to the restrictions of the Vaidika Āchāra. This last term is a common one and comes from the verbal root *char*, which means to move or to act, the prefix *Ā* being probably used in the sense of restriction. Āchāra thus means practice, way, rule of life governing a Sādhaka, or one who does Sādhanā or practice for some desired end (Siddhi).

The Āgamas are divided into three main groups according as the Ishṭadevatā worshipped is Shakti, Shiva or Vishṇu. The first is the Shākta Āgama, the second the Shaivāgama, and the third the Vaishṇava Āgama or Pañcharātra. This last is the Scripture to which the Shrīmad Bhāgavata (X. 90. 34) refers as Sāttvata Tantra in the lines,

Tenoktang sāttvatang tantram yaj jnāttvā muktibhāg bhavet
Yatra strīshūdradāsānāng sangskāro vaishṇavah smṛitah.

Some Āgamas are called Vaidik (Vaidika Āgama) and some non-Vaidik (Avaidika). The Kūrma Purāṇa (XVI. 1) mentions as belonging to the latter, Kapāla, Lākula, Vāma, Bhairava, Pūrva, Pashchima, Pañcharātra, Pāshupata and many others. Pāshupta again is said to be both Vaidika and Avaidika such as Lākula. Kūrma Purāṇa (Uttarabhāga, Ch. 38) says "By Me was first composed, for the attainment of Liberation, Shrauta (Vaidika) Pāshupata which is excellent, subtle, and secret, the essence of Veda (Vedasāra). The learned devoted to Veda should meditate on Shiva Pashupati. This is Pāshupata Yoga to be practised by seekers of Liberation. By Me also have been spoken Pāshupata, Soma, Lākula and Bhairava opposed to Veda (Vedavādaviruddhāni). These should not be practised. They are outside Veda." Sanatkumāra Saṁhitā says :

Shrautāshrautavibhedena dvividhastu shivāgamaḥ
Shrutisāramayah shrautah sah punar dvividho mataḥ
Svatantra itarash cheti svatantro dashadhā purā
Tathā'shṭadashadhā pashchāt siddhānta iti gīyate
Itaraḥ shrutisāras tu shatakoṭi-pravistaraḥ.

(See also Vāyu Saṁhitā, Ch. I. 28).

[Shaivāgama is of two kinds, Shrauta and Ashrauta. Shrauta is Shrutisāramaya, and of two kinds, Svatantra and Itara. Svatantra is first of ten kinds and then Siddhānta of eighteen kinds. (This is the Shaivasiddhānta

Āgama with 28 Mūla Āgamas and 207 Upāgamas. It is Shuddhādvaita because in it there is no Visheshaṇa.) Itara is Shrutisāra with numerous varieties.] Into this mass of sects I do not attempt to here enter, except in a general way. My subject is the doctrine and ritual of the Shāktas. There are said to be Shaiva, Vaishṇava, and Shākta Upanishads favouring one or another doctrine.

We must, however, in all cases distinguish between what a School says of itself and what others say of it. So far as I am aware all Āgamas, whatever be their origin, *claim* now to be based on Shruti, though of course as different interpretations are put on Shruti, those who accept one interpretation are apt to speak of differing Schools as heretical. These main divisions again have subdivisions. Thus there are several Schools of Shaivas; and there are Shāktas with their nine Āmnāyas, four Sampradāyas (Kerala, Kashmīra, Gauda and Vilāsa) each divided into two-fold division of inner and outer worship (Sammohana Tantra, Ch. V). There is for instance the Northern Shaiva School called Trika of Kashmir, in which country at one time Tantra Shāstras were very prevalent. There is again the Southern Shaiva School called Shaivasiddhānta. The Shāktas who are to be found throughout India are largely prevalent in Bengal and Assam. The Shāktas are rather allied with the Northern Advaita Shaiva than with the others, though in them also there is worship of Shakti. Shiva and Shakti are one and he who worships one necessarily worships the other. But whereas the Shaiva predominantly worships Shiva, the Shākta predominantly worships the Shakti side of the Ardhanārīshvara Mūrti, which is both Shiva and Shakti.

Mahāvishṇu and Sadāshiva are also one. As the Sammohana Tāntra (Ch. VIII) says "Without Prakṛiti the Saṁsāra (World) cannot be. Without Purusha true knowledge cannot be attained. Therefore should both be worshipped; with Mahākālī, Mahākāla." Some, it says, speak of Shiva, some of Shakti, some of Nārāyaṇa (Vishṇu). But the supreme Nārāyaṇa (Ādinārāyaṇa) is supreme Shiva (Parashambhu), the Nirguṇa Brahman pure as crystal. The two aspects of the Supreme reflect the one in the other. The Reflection (Pratibimba) is Māyā whence the World-Lords (Lokapālas) and the Worlds are born. The Ādyā Lalitā (Mahāshakti) at one time assumed the male form of Kṛishṇa and at another that of Rāma (Ch. IX). For all aspects are in Mahākālī, one with Bhairava Mahākāla, Who is Mahāvishṇu. "It is only a fool" it says, "who sees any difference between Rāma and Shiva." This is of course to look at the matter from the high Vedantik standpoint of Shākta doctrine. Nevertheless separate worship and rituals exist among the Sects. A common philosophical basis of the Shaivas and those of Shāktas, who are Āgamavādins, is the doctrine of the Thirty-six Tattvas. These are referred to in the Tantra (Ch. VII) so well known in Bengal which is called Kulārṇava. They are also referred to in other Shākta works and their commentaries such as the Ānandalaharī. The Shāradā Tilaka, a great authority amongst the Bengal Shāktas, is the work of Lakshmaṇāchārya, an author of the Kashmir Shaiva school. The latter school as also the Shāktas are Advaitins. The Shaiva Siddhānta and Pañcharātra are Shuddhādvaita and Vishishtādvaita respectively. There is also a great body of Buddhist Tantras of differing schools. [I have published one—the Srīchakra Sambhara Tantra as Vol. VII of Tāntrik Texts.] Now all these schools have Tantras of their own. The original connection of the Shaiva schools is said to be shown amongst other things, by the fact that some Tantras are common, such as Mṛigendra and Mātaṅga Tantras. It has been asserted that the Shākta school is not historically connected with the Shaivas. No grounds were given for this statement. Whatever be the historical origins of the former, the two appear to be in several respects allied at present, as any one who knows Shākta literature may find out for himself. In fact Shākta literature is in parts unintelligible to one unacquainted with some features of what is called the Shaiva Darshana. How otherwise is it that the 36 Tattvas and Ṣhaḍadhvā [see my "Garland of Letters"] are common to both?

The Shāktas have again been divided into three groups. Thus the esteemed Pandit R. Ananta Shāstri in the Introduction to his edition of Ānandalaharī speaks of the Kaula or Shākta Shāstras with sixty-four Tantras; the Mishra with eight Tantras; and the Samaya group which are said to be the most important of the Shākta Āgamas, of which five are mentioned. This classification purports to be based on the nature of the object pursued, according as it belongs to one or other of the Puruṣhārthas. Pancharātra literature is very considerable, one hundred and eight works being mentioned by the same Pandit in Vol. XIII, pp. 357-363 of the "Theosophist". I would refer the reader also to the very valuable edition of the Ahirbudhnya Samhitā by my friend Dr. Otto Schrader, with an Introduction by the learned Doctor on the Pancharātra system where many Vaiṣhṇava Tantras and Saṁhitās are cited. The Trika school has many Tantras of which the leading one is Mālinīvijaya. The Svachchhanda Tantra comes next. Jagadīsha Chandra Chattopādhyāya Vidyāvāridhi has written with learning and lucidity on this school. The Shaivasiddhānta has twenty-eight leading Tantras and a large number of Upāgamas, such as Tāraka Tantra, Vāma Tantra and others, which will be found enumerated in Schomerus' "Der Shaivasiddhānta", Nallasvami Pillai's "Studies in Shaivasiddhānta" (p. 294), and "Sivajñānasiddhiyar"

(p. 211). The Sammohana Tantra (Ch. VI) mentions 64 Tantras, 327 Upatantras, as also Yāmalas, Ḍāmaras, Saṁhitās and other Scriptures of the Shākta class; 32 Tantras, 125 Upatantras, as also Yāmalas, Ḍāmaras, Purāṇas and other Scriptures of the Shaiva class; 75 Tantras 205 Upatantras, as also Yāmalas, Ḍāmaras, Saṁhitās of the Vaiṣhṇava class; numerous Tantras and other scriptures of the Gāṇapatya and Saura classes, and a number of Purāṇas, Upapurāṇas and other variously named Scriptures of the Bauddha class. It then (Ch. VII) mentions over 500 Tantras and nearly the same amount of Upatantras, of some 22 Āgamas, Chīnāgama (see Ch. VI *post*), Buddhāgama, Jaina, Pāshupata, Kāpālika Pancharātra, Bhairava and others. There is thus a vast mass of Tantras in the Āgamas belonging to differing schools of doctrine and practice, all of which must be studied before we can speak with certainty as to what the mighty Āgama as a whole is. In this book I briefly deal with one section of it only. Nevertheless when these Āgamas have been examined and are better known, it will, I think, be found that they are largely variant aspects of the same general ideas and practices.

As instances of general ideas I may cite the following: the conception of Deity as a supreme Personality (Parāhantā) and of the double aspect of God in one of which He really is or becomes the Universe; a true emanation from Him in His creative aspect; successive emanations (Ābhāsa, Vyūha) as of "fire from fire" from subtle to gross; doctrine of Shakti; pure and impure creation; the denial of unconscious Māyā such as Shaṅkara teaches; doctrine of Māyā Koṣha and the Kanchukas (the six Shaiva Kanchukas being, as Dr. Schrader says, represented by the possibly earlier classification in the Pancharātra of the three Saṅkochas); the carrying of the origin of things up and beyond Purusha-Prakriti; acceptance at a later stage of Purusha-Prakriti, the Sānkhyān Guṇas, and evolution of Tattvas as applied to the doctrine of Shakti; affirmance of the reality of the Universe; emphasis on devotion (Bhakti); provision for all castes and both sexes.

Instances of common practice are for example Mantra, Bīja, Yantra, Mudrā, Nyāsa, Bhūtashuddhi, Kuṇḍalīyoga, construction and consecration of temples and images (Kriyā), religious and social observances (Charyā) such as Āhnika, Varṇāshramadharma, Utsava; and practical magic (Māyā-yoga). Where there is Mantra, Yantra, Nyāsa, Dīkṣhā, Guru and the like, there is Tantra Shāstra. In fact one of the names of the latter is Mantra Shāstra. With these similarities there are certain variations of doctrine and practice between the schools. Necessarily also, even on points of common similarity, there is some variance in terminology and exposition which is unessential. Thus when looking at their broad features, it is of no account whether with the Pancharātra we speak of Lakṣhmī Shakti, Vyūha, Saṅkocha; or whether in terms of other schools we speak of Tripurasundarī and Mahākālī, Tattvas and Kanchukas. Again there are some differences in ritual which are not of great moment except in one and that a notable instance. I refer to the well-known division of worshippers into Dakṣhiṇāchāra and Vāmāchāra. The secret Sādhanā of some of the latter (which I may here say is not usually understood) has acquired such notoriety that to most the term "The Tantra" connotes this particular worship and its abuses and nothing else. I may here also observe that it is a mistake to suppose that aberrations in doctrine and practice are peculiar to India. A Missionary wrote to me some years ago that this country was "a demon-haunted land". There are demons here, but they are not the only inhabitants; and tendencies to be found here have existed elsewhere. The West has produced many a doctrine and practice of an antinomian character. Some of the most extreme are to be found there. Moreover, though this does not seem to be recognized, it is nevertheless the fact that these Kaula rites are philosophically based on monistic doctrine. Now it is this Kaula doctrine and practice, limited probably, as being a secret doctrine, at all times to comparatively few, which has come to be known as "The Tantra". Nothing is more incorrect. This is but one division of worshippers who again are but one section of the numerous followers of the Āgamas, Shaiva, Shākta and Vaiṣhṇava. Though there are certain common features which may be called Tāntrik yet one cannot speak of "The Tantra" as though it were one entirely homogeneous doctrine and practice. Still less can we identify it with the particular practices and theories of one division of worshippers only. Further the Tantras are concerned with Science, Law, Medicine and a variety of subjects other than spiritual doctrine or worship. Thus Indian chemistry and medicine is largely indebted to the Tāntrikas.

According to a common notion the word "Tantra" is (to use the language of a well-known work) "restricted to the necromantic books of the latter Shivāic or Sakti mysticism" (Waddell's "Buddhism of Tibet," p. 164). As charity covers many sins, so "mystic" and "mysticism" are words which cover much ignorance. "Necromancy" too looms unnecessarily large in writers of this school. It is, however, the fact that Western authors generally so understand the term "Tantra". They are, however, in error in so doing as previously explained. Here I shortly deal with the significance of the Tantra Shāstra, which is of course also misunderstood, being generally spoken of as a jumble of "black magic," and "erotic mysticism," cemented together by a ritual which is "meaningless mummery". A large number of persons who talk in this strain have never had a Tantra in their hands, and such Orientalists as have read some portions of these Scriptures have not generally understood them, otherwise they would not have found them to be so "meaningless". They may be bad, or they may be good, but they have a meaning. Men are not such fools as to believe for ages in what is meaningless. The use of this term implies that their content had no meaning to them. Very likely; for to define as they do Mantra as "mystical words," Mudrā as "mystical gestures" and Yantra as "mystical diagrams" does not imply knowledge. These erroneous notions as to the nature of the Āgama are of course due to the mistaken identification of the whole body of the Scripture with one section of it. Further this last is only known through the abuses to which its dangerous practices as carried out by inferior persons have given rise. It is stated in the Shāstra itself in which they are prescribed that the path is full of difficulty and peril and he who fails upon it goes to Hell. That there are those who have so failed, and others who have been guilty of evil magic, is well-known. I am not in this Chapter concerned with this special ritual or magic but with the practices which govern the life of the vast mass of the Indian people to be found in the Tantras of the Āgamas of the different schools which I have mentioned.

A Western writer in a review of one of my books has expressed the opinion that the Tantra Shāstra (I think he meant the Shākta) was, at least in its origin, alien and indeed hostile to the Veda. He said "We are strongly of opinion that in their essence the two principles are fundamentally opposed and that the Tantra only used Vedic forms to mask its essential opposition." I will not discuss this question here. It is, however, the fact now, as it has been for centuries past, that the Āgamavādins claim to base their doctrine on Veda. The Vedānta is the final authority and basis for the doctrines set forth in the Tantras, though the latter interpret the Vedānta in various ways. The real meaning of Vedānta is Upaniṣhad and nothing else. Many persons, however, speak of Vedānta as though it meant the philosophy of Shaṅkara or whatever other philosopher they follow. This of course is incorrect. Vedānta is Shruti. Shaṅkara's philosophy is merely one interpretation of Shruti just as Rāmānuja's is another and that of the Shaivāgama or Kaulāgama is a third. There is no question of competition between Vedānta as Shruti and Tantra Shāstra. It is, however, the fact that each of the followers of the different schools of Āgama contend that their interpretation of the Shruti texts is the true one and superior to that of other schools. As a stranger to all these sects, I am not here concerned to show that one system is better than the other. Each will adopt that which most suits him. I am only stating the facts. As the Ahirbudhnya Saṁhitā of the Pancharātra Āgama says, the aspects of God are infinite, and no philosopher can seize and duly express more than one aspect. This is perfectly true. All systems of interpretation have some merits as they have defects, that of Shaṅkara included. The latter by his Māyāvāda is able to preserve more completely than any other interpretation the changelessness and stainlessness of Brahman. It does this, however, at the cost of certain defects, which do not exist in other schools, which have also their own peculiar merits and shortcomings. The basis and seat of authority is Shruti or experience and the Āgama interprets Shruti in its own way. Thus the Shaiva-Shākta doctrines are specific solutions of the Vedāntic theme which differ in several respects from that of Shaṅkara, though as they agree (I speak of the Northern Shaiva School) with him on the fundamental question of the unity of Jīvātmā and Paramātmā, they are therefore Advaita.

The next question is how the experience of which the Āgama speaks may be gained? This is also prescribed in the Shāstra in the form of peculiar Sādhanās or disciplines. In the first place there must be a healthy physical and moral life. To know a thing in its ultimate sense is to *be* that thing. To know Brahman, is according to Advaita, to *be* Brahman. One cannot realize Brahman the Pure except by being oneself pure (Shuddachitta). But to attain and keep this state, as well as progress therein, certain specific means, practice, rituals or disciplines are necessary. The result cannot be got by mere philosophical talk about Brahman. Religion is a practical activity. Just as the body requires exercise, training and gymnastic, so does the mind. This may be of a merely intellectual or spiritual kind. The means employed are called Sādhanā which comes from the root "*Sādh,*" to exert. Sādhanā is that which leads to Siddhi. Sādhanā is the development of Shakti. Man is Consciousness (Ātmā) vehicled by Shakti in the form of mind and body. But this Shakti is at base Pure Consciousness, just as Ātmā is; for Ātmā and Shakti are one. Man is thus a vast magazine of both latent and expressed power. The object of Sādhanā is to develop man's Shakti, whether for temporal or spiritual purposes. But where is Sādhanā to be found? Seeing that the Vaidika Āchāra has fallen in practical desuetude we can find it nowhere but in the Āgamas and in the Purāṇas which are replete with Tāntrik rituals. The Tantras of these Āgamas therefore contain both a *practical* exposition of spiritual doctrine and the means by which the truth it teaches may be *realized.* Their authority does not depend, as Western writers, and some of their Eastern followers, suppose on the date when they were revealed but on the question whether Siddhi is gained thereby. This too is the proof of Āyurveda. The test of medicine is that it cures. If Siddhi is not obtained, the fact that it is written "Shiva uvācha" (Shiva speaks) or the like counts for nothing. The Āgama therefore is a *practical* exposition and application of Doctrine varying according to its different schools.

The latest tendency in modern Western philosophy is to rest upon intuition, as it was formerly the tendency to glorify dialectic. Intuition has, however, to be led into higher and higher possibilities by means of Sādhanā. This term means work or practice, which in its result is the gradual unfolding of the Spirit's vast latent magazine of power (Shakti), enjoyment and vision which everyone possesses in himself. The philosophy of the Āgama is, as a friend and collaborator of mine Professor Pramathanātha Mukhyopādhyāya very well put it, a practical philosophy, adding, that what the intellectual world wants to-day is this sort of philosophy; a philosophy which not merely *argues* but *experiments.* The form which Sādhanā takes is a secondary matter. One goal may be reached by many paths. What is the path in any particular case depends on considerations of personal capacity and temperament, race and faith. For the Hindu there is the Āgama which contains forms of discipline which his race has evolved and are therefore *prima facie* suitable for him. This is not to say that these forms are unalterable or acceptable to all. Others will adopt other forms of Sādhanā suitable to them. Thus, amongst Christians, the Catholic Church prescribes a full and powerful Sādhana in its sacraments (Saṁskāra) and Worship (Pūjā Upāsanā), Meditation (Dhyāna), Rosary (Japa) and the like. But any system to be fruitful must *experiment* to gain *experience.* The significance of the Tantra Shāstra lies in this that it claims to afford a means available to all, of *whatever caste* and of *either sex*, whereby the truths taught may be *practically realized.*

The Tantras both in India and Tibet are the expression of principles which are of universal application. The mere statement of religious truths avails not. What is necessary for all is a *practical method* of realization. This too the occultist needs. Further the ordinary run of mankind can neither apprehend, nor do they derive satisfaction from mere metaphysical concepts. They accept them only when presented in personal form. They care not for Shūnyatā the Void, nor Sachchidānanda in the sense of mere Consciousness—Being—Bliss. They appeal to personal Bodhisattvas, Buddhas, Shiva, Viṣhṇu, Devī who will hear their prayer, and grant them aid. Next they cannot stand by themselves. They need the counsel and guidance of priest and Guru and the fortifying virtues of the sacraments. They need a definite picture of their object of worship, such as is detailed in the Dhyāna of the Devatās, an image, a Yantra, a Maṇḍala and so forth, a developed ritual and pictorial religion. This is not to say that they are wrong. These natural tendencies however become accentuated in course of time to a point where " superstition ", mechanical devotion and lifeless formalism and other abuses are produced. There then takes place what is called a " Reform," in the direction of a more spiritual religion. This too is accentuated to the point of barrenness. Religion becomes sterile to produce practical result and ritual and pictorial religion recurs. So Buddhism, which in its origin has been represented to be a reaction against excessive and barren ritualism, could not rest with a mere statement of the noble truths and the eightfold path. Something practical was needed. The Mahāyāna (Thegpa Chhenpo) was produced. Nāgārjuna in the second century A.D. (?) is said to have promulgated ideas to be found in the Tantras. In order to realize the desired end, use was made of all the powers of man, physical and mental. Theistic notions as also Yoga came again to the fore in the Yogacharyā and other Buddhist systems. The worship of images and an elaborate ritual was introduced. The worship of the Shaktis spread. The Mantrayāna and Vajrayāna found acceptance with, what an English writer ("The Buddhism of Tibet" by L. Waddell) describes in the usual style as its "silly mummery of unmeaning jargon and gibberish," the latter being said to be "the most depraved form of Buddhist doctrine". So-called Tāntrik Buddhisṁ became thus fully developed. A Tāntrik reformer in the person of Tsongkhapa arose, who codified the Tantras in his work Lam-rim Chhen-mo. The great code, the Kah-gyur, contains in one of its sections the Tantras (Rgyud) containing ritual, worship of the Divine Mothers, theology, astrology and natural science, as do their Indian counterparts. These are of four classes, the Kriyā, Charyā, Yoga, Anuttara Tantras, the latter comprising Mahā, Anu and Ati-Yoga Tantras. The Tan-gyur similarly contains many volumes of Tantras (Rgyud). Then, at length, Buddhism was driven from out of India. Brahmanism and its rituals survived and increased, until both in our day and the nearer past we see in the so-called reformed sects a movement towards what is claimed to be a more spiritual religion. Throughout the ages the same movements of action and reaction manifest. What is right here lies in the middle course. Some practical method and ritual is necessary if religion is not to be barren of result. The nature of the method and ritual will vary according to the capacity and devolopment of men. On the other hand, the "crooked influence of time" tends to overlay the essential spiritual truths with unintelligent and dead formalism. The Tantra Shāstra stands for a principle of high value though, like other things admittedly good, it is capable of, and has suffered, abuse. An important point in this connection should be noted. In Europe we see extreme puritan reaction with the result that the religious movements which embody them become one-sided and without provision for ordinary human needs. Brahmanism has ever been all-inclusive, producing a Sādhanā of varying kinds, material and mental, for the different stages of spiritual advancement and exempting from further ritual those for whom, by reason of their attainment, it is no longer necessary.

CHAPTER IV

TANTRA SHĀSTRA AND VEDA

In writing this Chapter I have in mind the dispute which some have raised upon the question whether the Āgamas, or some of them, are Vaidik or non-Vaidik.

I do not here deal with the nature and schools of Tantra or Āgama nor with their historical origin. Something has been said on these points in the Introductions to the English translations of Pandit Shiva Chandra Vidyārṇava's Tantratattva. I have also dealt with this subject in the two Chapters. "What are the Tantras and their significance?" and "Shakti and Shākta". I wish to avoid repetitions, except so far as is absolutely necessary for the elucidation of the particular subject in hand. On the disputed question whether the Āgamas are Vaidik or non-Vaidik I desire to point out that an answer cannot be given unless we keep apart two distinct matters, *viz.*, (1) what was the origin of the Āgamas and (2) what they are now. I am not here, however, dealing with the first or historical question, but with the second so far as the Shākta Āgama is concerned. Let us assume, for the sake of argument, that (to take a specific example) worship of Kālī and other Devīs by the Shāktas indicates the existence of non-Aryan elements in their Āgama. The question of real importance here, as always, is not as to what were the facts in remote past ages, but what they are now. The answer then is—let it be as you will regarding the origin of the Shākta Āgama; but at present Shākta worship is an integral part of the general Hinduism and as such admits the authority of Veda, accepting, as later explained, every other belief held by the general body of the Hindu people.

In a recent prosecution under Sections 292, 293 of the Indian Penal Code against an accused who had published a Tantra (but who was rightly acquitted), an Indian Deputy Magistrate who had advised the prosecution, and who claimed to be an orthodox Hindu, stated (I am informed) in the witness box, that he could not define what the Tantra Shāstra was, or state whether it was a Hindu scripture of the Kali age, or whether a well-known particular Shāstra shown to him was one of the Tantras. Such ignorance is typical of many at the present time and is a legacy from a vanishing age. How is it that a Shāstra which has had its followers throughout India from the Himālayas (the abode of Shiva and of Pārvatī Devī), to Cape Comorin (a corruption of Kumārī Devī) which ruled for centuries, so that we may speak of a Tāntrik epoch; which even to-day governs the household and temple ritual of every Hindu; how is it that such a Shāstra has fallen into complete neglect and disrepute amongst the larger body of the English-educated community? I remember a time when mention of the Shāstra was only made (I speak of course of the same class) with bated breath; and when any one who concerned himself therewith became thereby liable to the charge of giving licentious sway to drink and women. The answer is both a general and particular one. In the first place the English-educated people of this country were formerly almost exclusively, and later to a considerable extent, under the sway of their English educators. In fact they were in a sense their creation. They were, and some of them still are, the Mānasaputra of the English. For them what was English and Western was the mode. Hindu religion, philosophy and art were only, it was supposed, for the so-called "uneducated" women and peasants and for native Pandits who, though learned in their futile way, had not received the illuminating advantages of a Western training. In my own time an objection was (I am informed) taken by Indian Fellows of the Calcutta University to the appointment of the learned Pandit Chandrakānta Tarkālaṅkāra to a chair of Indian philosophy on the ground that he was a mere native Pandit. In this case English Fellows and the then Vice-Chancellor opposed this absurd and snobbish objection. When the authority of the English teachers was at its highest, what they taught was law, even though their judgments were, in respect of Indian subjects of which they had but a scant and imperfect knowledge, defective. If they said with, or in anticipation of, one Professor, that the Vedas were "the babbling of a child humanity" and the Brāhmaṇas "the drivel of madmen," or with another that the thought of the Upaniṣhads was so "low" that it could not be correctly rendered in the high English language; that in "treating of Indian philosophy a writer has to deal with thoughts of a lower order than the thoughts of the every-day life of Europe;" that Smṛiti was mere priestly tyranny, the Purāṇas idle legends and the Tantras mere wickedness and debauchery; that Hindu philosophy was (to borrow another English Professor's language concerning the Sāṅkhya) "with all its folly and fanaticism little better than a chaotic impertinence;" and that Yoga was, according to the same man of learning, "the fanatical vagaries of theocracy;" that Indian ritual was nothing but superstition, mummery, and idolatry, and (Indian) art, inelegant, monstrous, and grotesque—all this was with readiness accepted as high learning and wisdom, with perhaps here and there an occasional faint, and even apologetic, demur. I recollect in this connection a rather halting, and shamefaced, protest by the late Rajendra Lal Mitra. I do not say that none of these or other adverse criticisms had any ground whatever. There has been imperfection, folly, superstition, wickedness, here as elsewhere. There has been much of it, for example, in the countries whence these critics of India came. It is, however, obvious that such criticisms are so excessive as to be absurd.

Even when giving an account of Eastern thought the Western is apt to take up a "superior" attitude because he believes himself to be superior. The Bishop of Durham very clearly reveals this sense of superiority ("Christian Aspects of Life" by B. F. Westcott, 175) when after stating that the duty of the Christian missionary was to substitute for "the sterile theism of Islam and the shadowy vagueness of Hindu Philosophy a belief in a living and speaking God" he goes on to point out that "our very advantages" by way of "the consciousness of social and intellectual superiority with which we are filled" and "the national force which sets us as conquerors where we come as evangelists" constitute a danger in the mission field. It is this notion of "superiority" also which prevents a right understanding, and which notwithstanding the facts, insists on charges which, if established, would maintain the reputation for inferiority of the coloured races. It is this reiterated claim to superiority that has hypnotized many persons amongst Eastern races into the belief that the European is, amongst other things, always a safe and learned critic even of their own beliefs and practices.

Rājā Rammohan Roy was the first to take up the cause of his faith, divorcing it from the superstitious accretions which gather around all religions in the course of the ages. The same defence was made in recent times by that man of upstanding courage, Svāmī Vivekānanda. Foreign criticism on Indian religion now tends in some quarters to greater comprehension. I say in some quarters; for even in quite recent years English books have been published which would be amazing, were one not aware of the deep ignorance and prejudice which exist on the subject. In one of these books the Hindu religion is described as "a mixture of nightmare nonsense and time-wasting rubbish fulfilling no useful purpose whatever: only adding to the general burden of existence borne by Humanity in its struggle for existence." In another it is said to be "a weltering chaos of terror, darkness, and uncertainty". It is a religion without the apprehension of a moral evolution, without definite commandments, without a religious sanction in the sphere of morals, without a moral code and without a God: such so-called God, as there is, being "a mixture of Bacchus, Don Juan and Dick Turpin". It is there further described as the most material and childishly superstitious animalism that ever masqueraded as idealism; not another path to God but a pit of abomination as far set from God as the mind of man can go; staggering the brain of a rational man; filling his mind with wild contempt for his species and which has only endured "because it has failed". Except for the purpose of fanatical polemic, one would assume that the endurance of a faith was in some measure the justification of it. It is still more wonderful to learn from this work ("The Light of India" written by Mr. Harold Begbie and published by the Christian Literature Society for India) that out of this weltering chaos of all that is ignominious, immoral and crassly superstitious, come forth men who (in the words of the author) "standing at prayer startle you by their likeness to the pictures of Christ—eyes large, luminous and tranquil—the whole face exquisite with meekness and majestic with spirit." One marvels how these perfect men arise from such a worthless and indeed putrescent source. This absurd picture was highly coloured in a journalistic spirit and with a purpose. In other cases, faulty criticism is due to supercilious ignorance. As another writer says (the italics are mine) "For an Englishman to get a plain statement of what Brahmanism really means is far from easy. The only wonder is that people who *have to live on nine pence a week*, who marry when they are ten years old, are prevented from caste life from rising out of what is often, if not always, a degraded state, *have any religion at all*." As the Bishop of Peterborough has recently said it is difficult for some to estimate worth in any other terms than £. *s*. *d*. It is to be hoped that all such snobbish materialism will be hindered from entrance into this country. These quotations reveal the depths of ignorance and prejudice which still exist. As we are however aware, all English criticism is not as ignorant and prejudiced as these, even though it be often marred by essential error. On the contrary there are an increasing number who appreciate and adopt, or appreciate if they cannot accept, Indian beliefs. Further than this, Eastern thought is having a marked influence on that of the West, though it is not often acknowledged. Many have still the notion that they have nothing to learn in any domain from this hemisphere. After all, what any one else says should not affect the independence of our own judgment. Let others say what they will. We should ourselves determine matters which concern us. The Indian people will do so when they free themselves from that hypnotic magic, which makes them often place blind reliance on the authority of foreigners, who, even when claiming to be scholars, are not always free from bias, religious or racial. Such counsel, though by no means unnecessary to-day, is happily becoming less needed than in the past.

There are, however, still many Indians, particularly those of my own generation, whose English Gurus and their teaching have made them captives. Their mind has been so dominated and moulded to a Western manner of thinking (philosophical, religious, artistic, social and political) that they have scarcely any greater capacity to appreciate their own cultural inheritance than their teachers, be that capacity in any particular case more or less. Some of them care nothing for their Shāstra. Others do not understand it. The class of whom I speak are, in fact, as I have said, the Mānasaputra of the English in a strict sense of the term. The Indian who has lost his Indian soul must regain it if he would retain that independence in his thought and in the ordering of his life which is the mark of a man, that is of one who seeks Svarājyasiddhi. How can an imitator be on the same level as his original? Rather he must sit as a Chelā at the latter's feet. Whilst we can all learn something from one another, yet some in this land have yet to learn that their cultural inheritance with all its defects (and none is without such) is yet a noble one; an equal in rank, (to say the least), with those great past civilizations which have moulded the life and thought of the West. All this has been admitted by Indians who have discernment. Such value as my own remarks possess, is due to the fact that I can see and judge from without as an outsider, though (I will admit in one sense) interested observer—interested because I have at heart Indian welfare and that of all others which, as the world now stands, is bound up with it.

As regards the Tantra Shāstra in particular, greater ignorance prevailed and still exists. Its Vāmachāra practice however, seemed so peculiar, and its abuses were so talked of, that they captured attention to the exclusion of everything else; the more particularly that this and the rest of the Shāstra is hard to understand. Whilst the Shāstra provides by its Āchāras for all types from the lowest to the most advanced, its essential concepts, under whatever aspect they are manifested, and into whatever pattern they are woven, are (as Professor De La Vallée Poussion says of the Buddhist Tantra) of a metaphysical and subtle character. Indeed it is largely because of the subtlety of its principles, together with the difficulties which attend ritual exposition, that the study of the Tantras, notwithstanding the comparative simplicity of their Sanskrit, has been hitherto neglected by Western scholars. Possibly it was thought that the practices mentioned rendered any study of a system, in which they occurred, unnecessary. There was and still is some ground for the adverse criticism which has been passed on it. Nevertheless it was not a just appreciation of the Shāstra as a whole, nor even an accurate judgment in respect of the particular ritual thus singled out for condemnation. Let those condemn this Shāstra who will. That is their affair. But let them first study and understand it.

I have dealt with the subject of the Tantras in several papers. It is only necessary here to say that "the Tantra" as it is called was wrongly considered to be synonymous with the Shākta Tantras; that in respect of the latter the whole attention was given to the Vāmāchāra ritual and to magic (Shaṭkarma); that this ritual, whatever may in truth be said against it, was not understood; that it was completely ignored that the Tantras contained a remarkable philosophic presentment of religious teaching, profoundly applied in a ritual of psychological worth; and that the Shāstras were also a repertory of the alchemy, medicine, law, religion, art and so forth of their time. It was sufficient to mention the word "Tantra" and there was supposed to be the end of the matter.

I have often been asked why I had undertaken the study of the Tantra Shāstra, and in some English (as opposed to Continental) quarters it has been suggested that my time and labour might be more worthily employed. One answer is this: Following the track of unmeasured abuse I have always found something good. The present case is no exception. I protest and have always protested against unjust aspersions upon the Civilization of India and its peoples. If there be what is blameworthy, accuracy requires that criticism should be reduced to its true proportions. Having been all my life a student of the world's religions and philosophies, I entered upon a particular study of this Shāstra to discover for myself what it taught, and whether it was, as represented, a complete *reversal* of all other Hindu teaching with which I was acquainted. For it was said to be the cultivation or practice of gluttony, lust, and malevolence ("ferocity, lust, and mummery" as Brian Hodgson called it) which I knew the Indian Shāstra, like all the other religious Scriptures of the world, strictly forbid.

I found that the Shāstra was of high importance in the history of Indian religion. The Tantra Shāstra or Āgama is not, as some seem to suppose, a petty Shāstra of no account; one, and an unimportant sample, of the multitudinous manifestations of religion in a country which swarms with every form of religious sect. It is on the contrary with Veda, Smṛiti and Purāṇa one of the foremost important Shāstras in India, governing, in various degrees and ways, the temple and household ritual of the whole of India to-day and for centuries past. Those who are so strenuously averse to it, by that very fact recognize and fear its influence. From a historical point of view alone, it is worthy of study as an important part of Indian Culture, whatever be its intrinsic worth. History cannot be written if we exclude from it what we do not personally like. As Terence grandly said: "We are men and nothing which man has done is alien to us." There are some things in some of the Tantras and a spirit which they manifest of which their student may not personally approve. But the cause of history is not to be influenced by personal predilections. It is so influenced in fact. There are some who have found in the Shāstra a useful weapon of attack against Indian religion and its tendencies. Should one speak of the heights which Indian spiritual experience has reached, one might be told that the infamous depths to which it had descended in the Tantra Shāstra, the Puṣhṭimārga, the Vaiṣhṇava Sahajīya and so forth were more certainly established. Did one praise the high morality to be found in Indian Shāstra, it might be admitted that India was not altogether destitute of the light of goodness; but it might be asked, what of the darkness of the Tantra? And so on and so forth. Let us then grapple with and not elude the objection. There was of course something in all this. But such objectors and others had not the will (even if they had the capacity to understand) to give a true presentment of the teachings of the Shāstra. But the interests of fairness require both. Over and above the fact that the Shāstra is an historical fact, it possesses, in some respects, an intrinsic value which justifies its study. Thus it is the storehouse of Indian occultism. This occult side of the Tantras is of scientific importance, the more particularly having regard to the present revived interest in occultist study in the West. "New thought" as it is called and kindred movements are a form of Mantravidyā. Vashīkaraṇam is hypnotism, fascination. There is "Spiritualism" and "Powers" in the Tantras and so forth. For myself, however, the philosophical and religious aspect of the Scripture is more important still. The main question for the generality of men is not "Powers" (Siddhi). Indeed the study of occultism and its practice has its dangers; and the pursuit of these powers is considered an obstacle to the attainment of that true Siddhi which is the end of every Shāstra. A subject of greater interest and value is the remarkable presentation of Vedantic knowledge which the Shākta Tantra in particular gives (I never properly understood the Vedānta until after I had studied the Tantras) as also the ritual by which it is sought to gain realization (Aparokṣhajñāna). The importance of the Shākta Tantra may be summed up by the statement that it is a *Sādhana Shāstra of Advaitavāda.* I will develop this last matter in a future paper. I will only say now that the main question of the day everywhere is how to *realize* practically the truths of religion, whatever they be. This applies to all, whether Hindu, Mohamedan or Christian. Mere philosophical speculation and talk will avail nothing beyond a clarification of intellect. But, that, we all know, is not enough. It is not what we speculate about but what we are, which counts. The fundamental question is, how to realize (Sākṣhātkāra) religious teaching. This is the fruit of Sādhanā alone; whether the form of that Sādhanā be Christian, Hindu, Mohamedan, Buddhist or what else. The chief Sādhana-shāstra for the orthodox Hindu is the Tantra Shāstra or Āgama in its varying schools. In this fact lies its chief significance, and for Hindus its practical importance. This and the Advaitavādā on which the Shākta ritual rests is in my opinion the main reason why Shākta Darshana or doctrine is worthy of study.

The opinion which I had formed of the Shāstra has been corroborated by several to whom I had introduced the matter. I should like to quote here the last letter I had only a month ago from an Indian friend, both Sanskritist and philosopher (a combination too rare). He says " they (the Tantras) have really thrown before me a flood of new light. So much so, that I really feel as if I have discovered a new world. Much of the mist and haziness has now been cleared away and I find in the Tantras not only a great and subtle philosophy but many of the missing links in the development of the different systems of Hindu philosophy which I could not discover before but which I have been seeking for, for some years past." These statements might perhaps lead some to think that the Shāstra teaches something entirely, that is in every respect, new. As regards fundamental doctrines, the Tantra Shāstra (for convenience I confine myself to the Shākta form) teaches much which is to be found in the Advaita Vedānta. Therefore those who think that they will find in the Shāstra some fundamental truths concerning the world which are entirely new will be disillusioned. The observation does not apply to some doctrinal teaching, presentment, methods, and details, to which doubtless my friend's letter referred. He who has truly understood Indian Shāstra as a whole will recognize, under variety of form and degree of spiritual advancement, the same substance by way of doctrine.

Whilst the Shākta Tantra recognizes, with the four Vedas, the Āgamas and Nigamas, it is now based, as are all other truly Indian Shāstras on Veda. Veda, in the sense of Knowledge, is ultimately Spiritual Experience, namely Chit which Brahman is, and in the one partless infinite Ocean of Which the world, as a limited stress in Consciousness arises. So it is said of the Devī in the Commentary on the Trishatī:

Vedāntamahāvākya-janya sākṣhātkāra-rūpa-brahmavidyā.

She is Brahman-knowledge (Brahmavidyā) in the form of direct realization produced by the Vedāntic great saying (Mahāvākya)—that is "Tat tvam asi" ("That thou art") and all kindred sayings So'ham, ("He I am"), Brahmāsmi ("I am Brahman") and so forth. In other words,

Self-knowledge is self-luminous and fundamental and the basis of all other knowledge. Owing to its transcendency it is beyond both prover and proof. It is self-realized (Svānubhava). But Sruti is the source from which this knowledge arises, as Shaṅkara says, by removing (as also to some extent reason may do) false notions concerning it. It reveals by removing the superincumbent mass of human error. Again, Veda in a primary sense is the world as Idea in the Cosmic Mind of the creating Brahman and includes all forms of knowledge. Thus it is eternal, arising with and as the Saṁskāras at the beginning of every creation. This is the Vedamūrtibrahman. Veda in the secondary sense is the various partial revelations relating to Tattva, Brahman or God, and Dharma, morality, made at different times and places to the several Ṛṣhis which are embodied in the four Vedas, Ṛik, Yajus, Sāma and Atharva. Veda is not co-extensive therefore with the four Vedas. But are these, even if they be regarded as the "earliest," the only (to use an English term) revelations ? Revelation (Ākāshavāṇī) never ceases. When and wherever there is a true Ṛṣhi or Seer there is Revelation. And in this sense the Tantra Shāstra or Āgama claims to be a Revelation. The Shabdabrahmamūrti is Nigamādishāstramaya : it being said that Āgama is the Paramātmā of that Mūrti, the four Vedas with their Aṅgas are its Jīvātmā; the six philosophies its Indriyas; the Purāṇas and Upapurāṇas its gross body; Smṛiti its hands and other limbs and all other Shāstras are the hairs of its body. In the Heart-lotus are the fifty Tejoymayī Mātṛikā. In the pericarp are the Āgamas glittering like millions of suns and moons which are Sarvadharmamaya, Brahmajñānamaya, Sarvasiddhimaya, and Mūrtimān. These were revealed to the Ṛṣhis. In fact all Shāstras are said to constitute one great many-millioned collection (Shatakoṭi Saṁhitā) each being particular manifestations to man of the one, essential Veda. From this follows the belief that they do not contradict, but are in agreement with, one another: for Truth is one whatever be the degree in which it is received, or the form in which the Seers (Ṛishis) promulgated it to those whose spiritual sight has not strength enough to discern it directly and for themselves. But how, according to Indian notions, can that which is put forward as a Revelation be shown to be such? The answer is that of Ayurveda. A medicine is a good one if it cures. In the same way a Shāstra is truly such if the Siddhi which it claims to give is gained as the fruit of the practice of its injunctions, according to the competency and under the conditions prescribed. The principle is a practical and widely adopted one. The tree must be judged by its fruit. This principle may, if applied to the general life of to-day, lead to an adverse judgment on some Tāntrik practices. If so, let it be. It is, however, an error to suppose that even such practices as have been condemned, claim to rest on any other basis than Veda. It is by the learned in Tantra Shāstra said to be ignorance (Avidyā) to see a difference between Āgama and Veda.

Ignorant notions prevail on the subject of the relation of the Tantras to Veda and the Vedas. I read some years ago in a Bengali book by a Brahmo author that "the difference was that between Hell and Heaven". Now on what is such a condemnatory comparison based? It is safe to challenge production of the proof of such an assertion. Let us examine what the Shākta Tantra (to which allusion was made) teaches.

In the first place "Hell" recognizes "Heaven," for the Shākta Tantra, as I have said, acknowledged the authority of Veda. All Indian Shāstras do that. If they did not, they would not be Indian Shāstra. The passages on this point are so numerous, and the point itself is so plain that I will only cite a few.

Kulārṇava Tantra says (II. 85, 140, 141) that Kuladharma is based on and inspired by the Truth of Veda. *Tasmāt vedātmakam shāstram viddhi kaulātmakam priye.* In the same place Shiva cites passages from Shruti in support of His doctrine. The Prapanchasāra and other Tantras cite Vaidika Mahāvākya and Mantras; and as Mantras are a part of Veda, therefore, Meru Tantra says that Tantra is part of Veda (Prāṇatoṣhiṇī 70). Niruttara Tantra calls Tantra the Fifth Veda and Kūlāchāra is named the fifth Āshrama (*ib*); that is it follows all others. Matsyasūktamahātantra (XIII) says that that the disciple must be pure of soul (Shuddhātmā) and a knower of Veda. He who is devoid of Vaidika-kriyā (Vedakriyā-vivarjita) is disqualified (Mahārudrayāmala, I Khaṇḍa, Ch. 15; II Khaṇḍa, Ch. 2; Prāṇatoṣhiṇī 108). Gandharva Tantra (Ch. 2, Prāṇatoṣhiṇī 6) says that the Tāntrik Sādhaka must be a believer in Veda (Astika), ever attached to Brahman, ever speaking of Brahman, living in Brahman and taking shelter with Brahman; which, by the way, is a queer demand to make of those, the supposed object of whose rites is mere debauchery. The Kulārṇava says that there is no knowledge higher than that of Veda and no doctrine equal to Kaula (III. 113, *Nahivedādhikā vidyā na kaula-samadarshanam*). Here a distinction is drawn between Veda which is Vidyā and the Kaula teaching which he calls Darshana. See also Mahānirvāṇa Tantra (I. 18, 19; II. 8—15). In Mahānirvāṇa Tantra (III. 72) the Mantra Om sachchidekam Brahma is given and in the Prapanchasāra (Ch. XXIX) this (what it calls) " Secret of the Vedas " is explained.

That the Shākta Tantra claims to be based on Veda admits of no doubt. In fact Kulluka Bhaṭṭa, the celebrated commentator on Manu, says that Shruti is of two kinds, Vaidik and Tāntrik.

Vaidikī tāntrikī chaiva dvividhā shrutih kīrtitā.

It is of course the fact that different sects bandy words upon the point whether they in fact truly interpret Shruti and follow practice conformable to it. Statements are made by opposing schools that certain Shāstras are contrary to Shruti even though they profess to be based thereon. So a citation by Bhāskararāya in the Commentary to V. 46 of the Lalitāsahasranāma speaks of some Tantras as "opposed to Veda" (Vedaviruddhāni). The Vāyu Samhitā says "Shaivāgama is twofold, that which is based on Shruti and that which is not. The former is composed of the essence of Shruti. Shrauta is Svatantra and Itara (v. *ante* p. 19). *Shaivāgamo'pi dvividhah, shrauto' shrautash cha saṁsmritaḥ Shrutisāramayaḥ shrautaḥ svatantrastvitaro mataḥ.*

So again the Bhāgavata or Pancharātra Āgama has been said to be non-Vaidik. This matter has been discussed by Shaṅkarāchārya and Rāmānuja following Yamunāchārya.

We must in all cases distinguish between what a school says of itself and what others say of it. In Christianity both Catholicism and Protestantism claim to be based on the Bible and each alleges that the other is a wrong interpretation of it. Each again of the numerous Protestant sects says the same thing of the others.

But is Shākta Tantra contrary to Veda in fact? Let us shortly survey the main points in its doctrine. It teaches that Paramātmā Nirguṇa Shiva is Sachchidānanda (Prapanchasāra, Ch. XXIX: Kulārṇava, Ch. I, vv. 6-7). Kulārṇava says "Shiva is the impartite Supreme Brahman, the All-knowing (Sarvajña) Creator of all. He is the Stainless One and the Lord of all. He is One without a second (Advaya). He is Light itself. He changes not, and is without beginning or end. He is attributeless and above the highest. He is Sachchidānanda" (I. 6-7. And see the

Dhyāna and Pancharatnastotra in Mahānirvāna Tantra III. 50, 59-63). Brahman is Sachchidānanda, Eternal (Nitya), Changeless (Nirvikāra), Partless (Niṣhkala), Untouched by Māyā (Nirmala), Attributeless (Nirguṇa), Formless (Arūpa), Imperishable (Akṣhara), All-spreading like space (Vyomasannibha), Self-illuminating (Svyamjyotiḥ), Reality (Tattva) which is beyond mind and speech and is to be approached through spiritual feeling alone. (Bhāvanāgamya) (Kulārṇava I, 6-8; III. 92, 93; IX. 7). Mahānirvāṇa (III. 50, 59-63, 67-68, 74; III. 12). In His aspect as the Lord (Īshvara) of all, He is the All-knower (Sarvajña) Lord of all: whose Body is pure Sattva (Shuddhasattvamaya), the Soul of the universe (Vishvātmā) (Mahānirvāṇa I. 61, III. 68). Such definitions simply re-affirm the teaching of Veda. Brahman is That which pervades without limit the Universe (Prapanchasāra XXIX; Mahānirvāṇa III. 33-35) as oil the sesamum seed (Shāradā Tilaka I, Shāktānandataraṅgiṇī I, Prāṇatoṣhiṇī 13). This Brahman has twofold aspect as Parabrahma (Nirguṇa, Niṣhkala) and Shabdabrahman (Saguṇa, Sakala). Sammohana, a highly interesting Tantra, says (Ch. I) that Kubjikā is of twofold aspect, namely, Niṣhkalā when She is Chandra-vaktrā, and Sakalā when called Paramukhī). So too is Guhyakālī who as the first is Ekavaktrā mahāpashupatīshī advaitabhāvasampannā and as the second Dashavaktrā. So the Kulārṇava says Shabdabrahmaparamabrahmabhedena Brahmaṇo dvaividhyam uktam (Khanda V, Ullāsa 1). The same Tantra says that Sadāshiva is without the bonds (of Māyā) and Jīva is with them (Pāshabadho bhavej jīvah pāshamuktah Sadāshivahi, IX. 42) upon which the author of the Prāṇatoṣhinī, citing this passage says "thus the identity of Jīva and Shiva is shown (iti Shivajīvayoraikyam uktam). The Shākta Tantra is thus Advaitavāda: for it proclaims that Paramātmā and Jīvātmā are one. So it affirms the "grand words" (Mahāvākya) of Veda—"Tat tvam asi," "So'ham," "Brahmāsmi" (Mahānirvāṇa VIII. 264-265, V. 105; Prapanchasāra II; identifying Hrīm with Kuṇḍalī and Hangsaḥ and then with So'ham. Yah Sūkshmaḥ So'ham (*ib.* XXIV, Jnānārṇava Tantra XXI. 10. As to Brahmāsmi, see Kulārṇava IX. 32 and *ib.* 41. So hambhāvena pūjayet). The Mantra "all this is surely Brahman (Sarvam khalvidam Brahma) is according to the Mahānirvāṇa (VII. 98) the end and aim of Tāntrika Kulāchāra, the realization of which saying the Prapanchasāra Tantra describes as the fifth or Supreme State (Ch. XIX); for the identity of Jīvātmā and Paramātmā is Liberation which the Vedāntasāra defines to be Jïvabrahmanoraikyam). Kulārṇava refers to the Advaita of which Shiva speaks (Advaitantu shivenoktam I. 108. See also Mahānirvāṇa II. 33-34; III. 33-35; 50-64; Prapanchasāra II, XIX, XXIX). Gandharva Tantra says that the Sādhaka must be a nondualist (Dvaitahīna). (See Ch. II. *ib.* Prāṇatoṣhiṇī 108; Mahārudrayāmala I Khaṇḍa, Ch. 15; II Khaṇḍa, Ch. 2.) It is useless to multiply quotations on this point of which there is no end. In fact that particular form of worship which has earned the Shākta Tantras ill-fame claims to be a practical application of Advaitavāda. The Sammohana Tantra (Ch. VIII) gives high praise to the philosopher Shaṅkarāchārya saying that He was an incarnation of Shiva for the destruction of Buddhism. Kaulāchārya is said to properly follow a full knowledge of Vedāntic doctrine. Shiva in the Kulārṇava (I. 110) says "some desire dualism (Dvaita), others nondualism (Advaita) but my truth is beyond both (Dvaitādyaitavivarjita)."

Advaitavedānta is the whole day and life of the Shākta Sādhaka. On waking at dawn (Brahmamūhurta) he sits on his bed and meditates "I am the Devī and none other. I am Brahman who is beyond all grief. I am a form of Sachchidānanda whose true nature is eternal Liberation."

Aham Devī na chānyo'smi, Brahmaivāham na shokabhāk,
Sachchidānandarūpo'ham nityamuktasvabhāvavān.

At noon again seated in Pūjāsana at time of Bhūta-shuddhi he meditates on the dissolution of the Tattvas in Paramātmā. Seeing no difference between Paramātmā and Jīvātma he affirms Sā'ham "I am She". Again in the evening after ritual duties he affirms himself to be the Akhilātmā and Sachchidānanda, and having so thought he sleeps. Similarly (I may here interpose) in the Buddhist Tantra—the Sādhaka on rising in the state of Devadeha (hLayi-sku) imagines that the double drums are sounding in the heavens proclaiming the Mantras of the 24 Vīras (dPahvo), and regards all things around him as constituting the Maṇḍala of himself as Buddha Vajrasattva. When about to sleep he again imagines his body to be that of Buddha Vajrasattva and then merges himself into the tranquil state of the Void (Shūnyatā).

Gandharva Tantra says "having saluted the Guru as directed and thought 'So'ham' the wise Sādhaka the performer of the rite should ponder the unity of Jīva and Brahman."

Gurūn natvā vidhānena so'ham iti purodhasaḥ
Aikyam sambhāvayed dhīmān jīvasya Brahmaṇo'pi cha.

Kālī Tantra says "Having meditated in this way, a Sādhaka should worship Devī as his own Ātmā, thinking I am Brahman." Kubjikā Tantra says (Devī is called Kubjikā because She is Kuṇḍalī) "A Sādhaka should meditate on his own Self as one and the same with Her (Tayā sahitam ātmānam ekībhūtam vichintayet) : and so on.

The cardinal doctrine of these Shākta Tantras is that of Shakti whether in its Svarūpa (that is, as It is in Itself) as Chidrūpiṇī, the Parāprakṛiti of Paramātma (Mahānirvāṇa IV. 10) or as Māyā and Prakṛiti (see as to the latter the great

Hymn to Prakṛiti in Prapanchasāra, Ch. XI). Shakti as the Kubjikā Tantra says (Ch. I) is Consciousness (Chaitanyarūpiṇī) and Bliss (Ānandarūpiṇī). She is at the same time support of (Guṇāshrayā) and composed of the Guṇas (Guṇamayī). Māyā is however explained from the standpoint of Sādhanā, the Tantra Shāstra being a Sādhana Shāstra, and not according to the Māyāvāda, that is, transcendental standpoint, of Shaṅkara.

What is there in the great Devī Sūkta of the Ṛigveda (Maṇḍala X, Sūkta 125) which the Shākta Tantra does not teach? The Ṛiṣhi of this revelation was a woman the daughter of Ṛiṣhi Ambhṛiṇa. It was fitting that a woman should proclaim the Divine Motherhood. Her Hymn says "I am the Sovereign Queen the Treasury of all treasures; the chief of all objects of worship whose all-pervading Self all Devatās manifest; whose birthplace is in the midst of the causal waters: who breathing forth gives form to all created worlds and yet extends beyond them, so vast am I in greatness." (The full Hymn is translated in the French Edition of A. and E. Avalon's "Hymns to the Goddess," Bossard, Paris.)

It is useless to cite quotations to show that the Shākta Tantra accepts the doctrine of Karma which as the Kulārṇava (IX. 125) says Jīva cannot give up until he renounces the fruit of it; an infinite number of universes, and their transitoriness (Mahānirvāṇa III. 7), the plurality of worlds, Heaven and Hell, the seven Lokas, the Devas and Devīs, who as the Kulachūḍāmaṇi Nigama (following the Devī-Sūkta) says (Ch. I) are but parts of the great Shakti (Shāktānandataraṅgiṇī III). Being Advaitavāda, Moksha the state of Liberation and so forth is Paramātmā. It accepts Smṛiti and Purāṇas; the Mahānirvāṇa and other Tantras saying that they are the governing Shāstras of the Tretā and Dvāpara ages respectively, as Tantra is that of the Kaliyuga. So the Tārāpradīpa (Ch. I) says that in the Kaliyuga the Tāntrika and not the Vaidika Dharma is to be followed. It is said that in Satya, Veda was undivided. In Dvāpara, Kṛishṇadvaipāyana separated it into four parts. In Satya, Vaidika Upāsanā was Pradhāna, that is, prevailed; Sādhakas worshipping Indra for wealth, children and the like; though Nishkāma Ṛishis adored the Sarvashaktimān (Devīsukta is Advaitasiddhipūrna). In Tretā, worship according to Smṛiti prevailed. It was then that Vashishṭha is said to have done Sādhanā of Brahmavidyā according to Chīnāchārakrama. Though in the Dvāpara there was both Smṛiti and Purāṇa, rites were generally performed according to the Purāṇas. There was also then, as always, worshippers of the Pūrṇashaktimahāvidyā. At the end of Dvāpara and beginning of the Kali age the Tantra Shāstra was taught to men. Then the ten Saṁskāras, Shrāddha and Antyeshṭikriyā were, as they are now, performed according to the Vaidikadharma: Āshramachāra according to Dāyabhāga and other Smṛiti Texts; Vratas according to Purāṇa; Dīkshā and Upāsanā of Brahman with Shakti, and various kinds of Yoga Sādhanā, according to the Āgama which is divided into three parts Tantra (Sattvaguṇa), Yāmala (Rajoguṇa), and Ḍāmara (Tamoguṇa). There were 64 Tantras for each of the three divisions Ashvakrāntā, Rathakrāntā, Vishṇukrāntā.

Such is a Tāntrik tradition concerning the Ages and their appropriate Scriptures. Whether this tradition has any historical basis still awaits inquiry, which is rendered difficult by the fact that many Tantras have been lost and others destroyed by those inimical to them. It is sufficient for my purpose to merely state what is the belief; that purpose being to show that the Tantra Shāstra recognizes, and claims not to be in conflict with, Veda or any other recognized Shāstra. It accepts the six Philosophies

(Darshana) which Shiva says are the six limbs of Kula and parts of his body, saying that he who severs them severs His limbs (Kulārṇava II. 84, 84-85). The meaning of this is that the Six Philosophies and the Six Minds, as all else, are parts of His body. It accepts the Shabda doctrine of Mīmāṁsā subject to certain modifications to meet its doctrine of Shakti. It, in common with the Shaiva Tantra, accepts the doctrine of the 36 Tattvas, and Ṣhaḍadhvā [Tattva, Kalā, Bhuvana, Varṇa, Pada, Mantra; see my "Garland of Letters"]. This is an elaboration in detail which explains the origin of the Purusha and Prakṛiti Tattvas of the Sāṅkhya. These are shown to be twin facets of the One and the "development" of Shakti into Purusha-Prakṛiti Tattva, is shown. These Tattvas include the ordinary 24, Prakṛiti with its Guṇas to Pṛithivī. It accepts the doctrine of three bodies (causal, subtle, gross) and the three states (Jāgrat, Svapna, Suṣhupti) in their individual and collective aspects. It follows the mode of evolution (Pariṇāma) of Sāṅkhya in so far as the development of Jīva is concerned, as also an Ābhāsa, in the nature of Vivartta, "from Fire to Fire" in the Pure Creation. Its exposition of the body includes the five Prāṇas, the seven Dhātus, the Doṣhas (Vāyu, Pitta, Kapha) and so forth (Prapanchasāra II). On the ritual side it contains the commonly accepted ritual of present-day Hinduism; Mantra, Yantra, Pratimā, Liṅga, Shālagrāma, Nyāsa, Japa, Pūjā, Stotra, Kavacha, Dhyāna and so forth, as well as the Vaidik rites which are the ten Saṁskāras, Homa and the like. Most of the commonly accepted ritual of the day is Tāntrik. It accepts Yoga in all its forms Mantra, Haṭha, Laya, Jñāna; and is in particular distinguished by its practice of Laya or Kuṇḍalī-yoga and other Haṭha processes.

Therefore not only is the authority of the Veda acknowledged along with the Āgamas, Nigamas and Tantras but there is not a single doctrine or practice, amongst those hitherto mentioned, which is either not generally held, or which has not the adherence of large numbers of Indian worshippers. It accepts all the notions common to Hinduism as a whole. Nor is there a single doctrine previously mentioned which is contrary to Veda, that is on the assumption of the truth of Advaitavāda. For of course it is open to Dualists and Vishiṣhṭādvaitins to say that its Monistic interpretation of Vedānta is not a true exposition of Vaidik truth. No Shākta will however say that. Subject to this, I do not know of anything which it omits and should have included, or states contrary to the tenor of Vaidik doctrine. If there be anything I shall be obliged, as a student of the Shāstra, to any one who will call my attention to it. The Shāstra has not, therefore, up to this point shown itself as a "Hell" in opposition to the Vaidik "Heaven".

But it may be said that I have omitted the main thing which gives it its bad and un-Vaidik character namely the ill-famed Panchatattva or worship with meat, wine, fish, grain and woman. I have also omitted the magic to be found in some of the Shāstras.

The latter may be first shortly dealt with. Magic is not peculiar to the Tantras. It is to be found in plenty in the Atharvaveda. In fact the definition of Abhichāra is "the Karma described in the Tantras and Atharvaveda". Abhichāra is magical process with intent to destroy or injure. It is Hiṁsā-karma, or act injurious to others. There is nothing anti-Vaidik then in Magic. I may, however, here also point out that there is nothing wrong in Magic (Ṣhaṭkarma) *per se.* As with so many other things it is the use or abuse of it which makes it right or wrong. If a man kills, by Māraṇa Karma, a rival in his business to get rid of competition and to succeed to his clients' custom, he commits a very grave sin—one of the most grievous of sins.

Suppose, however, that a man saw a tiger stalking a child, or a dacoit about to slay it for its golden ornament; his killing of the tiger or dacoit would, if necessary for the safety of the child, be a justifiable act. Magic, is however, likely to be abused and has in fact been abused by some of the Tāntriks. I think this is the most serious charge established against them. For evil magic which proceeds from malevolence is a greater crime than any abuse of natural appetite. But in this, as in other matters, we must distinguish between what the Shāstra says and the practices of its followers. The injunction laid upon the Sādhaka is that he "should do good to other beings as if they were his own self". *Ātmavat sarvabhūtebhyo hitam kuryāt kuleshvari* (Kulārṇava Tantra XII. 63). In the Kulārṇava Samhitā (a different and far inferior work to the Tantra of that name) Shiva recites some horrible rites with the flesh of rat and bat; with the soiled linen of a Chaṇḍāla woman, with the shroud of a corpse, and so forth; and then he says "My heart trembles (hṛidayam kampate mama), my limbs tremble (gātrāṇi mama kampante), my mouth is dry oh Pārvatī! (mukham shuṣhyate Pārvatī!) Oh gentle one my mind is all disturbed (kṣhobho me jāyate bhadre). What more shall I say? Conceal it (Na vaktavyam) "conceal it, conceal it." He then says: "In the Kali age Sādhakas are generally greedy of money. Having done greatly sinful acts they destroy living beings. For them there is neither Guru nor Rudra, nor Thee nor Sādhikā. My dear life! they are ready to do acts for the destruction of men. Therefore it is wrong to reveal these matters, oh Devi. I have told Thee out of affection for Thee, being greatly pleased by Thy kisses and embrace. But it should be as carefully concealed by Thee as thine own secret body. Oh Pārvati! all this is greatly sinful and a very bad Yoga. (Mahāpātakayuktam tat kuyogo'yam udāhṛitah.)"

Kalikāle sādhakāstu prāyasho dhanalolupāḥ
Mahākṛityām vidhāyaiva prāṇinām badhabhāginaḥ
Na gurur nāpi Rudro vā naiva tvam naiva sādhikā
Mahāpraṇivināshāya samarthaḥ prāṇavallabhe
Etat prakāshanam devi doṣhāya parikalpyate
Snehena tava deveshi chumbanālinganaistathā
Santuṣhyaiva mayā devi sarvam etat prakāshitam
Tvayā gopyam prayatnena svayoniriva Pārvati
Mahāpātaka-yuktam tat kuyogo'yam udāhritaḥ.

"None of these things are ever to be done by Thee Oh Daughter of the Mountain (*Sarvathā naiva kartavyas tvayā Parvatanandini*). Whoever does so, incurs the sin of destroying Me. I destroy all such, as does fire, dry grass. Of a surety such incur the sin of slaying a Brāhmaṇa. All such incur the sin of slaying a Brāhmaṇa."

Sarvathā naiva kartavyas tvayā Parvatanandini
Badhabhāk mama deveshi kṛityāmimām samācharet
Tasya sarvam harāmyāshu vahniḥ shuṣhkatṛiṇam yathā
Avyārthām brahmahatyāncha brahmahatyām savindatī.

When therefore we condemn the sin of evil magic it is necessary to remember both such teaching as is contained in this quotation, and the practice of those of good life who follow the Shāstra. To do so is to be both fair and accurate. There is nothing, in any event, in the point that the magical contents of the Tantra Shāstra make it contrary to Veda. Those who bring such a charge must also prefer it against the Atharvaveda.

As a matter of fact Magic is common to all early religions. It has been practised, though condemned, in Christian Europe. It is not necessary to go back to the old witchcraft trials. There are some who protest against its recrudescence to-day. It has been well observed that there are two significant facts about occultism, namely its catholicity (it is to be found in all lands and ages) and its amazing power of recuperation after it has been supposed to have been disproved as mere "superstition". Even some quarter of a century ago (I am quoting from the same author) there were probably not a score of people in London (and those kept their preoccupation to themselves) who had any interest at all in the subject except from a purely antiquarian standpoint. Magic was dismissed by practically all educated men as something too evidently foolish and nonsensical to deserve attention or inquiry. In recent years the position has been reversed in the West, and complaint is again made of the revival of witchcraft and occultism to-day. The reason of this is that modern scientific investigation has established the objectivity of some leading phenomena of occultism. For instance a little more than a century or so ago it was still believed that a person could inflict physical injury on another by means other than physical. And this is what is to be found in that portion of the Tantra Shāstras which deal with the Ṣhaṭkarma. Witches confessed to having committed this crime and were punished therefor. At a later date the witchcraft trials were held to be evidence of the superstition both of the accused and accusers. Yet psychology now allows the principle that Thought is itself a Force, and that by Thought alone, properly directed, without any known physical means the thought of another, and hence his whole condition, can be affected. By physical means I mean direct physical means, for occultism may, and does avail, itself of physical means to stimulate and intensify the force and direction of thought. This is the meaning of the magic rituals which have been so much ridiculed. Why is black the colour of Māraṇa Karma? Because that colour incites and maintains and emphasizes the will to kill. So Hypnotism (Vashīkaraṇam), as an instance of the exercise of the Power of

Thought, makes use of gestures, rotatory instruments and so forth.

The Magician having a firm faith in his (or her) power (for faith in occultism as in Religion is essential) surrounds himself with every incentive to concentrated, prolonged and (in malevolent magic), malevolent thought. A figure or other object such as part of the clothing, hair, nails and so forth of the victim represents the person to be attacked by magic. This serves as the 'immediate object' on which the magical thought is expended. The Magician is helped by this and similar aids to a state of fixed and malignant attention which is rendered intense by action taken on the substituted object. It is not of course the injuries done to this object which are the direct cause of injury to the person attacked, but the thought of the magician of which these injuries are a materialization. There is thus present the circumstances which a modern psychologist would demand for success in a telepathic experiment. As the witchcraft trials show, the victim is first affected in thought and then in body by the malignant thought thus focussed upon him. Sometimes no apparent means are employed, as in a case reported to me by a friend of mine as occurring in a Bombay Hotel when a man well-known in India for his "Powers" (Siddhi) drove away, by the power of his thought only, a party of persons sitting at a neighbouring table whose presence was greatly distasteful to one of his companions. This, if the effect of magical power, was an instance of what the Tantras call Uchchāṭana. In all cases the general principle is the same, namely the setting in motion and direction of powerful thought by appropriate means.

This is the view of those who give what may be called a psychological explanation of these phenomena. These would hold that the magical symbolisms are without inherent force but work according to race and individual characteristics on the mind which does the rest. Others believe that there is an inherent power in Symbolism itself, that the "Symbol" is not merely such but an actual expression of, and instrument by which, certain occult laws are brought into play. In other words the power of "Symbolism" derives not merely from the effect which it may have on particular minds likely to be affected by it but from itself as a law external to human thought. Some again (and Indian magicians amongst others) believe in the presence and aid of discarnate personalities (such as the unclean Pishāchas) given in the carrying out of occult operations. Similarly it is commonly held by some that where so-called "spiritualistic" phenomena are real and not fraudulent (as they sometimes are) the action is not that of the dead but of Infernal Spirits simulating them and misleading men to their ruin. Occultism in the sense of a belief in, and claim to be able to use, a certain range of forces which may be called preternatural, has the adherence not only of savage and barbarous people (who always believe in it) but also of an increasing number of "civilized" Londoners, Berliners, Americans, Parisians and other Western peoples. They differ in all else but they are united in this. Even what most would regard as downright superstition still abundantly flourishes in the West. Witness the hundreds of thousands of "touchwood" figures and the like sent to the troops in the recent war, the horror of sitting 13 to a table, and so on. In fact, from the earliest ages, magic has gone hand-in-hand with religion, and if for short periods the former has been thought to be dead it always rises again. Is this, as some say, the mark of the inherent silly credulity of mankind, or does the fact show that there is something in the claims which occultism has made in all ages? India (I do not speak of the English-educated community which shares in the rise and fall of

English opinion) has always believed in occultism and some of the Tantra Shāstras are repertories of its ritual. Magic and superstition proper exist in this country but are also to be found in the West. The same remark applies to every depreciatory criticism passed upon the Indian people. Some have thought that occultism is the sign both of savagery and barbarism on the one hand and of decadent civilization on the other. In India it has always existed and still exists. It has been well said that there is but one mental attitude impossible to the educated man, namely blank incredulity with regard to the whole subject. There has been, and is, a change of attitude due to an increase of psychological knowledge and scientific investigation into objective facts. Certain reconciliations have been suggested, bringing together the ancient beliefs, which sometimes exist in crude and ignorant forms. These reconciliations may be regarded as insufficiently borne out by the evidence. On the other hand a proposed reconciliation may be accepted as one that on the whole seems to meet the claims made by the occultist on one side and the scientific psychologist on the other. But in the present state of knowledge it is no longer possible to reject both claims as evidently absurd. Men of approved scientific position have, notwithstanding the ridicule and scientific bigotry to which they have been exposed, considered the facts to be worthy of their investigation. And on the psychological side successive and continuous discoveries are being made which corroborate ancient beliefs in substance, though they are not always in consonance with the mode in which those beliefs were expressed. We must face the fact that (with Religion) Occultism is in some form or another a widely diffused belief of humanity. All however will be agreed in holding that malevolent Magic is a great Sin. In leaving the subject of Magic I may here add that modern psychology and its data afford remarkable corroboration of some other Indian beliefs such as that Thought is a Force, and that its operation is in a field of Consciousness which is wider than that of which the mind is ordinarily aware. We may note also the aid which is derived from the establishment of dual and multiple personalities in understanding how it may be possible that in one unity there may be yet varying aspects.

The second charge is the alleged Avaidik character of the secret Panchatattva Sādhanā, with wine, flesh and woman, its alleged immorality of principle, and the evil lives of those who practise it. I am not in the present paper dealing in full with this subject; not that I intend by any means to shirk it; but it is more appropriately the subject of consideration in future Chapters on the subject of Shākta Tāntrik Sādhanā of which it forms a part. What I wish to say now is only this: We must distinguish in the first place between a *principle* and its *application*. A principle may be perfectly right and sound and yet a supposed application may not be an application in fact; or if there be an application, the latter may violate some other moral or physical law, or be dangerous and inexpedient as leading to abuse. I will show later that the principle involved is one which is claimed to be in conformity with Vaidik truth, and to be in fact recognized in varying forms by all classes of Hindus. Some do so dualistically. The Sādhanā of the Shākta Tantra is, whether right or wrong, an application of the principles of Advaitavāda and in its full form should not, it is said, be entered upon until after Vedāntic principles have been mastered. For this reason Kauladharma has been called the fifth Āshrama. Secondly I wish to point out that this ritual with wine and meat is not as some suppose a new thing; something introduced by the Shākta Tāntriks. On the contrary it is very old and has sanction in Vaidik practice as will appear from the authorities cited in the Appendix to this Chapter. So much is this so, that a Tāntrik Sādhu discussing the matter with a Bengali friend of mine said of himself, as a follower of this ritual, that he was a Hindu and that those who were opposed to it were Jainas. What he meant, and what seems to be the fact, is that the present-day general prohibition against the use of wine, and the generally prevalent avoidance, or limitation of an animal diet, are due to the influence of Jainism and Buddhism which arose after, and in opposition to, Vaidik usage. Their influence is most marked of course in Vaishnavism but has not been without effect elsewhere. When we examine ancient Vaidik usage we find that meat, fish and Mudrā (the latter in the form of Purodāsha) were consumed, and intoxicating liquor (in the form of Soma) was drunk, in the Vaidik Yajñas. We also discover some Vaidik rites in which there was Maithuna. This I have dealt with in my article on "Shakti and Shākta".

The abovementioned facts show in my opinion that there is ground for the doctrine of the Tāntrikas that it is a mark of ignorance (Avidyā) to sever Veda and Tantra. My conclusion is not however a counsel to follow this nor to any other particular form of ritual. I am only concerned to state the facts. I may, however, here add two observations.

From an outside point of view (for I do not here deal with the subject otherwise) we must consider the age in which a particular Shāstra was produced and consequently the conditions of the time, the then state of society, its moral and spiritual development and so forth. To understand some rites in the past history of this and other countries one must seek, in lieu of surface explanations, their occult significance in the history of the human race; and the mind must cast itself back into the ages whence it has emerged, by the aid of those traces which it still bears in the depths of its being of that which outwardly expressed itself in ancient custom.

Take for instance the rite of human sacrifice which the Kālikalpalatā says that the Rājā alone may perform (*Rājā naravalim dadāyenna yo'pi parameshvari*) but in which, as the Tantrasāra states, no Brāhmaṇa may participate (*Brāhmaṇānāng naravalidāne nādhikāraḥ*) Such an animal sacrifice is not peculiarly "Tāntrik" but an instance of the survival of a rite widely spread in the ancient world; older than the day when Jehovah bade Abraham sacrifice his son (Gen. XXII) and that on which Sunaḥsepa (Aitareya Brāhmaṇa VII, 3) like Isaāc was released. Reference, it is true, is made to this sacrifice in the Shāstras, but save as some rare exception (I myself judged a case in Court some years ago) it does not exist to-day and the vast mass of men do not wish to see it revived. The Chakra ritual similarly is either disappearing or becoming in spirit transformed where there had been abuse.

What is of primary value in the Tantra Shāstra are certain principles with which I have dealt elsewhere, and with which I deal again in part in this and the following lectures. The application of these principles in ritual is a question of form. All form is a passing thing. In the shape of ritual its validity is limited to place and time. As so limited, it will continue so long as it serves a useful purpose and meets the needs of the age, and the degree of its spiritual advancement, or that of any particular body of men who practise it; otherwise it will disappear, whilst the foundations of Vedānta on which it rests may remain. In the same way it is said that we ourselves come and go with our merits and demerits, but that the Spirit ever abides beyond both good and evil.

NOTE TO CHAPTER IV

The following note as to Tantra Shāstra and Veda was kindly prepared for me at my request by Sj. Braja Lal Mukherji, M.A.:

My purpose in this paper is not to give to the public any pre-conceived opinion, but is simply to put together certain facts which will enable it to form a correct opinion on the subject.

These facts have been collected from sources as to the authenticity of which there is no doubt. There is no dispute that most of these works disclose the state of Vaidik society prior to the 6th century B.C. and that at the time when the said works were composed the Vaidik rituals were being observed and performed. Certain elements which have been *assumed* to be non-Vaïdik, appear in the said works or at least in many of them, and they have been summarily disposed of by some scholars as supplementary (Parishishta), or interpolations (Prakshipta). The theory that these portions are interpolations is based on the *assumption* that the said elements are non-Vaidik or post-Vaidik and also on the *assumption* that at the times when the said works were composed, the Anushtup-chhandah was not known; and that therefore, those portions of the said works which appear in Anushtubh, must be later interpolations. We need not go into the propriety of these assumptions in this paper; but suffice it to say, that the first assumption simply begs the question, and the second one is not of any importance in connection with the subject of this paper; inasmuch as, the statements made in the Anushtubh portions are corroborated by earlier authorities as to whose antiquity there is no question, and in any case, the fact that the statements have been made are proof of earlier usage or custom.

Vaidik sacrifices are divided into three classes: (1) Pākayajnas, (2) Haviryajnas and (3) Soma sacrifices; and there are sub-divisions under each of the said classes. The

Soma sacrifices are classed under three heads according to the number of days required for performance, *viz.*, Ekāha, Ahina and Satra. Ekāha sacrifices are those which are performed in one day by three Savanas, exactly as in the Jagaddhātrī Pūjā; Ahina sacrifices are performed from two to eleven days and Satras are performed during a long period, the minimum number of days required being thirteen and the maximum being a thousand years. The twelve-day sacrifices are arranged as a separate class. The principal Somayajnas are (1) Agnishtoma, (2) Atyagnishtoma, (3) Ukthyah, (4) Shodashī, (5) Vājapeyah, (6) Atirātrah, (7) Āptoryāma. The Ishtis or Haviryajnas are also principally seven in number, namely, (1) Agnyādheyam, (2) Agnihotram, (3) Darsha-paurnamāsa, (4) Chāturmāsyam, (5) Āgrayaneshti, (6) Niruddhapashubandha, and (7) Sautrāmani. The Pākayajnas are also seven in number, namely, (1) Ashtakā, (2) Pārvanam, (3) Srāddham, (4) Srāvani, (5) Āgrahāyani, (6) Chaitri, and (7) Āshvayuji. The last seven are to be performed with the help of the Grihya fire and are described in the Grihya works. The others are described in the Srauta works.

Whatever be the difference among these Yajnas in regard to the number of stomas or stotras and the Sāmans to be sung and the Kapālas, Grahas, or the number and nature of sacrifices or as to other particulars, there are some ideas which prevail in all of them. All Yajnas are based on the idea that Mithunīkarana leads to spiritual happiness. Sexual intercourse is Agnihotra (S.B. XI. 6. 2. 10). Mithunīkarana is consecration (S.B. III. 2. 1. 2, etc.) They enclose the Sadas secretly, for enclosing is Mithunīkarana and therefore it must be done secretly (S.B. IV. 6, 7, 9 and 10). Bricks (Vishvajyotis) are made because the making of the bricks causes generation (S.B. VI. 5. 3. 5). Two Pādas or Charanas of an Anushtubh verse are read in a detached manner and the two remaining are read together to imitate the manner of sexual union (A.B. II. 5. 3); they do not worship a female Devatā unless she is coupled with a male Deva (A.B. III. 5. 4); they use a couple of Chhandas distinguishing the one as male from the other as female and the two are taken together and believed to be the symbol of Maithuna, and by such Maithuna the desired result of a ritual is achieved (A.B. V. 3. 1); they believe that the reading of the Āhanasyā mantra (S.S.S. XII. 24. 1-10; A.V. XX. 136) will confer bliss (A.B. VI. 5. 10); they say that the highest and best form of Maithuna is that of Shraddhā and Satya, Piety and Truth (A.B. VII. 2. 9) and this kind of Maithuna in the abstract is directed for Agnihotrīs who have purified themselves by actual performances and observances in a religious spirit.

They direct the observance and performance of Maithuna as a religious rite or part of a religious rite (L.S.S. IV. 3. 17; K.S.S. XIII. 42; T.A. IV. 7. 5; X. 62, 7; A.A. I. 2. 4. 10; V. 1. 5. 13; G.G.S. II. 5, 6, 9, 10; S.G.S. I. 19. 2-6; K.G.S. I. 4. 15; H.G.S. I. 24. 3; Ap. G.S. III. 8. 10; P.G.S. I. 11. 7; Ap. S.S. V. 25. 11; Tan. Br. VIII. 7. 12; Chh. Up. II. 13. 1-2) and they direct that Mantras are to be uttered during the observance of this rite (Br. D.V. 90; VIII. 82; R.V. V. 82. 4; R.V. X. 85. 37; R.V. Kh. 30. 1; Rik P. II. 15. 1-8; As. S.S. VIII. 3. 28: G.B. VI. 15). One of the articles of faith of the Vaidik people therefore was, the sexual union led the way to bliss hereafter and must be perfomed in a true religious spirit to ensure spiritual welfare; wanton indulgence being severely deprecated. Idā (a woman) said: " if thou wilt make use of me at the sacrifice, then whatever blessing thou shalt invoke through me, shall be granted to thee." (S.B. I. 8—1. 9, etc.)

The Vaidik people performed their Somayajnas and Haviryajnas which included the Sautrāmani, with libations and drinks of intoxicating liquor (L.S.S. V. 4, 11; K.S.S. XIX. 1, etc.; S.S.S. XV. 15; XIV. 13. 4; S.B. V. 1. 2. 12; V. 1. 5. 28; XII. 7. 3. 14, etc.; XII. 8. 1, etc.; XII. 8. 2. 21, 22; V. 5. 4. 19, etc.; XII. 7. 3. 8; Ap. S.S. XVIII. 1. 9). Surā purifies the sacrificer whilst itself is purified (S.B. XII. 8. 1. 16). Rishi Kakshivān sings the praises of Surā (R.V. I. 116. 7). It is said to be a desirable thing (R.V. X. 107. 9; VIII. 2. 12). They prefer Soma, the sweet drink. Soma is Paramāhutih (S.B. VI. 6. 3. 7); it is the nectar of immortality (S.B. IX. 4. 4. 8). They deprecate and punish the wanton use of intoxicating liquor (Ap. Dh. S. I. 25. 3; Ga. Dh. S. XXIII. 10; Va. Dh. S. XX. 19; Ba. Dh. S. II. 1. 18, etc.; S.V.B. I. 5). They direct the use of Surā and Soma for attainment of happiness and prescribe the manner and purpose of drinking the same; they prescribe the measure and number of drinks to be offered or taken at a sacrifice (S.B. V. 1. 2. 9, etc., V. 5. 4), and they add that a breach of these rules destroys the efficacy of the rite. They offer libations of Surā to the Fathers (A.B. III. 1. 5; S.B. V. 5. 4. 27, etc.). They offer Surā to the Ashwins (R.V.B. I. 44). They offer Surā to Vināyāka's mother (Yag. I. 288). During the performance of a sacrifice, the priests and the householder sit together; they all touch their cups, and raise them to their mouths, all the while reciting proper Mantras addressed to Devas (A.B. VI. 3. 1) and then they drink (A.B. VII. 5. 7).

The Vaidik people used to offer to their Devatās at their sacrifices animal and vegetable food. The vegetable substances are Tandula, Pishtaka, Phalīkarana, Purodāsha, Odana, Yavāgūh, Prithuka, Lāja, Dhāna and Saktu, and the animal food was Payah, Dadhi, Ājyam, Āmikshā Vājinam, Vapā, Māmsam, Lohitam, Pashurasah; the principal of these being Dhāna, Karambha, Paribāha, Purodāsha and Payasyā (A.B. II. 3. 6). Indeed it would not be incorrect to say that no Vaidik rite can be performed without these offerings; the forms and the mode of preparation and the number of cakes to be offered, differing in each case (A.B. I. 1. 1; II. 1-9; II. 3. 5; II. 3-6; S.B. I. 2. 2; L.S.S. V. 4. 1, etc.; Ap. S.S. XII. 3. 12; XII. 4, 9. 14.; K.S.S. V. 309; Tait. Br. III. 2. 6, etc.). They offer animal sacrifices (Kat. S.S. Chap. VI; S.B. III. 6. 4; III. 8. 1; V. 1. 3. 2. 14; V. 3. 1. 10; VI. 2. 2. 15. Kanda XIII; As. G.S. I. 11; P.G.S. III. 11; G.G.S. III. 10. 18; Kh. G.S. III. 4; H.G.S. II. 15), which include the horse, goats, sheep, oxen (Tait. Br. II. 8. 1, etc.) and human beings (Tait. Br. III. 4. 1). They believe that by performing animal sacrifices, the sacrificer ransoms himself (S.B. XI. 7. 1. 3; A.B. II. 1. 3) or wins all these worlds (Ap. S.S. VII. 1. 1). The animal is the sacrificer himself (A.B. II. 2. 1). They direct by special rules, in what manner the animal should be killed, cut and offered (A.B. II. 6; S.B. III. 8. 1. 15). They were aware that wanton killing of animals was wrong (A.B. II. 1. 7) and believed that offering animal sacrifices to the Devatās, was one of the means whereby bliss hereafter could be attained (Ba. Dh. S. II. 4. 23). And it was only for certain Yajnas that animals could be slain (Va. Dh. S. IV. 5-8; S.G.S. II. 16; 1 Ba. S.S. IV). Wanton killing of animals was very severely punished (Ap. Dh. S.I. 25. 13-26; Ga. Dh. S. XXII. 18, etc.; Va. Dh. S. 18. 23, etc.; Ba. Dh. S. I. 19. 6).

The Vaidik people from the time of the earliest Yajnas severely deprecated lust of any kind whatsoever; and they allowed Maithuna, Māmsa, Madya and Mudrā for religious purposes only and as offerings to the Devas. The Chakra sittings of the Tāntriks (M.N.T. Ch. VI) have unmistakable similarities with the Vājapeya and Sautrāmani (S. B. V; K.S.S. XIV; A.B. III. 4. 3; S.B. XII. 7. 1, etc.; K.S.S. XIX) and even the manner of drinking in company has been preserved as will appear from the references given above.

When performing Yajna in company, the members of the company become Brāhmaṇas and there is no distinction of caste (A.B. VII. 4. 1).

The worship in both Vaidik and Tāntrik rites begins with Āchamana, which is a form of ablution, in which certain parts of the body are touched with water. In this respect, the Vaidik and the Tāntrik practices are exactly similar (G.G.S. 1. 2. 5; Tait. A. II. 11; M.N.T. Chap. V). They purify themselves by uttering some mantras as Bijas while contemplating the Deities of certain parts of their bodies and touching such parts with their fingers (A.A. III. 2. 1. 2; III. 2. 5. 2; R.V.B. II. 16). They contemplate each Deva through his or her particular Mantras (R.V. III. 62. 10) which will be found collected in the Parishishta to the Taittirīya Āranyaka. They make use of certain sounds for removing unclean spirits, *e.g.*, Khat. Phat. Hum. (T.A. IV. 27; S.V. St. I. 2. 1; I. 1. 3; Aranyagāna VI. 1-8; IV. 2. 19; S.B. I. 5. 2. 18; I. 3. 3. 14; I. 7. 2. 11-14; I. 7. 2. 21; XI. 2. 2. 3 and 5; M.N.T. Chap. III) and for other purposes (A.B. II. 3. 6). They attribute a Deity to each letter in a Mantra (A.B. II. 5. 5).

They make gestures with their fingers as part of their religious rites (S.B. III. 1. 3. 25; III. 4. 3. 2) and locate the Devatās of particular sounds in particular parts of their bodies (P.S. 54, 56; K.S.S. VII. 71, 73). They perform their baths as a means of and with the view of pleasing their Devas (G. Sn. S. and M.N.T.) and in performing the Āchamana they sacrifice unto themselves conceiving that they are part and parcel of the Great Brahma (T.A. X. i). They worship the Great Brahma thrice daily, such worship being called Sandhyā-bandanā or Āhnika-kriyā, twilight prayers or daily rites. How and when the forms of Vaidik Sandhyā now practised by Vaidikas commenced has not yet been ascertained but, there is no doubt that prior to the time when the Taittirīya Āranyaka was composed the practice existed in its present form. It will be remembered that it is only in that work that we find the Sandhyā-mantras recorded. The practice of Prānāyāma and Tarpana to Rishis, Fathers, and Devas also existed before Baudhāyana. This practice of Vaidik Sandhyā worship should be compared with the Tāntrik mode, to gain an insight into the relationship of the Vedas and the Tantras.

In the Yajnas, the Vaidik people principally worshipped (1) Sarasvatī (S.B. II. 5. 4. 6; III. 1. 4. 9; III. 9. 1. 7; V. 2. 2. 14; V. 3. 5. 8; V. 4. 5. 7; V. 5. 2. 7) to whom animals are sacrificed (S.B. III. 9. 1. 7; V. 5. 4. 1; XII. 7. 2. 3) and who is the same as Vāk or Vāgdevī who became a lioness and went over to the Devatās, on their undertaking that to her offerings should be made before they were made to Agni (S.B. III. 5. 1. 21) and who bestows food (S.B. XII. 8. 2. 16); (2) Mahādeva or Mahesha, another form of Agni, in all his eight forms (S.B. VI. 1. 3. 10 *et seq.*); (3) Rudra, (4) Vishnu, (5) Vināyaka (Ganesha), (6) Skanda (Kārtikeya) (S.V.B. I. 4. 31 *et seq.*); (7) the Lingam or Phallus (T.A. X. 17) on whom they meditated during the daily Sandhyā worship and who is the same as Shambhu riding on a bull, (8) Shiva (S.V.B. I, 2. 2). They also worshipped (9) the cow whom they called Bhagavatī (A.B. V. 5. 2) and also (10) Indra, Varuna, Agni, Soma, Rudra, Pushan, the Ashwins, Sūryya and some other Deities. For purposes of attaining eternal bliss they worshipped Rātridevī (S.V.B. III. 8) and this Rātridevī is described as a girl growing into womanhood who bestows happiness. She has long and flowing hair, has in her hand a noose. If she is pleased, then all other Devas are pleased. She being pleased offers boons, but the worshipper must reject the same and then he will gain freedom from re-birth. This is the worship of Rātri; it requires no fasting and must be performed at night. The Mantras to be recited, is the Rātri Sūkta which commences with Rātrir bakhyad (Rig Veda X. 127. 1) to be followed by āratri pārthivam rajas.

The Rig-Vidhāna-Brāhmana (IV. 19) which follows the Sāma-Vidhāna-Brāhmana declares that the Rātri Sūkta must be recited; the worship must be peformed as a Sthālipāka Yajna. Rātri is substantially the same with, but in form different from, Vāgdevī; and they are sometimes worshipped as one and the same (Tait. Br. II. 4. 6. 10 *et seq.*). The Rātri Sūkta describes her as black (R. V. X. 127. 2-3). The portion of the Rātri Sūkta which is included in the Khila portion of the Rig-Veda (R.V. Kh. 25) calls Rātri Devī by the name of Durgā and this Mantra appears in Taittirīya Āranyaka (X. 1). She is described here, as the bearer of oblations; therefore, she is the same as Agni (Fire) and as such she has tongues which are named as follows: (1) Kālī, (2) Karālī, (3) Manojaba, (4) Sulohitā, (5) Sudhūmravarnā, (6) Sphulingini, (7) Shuchismitā and these tongues loll out and by these tongues offerings are received (Grihya-Sangraha I. 13. 14). The Brihad-devatā mentions that Aditi, Vāk, Sarasvatī and Durgā are the same (II. 79).

In conformity with the Vaidik system the Tāntrik-system of worship acknowledges that Om is the supreme Bīja (A.B. VII. 3. 6; II. 1. 2; V. 5. 7 ; A.A. II. 3. 8; Chh. Up. I. 1. 1 *et seq.*; T.A. VII. 8; X. 63. 21 *et seq.*; Shakatāyana, p. 106 (Oppert); Pānini VIII. 2. 87; Br. D. II. 127, 133; G.B. IX. 1. 24; I. 1. 17. 19; M.N.T. II. 32) and they also acknowledge and use the Hinkāra of the Vedas pronounced Hum (S.B. I. 4. 1. 2; IX. 1. 2. 3. 4; A.B. III. 2. 12; L.S.S. I. 10. 25; I. 1. 27; II. 1. 4; IV. 3. 22). The rules and practice of Āchamana, and the bath are exactly the same as will be found on a comparison of chapter V of the Mahānirvāna Tantra with the Snānasūtra of Gobhila. The Tantras prefer to use single compounds instead of long sentences to express an idea and form one letter Mantras very much according to the Vaidik method. We also find the practice of Nyāsa and Shuddhi foreshadowed in the Vedas as has been already mentioned. (See also S.B. VII. 5. 2. 12). The principal Devī of the Veda is Sarasvatī, who is called Nagna in the Nighantu, expressing nudeness, and also referring to that age of a woman when womanhood has not expressed itself. If we again, take these ideas with that of the Sāma-Vidhāna-Brāhmana, we have the almost complete form of a Devī who is called at the present day by the name of Kālī. Another Devī whose worship is very popular at the present day is Durgā, who has a lion for her carrier. It will have been observed, that Vāch turned herself into a lion, and after earnest solicitations went over to the Devas; and therefore, Vāch and the lion are identically the same. We have already given references which show that Vāch and Durgā were the same; and these facts explain how Durgā has a lion to carry her. The worship of Rātri is to be performed at night and therefore the worship of Kālī must be a night performance; and therefore, must partake of all the features of a night performance; and these elements must be sought for in the Vaidik Atirātra. The Atirātra is a performance of three Paryyāyas or rounds of four Stotras and Shāstras in each and at the end of each libations are offered, followed by drinking of Soma. The same rules and practices as in the Atirātra are substantially followed in the worship of the Devī Kālī, *bhāng* being very largely used under the name of Vijayā and Amrita. It will be remembered that the Devī of the Atirātra is Sarasvatī. The principal male Devatā of the Tantras is Mahādeva named also Shiva, Mahesha, Shambhu, Soma and also in a different aspect Rudra. Rudra and Mahādeva are admittedly Vaidik gods. Rudra is described as having bows and arrows and has hundred heads and thousand eyes (S.B. IV. 1. 1. 6; Yajur Veda III. 27). Mahādeva is Mahān devah, the great God (S.B. VI. 1. 3. 16). It appears that the Mantras of the different aspects of Mahādeva, which are even now used by Tāntrikas, were known and used by the Vaidik people. I cannot, however, trace the name Mahesha in Vaidik literature. Shiva can be identified with Rudra Susheva, who is a kind god (S.B. V. 4. 4. 12). Mahādeva (Soma) is clad in a tiger skin which can be traced in Vaidik literature (S.B. V. 3. 5. 3; V. 4. 1. 11). Rudra is black, in the Tantras as well as in the Vedas. He is the same as Manyu with a Devī on each side of him (S.B. IX. 1. 1. 6; XI. 6. 1. 12 and 13). In this connection, we must not fail to note some of the attributes of Vaidik Nirritti. Nirritti is black and is a terrible Devī and punishes those who do not offer Soma to her. She is the Devī of misfortunes and removes all misfortune. She is the genetrix and she is fond of the cremation ground (S.B. VII. 2. 1; A.B. IV. 2. 4).

The Tantras direct the worship also of Ganesha, Kārtika and Vishnu, for whose worship the Sāma-Vidhāna-Brāhmana prescribes the singing of certain Sāmans, known as the Vināyaka Samhitā (S.V. 4. 5. 3. 3), Skanda-Samhitā (S. V. 3. 2. 1. 4) and the Vishnu-Samhitā (S. V. 3. 1. 3. 9) respectively.

The Tantras also direct the use of certain figures which are called Yantras. These may be of various kinds and forms and may be used for various purposes. One of these which is constantly used, is a triangle within a square (M.N.T. Chap. V) and this can be traced to the rules for the preparation of the Agnikshetra, or the Fire Altar of the Vaidik people (S.B. VI. 1. 1. 6). Another curious circumstance in connection with the altar is, that both in the Vaidik and the Tāntrik ritual, the heads of five animals are used in its preparation (S.B. VI. 2. 1. 5-8). The worship of the Lingam is foreshadowed by the Vaidik Deity Vishnu Sipivishta (R.V. VII. 1001, etc.; Nirukta V. 2. 2) and the serpent which twines round Devas or Devīs is foreshadowed by the Sarparājnī, the Serpent Queen (S.B. IV. 6. 9. 17) who is the same as Vāch.

The facts collected here will, it is hoped, enable impartial readers tó come to a definite conclusion as to the relationship of the Vaidik to the Tāntrik ritual.

ABBREVIATIONS

A.A. = Aitareya Āranyaka. A.B. = Aitareya Brāhmana. As. S.S. = Āshvalāyana Shrauta Sūtra. Ap. S.S. = Āpastamba Shrauta Sūtra. Ap. Dh. S. = Āpastamba Dharma Sūtra. Ap. G.S. = Āpastamba Grihya Sūtra. A.V. = Atharva Veda. Ba. Dh. S. = Baudhāyana Dharma Sūtra. Ba. S.S. = Baudhāyana Shrauta Sūtra. Br. D. = Brihaddevatā (Calcutta edition). Chh. Up. = Chhāndatra Upanishad. Ga. Dh. S. = Gautama Dharma Sūtra. G.B. = Gopatha Brāhmana. G. G. S. = Gobhila Grihya Sūtra. G. Sn. S. = Gobhila Snāna Sūtra. H. G. S. = Hiranyakeshīya Grihya Sūtra. K.S.S. = Kātyāyana Shrauta Sūtra. Kh. G.S. = Khādira Grihya Sūtra. L.S.S. = Lātyāyana Srauta Sūtra. M.N.T. = Mahānirvāna Tantra. N.S. = Nāradīya Shikshā. Ngh. = Nighantu. Nir. = Nirukta. P.S. = Pāninīya Shikshā. P.G.S. = Parāshara Grihya Sūtra. R.V. = Rig Veda. R.V.B. = Rig Vidhāna Brāhmana. Rik. P. = Rik-Parishishta. R.V.Kh. = Rig Veda Khila. S.B. = Shatapatha Brāhmana. S.G.S. = Sānkhyāyana Grihya Sūtra. S.V.B. = Sāma Vidhāna Brāhmana. S.V.St. = Sāma Veda Stobha portion. S.V. = Sāma Veda. S.S.S. = Sankhyāyana Shrauta Sūtra. T.A. = Taittirīya Āranyaka. Tait. Br. = Taittirīya Brāhmana. Tan. Br. = Tāndya Brāhmana. Va. Dh. S. = Vashistha Dharma Sūtra. Yag. = Yājnavalkya.

CHAPTER V

THE TANTRAS AND RELIGION OF THE SHĀKTAS

[What follows this bracket is a translation, done in literal fashion, from the German, of an article by the learned Sanskritist, Professor Winternitz, entitled "Die Tantras und die Religion der Saktas" published in the Berlin monthly, the "Ostasiatische Zeitschrift," 1916, Heft 3. The article does not show a complete comprehension of its subject-matter, nor was this to be expected. In European fashion Sādhaka is translated "Magician" and Sādhanā is thought of as "magical evocation" and Mahāyogini as "Great Magician". This is the more unfortunate, as the Professor evidently does not like "magic". It is true that in Indrajalavidyā there is Sādhanā to achieve its purposes, but what is of course meant is Sādhanā in its religious sense. We hear again of "idolatry" though idolatry is not (in the sense in which those who make the charge use the word) to be found in any part of the world. Mantra is still "gibberish," "trash" and so on. After all, many of these matters are as much a question of temperament as argument. The mind which takes these views is like that of the Protestant who called the Catholic Mass "Hocus Pocus". It is superstitious trash to him but a holy reality to the believer. Such criticism involves the fallacy of judging others from one's own subjective standpoint. Moreover, not one man in thousands is capable of grasping the inner significance of this doctrine and for this reason it is kept secret nor does any writing reveal it to those without understanding. The learned Professor has also evidently no liking for "Occultism" and "India-faddists" (Indiensschwarmern). But the former exists whether we like its facts or not. Nevertheless, in reading this article one feels oneself in the presence of a learned mind which wills to be fair and is not to be stampeded from investigation on hearing the frightful word "Tantra". Several appreciations are just. Particularly noteworthy is the recognition that the Tantra Shāstras or Āgamas are not merely some pathological excrescence on "Hinduism" but simply one of its several presentations. Nor are they simply Scriptures of the Shāktas. Their metaphysics and ethics are those of the common Brahmanism of which all the sects are offshoots, whatever be the special peculiarities in presentment of doctrine or in its application. Before this Professor Albert Grunwedelhad said (in his "Der Weg Nach Sambhala," Munchen 1915): "The Tantras are nothing but the continuation of the Veda" (Die Tantras, sind eben die fortsetzung des Veda). He calls also the Tantras the "model-room" (Akt-saal) of Indian Art (the Aktsaal is a room in an Academy of Art in which casts are kept as models for the students). These Scriptures, he adds, "furnish the æsthetics and in fact we find that in the later books (of the Kalachakra) the whole figurative mythology (of that system) has been built up on this scheme. Whence this evolution of forms arises is indeed another question which will bring many a surprise to the friends of 'National Indian Art' (sic!). Talking is easier. The Jains too have such things." I may add that the fact that some Jains carry out some so-called "Tāntrik rites" is not generally known. Vaishnavas and Bauddhas also have these rites. Notions and practices generally charged to the Shāktas only are held and carried out by other sects. It is to be remembered also that there are many schools of Āgama. Some of them state that other Āgamas were promulgated "for the delusion of men". It is needless to add that, here as elsewhere, to the adherent of a particular Āgama his particular scripture is good, and it is the scripture of his opponent which is "for delusion". Orthodoxy is "my doxy" in India also amongst some sects. Shākta liberalism (being Advaita Vedanta) finds a place for all.

It cannot, therefore, be said that the Āgamas are wholly worthless and bad without involving all Hinduism in that charge. On the contrary the Professor discovers that behind the "nonsense" there may be a deep sense and that "immorality" is not the end or aim of the Cult of the Mother.[1] He also holds that if the Tāntrik Scriptures contain some things to which he and others take objection, such things in no wise exhaust their contents. There is nothing wonderful about this discovery, which anyone may make for himself by simply reading and understanding the documents, but the wonder, consists in this that it has not hitherto been thought necessary (where it has been possible) to read and understand the Tantra Shāstras first and then to criticise them. All the greater then are our thanks to the learned Sanskritist for his share in this work of justice.—J. W.]

INDIA remains still the most important country on earth for the student of religion. In India we meet with all forms of religious thought and feeling which we find on earth, and that not only at different times but also all together even to-day. Here we find the most primitive belief in ancestral Spirits, in Demons and Nature Deities with a primeval, imageless sacrificial cult. Here also is a polytheism passing all limits, with the most riotous idolatry, temple cult, pilgrimages, and so forth. And, side by side with and beyond these crudest forms of religious life, we find what is deepest and most abstract of what religious thinkers of all times have ever thought about the Deity, the noblest pantheistic and the purest monotheistic conceptions. In India we also find a priestcraft as nowhere else on earth side by side with a religious tolerance which lets sect after sect, with the most wonderful saints, exist together. Here there were and still are forest recluses, ascetics, and

[1] See as to the Secret Ritual and its Objects, Chapter XXVII, *ibid.*

mendicant monks, to whom renunciation of this world is really and truly a matter of deepest sincerity, and together with them hosts of idle mendicant monks, vain fools and hypocrites, to whom religion is only a cloak for selfish pursuits for the gratification of greed for money, of greed for fame or the hankering after power.

From India also a powerful stream of religious ideas has poured forth over the West, and especially over the East, has flooded Central Asia, has spread over Tibet, China, Korea and Japan, and has trickled through the further East down to the remotest islands of the East Indian Archipelago. And finally, in India as well as outside India, Indian religions have often mixed with Christianity and with Islam, now giving and now taking.

Indeed, sufficient reason exists to welcome every work which contributes in one way or other to a richer, deeper or wider knowledge of Indian religion. I would like, therefore, to draw attention in what follows to some recently published works of this nature.

These are the exceedingly meritorious publications of Arthur Avalon with reference to the literature of the Tantras. Through these works we obtain, for the first time, a deeper insight into the literature of the Tantras, the holy books of Shāktism, and into the nature of this much abused religion itself. It is true that H. H. Wilson[1] in his essays on the religious sects of the Hindus which appeared from 1828 to 1832 has given a brief but relatively reliable and just exposition of this religion. M. Monier-Williams[2] who has treated more fully of Shāktism, worship of the Goddess, and the contents of the Tantras, has only to tell terrible and horrible things. He describes the faith

[1] Works, Vol. I, London, 1862, pp. 240-265.

[2] Brahmanism and Hinduism, 4th ed., London, 1891, p. 180 ff.

of the Shāktas, of the worshippers of the feminine Deities, as a mixture of sanguinary sacrifices and orgies with wine and women. Similar is the picture of this sect presented by A. Barth[1] who on the one hand indeed admits that the Cult of the Mother is based on a deep meaning and that the Tantras are also full of theosophical and moral reflections and ascetic theories, but is not thereby prevented from saying that the Shākta is "nearly always a hypocrite and a superstitious debauchee," even though many amongst the authors of the Tantras may have really believed that they were performing a sacred work.[2] R. G. Bhandarkar,[3] to whom we owe the latest and most reliable exposition of Indian sectarianism, happens in fact to deal with the Shāktas very summarily. Whereas the greater part of his excellent book deals with the religion of the Vaishnavas and with the sects of the Shaivas, he only devotes a few pages to the sect of the Shāktas which evidently seems unimportant to him. He speaks, however, both about the metaphysical doctrines and about the cult of this sect, with in every way, the cool, quiet objectivity of the historian. The exposition is only a little too brief and meagre. So, all the more are Avalon's books welcome.

The most valuable is the complete English translation of a Tantra, the Mahānirvāṇa Tantra,[4] with an Introduction of 146 pages which introduces us to the chief doctrines

---

[1] The Religions of India, 2nd ed., London, 1889, p. 199 ff.

[2] Op. Cit., p. 204.

[3] Vaishnavism, Shaivism and Minor Religious Systems. (Grundriss der indo-arischen Philologie und Altertumskunde III (6), Strassburg, 1913, p. 142 ff.) I (Dr. W.) have spoken more fully about this work in the Deutsche Literaturzeitung, 1915, No. 2. [To the above Professor Winternitz might have added Professor Vallée Poussins Studies—J. W.]

[4] Tantra of the Great Liberation (Mahānirvāṇa Tantra), a Translation from the Sanskrit, with Introduction and Commentary by Arthur Avalon.

of the Shāktas and with the exceedingly complicated, perhaps purposely confused, terminology of the Tantras. If we have been accustomed, up till the present, to see nothing else in Shāktism and in the Tantras, the sacred books of this sect, than wild superstition, occult humbug, idiocy, empty magic and a cult with a most objectionable morality, and distorted by orgies—then a glimpse at the text made accessible to us by Avalon, teaches us that—all these things are indeed to be found in this religion and in its sacred texts, but that by these their contents are nevertheless, in no wise exhausted.

On the contrary, we rather find that behind the nonsense there lies hidden after all much deep sense and that immorality is not the end and aim of the cult of the Mother. We find that the mysticism of the Tantras has been built up on the basis of that mystic doctrine of the unity of the soul and of all with the Brahman, which is proclaimed in the oldest Upanishads and which belongs to the most profound speculations which the Indian spirit has imagined. This Brahman, however, the highest divine principle, is, according to the doctrines of the Shākta philosophers, no "nothing", but the eternal, primeval Energy (Shakti) out of which everything has been created, has originated, has been born. Shakti, "Energy," however is not only grammatically feminine. Human experience teaches also that all life is born from the womb of the woman, from the mother. Therefore the Indian thinkers, from whom Shāktism has originated, believed that the highest Deity, the supremest creative principle, should be brought nearest to the human mind not through the word "Father", but through the word "Mother". And all philosophical conceptions to which language has given a feminine gender, as well as all mythological figures which appear feminine in popular belief, become Goddesses, Divine Mothers. So, before all, there is Prakṛiti, taken from the Sangkhya philosophy, primeval matter, "Nature", who stands in contrast to Purusha, the male spirit, and is identical with Shakti. And this Shakti is, again, mythologically conceived as the spouse of God Shiva, Mahādeva, the "Great God". Mythology, however, knew already Umā or Pārvatī, "the daughter of the Mountain", the daughter of the Himālaya, as the spouse of Shiva. And so Prakṛiti, Shaktī, Umā, Pārvatī, are ever one and the same. They are only different names for the one great All-Mother, the Jaganmātā, "the Mother of all the living". The Indian mind had been long since accustomed to see Unity in all Multiplicity. Just as one moon reflects itself in innumerable waters, so Devi, the "Goddess", by whatever other names she may be otherwise called, is the embodiment of all Gods and of all "energies" (Shaktis) of the Gods. Within her is Brahmā, the Creator, and his Shakti; within her is Viṣhnu, the Preserver, and his Shakti; within her is also Shiva as Mahākāla, "great Father Time", the great Destroyer. But as this one is swallowed up by herself, she is also Ādyakālikā, the "primordial Kālī"; and as a "great magician", Mahāyoginī, she is at the same time Creatrix, Preservatrix, and Destroyer of the world. She is also the mother of Mahākāla, who dances before her, intoxicated by the wine of Madhuka blossoms.[1] As, however, the highest Deity is a woman, every woman is regarded as an embodiment of this Deity. Devī, "the Goddess", is within every feminine being. This conception it is, which has led to a woman worship which, undoubtedly, has taken the shape, in many circles, of wild orgies, but which also—at least according to the testimony of the Mahānirvāṇa Tantra—could appear in a purer and nobler form, and has as surely done so.

[1] As all "five true things" begin with an M, they are also called "the five M".

To the worship of the Devī, the Goddess, who is the joyously creative energy of nature, belong the "five true things" (Panchatattva) through which mankind enjoy gladly, preserve their life and procreate; intoxicating drink which is a great medicine to man, a breaker of sorrows and a source of pleasure; meat of the animals in the villages, in the air and in the forests, which is nutritious and strengthens the force of body and mind; fish which is tasty and augments procreative potency; roasted corn which, easily obtained, grows in the earth and is the root of life in the three worlds; and fifthly physical[1] union with Shakti "the source of bliss of all living beings, the deepest cause of creation and the root of the eternal world".[2] But these "five true things" may only be used in the circle of initiates, and only after they have been consecrated by sacred formulas and ceremonies. The Mahānirvāṇa Tantra lays stress on the fact that no abuse may be made of these five things. Who drinks immoderately is no true worshipper of the Devī. Immoderate drinking, which disturbs seeing and thinking, destroys the effect of the sacred action. In the sinful Kali age also, only the own spouse should be enjoyed as Shakti. In everything the Tantra takes all imaginable trouble to excuse the Panchatattva ceremonies and to prevent their abuse. In the Kali age sweets (milk, sugar, honey) must be used instead of intoxicating drink, and the adoration of the lotus feet of the Devī should be substituted for the physical union. The worship should not be secret, indecencies should not occur, and evil, impious people should not be admitted to the circle of the worshippers.[3] True, it is permissible for the "Hero" (Vīrà)

---

[1] Mahānirvāṇa Tantra, VIII, 108 ff. (p. 156).

[2] Mahānirvāṇa Tantra, IV, 29-31, V, 141.

[3] Mahānirvāṇa Tantra, VI, 186 ff. (p. 185 ff.); VI, 14 ff. (p. 104 f.); VIII, 171 ff., 190 ff. (pp. 177, 180).

who is qualified to be Sādhaka or "magician" to unite in secret worship with other Shaktis. Only in the highest "heavenly condition" (Divyabhāva) of the saint do purely symbolical actions take the place of the "five true things".

But to the worship of the Devī belong in the first place Mantras (formulas) and Bījas (monosyllabic mysterious words like Aim, Klīm, Hrīm, etc.); further also Yantras (diagrams of a mysterious meaning, drawn on metal, paper or other material), Mudrās (special finger positions and hand movements) and Nyāsas. (These last consist in putting the tips of the fingers and the flat of the right hand, with certain mantras, on the various parts of the body, in order by that to fill one's own body with the life of the Devī.) By the application of all these means the worshipper renders the Deity willing and forces him into his service, and becomes a Sādhaka, a magician. For Sādhanā, "Magic", is the chief aim, though not the final aim of Devī worship.

This highest and final aim is the same as that of all Indian sects and religious systems; Mokṣha or deliverance, the unification with the Deity in Mahānirvāṇa, the "great extinction". The perfected saint, the Kaula, reaches this condition already in the present life and is one who is liberated whilst living (Jīvanmukta). But the way to deliverance can only be found through the Tantras. For Veda, Smṛiti, Purāṇas and Itihāsa are each the sacred books of past ages of the world, whilst for our present evil age, the Kali age, the Tantras have been revealed by Shiva for the salvation of mankind (I, 20 ff.) The Tantras thus on the strength of their own showing indicate themselves to be relatively modern works.[1] In the present

[1] In the present cycle these Scriptures come last before the Satya Yuga of the next cycle.

age Vedic and other rites and prayers have no value but only the mantras and ceremonies taught in the Tantras (II, 1 ff.). And just as the worship of the Devī leads equally to thoroughly materialistic results through magic and to the highest ideal of Nirvāṇa, so there is a strong mixture in the worship itself of the sensuous and the spiritual. Characteristic is Mahānirvāṇa Tantra V, 139-151 (P. 86 ff.): The worshipper first offers to the Devī spiritual adoration, dedicating to her his heart as her seat, the nectar of his heart as the water for washing her feet, his mind as a gift of honour, the restlessness of his senses and thoughts as a dance, selflessness, dispassionateness, and so forth as flowers, but then he offers to the Devī an ocean of introxicating drink, a mountain of meat and dried fish, a heap of roasted corn in milk, with sugar and butter, "nectar" and other things. Besides the "five true things" and other elements of this most sensuous worship which is calculated to produce the intoxication of the senses, and in which also bells, incense, flowers, lights and rosaries are not lacking, there is also the quiet contemplation (Dhyāna) of the Deity. And likewise, we find side by side with mantras which are completely senseless and insipid such beautiful sayings as, for instance, V, 156: "O Adyā Kālī, who dwellest in the innermost soul of all, who art the innermost light, O Mother! Accept this prayer of my heart. I bow down before thee."

The Shāktas are a sect of the religion which is commonly designated "Hinduism," a term which is a facile one but which has not been chosen very happily. The word embraces all the sects and creeds which have originated from Brahmanism through a mixture with the cults of the aborigines of India and thus represent a kind of degeneration of the old Brahmanical religion, but which still hold fast more or less, to orthodox Brahmanism [1] and so distinguish themselves from the heretical sects (Buddhists and Jains). In reality there is strictly no sense in speaking of "Hinduism" as a "system" or as one "religion". For it is impossible to say where Brahmanism ends and where "Hinduism" begins. We are also altogether ignorant as to how much the old Brahmanic religion had already assimilated from the faith and the customs of the non-Aryan populace. For it is not admissible to classify without further ado all animal worship, all demon worship, all fetichism and so on as "non-Aryan". In reality all sects of "Hinduism" which are related to a worship of Viṣhnu or of Shiva, are nothing but offshoots of the original Brahmanism, which they never, however, deny. So also Shāktism has as a special characteristic merely the worship of the Shaktis, of the female deities, with its accessory matter (of the "five true things," the worship in the chakra or "circle" of the initiates, and so on). For the rest, its dogmatics—or if it be preferred, its metaphysics—as well as its ethics are altogether those of Brahmanism, of which also the essential ritual institutions have been preserved. In dogmatics it is the teachings of the orthodox systems of the Vedanta and the Sāṅkhya, which meet us also in the Tantras clearly enough, sometimes even under the trash of senseless magic formulas. And as far as ethics are concerned, the moral teaching in the VIII chapter of the Mahānirvāṇa Tantra reminds us from beginning to end of Manu's Code, the Bhagavad Gita, and the Buddhist sermons. Notwithstanding the fact that in the ritual proper of the Shākta there are no caste differences but in Shakti worship all castes as well as the sexes are equal, yet, in

[1] Compare the definition of "Hinduism" in Monier Williams' "Hinduism", London (Society for Promoting Christian Knowledge), 1882, p. 84 ff.

harmony with Brahmanism, the castes are recognized, with this modification that a fifth caste is added to the four usual ones, which springs from the mixture of the four older ones, namely, the caste of the Sāmanyas. Whilst Manu, however, distinguishes four Ashramas or statuses of life, the Mahānirvāṇa Tantra teaches that there are only two Ashramas in the Kali age, the status of the householder and that of the ascetic. For the rest, everything which is taught in our Tantra about the duties towards parents, towards wife and child, towards relations and in general towards fellowmen, might find a place, exactly in the same way, in any other religious book or even in a profane manual of morals. As an example we may quote only a few verses from this Chapter VIII: (*vv.* 24, 25, 33, 35, 39, 45-47, 63-67).

The duties of each of the castes as well as the duties of the king are not prescribed much differently from Manu. Family life is estimated very highly by the Mahānirvāṇa Tantra. So it is rigorously prescribed that no one is allowed to devote himself to the ascetic life who has children, wives, or such like near relations to maintain.[1] Entirely in consonance with the prescriptions of the Brahmanic texts also are the "sacraments from conception until the marriage which are described in the 9th chapter of the Mahānirvāṇa Tantra (*Samskāras*). Likewise in the 10th chapter the direction for the disposal and the cult of the dead (*Shrāddha*) are given. A peculiarity of the Shāktas in connection with marriage consists in the fact that side by side with the *Brahma* marriage for which the Brahmanic prescriptions are valid, there is also a Shaiva marriage, that is a kind of marriage for a limited period which is only permitted to the

[1] In the Kautilya-Arthashāstra, the oldest manual of politics (11-1-1919, p. 48) a fine is prescribed for him who becomes an ascetic without having previously made provision for wife and child.

members of the circle (*Chakra*) of the initiates. But children out of such a marriage are not legitimate and do not inherit.[1] So far Brahmanic law applies also to the Shāktas, and so the section concerning civil and criminal law in the 11th and 12th chapters of the Mahānirvāṇa Tantra substantially agree with Manu.

Of course, notwithstanding all this, the Kauladharma expounded in the Tantra is declared the best of all religions in an exuberant manner and the veneration of the *Kula*-saint is praised as the highest merit. It is said in a well-known Buddhist text: "As, ye monks, there is place for every kind of footprints of living beings that move in the footprint of the elephant, because, as is known indeed, the footprint of the elephant is the first in size amongst all, so, ye monks, all salutary doctrines are contained in the four noble truths." So it is said in the Mahānirvāṇa Tantra,[2] (probably in recollection of the Buddhist passage): "As the footprints of all animals disappear in the footprint of the elephant, so disappear all other religions (*dharma*) in the Kula religion (*kula-dharma*)."

From what has been said it is clear that Avalon is right when he declares that uptill now this literature has been only too often judged and still more condemned without knowing it, and that the Tantras deserve to become better known than has been the case hitherto. From the point of view of the history of religion they are already important for the reason that they have strongly influenced Mahāyāna Buddhism and specially the Buddhism of Tibet. It is, therefore, much to be welcomed that Avalon has undertaken to publish a series of texts and translations from this literature. It is true that we have no desire to be made

[1] It is incorrect to call them illegitimate children. But offsprings of a Brahma marriage are preferential inheritors.—J. W.

[2] XIV, 180, *cf.* Majjimanikaya 28.

acquainted with all the 3×64 Tantras which are said to exist. For—this should not be denied, that for the greatest part these works contain, after all, only stupidity and gibberish ("doch nur Stumpfsinn und Kauderwelsch"). This is specially true of the Bījas and Mantras, the mysterious syllables and words and the magic formulas which fill these volumes. To understand this gibberish only to a certain degree and to bring some sense into this stupidity, it is necessary to know the Tāntric meaning of the single vowels and consonants. For, amongst the chief instruments of the magic which plays such a great part in these texts, belongs the spoken word. It is not the meaning embedded in the mantra which exercises power over the deity, but the word, the sound. Each sound possesses a special mysterious meaning. Therefore, there are special glossaries in which this mysterious meaning of the single vowels and consonants is taught. A few of such glossaries, indispensable helps for the Sādhaka, or rather the pupil who wants to develop himself into a Sādhaka, have been brought to light in the first volume of the series of Tāntric Texts,[1] published by Avalon: The Mantrābhidhāna belonging to the Rudrayāmala, Ekāksharakosha ascribed to Purushottamadeva the Bījanighantu of Bhairava and two Mātrikanighantus, the one by Mahīdhara, the other by Mādhava.[2] Added to these is one other auxiliary text of this same kind, the Mudrānighantu, belonging to the Vāmakeṣhvara Tantra, an enumeration of the finger positions as they are used in Yoga.

[1] Tāntrik Texts published by Arthur Avalon : Vol. I. Tantrābhidāna, II. Shatchakra Nirūpaṇa, III. Prapañchasāra (since published and not before Professor Winternitz when he wrote this review), IV. Kulachūdāmaṇi, V. Kulārṇava, VI. Kālīvilāsa, VII. Shrichakra Sambhara, VIII. Tantrarāja, IX. Kāmakalāvilāsa. (A.A.)

[2] *Cf.* in connection with these glossaries also Th Zachariæ, Die indischen Worterbucher (Grundriss der indo-arischen Phil. 1, 3B, 1897) Sec. 27.

The second volume of the same series of Texts contain the text of the Shaṭchakranirūpaṇa, the "description of the six circles," together with no less than three commentaries. The "six circles" are six places in the human body, imagined as lotus-shaped, of great mystical significance and therefore of great importance for Yoga. The first of these circles is Mūlādhāra, which is described as a triangle in the middle of the body with its point downwards and imagined as a red lotus with four petals on which are written the four golden letters Vam, Sham, Sam and Sham. In the centre of this lotus is Svayambhuliṅga. At the root of this reddish brown liṅga the Chitrinīnadi opens, through which the Devī Kundalinī ascends, more delicate than a lotus fibre and more effulgent than lightning, and so on.[1] The Shaṭchakranirūpaṇa is the VI chapter of the Shritattva-chintāmani composed by Purnānanda Swāmi. In addition the volume contains the text of a hymn, entitled Pāduka-panchakam, which is said to have been revealed by Shiva, and a voluminous commentary.

The third volume of the Series contains the text of the Prapañchasāratantra which is ascribed to the Vedantic philosopher Shaṅkarāchārya, and by others to the deity Shiva in his incarnation as Shaṅkarāchārya.

The name Shaṅkara appears fairly often in Tantra literature, but it is not at all sure that the works in question really come from the Philosopher. Avalon prefaces the text by a detailed description of the contents of the work. *Prapancha* means "extension," "the extended Universe" from which "Prapañchasāra" "the innermost being of the universe". The work begins with a description of creation,

[1] Any one interested in these "Six Circles" Chakra will find them described in Avalon's Introduction to the Mahānirvāṇa Tantra, pp. lxii-lxiii (and later and more fully in "The Serpent Power".—J. W.)

accompanied, in the first two chapters, by detailed expositions of Chronology, Embryology, Anatomy, Physiology and Psychology, which are exactly as "scientific" as both the following chapters which treat of the mysterious meaning of the letters of the Sanskrit alphabet and of the Bījas. The further chapters which partly contain rituals, partly prayers, meditations and Stotras, are of greater importance from the standpoint of the history of religion. To how high a degree in the Shakti cult the erotic element predominates, is shown in IX, 23 ff., where a description is given, "how the wives of the gods, demons, and demi-gods impelled by mantras come to the magician, the Sādhaka, oppressed by the greatness of their desires." In the XVIII chapter, the mantras and the dhyānas (meditations) for the adoration of the God of love and his Shaktis are taught, and the union of man and woman is represented as a mystic union of the "I" (*Ahamkāra*) with perception (*Buddhi*) and as a sacred sacrificial action. When a man honours his beloved wife in such a way, she will, struck by the arrows of the God of love, follow him like a shadow even in the other world (XVIII, 33). The XXVIII chapter is devoted to *Ārdhanarīṣhvara*, the God who is half woman —Shiva, represented as a wild looking man, forms the right-hand half of the body, and his Shakti represented as a voluptuous woman, the left-hand half. The XXXIII chapter which seems to have originally closed the work describes in its first part ceremonies against childlessness, the cause of which is indicated as lack of veneration of the Gods and neglect of the wife. The second part is connected with the relation between teacher and pupil which is of extreme importance for the Shākta religion. Indeed, worship of the Guru, the teacher, plays a prominent part in this sect.

However, the rituals and Mantras described in this Tantra are not exclusively connected with the different forms of the Devī and Shiva, but Viṣhnu and his Avatāras are also often honoured. The XXXVI chapter contains a disquisition on Viṣhnu Trilokyamohana (the Enchanter of the triple world) in verses 35-47 translated by Avalon.[1] It is a description glowing and sensuous (Voll sinnlicher Glut.): Viṣhnu shines like millions of suns and is of infinite beauty. Full of goodness his eye rests on Shrī, his spouse, who embraces him, full of love. She too is of incomparable beauty. All the Gods and Demons and their wives offer homage to the August Pair. The Goddesses, however, press themselves in a burning yearning of love towards Viṣhnu, whilst exclaiming: "Be our husband, our refuge, August Lord!" In addition to this passage Avalon has also translated the hymns to Prakṛiti (Chapter XI), to Viṣhnu (Chapter XXI) and to Shiva (Chapter XXVI).[2] Of these hymns the same holds good as of the collection of hymns to the Devī, which Avalon, together with his wife, has translated in a separate volume.[3] Whilst many of these texts are mere insipid litanies of names and epithets of the worshipped deities, there are others, which, as to profoundness of thought and beauty of language may be put side by side with the best productions of the religious lyrics of the Indians. So the hymn to Prakṛiti in the Prapañchasāra XI, 48, begins with the words:

"Be gracious to me, O Pradhāna, who art Prakṛiti in the form of the elemental world. Life of all that lives. With folded hands I make obeisance to thee our Lady, whose very nature it is to do that which we cannot understand."

---

[1] Introduction, p. 61 ff.

[2] Introduction, p. 29 ff., 45 ff. and 52 ff.

[3] Hymns to the Goddess translated from the Sanskrit by Arthur and Ellen Avalon (1913).

It is intelligible that the poets have found much more intimate cries of the heart when they spoke of the Deity as their "Mother" than when they addressed themselves to God as Father. So, for instance, it is said in a hymn to the Goddess[1] ascribed to Shaṅkara:

2

By my ignorance of Thy commands
By my poverty and sloth
I had not the power to do that which I should have done
Hence my omission to worship Thy feet.
But Oh Mother, auspicious deliverer of all,
All this should be forgiven me
For, a bad son may sometimes be born, but a bad mother never.

3

Oh Mother! Thou hast many sons on earth,
But I, your son, am of no worth;
Yet it is not meet that Thou shouldst abandon me
For, a bad son may sometimes be born, but a bad mother never.

4

Oh Mother of the world, Oh Mother!
I have not worshipped Thy feet,
Nor have I given abundant wealth to Thee,
Yet the affection which Thou bestowest on me is without compare,
For, a bad son may sometimes be born, but a bad mother never.

Avalon looks with great sympathy on the Shākta religion which has found the highest expression for the

[1] Hymns to the Goddess, p. 94 ff., Verse 24.

divine principle in the conception "Mother". He is of opinion[1] that when the European thinks that it is a *debasement* of the deity to conceive of it as feminine, then this can only be because he "looks upon his mother's sex as lower than his own" and because he thinks it unworthy of the deity to conceive it otherwise than masculine. That the conception of the Indian and especially of the Shākta is, in this connection, the more unbiased and unprejudiced one, we will freely concede to Avalon. He, however, goes still further and believes that the Tantras not only have an interest from the point of view of the history of religion, but that they also possess an independent value as manuals of Sādhanā, that is magic.[2] However grateful we might be to the editor and translator of these texts for having made us better acquainted with a little known and much misunderstood Indian system of religion, we yet would hope to be saved from the possibility of seeing added to the Vedantists, Neo-Buddhists, Theosophists and other India-faddists (Indienschwarmern) in Europe and America, adherents of the Sādhanā of the Shakti cult. The student of religion cannot and may not leave the Tantras and Shāktism unnoticed. They have their place in the history of religion. But, may this occultism, which often flows from very turbid sources—(this word should not be translated as "Secret Science" thus abusing the sacred name of Science, but rather as "Mystery Mongering" (Geheimtuerei) remain far away from our intellectual life.

[To the above may be added a recent criticism of M. Masson Oursel of the College de France in the Journal "Isis" (iii, 1920) which is summarized and translated from the French: "The obscurity of language, strangeness of

---

[1] Hymns to the Goddess, Preface.

[2] Tāntrik Text, Vol. I, p. 4.

thought and rites sometimes adjudged scandalous, have turned away from the study of the immense Tāntrik literature even the most courageous savants. If, however, the Tantras have appeared to be a mere mass of aberrations, it is because the key to them was unknown. The Tantras are the culmination of the whole Indian literature. Into them flow both the Vedic and popular cults. Tāntricism has imposed itself on the whole Hindu mentality (le Tantrisme, est imposé à toute la mentalité hindoue). Arthur Avalon has undertaken with complete success a task which in appearance seems to be a thankless one but is in reality fecund of results."

The article of Dr. Winternitz deals largely with the Mahānirvāṇa Tantra. Because objections cannot be easily found against this Tantra, the theory has been lately put forward by Dr. Farquhar in his last work on Indian Literature that this particular scripture is exceptional and the work of Ram Mohun Roy's Guru Hariharānanda Bhārati. The argument is in effect " All Tantras are bad; this is not bad: therefore it is not a Tantra." In the first place, the MS. referred to in the Preface to A. Avalon's translation of this Tantra as having been brought to Calcutta, was an old MS. having the date Shakābda 1300 odd, that is, several hundreds of years ago. Secondly, the Mahānirvāṇa which belongs to the Viṣhnukrāntā, or as some say Rathakrāntā, is mentioned in the Mahāsiddhisāra Tantra, an old copy of which was the property of Rāja Sir Radhakant Dev (b. 1783—d. 1867), a contemporary of Raja Ram Mohun Roy (1774-1833) who survived the latter's son. The earliest edition of that Tantra by Ānandachandrā Vedāntavāgīsha was published from a text in the Sānskrit College Library which is not likely to have had amongst its MSS. one which was the work of a man who, whatever be the date of his death, must have died within a comparatively short period of the publication of this edition. In fact, the Catalogue describes it as an old MS. and an original Tantra. Dr. Rajendralala Mitra in his notice of a MS. of the Tagore collection speaks of it as containing only the first half of fourteen chapters. This is so. The second half is not published and is very rare. The Pandit's copy to which reference was made in the Preface to A. A.'s translation of the Mahānirvāṇa contained both parts. How comes it that if the Tantra was written by Raja Ram Mohun Roy's Guru that we only have the first half and not the second containing amongst other things the so-called magic or Shaṭkarma. It should be mentioned that there are three Tantras—the Nirvāṇa, Bṛihannirvāṇa and Mahānirvāṇa Tantras, similar to the group Nila, Brihannila and Mahānila Tantras. It is to be noted also that in the year 1293 B.S. or 1886 an edition of the Mahānirvāṇa was published with commentary by a Sannyasin calling himself Shaṅkarācharacharya under the auspices of the Danda Sabha of Maṇikarnika Ghat, Benares, which contains more verses than is contained in the text, commented upon by Hariharānanda and the interpretation of the latter as also that of Jagamohan Tarkālaṅkara, are in several matters controverted. We are asked to suppose that Hariharānanda was both the author of, and commentator on, the Tantra. That the Mahānirvāṇa has its merits is obvious, but there are others which have theirs. The same critic speaks of the Prapañchasâra as a "rather foul work". This criticism is ridiculous. The text is published for any one to judge. All that can be said is what Dr. Winternitz has said, namely, that there are a few passages with sensuous erotic imagery. These are descriptive of the state of women in love. What is wrong here? There is nothing "foul" in this except for people to whom all erotic phenomena are foul. "This is a very indecent picture," said an elderly lady to Byron, who retorted " Madam, the indecency consists in your remark." It cannot be too often asserted that the ancient East was purer in these matters than the modern West, where, under cover of a pruriently modest exterior, a cloaca of extraordinarily varied psychopathic filth may flow. This was not so in earlier days, whether of East or West, when a spade was called a spade and not a horticultural instrument. In America it is still, I am told, considered indecent to mention the word "leg". One must say "limb". Said Tertullian: " Natura veneranda et non erubescenda "; that is, where the knower venerates his unknowing critic blushes.

The Prapañchasāra which does not even deal with the rite against which most objection has been taken (while the Mahānirvāṇa does), treats of the creation of the world, the generation of bodies, physiology, the classification of the letters, the Kalās, initiation, Japa, Homa, the Gāyatri Mantra, and ritual worship of various Devatas and so forth; with facts in short which are not "foul" with or without the qualifying "rather".

J. W.]

CHAPTER VI

SHAKTI AND SHĀKTA

SHAKTI who is in Herself pure blissful Consciousness (Chidrūpiṇī) is also the Mother of Nature and is Nature itself born of the creative play of Her thought. The Ṣhākta faith, or worship of Shakti, is, I believe, in some of its essential features one of the oldest and most wide-spread religions in the world. Though very ancient, it is yet, in its essentials, and in the developed form in which we know it to-day, harmonious with some of the teachings of modern philosophy and science; not that this is necessarily a test of its truth. It may be here noted that in the West, and in particular in America and England, a large number of books are now being published on "New Thought," "Will Power," "Vitalism," "Creative Thought," "Right Thought," "Self Unfoldment," "Secret of Achievement," "Mental Therapeutics" and the like, the principles of which are essentially those of some forms of Shakti Sādhanā both higher and lower. There are books of disguised magic as how to control others (Vashīkaraṇa) by making them buy what they do not want, how to secure "affection" and so forth which, notwithstanding some hypocrisies, are in certain respects on the same level as the Tāntrik Shavara as a low class of books on magic are called. Shavara or Chaṇḍāla are amogst the lowest of men. The ancient and at the same time distinguishing character of the faith is instanced by temple worship (the old Vaidik worship was generally in the home or in the open by the river), the cult of images, of Linga and Yoni (neither of which, it is said, were part of the original Vaidik practice), the worship of Devīs and of the Magna Mater (the great Vaidik Devatā was the male Indra) and other matters of both doctrine and practice.

Many years ago Edward Sellon, with the aid of a learned Orientalist of the Madras Civil Service, attempted to learn its mysteries, but for reasons, which I need not here discuss, did not view them from the right standpoint. He, however, compared the Shāktas with the Greek Telestica or Dynamica, the Mysteries of Dionysus "Fire born in the cave of initiation" with the Shakti Pūjā, the Shakti Shodhana with the purification shown in d'Hancarvilles' "Antique Greek Vases"; and after referring to the frequent mention of this ritual in the writings of the Jews and other ancient authors, concluded that it was evident that we had still surviving in India in the Shākta worship a very ancient, if not the most ancient, form of Mysticism in the whole world. Whatever be the value to be given to any particular piece of evidence, he was right in his general conclusion. For, when we throw our minds back upon the history of this worship we see stretching away into the remote and fading past the figure of the Mighty Mother of Nature, most ancient among the ancients; the Ādyā Shakti, the dusk Divinity, many breasted crowned with towers whose veil is never lifted, Isis, "the one who is all that has been, is and will be," Kālī, Hathor, Cybele, the Cowmother Goddess Ida, Tripurasundarī, the Ionic Mother, Tef the spouse of Shu by whom He effects the birth of all things, Aphrodite, Astarte in whose groves the Baalim were set, Babylonian Mylitta, Buddhist Tārā, the Mexican Ish, Hellenic Osia, the consecrated, the free and pure, African Salambo who like Pārvatī roamed the Mountains,

Roman Juno, Egyptian Bast the flaming Mistress of Life, of Thought, of Love, whose festival was celebrated with wanton joy, the Assyrian Mother Succoth Benoth, Northern Freia, Mūlaprakriti, Semele, Māyā, Ishtar, Saitic Neith Mother of the Gods, eternal deepest ground of all things, Kundalī, Guhyamahābhairavī and all the rest.

And yet there are people who allege that the "Tāntrik" cult is modern. To deny this is not to say that there has been or will be no change or development in it. As man changes, so do the forms of his beliefs. An ancient feature of this faith and one belonging to the ancient Mysteries is the distinction which it draws between the initiate whose Shakti is awake (Prabuddha) and the Pashu the unillumined or "animal" and, as the Gnostics called him, "material" man. The Natural, which is the manifestation of the Mother of Nature, and the Spiritual or the Mother as She is in and by Herself are one, but the initiate alone truly recognizes this unity. He knows himself in all his natural functions as the one Consciousness whether in enjoyment (Bhukti), or Liberation (Mukti). It is an essential principle of Tāntrik Sādhanā that man in general must rise through and by means of Nature, and not by an ascetic rejection of Her. A profoundly true principle is here involved whatever has been said of certain applications of it. When Orpheus transformed the old Bacchic cult, it was the purified who in the beautiful words of Euripides "went dancing over the hills with the daughters of Iacchos". I cannot, however, go into this matter in this paper which is concerned with some general subjects and the ordinary ritual. But the evidence is not limited to mysteries of the Shakti Pūjā. There are features in the ordinary outer worship which are very old and widespread, as are also other parts of the esoteric teaching. In this connection, a curious instance of the existence, beyond India, of Tāntrik doctrine and practice is here given. The American Indian Maya Scripture of the Zunis called the Popul Vuh speaks of Hurakan or Lightning, that is (I am told) Kundalīshakti; of the "air tube" or "White-cord" or the Sushumnā Nādi; of the "two-fold air tube" that is Idā and Pingalā; and of various bodily centres which are marked by animal glyphs.

Perhaps the Panchatattva Ritual followed by some of the adherents of the Tantras is one of the main causes which have operated in some quarters against acceptance of the authority of these Scriptures and as such responsible for the notion that the worship is modern. On the contrary, the usage of wine, meat, and so forth is itself very old. There are people who talk of these rites as though they were some entirely new and comparatively modern invention of the "Tantra", wholly alien to the spirit and practice of the early times. If the subject be studied it will, I think, be found that in this matter those worshippers who practise these rites are (except possibly as to Maithuna) the continuators of very ancient practices which had their counterparts in the earlier Vaidikāchāra, but were subsequently abandoned, possibly under the influence of Jainism and Buddhism. I say "counterpart", for I do not mean to suggest that in every respect the rites were the same. In details and as regards, I think, some objects in view, they differed. Thus we find in this Panchatattva Ritual a counterpart to the Vaidik usage of wine and animal food. As regards wine, we have the partaking of Soma; meat was offered in Māṁsāshṭaka Shrāddha; fish in the Ashtakashrāddha and Pretashrāddha; and Maithuna as a recognized rite will be found in the Vāmadevya Vrata and Mahāvrata of universally recognized Vaidik texts, apart from the alleged, and generally unknown, Saubhāgyakānda of the Atharvaveda to which the Kālikopanishad and other "Tāntrik" Upanishads are said to belong. Possibly, however, this element of Maithuna may be foreign and imported by Chīnāchāra (see Ch. V). So again, as that distinguished scholar Professor Ramendra Sundara Trivedi has pointed out in his Vichitraprasanga, the Mudrā of the Panchatattva corresponds with the Purodāsha cake of the Soma and other Yāgas. The present rule of abstinence from wine, and in some cases, meat is due, I believe, to the original Buddhism. It is so-called "Tāntriks", who follow (in and for their ritual only) the earlier practice. It is true that the Samhitā of Ushanāh says, "Wine is not to be drunk, given or taken (Madyam apeyam adeyam agrāhyam)" but the yet greater Manu states, "There is no wrong in the eating of meat or the drinking of wine (Na māṁsabakshane dosho na madye)" though he rightly adds, as many now do, that abstention therefrom is productive of great fruit (Nivrittistu mahāphalā). The Tāntrik practice does not allow extra-ritual or "useless" drinking (Vrithāpāna).

Further, it is a common error to confound two distinct things, namely, belief and practice and the written records of it. These latter may be comparatively recent, whilst that of which they speak may be most ancient. When I speak of the ancient past of this faith I am not referring merely to the *writings* which exist to-day which are called Tantras. These are composed generally in a simple Sanskrit by men whose object it was to be understood rather than to show skill in literary ornament. This simplicity is a sign of age. But at the same time it is Laukika and not Ārsha Sanskrit. Moreover, there are statements in them which (unless interpolations) fix the limits of their age. I am not speaking of the writings themselves but of what they say. The faith that they embody, or at least its earlier forms, may have existed for many ages before it was reduced to writing amongst the Kulas or family folk, who received it as handed down by tradition (Pāramparyya) just as did the Vaidik Gotras. That such beliefs and practices, like all other things, have had their development in course of time is also a likely hypothesis.

A vast number of Tantras have disappeared probably for ever. Of those which survive a large number are unknown. Most of those which are available are of a fragmentary character. Even if these did appear later than some other Shāstras, this would not, on Indian principles, affect their authority. According to such principles the authority of a Scripture is not determined by its date; and this is sense. Why, it is asked, should something said 1,000 years ago be on that account only truer than what was said 100 years ago? It is held that whilst the teaching of the Āgama is ever existent, particular Tantras are constantly being revealed and withdrawn. There is no objection against a Tantra merely because it was revealed to-day. When it is said that Shiva spoke the Tantras, or Brahmā wrote the celebrated Vaiṣhnava poem called the Brahmasamhitā, it is not meant that Shiva and Brahmā materialised and took a reed and wrote on birch bark or leaf, but that the Divine Consciousness to which men gave these and other names inspired a particular man to teach, or to write, a particular doctrine or work touching the eternally existing truth. This again does not mean that there was any one whispering in his ear, but that these things arose in his consciousness. What is done in this world is done through man. There is a profounder wisdom than is generally acknowledged in the saying "God helps those who help themselves". Inspiration too never ceases. But how, it may be asked, are we to know that what is said is right and true? The answer is "by its fruits". The authority of a Shāstra is determined by the question whether Siddhi is gained through its provisions or not. It is not enough that "Shiva uvācha" (Shiva says) is writ in it.

The test is that of Āyurveda. A medicine is a true one if it cures. *The Indian test for everything is actual experience.* It is from Samādhi that the ultimate proof of Advaitavāda is sought. How is the existence of Kalpas known? It is said they have been remembered, as by the Buddha who is recorded as having called to mind 91 past Kalpas. There are arguments in favour of rebirth but that which is tendered as real proof is both the facts of ordinary daily experience which can, it is said, be explained only on the hypothesis of pre-existence; as also actual recollection by self-developed individuals of their previous lives. Modern Western methods operate through magnetic sleep producing "regression of memory". (See A. de Rochas "Les Vies Successives" and Lancelin "La Vie posthume".) Age, however, is not wholly without its uses: because one of the things to which men look to see in a Shāstra is whether it has been accepted or quoted in works of recognized authority. Such a test of authenticity can, of course, only be afforded after the lapse of considerable time. But it does not follow that a statement is in fact without value because, owing to its having been made recently, it is not possible to subject it to such a test. This is the way in which this question of age and authority is looked at on Indian principles.

A wide survey of what is called orthodox "Hinduism" *to-day* (whatever be its origins) will disclose the following results: Vedānta in the sense of Upanishad as its *common doctrinal basis*, though variously interpreted, and a great number of differing disciplines or *modes of practice* by which the Vedānta doctrines are realized in actual fact. We must carefully distinguish these two. Thus the Vedānta says "So'ham"; which is Haṁsa. "Hakāra is one wing; Sakāra is the other. When stripped of both wings She Tāra is Kāmakalā." (Tantrarāja Tantra.) The Āchāras set forth the means by which "So'ham" is to be translated into actual fact for the particular Sādhaka. Sādhanā comes from the root "Sādh" which means effort or striving or accomplishment. Effort for and towards what? The answer for those who desire it is liberation from every form in the hierarchy of forms, which exist as such, because consciousness has so limited itself as to obscure the Reality which it is, and which "So'ham" or "Shivo'ham" affirm. And why should man liberate himself from material forms? Because it is said, that way only lasting happiness lies: though a passing yet, fruitful bliss may be had here by those who identify themselves with the active Brahman (Shakti). It is the actual experience of this declaration of "So'ham" which in its fundamental aspect is Veda: knowledge (Vid) or actual Spiritual Experience, for in the monistic sense to truly know anything is to *be* that thing. This Veda or experience is not to be had sitting down thinking vaguely on the Great Ether and doing nothing. Man must *transform* himself, that is, *act* in order to know. Therefore, the watchword of the Tantras is Kriyā or action.

The next question is what Kriyā should be adopted towards this end of Jnāna. "Tanyate, vistāryate jnānam anena iti Tantram." According to this derivation of the word Tantra from the root "Tan" "to spread", it is defined as the Shāstra by which knowledge (Jnāna) is spread. Mark the word Jnāna. The end of the practical methods which these Shāstras employ is to spread Vedāntic Jnāna. It is here we find that variety which is so puzzling to those who have not gone to the root of the religious life of India. The *end* is substantially one. The *means* to that end necessarily vary according to knowledge, capacity, and temperament. But here again we may analyse the means into two main divisions, namely, Vaidik and Tāntrik, to which may be added a third or the mixed (Mishra). The one body of Hinduism reveals as it were, a double framework represented by the Vaidik and Tāntrik Āchāras, which have in certain instances been mingled.

The word "Tantra" by itself simply means as I have already said "treatise" and not necessarily a religious scripture. When it has the latter significance, it may mean the Scripture of several divisions of worshippers who vary in doctrine and practice. Thus there are Tantras of Shaivas, Vaiṣhnavas, and Shāktas and of various sub-divisions of these. So amongst the Shaivas there are the Shaivas of the Shaiva Siddhānta, the Advaita Shaiva of the Kashmir School, Pāshupatas and a multitude of other sects which have their Tantras. If "Tāntric" be used as meaning an adherent of the Tantra Shāstra, then the word, in any particular case, is without definite meaning. A man to whom the application is given may be a worshipper of any of the Five Devatās (Sūrya, Ganeṣha, Viṣhnu, Shiva, Shakti) and of any of the various Sampradāyas worshipping that Devatā with their varying doctrine and practice. The term is a confusing one, though common practice compels its use. So far as I know, those who are named "Tāntrics" do not themselves generally use this term but call themselves Shāktas, Shaivas and the like, of whatever Sampradāya they happen to be.

Again Tantra is the name of only one class of Scripture followed by "Tāntrics". There are others, namely, Nigamas, Āgamas, Yāmalas, Dāmaras, Uddīshas, Kakṣhapūtas and so forth. None of these names are used to describe the adherents of these Shāstras except, so far as I am aware, Āgama in the use of the term Āgamavādin, and Āgamānta in the descriptive name of Āgamānta Shaiva. I give later a list of these Scriptures. as contained in the various Āgamas. If we summarise them shortly under the term Tantra Shāstra, or preferably Āgama, then we have four main classes of Indian Scripture, namely, Veda (Samhitā, Brāhmaṇa, Upanishad), Āgama or Tantra Shāstra, Puraṇa, Smṛiti. Of these Shāstras the authority of the Āgama or Tantra Shāstra has been denied in modern times. This view may be shown to be erroneous by reference to Shāstras of admitted authority. It is spoken of as the Fifth Veda. Kulluka Bhatta, the celebrated commentator on Manu, says: "Shṛuti is twofold, Vaidik and Tāntrik (Vaidikī tāntrikī chaiva dvividhā shrutih kīrtitā)". This refers to the Mantra portion of the Āgamas. In the Great Vaiṣhnava Shāstra, the Shrimad Bhāgavata, Bhagavān says: "My worship is of the three kinds—Vaidik, Tāntrik and Mixed (Mishra)" and that, in Kaliyuga, "Keshava is to be worshipped according to the injunction of Tantra." The Devībhāgavata speaks of the Tantra Shāstra as a Vedānga. It is cited as authority in the Ashtaviṁshati Tattva of Raghunandana who prescribes for the worship of Durgā as before him had done Shrīdatta, Harināthа, Vidyādhara and many others. Some of these and other references are given in Mahāmahopādhyaya Yādaveshvara Tarkaratna's Tantrer Prāchīnatva in the Sāhitya Samhitā of Aswin 1317. The Tārāpradīpa and other Tāntrik works say that in the Kaliyuga the Tāntrika and not the Vaidika Dharma is to be followed. This objection about the late character and therefore unauthoritativeness of the Tantra Shāstras generally (I do not speak of any particular form of it) has been taken by Indians from their European Gurus.

According to the Shākta Scriptures, Veda in its wide sense does not only mean Ṛik, Yajus, Sama, Atharva as now published but comprises these together with the generally unknown and unpublished Uttara Kāṇḍa of the Atharva Veda, called Saubhāgya, with the Upanishads attached to this. Sāyana's Commentary is written on the Purva Kāṇḍa. These are said (though I have not yet verified the fact) to be 64 in number. Some of these, such as Advaitabhāva, Kaula, Kālikā, Tripura, Tārā, Aruṇā Upanishads and Bahvrichopanishad, Bhāvanopanishad, I have published as the XI volume of Tāntrik Texts. Aruṇā means "She who is red". Redness (Lauhityam) is Vimarsha. (See Vol. XI, Tāntrik Texts. Ed. A. Avalon.) I may also here refer my reader to the Kaulāchārya Sadānanda's Commentary on the great Īsha Upanishad. Included also in "Veda" (according to the same view) are the Nigamas, Āgamas, Yāmalas and Tantras. From these all other Shāstras which explain the meaning (Artha) of Veda such as Purāṇa and Smṛiti, also Itihāsa and so forth are derived. All these Shāstras constitute what is called a "Many million-ed" (Shatakoti) Samhitā which are developed, the one from the other as it were an unfolding series. In the Tāntrik Sangraha called Sarvollāsa by the Sarvavidyāsiddha Sarvānandanātha the latter cites authority (Nārāyaṇī Tantra) to show that from Nigama came Āgama. Here I pause to note that the Sammohana says that Kerala Sampradāya is Dakshiṇa and follows Veda (Vedamārgastha), whilst Gauda (to which Sarvānandanātha belonged) is Vāma and follows Nigama. Hence apparently the pre-eminence given to Nigama. He then says from Āgama came Yāmala, from Yāmala the four Vedas, from Vedas the Purāṇas, from Purāṇas Smṛiti, and from Smṛiti all other Shāstras. There are, he says, five Nigamas and 64 Āgamas. Four Yāmalas are mentioned, which are said to give the gross form (Sthūlarūpa). As some may be surprised to learn that the four Vedas came from the Yāmalas (*i.e.*, were Antargata of the Yāmalas) which literally means what is uniting or comprehensive, I subjoin the Sanskrit verse from Nārāyaṇī Tantra.

Brahmayāmalasambhūtam sāmaveda-matam shive
Rudrayāmalasamjāta rigvedo paramo mahān

Vishnuyāmalasambhūto yajurvedah kuleshvari
Shaktiyāmalasambhūtam atharva paramam mahat.

Some Tantras are called by opposing sects Vedaviruddhāni (opposed to Veda), which of course those who accept them deny, just as the Commentary of the Nityāshodashikārnava speaks of the Pancharātrin as Vedabhrashṭa. That some sects were originally Avaidika is probable, but in process of time various amalgamations of scriptural authority, belief and practice took place.

Whether we accept or not this theory, according to which the Āgamas and kindred Shāstras are given authority with the four Vedas we have to accept the facts. What are these?

As I have said, on examination the one body of Hinduism reveals as it were a double framework. I am now looking at the matter from an outside point of view which is not that of the Shākta worshipper. We find on the one hand the four Vedas with their Samhitās, Brāhmaṇas, and Upanishads and on the other what has been called the "Fifth Veda," that is Nigama, Āgama and kindred Shāstras and certain especially "Tāntrik" Upanishads attached to the Saubhāgya Kāṇḍa of the Atharvaveda. There are Vaidik and Tāntrik Kalpa Sūtras and Sūktas such as the Tāntrika Devī and Matsya Sūktas. As a counterpart of the Brahmasūtras, we have the Shakti Sūtras of Agastya. Then there is both Vaidik and "Tāntrik" ritual such as the ten Vaidik Saṁskāras and the Tāntrik Saṁskāras, such as Abhisheka; Vaidik and Tāntrik initiation (Upanayana and Dīkshā); Vaidik and Tāntrik Gāyatrī; the Vaidik Om, the so-called "Tāntrik" Bījas such as Hrīng; Vaidika Guru and Deshika Guru and so forth. This dualism may be found carried into other matters as well, such as medicine, law, writing. So, whilst the Vaidik Āyurveda employed generally vegetable drugs, the "Tāntriks" used metallic substances.

A counterpart of the Vaidika Dharmapatnī was the Shaiva wife, that is, she who is given by desire (Kāma). I have already pointed out the counterparts of the Panchatattva in the Vedas. Some allege a special form of Tāntrik script at any rate in Gauda Desha and so forth.

What is the meaning of all this? It is not at present possible to give a certain answer. The subject has been so neglected and is so little known. Before tendering any conclusions with any certainty of their correctness, we must examine the Tāntrik Texts which time has spared. It will be readily perceived, however, that if there be such a double frame as I suggest, it indicates that there were originally two sources of religion one of which (possibly in some respects the older) incorporated parts of, and in time largely superseded the other. And this is what the "Tāntriks" impliedly allege in their views as to the relation of the four Vedas and Āgamas. If they are not both of authority, why should such reverence be given to the Deshika Gurus and to Tāntrik Dīkshā?

Probably, there were many Avaidika cults, not without a deep and ancient wisdom of their own, that is, cults outside the Vaidik religion (Vedabāhya) which in the course of time adopted certain Vaidik rites such as Homa: the Vaidikas, in their own turn, taking up some of the Avaidika practices. It may be that some Brāhmanas joined these so-called Anārya Sampradāyas just as we find to-day Brāhmanas officiating for low castes and being called by their name. At length the Shāstras of the two cults were given at least equal authority. The Vaidik practice then largely disappeared, surviving chiefly both in the Smārta rites of to-day and as embedded in the ritual of the Āgamas. These are speculations to which I do not definitely commit myself. They are merely suggestions which may be worth consideration when search is made for the origin of the Āgamas.

If they be correct, then in this, as in other cases, the beliefs and practices of the Soil have been upheld until to-day against the incoming cults of those "Āryas" who followed the Vaidik rites and who in their turn influenced the various religious communities without the Vaidik fold.

The Smārtas of to-day represent what is generally called the Shrauta side, though in these rites there are mingled many Pauranic ingredients. The Ārya Samāja is another present-day representative of the old Vaidika Āchāra, mingled as it seems to me with a modernism, which is puritan and otherwise. The other, or Tāntrik side, is represented by the general body of present-day Hinduism, and in particular by the various sectarian divisions of Shaivas, Shāktas, Vaiṣhnavas and so forth which go to its making.

Each sect of worshippers has its own Tantras. In a previous Chapter I have shortly referred to the Tantras of the Shaivasiddhānta, of the Pancharātra Āgama, and of the Northern Shaivaism of which the Mālinīvijaya Tantra sets the type. The old fivefold division of worshippers was, according to the Panchopāsana, Saura, Gānapatya, Vaiṣhnava, Shaiva, and Shākta whose Mūla Devatās were Sūrya, Ganapati, Viṣhnu, Shiva and Shakti respectively. At the present time the threefold division, Vaiṣhnava, Shaiva, Shākta, is of more practical importance, as the other two survive only to a limited extent to-day. In parts of Western India the worship of Ganesha is still popular and I believe some Sauras or traces of Sauras here and there exist, especially in Sind.

Six Āmnāyas are mentioned in the Tantras. (Shaḍāmnāyāh). These are the six Faces of Shiva, looking East (Pūrvāmnāya), South (Dakshināmnāya), West (Pashchimāmnāya), North (Uttarāmnāya), Upper (Urddhvāmnāya), Lower and concealed (Adhāmnāya). The six Āmnāyas are thus so called according to the order of their origin. They are thus described in the Devyāgama cited in the Tantrarahasya (see also, with some variation probably due to corrupt text, Patala II of Samayāchāra Tantra): "(1) The face in the East (that is in front) is of pearl-like lustre with three eyes and crowned by the crescent moon. By this face I (Shiva) revealed (the Devīs) Shrī Bhuvaneshvarī, Triputā, Lalitā, Padmā, Shūlinī, Sarasvatī, Tvaritā, Nityā, Vajraprastārinī, Annapūrna, Mahālakshmī, Lakshmī, Vagvādinī with all their rites and Mantras. (2) The Southern face is of a yellow colour with three eyes. By this face I revealed Prasādasadāshiva, Mahāprāsadamantra, Dakshināmurti, Vatuka, Manjughosha, Bhairava, Mritasanjīvānividyā, Mrityunjayā with their rites and Mantras. (3) The face in the West (that is at the back) is of the colour of a freshly formed cloud. By this face I revealed Gopāla, Krishṇa, Nārāyaṇa, Vāsudeva, Nṛisiṁha, Vāmana, Varāha, Rāmachandra, Vishṇu, Harihara, Ganesha, Agni, Yama, Sūrya, Vidhu (Chandra) and other planets, Garuda, Dikpālas, Hanumān and other Suras, their rites and Mantras. (4) The face in the North is blue in colour and with three eyes. By this face, I revealed the Devīs, Dakshinakālikā, Māhākālī, Guhyakālī, Smashānakālikā, Bhadrakālī, Ekajatā, Ugratārā, Tāritnī, Kātyāyanī, Chhinnamastā, Nīlasarasvatī, Durgā, Jayadurgā, Navadurgā, Vāshulī, Dhūmāvātī, Vishālākshī, Gaurī, Bagalāmukhī, Pratyangirā, Mātanggī, Mahīshamardinī, their rites and Mantras. (5) The Upper face is white. By this face I revealed Shrīmattripurasundarī, Tripureshī, Bhairavī, Tripurabhairavī, Smashānabhairavī, Bhuvaneshībhairavī, Shatkutabhairavī, Annapūrnābhairavī, Panchamī, Shodashī, Mālinī, Valāvalā, with their rites and Mantras. (6) The sixth face (Below) is lustrous of many colours and concealed. It is by this mouth that I spoke of Devatāsthāna, Āsana, Yantra, Mālā, Naivedya, Validāna, Sādhanā, Purashcharana, Mantrasiddhi. It is called Īshānāmnāya." The Samayāchāra Tantra (Ch. 2) says that whilst the first four Āmnāyas are for the Chaturvarga or Dharma, Artha, Kāma, Moksha, the upper (Urdhvāmnāya) and lower (Adhāmnāya) are for liberation only. The Sammohana Tantra (Ch. V) first explains Pūrvāmnāya, Dakshināmnāya, Pashchimāmnāya, Uttarāmnāya, Urdhvāmnāya according to what is called Deshaparyyāya. I am informed that no Pūja of Adhāmnāya is generally done but that Shadanvaya Shāmbhavas, very high Sādhakas, at the door of Liberation do Nyāsa with this sixth concealed Face. It is said that Pātāla Āmnāya is Sambhogayoga. The Nishkala aspect in Shaktikrama is for Pūrva, Tripurā; for Dakshina, Saura, Gānapatya and Vaiṣhnava; for Pashchima, Raudra, Bhairava; for Uttara, Ugrā, Āpattārinī. In Shaivakarma the same aspect is for the first, Sampatpradā and Mahesha; for the second, Aghora, Kālikā and Vaiṣhnava Darshana; for the third, Raudra, Bhairava, Shaiva; for the fourth, Kuvera, Bhairava, Saudarshaka; and for Urddhvāmnāya, Ārddhanārisha and Pranava. Niruttara Tantra says that the first two Āmnāyas contain rites for the Pashu Sādhaka (see as to the meaning of this and the other classes of Sādhakas, the Chapter on Panchatattva ritual *Pūrvāmnāyoditam karma pāshavam kathitam priye*, and so with the next). The third or Pashchimāmnāya is a combination of Pashu and Vīra (*Pashchimāmnāyajam karma pashu-vīrasamāshritam*). Uttarāmnāya is for Vīra and Divya (*Uttarāmnāyajam karma divya-vīrāshritam priye*). The upper Āmnāya is for the Divya (*Urddhvāmnāyoditam karma divyabhāvāshritam priye*). It adds that even the Divya does Sādhanā in the cremation ground in Vīrabhāva (that is, heroic frame of mind and disposition) but he does such worship without Vīrāsana.

The Sammohana also gives a classification of Tantras according to the Āmnāyas as also special classifications, such as the Tantras of the six Āmnāyas according to Vatukāmnāya. As only one Text of the Sammohana is available whilst I write, it is not possible to speak with certainty of accuracy as regards all these details.

Each of these divisions of worshippers have their own Tantras, as also had the Jainas and Bauddhas. Different sects had their own particular subdivisions and Tantras of which there are various classifications according to Krāntās, Deshaparyāya, Kālaparyāya and so forth.

The Sammohana Tantra mentions 22 different Āgamas including Chināgama (a Shākta form), Pāshupata (a Shaiva form), Pancharātra (a Vaiṣhnava form), Kāpālika, Bhairava, Aghora, Jaina, Bauddha; each of which is said there to contain a certain number of Tantras and Upatantras.

According to the Sammohana Tantra, the Tantras according to Kālaparyāya are the 64 Shākta Tantras, with 327 Upatantras, 8 Yāmalas, 4 Dāmaras, 2 Kalpalatās and several Samhitās, Chūdāmaṇis (100) Arnavas, Purāṇas, Upavedas, Kakshapūtas, Vimarshinī and Chintāmaṇis. The Shaiva class contains 32 Tantras with its own Yāmalas, Dāmaras and so forth. The Vaiṣhnava class contains 75 Tantras with the same, including Kalpas and other Shāstras. The Saura class has Tantras with its own Yāmalas, Uddīshas and other works. And the Gānapatya class contains 30 Tantras with Upatantras, Kalpas and other Shāstras, including one Dāmara and one Yāmala. The Bauddha class contains Kalpadrumas, Kāmadhenus, Sūktas, Kramas, Ambaras, Purāṇas and other Shāstras.

According to the Kulārṇava and Jnānadīpa Tantras there are seven Āchāras of which the first four, Veda, Vaiṣhnava, Shaiva and Dakshina belong to Pashvāchāra; then comes Vāma, followed by Siddhānta, in which gradual approach is made to Kaulāchāra the reputed highest. Elsewhere six and nine Āchāras are spoken of and different kinds of Bhāvas, Sabhāva, Vibhāva and Dehabhāva and so forth which are referred to in Bhāvachudāmaṇi.

An account of the Āchāras is given in the Haratattvadīdhiti [pp. 339-342. See in particular Vishvasāra Tantra (Ch. 24) and Nityā Tantra and Prāṇatoshinī. The first is the best account].

Vedāchāra is the lowest and Kaulāchāra the highest. (Kulārṇava Tantra II). Their characteristics are given in the 24th Patala of Vishvasāra Tantra. The first four belong to Pashvāchāra (see Chapter on Shākta Sādhanā) and the last three are for Vīra and Divya Sādhakas. Summarising the points of the Vishvasāra: a Sādhaka in Vedāchāra should carry out the prescriptions of the Veda, should not cohabit with his wife except in the period following the courses. He should not eat fish and meat on the Parva days. He should not worship the Deva at night. In Vaiṣhnavāchāra he follows the injunctions (Niyama) of Vedāchāra. He must give up eating of flesh (Nityā Tantra says he must not kill animals), avoid sexual intercourse and even the talk of it. This doubtless means a negation of the Vīra ritual. He should worship Viṣhṇu. This Āchāra is distinguished from the last by the great endurance of Tapas and the contemplation of the Supreme everywhere. In Shaivāchāra, Vedāchāra is prescribed with this difference that there must be no slaughter of animals and meditation is on Shiva. Dakshiṇāchāra is said to have been practised by Rishi Dakshināmūrti and is therefore so called. This Āchāra is preparatory for the Vīra and Divya Bhāvas. Meditation is on the Supreme Īshvarī after taking Vijayā (Hemp). Japa of Mantra is done at night. Siddhi is attained by using a rosary of human bone (Mahāshaṅkha) at certain places including a Sḥaktipītha. Vāmāchāra is approved of Vīras and Divyas. One should be continent (Brahmachārī) at day and worship with the Panchatattva at night ("*Panchatattvākramenaiva rātrau devīm prapūjayet*"). The statement of Nityā (*Panchatattvānukalpena ratrau devīng prapūjayet*) is, if correctly reported, I think, incorrect. This is Vīra Sādhanā and the Vīra should generally only use substitutes when the real Tattvas cannot be found. Chakra worship is done. Siddhi is destroyed by revelation thereof; therefore the Vāma path is hidden. The Siddhāntāchārī is superior to the last by his knowledge "hidden in the Vedas, Shāstras and Purāṇas like fire in wood, by his freedom from fear of the Pashu, by his adherence to the truth, and by his open performance of the Panchatattva ritual. Open and frank, he cares not what is said." He offers the Panchatattvas openly. Then follows a notable passage. "Just as it is not blameable to drink openly in the Sautramani Yajna (Vaidik rite), so in Siddhāntāchāra wine is drunk openly. As it is not blameable to kill horses in the Ashvamedha Yajna (Vaidik rite), so no offence is committed in killing animals in this Dharma." Nityā Tantra says that an article, be it pure or impure, becomes pure by purification. Holding a cup made of human skull, and wearing the Rudrāksha, the Siddhāntāchārī moves on earth in the form of Bhairava Himself. The knowledge of the last Āchāra, that of the Kaula, makes one Shiva. Just as the footprint of every animal disappears in that of the elephant, so every Dharma is lost in the greatness of Kuladharma. Here there are no injunctions or prohibitions, no restriction as to time or place, in fact no rule at all. A Kaula is himself Guru and Sadāshiva and none are superior to him. Kaulas are of three classes, inferior (the ordinary or Prākrita Kaula), who is ever engaged in ritual such as Japa, Homa, Pūja, follows Vīrāchāra (with Panchatattva) and strives to attain the highland of knowledge; middling is the Kaula who does Sādhanā with the Panchatattva, is deeply immersed in meditation (Dhyāna) and Samādhi; superior, the Kaula who "Oh Mistress of the Kaulas sees the imperishable, and all-pervading Self in all things and all things in the Self." He is a good Kaula who makes no distinction between mud and sandal-paste, gold and straw, a home and the cremation ground. He is a superior Kaula who meditates on the Self with the self, who has equally regard for all, who is full of contentment, forgiveness and compassion. Nityā Tantra (Patala III) says that Kaulas move about in various shapes, now as an ordinary man of the world adhering to social rules (Shishta), at other times as one who has fallen therefrom (Brashta). At other times he seems to be as weird and unearthly as a ghost (Bhūta). Kaulāchāra is, it says, the essence which is obtained from the ocean of Veda and Āgama after churning it with the staff of knowledge.

In a modern account of the Āchāras (see Sanātana-sādhana-Tattva or Tantra-rahasya by Sachchidānanda Svāmi) it is said that some speak of Aghorāchāra and Yogāchāra as two further divisions between the last but one and last. However this may be, the Aghoras of to-day are a separate sect who, it is alleged, have degenerated into mere eaters of corpses, though Aghora is said to only mean one who is liberated from the terrible (Ghora) Saṁsāra. In Yogāchāra was learnt the upper heights of Sādhana and the mysteries of Yoga such as the movements of the Vāyu in the bodily microcosm (Kshudrabrahmāṇḍa), the regulation of which controls the inclinations and propensities (Vritti), Yogāchāra is entered by Yoga-dīkshā and achievement in Ashtāngayoga qualifies for Kaulāchāra. Whether there were such further divisions I cannot at present say. I prefer for the time being to follow the Kulārṇava. The Svāmī's account of these is as follows: Vedāchāra which consists in the daily practice of the Vaidik rites (with, I may add, some Tāntrik observances) is the gross body (Sthūla-deha) which comprises within it all the other Āchāras, which are as it were its subtle body (Sūkshma-deha) of various degrees. The worship is largely of an external character, the object of which is to strengthen Dharma. This is the path of action (Kriyāmārga). This and some other observations may be a modern reading of the old facts but are on the whole, I think, justified. The second stage of Vaiṣhnavāchāra is the path of devotion (Bhaktimārga) and the aim is union of devotion with faith previously acquired. The worshipper passes from blind faith to an understanding of the supreme protecting Energy of the Brahman, towards which his devotion goes forth. With an increasing determination to uphold Dharma and to destroy Adharma, the Sādhaka passes into the third stage or Shaivāchāra which the author cited calls the militant (Kshattriya) stage, wherein to love and mercy are added strenuous striving and the cultivation of power. There is union of faith, devotion, and inward determination (Antarlaksha). Entrance is here made upon the path of knowledge (Jnānamārga). Following this is the fourth stage or Dakshināchāra, which originally and in Tantra Shāstra does not mean "right-hand worship" but according to the author cited is the Āchāra "favourable" to the accomplishment of the higher Sādhanā of which Dakshina-Kālika is Devī. (The Vishvasāra already cited derives the word from Dakshināmūrthi muni, but Dakshina in either case has the same meaning. Dakshinakālī is a Devī of Uttarāmnāya and approach is here made to Vīrā rituals.) This stage commences when the worshipper can make Dhyāna and Dhārāṇa of the threefold Shakti of the Brahman (Ichchhā, Kriyā, Jnāna), and understands the mutual connection of the three and of their expression as the Guṇas, and until he receives the rite of initiation called Pūrnabhishekha. At this stage the Sādhaka is Shākta and qualified for the worship of the threefold Shakti of Brahman (Brahmā, Vishnu, Maheshvara). He worships the Ādya-Shakti as Dakshina-Kālikā in whom are united the three Shaktis. The aim of this stage is the union of faith, devotion, and determination with a knowledge of the threefold energies. (Passage is thus made from the Deva-aspect to the Deva-whole.) Up to this stage the Sādhaka has followed Pravritti Mārga, or the outgoing path, the path of worldly enjoyment, albeit curbed by Dharma. The Sādhaka now, upon the exhaustion of the forces of the outward current, makes entry on the path of return (Nivrittimārga). As this change is one of primary importance, some have divided the Āchāras into the two broad divisions of Dakshināchāra (including the first four) and Vāmāchāra (including the last three). Strictly, however, the first three can only be thus included in the sense that they are preparatory to Dakshināchāra proper and are all in the Pravritti Mārga and are not Vāmāchāra. It is thus said that men are born into Dakshināchāra but are received by initiation into Vāmāchāra. As Dakshināchāra does not mean "right-hand worship" so Vāmāchāra does not mean, as is vulgarly supposed, "left-hand worship". "Left-hand" in English has a bad sense and it is not sense to suppose that the Shāstra, which prescribes this Āchāra, itself gives it a bad name. Vāma is variously interpreted. Some say it is the worship in which woman (Vāmā) enters that is Latāsādhanā. Vāma, this author says, means "adverse" that is the stage adverse to the Pravritti, which governs in varying degrees the previous Āchāras. For, entry is here made on the Nivritti path of return to the Source of outgoing. (In this Āchāra also there is worship of the Vāmā Devī.) In Vāmāchāra the Sādhaka commences to directly destroy Pravritti and, with the help of the Guru, to cultivate Nivritti. The help of the Guru throughout is necessary. It is comparatively easy to lay down rules for the Pravritti Mārga but nothing can be achieved in Vāmāchāra without the Guru's help. Some of the disciplines are admittedly dangerous and, if entered upon without authority and discretion, will probably lead to abuse. The method of the Guru at this stage is to use the forces of Pravritti in such a way as to render them self-destructive. The passions which bind (notably the fundamental instincts for food, drink, and sexual satisfaction) may be it is said so employed as to act as forces whereby the particular life, of which they are the strongest physical manifestation, is raised to the universal life. Passion which has hitherto run downward and outwards (often to waste) is directed inwards and upwards and transformed to power. But it is not only the lower physical desires of eating, drinking, and sexual intercourse which must be subjugated. The Sādhaka must at this stage commence (the process continues until the fruit of Kaulā chāra is obtained) to cut off all the eight bonds (Pāsha) which have made him a Pashu, for up to and including Dakshināchāra is Pashu worship. These Pāsha, bonds or "afflictions" are variously enumerated but the more numerous classifications are merely elaborations of the smaller divisions. Thus, according to the Devī-bhāgavata, Moha is ignorance or bewilderment, and Mahāmoha is the desire for worldly pleasure which flows from it. The Kulārṇava Tantra mentions eight primary bonds, Dayā (that is pity as the feeling which binds as opposed to divine compassion or Karuṇā), Moha (ignorance), Lajjā (shame, which does not mean that a man is to be a shameless sinner but weak worldly shame of being looked down upon, of infringing conventions and so forth), family (Kula, which ceases to be a tie), Shīla (here usage, convention) and Varna (caste; for the enlightened is beyond all its distinctions). When, to take the Svāmī's example, Shrī Kṛishna stole the clothes of the bathing Gopīs or milkmaids and cowherds and made them approach Him naked, He removed the artificial coverings which are imposed on man in the Saṁsāra. The Gopīs were eight, as are the Bonds, and the errors by which the Jīva is misled are the clothes which Krishna stole. Freed of these the Jīva is liberated from all bonds arising from his desires, family and society. Formerly it was sufficient to live in worldly fashion according to the morality governing life in the world. Now the Sādhaka must go further and transcend the world, or rather seek to do so. He rises by those things which are commonly the cause of fall. When he has completely achieved his purpose and liberated himself from all bonds, he reaches the stage of Shiva (Shivatva). It is the aim of the Nivritti Sādhanā to liberate man from the bonds which bind him to the Saṁsāra and to qualify the Vīra Sādhaka, through Rājasika Upāsanā (see Chapter on Panchatattva) of the highest grades of Sādhanā in which the Sāttvika Guna predominates. He is then Divya or divine. To the truly Sāttvik there is neither attachment, fear or disgust (Ghrinā). What is thus commenced in Vāmāchāra, is gradually completed by the rituals of Siddhāntāchāra and Kaulāchāra. In the last three Āchāras the Sādhaka becomes more and more freed from the darkness of Saṁsāra and is attached to nothing, hates nothing, is ashamed of nothing (really shameful acts being *ex hypothesi* below his acquired stage), and has freed himself of the artificial bonds of family, caste, and society. He becomes an Avadhūta, that is, one who has "washed off" everything and has relinquished the world. Of these, as stated later, there are several classes. For him there is no rule of time or place. He becomes, like Shiva himself, a dweller in the cremation ground (Smashāna). He attains Brahmajnāna or the Gnosis in perfect form. On receiving Mahāpūrnadīkshā, he performs his own funeral rites and is dead to the

Saṁsāra. Seated alone in some quiet place, he remains in constant Samādhi (ecstasy), and attains it in its highest or Nirvikalpa form. The Great Mother the Supreme Prakṛiti Mahāshakti dwells in his heart which is now the inner cremation ground wherein all passions have been burnt away. He becomes a Paramahaṁsa who is liberated whilst yet living (Jīvanmukta).

From the above it will be seen that the Āchāras are not various sects in the European sense, but stages in a continuous process through which the Sādhaka must pass before he reaches the supreme state of the highest Kaula (for the Kaulas are of differing degrees). Passing from the gross outer body of Vedāchāra, he learns its innermost core of doctrine, not expressed but latent in it. These stages need not be and are not ordinarily passed through by each Jīva in the course of a single life. On the contrary they are as a rule traversed in the course of a multitude of births, in which case the weaving of the spiritual garment is recommenced where, in a previous birth, it was dropped on death. In one life the Sāḍhaka may commence at any stage. If he is a true Kaula now it is because in previous births he has by Sādhanā in the preliminary stages won his entrance into it. Knowledge of Shakti is, as the Niruttara Tantra says, acquired after many births; and according to the Mahānirvāṇa Tantra it is by merit acquired in previous births that the mind is inclined to Kaulāchāra.

Kauladharma is in no wise sectarian but on the contrary claims to be the head of all sects. It is said "at heart a Shākta, outwardly a Shaiva, in gatherings a Vaiṣhnava (who are wont to gather together for worship in praise of Hari) in thus many a guise the Kaulas wander on earth."

Antah-shāktah vahih-shaivāh sabhāyām vaishnavāmatāh
Nānā-rūpadharāh Kaulāh vicharanti mahitāle.

The saying has been said to be an expression of this claim which is I think involved in it. It does however also I think indicate secrecy, and adaptability to sectarian form, of him who has pierced to the core of that which all sects in varying, though partial, ways present. A Kaula is one who has passed through these and other stages, which have as their own inmost doctrine (whether these worshippers know it or not) that of Kaulāchāra. It is indifferent what the Kaulas apparent sect may be. The form is nothing and everything. It is nothing in the sense that it has no power to narrow the Kaulas inner life. It is everything in the sense that knowledge may infuse its apparent limitations with an universal meaning. A man may thus live in all sects, without their form being ever to him a bond.

In Vaidik times there were four Āshramas, that is, states and stages in the life of the Ārya, namely (in their order) that of the chaste student (Brahmachārya), secular life as a married house-holder (Grihastha), the life of the forest recluse with his wife in retirement from the world (Vānaprastha), lastly that of the beggar (Bhikshu or Avadhūta), wholly detached from the world, spending his time in meditation on the Supreme Brahman in preparation for shortly coming death. All these four were for the Brāhmana caste, the first three for the Kshattriya, the first two for the Vaishya and for the Shūdra the second only (Yogiyājnavalkya, Ch. I). As neither the conditions of life nor the character, capacity and powers of the people of this age allow of the first and third Āshrama, the Mahānirvāṇa Tantra states (VIII. 8) that in the Kali age there are only two Āshramas, namely, the second and last, and these are open tc all castes indiscriminately (*ib.* 12). The same Tantra (XIV. 141 *et seq.*) speaks of four classes of Kulayogis or Avadhūtas namely the Shaivāvadhūta and Brahmāvadhūta, which are each of two kinds, imperfect (Apūrna) and perfect (Pūrna). The first three have enjoyment and practise Yoga. The fourth or Paramahaṁsa should be absolutely chaste and should not touch metal. He is beyond all household duties and caste, and ritual, such as the offering of food and drink to Devatā. The Bhairavadāmara classes the Avadhūta into (*a*) Kulāvadhūta, (*b*) Shaivāvadhūta, (*c*) Brahmāvadhūta, (*d*) Haṁsāvadhūta. Some speak of three divisions of each of the classes Shaivāvadhūta and Brahmāvadhūta (see pp. XLIII, XLIV of Introduction to A. Avalon's Ed. of Mahānirvāṇa). The Shaivāvadhūtas are not, either, from a Western or Shāstric standpoint, as high as the Brahmāvadhūta. The lowest of the last class can have intercourse only with the own wife (Svakīya Shakti as opposed to the Shaiva Shakti); the middling has ordinarily nothing to do with any Shakti, and the highest must under no circumstance touch a woman or metal, nor does he practise any rites or keep any observances.

The main divisions here are Vedāchāra, Dakshināchāra and Vāmāchāra. Vedāchāra is not Vaidikāchāra, that is, in the Shrauta sense, for the Shrauta Vaidikāchāra appears to be outside this sevenfold Tāntrik division of which Vedāchāra is the Tāntrik counterpart. For it is Tāntrik Upāsanā with Vaidik rites and mantras, with (I have been told) Agni as Devatā. As a speculation we may suggest that this Āchāra was for those not Adhikārī for what is called the Shrauta Vaidikāchāra. The second and third belong and lead up to the completed Dakshināchāra. This is Pashvāchāra. Vāmāchāra commences the other mode of worship, leading up to the completed Kaula the Kaulāvadhūta, Avadhūta, and Divya. Here, with the attainment of Brahmajnāna, we reach the region which is beyond all Āchāras which is known as Svechchhāchāra. All that those belonging to this state do or touch is pure. In and after Vāmāchāra there is eating and drinking in, and as part of, worship and Maithuna. After the Pashu there is the Vīra and then the Divya. Pashu is the starting point, Vīra is on the way and Divya is the goal. Each of the sects has a Dakshina and Vāma division. It is commonly thought that this is peculiar to Shāktas: but this is not so. Thus there are Vāma, Gānapatyas and Vaiṣhnavas and so forth. Again Vāmāchāra is itself divided again into a right and left side. In the former wine is taken in a cup of stone or other substance, and worship is with the Svakīya Shakti or Sādhaka's own wife; the latter and more advanced stage drinking is done from a skull and worship may be with Parastrī, that is, some other Shakti. In the case however of some sects which belong to the Vāmāchāra division, whilst there is meat and wine, there is, I am told, no Shakti for the members are chaste (Brahmachārī). So far as I can ascertain these sects which are mentioned later seem to belong to the Shaiva as opposed to the Shākta group.

The Tāntrik Sangraha called Shāktānanda-Taranginī by Brahmānanda Svāmī says (Ch. 2) that Āgama is both Sadāgama and Asadāgama and that the former alone is Āgama according to the primary meaning of the word (*Sadāgama eva āgamashabdasya mukhyatvāt*). He then says that Shiva in the Āgama Samhita condemns the Asadāgama saying "Oh Deveshi, men in the Kali age are generally of a Rājasik and Tāmasik disposition and being addicted to forbidden ways deceive many others. Oh Sureshvari, those who *in disregard of their Varnāshrama Dharma* offer to us flesh, blood and wine become Bhūtas, Pretas, and Brahmarākshasas," that is, various forms of evil spirits. This prohibits such worship as is opposed to Varnāshrama-dharma. It is said, however, by the Vāmāchārīs, who take consecrated wine and flesh as a Yajna, not to cover their case.

It is not uncommonly thought that Vāmāchāra is that Āchāra into which Vāmā or woman enters. This is true only to a certain extent: that is, it is a true definition of those Sādhakas who do worship with Shakti according to Vāmāchāra rites. But it seems to be incorrect, in so far as there are, I am told, worshippers of the Vāmāchāra division who are chaste (Brahmachārī). Vāmāchāra means literally "left" way, not "left-handed" in the English sense which means what is bad. As the name is given to these Sādhakas by themselves it is not likely that they would adopt a title which condemns them. What they mean is that this Āchāra is the opposite of Dakshināchāra. Philosophically it is more monistic. It is said that even in the highest Siddhi of a Dakshināchārī "there is always some One above him"; but the fruit of Vāmāchāra and its subsequent and highest stages is that the Sādhaka "becomes the Emperor Himself". The Bhāva differs, and the power of its method compared with Dakshināchāra is said to be that between milk and wine.

Moreover it is to be noted that the Devī whom they worship is on the left of Shiva. In Vāmāchāra we find Kāpālikas, Kālamukhas, Pāshupatas, Bhāndikeras, Digambaras, Aghoras, followers of Chīnāchāra and Kaulas generally who are initiated. In some cases, as in that of the advanced division of Kaulas, worship is with all five Tattvas (Panchatattva). In some cases there is Brahmacharya as in the case of Aghora and Pāshupata, though these drink wine and eat flesh food. Some Vāmāchārīs, I am informed, never cease to be chaste (Brahmachārī), such as Oghada Sadhus, worshippers of Batuka Bhairava, Kaṇthadhārī and followers of Gorakshanātha, Sitanātha and Matsyendranātha. In Nīlakrama there is no Maithuna. In some sects there are differing practices. Thus, I am told, amongst the Kālamukhas the Kālavīras only worship Kumārīs up to the age of nine, whereas the Kāmamohanas worship with adult Shaktis.

Some advanced members of this (in its general sense) Vāmāchāra division do not, I am informed, even take wine and meat. It is said that the great Vāmāchārī Sādhaka Rājā Krishnachandra of Nadia, Upāsaka of the Chhinnamastā Mūrti, did not take wine. Such and similar Sādhakas have passed beyond the preliminary stage of Vāmāchāra, and indeed (in its special sense) Vāmāchāra itself. They may be Brāhma Kaulas. As regards Sādhakas generally it is well to remember what the Māhākāla Samhitā, the great Shāstra of the Madhyastha Kaulas, says in the 11th Ullāsa called Sharīra-yoga-kathanam : "Some Kaulas there are who seek the good of this world (*Aihikārthadhritātmānah*). So also the Vaidikas enjoy what is here (*Aihikārtham kāmayante*: as do, I may interpose, the vast bulk of present humanity) and are not seekers of liberation (*Amrite ratim na kurvanti*). Only by Nishkāmasādhanā is liberation attained."

The Panchatattva are either real (Pratyaksha. "Idealising" statements to the contrary are, when not due to ignorance, false), substitutional (Anukalpa) or esoteric (Divyatattva). As regards the second, even a vegetarian would not object to "meat" which is in fact ginger, nor the abstainer to "wine" which is cocoanut water in a bell-metal vessel. As for the Esoteric Tattva they are not material articles or practices, but the symbols for Yogic processes. Again some notions and practices are more moderate and others extreme. The account given in the Mahānirvāṇa of the Bhairavī and Tattva Chakras may be compared with some more unrestrained practice; and the former again may be contrasted with a modern Chakra described in the 13th Chapter of the Life of Bejoy Krishna Gosvāmī by Jagadbandu Maitra. There a Tāntrika Siddha formed a Chakra at which the Gosvāmī was present. The latter says that all who were there, felt as if the Shakti was their own

Mother who had borne them, and the Devatās whom the Chakreshvara invoked appeared in the circle to accept the offerings. Whether this is accepted as a fact or not, it is obvious that it was intended to describe a Chakra of a different kind from that of which we have more commonly heard. There are some practices which are not correctly understood; there are some principles which the bulk of men will not understand; for to so understand there must be besides knowledge that undefinable Bhāva, the possession of which carries with it the explanation which no words can give. I have dealt with this subject in the Chapter on the Panchatattva. There are expressions which do not bear their surface meaning. *Gomāngsa-bhakshana* is not "beef-eating" but putting the tongue in the root of the throat. What some translate as "Ravishing the widow" refers not to a woman but to a process in Kundalī Yoga and so forth. Lastly and this is important; a distinction is seldom, if ever, made between Shāstric principles and actual practice, nor is count taken of the conditions properly governing the worship and its abuse. It is easy to understand that if Hinduism has in general degenerated, there has been a fall here. It is, however, a mistake to suppose that the sole object of these rites is enjoyment. It is not necessary to be a "Tāntrik" for that. The moral of all this is, that it is better to know the facts than to make erroneous generalizations.

There are said to be three Krāntās or geographical divisions of India, of which roughly speaking the North-Eastern portion is Viṣhnukrāntā, the North-Western Rathakrāntā and the remaining and Southern portion is Ashvakrāntā. According to the Shāktamangala and Mahāsiddhisāra Tantras, Vishnukrāntā (which includes Bengal) extends from the Vindhya range to Chattala or Chittagong. From Vindhya to Thibet and China is Rathakrāntā. There is then some difference between these two Tantras as to the position of Ashvakrāntā. According to the first this last Krāntā extends from the Vindhya to the sea which perhaps includes the rest of India. According to the Mahāsiddhisāra Tantra it extends from the Karatoyā River to a point which cannot be identified with certainty in the text cited, but which may be Java. To each of these 64 Tantras have been assigned. One of the questions awaiting solution is whether the Tantras of these three geographical divisions are marked by both doctrinal and ritual peculiarities and if so what they are. This subject has been referred to in the first volume of the "Principles of Tantra" wherein a list of Tantras is given.

In the Shākta division there are four Sampradāyas, namely, Kerala, Kāshmīra, Gauda and Vilāsa, in each of which there is both outer and inner worship. The Sammohana Tantra gives these four Sampradāyas, also the number of Tantras, not only in the first three Sampradāyas, but in Chīna and Drāvida. I have been informed that out of 56 Deshas (which included beside Hunas, places outside India, such as Chīna, Mahāchīna, Bhota, Siṁhala), 18 follow Gauda extending from Nepāla to Kalinga and 19 follow Kerala extending from Vindhyāchala to the Southern Sea, the remaining countries forming part of the Kāshmīra Desha; and that in each Sampradāya there are Paddhatis such as Shuddha, Gupta, Ugra. There is variance in Devatās and Rituals some of which are explained in the Tārasukta and Shaktisangama Tantra.

There are also various Matas such as Kādi Mata, called Virādanuttara of which the Devatā is Kālī [see Introduction to Vol. 8. (Tantrarāja) Tāntrik Texts]; Hādi Mata called Haṁsarāja of which Tripurasuṇdarī is Devatā and Kahādi Mata the combination of the two of which Tārā is Devatā that is Nīlasarasvatī. Certain Deshas are called Kādi,

Hādi, Ka-hādi Deshas and each Mata has several Āmnāyas. It is said that the Haṁsatārā Mahāvidyā is the Sovereign Lady of Yoga whom Jainas call Padmāvatī, Shāktas Shakti, Bauddhas Tārā, Chīna Sādhakas Mahogrā, and Kaulas Chakreshvarī. The Kādis call her Kālī, the Hādis Shrīsundarī and the Kādi-Hādis Haṁsah. Volumes VIII and XII of "Tāntrik Texts" contain that portion of the Tantrarāja which belongs to Kādi Mata and in the English Introduction I have dealt with this subject.

Gauda Sampradāya considers Kādi the highest Mata, whilst Kāshmīra and Kerala worship Tripurā and Tārā. Possibly there may have been originally Deshas which were the exclusive seats of specific schools of Tantra, but later and at present, so far as they exist, this cannot be said. In each of the Deshas different Sampradāyas may be found, though doubtless at particular places, as in Bengal, particular sects may be predominant.

In my opinion it is not yet possible to present, with both accuracy and completeness, the doctrine and practice of any particular Tāntrik School, and to indicate wherein it differs from other Schools. It is not possible at present to say fully and precisely who the original Shāktas were, the nature of their sub-divisions and of their relation to, or distinction from, some of the Shaiva group. Thus the Kaulas are generally in Bengal included in the Brahmajnānī Shākta group but the Sammohana in one passage already cited mentions Kaula and Shākta separately. Possibly it is there meant to distinguish ordinary Shāktas from the special group called Kaula Shāktas. In Kashmir some Kaulas, I believe, call themselves Shaivas. For an answer to these and other questions we must await a further examination of the texts. At present I am doing clearing of mud (Paṅkoddhara) from the tank, not in the expectation that I can wholly clear away the mud and weeds, but with a desire to make a beginning which others may complete.

He who has not understood Tantra Shāstra has not understood what "Hinduism" is as it exists to-day. The subject is an important part of Indian culture and therefore worth study by the duly qualified. What I have said should be sufficient to warn the ignorant from making rash generalizations. At present we can say that he who worships the Mantra and Yantra of Shakti is a Shākta, and that there were several Sampradāyas of these worshippers. What we can, and should first, do is to study the Shākta Darshana as it exists to-day, working back from the known to the unknown. What I am about to describe is the Shākta faith as it exists *to-day*, that is Shaktivāda, not as something entirely new but as the development and amalgamation of the various cults which were its ancestors.

Summarizing Shākta doctrine we may first affirm that it is *Advaitavāda* or Monism. This we might expect seeing that it flourished in Bengal which, as the old Gauda Desha, is the Guru both of Advaitavāda and of Tantra Shāstra. From Gauda came Gaudapādāchārya, Madhusūdana Sarasvatī, author of the great Advaitasiddhi, Rāmachandratīrthabhāratī, Chitsukhāchārya and others. There seems to me to be a strong disposition in the Brahmaparāyana Bengali temperament towards Advaitavāda. For all Advaitins the Shākta Āgama and Advaita Shaivāgama must be the highest form of worship. A detailed account of the Advaita teachings of the Shāktas is a matter of great complexity and of a highly esoteric character, beyond the scope of this paper. I may here note that the Shākta Tantras speak of 94 Tattvas made up of 10, 12 and 16 Kalās of Fire, Sun and Moon constituting the Kāmakalā respectively; and 19 of Sadāshiva, 6 of Īshvara, 10 each of Rudrā, Viṣhṇu and Brahma. The 51 Kalās or Mātrikās which are the

Sūkshmarūpa of the 51 letters (Varṇa) are a portion of these 94. These are the 51 coils of Kundali from Bindu to Shrīmātrikotpatti-Sundarī mentioned in my " Garland of Letters " or Studies on the Mantra Shāstra. These are all worshipped in the wine jar by those Shāktas who take wine. The Shāstras also set out the 36 Tattvas which are common of Shāktas and Shaivas ; the five Kalās which are Sāmānya to the Tattvas, namely, Nivritti, Pratishtha, Vidyā, Shāntā, Shāntyatīta, and the Shadadhvā, namely, Varṇa, Pada, and Mantra, Kalā, Tattva, Bhuvana, which represent the Artha aspect and the Shabda aspect respectively. (See " Garland of Letters ".)

To pass to more popular matters, a beautiful and tender concept of the Shāktas is the *Motherhood of God*, that is, God as Shakti or the Power which produces, maintains and withdraws the universe. This is the thought of a worshipper. Though the Sammohana Tantra gives high place to Shaṅkara as conqueror of Buddhism (speaking of him as a manifestation of Shiva and identifying his four disciples and himself with the five Mahāpretas), the Āgamas as Shāstras of worship do not teach Māyāvāda as set forth according to Shaṅkara's transcendental method. Māyā to the Shākta worshipper is not an unconscious something, not real, not unreal, not real-unreal, which is associated with Brahman in its Īshvara aspect, though it is not Brahman. Brahman is never associated with anything but Itself. Māyā to the Shākta is Shakti; Shakti veiling Herself as Consciousness, but which, as being Shakti, is Consciousness. To the Shākta all that he sees is the Mother. *All* is Consciousness. This is the standpoint of Sādhanā. The Advaitins of Shaṅkara's School claim that their doctrine is given from the standpoint of Siddhi. I will not argue this question here. When Siddhi is obtained there will be no argument. Until that event Man is, it is admitted, subject to Māyā and must think and act according to the forms which it imposes on him. It is more important after all to realize in fact the universal presence of the Divine Consciousness, than to attempt to explain it in philosophical terms.

The Divine Mother first appears in and as Her worshipper's earthly mother, then as his wife; thirdly as Kālikā, She reveals Herself in old age, disease and death. It is she who manifests, and not without a purpose, in the vast outpouring of Saṁhāra Shakti which was witnessed in the great world-conflict of our time. The terrible beauty of such forms is not understood. And so we get the recent utterance of a Missionary Professor at Madras who being moved to horror at the sight of (I think) the Chāmundāmūrti called the Devī a " She-Devil ". Lastly She takes to Herself the dead body in the fierce tongues of flame which light the funeral pyre.

The Monist is naturally unsectarian and so the Shākta faith, as held by those who understand it, is *free from a narrow sectarian spirit.*

Nextly it, like the other Āgamas, makes provision for *all castes* and *both sexes.* Whatever be the true doctrine of the Vaidikas, their practice is in fact marked by exclusiveness. Thus they exclude woman and Shūdras. It is easy to understand why the so-called Anārya Sampradāyas did not do so. A glorious feature of the Shākta faith is the *honour which it pays to woman.* And this is natural for those who worship the Great Mother, whose representative (Vigraha) all earthly women are. *Striyo devāh striyah prānāh.* " Women are Devas; women are life itself," as an old Hymn in the Sarvollasa has it. It is because Woman is a Vigraha of the Ambā Devī, Her likeness in flesh and blood, that the Shākta Tantras enjoin the honour and worship of women and girls (Kumārīs), and forbade all harm to them such as the Sati rite, enjoining that not even a female animal is to be sacrificed. With the same solicitude for women, the Mahānirvāṇa prescribes that even if a man speaks rudely (Durvvachyang kathayan) to his wife, he must fast for a whole day, and enjoins the education of daughters before their marriage. The Moslem Author of the Dabistan (ii. 154. Ed. 1843) says "The Āgama favours both sexes equally. Men and women equally compose mankind. This sect hold women in great esteem and call them Shaktis and to ill-treat a Shakti that is a woman is a crime." The Shākta Tantras again *allow of women being Guru*, or Spiritual Director, a reverence which the West has not (with rare exceptions) yet given them. Initiation by a Mother bears eightfold fruit. Indeed to the enlightened Shākta the whole universe is Strī or Shakti. "Aham strī" as the Advaitabhāva Upanishad says. A high worship therefore which can be offered to the Mother to-day consists in getting rid of abuses which have neither the authority of ancient Shāstra, nor of modern social science and to honour, cherish, educate and advance women (Shakti). *Striyo devāh striyah prānāh.* Gautamīya Tantra says *Sarva-varnādhikārashcha nārīnām yogya eva cha;* that is, the Tantra Shāstra is for all castes and for women: and the Mahānirvāṇa says that the low Kaula who refuses to initiate a Chaṇḍāla or Yavana or a woman out of disrespect goes the downward path. No one is excluded from anything except on the grounds of a real and not artificial or imagined incompetency.

An American Orientalist critic, in speaking of "the worthlessness of Tāntric philosophy", said that it was "*Religious Feminism run mad,*" adding "What is all this but the *feminisation* of orthodox Vedānta? It is a doctrine for *suffragette* Monists: the dogma unsupported by any evidence that *the female principle antedates and includes the male principle,* and that this female principle is supreme Divinity." The "worthlessness" of the Tāntrik philosophy is a personal opinion on which nothing need be said, the more particularly that Orientalists who, with insufficient knowledge, have already committed themselves to this view are not likely to easily abandon it. The present criticism, however, in disclosing the grounds on which it is based, has shown that they are without worth. Were it not for such ignorant notions, it would be unnecessary to say that the Shākta Sādhaka does not believe that there is a Woman Suffragette or otherwise, in the sky, surrounded by the members of some celestial feminist association who rules the male members of the universe. As the Yāmala says for the benefit of the ignorant "*neyam yoshit na cha pumān na shando na jadah smritah*". That is, God is neither female, male, hermaphrodite or unconscious thing. Nor is his doctrine concerned with the theories of the American Professor Lester Ward and others as to the alleged pre-eminence of the female principle. We are not here dealing with questions of science or sociology. It is a common fault of western criticism that it gives material interpretations of Indian Scriptures and so misunderstands it. The Shākta doctrine is concerned with those Spiritual Principles which exist before, and are the origin of, both men and women. Whether, in the appearance of the animal species, the female "antedates" the male is a question with which it is not concerned. Nor does it say that the "female principle" is the supreme Divinity. Shiva the "male" is co-equal with Shivā the "female," for both are one and the same. An Orientalist might have remembered that in the Sāṅkhya, Prakṛiti is spoken of as "female", and Purusha as "male". And in Vedānta, Māyā and Devī are of the feminine gender. Shakti is not a male nor a female "person", nor a male nor a female "principle", in the sense in which sociology, which is concerned with gross matter, uses those terms. Shakti is symbolically "female" because it is the productive principle. Shiva, in so far as He represents the Chit or consciousness aspect, is actionless (Nishkriya), though the two are inseparably associated even in creation. The Supreme is the attributeless (Nirguṇa) Shiva, or the neuter Brahman which is neither "male" nor "female". With such mistaken general views of the doctrine, it was not likely that its more subtle aspects by way of relation to Shaṅkara's Māyāvāda, or the Sāṅkhya Darshana should be appreciated. The doctrine of Shakti has no more to do with "Feminism" than it has to do with "old age pensions" or any other sociological movement of the day. This is a good instance of those apparently "smart" and cocksure judgments which Orientalists and others pass on things Indian. The errors would be less ridiculous if they were on occasions more modest as regards their claims to know and understand. What is still more important, they would not probably in such case give unnecessary ground for offence.

The characteristic features of Shākta-dharma are thus its Monism; its concept of the Motherhood of God; its unsectarian spirit and provision for Shūdras and women, to the latter of whom it renders high honour, recognizing that they may be even Gurus; and lastly its Sādhanā skilfully designed to realize its teachings.

As I have pointed out on many an occasion this question of *Sādhanā* is of the highest importance, and has been in recent times much overlooked. It is that which more than anything else gives value to the Āgama or Tantra Shāstra. Mere talk about religion is only an intellectual exercise. Of what use are grand phrases about Ātmā on the lips of those who hate and injure one another and will not help the poor. Religion is kindness. Religion again is a practical activity. Mind and body must be trained. There is a spiritual as well as a mental and physical gymnastic. According to Shākta doctrine each man and woman contains within himself and herself a vast latent magazine of Power or Shakti, a term which comes from the root "Shak" to be able, to have force to do, to act. They are each Shakti and nothing but Shakti, for the Svarūpa of Shakti that is Shakti as it is in itself is Consciousness, and mind and body are Shakti. The problem then is how to raise and vivify Shakti. This is the work of Sādhanā in the Religion of Power. The Āgama is a practical philosophy, and as the Bengali friend and collaborator of mine, Professor Pramathanātha Mukhyopādhyāya, whom I cite again, has well put it, what the intellectual world wants to-day is the sort of philosophy which not merely *argues* but *experiments*. This is Kriyā. The form which Sādhanā takes necessarily varies according to faith, temperament and capacity. Thus, amongst Christians, the Catholic Church, like Hinduism, has a full and potent Sādhanā in its sacraments Saṁskāra, temple (Church) and private worship (Pūjā, Upāsanā) with Upachāra "bell, light and incense" (Ghantā, Dīpa, Dhūpa) Images or Pratimā (hence it has been called idolatrous), devotional rites such as Novenas and the like (Vrata), the threefold "Angelus" at morn, noon and evening (Sandhyā), rosary (Japa), the wearing of Kavachas (Scapulars, Medals, Agnus Dei), pilgrimage (Tīrtha), fasting, abstinence and mortification (Tapas), monastic renunciation (Sannyāsa), meditation (Dhyāna), ending in the union of mystical theology (Samādhi) and so forth. There are other smaller details such for instance as Shānti-abhisheka (Asperges) into which I need not enter here. I may, however, mention the Spiritual Director who occupies the place of the Guru; the worship (Hyperdulia) of the Virgin-Mother which made Svāmī Vivekānanda call the Italian Catholics, Shāktas; and the use of wine (Madya) and bread (corresponding to Mudrā) in the Eucharist or Communion Service. Whilst however the Blessed Virgin evokes devotion as warm as that which is here paid to Devī, she is not Devī for she is not God but a creature selected as the vehicle of His incarnation (Avatāra). In the Eucharist the bread and wine are the body and blood of Christ appearing under the form or "accidents" of those material substances; so also Tārā is Dravamayī, that is, the "Saviour in liquid form." (Mahānirvāna Tr. xi. 105-107.) In the Catholic Church (though the early practice was otherwise) the laity no longer take wine but bread only, the officiating priest consuming both. Whilst however the outward forms in this case are similar, the inner meaning is different. Those however who contend that eating and drinking are inconsistent with the "dignity" of worship may be reminded of Tertullian's saying that Christ instituted His great sacrament at a meal. These notions are those of the dualist with all his distinctions. For the Advaitin every function and act may be made a Yajna. Agape or "Love Feasts," a kind of Chakra, were held in early times, and discontinued as orthodox practice, on account of abuses to which they led; though they are said still to exist in some of the smaller Christian sects of the day. There are other points of ritual which are peculiar to the Tantra Shāstra and of which there is no counterpart in the Catholic ritual such as Nyāsa and Yantra. Mantra exists in the form of prayer and as formulæ of consecration, but otherwise the subject is conceived of differently here. There are certain gestures (Mudrā) made in the ritual, as when consecrating, blessing, and so forth, but they are not so numerous or prominent as they are here. I may some day more fully develop these interesting analogies, but what I have said is for the present sufficient to establish the numerous similarities which exist between the Catholic and Indian Tāntrik ritual. Because of these facts the "reformed" Christian sects have charged the Catholic Church with "Paganism". It is in fact the inheritor of very ancient practices but is not necessarily the worse for that. The Hindu finds his Sādhanā in the Tantras of the Āgama in forms which his race has evolved. In the abstract there is no reason why his race should not modify these forms of Sādhanā or evolve new ones. But the point is that *it must have some form of Sādhanā.* Any system to be fruitful must *experiment* to gain *experience.* It is because of its powerful sacraments and disciplines that in the West the Catholic Church has survived to this day, holding firm upon its "Rock" amid the dissolving sects, born of what is called the "Reform". It is likely to exist when these, as presently existing sects, will have disappeared. All things survive by virtue of the truth in them. The particular truth to which I here refer is that a faith cannot be maintained by mere hymn-singing and pious addresses. For this reason too Hinduism has survived.

This is not necessary to say that either of these will, as presently existing forms, continue until the end of time. The so-called Reformed or Protestant sects, whether of West or East, are, when viewed in relation to man in general, the imperfect expression of a truth misunderstood and misapplied, namely that the higher man spiritually ascends the less dependent is he on form. The mistake which such Sects make is to look at the matter from one side only, and to suppose that all men are alike in their requirement. The Āgama is guilty of no such error. It offers form in all its fullness and richness to those below the stage of Yoga, at which point man reaches what the Kulārnava Tantra calls the Varna and Āshrama of Light (Jyotirvarnāshramī), and gradually releases himself from all form that he may unite his self with the Formless One. I do not know which most to admire—the colossal affirmations of Indian doctrine, or the wondrous variety of the differing disciplines which it prescribes for their realization in fact.

The Buddhists called Brāhmanism Shīlavrataparāmarsha, that is, a system believing in the efficacy of ritual acts. And so it is, and so at length was Buddhism, when passing through Mahāyāna it ended up with the full Tāntrik Sādhanā of the Vajrayāna School. There are human tendencies which cannot be suppressed. Hinduism will, however, disappear, if and when Sādhanā (whatever be its form) ceases; for that will be the day on which it will no longer be something real, but the mere subject of philosophical and historical talk. Apart from its great doctrine of Shakti, the main significance of the Shākta Tantra Shāstra lies in this, that it affirms the principle of the *necessity of Sādhanā* and claims to afford a *means* available to all of whatever *caste* and of either *sex* whereby the teachings of Vedānta may be practically *realized.*

But let no one take any statement from any one, myself included, blindly, without examining and testing it. I am only concerned to state the facts as I know them. It is man's prerogative to think. The Sanskrit word for "man" comes from the root *man* "to think". Those who are Shāktas may be pleased at what I have said about their faith. It must not, however, be supposed that a doctrine is necessarily true simply because it is old. There are some hoary errors. As for science, its conclusions shift from year to year. Recent discoveries have so abated its pride that it has considerably ceased to give itself those pontifical airs which formerly annoyed some of us. Most will feel that if they are to bow to any Master it should be to a spiritual one. A few will think that they can safely walk alone. Philosophy again is one of the noblest of life's pursuits, but here too we must examine to see whether what is proposed for our acceptance is well-founded. The maxim is current that there is nothing so absurd but that it has been held by some philosopher or another. We must each ourselves judge and choose, and if honest, none can blame our choice. We must put all to the test. We may here recollect the words of Shruti—"*Shrotavyah, Mantavyah, Nididhyāsitavyah,*"—"listen, reason and ponder"; for as Manu says "*Yastarkenānusandhatte sa dharmam veda, netarah*"—"He who by discussion investigates, he knows Dharma and none other." Ultimately there is experience alone which in Shākta speech is *Sāham*—"She I am".

NOTE TO CHAPTER VI

I have referred to the Vaidik and Āgamic strands in Indian Dharma. I wish to add some weighty remarks made by the well-known Vedāntic Monthly *The Prabuddha Bhārata* (Māyāvati, U. P., July 1914). They were elicited by the publication of Arthur Avalon's "Principles of Tantra". After pointing out that a vindication of the Tantras rebounds directly to the benefit of Hinduism as a whole, for Tāntrikism in its real sense is nothing but the Vedic religion struggling with wonderful success to reassert itself amidst all those new problems of religious life and discipline which historical events and developments thrust upon it, and after referring to the Introduction to that work, the author of the review wrote as follows:

"In this new publication the most noteworthy feature of this new Introduction he has written for the Tantratattva is his appreciative presentation of the orthodox views about the antiquity and the importance of the Tantras, and it is impossible to overestimate the value of this presentation.

For hitherto all theories about the origin and the importance of the Tantras have been more or less prejudiced by a wrong bias against Tāntrikism which some of its own later sinister developments were calculated to create. This bias has made almost every such theory read either like a condemnation or an apology. All investigation being thus disqualified, the true history of Tāntrikism has not yet been written; and we find cultured people mostly inclined either to the view that Tāntrikism originally branched off from the Buddhistic Mahāyāna or Vajrayāna as a cult of some corrupted and self-deluded monastics, or to the view that it was the inevitable dowry which some barbarous non-Aryan races brought along with them into the fold of Hinduism. According to both these views, however, the form which this Tāntrikism—either a Buddhistic development or a barbarous importation—has subsequently assumed in the literature of Hinduism, is its improved edition as issuing from the crucibles of Vedic or Vedāntic transformation. But this theory of the curious co-mingling of the Vedas and Vedānta with Buddhistic corruption or with non-Aryan barbarity is perfectly inadequate to explain the all-pervading influence which the Tantras exert on our present-day religious life. Here it is not any hesitating compromise that we have got before us to explain, but a bold organic synthesis, a legitimate restatement of the Vedic culture for the solution of new problems and new difficulties which signalized the dawn of a new age.

In tracing the evolution of Hinduism, modern historians take a blind leap from Vedic ritualism direct to Buddhism, as if to conclude that all those newly formed communities, with which India had been swarming all over since the close of the fateful era of the Kurukshetra war and to which was denied the right of Vedic sacrifices, the monopoly of the higher threefold castes of pure orthodox descent, were going all the time without any religious ministrations. These Aryanised communities, we must remember, were actually swamping the Vedic orthodoxy, which was already gradually dwindling down to a helpless minority in all its scattered centres of influence, and was just awaiting the final blow to be dealt by the rise of Buddhism. Thus the growth of these new communities and their occupation of the whole land constituted a mighty event that had been silently taking place in India on the outskrits of the daily shrinking orthodoxy of Vedic ritualism, long before Buddhism appeared on the field, and this momentous event our modern historians fail to take due notice of either, it may be because, of a curious blindness of self-complacency or because of the dazzle which the sudden triumph of Buddhism and the overwhelming mass of historical evidences left by it, create before their eyes. The traditional Kali Yuga dates from the rise of these communities and the Vedic religious culture of the preceding Yuga underwent a wonderful transformation along with a wonderful attempt it made to Aryanise these rising communities.

History, as hitherto understood and read, speaks of the Brahmins of the pre-Buddhistic age,—their growing alienation from the Jnāna-kāṇḍa or the Upanishadic wisdom, their impotency to save the orthodox Vedic communities from the encroachments of the non-Vedic hordes and races, their ever-deepening religious formalism and social exclusiveness. But this history is silent on the marvellous feats which the Upanishadic sects of anchorites were silently performing on the outskirts of the strictly Vedic community with the object of Aryanising the new India that was rising over the ashes of the Kurukshetra conflagration. This new India was not strictly Vedic like the India of the bygone ages, for it could not claim the religious ministrations of the orthodox Vedic Brahmins and could not, therefore, perform Yajnas like the latter.

The question, therefore, is as to how this new India became gradually Aryanised, for Aryanisation is essentially a spiritual process, consisting in absorbing new communities of men into the fold of the Vedic religion. The Vedic ritualism that prevailed in those days was powerless, we have seen, to do anything for these new communities springing up all over the country. Therefore, we are obliged to turn to the only other factor in Vedic religion besides the Karma-kāṇḍa for an explanation of those changes which the Vedic religion wrought in the rising communities in order to Aryanise them. The Upanishads represent the Jnāna-kāṇḍa of the Vedic religion and if we study all of them, we find that not only the earliest ritualism of Yajnas was philosophised upon the earlier Upanishads, but the foundation for a new, and no less elaborate, ritualism was fully laid in many of the later Upanishads. For example, we study in these Upanishads how the philosophy of Pancha-upāsana (fivefold worship, *viz.*, the worship of Shiva, Devī, Sun, Ganesh and Viṣhnu) was developed out of the mystery of the Praṇava (" Om "). This philosophy cannot be dismissed as a post-Buddhistic interpolation, seeing that some features of the same philosophy can be clearly traced even in the Brahmanas (*e.g.*, the discourse about the conception of Shiva).

Here, therefore, in some of the later Upanishads we find recorded the attempts of the pre-Buddhistic recluses of the forest to elaborate a post-Vedic ritualism out of the doctrine of the Praṇava and the Vedic theory of Yogic practices. Here in these Upanishads we find how the Bīja-mantras and the Shaṭchakra of the Tantras were being originally developed, for on the Praṇava or Udgītha had been founded a special learning and a school of philosophy from the very earliest ages and some of the " spinal " centres of Yogic meditation had been dwelt upon in the earliest Upanishads and corresponding Brahmanas. The Upakaranas of Tāntrik worship, namely, such material adjuncts as grass, leaves, water and so on, were most apparently adopted from Vedic worship along with their appropriate incantations. So even from the Brahmanas and the Upanishads stands out in clear relief a system of spiritual discipline,—which we would unhesitatingly classify as Tāntrik—having at its core the Pancha-upāsana and around it a fair round of rituals and rites consisting of Bīja-mantras and Vedic incantations, proper meditative processes and proper manipulation of sacred adjuncts of worship adopted from the Vedic rites. This may be regarded as the earliest configuration which Tāntrikism had on the eve of those silent but mighty social upheavals through which the Aryanisation of vast and increasing multitudes of new races proceeded in pre-Buddhistic India and which had their culmination in the eventful centuries of the Buddhistic *coup de grace*.

Now this pre-Buddhistic Tāntrikism, perhaps, then recognized as the Vedic Pancha-upāsana, could not have contributed at all to the creation of a new India, had it remained confined completely within the limits of monastic sects. But like Jainism, this Pancha-upāsana went forth all over the country to bring ultra-Vedic communities under its spiritual ministrations. Even if we enquire carefully into the social conditions obtaining in the strictly Vedic ages, we find that there was always an extended wing of the Aryanised society where the purely Vedic Karma-kāṇḍa could not be promulgated, but where the moulding influence of Vedic ideals worked through the development of suitable spiritual activities. It is always to the Jnāna kāṇḍa and the monastic votaries thereof, that the Vedic religion owed its wonderful expansiveness and its progressive self-adaptability, and every religious development within the Vedic fold, but outside, the ritualism of Homa sacrifices, is traceable to the spiritual wisdom of the all-renouncing forest recluses. This 'forest' wisdom was most forcibly brought into requisition when after the Kurukshetra a new age was dawning with the onrush and upheaval of non-Aryan and semi-Aryan races all over India —an echo of which may be found in that story of the Mahābhārata where Arjuna fails to use his Gāndiva to save his protegés from the robbery of the non-Aryan hordes.

The greatest problem of the pre-Buddhistic ages was the Aryanisation of the new India that rose and surged furiously from every side against the fast-dwindling centres of the old Vedic orthodoxy struggling hard, but in vain, by social enactments to guard its perilous insulation. But for those religious movements, such as those of the Bhāgavatas, Shāktas, Sauryas, Shaivas, Gānapatyas and Jainas, that tackled this problem of Aryanisation most successfully, all that the Vedic orthodoxy stood for in the real sense would have gradually perished without trace. These movements, specially the five cults of Vedic worship, took up many of the non-Aryan races and cast their life in the mould of the Vedic spiritual ideal, minimizing in this way the gulf that existed between them and the Vedic orthodoxy and thereby rendering possible their gradual amalgamation. And where this task remained unfulfilled owing to the mould proving too narrow still to fit into the sort of life which some non-Aryan races or communities lived, there it remained for Buddhism to solve the problem of Aryanisation in due time. But still we must remember that by the time Buddhism made its appearance, the pre-Buddhistic phase of Tāntrik worship had already established itself in India so widely and so firmly that instead of dislodging it by its impetuous onset—all the force of which, by the bye, was mainly spent on the tattering orthodoxy of Vedic ritualism—Buddhism was itself swallowed up within three or four centuries by its perhaps least suspected opponent of this Tāntrik worship and then wonderfully transformed and ejected on the arena as the Mahāyāna.

The publication of these two volumes is an event of great interest and importance. The religious beliefs of the modern Hindus have been represented to English readers from various points of view, but the peculiar mould into which they have been sought to be cast in comparatively modern centuries has not received adequate attention. The exponents of the religion of modern Hindus take cognizance more of the matter and source of their beliefs than of the change of form they have been undergoing through the many centuries. The volumes under review, as well as other publications brought out by Arthur Avalon, serve to carry this important question of form to such a prominence as almost makes it obligatory for every exhaustive exposition of Hindu doctrines in future to acknowledge and discriminate in them the formative influences of the Tāntrik restatement. In the Tantratattva, the presentation and vindication of the Hindu religious beliefs and practices avowedly and closely follow the methodology of the Tantras, and the learned pundit has fully succeeded in establishing the fact that what lies behind these beliefs and practices is not mere prejudice or superstition but a system of profound philosophy based on the Vedas. Every student of modern Hinduism should acquaint himself with this, namely, its immediate background of Tāntrik philosophy and ritualism.

The Hindu religious consciousness is like a mighty Ganges emerging from the Himalayas of Vedic wisdom, receiving tributaries and sending out branch streams at many points in its course. And though the nature of the current, its colour, velocity or uses may vary at different places, the Ganges is the same Ganges whether at Hardwar, Allahabad or Calcutta. The stream is not only one but it has also its one main channel in spite of all the many tributaries and branches. And the whole of the stream is sacred, though different sects may choose special points and confluences as of special sanctity to themselves, deriving inspiration thence for their special sectarian developments. Now, though the rise of Tāntrik philosophy and ritualism created in former times new currents and backwaters along the stream of Hinduism, it was essentially an important occurrence in the main stream and channel; and instead of producing a permanent bifurcation in that stream, it coalesced with it, colouring and renovating, more or less, the whole tenour of the Hindu religious consciousness. As a result, we find Tāntrik thought and sentiment equally operative in the extreme metaphysical wing of Hinduism as well as in its lower matter-of-fact phases.

This actual permeation of Hindu religious consciousness by Tāntrik thought and sentiment should receive the fullest recognition at the hands of every up-to-date exponent. His predecessors of former generations might have to strengthen their advocacy of Tāntrik doctrines by joining issue with the advocates of particular phases of Hindu religion and philosophy. But the present epoch in the history of our religious consciousness is pre-eminently an epoch of wonderful synthetic mood of thought and sentiment, which is gradually pervading the Hindu religious consciousness ever since Srī Rāmakrishna Paramahamsa embodied in himself its immediate possibilities, to find in the literature that is being so admirably provided for English readers by Arthur Avalon an occasional tendency to use Tāntrik doctrines as weapons for combating certain phases of Hindu belief and practice. This tendency seems to betray quite a wrong standpoint in the study of the Tantras, their relation to other Scriptures and their real historical significance."

CHAPTER VII

IS SHAKTI FORCE?

THERE are some persons who have thought, and still think, that Shakti means force and that the worship of Shakti is the worship of force. Thus Keshub Chunder Sen (*New Dispensation*, p. 108), wrote:

Four centuries ago the Shāktas gave way before the Bhaktas. Chaitanya's army proved invincible, and carried all Bengal captive. Even to-day his gospel of love rules as a living force, though his followers have considerably declined both in faith and in morals. Just the reverse of this we find in England and other European countries. There the Shāktas are driving the Bhaktas out of the field. Look at the Huxleys, the Tyndalls and the Spencers of the day. What are they but Shāktas, worshippers of Shakti or Force? The only Deity they adore, if they at all adore one, is the Prime Force of the universe. To it they offer dry homage. Surely then the scientists and materialists of the day are a sect of Shakti-worshippers, who are chasing away the true Christian devotees who adore the God of Love. Alas! for European Vaiṣhnavas they are retreating before the advancing millions of Western Shāktas. We sincerely trust, however, the discomfiture of devotion and Bhakti will be only for a time, and that a Chaitanya will yet arise in the West, crush the Shāktas, who only recognize Force as Deity and are sunk in carnality and voluptuousness, and lead natures into the loving faith, spirituality, simplicity, and rapturous devotion of the Vaiṣhnava.

Professer Monier Williams ("*Hinduism*") also called it a doctrine of Force.

Recently the poet Rabindranath Tagore has given the authority of his great name to this error (*Modern Review*, July, 1919). After pointing out that Egoism is the price paid for the fact of existence and that the whole universe is assisting in the desire that the "I" should be, he says that man has viewed this desire in two different ways, either as a whim of Creative Power, or a joyous self-expression of Creative Love. Is the fact then of his *being*, he asks, a revealment of Force or of Love? Those who hold to the first view must also, he thinks, recognize conflict as inevitable and eternal. For according to them Peace and Love are but a precarious coat of armour within which the weak seek shelter, whereas that which the timid anathematise as unrighteousness, that alone is the road to success. "The pride of prosperity throws man's mind outwards and the misery and insult of destitution draws man's hungering desires likewise outwards. These two conditions alike leave man unashamed to place above all other gods, Shakti the Deity of Power—the Cruel One, whose right hand wields the weapon of guile. In the politics of Europe drunk with Power we see the worship of Shakti."

In the same way the poet says that in the days of their political disruption, the cowed and down-trodden Indian people through the mouths of their poets sang the praises of the same Shakti. "The Chandi of Kavikangkan and of the Annadāmangala, the Ballad of Mānasā, the Goddess of Snakes, what are they but Pæans of the triumph of Evil? The burden of their song is the defeat of Shiva the *good* at the hands of the cruel deceitful *criminal* Shakti." "The male Deity who was in possession was fairly harmless. But all of a sudden a feminine Deity turns up and demands to be worshipped in his stead. That is to say that she insisted on thrusting herself where she had no right. Under what title? Force! By what method? Any that would serve."

The Deity of Peace and Renunciation did not survive. Thus he adds that in Europe the modern Cult of Shakti says that the pale anæmic Jesus will not do. But with high pomp and activity Europe celebrates her Shakti worship.

"Lastly the Indians of to-day have set to the worship of Europe's Divinity. In the name of religion some are saying that it is cowardly to be afraid of wrong-doing. Both those who have attained worldly success, and those who have failed to attain it are singing the same tune. Both fret at righteousness as an obstacle which both would overcome by physical force." I am not concerned here with any popular errors that there may be. After all, when we deal with a Shāstrik term it is to the Shāstra itself that we must look for its meaning. Shakti comes from the root *Shak* "to be able," "to do". It indicates both activity and capacity therefor. The world, as world, is activity. But when we have said that, we have already indicated that it is erroneous to confine the meaning of the term Shakti to any special form of activity. On the contrary Shakti means both power in general and every particular form of power. Mind is a Power: so is Matter: Mind is constantly functioning in the form of *Vritti*, Reasoning, Will and Feeling (Bhāva) such as love, aversion and so forth are all aspects of Mind-power in its general sense. Force is power translated to the material plane, and is therefore only one and the grossest aspect of Shakti or power. But all these special powers are limited forms of the great creative Power which is the Mother (Ambikā) of the Universe. Worship of Shakti is not worship of these limited forms but of the Divine will, knowledge and action, the cause of these effects. That Mahāshakti is perfect consciousness (Chidrūpinī) and Bliss (Ānandamayī) which produces from Itself the contracted consciousness experiencing both pleasure and pain. This production is not at all a "whim". It is the nature (Svabhāva) of the ultimate.

Bliss is Love (*Niratishayapremāspadatvam ānandatvam*). The production of the Universe is according to the Shākta an act of love, illustrated by the so-called erotic imagery of the Shāstra. The Self loves itself whether before, or in, creation. The thrill of human love which continues the life of humanity is an infinitesimally small fragment and faint reflection of the creative act in which Shiva and Shakti join to produce the Bindu which is the seed of the Universe.

I quite agree that the worship of mere Force is Āsurik and except in a transient sense futile. Force, however, may be moralized by the good purpose which it serves. The antithesis is not rightly between Might and Right but between Might in the service of Right and Might in the service of Wrong. To worship force merely is to worship matter. He however who worships the Mother in Her Material forms (Sthūlarūpa) will know that She has others, and will worship Her in all such forms. He will also know that She is beyond all limited forms as that which gives being to them all. We may then say that Force is a gross form of Shakti, but Shakti is much more than that "here" (Iha), and the infinite Power of Consciousness "there" (Amutra). This last, the Shakti of worship, is called by the Shāstra the Pūrnāhambhāva or the experience "All I am".

CHAPTER VIII

CHĪNĀCHĀRA

(VASHISHTHA AND BUDDHA)

IT has been the subject of debate whether the Tāntrik Panchatattva ritual with wine and so forth is a product of Buddhism, and whether it is opposed to Vaidika Dharma. Some have supposed that these rites originally came from yellow Asia, penetrated into India where they received its impress, and again made their way to the north to encounter earlier original forms. I have elsewhere put forward some facts which suggest that these rites may be a continuance, though in another form, of ancient Vaidik usage in which Soma, Meat, Fish and Purodāsha formed a part. Though there are some Maithuna rites in the Vedas it is possible that the Bengal Shākta ritual in this respect has its origin in Chīnāchāra. Possibly the whole ritual comes therefrom. I have spoken of Bengal because we should distinguish it from other forms of Shākta worship. The matter is so obscure at present that any definite affirmation as to historical origins lacks justification. Most important however in the alleged Buddhist connection is the story of Vashishtha to be found in the Tantras. He is said to have gone to Mahāchīna (Tibet), which, according to popular belief, is half way to heaven. Mahādeva is said to be visible at the bottom of the Manasarova Lake near Kailāsa. Some of the Texts bearing on it have been collected in the Appendix to the edition of the Tārā Tantra which has been published by the Varendra Anusandhāna Samiti. The Tārā Tantra opens (I. 2) with the following question of Devī Tārā or Mahānīla-Sarasvatī : "Thou didst speak of the two Kula-bhairavas, Buddha and Vashishtha. Tell me by what Mantra they became Siddha." The same Tantra (IV. 10) defines a Bhairava as follows : "He who purifies these five (*i.e.*, Panchatattva) and after offering the same (to the Devatā) partakes thereof is a Bhairava." Buddha then is said to be a Kula-bhairava. It is to be noted that Buddhist Tāntriks who practise this ritual are accounted Kaulas. Shiva replied, "He Janārdana (Viṣhnu) is the excellent Deva in the form of Buddha (Buddharūpī)." It is said in the Samayāchāra Tantra that Tārā and Kālikā, in their different forms, as also Mātangī, Bhairavī, Chhinnamastā, and Dhūmāvatī belong to the northern Āmnāya. The sixth Chapter of the Sammohana Tantra mentions a number of Scriptures of the Bauddha class, together with others of the Shākta, Shaiva, Vaiṣhnava, Saura and Gānapatya classes.

Vashishtha is spoken of in the XVII Chapter of the Rudrayāmala and the 1st Patala of the Brahmayāmala. The following is the account in the former Tāntrik Scripture :

Vashishtha, the self-controlled, the son of Brahmā, practised for ages severe austerities in a lonely spot. For six thousand years he did Sādhanā, but still the Daughter of the Mountains did not appear to him. Becoming angry he went to his father and told him his method of practice. He then said, "Give me another Mantra Oh Lord since this Vidya (Mantra) does not grant me Siddhi (success) otherwise in your presence I shall utter a terrible curse."

Dissuading him Brahmā said, "Oh son, who art learned in the Yoga path, do not do so. Do thou worship Her again with wholehearted feeling, when She will appear and grant you boons. She is the Supreme Shakti. She saves from all dangers. She is lustrous like ten million suns. She is dark blue (Nīlā). She is cool like ten million moons. She is like ten million lightning-flashes. She is the spouse of Kāla (Kālakāminī). She is the beginning of all. In Her there is neither Dharma nor Adharma. She is in the form of all. *She is attached to pure Chīnāchāra* (Shuddhachīnāchāraratā. She is the initiator (Pravarttikā) of Shakti-chakra. Her greatness is infinitely boundless. She helps in the crossing of the ocean of the Saṁsāra. *She is Buddheshvari* (possibly Buddhīshvarī, Lord of Buddhi). She is Buddhi (intelligence) itself (Buddhirūpā). *She is in the form of the Atharva branch of the Vedas* (Atharvavedashākhinī). Numerous Shāstric references connect the Tantra Shāstra with the Atharvaveda. (See in this connection my citation from Shaktisangama Tantra in "Principles of Tantra".) She protects the beings of the worlds. Her action is spread throughout the moving and motionless. Worship Her, my son. Be of good cheer. Why so eager to curse? Thou art the jewel of kindness. Oh son, worship Her constantly with thy mind (Chetas). Being entirely engrossed in Her, thou of a surety shalt gain sight of Her."

Having heard these words of his Guru and having bowed to him again and again the pure one (Vashishtha), *versed in the meaning of Vedānta,* betook himself to the shore of the ocean. For full a thousand years he did Japa of Her Mantra. Still he received no message (Ādesha). Thereupon the Muni Vashishtha grew angry, and being perturbed of mind prepared to curse the Mahāvidyā (Devī). Having sipped water (Āchamana) he uttered a great and terrible curse. Thereupon Kuleshvarī (Lady of the Kaulas) Mahāvidyā appeared before the Muni.

She who dispels the fear of the Yogins said, "How now Vipra (Are Vipra), why have you terribly cursed without cause? Thou dost not understand *My Kulāgama* nor knowest how to worship. How *by mere Yoga practice* can either man or Deva get sight of My Lotus-Feet. *My worship* (Dhyāna) *is without austerity and pain.* To him who desires My Kulāgama, who is Siddha in My Mantra, and knows *My pure Vedāchāra,* My Sādhanā is pure (Punya) *and beyond even the Vedas* (Vedānāmapyagochara). [This does not mean unknown to the Vedas or opposed to them but something which surpasses the Vaidik ritual of the Pashu. This is made plain by the following injunction to follow the Atharvaveda.] *Go to Mahāchīna* (Tibet) *and the country of the Bauddhas and always follow the Atharvaveda* (*Bauddha deshe'tharvavede Mahāchīne sadā braja*). Having gone there and seen My Lotus-Feet which are Mahābhāva (the great blissful feeling which in Her true nature She is) thou shalt, Oh Maharshi, become versed in My Kula and a great Siddha."

Having so said, She became formless and disappeared in the ether and then passed through the ethereal region. The great Rishi having heard this from the Mahāvidyā Sarasvati *went to the land of China* where *Buddha is established* (Buddhapratishthita). Having repeatedly bowed to the ground, Vashishtha said, "Protect me, Oh Mahādeva who art the Imperishable One in the form of Buddha (Buddharūpa). I am the very humble Vashishtha, the son of Brahmā. My mind is ever perturbed. I have come here (Chīna) for the Sādhanā of the Mahādevī. I know not the path leading to Siddhi. Thou knowest the path of the Devas. Seeing however thy way of life (Āchāra) *doubts assail my mind* (*Bhayāni santi me hridi*: because he saw the (to him) extraordinary ritual with wine and woman). Destroy them and my wicked mind which inclines to Vaidik ritual

(Vedagāminī ; that is, the ordinary Pashu ritual) Oh Lord in Thy abode there are ever rites *which are outside Veda* (Veda-vahishkrita : that is, the Vaidik ritual and what is consistent with Veda as Vashishtha then supposed). How is it that wine, meat, woman (Anganā) are drunk, eaten and enjoyed by naked (Digambara) Siddhas who are high (Vara), and awe-inspiring (Raktapānodyata). They drink constantly and enjoy (or make enjoy) beautiful woman (*Muhurmuhuh prapivanti ramayanti varānganām*). With red eyes they are ever exhilarated and replete with flesh and wine (*Sadā-māngsāsavaih pūrnāh*). They are powerful to favour and punish. They *are beyond the Vedas* (Vedasyagocharāh). They enjoy wine and women (Madyastrīsevane ratāh)" (Vashishtha merely saw the ritual surface).

Thus spoke the great Yogī having seen the rites which *are outside the Veda* (Veda-vahishkrita. v. *ante*). Then bowing low with folded hands he humbly said, "*How can inclinations such as these be purifying to the mind? How can there be Siddhi without Vaidik rites?*"

Manah-pravrittireteshu katham bhavati pāvani
Kathang vā jāyate siddhir veda kāryyang vinā prabho.

Buddha said, "Oh Vashishtha, listen the while I speak to thee of the excellent Kula path, by the mere knowing of which one becomes in a short time like Rudra Himself. I speak to thee in brief of the Āgama which is the essence of all and which leads to Kulasiddhi. *First of all, the Vira (hero) should be pure* (Shuchi. Buddha here states the conditions under which only the rites are permissible). His mind should be penetrated with discrimination (Viveka) and freed of all Pashubhāva (state of an uninitiate Pashu or animal man). Let him avoid the company of the Pashu and remain alone in a lonely place, *free from lust,* anger and other passions. He should constantly devote himself to Yoga practice. He should be firm in his resolve to learn Yoga; he should ever tread the Yoga path and *fully know the meaning of the Veda* (Vedārthanipuno mahān). In this way the pious one (Dharmātma) of good conduct and largeness of heart (Audārya) should, by gradual degrees, restrain his breath, and through the path of breathing compass the destruction of mind. Following this practice the self-controlled (Vashī) becomes Yogī. In slow degrees of practice the body firstly sweats. This is the lowest stage (Adhama). The next is middling (Madhyama). Here there is trembling (Kampa). In the third or highest (Para) stage one is able to levitate (Bhūmityāga). By the attainment of Siddhi in Prānāyāma one becomes a master in Yoga. Having become a Yogī by practice of Kumbhaka (restraint of breath) he should be Maunī (given over to silence) and full of intent devotion (Ekānta-bhakti) to Shiva, Krishna and Brahmā. The pure one should realize by mind, action, and speech that Brahmā, Vishnu and Shiva are restless like the moving air (Vāyavīgatichanchalah. *Quaere.* Perhaps the transient nature of these Devatās, as compared with the supreme Shakti, is indicated.) The man of steady mind should fix it on Shakti, who is consciousness (Chidrūpā). Thereafter the Mantrin should practise Mahāvīrabhāva (the feeling of the great hero) and follow the Kula path, the Shakti-chakra, the Vaiṣhnava Sattva-chakra and Navavigraha and should worship Kulakātyāyanī, the excellent one, the Pratyaksha Devatā (that is, the Deity who responds to prayer) who grants prosperity and destroys all evil. She is consciousness (Chidrūpā), She is the abode of knowledge (Jnāna) and is Consciousness and Bliss, lustrous as ten million lightnings, of Whom all Tattvas are the embodiment, who is Raudrī with eighteen arms, fond of wine and mountains of flesh (the text is *Shivāmāngsāchalapriyām*, but the first word should be *Surā*). Man should do Japa of the Mantra, taking refuge with Her, and following the Kula path. Who in the three worlds knows a path higher than this? By the grace gained therein, the great Brahmā Himself became the Creator, and Viṣhnu, whose substance is Sattva-guṇa, the object of adoration of all, highly deserving of worship, the great, and Lord of Yajurveda, became able to protect. By it Hara the Lord of Vīras, the wrathful one, Lord of wrath and of mighty power, became the Destroyer of all. By the grace of Vīrabhāva the Dikpālas (Protectors of the quarters) became like unto Rudra. By a month's practice power to attract (Ākarshanasiddhi) is attained. In two months one becomes the Lord of Speech. In four months one becomes like unto the Dikpālas, in five months one becomes the five arrows (probably masters the five Tanmātras), and in six months he becomes Rudra Himself. The fruit of this method (Āchāra) is beyond all others. This is Kaulamārga. There is nothing which surpasses it. If there be Shakti, the Vipra becomes a complete Yogī by six months' practice. Without Shakti even Shiva can do nought. What then shall we say of men of small intelligence."

Having said this, He whose form is Buddha (Buddharūpī) made him practise Sādhanā. He said, "Oh Vipra, do thou serve Mahāshakti. Do thou practise Sādhanā with wine (Madyasādhanā) and thus shalt thou get sight of the Lotus-Feet of the Mahāvidya." Vashishtha having heard these words of the Guru and meditating on Devī Sarasvatī went to the Kulamandapa to practise the wine ritual (Madirāsādhanā) and having repeatedly done Sādhanā with wine, meat, fish, parched grain and Shakti he became a complete Yogī (Pūrnayogī).

A similar account is given in the Brahmayāmala. There are some variants however. Thus while in the Rudrayāmala, Vashistha is said to have resorted to the shore of the ocean, in the Brahmayāmala he goes to Kāmākhyā, the great Tāntrik Pītha and shrine of the Devī. (The prevalence of Her worship amongst the Mongolian Assamese is noteworthy.) It may be here added that this Yāmala states that, except at time of worship, wine should not be taken nor should the Shakti be unclothed. By violation of these provisions life, it says, is shortened, and man goes to Hell.

According to the account of the Brahmayāmala, Vashishtha complaining of his ill-success was told to go to the Blue Mountains (Nīlāchala) and worship Parameshvarī near Kāmākhyā (Kamrup in Assam). He was told that Viṣhnu in the form of Buddha (Buddharūpī) alone knew this worship according to Chīnāchāra. Devī said, "without Chīnāchāra you cannot please Me. Go to Viṣhnu who is Udbodharūpī (illumined) and worship Me according to the Āchāra taught by Him." Vashishtha then went to Viṣhnu in the country Mahāchīna, which is by the side of the Himālaya (Himavatpārshve), a country inhabited by great Sādhakas and thousands of beautiful and youthful women whose hearts were gladdened with wine, and whose minds were blissful with enjoyment (Vilāsa). They were adorned with clothes which inspired love (Shringāravesha) and the movement of their hips made tinkle their girdles of little bells. Free of both fear and prudish shame they enchanted the world. They surround Īshvara and are devoted to the worship of Devī. Vashishtha wondered greatly when he saw Him in the form of Buddha (Buddharūpī) with eyes drooping from wine. "What" he said, "is Viṣhnu doing in His Buddha form? *This way* (*Āchāra*) *is opposed to Veda* (Vedavādaviruddha). I do not approve of it (*Asammato mama*)." Whilst so thinking, he heard a voice coming from the ether saying, "Oh thou who art devoted to good acts, think not like this. This Āchāra is of excellent result in the Sādhanā of Tārinī. She is not pleased with anything which is the contrary of this. If thou dost wish to gain Her grace speedily, then worship Her according to Chīnāchāra." Hearing this voice, Vashishtha's hairs stood on end and he fell to the ground. Being filled with exceeding joy he prayed to Viṣhnu in the form of Buddha (Buddharūpa). Buddha, who had taken wine, seeing him was greatly pleased and said, "Why have you come here?" Vashishtha bowing to Buddha told him of his worship of Tārinī. Buddha who is Hari and full of knowledge (Tattvajnāna) spoke to him of the *five Makāras* (M: that is, the five commencing with the letter M or Madya, or wine and so forth) *which are in Chīnāchāra* (*Majnānam Chīnachārādikāranam*) *saying that this should not be disclosed* (a common injunction as regards this ritual and renders it from the opponents' standpoint suspect). "By practising it thou shalt not again sink into the ocean of being. It is full of knowledge of the Essence (Tattvajnāna) and gives immediate liberation (Mukti)." He then goes on to explain a principal feature of this cult, namely, its freedom from the ritual rules of the ordinary worship above which the Sādhaka has risen. It is mental worship. In it bathing, purification, Japa, and ceremonial worship is by the mind only. (No outward acts are necessary; the bathing and so forth is in the mind and not in actual water, as is the case in lower and less advanced worship.) There are no rules as to auspicious and inauspicious times, or as to what should be done by day and by night. Nothing is pure or impure (there is no ritual defect of impurity) nor prohibition against the taking of food. Devī should be worshipped even though the worshipper has had his food, and even though the place be unclean. Woman who is Her image should be worshipped (Pūjanam striyah) and never should any injury be done to her (*Strīdvesho naiva kartavyah*).

Are we here dealing with an incident in which Shākyamuni or some other Buddha of Buddhism was concerned?

According to Hindu belief the Rāmāyaṇa was composed in the Tretā age, and Vashishtha was the family priest of Dasharatha and Rāma (Ādikanda VII. 4. 5, VIII. 6, Ayodhyākanda V. 1). The Mahābhārata was composed in Dvāpara. Krishna appeared in the Sandhyā between this and the Kaliyuga. Both Kurukshetra and Buddha were in the Kali age. According to this chronology, Vashishtha who was the Guru of Dasharatha was earlier than Shākyamuni. There were, however, Buddhas before the latter. The text does not mention Shākyamuni or Gautama Buddha. According to Buddhistic tradition there were many other Buddhas before him such as Dīpankara "The Luminous One", Krakuchhanda and others, the term Buddha being a term applicable to the enlightened, whoever he be. It will no doubt be said by the Western Orientalist that both these Yāmalas were composed after the time of Shākyamuni. But if this be so, their author or authors, as Hindus, would be aware that according to Hindu Chronology Vashishtha antedated Shākyamuni. Apart from the fact of there being other Buddhas, according to Hinduism "types" as distinguished from "forms" of various things, ideas, and faiths, are persistent, though the forms are variable, just as is the case with the Platonic Ideas or eternal archtypes. In this sense neither Veda, Tantrashāstra nor Buddhism had an absolute beginning at any time. As types of ideas or faiths they are beginningless (Anādi), though the forms may have varied from age to age, and though perhaps some of the types may have been latent in some of the ages. If the Vedas are Anādi so are the Tantra-shāstras. To the Yogic vision of the Rishi which makes latent things patent, variable forms show their hidden types. Nothing is therefore absolutely new. A Rishi in the Tretā Yuga will know that which will apparently begin in Kali or Dvāpara but which is already really latent in his own age. Viṣhnu appears to his vision as the embodiment of that already latent, but subsequently patent, cult. Moreover in a given age, what is latent in a particular land (say Āryāvarta) may be patent in another (say Mahāchīna). In this way, according to the Hindu Shāstra, there is an essential conservation of types subject to the conditions of time, place, and person (Deshakālapātra). Moreover, according to these Shāstras, the creative power is a reproducing principle. This means that the world-process is cyclic according to a periodic law. The process in one Kalpa is substantially repeated in another and Vashishtha, Buddha, and the rest appeared not only in the present but in previous grand cycles or Kalpas. Just as there is no absolute first beginning of the Universe, so nothing under the sun is absolutely new. Vashishtha, therefore, might have remembered past Buddhas, as he might have foreseen those to come. In Yogic vision both the past and the future can project their shadows into the present. Every Purāṇa and Samhitā illustrates these principles of Yogic intuition backwards and forwards. To the mind of Īshvara both past and future are known. And so it is to such who, in the necessary degree, partake of the qualities of the Lord's mind. The date upon which a particular Shāstra is compiled is, from this viewpoint, unimportant. Even a modern Shāstra may deal with ancient matter. In dealing with apparent anachronisms in Hindu Shāstra, it is necessary to bear in mind these principles. This of course is not the view of "Oriental scholars" or of Indians whom they have stampeded into regarding the beliefs of their country as absurd. It is however the orthodox view. And as an Indian friend of mine to whose views I have referred has said, "What the Psychic research society of the West is conceding to good 'mediums' and 'subjects' cannot be withheld from our ancient supermen—the Rishis."

The peculiar features to be noted of this story are these. Vashishtha must have known what the Vedas and Vaidik rites were, as ordinarily understood. He is described as *Vedāntavit.* Yet he was surprised on seeing Chīnāchāra rites and disapproved of them. He speaks of it as "outside Veda" (Vedavahishkrita) and even opposed to it (Vedavāda-viruddha). On the other hand the connection with Veda is shown, in that the Devī who promulgates this Āchāra is connected with the Atharvaveda, and directs Vashishtha always to follow that Veda, and speaks of the Āchāra not as being opposed to, but as something so high as to be beyond, the ordinary Vaidik ritual (Vedānāmapyagocharah). He is to be fully learned in the import of Veda (Vedārtha-nipuno). It was by the grace of the doctrine and practice of Chīnāchāra that Viṣhnu became the Lord of Yajurveda. The meaning therefore appears to be, that the doctrine and practice lie implict in the Vedas, but go beyond what is ordinarily taught. Viṣhnu therefore says that it is not to be disclosed. What meaning again are we to attach to the word Viṣhnubuddharūpa. Buddha means "enlightened" but here a particular Buddha seems indicated, though Viṣhnu is also spoken of as Udbodharūpī and the Devī as Buddhesh-varī. The Tārā Tantra calls him a Kulabhairava. As is well known, Buddha was an incarnation of Viṣhnu. Vashish-tha is told to go to Mahāchīna by the Himālaya and the country of the Bauddhas (Bauddhadesh). The Bauddhas who follow the Panchatattva ritual are accounted Kaulas. It is a noteworthy fact that the flower of the Devī is Jabā, the scarlet hibiscus or China rose. As the last name may indicate it is perhaps not indigenous to India but to China whence it may have been imported possibly through Nepal. This legend, incorporated as it is in the Shāstra itself, seems to me of primary importance in determining the historical origin of the Panchatattva ritual.

CHAPTER IX

THE TANTRA SHĀSTRAS IN CHINA

ADOPTING for the purpose of this essay, and without discussion as to their accuracy, the general views of Orientalists on chronology and the development of the Buddhistic schools, the history of the Buddhistic Tantra is shortly as follows. The Mahāyāna (which commenced no one knows exactly when) was represented in the first and second centuries by the great names of Ashvaghosha and Nāgārjuna. Its great scripture is the Prajnāpāramitā. Its dominance under the protection of Kanishka marks the first steps towards metaphysical, theistic, and ritualistic religion, a recurring tendency amongst men to which I have previously referred. In the second half of the first century A.D., Buddhism, apparently in its Mahāyāna form, spread to China, and thence to Corea, then to Japan in the sixth century A.D. and to Tibet in the seventh. Some time between the 4th and 5th centuries A.D. Asanga, a Buddhist monk of Gāndhāra, is said to have promulgated the Buddhist Yogāchāra which, as its name imports, was an adaptation of the Indian Patanjali's Yoga Darshana. Dr. Waddell says that "this Yoga parasite (most Europeans dislike what they understand of Yoga) containing within itself the germs of Tāntrism" soon developed "monster out-growths" which "cankered" "the little life of purely Buddhistic stock" in the Mahāyāna, which is itself characterized as merely "sophistic nihilism". Whatever that may mean, it certainly has the air of reducing the Mahāyāna to nothingness. We are then told that at the end of the sixth century "Tāntrism or Sivaic mysticism (a vague word) with its worship of female energies (Shakti) and Fiendesses began to tinge both Hinduism and Buddhism, the latter of which "became still more debased with silly contemptible mummery of unmeaning jargon, gibberish, charmed sentences (Dhāranī) and magic circles (Mandalā)" in the form of the "Vehicle" called Mantrayāna alleged to have been founded by Nāgārjuna who received it from the Dhyāni Buddha Vairochana through the Bodhisattva Vajrasattva at the "Iron tower" in Southern India. Continuing he says "that on the evolution in the tenth century of the demoniacal Buddhas of the Kālachakra (system) the Mantrayāna developed into the Vajrayāna "the most depraved form of Buddhist doctrine" wherein the "Devotee" endeavours with the aid of the "Demoniacal Buddhas" and of "Fiendesses" (Dākinī) "to obtain various Siddhis". The missionary author the Revd. Graham Sandberg, who is so little favourable to Buddhism that he can discover (p. 260) in it "no scheme of metaphysics or morality which can be dignified with the title of an ethical system," when however speaking of this "most depraved form" in a short Chapter on the Tantras and Tāntrik rites ("Tibet and the Tibetans", 218) says that this new vehicle (Ngag-kyi Thegpa) did not profess to supersede the time-honoured Vajrayāna (Dorje-Thegpa) but it claimed "by its expanded mythological scheme and its fascinating and even sublime mystic conceptions to crystallize the old Tāntrik methods into a regular science as complicated as it was resourceful." We are all naturally pleased at finding resemblances in other doctrines to teachings of our own, and so the reverend author, after pointing out that a leading feature of the Kālachakra (Dus-Kyi-khorlo) was the evolution of the idea of a Supreme

Personal Being, says that "many fine and distinctively theistic characteristics of the Deity, His disposition, purity, fatherliness, benevolence and isolated power are set out in the Kālachakra treatises." But he is, as we might expect, of the opinion that this was only an effort towards the real thing, probably influenced by the fact of Christian and Mahomedan teaching. We commonly find that a Semitic source is alleged for what cannot be denied to be good in Hinduism, or its child Buddhism. One wonders however how the "demoniacal Buddhas" and "Fiendesses" work themselves into this be-praised effort to teach Christian ideas. At the risk of straying from my subject, I may point out that in Buddhism the Devatās are given both peaceful (Zhi) and wrathful (Khro) aspects. The latter denotes the terrible (what in India is called Bhairava) aspects of the Divinity, but does not change Him or her into a Demon, at least in Buddhist or Indian belief. Even to the Christian, God has both a terrible and benign aspect. It is true that some of the representations of the former aspect in Northern Buddhism are, to most Westerns, demoniac in form, but that is the way the Tibetan mind works in endeavouring to picture the matter for itself, as the Hindus do with their Devīs Kālī, Chhinnamastā and Chandī. Another and artistically conceived idea of Bhairava is pictured in a beautiful Indian Kangra painting in my possession in which a smouldering restrained wrath, as it were a lowering dark storm-cloud, envelopes the otherwise restrained face and immobile posture of the Devatā. As regards the esoteric worship of Dākinīs I have said a word in the Foreword to the seventh volume of my "Tāntrik Texts". Without having recourse to abuse, we can better state the general conclusion by saying that the Tāntrik cult introduced a theistical form of organized worship with prayers, litanies, hymns, music, flowers, incense, recitation of Mantra (Japa),

Kavachas or protectors in the form of Dhāranīs, offerings, help of the dead: in short, with all practical aids to religion for the individual together with a rich and pompous public ritual for the whole body of the faithful.

For the following facts, so far as China is concerned, I am indebted in the main to the learned work of the Jesuit Father L. Wieger "Histoire des Croyances religieuses et des opinions philosophiques en Chine" (Paris Challamel 1917). The author cited states that Indian Tāntrism "the school of efficacious formula" developed in China in the seventh and eighth centuries of our era, as a Chinese adaptation of the old Theistic Yoga of Patanjali (Second century B.C.) recast by Samanta Bhadra, "and fixed in polytheistic (?) form" by Asamgha (circ. 400 A.D. or as others say 500 A.D.). A treatise of the latter translated into Chinese in 647 A.D. had but little success. But in 716 the Indian Shubhakara came to the Chinese Court, gained the support of the celebrated Tchang-soei, known under his monastic name I-hing to whom he taught Indian doctrine, the latter in return giving aid by way of translations. Shubhakara, in the Tāntrik way, thought that the Buddhist Monks in China were losing their time in mere philosophising since (I cite the author mentioned) the Chinese people were not capable of abstract speculations. Probably Shubhakara, like all of his kind, was a practical man, who recognized, as men of sense must do, that in view of the present character of human nature, religion must be organized and brought to the people in such a form as will be fruitful of result. Metaphysical speculations count with them for little either in China or elsewhere. Shubhakara and his school taught the people that "man was not like the Banana a fruit without kernel". His body contained a Soul. A moral life was necessary; for after death the Soul was judged and if found wicked was cast into Hell. But how was man to guard against this and the evil spirits around him? How was he to secure health, wealth, pardon for his sins, good being in this world and the hereafter? The people were then taught the existence of Divine Protectors, including some forms of Hindu Divinities as also the manner in which their help might be invoked. They were instructed in the use of Mantras, Dhāranīs, and Mudrās the meaning of which is not explained by Dr. Waddell's definition "certain distortions of the fingers". They were taught to pray, to make offerings, and the various other rituals everywhere to be found in Tantra Shāstra. Father Wieger says that pardon of sins and saving from the punishment of Hell was explained by the Chinese Tāntriks of this school not as a derogation from justice, but as the effect of the appeal to the Divine Protector which obtained for the sinful man a fresh lease of life, a kind of respite during which he was enabled to redeem himself by doing good in place of expiating his sins by torture in Hell. The devout Tāntrik who sought after his death to be born in the heaven of such and such Buddha, obtained his wish. Sinners who had done nothing for themselves might be helped even after their death by the prayers of relatives, friends and priests. The devotion of the Tāntriks for the salvation of the deceased was very great. "Let us suppose" says one of the Texts "that a member of your family is thrown in prison. What will you not do to relieve him there, or to get him out from it. In the same way we must act for the dead who are in the great Prison of Hell." Prayer and charity with the view to aid them is accounted to their merit. Above all it is necessary to obtain the aid of the priests who deliver these bound souls by the ritual *ad hoc*, accompanied by music which forms an important part of the Buddhist Tāntrik rites. The resemblance of all this to the Catholic practice as regards the souls in purgatory is obvious. As in the

Indian Compendia, such as the Tantrasāra, there were prayers, Mantras and Dhāranīs to protect against every form of evil, against the bad Spirits, wild beasts, natural calamities, human enemies, and so forth, which were said to be effective, provided that they were applied in the proper disposition and at the right time and in the right manner. But more effective than all these was the initiation with water (Abhisheka). For innumerable good Spirits surround the initiates in all places and at all times so that no evil touches them. It was recommended also to carry on the body the written name of one's protector (Ishtadevatā) or one of those signs which were called "Trancendent seals, conquerors of all Demons". This practice again is similar to that of the use by the Indian Tāntriks of the Kavacha, and to the practice of Catholics who wear scapulars, "Agnus Dei", and consecrated medals. In order to encourage frequent invocations, as also to count them, the Buddhist Tāntriks had Buddhistic chaplets like the Indian Mālā and Catholic Rosary. The beads varied from 1080 (Quaere 1008) to 27. In invoking the Protectors the worshipper held firmly one bead with four fingers (the thumb and first finger of both hands) and then centred his mind on the formula of invocation. Carried on the body, these Rosaries protected from every ill, and made all that one said, a prayer. To use the Indian phrase all that was then said, was Mantra.

Tāntricism was reinforced on the arrival in 719 A.D. of two Indian Brāhmanas, Vajrabodhī and Amogha. The demand for Tantras then became so great that Amogha was officially deputed by the Imperial Government to bring back from India and Ceylon as many as he could. Amogha who was the favourite of three Emperors holding the rank of minister and honoured with many titles lived till 774. He made Tāntricism the fashionable sect. Father Wieger says that in the numerous works signed by him, there is not to be found any of those rites, Indian or Tibetan, which come under the general term Vāmāchāra, which includes worship with wine and women. He has it from Buddhist sources that they deplore the abuses which as regards this matter have taken place in India. In the state of decadence witnessed to-day there largely remains only a liturgy of invocations accompanied by Mudrā and Music, with lanterns and flags from which Bonzes of low degree making a living when called upon by householders to cure the sick, push their business and so forth. Amogha, however, demanded more of those who sought initiation. In the Indian fashion he tested (Parīkshā) the would-be disciple and initiated only those who were fit and had the quality of Vajra. To such only was doubtless confided the higher esoteric teachings and ritual. Initiation was conferred by the ritual pouring of water on the head (Abhisheka), after a solemn act of contrition and devotion.

The following is a description of the rite of initiation (Abhisheka). It is the Buddha who speaks. "Just as an imperial prince is recognized as he who shall govern so my disciples, tested and perfectly formed, are consecrated with water. For the purpose of this ceremony one places on a height, or at least on rising ground, a platform seven feet in diameter strewn with flowers and sprinkled with scented water. Let silence be kept all around. Persian incense is burnt. Place a mirror of bronze and seven arrows to keep away demoniac spirits. The candidate who has been previously prepared by a rigorous abstinence, fully bathed and clad in freshly washed garments kneels on the platform and listens to a lecture explaining the meaning of the rite. His right shoulder is uncovered and his two hands joined. He forms interiorly the necessary intention. Then the Master of the ceremony, holding him firmly by the right hand, pours with the left on the head of the candidate for initiation the ritual water." This initiation made the Chela a son of Buddha and a depository of the latter's doctrine, for the Tantras were deemed to represent the esoteric teaching of the Buddha, just as in India they contain the essence of all knowledge as taught by Shiva or Devī.

The initiates of Amogha were distinguished by their retired life and secret practices, which gained for them the name of "School of Mystery". It transpired that they were awaiting a Saviour in a future age. This rendered them suspect in the eye of Government who thought that they were perhaps a revolutionary society. The sect was accordingly forbidden. But this did not cause it to disappear. On the contrary, for, as the Reverend Father says, in China (and we may add elsewhere) the forbidden fruit is that which is of all the most delicious. The lower ranks avoided this higher initiation and largely lapsed into mechanical formalism, and the true adepts wrapt themselves in a mystery still more profound, awaiting the coming of the future Buddha Maitreya, who, they taught, had inspired Asaṅgha with the doctrine they held. Father Wieger says that their morality is severe and their life very austere. (Leur morale est sévére, leur vie trés austére.) There is a hierarchy of teachers who visit the households at appointed intervals, always after nightfall, leaving before daybreak and supported by the alms of those whom they thus teach. The learned missionary author adds that Tāntrik adepts of this class are often converted to Christianity and quickly become excellent Christians "since their morals are good and they have a lively belief in the supernatural". ("Leurs moeurs ayant été bonnes et leur croyance au surnaturel étant trés vive.")

Here I may note on the subject of Dhāraṇīs, that it has been said that these were only introduced into China during the Tang Dynasty. Father Wieger, however, (p. 385) says that an authentic Riddhi-mantra is to be found in translations made by Leou-Keatch'an in the second century A.D. Buddha is said to have announced to Ānanda, who accompanied him, that five hundred years after his Nirvana, a sect of magicians (whom the author calls Sivaite Tāntrics) would be the cause of the swarming of evil spirits. Instructions were then given for their exorcism. This puts the "Sivaites" far back.

CHAPTER X

A TIBETAN TANTRA

[This Chapter is an admirably understanding review (reprinted from the "Theosophist" of July 1919) by Mr. Johan Van Manen, the Tibetan scholar. It was written on the seventh volume of Tāntrik Texts which contains the first Tibetan Tantra to be published. The Tantra which was selected for the series was the Shrīchakra-Sambhara, because the Editor happened to have manuscripts of this and other works of the same school.]

ALL lovers of Indian philosophy are familiar with the magnificent series of works on the Tantra which, under the general editorship of "Arthur Avalon", have seen the light within the last few years. Some 15 volumes, either texts, translations, or studies, have hitherto been published, and the titles of a number of further works are announced as in preparation or in the press. Just now a new volume has been added to the series, constituting Vol. VII of the "Texts", and this book is undoubtedly one of the most interesting of all those hitherto issued.

Up till now the series has only dealt with works and thoughts originally written down in Sanskrit; this new volume goes further afield and brings us the text and translation of a Tibetan work, dealing with the same subject the whole series is intended to study. Tibetan Tāntrism is undoubtedly a development of its Indian prototype, and at a further stage of our knowledge of the whole subject, the historical development of this school of thought will be, no doubt, studied minutely. Though this present volume brings valuable material towards such an historical study, our knowledge of the Tantra under this aspect is as yet far too limited to enable us to say much about this side of the questions raised by its publication or to find a place for it in the present review of the work. What is more urgent now is to examine this book as it stands, to try to define the general trend of its contents, and to attempt to value it generally in terms of modern speech and thought. In our discussion of the book, therefore, we shall not concern ourselves with questions of technical scholarship at all, but attempt to go to the heart of the subject in such a manner as might be of interest to any intelligent man attracted towards philosophical and religious thought. And it is perhaps easier to do so with the present work than with many others in the series to which it belongs, for more than these others this work makes an appeal to the intellect direct, and proves very human and logical, so as to evoke a response in even such readers as are not prepared by a detailed knowledge of system and terminology, to disentangle an elaborate outer form from the inner substance. It is true that here also, every page and almost every line bristles with names and terms, but the thought connecting such terms is clear, and these, serving much the purposes of algebraical notations in mathematical formulæ, can be easily filled in by any reader with values derived from his own religious and philosophical experience.

The Tantras have, often, not been kindly spoken of. It has been said that they have hitherto played, in Indology, the part of a jungle which everybody is anxious to avoid. Still stronger, a great historian is quoted as having said that it would be " the unfortunate lot of some future scholar to wade through the disgusting details of drunkenness and debauchery which were regarded as an essential part of their religion by a large section of the Indian community not long ago ". And Grünwedel, speaking especially of the Tibetan

Tantras (*Mythology*, p. 106), from the immense literature of which as yet nothing had been translated, says: " To work out these things will be, indeed, a *sacrificium intellectus*, but they are, after all, no more stupid than the Brahmanas on which so much labour has been spent." But here we have the first translation into a European language of one of these Tāntrik texts; and far from being obscene or stupid, it strikes us as a work of singular beauty and nobility, and as a creation of religious art, almost unique in its lofty grandeur. It is so totally unlike any religious document we are acquainted with, that it is almost inconceivable that this is only a brief specimen, a first specimen, made accessible to the general public, of a vast literature of which the extent (as existing in Tibet) cannot yet even be measured. Yet, in saying that the nature of our book is unique, we do not mean to imply that close analogies cannot be found for it in the religious literatures and practices of the world. Such an aloofness would be rather suspicious, for real religious experience is, of course, universal, and, proceeding from the same elements in the human heart, and aspiring to the same ends, must always show kinship in manifestation. Yet this Tibetan product has a distinctive style of its own, which singles it out in appearance as clearly, let us say, as the specific character of Assyrian or Egyptian art is different from that of other styles.

When we now proceed to examine the document before us, at the outset a verdict of one of the critics of Tāntrism comes to our mind, to the effect that the Tantra is perhaps the most elaborate system of auto-suggestion in the world. This dictum was intended as a condemnation; but though accepting the verdict as correct, we ourselves are not inclined to accept, together with it, the implied conclusion. Auto-suggestion is the establishment of mental states and moods from within, instead of as a result of impressions received from without. Evidently there must be two kinds of this auto-suggestion, a true and a false one. The true one is that which produces states of consciousness corresponding to those which may be produced by realities in the outer world, and the false one is that which produces states of consciousness not corresponding to reactions to any reality without. In the ordinary way the consciousness of man is shaped in response to impressions from without, and so ultimately rests on sensation, but theoretically there is nothing impossible in the theory that these "modifications of the thinking principle" should be brought about by the creative will and rest rather on imagination and intuition than on sensation. This theory has not only been philosophically and scientifically discussed, but also practically applied in many a school of mysticism or Yoga. If I remember well, there is a most interesting book by a German (non-mystic) Professor, Staudenmeyer, dealing with this subject, under the title of *Magic as an Experimental Science* (in German), and the same idea seems also to underlie Steiner's theory of what he calls "imaginative clairvoyance." In Christian mysticism this has been fully worked out by de Loyola in his "Spiritual Exercises" as applied to the Passion of the Christ. In what is now-a-days called New Thought, this principle is largely applied in various manners. In our book we find it applied in terms of Tāntrik Buddhism with a fulness and detail surpassing all other examples of this type of meditation. In order to present the idea in such a way that it may look plausible in itself, we have first to sketch out the rational underlying any such system. This is easily done.

We can conceive of this universe as an immense ocean of consciousness or intelligence in which the separate organisms, human beings included, live and move and have their being. If we conceive of this mass of consciousness as subject to laws analogous to those of gravity, and at the same time as being fluidic in nature, then the mechanism of all intellectual activity might well be thought of, in one of its aspects, as hydraulic in character. Let any organism, fit to be a bearer of consciousness, only open itself for the reception of it, and the hydraulic pressure of the surrounding sea of consciousness will make it flow in, in such a form as the construction of the organism assumes. The wave and the sea, the pot and the water, are frequent symbols in the East, used to indicate the relation between the all-consciousness and the individual consciousness. If the human brain is the pot sunk in the ocean of divine consciousness, the form of that pot will determine the form which the all-consciousness will assume within that brain.

Now imagination, or auto-suggestion, may determine that form. Through guess, intuition, speculation, tradition, authority, or whatever the determinant factor may be, any such form may be chosen. The man may create any form, and then, by expectancy, stillness, passivity, love, aspiration or whatever term we choose, draw the cosmic consciousness within him, only determining its form for himself, but impersonally receiving the power which is not from himself, but from without. The process is like the preparation of a mould in which molten metal is to be cast, with this difference, that the metal cast into the mould is not self-active and alive, and not ever-present and pressing on every side, as the living consciousness is which constitutes our universe.

We may take an illustration from the mechanical universe. This universe is one seething mass of forces in constant interplay. The forces are there and at work all the time, but only become objectified when caught in suitable receivers. The wind-force, if not caught by the arms of the windmill, the forces of stream or waterfall, if not similarly gathered in a proper mechanism, disperse themselves in space and are not focused in and translated into objective units of action. So with the vibrations sent along the wire, in telegraphic or telephonic communication, or with the other vibràtions sent wirelessly. In a universe peopled with intelligences, higher beings, gods, a whole hierarchy of entities, from the highest power and perfection to such as belong to our own limited class, constant streams of intelligence and consciousness must continuously flash through space and fill existence. Now it seems, theoretically indeed, very probable, assuming that consciousness is one and akin in essence, that the mechanical phenomenon of sympathetic vibration may be applied to that consciousness as well as to what are regarded as merely mechanical vibrations. So, putting all the above reasonings together, it is at least a plausible theory that man, by a process of auto-suggestion, may so modify the organs of his consciousness, and likewise attune his individual consciousness in such a way, as to become able to enter into a sympathetic relation with the forces of cosmic consciousness ordinarily manifesting outside him and remaining unperceived, passing him as it were, instead of being caught and harnessed. And this is not only a theory, but more than that—a definite statement given as the result of experience by mystics and meditators of all times and climes.

Now we may ask: how has this method been applied in our present work? A careful analysis of its contents makes us discover several interesting characteristics. First of all we have to remember that our text presupposes a familiarity with the religious conceptions, names, personalities and philosophical principles of Northern Buddhism, which are all freely used in the composition. What is strange and foreign in them to the Western reader is so only because he moves in unfamiliar surroundings. But the character of the composition is one which might be compared to such analogous Western productions (with great differences, however) as the Passion Play at Oberammergau or the mediæval mystery-plays. Only, in some of the latter the historical element predominates, whilst in the Tibetan composition the mythological element (for want of a better word) forms the basis and substance. In other words, in this ritual of meditation the Gods, Powers and Principles are the actors, and not historical or symbolical personages of religious tradition. Secondly the play is enacted in the mind, inwardly, instead of on the scene, outwardly. The actors are not persons, but conceptions.

First, the meditator has to swing up his consciousness to a certain pitch of intensity, steadiness, quiet, determination and expectancy. Having tuned it to the required pitch, he fixes it on a simple centre of attention which is to serve as a starting-point or gate through which his imagination shall well up as the water of a fountain comes forth through the opening of the water-pipe. From this central point the mental pictures come forth. They are placed round the central conception. From simple to complex in orderly progression the imaginative structure is elaborated. The chief Gods appear successively, followed by the minor deities. Spaces, regions, directions are carefully determined. Attributes, colours, symbols, sounds are all minutely prescribed and deftly worked in, and explications carefully given. A miniature world is evolved, seething with elemental forces working in the universe as cosmic forces and in man as forces of body and spirit. Most of the quantities in this elaborate notation are taken from the body of indigenous religious teaching and mythology. Some are so universal and transparent that the non-Tibetan reader can appreciate them even without a knowledge of the religious technical terms of Tibet. But anyhow, an attentive reading and re-reading reveals something, even to the outsider, of the force of this symbological structure, and makes him intuitively feel that here we are assisting in the unfolding of a grand spiritual drama, sweeping up the mind to heights of exaltation and nobility.

As to the terminological side of the text, the Editor's abundant notes prove as valuable as useful. They may disturb the elevated unity of the whole at first, but after some assiduous familiarizing, lead to fuller and deeper comprehension. Even a single reading is sufficient to gain the impression that a stately and solemn mental drama is enacted before us with an inherent impressiveness which would attach, for instance to a Christian, to the performance of a ritual in which all the more primary biblical persons, human and superhuman, were introduced, in suitable ways, as actors. And the superlative cleverness of this structure! Starting from a single basic note, this is developed into a chord, which again expands into a melody, which is then elaborately harmonised. Indeed the meditation is in its essence both music and ritual. The initial motives are developed, repeated, elaborated, and new ones introduced. These again are treated in the same way. A symphony is evolved and brought to a powerful climax, and then again this full world of sound, form, meaning, colour, power is withdrawn, limited, taken back into itself, folded up and dissolved, turned inwards again and finally returned into utter stillness and rest, into that tranquil void from which it was originally evoked and which is its eternal mother. I do not know of any literature which in its nature is so absolutely symphonic, so directly akin to music, as this sample of a Tibetan meditational exercise. And curiously enough, it makes us think of another manifestation of Indian religious art, for in words this document is akin to the Indian temple decoration, especially the South Indian gopura, which in its endless repetitions and elaborations seems indeed instinct with the same spirit which has given birth to this scheme of imagination taught in these Tantras. Only, in stone or plaster, the mythological host is sterile and immovable, whilst, as created in the living mind, the similar structure partakes of the life of the mind within and without. The sculptural embodiment is, therefore, serviceable to the less evolved mind. The Tantra is for the religious thinker who possesses power.

But we said that our meditational structure was also akin to ritual. What we mean by this is that all the figures and images evoked in the mind in this meditation are, after all, only meant, as the words, vestures and gestures in a ritual, to suggest feelings, to provoke states of consciousness, and to furnish (if the simile be not thought too pathetic) pegs to hang ideas upon.

Like as a fine piece of music, or a play, can only be well rendered when rehearsed over and over again, and practised so that the form side of the production becomes almost mechanical, and all power in the production can be devoted to the infusion of inspiration, so can this meditation only be perfectly performed after untold practice and devotion. It would be a totally mistaken idea to read this book as a mere piece of literature, once to go through it to see what it contains, and then to let it go. Just as the masterpieces of music can be heard hundreds of times, just as the great rituals of the world grow in power on the individual in the measure with which he becomes familiar with them and altogether identifies himself with the most infinitely small minutiæ of their form and constitution, so this meditation ritual is one which only by repetition can be mastered and perfected. Like the great productions of art or nature, it has to "grow" on the individual.

This meditational exercise is not for the small, nor for the flippant, nor for those in a hurry. It is inherently an esoteric thing, one of those teachings belonging to the regions of "quiet" and "tranquillity" and "rest" of Taoistic philosophy. To the ignorant it must be jabber, and so it is truly esoteric, hiding itself by his own nature within itself, though seemingly open and accessible to all. But in connection with this meditation we do not think of pupils who read it once or twice, or ten times, or a hundred, but of austere thinkers who work on it as a life-work through laborious years of strenuous endeavour. For, what must be done to make this meditation into a reality? Every concept in it must be vivified and drenched with life and power. Every god in it must be made into a living god, every power manipulated in it made into a potency. The whole structure must be made vibrant with forces capable of entering into sympathetic relation with the greater cosmic forces in the universe, created in imitation on a lower scale within the individual meditator himself. To the religious mind the universe is filled with the thoughts of the gods, with the powers of great intelligences and consciousnesses, radiating eternally through space and really constituting the world that is. "The world is only a thought in the mind of God." It must take years of strenuous practice even to build up the power to visualize and correctly produce as an internal drama this meditation given in our book. To endow it with life and to put power into this life is an achievement that no small mind, no weak devotee, can hope to perform. So this meditation is a solemn ritual, like the Roman Catholic Mass; only it is performed in the mind instead of in the church, and the mystery it celebrates is an individual and not a general sacrament.

In what we have said above we have tried to give some outlines of the chief characteristics of this remarkable work, now brought within the reach of the general reading public, and especially of benefit to those among them interested in the study of comparative religion along broad lines. We owe, indeed, a debt of gratitude to Arthur Avalon, whose enthusiasm for and insight into the Indian religious and philosophical mind have unearthed this particular gem for us. We may be particularly grateful that his enthusiasm has not set itself a limit, so as to prevent him from dealing with other than Sanskrit lore alone, and from looking for treasure even beyond the Himalayas. In this connection we may mention that it is his intention to maintain this catholic attitude, for he is now taking steps to incorporate also an important Japanese work on the *Vajrayāna* in his Tāntrik series. As far as this first Tibetan text is concerned, the choice has been decidedly happy, and he has been no less fortunate in having been able to secure a competent collaborator to undertake the philological portion of the work, the translating and editing labour. The result of thus associating himself with a capable indigenous scholar to produce the work, has been a great success, a production of practical value which will undoubtedly not diminish in all essentials for a long time to come. For not only is this particular work in and for itself of interest, with a great beauty of its own; it has another value in quite other directions than those connected with the study of meditation or of religious artistic creation.

The work furnishes a most important key to a new way of understanding many phases and productions of Indian philosophy. The projection of the paraphernalia of Hindu mythology inwards into the mind as instruments of meditation, the internalising of what we find in the Purāṇas or the Epic externalised as mythology, has seemed to me to throw fresh and illuminating light on Indian symbology. To give an illustration: In this Tantra we find an elaborate manipulation of weapons, shields, armour, as instruments for the protection of the consciousness. Now all these implements figure, for instance, largely and elaborately in such a work as the *Ahirbudhnya Samhitā*, of which Dr. Schrāder has given us a splendid summary in his work, *Introduction to the Pancharātra.* But in the *Pancharātra* all these implements are only attributes of the gods. In our text we find a hint as to how all these external mythological data can also be applied to and understood as internal workings of the human consciousness, and in this light Indian mythology assumes a new and richer significance. I do not want to do more here than hint at the point involved, but no doubt any student of Hindu mythology who is also interested in Hindu modes of thought, in the Hindu Psyche, will at once see how fruitful this idea can be.

One of the riddles of Indian thought is that its symbology is kinetic and not static, and eludes the objective formality of Western thought. That is why every Hindu god is another, who is again another, who is once more another. Did not Kipling say something about "Kāli who is Pārvati, who is Sitala, who is worshipped against the small-pox"? So also almost every philosophical principle is an "aspect" of another principle, but never a clear-cut, well-circumscribed, independent thing by itself. Our text goes far towards giving a hint as to how all these gods and principles, which in the Purāṇas and other writings appear as extra-human elements, may perhaps also be interpreted as aspects of the human mind (and even human body) and become a psychological mythology instead of a cosmic one.

The idea is not absolutely new, but has been put forward by mystics before. The Cherubinic Wanderer sang that it would be of no avail to anyone, even if the Christ were born a hundred times over in Bethlehem, if he were not born within the man himself. It has been said of the *Bhagavad-Gītā* that it is in one sense the drama of the soul, and that meditation on it, transplanting the field of Kurukshetra within the human consciousness, may lead to a direct realization of all that is taught in that book, and to a vision of all the glories depicted therein. That idea is the same as that which is the basis of our text. Its message is: "Create a universe within, in order to be able to hear the echoes of the universe without, which is one with that within, in essence." If seers, occultists, meditators really exist, they may be able to outline the way and method by which they themselves have attained. So it was with de Loyola and his "Spiritual Exercises," and there is no reason why it should not be the same with the book we are discussing here.

As to how far we have here a result of practical experience, or only an ingenious theory, a great "attempt," as it were, we will not and cannot decide. To make statements about this needs previous experiment, and we have only read the book from the outside, not lived its contents from within. But however this may be, even such an outer reading is sufficient to reveal to us the grandeur of the conception put before us, and to enable us to feel the symphonic splendour of the creation as a work of religio-philosophic art; and that alone is enough to enable us to judge the work a masterpiece and a document of first-class value in the field of religious and mystical literature. The form is very un-Western indeed, and in many ways utterly unfamiliar and perhaps bewildering. But the harmony of thought, the greatness of the fundamental conceptions, the sublimity of endeavour embodied in it, are clear; and these qualities are certainly enough to gain for it admirers and friends—perhaps here and there a disciple—even in our times so badly prepared to hear this Tibetan echo from that other world, which in many ways we in the West make it our strenuous business to forget and to discount.

CHAPTER XI

SHAKTI IN TAOISM

THE belief in Shakti or the Divine Power as distinguished from the Divine Essence (Svarūpa), the former being generally imagined for purposes of worship as being in female form, is very ancient. The concept of Shakti in Chinese Taoism is not merely a proof of this (for the Shakti notion is much older) but is an indication of the ancient Indian character of the doctrine. There are some who erroneously think that the concept had its origin in "Sivaic mysticism," having its origin somewhere in the sixth century of our era. Lao-tze or the "old master" was twenty years senior to Confucius and his life was said to have been passed between 570-490 B.C. A date commonly accepted by European Orientalists as that of the death of Buddha (Indian and Tibetan opinions being regarded, as "extravagant") would bring his life into the sixth century B.C., one of the most wonderful in the world's history. Lao-tze is said to have written the Tao-tei-king, the fundamental text of Taoism. This title means Treatise on Tao and Tei. Tao which Lao-tze calls "The great" is in its Sanskrit equivalent Brahman and Tei is Its power or activity or Shakti. As Father P. L. Wieger, S.J., to whose work (Histoire des croyances religieuses et des opinions philosophiques en Chine, p. 143 *et seq.* 1917) I am here indebted, points out, Lao-tze did not invent Taoism no more than Confucius (557-419 B.C.) invented Confucianism. It is characteristic of these and other Ancient Eastern Masters that they do not claim to be more than "transmitters" of a wisdom older than themselves. Lao-tze was not the first to teach Tao-ism. He had precursors who, however, were not authors. He was the writer of the first book on Taoism which served as the basis for the further development of the doctrine. On this account its paternity is attributed to him. There was reference to this doctrine it is said in the official archives (p. 743). The pre-Taoists were the annalists and astrologers of the Tcheou. Lao-tze who formulated the system was one of them (*ib.* 69). The third Ministry containing these archives registered all which came from foreign parts, as Taoism did. For as Father Wieger says, *Taoism is in its main lines a Chinese adaptation of the contemporary doctrine of the Upanishads* ("or le Taoisme est dans ses grandes lignes une adaptation Chinoise de la doctrine Indienne contemporaine des Upanishads"). The actual fact of importation cannot in default of documents be proved but as the learned author says, the fact that the doctrine was not Chinese, that it was then current in India, and its sudden spread in China, creates in favour of the argument for foreign importation almost a certain conclusion. The similarity of the two doctrines is obvious to any one acquainted with that of the Upanishads and the doctrine of Shakti. The dualism of the manifesting Unity (Tao) denoted by Yinn-Yang appears for the first time in a text of Confucius, a contemporary of Lao-tze, who may have informed him of it. All Chinese Monism descends from Lao-tze. The patriarchal texts were developed by the great Fathers of Taoism Lie-tzeu and Tchong-tzeu (see "Les Péres du systéme Taoiste" by the same author) whom the reverend father calls the only real thinkers that China has produced. Both were practically prior to the contact of Greece and India on the Indus under Alexander.

The first development of Taoism was in the South. It passed later to the North where it had a great influence.

According to Taoism there was in the beginning, now, and ever will be an ultimate Reality, which is variously called *Huan* the Mystery, which cannot be named or defined, because human language is the language of limited beings touching limited objects, whereas Tao is imperceptible to the senses and the unproduced cause of all, beyond which there is nothing: *Ou* the Formless, or *Tao* the causal principle the unlimited inexhaustible source from which all comes, ("Tao le principe parceque tout derive de lui") Itself proceeds from nothing but all from It. So it is said of Brahman that It is in Itself beyond mind and speech, formless and (as the Brahmasūtra says) That from which the Universe is born, by which it is maintained and into which it is dissolved. From the abyss of Its Being, It throws out all forms of Existence and is never emptied. It is an infinite source exteriorising from Itself all forms, by Its Power (Tei). These forms neither diminish nor add to Tao which remains ever the same. These limited beings are as a drop of water in Its ocean. Tao is the sum of, and yet as infinite, beyond all individual existences. Like Brahman, Tao is one, eternal, infinite, self-existent, omnipresent, unchanging (Immutable) and complete (Pūrna). At a particular moment (to speak in our language for It was then beyond time) Tao threw out from Itself Tei Its Power (Vertu or Shakti) which operates in alternating modes called *Yinn* and *Yang* and produces, as it were by condensation of its subtility (Shakti ghanībhūta), the Heaven and Earth and Air between, from which come all beings. The two modes of Its activity, Yinn and Yang, are inherent in the Primal That, and manifest as modes of its *Tei* or Shakti. *Yinn* is rest, and therefore after the creation of the phenomenal world a going back, retraction, concentration towards the original Unity (Nivritti), whereas *Yang* is action and therefore the opposite principle of going forth or expansion (Pravritti). These modes appear in creation under the sensible forms of Earth (Yinn) and Heaven (Yang). The one original principle or Tao, like Shiva and Shakti, thus becomes dual in manifestation as Heaven-Earth from which emanate other existences. The state of *Yinn* is one of rest, concentration and imperceptibility which was the own state (Svarūpa) of Tao before time and things were. The state of *Yang* is that of action, expansion, of manifestation in sentient beings and is the state of Tao in time, and that which is in a sense not Its true state ("L'etat *Yinn* de concentration, de repos, d'imperceptibilité, qui fut celui du Principe avant le temps, est son état propre. L'etat *Yang* d'expansion et d'action, de manifestation dans les êtres sensibles, est son état dans le temps, en quelque sorte impropre"). All this again is Indian. The primal state of Brahman or Shiva-Shakti before manifestation is that in which It rests in Itself (Svarūpa-vishrānti), that is, the state of rest and infinite formlessness. It then by Its Power (Shakti) manifests the universe. There exists in this power the form of two movements or rhythms, namely, the going forth or expanding (Pravritti) and the return or centering movement (Nivritti). This is the Eternal Rhythm, the Pulse of the universe, in which it comes and goes from that which in Itself, does neither. But is this a real or ideal movement? According to Father Wieger, Taoism is a realistic and not idealistic pantheism in which Tao is not a Conscious Principle but a Necessary Law, not Spiritual but Material, though imperceptible by reason of its tenuity and state of rest ("Leur systéme est un pantheisme realīste, pas idêaliste. Au commencement était un étre unique non pas intelligent mais loi fatale, non spirituel mais matériel, imperceptible a force de tenuité, d' abord immobile "). He also calls Heaven and Earth unintelligent agents of production of sentient beings (Agent non-intelligents de la production de tous les êtres sensibles). I speak with all respect for the opinion of one who has made a special study of the subject which I have not so far as its Chinese aspect is concerned. But even if, as is possible, at this epoch the full idealistic import of the Vedānta had not been developed, I doubt the accuracy of the interpretation which makes Tao material and unconscious. According to Father Wieger, Tao prolongates Itself. Each being is a prolongation (Prolongement) of the Tao, attached to it and therefore not diminishing It. Tao is stated by him to be Universal Nature, the sum (Samashti) of all individual natures which are terminal points (Terminaisons) of Tao's prolongation. Similarly in the Upanishads, we read of Brahman producing the world from Itself as the spider produces the web from out itself. Tao is thus the Mother of all that exists (" la mére de tout ce qui est "). If so, it is the Mother of mind, will, emotion and every form of consciousness. How are these derived from merely a "material" principle? May it not be that just as the Upanishads use material images to denote creation and yet posit a spiritual conscious (though not in our limited sense) Principle, Lao-tze, who was indebted to them, may have done the same. Is this also not indicated by the Gnostic doctrine of the Taoists? The author cited says that to the cosmic states of Yinn and Yang correspond in the mind of man the states of rest and activity. When the human mind thinks, it fills itself with forms or images and is moved by desires. Then it perceives only the effects of Tao, namely, distinct sentient beings. When on the contrary the action of the human mind stops and is fixed and empty of images of limited forms, it is then the Pure Mirror in which is reflected the ineffable and unnameable Essence of

Tao Itself, of which intuition the Fathers of Taoism speak at length. (" Quand an contraire l'esprit humain est arrêté est vide et fixe, alors miroir net et pur, il mire l'essence ineffable et innomable du Principe lui-meme. Les Pêres nous parleront au long de cette intuition.") This common analogy of the Mirror is also given in the Kāmakalāvilāsa (v. 4) where it speaks of Shakti as the pure mirror in which Shiva reflects Himself (*pratiphalati vimarsha darpane vishade*). The conscious mind does not reflect a material principle as its essence. Its essence must have the principle of consciousness which the mind itself possesses. It is to Tei the Virtue or Power which Tao emits from Itself (" ce Principe se mit a êmettre Tei sa vertu ") that we should attribute what is apparently unconscious and material. But the two are one, just as Shiva the possessor of power (Shaktimān) and Shakti or power are one, and this being so distinctions are apt to be lost. In the same way in the Upanishads statements may be found which have not the accuracy of distinction between Brahman and its Prakriti, which we find in later developments of Vedānta and particularly in the Shākta form of it. Moreover we are here dealing with the One in Its character both as cause and as substance of the World Its effect. It is of Prakriti-Shakti and possibly of *Tei* that we may say that it is an apparently material unconscious principle, imperceptible by reason of its tenuity and (to the degree that it is not productive of objective effect) immobile. Further Father Wieger assures us that all contraries issue from the same unchanging Tao and that they are only *apparent* (Toute contrariété n'est qu' apparente "). But relative to what? He says that they are not subjective illusions of the human mind, but objective appearances, double aspects of the unique Being, corresponding to the alternating modalities of *Yinn* and *Yang*. That is so. For as

Shaṅkara says, external objects are not merely projections of the individual human mind but of the cosmic mind, the Īshvarī Shakti.

We must not, of course, read Taoism as held in the sixth century B.C. as if it were the same as the developed Vedānta of Shaṅkara who, according to European chronology, lived more than a thousand years later. But this interpretation of Vedānta is an aid in enabling us to see what is at least implicit in earlier versions of the meaning of their common source—the Upanishads. As is well-known, Shaṅkara developed their doctrine in an idealistic sense, and therefore his two movements in creation are Avidyā, the primal ignorance which produces the appearance of the objective universe, and Vidyā or knowledge which dispels such ignorance, ripening into that Essence and Unity which is Spirit-Consciousness Itself. Aupanishadic doctrine may be regarded either from the world or material aspect, or from the non-world and spiritual aspect. Men have thought in both ways and Shaṅkara's version is an attempt to synthesize them.

The Taoist master Ki (*Op. cit.*, 168) said that the celestial harmony was that of all beings in their common Being. All is one as we experience in deep sleep (Sushupti). All contraries are sounds from the same flute, mushrooms springing from the same humidity, not real distinct beings but differing aspects of the one universal "Being". "I" has no meaning except in contrast with "you" or "that". But who is the Mover of all? Everything happens *as if* there were a real governor. The hypothesis is acceptable provided that one does not make of this Governor a *distinct being*. He (I translate Father Wieger's words) is a tendency without palpable form, the inherent norm of the universe, its immanent evolutionary formula. The wise know that the only Real is the Universal Norm. The unreflecting vulgar believe in the existence of distinct beings. As in the case of the Vedānta, much misunderstanding exists because the concept of Consciousness differs in East and West as I point out in detail in the essay dealing with Chit-Shakti.

The space between Heaven and Earth in which the Power (Vertu, Shakti, Tei) is manifested is compared by the Taoists to the hollow of a bellows of which Heaven and Earth are the two wooden sides; a bellows which blows without exhausting itself. The expansive power of Tao in the middle space is imperishable. It is the mysterious Mother of all beings. The come and go of this mysterious Mother, that is, the alternating of the two modalities of the One, produce Heaven and Earth. Thus acting, She is never fatigued. From Tao was exteriorized Heaven and Earth. From Tao emanated the producing universal Power or Shakti, which again produced all beings without self-exhaustion or fatigue. The one having put forth its Power, the latter acts according to two alternating modalities of going forth and return. This action produces the middle air or *Ki* which is tenuous Matter, and through Yinn and Yang, issue all gross beings. Their coming into existence is compared to an unwinding (Dèvidage) from That or Tao, as it were a thread from reel or spool. In the same way the Shākta Tantra speaks of an "uncoiling". Shakti is coiled (Kundalinī) round the Shiva-point (Bindu), one with It in dissolution. On creation She begins to uncoil in a spiral line movement which is the movement of creation. The Taoist Father Lieu-tze analysed the creative movement into the following stages: "The Great Mutation" anterior to the appearance of tenuous matter (Movement of the two modalities in undefined being), "the Great Origin" or the stage of tenuous matter, "the Great Commencement" or the stage of sensible matter, "the Great Flux" or the stage of plastic matter and actual present material compounded existences. In the primitive state, when matter was imperceptible, all beings to come were latent in an homogeneous state.

I will only add as bearing on the subject of consciousness that the author cited states that the Taoists lay great stress on intuition and ecstasy which is said to be compared to the unconscious state of infancy, intoxication, and narcosis. These comparisons may perhaps mislead just as the comparison of the Yogi state to that of a log (Kāshṭhavat) has misled. This does not mean that the Yogi's consciousness is that of a log of wood, but that he no more perceives the external world than the latter does. He does not do so because he has the Samādhi conscious, that is, Illumination and true being Itself. He is one then with Tao and Tei or Shakti in their true state.

CHAPTER XII

ALLEGED CONFLICT OF SHĀSTRAS[1]

A NOT uncommon modern criticism upon the Indian Shāstras is that they mutually conflict. This is due to a lack of knowledge of the doctrine of Adhikāra and Bhūmikā, particularly amongst Western critics, whose general outlook and mode of thought is ordinarily deeply divergent from that which has prevailed in India. The idea that the whole world should follow one path is regarded by the Hindus as absurd, being contrary to Nature and its laws. A man must follow that path for which he is fit, that is, for which he is Adikhārī. Adhikāra or competency literally means "spreading over" that is "taking possession of". What is to be known (Jnātavya), done (Kartavya), acquired (Prāptavya) is determined not once and generally for all, but in each case by the fitness and capacity therefor of the individual. Each man can know, do, and obtain not everything, nor indeed one common thing, but that only of which he is capable (Adhikārī). What the Jīva can think, do, or obtain, is his competency or Adhikāra, a profound and practical doctrine on which all Indian teaching and Sādhanā is based. As men are different and therefore the Adhikāra is different, so there are different forms of teaching and practice for each Adhikāra. Such teaching may be Shrauta or Ashrauta. Dealing here with the first, it is said that of

[1] This Chapter originally appeared in the *Indian Philosophical Review*, Vol. II, No. 4 (April 1919).

all Vidyās the Lord is Īshāna, and that these differing forms are meant for differing competencies, though all have one and the same object and aim. This has been well and concisely worked out by Bhāskararāya, the Commentator on Tāntric and Aupanishadic Texts in his Bhāshya upon the *Nityāshodashikārṇava*, which is, according to him, a portion of the great Vāmakeshvara Tantra. The second portion of the *Nityāshodashikārṇava* is also known as the *Yoginīhṛidaya*. These valuable Tāntrik Texts have been published as the 56th Volume of the Poona Ānandāshrama Series which includes also (Vol. 69) the Jnānārṇava Tantra. The importance of the Vāmakeshvara is shown by the fact that Bhāskararāya claims for it the position of the independent 65th Tantra which is mentioned in the 31st verse of the *Ānandalaharī*. Others say that the Svatantra there spoken of, is the Jnānārṇava Tantra, and others again are of the opinion that the *Tantrarāja* is the great independent Tantra of which the *Ānandalaharī* (ascribed to Shrīmadāchāryyabhagavatpāda, that is, Shaṅgkarāchāryya) speaks. Bhāskararāya who lived in the first half of the eighteenth century, gives in his Commentary the following exposition:

In this world all long for happiness which is the sole aim of man. Of this there is no doubt. This happiness again is of two kinds, namely, that which is produced and transient (Kṛitrima) and that which is unproduced and enduring (Akṛitrima), called respectively Desire (Kāma) and Liberation (Moksha). Dharma procures happiness of both kinds, and Artha helps to the attainment of Dharma. These therefore are desired of all. There are thus four aims of man (Purushārtha) which though, as between themselves, different, are yet intimately connected, the one with the other. The Kalpasūtra says that self-knowledge is the aim and end of man (Svavimarshah purushārthah). This is said of Liberation as being the highest end, since it alone gives real and enduring happiness. This saying, however, does not raise any contradiction. For, each of the four is to be had by the Jnāna and Vijnāna appropriate for such attainment. These (Purushārtha) are again to be attained according to the capacity of the individual seeking them (Tādṛisha-tādṛisha-chittaikasādhyāni). The competency of the individual Chitta depends again on the degree of its purity.

The very merciful Bhagavān Parameshvara desirous of aiding men whose mind and disposition (Chitta) differ according to the results produced by their different acts, promulgated different kinds of Vidyā which, though appearing to be different as between themselves, yet have, as their common aim, the highest end of all human life, that is, Liberation.

Shruti also says (Nṛisinghapūrvatāpanī Up. I-6; Mahānārāyaṇa Up. XVII-5): "Of all Vidyās the Lord is Īshāna" (Īshānah sarvavidyānām) and (Sveta. Up. VI-18) "I who desire liberation seek refuge in that Deva who creates Brahmā who again reveals the Vedas and all other learning" (Yo Brahmāṇam vidadhātī pūrvam yo vai vedāngshcha prahinoti). The particle "cha" impliedly signifies the other Vidyās collectively. We also find it said in furtherance of that statement "To him the first born He gave the Vedas and Purāṇas." *Smriti* also states that the omniscient Poet (Kavi), Carrier of the Trident (Shiva shūlapāṇi), is the first Promulgator of these eighteen Vidyās which take differing paths (Bhinnavartma). It follows that, inasmuch as Paramashiva, the Benefactor of the Worlds, is the Promulgator of all Vidyās, they are all authoritative, though each is applicable for differing classes of competency (Adhikāribhedena). This has been clearly stated in *Sūtasamhitā* and similar works.

Capacity (Adhikāra) is (for example) of this kind. The unbeliever (Nāstika *i.e.*, in Veda) has Adhikāra in Darshanas such as Ārhata (Jaina) and the like. Men of the first three castes have Adhikāra in the path of Veda. Similarly the Adhikāra of an individual varies according to the purity of his Chitta. For we see that the injunctions relating to Dharma vary according to Āshrama and caste (Varna-bheda). Such texts as praise any particular Vidyā are addressed to those who are Adhikārī therein, and their object is to induce them to follow it. Such texts again as disparage any Vidyā are addressed to those who are not Adhikarī therein, and their object is to dissuade them from it. Nor again should these words of blame (or praise) be taken in an absolute sense, that is otherwise than relatively to the person to whom they are addressed.

Yāni tattad vidyāprashaṅgsakāni vachanāni tāni tattadadhikāriṇaṁ pratyeva pravartakāni. Yāni cha tannindakāni tāni tattadanadhikāriṇaṁ prati nivartakāni. Na punarnahi nindānyāyena vidheyastāvakāni (Bhāskararāya's Introductory Commentary to *Nityāshodashikārṇava* Tantra. p. 2).

In early infancy, parents and guardians encourage the play of the child in their charge. When the age of study is reached, the same parents and guardians chastise the child who inopportunely plays. This we all see. A male of the three higher castes should, on the passing of the age of play, learn his letters and then metre (Chhandas) in order to master language. The Agnī Purāṇa has many texts such as "Faultless is a good Kāvya"; all of which encourage the study of Kāvya. We also come across prohibitions such as "He who has mastered the subject should avoid all discussion relating to Kāvya". When the object to be gained by the study of Kāvya is attained and competency is gained for the next higher stage (Uttarabhūmikā), it is only a harmful waste of time to busy oneself with a lower stage (Pūrvabhūmikā), in neglect of that higher stage for the Sādhanā of which one has become competent. This is the meaning of the prohibition. Again the injunction is to study Nyāyashāstra so as to gain a knowledge of the Ātmā as it is, and other than as it appears in the body and so forth. The texts are many such as "By reasoning (Shungga) seek the Ātmā." Shungga = Hetu = Avayavasamudayātmakanyāya, that is Logic with all its five limbs. When it is known that the Ātmā, as such is other than the, body, is separate from the body and so forth, and the means which lead to that knowledge are mastered, then man is prohibited from occupying himself with the subject of the former stage (Pūrvabhūmikā) by such texts as "Anvīkshikī and Logic (Tarkavidyā) are useless" (Anvīkshikīm tarkavidyāmanurakto nirarthikām). Injunctions such as "The wise should practise Dharma alone (Dharmam evācharet prājnah)" urge man towards the next stage (Uttarabhūmikā). The study of the Pūrvamīmāngsā and the Karmakāṇḍa in the Vedas is useful for this purpose. When by this means Dharma, Artha and Kāma are attained, there arises a desire for the fourth Purushārtha (Liberation or Moksha). And therefore to sever men from the former stage (Pūrvabhūmikā) there are texts which deprecate Karma such as (Mund. Up. 1-2, 12) "By that which is made cannot be attained that which is not made" (Nāstyakṛitah kṛitena). Vashishtha says that these (earlier stages) are seven and that all are stages of ignorance (Ajnānabhūmikā). Beyond these are stages of Jnāna. For the attainment of the same there are injunctions relating to Brahmajnāna which lead on to the next higher stage, such as (Mund. Up. I. 2, 12) "He should go to the Guru alone" (Sa gurum evābhigachchhet) "Listen (Br. Ar. II. 4, 5, IV, 5, 6), oh Maitreyi, the Ātmā should be realised" (Ātmā vā are drashtavyah). Some say that the Jnāna-bhūmikās are many and rely on the text "The wise say that the stages of Yoga are many". The holy Vashishtha says that there are seven, namely, Vividishā (desire to know), Vichāranā (reflection,), Tanumānasa (concentration), Sattvāpatti (commencement of realisation), Asamsakti (detachment), Padārthābhāvinī (realisation of Brahman only) and Turyagā (full illumination in the fourth state). The meaning of these is given in, and should be learnt from, the Jnānashāstra of Vashishtha.

These terms are also explained in Brahmānanda's Commentary on the Hathayoga Pradīpikā (1-3). His account differs from that of Bhāskararāya as regards the name of the first Bhūmikā which he calls Jnānabhūmi or Subhechchhā, and the sixth is called by him Parārthābhāvinī and not Padārthābhāvinī. The sense in either case is the same. According to Brahmānanda, Jnānabhūmi is the initial stage of Yoga characterised by Viveka, Vairāgya, and the six Sādhanās beginning with Shama and leading to Mumukshā. Vichāranā is Shravana and Manana (Shravanamananātmikā) Tanumānasā = Nididhyāsana when the mind, the natural characteristic of which is to wander, is directed towards its proper Yoga-object only. These three preliminary stages are known as Sādhanābhūmikā. The fourth stage Sattvāpatti is Samprajnātayoga-bhūmikā. The mind having been purified by practice in the three preceding Bhūmikās the Yogī commences to realise and is called Brahmavit. The last three stages belong to Asamprajnātayoga. After attainment of Sattvāpatti Bhūmikā, the Yogī reaches the fifth stage called Asamsakti. Here he is totally detached and in the state of wakening (Vyuttishthate). As such he is called Brahmavid-vara. At the sixth, or Parārthābhāvinī Bhūmikā, he meditates on nothing but Parabrahman (Parabrahmātiriktam na bhāvayati). He is supremely awakened (Paraprabodhita) and is awake (Vyutthita). He is then called Brahmavid-varīyān. In the last or seventh stage (Tūryyaga) he is Brahmavidvarishta, and then truly attains illumination in itself (Svatahparato vā vyutthānam prāpnoti)

The Upanishads and Uttaramīmāngsā are helpful for this purpose (Upayogī) and should therefore be studied.

Brahmajnāna again is of two kinds: namely, Shābda and Aparokshānubhavarūpa. Understanding of the meaning of Shāstra (Shāstradrishti), the word of the Guru (Gurorvākyam) and certainty (Nishchaya) of the unity of the individual self (Sva) and the Ātmā are powerful to dispel inward darkness, but not the mere knowledge of words (Shābdabodha). See Yogavāshishṭha Utpatti, Kh. IX. 7-16.) Therefore, when the Shābdabhūmikā is attained one should not waste one's time further at this stage, and there are texts which prohibit this. Thus (Br. Ar. III, 5-1) "Having become indifferent to learning let him remain simple as in childhood" (Pāndityānnirvidya bālyena tishṭhāset).

Between the second and third of the seven stages (Bhūmikā) there is the great stage Bhakti. Bhaktimīmāmsā (*e.g.*, Nārada Sūtra, Sanatsujātīya) is helpful and should be studied. Bhakti continues to the end of the fifth Bhūmikā. When this last is attained the Sādhaka gains the fifth stage which is Aparokshānubhavarūpa. This is Jīvanmukti. Following closely upon this is Videhakaivalya. In the text "From Jnāna alone Kaivalya comes (Jnānād eva tu kaivalyam), the word Jnāna signifies something other and higher than Anubhava (Anubhavaparatva). In Nyāya and other Shāstras it is stated that Moksha will be attained by mastery in such particular Shāstra, but that is merely a device by which knowledge of the higher stage is not disclosed. This is not blameworthy because its object is to remove the disinclination to study such Shāstra by reason of the delay thereby caused in the attainment of Purushārtha (which disinclination would exist if the Sādhaka knew that there was a higher Shāstra than that which he was studying). There are texts such as "By Karma alone (eva) is achievement" (Karmanaiva tū samsiddhih); "Him whom he selects by him he is attainable" (Yamevaisha vrinnute tena labhyah). The word "eva" refers to the Bhūmikā which is spoken of and prohibits Sādhanā for the attainment of fruit which can only be gained by mastery of, or competency in (Adhikāra), the next higher Bhūmikā (Uttarabhūmikā). The words do not deny that there is a higher stage (Bhūmikā). The word alone (eva) in "Jnānād eva tu" ("from Jnāna alone") indicates, however, that there is a stage of Sādhanā subsequent to that here spoken of. There is thus no conflict between the Rishis who are teachers of the different Vidyās. Each one of these Bhūmikās has many sub-divisions (Avāntarabhūmikā) which cannot be altogether separated the one from the other, and which are only known by the discerning through experience (Anubhava). So it has been said: "Oh Rāghava, I have spoken to thee of the seven States (Avasthā) of ignorance (Ajnāna). Each one is hundredfold (that is many) and yields many fruits (Nānāvibhavarūpinī). Of these many Bhūmikās, each is achieved by Sādhanā through many births. When a man by great effort prolonged through countless lives, and according to the regular order of things (Kramena), gains a full comprehension of the Bhūmikā in which he has certain knowledge of the Shabdatattva of Parabrahman, he ceases to have any great attachment to, or aversion for, Sangsāra and this is a form of excellent Chittashuddhi. Such an one is qualified for the path of Devotion (Bhakti)." For, it has been said: "Neither indifferent (Nirvinna) nor attached; for such an one Bhaktiyoga grants achievement (Siddhida)."

Bhakti again is of two kinds: Gaunī (secondary) and Para (supreme). The first comprises Dhyāna, Archana, Japa, Nāmakīrtana and the like of the Saguna Brahman. Parabhakti is the special state (Anurāgavisheshartūpa) which is the product of these. The first division of Bhakti includes several others (Avāntara-Bhūmika). The first of these is Bhāvanāsiddhi illustrated by such texts "Let him meditate on woman as fire" (Yoshāmagnim dhyāyīta). The second is worship (Upāsti) as directed in such texts (Chhā. Up. III. 18-1) as "Mano brahmetyupāsīta". The third is Ishvaropāsti (worship of the Lord). Since the aspects of the Lord vary according as He is viewed as Sūryya, Ganesha, Vishnu, Rudra, Parashiva and Shakti, the forms of worship belong to different Bhūmikās. The forms of Shakti again are endless such as Chhāyā, Ballabhā, Lakshmī and the like. In this manner, through countless ages all these Bhūmikās are mastered, when there arises Gaunabhakti for Tripurasundarī. On perfection of this there is Parabhakti for Her. This is the end, for it has been said (Kulārṇava Tantra III. 82): "Kaulajnāna is revealed for him whose Chitta has been fully purified, Ārka, Gānapatya, Vaishnava, Shaiva, Daurgā (Shākta) and other Mantras in their order." Bhāskararāya also quotes statement in the Kulārṇava Tantra (II. 7, 8): "Higher than Vedāchāra is Vaishnavāchāra, higher than Vaishnavāchāra is Shaivāchāra, higher than Shaivāchāra is Dakshināchāra, higher than Dakshināchāra is Vāmāchāra, higher than Vāmāchāra is Siddhāntāchāra, higher than Siddhāntāchāra is Kaulāchāra than which there is nothing higher nor better."

Many original texts might be cited relative to the order of stages (Bhūmikākrama) but which are not quoted for fear of prolixity. Some of these have been set out in Saubhāgya-bhāskara, (that is, Bhāskararāya's Commentary on the Lalitāsahasranāma). The Sundarī tāpanīpanchakā, Bhāvanopanishad, Kaulopanishad, Guhyopanishad, Mahopanishad, and other Upanishads (Vedashirobhāga) describe in detail the Gaunī Bhakti of Shrī Mahātripurasundarī and matter relating thereto. The Kalpasūtras of Āshvalāyana and others, the Smritis of Manu and others come after the Pūrvakānda (Karmakānda) of the Veda. In the same way the Kalpasūtras of Parashurāma and others and the Yāmalas and other Tantras belong to the latter part of the Veda or the Upanishadkānda. The Purāṇas relate to, and follow both, Kāndas. Therefore the authority of the Smritis, Tantras, and Purāṇas is due to their being based on Veda (Smrititantra purānām vedamūlakatvenaiva prāmānyam). Those which seem (Pratyaksha) opposed to Shruti (Shrutiviruddha) form a class of their own and are without authority and should not be followed unless the Veda (Mūlashruti) is examined (and their conformity with it established). There are some Tantras, however, which are in every way in conflict with Veda (Yānitu sarvāmshena vedaviruddhānyeva). They are some Pāshupata Shāstras and Pancharātra. They are not for those who are in this Bhūmikā (*i.e.*, Veda Panthā). He who is qualified for rites enjoined in Shruti and Smriti (Shrautasmārta-karmādhikāra) is only Adhikārī for these (Pāshupata and Pancharātra) if by reason of some sin (Pāpa) he falls from the former path. It has therefore been said: "The Lord of Kamala (Vishnu) spoke the Pancharātras, the Bhāgavata, and that which is known as Vaikhānasa (Vaikhānasābhidhama form of Vaishnavism) for those who have fallen away from the Vedas (Vedabhrashta)." The following Texts relate only to some of the Shāstras of the classes mentioned. So we have the following: "He who has fallen from Shruti, who is afraid of the expiatory rites (Prāyashchitta) prescribed therein, should seek shelter in Tantra so that by degrees he may be qualified for Shruti (Shruti-siddhyartham)." Though the general term "Tantra" is employed, particular Tantras (that is, those opposed to Shruti or Ashrauta) are here meant. The Adhikarana (Sūtra) Patyurasāmanjasyāt (II. 2. 37) applies to Tantras of this class. The Agastya and other Tantras which describe the worship of Rāma, Krishna, Nrisingha, Rudra, Parashiva, Sundarī (Shakti) and others evidently derive from the Rāmatāpani and other Upanishads. There is therefore no reason to doubt but that they are authoritative.

Worship (Upāsti) of Sundarī Shakti is of two kinds: Bahiryāga or outer, and Antaryāga or inner, worship. Antaryāga is again of three kinds: Sakala, Sakala-Nishkala, and Nishkala, thus constituting four Bhūmikās. As already stated, the passage is from a lower to a higher and then to a yet higher Bhūmikā. Five forms of Bahiryāga are spoken of, namely, Kevala, Yāmala, Mishra, Chakrayuk and Virasangkara, which have each five divisions under the heads Abhigamana and others and Daurbodhya and others in different Tantras. Bahiryāga with these distinctions belongs to one and the same Bhūmikā. Distinctions in the injunctions (Vyavasthā) depend entirely on differences as to place, time, and capacity, and not on the degree of Chittashuddhi (Na punashchittashuddhi-bhedena). On the other hand injunctions given according to difference of Bhūmikā, which is itself dependent on the degree of purity of the Chitta, are mandatory.

To sum up the reply to the question raised by the title of this paper: The Shāstras are many and are of differing form. But Īshvara is the Lord of all the Vidyās which are thus authoritative and have a common aim. The Adhikāra of men varies. Therefore so does the form of the Shāstra. There are many stages (Bhūmikā) on the path of spiritual advance. Man makes his way from a lower to a higher

Bhūmikā. Statements in any Shāstra which seem to be in conflict with some other Shāstra must be interpreted with reference to the Adhikāra of the persons to whom they are addressed. Texts laudatory of any Vidyā are addressed to the Adhikārī therein with the object of inducing him to follow it. Texts in disparagement of any Vidyā are addressed to those who are not Adhikārī therein, either because he has not attained, or has surpassed, the Bhūmikā applicable, and their object is to dissuade them from following it. Neither statements are to be taken in an absolute sense, for what is not fit for one may be fit for another. Evolution governs the spiritual as the physical process, and the truth is in each case given in that form which is suitable for the stage reached. From step to step the Sādhaka rises, until having passed through all presentments of the Vaidik truth which are necessary for him, he attains the Vedasvarūpa which is knowledge of the Self.

These ancient teachings are in many ways very consonant with what is called the "modernist" outlook. Thus, let it be noted that there may be (as Bhāskararāya says) Adhikāra for Ashrauta Shāstra such as the Ārhata, and there is a Scripture for the Vedabhrashta. These, though non-Vaidik, are recognised as the Scriptures of those who are fitted for them. This is more than the admission that they are the Scriptures in fact of such persons. The meaning of such recognition is brought out by an incident some years ago. An Anglican clergyman suggested that Mahomedanism might be a suitable Scripture for the Negro who was above "fetichism" but not yet fit to receive Christian teaching. Though he claimed that the latter was the highest and the most complete truth, this recognition (quite Hindu in its character) of a lower and less advanced stage, brought him into trouble. For those who criticised him gave no recognition to any belief but their own. Hinduism does not deny that other faiths have their good fruit. For this reason, it is tolerant to a degree which has earned it the charge of being "indifferent to the truth". Each to his own. Its principles admit a progressive revelation of the Self to the self, according to varying competencies (Adhikāra) and stages (Bhūmikā) of spiritual advance. Though each doctrine and practice belongs to varying levels, and therefore the journey may be shorter or longer as the case may be, ultimately all lead to the Vedasvarūpa or knowledge of the Self, than which there is no other end. That which immediately precedes this complete spiritual experience is the Vedāntik doctrine and Sādhanā for which all others are the propædeutik. There is no real conflict if we look at the stage at which the particular instructions are given. Thought moves by an immanent logic from a less to a more complete realization of the true nature of the thinker. When the latter has truly known what he is, he has known what all is. Vedayite iti Vedah. "Veda is that by which what is, and what is true, is made known."

Whilst the Smritis of the Seers vary and therefore only those are to be accepted which are in conformity with the Standard of true experience or Veda, it is to be remembered that because a Seer such as Kapila Ādividvan (upon whose Smriti or experience the Sāṅgkhya is assumed to be founded) teaches Dvaitavāda, it does not (in the Hindu view) follow that he had not himself reached a higher stage, such as Advaitavāda is claimed to be. A Seer may choose to come down to the level of more ordinary people and teach a Dvaitavāda suited to their capacity (Adhikāra). If all were to teach the highest experience there would be none to look after those who were incapable of it, and who must be led up through the necessary preliminary stages. Sāṅgkhya is the science of analysis and discrimination, and therefore the preparation for Vedānta which is the science of synthesis and assimilation. Kapila, Gotama and Kanāda mainly built on reason deepened and enlarged, it may be, by Smriti or subjective experience. We do not find in them any complete synthesis of Shruti. A general appeal is made to Shruti and a few texts are cited which accord with what (whether it was so in fact to them or not) is in fact a provisionally adopted point of view. They concentrate the thoughts and wills of their disciples on them, withholding (if they themselves have gone further) the rest, as not at present suited to the capacity of the Shishya, thus following what Shangkara calls Arundhatī-darshana-nyāya. Nevertheless the higher truth is immanent in the lower. The Differential and Integral Calculus are involved in elementary Algebra and Geometry because the former generalize what the latter particularize. But the teacher of elementary Mathematics in the lower forms of a school would only confound his young learners if he were to introduce such a general theorem (as say Taylor's) to them. He must keep back the other until the time is ripe for them. Again the great Teachers teach whole-heartedness and thoroughness in both belief and action, without which the acceptance of a doctrine is useless. Hence a teacher of Dvaitavāda, though himself Advaita-darshī, presents Dvaita to the Adhikārī Shishya in such a forcible way that his reason may be convinced and his interest may be fully aroused. It is useless to say to a Sādhaka on the lower plane "Advaita is the whole truth. Dvaita is not; but though it is not, it is suited to your capacity and therefore accept it." He will of course say that he does not then want Dvaita, and, being incapable of understanding Advaita, will lose himself. This, I may observe, is one of the causes of Scepticism to-day. In the olden time it was possible to teach a system without anything being known of that which was higher. But with the printing of books some people learn that all is Māyā, that Upāsanā is for the "lower" grades and so forth, and, not understanding what all this means, are disposed to throw Shāstric teaching in general overboard. This they would not have done if they had been first qualified in the truth of their plane and thus become qualified to understand the truth of that which is more advanced. Until Brahma-sākshātkāra, all truth is relative. Hence, Bhagavān in the Gītā says: "Na buddhi-bhedam janayed ajnānam karma sanginām." Tradition supports these views. Therefore Vyāsa, Kapila, Gautama, Jaimini, Kanāda and others have differently taught, though they may have possibly experienced nearly similarly. Jaimini in his Pūrva Mīmāmsā differs in several respects from Vyāsa or Bādarāyana in his Uttara-Mīmāmsā though he was the disciple of the latter. Vyāsa is Advaita-darshī in Vedānta but Dvaita-darshī in Yogabhāshya. Is it to be supposed, that the Shishya was Anadhikārī, and that his Guru, therefore, withheld the higher truth from him, or was the Guru jealous and kept his Shishya in actions, withholding Brahma-jnāna?

A Rishi who has realized Advaita may teach Āyur-veda or Dhanuveda. He need not be Sthūla-darshī, because he teaches Sthūla-vishaya. Again Shāstras may differ, because their standpoint and objective is different. Thus the Pūrvamīmāmsa deals with Dharma-jignāsā, stating that Veda is practical and enjoins duties, so that a Text which does not directly or indirectly mean or impose a duty is of no account. The Uttara-mīmāmsā, on the other hand, deals with Brahmajignāsā and therefore in the Sūtra 'Tattu samanvayāt' it is laid down that a Mantra is relevant, though it may not impose a duty ("Do this or do not do this") but merely produces a Jnāna (Know this, "That Thou art"). The difference in interpretation is incidental to difference in standpoint and objective. The same remarks apply to the various forms of Advaita such as Vishishtādvaita, Shuddhādvaita; between the Shaktivāda of the Shākta Āgama and Vivarttavāda. In some Shāstras stress is laid on Karma, in others on Bhakti, and yet in others on Jnāna as in the case of Māyāvāda. But though the emphasis is differently placed, each is involved in the other and ultimately meet and blend. The Mahimnastava says: "Though men, according to their natures, follow differing paths, Thou art the end of all, as is the ocean of all the rivers which flow thereto." Madhusūdana Sarasvatī commenting on this, has written his Prasthānabheda, the reconciliation of varying doctrines. To-day the greatest need in these matters is (for those who are capable of understanding) the establishment of this intellectual and spiritual Whole (Pūrna). The Seers who live in the exalted Sphere of Calm, understand the worth and significance of each form of spiritual culture as also their Synthesis, and to the degree that lesser minds attain this level to this extent they will also do so. Whilst the lower mind lives in a section of the whole fact and therefore sees difference and conflict, the illumined who live in and have in varying degrees experience of the Fact itself, see all such as related parts of an Whole.

CHAPTER XIII

SARVĀNANDANĀTHA[1]

THE Sarvollāsa, a copy of which came into my possession some three years ago, is a rare MS. It is a Saṅgraha by the Sarvavidyāsiddha Sarvānandanātha who, though celebrated amongst the Bengal followers of the Āgama, is, I should think, almost unknown to the general public. There is a life in Sanskrit of Sarvānandanātha entitled Sarvānandataranginī by his son Shivanātha in which an account of the attainment of his Siddhi is given and I am indebted in respect of this article to a short unpublished memoir by Sj. Dinesha Chandra Bhattāchāryya, formerly Research Scholar, who as a native of Tipperah has had the desire to see Sarvānandanātha's place in the History of the so-called "Tāntricism" in Bengal duly recognized.

It is said that Sarvānanda had striven for Siddhi for seven previous births and a verse preserves the names of the places where he died in these successive lives. His grandfather Vāsudeva originally lived at Purvasthali in the Burdwan district but was led by a divine call to Mehar in Tipperah where in ages past Mātanga Muni had done Tapas. A deep hole is still shown as being of Mātanga's time. It is also said that round about the place where Sarvānandanātha performed his Shavasādhanā, adept Sādhakas even

[1] Reprinted from *The Hindustan Review*, Vol. 41, January 1920.

now discover the hidden Linga established by Mātanga marked out by equally hidden barriers or Kīlakas.

Vāsudeva then went to Kāmākhyā where he died after undergoing severe Tapas. He left his son at Mehar who himself afterwards had a son, the grandson of Vāsudeva. In fact it is said that the grandfather Vāsudeva was reborn as the son of his own son, that is, as Sarvānanda. In early life the latter was stupid and illiterate. He was sharply rebuked by the local Rajah for his ignorance in proclaiming a New Moon day to be Full Moon day. Being severely punished by his relatives he determined to begin his letters and went out to search for the necessary palm-leaves. There in the jungle he met a Sannyasi, who was Mahādeva himself in that form and who whispered in his ears a Mantra and gave him certain instructions. His servant Puna was an advanced Sādhaka, who had been psychically developed under Vāsudeva. Puna separating the subtle (Sūkshmadeha) from the gross body, served as a corpse on the back of which Sarvānanda performed Shavasādhanā and attained Siddhi that same new moon night on which to the amazement of all a perfect moon shone over Mehar. This full moon episode is popularly the most famous of Sarvānanda's wonders.

Some time after Sarvānanda left Mehar after having given utterance to the curse that his own family would die out in the 22nd, and that of the local chief in the 15th generation. This last announcement is said to have come true as the Rajah's descendant in the fifteenth generation actually died without issue, though the family survives through his adopted son. Sarvānanda started for Benares but stopped at Senhati in Jessore where he was compelled to marry again and where he lived for some years. His place of worship at Senhati is still shown. At the age of 50 he went to Benares with his servant Puna and nephew Sadānanda. At

Benares the Shaiva Dandins were then, as now, predominant. He quarrelled with them, or they with him, on account of his doctrines and practice.

In return for their treatment of him he to their awe and possibly disgust converted (so it is said) their food into meat and wine. Of course the Benares Dandins, as is usual in such cases, give a different account of the matter. Their tradition is that, after a Shāstric debate, Sarvānanda was convinced by the Dandins that the Siddhi which he boasted of was no real Siddhi at all and was then made a convert to their own doctrines, which is the most satisfactory of all results for the men of piety who wrangle with others and try to make them come over to their views. It is worthy of note how quarrelsome in all ages many of the pious and wonder-workers have been. But perhaps we do not hear so much of the quieter sages who lived and let others live, diffusing their views not amongst those who were satisfied with what they knew or thought they knew, but among such as had not found and therefore sought.

After this event Sarvānanda disappeared from Benares which rather points to the fact that the Dandins did not acquire a distinguished adversary for their community. Tradition is silent as to what happened to him later and as to the date and place of his end.

Sj. Dinesh Chandra Bhattāchāryya has made for me a calculation as to the date of Sarvānanda's Siddhi which fell on a Pausha Samkrānti corresponding to Chaturdasi or Amāvāsya falling on a Friday. Between 1200 and 1700 A.D. there are three dates on which the above combination took place, *viz.*, 1342, 1426 and 1548 A.D. The first date is too early as 15 or 16 generations, to which his family descends at present, does not carry us so far back. The last date seems too late. For according to tradition Jānakīvallabha Gurvvāchāryya, himself a famous Siddha, and fifth in descent from Sarvānanda, was a contemporary of one of the "twelve Bhuiyas" of Bengal late in the reign of Akbar (*circ.* 1600 A.D.). The date 1426 A.D. is therefore adopted. It will thus appear that he lived about a century before the three great Bengal Tāntrikas, namely, Krishnānanda, Brahmānanda and Purnānanda, all of whom are of the 16th century. But this calculation has still to be verified by data culled from an examination of the Sarvollāsa such as the authorities which its author cites.

This last work, I am told, is that by which he is best known. Two other short Tāntrika works are ascribed to a Sarvānanda though whether it is the same Siddha is not certain. There is, I am told, a Navārnapūjapaddhati by Sarvānandanātha in a MS. dated 1668 Vikramābda in the Raghunāth Temple Library in Kashmir and another work the Tripurārchanadīpikā is reported from the Central Provinces.

As is usual in such cases there is a legend that Sarvānanda is still living by Kāyavyuha in some hidden resort of Siddha-purushas. The author of the memoir from which I quote, tells of a Sādhu who said to my informant that some years ago he met Sarvānandanātha in a place called Champakāranya but only for a few minutes, for the Sādhu was himself miraculously wafted elsewhere.

Some very curious reading of deep interest to the psychologist, the student of psychic phenomena and the historian of religions is to be found in the stories which are told of Sādhus and Siddhas of Sarvānanda's type who, whether they did all that is recounted of them or not, yet lived so strangely, as for instance, to take another case, that of Brahmānanda the author of the Shāktānandatarangini who going in his youth in quest of a prostitute, found in the house he entered and in the woman who came to him his own mother, herself the victim of a Mussulman ravisher. It was the horror of this encounter which converted his mind and led him to become a Sādhu, during which life he did Dhyāna in the body of a dead and rotting elephant and the other things related of him. They await collection. But when their value has been discovered possibly these traditions may have disappeared. Even if all the facts related of these Sādhus and Siddhas were the work of imagination (and whilst some of them may be so, others are in all probability true enough) they are worth preservation as such. The history of the human mind is as much a fact as anything which is reverenced because it is "objective" This last class of fact is generally only the common experience. It is attractive, yet sometimes fearsome, to follow the mind's wanderings both in the light and in that curious dark, which only explorers in these paths know. If one does not lose one's way (and in this lies a peril) we emerge with a confidence in ourselves at having passed a test—a confidence which will serve our future. In any case as I have said there is an opportunity of research for those whose workings are in the outer crust of mere historical fact.

CHAPTER XIV

CHIT-SHAKTI

(THE CONSCIOUSNESS ASPECT OF THE UNIVERSE)

CHIT-SHAKTI is Chit, as Shakti, that is as Power, or that aspect of Chit in which it is, through its associated Māyā-Shakti, operative to create the universe. It is a commonly accepted doctrine that the ultimate Reality is Samvid, Chaitanya or Chit.

But what is Chit? There is no word in the English language which adequately describes it. It is not mind: for mind is a limited instrument through which Chit is manifested. It is that which is behind the mind and by which the mind itself is thought, that is created. The Brahman is mindless (Amanah). If we exclude mind we also exclude all forms of mental process, conception, perception, thought, reason, will, memory, particular sensation and the like. We are then left with three available words, namely, Consciousness, Feeling, Experience. To the first term there are several objections. For if we use an English word, we must understand it according to its generally received meaning. Generally by "Consciousness" is meant self-consciousness, or at least something particular, having direction and form, which is concrete and conditioned; an evolved product marking the higher stages of Evolution. According to some, it is a mere function of experience, an epiphenomenon, a mere accident of mental process. In the sense it belongs only to the highly developed organism and involves a subject attending to an object of which, as of itself, it is conscious. We are thus said to have most consciousness when we are awake (Jāgrat avasthā) and have full experience of all objects presented to us; less so when dreaming (Svapna avasthā) and deep anæsthesia in true dreamless sleep (Sushupti). I may here observe that recent researches show that this last state is not so common as is generally supposed. That is complete dreamlessness is rare; there being generally some trace of dream. In the last state it is commonly said that consciousness has disappeared, and so of course it has, if we first define consciousness in terms of the waking state and of knowledge of objects. According to Indian notions there is a form of conscious experience in the deepest sleep expressed in the well-known phrase "Happily I slept I knew nothing". The sleeper recollects on waking that his state has been one of happiness. And he cannot recollect unless there has been a previous experience (Anubhava) which is the subject-matter of memory. In ordinary parlance we do not regard some low animal forms, plants or mineral as "conscious". It is true that now in the West there is (due to the spread of ideas long current in India) growing up a wider use of the term "consciousness" in connection not only with animal but vegetable and mineral life, but it cannot be said that the term "consciousness" has yet generally acquired this wide signification. If then we use (as for convenience we do) the term "Consciousness" for Chit, we must give it a content different from that which is attributed to the terms in ordinary English parlance. Nextly, it is to be remembered that what in either view we understand by consciousness is something manifested, and therefore limited, and derived from our finite experience. The Brahman as Chit is the infinite substratum of that. Chit in itself (Svarūpa) is not particular, nor conditioned and concrete. Particularity is that aspect in which it manifests as, and through, Māyā-Shakti. Chit manifests as Jnāna-Shakti which, when used otherwise than as a loose synonym for Chit, means knowledge of objects. Chit-Svarūpa is neither knowledge of objects nor self-consciousness in the phenomenal sense. Waking, dreaming and dreamless slumber are all phenomenal states in which experience varies; such variance being due not to Chit but to the operation or cessation of particular operation of the vehicles of mind (Antahkarana) and sense (Indriya). But Chit never disappears nor varies in either of the three states, but remains one and the same through all. Though Chit-Svarūpa is not a knowledge of objects in the phenomenal sense, it is not, according to Shaiva-Shākta views (I refer always to Advaita Shaiva-darshana), a mere abstract knowing (Jnāna) wholly devoid of content. It contains within itself the Vimarsha-Shakti which is the cause of phenomenal objects, then existing in the form of Chit (Chidrūpinī). The Self then knows the Self. Still less can we speak of mere "awareness" as the equivalent of Chit. A worm or meaner form of animal may be said to be vaguely aware. In fact mere "awareness" (as we understand that term) is a state of Chit in which it is seemingly overwhelmed by obscuring Māyā-Shakti in the form of Tamoguna. Unless therefore we give to "awareness", as also to consciousness, a content, other than that with which our experience furnishes us, both terms are unsuitable. In some respects Chit can be more closely described by Feeling, which seems to have been the most ancient meaning of the term Chit. Feeling is more primary, in that it is only after we have been first affected by something that we become conscious of it. Feeling has thus been said to be the raw material of thought, the essential element in the Self, what we call personality being a particular form of feeling. Thus in Sāṅkhya, the Gunas are said to be in the nature of happiness (Sukhā), sorrow (Duhkha) and illusion (Moha) as they are experienced by the Purusha-Consciousness. And in Vedānta, Chit and Ānanda or Bliss or Love are one. For Consciousness then is not consciousness *of* being (Sat) but Being-consciousness (Sat-Chit): nor a Being which is conscious *of* Bliss (Ānanda) but Being-Consciousness-bliss (Sachchidānanda). Further "feeling" has this advantage that it is associated with all forms of organic existence even according to popular usage, and may scientifically be aptly applied to inorganic matter. Thus whilst most consider it to be an unusual and strained use of language, to speak of the consciousness of a plant or stone, we can and do speak of the feeling or sentiency of a plant. Further the response which inorganic matter makes to stimuli is evidence of the existence therein of that vital germ of life and sentiency (and therefore Chit) which expands into the sentiency of plants, and the feelings and emotions of animals and men. It is possible for any form of unintelligent being to feel however obscurely. And it must do so, if its ultimate basis is Chit and Ānanda, however veiled by Māyā-Shakti these may be. The response which inorganic matter makes to stimuli is the manifestation of Chit through the Sattvaguna of Māyā-Shakti, or Shakti in its form as Prakriti-Shakti. The manifestation is slight and apparently mechanical because of the extreme predominance of the Tamoguna in the same Prakriti-Shakti. Because of the limited and extremely regulated character of the movement which seems to exclude all volitional process as known to us, it is currently assumed that we have merely to deal with what is an unconscious mechanical energy. Because vitality is so circumscribed and seemingly identified with the apparent mechanical process, we are apt to assume mere unconscious mechanism. But as a fact this latter is but the form assumed by the conscious Vital Power which is in and works in all matter whatever it be. To the eye, however, unassisted by scientific instruments, which extend our capacity for experience, establishing artificial organs for the gaining thereof, the matter appears Jada (or unconscious); and so both in common English and Indian parlance we call that alone living or Jīva which, as organized matter, is endowed with body and senses. Philosophically, however, as well as scientifically, all is Jīvātmā which is not Paramātmā: everything in fact with form, whether the form exists as the simple molecule of matter, or as the combination of these simple forms into cells and greater organisms. The response of metallic matter is a form of sentiency—its germinal form—a manifestation of Chit intensely obscured by the Tamoguna of Prakriti-Shakti.

In plants Chit is less obscured, and there is the sentient life which gradually expands in animals and men, according as Chit gains freedom of manifestation through the increased operation of Sattvaguna in the vehicles of Chit; which vehicles are the mind and senses and the more elaborate organization of the bodily particles. What is thus mere incipient or germinal sentiency, simulating unconscious mechanical movement in inorganic matter, expands by degrees into feeling akin, though at first remotely, to our own, and into all the other psychic functions of consciousness, perception, reasoning, memory and will. The matter has been very clearly put in a Paper on "The Four Cosmic Elements" by C. G. Sander which (subject to certain reservations stated) aptly describes the Indian views on the subject in hand. He rightly says that sentiency is an integrant constituent of all existence, physical as well as metaphysical and its manifestation can be traced throughout the mineral and chemical as well as vegetable and animal worlds. It essentially comprises the functions of relationship to environment, response to stimuli, and atomic memory in the lower or inorganic plane; whilst in the higher or organic planes it includes all the psychic functions such as consciousness, perception, thought, reason, volition and individual memory. Inorganic matter through the inherent element of sentiency is endowed with æsthesia or capacity of feeling and response to physical and chemical stimuli such as light, temperature, sound, electricity, magnetism and the action of chemicals. All such phenomena are examples of the faculty of perception and response to outside stimuli of matter. We must here include chemical sentiency and memory; that is the atom's and molecule's remembrance of its own identity and behaviour therewith. Atomic memory does not, of course, imply self-consciousness, but only inherent group-spirit which responds in a characteristic way to given outside stimuli. We may call it atomic or physical consciousness. The consciousness of plants is only trance-like (what the Hindu books call 'Comatose') though some of the higher aspects of sentiency (and we may here use the word 'consciousness') of the vegetable world are highly interesting; such as the turning of flowers to the sun; the opening and shutting of leaves and petals at certain times, sensitiveness to the temperature and the obvious signs of consciousness shewn by the sensitive and insectivorous plants, such as the Sundew, the Venus Fly-trap, and others. The sentiency of micro-organisms which dwell on the borderland between the vegetable and animal worlds have no sense organs, but are only endowed with tactile irritability, yet they are possessed of psychic life, sentiency, and inclination, whereby they perceive their environment and position, approach, attack and devour food, flee from harmful substances and reproduce by division. Their movements appear to be positive, not reflex. Every cell, both vegetable and animal, possesses a biological or vegetative consciousness, which in health is polarized or subordinate to the government of the total organism of which it forms an integral part; but which is locally impaired in disease and ceases altogether at the death of the organism. In plants, however, (unlike animals) the cellular consciousness is diffused or distributed amongst the tissues or fibres; there being apparently no special conducting or centralizing organs of consciousness such as we find in higher evolutionary forms. Animal consciousness in its highest modes becomes self-consciousness. The psychology of the lower animals is still the field of much controversy; some regarding these as cartesian machines and others ascribing to them a high degree of psychic development. In the animals there is an endeavour at centralization of consciousness which reaches its most complex stage in man, the possessor of the most highly organized system of consciousness, consisting of the nervous system and its centres and functions, such as the brain and solar plexus, the site of Ājnā and upper centres, and of the Manipūra Chakra. Sentiency or feeling is a constituent of all existence. We may call it consciousness however, if we understand (with the author cited) the term "consciousness" to include atomic or physical consciousness, the trance consciousness of plant life, animal consciousness and man's completed self-consciousness.

The term Sentiency or Feeling, as the equivalent of manifested Chit, has, however, this disadvantage: whereas intelligence and consciousness are terms for the highest attributes of man's nature, mere sentiency, though more inclusive and common to all, is that which we share with the lowest manifestations. In the case of both terms, however, it is necessary to remember that they do not represent the Chit-Svarūpa or Chit as It is in itself. The term

Svarūpa (own form) is employed to convey the notion of what constitutes anything what it is, namely, its true nature as it is in itself. Thus, though the Brahman or Shiva manifests in the form of the world as Māyā-Shakti, its Svarūpa is pure Chit.

Neither sentiency nor consciousness, as known to us, is Chit-Svarūpa. They are only limited manifestations of Chit just as reason, will, emotion and memory, their modes are. Chit is the back-ground of all forms of experience which are its modes, that is Chit veiled by Māyā-Shakti. Chit-Svarūpa is never to be confounded with, or limited to, its particular modes. Nor is it their totality, for whilst it manifests in these modes It yet, in Its own nature, infinitely transcends them. Neither sentiency, consciousness, nor any other term borrowed from a limited and dual universe adequately describe what Chit is in Itself (Svarūpa). Vitality, mind, matter are its limited manifestations in form. These forms are ceaselessly changing, but the undifferentiated substratum of which they are particularized modes is changeless. That eternal, changeless, substratum is Chit, which may thus be defined as the *changeless principle of all our changing experience.* All is Chit, clothing itself in forms by its own Power of Chit-Shakti and Māyā-Shakti: and that Power is not different from Itself. Chit is not the subject of knowledge or speech. For as the Varāha Upanishad (Chap. IV) says it is "The Reality which remains after all thoughts are given up." What it is in Itself is unknown but to those who become It. It is fully realized only in the highest state of Ecstasy (Samādhi) and in bodiless liberation (Videha Mukti) when Spirit is free of its vehicles of mind and matter. A Modern Indian Philosopher has (See "Approaches to Truth" and the "Patent Wonder" by Professor Pramathanātha Mukhyopādhyāya) very admirably analysed the notion of the universal Ether of Consciousness

(Chidākāsha) and the particular Stress formed in it by the action of Māyā-Shakti. In the first place, he points out that logical thought is inherently dualistic and therefore presupposes a subject and object. Therefore to the pragmatic eye of the western, viewing the only experience known to him, consciousness is always particular having a particular form and direction. Hence where no direction or form is discernible, they have been apt to imagine that consciousness as such has also ceased. Thus if it were conceded that in profound sleep there were no dreams, or if in perfect anæsthesia it were granted that nothing particular was felt, it was thereby considered to be conceded that consciousness may sometimes cease to exist in us. What does in fact cease is the consciousness of objects which we have in the waking and dreaming states. Consciousness as such is neither subjective nor objective and is not identical with intelligence or understanding—that is with directed or informed consciousness. Any form of unintelligent being which feels, however chaotically it may be, is yet, though obscurely so (in the sense here meant) conscious. Pure consciousness, that is consciousness as such, is the background of every form of experience.

In practical life and in Science and Philosophy when swayed by pragmatic ends, formless experience has no interest, but only certain forms and tones of life and consciousness. Where these are missed we are apt to fancy that we miss life and feeling-consciousness also. Hence the essential *basis* of existence or Chit has been commonly looked upon as a very much specialized and peculiar manifestation in nature.

On the contrary, Chit is Being or Reality itself. Chit as such is identical with Being as such. The Brahman is both Chit and Sat. Though in ordinary experience Being and Feeling-Consciousness are essentially bound up together, they still seem to diverge from each other. Man by his very constitution inveterately believes in an objective existence beyond and independent of his self. And this is so, so long as he is subject to the veil (Māyā-Shakti). But in that ultimate basis of experience which is the Paramātma the divergence has gone; for the same boundless substratum which is the continuous mass of experience is also that which is experienced. The self is its own object. To the exalted Yogin the whole universe is not different from himself as Ātmā. This is the path of the " upward-going " Kundalī (Urddhva-Kundalinī).

Further, there has been a tendency in fact to look upon consciousness as a mere function of experience; and the Philosophy of unconscious ideas and mind-stuff would even go so far as to regard it as a mere accident of mental process. This is to reverse the actual facts.

Consciousness should rather be taken as an original datum than as a later development and peculiar manifestation. We should begin with it in its lowest forms, and explain its apparent pulse-life by extending the principle of veiling (Māyā-Shakti) which is ceaselessly working in man, reducing his life to an apparent series of pulses also. An explanation which does not start with this primordial extensity of experience cannot expect to end with it. For if it be not positive at the beginning, it cannot be derived at the end.

But what, it may be asked, is the proof of such pure experience? Psychology which only knows changing states does not tell us of it. This is so. Yet from those states, some of which approach indifferentiation, inferences may be drawn; and experience is not limited to such states, for it may transcend them.

It is true that ordinarily we do not meet with a condition of consciousness which is without a direction or form;

but tests drawn from the incidents of ordinary normal life are insufficient, it has been argued, to prove that there is no consciousness at all when this direction and form are supposed to have gone. Though a logical intuition will not tell its own story, we can make reflection on intuition render us some sort of account, so that the intuitive fact appears in review, when it will appear that consciousness is the basis of, indeed, existence itself, and not merely an attendant circumstance. But the only proof of pure consciousness is an instance of it. This cannot be established by mere reflection. The bare consciousness of this or that, the experience of just going to sleep and just waking, and even the consciousness of being as such, are but approximations to the state of consciousness as such, that is pure consciousness, but are not identical with it. Then, what evidence, it may be asked, have we of the fact that pure consciousness is an actual state of being? In normal life as well as in abnormal pathological states, we have occasional stretches of experience in which simplicity of feature or determination has advanced near to indifferentiation, in which experience has become almost structureless. But the limit of pure experience is not there reached. On the other hand, there is no conclusive proof that we have ever had a real lapse of consciousness in our life, and the extinction of consciousness as such is inconceivable in any case. The claim, however, that consciousness as such exists, rests not so much on logical argument as on intuitive grounds, on revelation (Shruti) and spiritual *experience* of the truth of that revelation.

According to Indian Monism, a Pure Principle of Experience not only is, but is the one and only ultimate permanent being or reality. It does not regard Chit as a mere function, accident, or epiphenomenon, but holds it to be the ever existing *plenum* which sustains and vitalizes all phenomenal existence, and is the very *basis* on which all forms of multiple experience, whether of sensation, instinct, will, understanding, or reason, rest. It is, in short, the unity and unchanging Reality behind all these various changing forms which, by the veil or Māyā-Shakti, Jīva assumes.

The Chit-Svarūpa, inadequately described as mere blissful awareness of feeling, exists, as the basis and appears in the form of, that is clothed with, mind; a term which in its general sense is not used merely in the sense of the purely mental function of reason but in the sense of all the forms in which consciousness is displayed, as distinguished from Chit Itself, which is the unity behind all these forms whether reason, sensation, emotion, instinct, or will. All these are modes wherein the plastic unformed clay of life is determined. For every conception or volition is essentially an apparent circumscription or limitation of that Sat which is the basis of phenomenal life.

Professor P. N. Mukhyopādhyāya has described pure consciousness to be an infinitude of "awareness," lacking name and form and every kind of determination, which is a state of complete quiescence where the potential is zero or infinity—a condition without strain or tension which is at once introduced when the slightest construction is put upon it, resulting in a consciousness of bare "this" and "that". It is not a consciousness of anything. It is an experience of nothing *in particular*. But this must not be confounded with *no* experience. The former is taken to be the latter because life is pragmatic, interest being shown in particular modes of awareness. To man's life, which is little else than a system of partialities, pure experience in which there is nothing particular to observe or shun, love or hate seems practically to be no experience at all. Pure Consciousness is impartial. There is no difference (Bheda) so far as pure Awareness is concerned. Pure Consciousness is a kind of experience which stands above all antithesis of motion and rest. It does not know Itself either as changing or statical, since it is consciousness *as such* without any determinations or mode whatever. To know itself as changing or permanent, it must conceal its alogical and unspeakable nature in a veil (Māyā). Every determination or form makes experience a directive magnitude. Consciousness then assumes a direction or special reference. It is not possible to direct and refer in a special way without inducing such a feeling of strain or tension, whether the conditions be physiological or psychological. Pure consciousness has, thus, been compared to an equipotential surface of electrical distribution. There is no difference of potentials between any two points A and B over this surface. It is a stretch of consciousness, in which there is, apparently, no sensible diversity of features, no preference, no differential incidence of subjective regard. Like the equipotential surface, such consciousness is also quiescent. To secure a flow on it, there must be a difference of potentials between any two points. Similarly, to have a reference, a direction, a movement of attention, there must be a determination in the total experience of the moment in the given mass of consciousness. Absolute quiescence is a state of consciousness which is pure being with no special subjective direction and reference; with no difference of level and potential between one part of the experience and another. Experience will show special subjective direction and reference if it assumes at least form or determination, such as "this" or "that"; to have no difference of level or potential, experience must be strictly undifferentiated—that is to say, must not involve the least ideal or representative structure. Absolute quiescence exists only with that Consciousness which is pure Being, or Paramātmā.

With regard, however, to all descriptions of this state, it must be borne in mind that they only negatively correspond with their subject-matter by the elimination of characteristics which are peculiar to, and constitute the human consciousness of, the Jīva, and are therefore alien to the Supreme Consciousness. They give us no positive information as to the nature of pure Chit, for this is only known in Yoga by the removal of ignorance (Avidyā) under which all logical thinking and speaking is done. This "ignorance" is nothing but a term for those limitations which make the creature what he is. It is a commonplace in Indian religion and philosophy that the Brahman as It exists in Itself is beyond all thought and words, and is known only by the Samādhi of Yoga. As the Mahānirvāna Tantra says (III. V. 6. *et seq.*): "The Brahman is known in two ways: from His manifestations which are the object of Sādhanā or as It is in itself in Samādhiyoga:" for, as Ch. XIV, V. 135 *Ibid.*, says, Ātmajnāna is the one means of liberation in which Its nature is realized. It is, perhaps in part at least, because the merely negative and imperfect character of such description is not sufficiently noted that pure consciousness, as the author cited points out, has in general awakened no serious interest in the practical West; though it has been the crown of glory for some of, what have been said to be, the stateliest forms of Eastern thought, which asserts itself to be in possession of an *experimental* method by which the condition of pure consciousness may be realized. The question is, thus, not one of mere speculation, but of *demonstration.* This state, again, is believed by the East to be not a dull and dreary condition, a dry abstraction or *reductio ad absurdum* of all which imparts to our living its worth and significance. Not at all; since it is the first Principle in which as Power all existence is potential and from which it proceeds. It is reasonable, therefore, it is contended, to assume that all which life possesses of real worth exists in the Source of life itself. Life is only a *mode* of infinite Supremacy with beatitude, which is Being and Consciousness in all its metaphysical grandeur, an absolutely understandable condition which no imagination can depict and no categories can reach and possess.

Owing to the necessarily negative character of some of the descriptions of the Supreme Brahman we find such questions "How can it differ from a nullity?" ("Dialogues on Hindu Philosophy," 259, by Rev. K. M. Banerjee): and the statement of the English Orientalist Colonel Jacob (whose views are akin to those of others) that "Nirvāna is an unconscious (*sic*) and stone-like (*sic*) existence". Such a misconception is the more extraordinary in that it occurs in the work of an author who was engaged in the translation of a Vedāntic treatise. These and many similar statements seem to establish that it is possible to make a special study of Vedānta and yet to misunderstand its primary concepts. It is true that the Brahman is unconscious in the sense that It is not our consciousness; for, if so, It would be Jīva and not Paramātmā. But this is only to say that it has not our limitations. It is unlimited Chit. A stone represents its most veiled existence. In its Self it is all light and self-illumining (Svaprakāsha). As Shruti says (Katha Up. 5-15) "All things shed lustre by His lustre. All things shine because He shines." All things depend on It: but It has not to depend on anything else for Its manifestation. It is therefore better to say with the Hañsopanishad and the Christian Gospel that It is the Peace beyond all understanding. It has been drily remarked that "The idea that Yoga means a dull state is due, perhaps, to the misunderstanding of Patanjali's definition of it."

Man, however, ordinarily and by his nature craves for modes and forms (Bhaumānanda); and though all enjoyment comes from the pure Supreme Consciousness, it is supposed that dualistic variety and polarity are necessary for enjoyment. What, thus, in its plentitude belongs to the sustaining spirit of all life is transferred to life alone. All knowledge and existence are identified with variety, change, polarity. Whilst skimming over the chequered surface of the sea, we thus, it is said, ignore the unfathomed depths which are in repose and which nothing stirs, wherein is the Supreme Peace (Shāntā) and Bliss (Paramānanda).

The Brihadāranyaka Upanishad says "Other beings live on a fraction of this great Bliss." The Bliss of Shiva and Shakti are one, for they are inseparate. Hence she is called (Trishatī II. 32) Ekabhoga: for Eka = Ishvara and Bhoga = Svasvarūpānanda.

Nyāya and Sāṅkhya say that the chief end of man is the absolute cessation of pain, but Vedāntins, going beyond this negative definition, say that, all pain having surceased on Unity with the Supreme, the chief end is that positive Bliss which is of its essence. The Devī Kalyānī, the Mother of all, is Herself Bliss—that is, all bliss from earthly bliss (Bhaumānanda) to Brahman-bliss (Brahmānanda). As the Commentator Shaṅkara in his commentary on the Trishatī says (citing Shruti): "Who else can make us breathe, who else can make us live, if this blissful Ether were not?"

If, further, it be asked *what* is pure Experience which manifests itself in all these diverse forms, it must be said that from Its very definition pure Chit, or the Supreme Brahman (Parabrahman), is that about which nothing in particular can be predicated: for predication is possible only in relation to *determinations* or modes in consciousness. And in this sense Yogatattva Upanishad says that those who seek a knowledge of it in Shāstras are deluded;

"How can that which is self-shining be illuminated by the Shāstras? Not even the Devas can describe that indescribable state." The Māndukya Upanishad, speaking of the fourth aspect (Pāda) of Ātmā, says that it is the non-dual Shiva which is not an object which can be sensed, used, taken, determined (by any marks), or of which an account can be given, but is unthinkable and knowable only by the realization of Ātmā. Negative predication may, however, clear away improper notions. It is really inscrutable Being upon which no category can be fastened. This must always be borne in mind in any attempted definition of this transcendent state. It is of a self-existent (Nirādhāra), unending (Nitya), changeless (Avikāri), undifferentiated (Abhinna), spaceless (Pūrna), timeless (Shāsvata), all-pervading (Sarvatrāvastha), self-illumining (Svayamjyotih), pure (Shuddha) experience. As the Kulārnava Tantra says (I—6, 7): "Shiva is the impartite Supreme Brahman, the all-knowing Creator of all. He is the stainless One and the Lord of all. He is one without a second (Advaya). He is light itself. He changes not, and is without beginning or end. He is without attribute and above the highest. He is Being (Sat), Consciousness (Chit), and Bliss (Ānanda). As Sat, It is unity of being beyond the opposites of "this" and "that," "here and there," "then and now". As Chit, It is an experiencing beyond the opposites of worldly knowledge and ignorance. As Supreme Ānanda, It is the Bliss which is known upon the dissolution of the dualistic state which fluctuates between, and is composed of, happiness and sorrow; for created happiness is only an impermanent change of state (Vikāra) or Becoming, but the Supreme Bliss (Paramānanda) endures. Bliss is the very Nature (Svarūpa) of this Supreme Consciousness, and not, as with the creature, a mere changing attribute of some form of Becoming. Supreme Being (Sat) is a unity without parts (Nishkala).

Supreme Feeling-Consciousness (Chit) is immediacy of experience. In the Jīvā, Consciousness of Self is set over against the not-self; for logical thought establishes a polarity of subject and object. Thus the undifferentiated Supreme Consciousness transcends, and the Supreme Bliss (Paramānanda) is beyond, the changing feelings of happiness and sorrow. It is the great Peace (Shāntā) which, in the words of the Hañsopanishad (V. 12, Ed. Ānandāshrama, XXIX, p. 593) as of the New Testament, passes all worldly understanding. Sachchidānanda, or Pure Being, persists in all the states of Becoming which are its manifestation as Shakti. It may be compared to a continuous, partless, undifferentiated Unity universally pervading the manifested world like ether or space, as opposed to the limited, discontinuous, discrete character of the forms of "matter" which are the products of its power of Shakti. It is a state of quiescence free of all motion (Nihspanda), and of that vibration (Spandana) which, operating as the Primordial Energy, evolves the phenomenal world of names and forms. It is, in short, said to be the innermost Self in every being—a changeless Reality of the nature of a purely experiencing principle (Chaitanyam Ātmā) as distinguished from whatever may assume the form of either the experienced, or of the means of experience. This Chit in bodies underlies as their inner-most Self all beings. The Chit or Ātmā as the underlying Reality in all is, according to Vedānta, one, and the same in all: undivided and unlimited by any of them, however much they may be separated in time and space. It is not only all-pervading, but all-transcending. It has thus a two-fold aspect: an immanent aspect as Shakti (Power), in which It pervades the universes (Saguna Brahman); and a transcendental aspect, in which It exists beyond all Its worldly manifestations (Nirguna Brahman). Chit, as it is in itself, is spaceless and timeless, extending beyond all limitations of time and space and all other categories of existence. We live *in* the Infinite. All limits exist *in* Chit. But these limits are also another aspect of *It* that is Shakti. It is a boundless tranquil ocean on the surface of which countless varied modes, like waves, are rising, tossing and sinking. Though It is the one Cause of the universe of relations, in itself It is neither a relation nor a totality of relations, but a completely relationless Self-identity unknowable by any logical process whatever.

Chit is the boundless permanent *plenum* which sustains and vitalizes everything. It is the universal Spirit, all-pervading like the Ether, which is, sustains, and illumines all experience and all process in the *continuum* of experience. In it the universe is born, grows and dies. This *plenum* or *continuum* is as such all-pervading, eternal, unproduced, and indestructible: for production and destruction involve the existence and bringing together and separation of parts which in an absolute partless *continuum* is impossible. It is necessarily in itself, that is as Chit, motionless, for no parts of an all-filling *continuum* can move from one place to another. Nor can such a *continuum* have any other form of motion, such as expansion, contraction, or undulation since all these phenomena involve the existence of parts and their displacement. Chit is one undifferentiated, partless, all-pervading, eternal, spiritual substance. In Sanskrit, this *plenum* is called Chidākāsha; that is, just as all material things exist in the all-pervading physical Ether, so do they and the latter exist in the infinitely extending Spiritual "Ether" which is Chit. The Supreme Consciousness is thought of as a kind of permanent spiritual "Space" (Chidākāsha) which makes room for and contains all varieties and forms appearing and disappearing. Space itself is an aspect of spiritual substance,

It is a special posture of that stress in life which takes place in unchanging consciousness (P. Mukhyopādhyāya "The Patent Wonder," 21—24). In this Ocean of Being-Consciousness we live, move and have our being. Consciousness as such (that is, as distinguished from the products of Its power or Shakti), is never finite. Like space, it cannot be limited, though, through the operation of its power of self-negation or Māyā-Shakti, it may appear as determined. But such apparent determinations do not ever for us express or exhaust the whole consciousness, any more than space is exhausted by the objects in it. Experience is taken to be limited because the Experiencer is swayed by a pragmatic interest which draws his attention only to particular features in the *continuum*. Though what is thus experienced is a part of the whole experience, the latter is felt to be an infinite expanse of consciousness or awareness in which is distinguished a definite mass of especially determined feeling.

As Chit is the infinite *plenum*, all limited being exists *in* it, and it is in all such beings as the Spirit or innermost Self and as Māyā-Shakti it is their mind and body. When the existence of anything is affirmed, the Brahman is affirmed, for the Brahman is Being itself. This pure Consciousness, or Chit is the Paramātmā Nirguna Shiva who is Being-Consciousness-Bliss (Sachchidānanda). Consciousness is Being. Paramātmā, according to Advaita Vedānta, is not a consciousness *of* being, but Being-Consciousness. Nor it is a consciousness *of* Bliss, but it *is* Bliss. All these are one in pure Consciousness. That which is the nature of Paramātmā never changes, notwithstanding the creative ideation (Srishtikalpanā) which is the manifestation of Shakti as Chit-Shakti and Māyā-Shakti. It is this latter Shakti which, according to the Shākta Tantra, evolves. To adopt a European analogy which is yet not complete, Nishkala Paramātmā is Godhead (Brahmatva). Sakala, or Saguna Ātmā, is God (Īshvara). Each of the three systems Sāṅkhya, Māyāvāda Vedānta, and Shākta monism agrees in holding the reality of pure consciousness (Chit). The question upon which they differ is as to whether unconsciousness is a second independent reality, as Sāṅkhya alleges; and, if not, how the admitted appearance of unconsciousness as the Forms is to be explained consistently with the unity of the Brahman.

Such then is Chit, truly known as it is in Itself only in completed Yoga or Moksha; known only through Its manifestations in our ordinary experience, just as to use the simile of the Kaivalya Kālikā Tantra, we realize the presence of Rāhu or Bhūchchhāyā (the Eclipse) by his actions on the sun and moon. The Eclipse is seen but not the cause of it. Chit-Shakti is a name for the same changeless Chit when associated in creation with its operating Māyā-Shakti. The Supreme Chit is called Parāsamvit in the scheme of the Thirty-six Tattvas which is adopted by both the Shaiva and Shākta Āgamas.

According to Shaṅkara, the Supreme Brahman is defined as pure Jnāna without the slightest trace of either actual or potential objectivity. The Advaita Shaiva-Shāktas regard this matter differently in accordance with an essential principle of the Āgamic School with which I now deal.

All occultism whether of East or West posits the principle that there is nothing in any one state or plane which is not in some other way, actual or potential, in another state or plane. The Western Hermetic maxim runs "As above so below". This is not always understood. The saying does not mean that what exists in one plane exists *in that form* in another plane. Obviously if it did the planes would be the same and not different. If Īshvara thought and felt and saw objects, in the human way, and if he was loving and wrathful, just as men are, He would not be Īshvara but Jīva. The saying cited means that a thing which exists on one plane exists on all other planes, according either to the form of each plane, if it be an intermediate causal body (Kāranāvāntarasharīra) or ultimately as the mere potentiality of becoming which exists in Ātmā in its aspect as Shakti. The Hermetic maxim is given in another form in the Vishvasāra Tantra: "What is here is elsewhere. What is not here is nowhere" (*Yadihāsti tad anyatra. Yannehāsti na tat kvachit*). Similarly the northern Shaiva Shāstra says that what appears *without* only so appears *because* it exists *within*. One can only take out of a receptacle what is first assumed to be within it. What is in us must in some form be in our cause. If we are living, though finite forms, it is because that cause is infinite Being. If we have knowledge though limited, it is because our essential substance is Chit the Illuminator. If we have bliss, though united with sorrow, it is because It is Supreme Bliss. In short, our experience must exist in germ in It. This is because in the Shākta Āgama, there is for the worshipper a real creation and, therefore, a real nexus between the Brahman as cause and the world as effect. According to the transcendent method of Shaṅkara, there is not in the absolute sense any such nexus. The notion of creation by Brahman is as much Māyā as the notion of the world created.

Applying these principles we find in our dual experience an "I" (Aham or subject) which experiences as object a "This" (Idam): that is the universe or any particular object of the collectivity which compose it. Now it is said that the duality of "I" and "This" come from the One which is in its essential nature (Svarūpa) an unitary experience without such conscious distinction. For Vedānta, whether in its Māyāvāda or Shākta form, agrees in holding that in the Supreme there is no consciousness of objects such as exists on this plane. The Supreme does not see objects outside Itself, for it is the whole and the experience of the whole as Īshvara. It sees all that is as Itself. It is Pūrna or the Whole. How then, it may be asked, can a supreme, unchanging, partless, formless, Consciousness produce from Itself something which is so different from Itself, something which is changing, with parts, form and so forth. Shankara's answer is that, transcendentally, it does not produce anything. The notion that it does so is Māyā. What then is his Māyā? This I have more fully explained in my papers on "Māyā-Shakti" and on "Māyā and Shakti". I will only here say that his Māyā is an unexplainable (anirvachanīya) principle of unconsciousness which is not real, not unreal, and not partly either; which is an eternal falsity (Mithyābhūtā sanātanī), which, though not Brahman, is inseparably associated with It in Its aspect as Īshvara; which Māyā has Brahman for its support (Māyā Brahmāshritā); from which support it draws an appearance of separate independent reality which in truth it does not possess. The Parabrahman aspect of the One is not associated with Māyā.

According to the Shākta exposition of Advaitavāda, Māyā is not an unconscious (jada) principle but a particular Shakti of Brahman. Being Shakti, it is at base consciousness, but as Māyā-Shakti it is Consciousness veiling Itself. Shakti and Shaktimān are one and the same: that is, Power and its Possessor (Shaktimān). Therefore Māyā-Shakti is Shiva or Chit in that particular aspect which He assumes as the material cause (Upādāna-kārana) in creation. Creation is real; that is, there is a direct causal nexus between Shiva as Shakti (Chit Shakti and Māyā Shakti) and the universe. In short Shiva as Shakti is the cause of the universe, and as Shakti, in the form of Jīva (all manifested forms), He actually evolves. Comparing these two views;—Shankara says that there is in absolute truth no creation and therefore there can be no question how it arose. This is because he views the problem from the transcendental (Paramārthika) standpoint of self-realization or Siddhi. The Shākta Shāstra, on the other hand, being a practical Sādhanā Shāstra views the matter from our, that is the Jīva, standpoint. To us the universe and ourselves are real. And Īshvara the Creator is real. Therefore there is a creation, and Shiva as Shakti creates by evolving into the Universe, and then appearing as all Jīvas. This is the old Upanishadic doctrine of the spider actually evolving the web from itself, the web being its substance in that form. A flower cannot be raised from seed unless the flower was in some way already there. Therefore as there is an "Aham" and "Idam" in our experience, in some way it is in the supreme experience of Parashiva or Parāsamvit. But the Idam or Universe is not there as with us; otherwise It would be Jīva. Therefore it is said that there are two principles or aspects in the Brahman, namely, that Prakāsha or Chit aspect, and Vimarsha Shakti, the potential Idam, which in creation explicates into the Universe. But in the supreme experience or Āmarsha, Vimarsha Shakti (which has two states) is in Its supreme form. The subtler state is in the form of consciousness (Chidrūpinī); the gross state is in the form of the Universe (Vishvarūpinī.) The former is beyond the universe (Vishvottīrnā). But if Vimarsha Shakti is there in the form of consciousness (Chidrūpinī), it is one with Chit. Therefore it is said that the Aham and Idam, without ceasing to be in the supreme experience, are in supreme Shiva in undistinguishable union as Chit and Chidrūpinī. This is the Nirguna state of Shivashakti. As She is then in undistinguishable union with Shiva, She is then also simple unmanifested Chit. She is then Chaitanya-rūpā or Chidrūpinī: a subtle Sanskrit expression which denotes that She is the same as Chit and yet suggests that though in a present sense She is one with Him, She is yet in a sense (with reference to Her potentiality of future manifestation) different from Him. She is Sachchidānandamayī and He is Sachchidānanda. She is then the unmanifested universe in the form of undifferentiated Chit. The mutual relation, whether in manifestation or beyond it, whether as the imperfect or Ideal universe, is one of inseparable connection or inherence (Avinābhāva-sambandha, Samanvaya) such as that between "I-ness" (Ahantā) and "I" (Aham), existence and that which exists (Bhāva, Bhavat), an attribute and that in which it inheres (Dharma, Dharmin), sunshine and the sun and so forth. The Pancharātra School of the Vaishnava Āgama or Tantra, speaking of the Mahāshakti Lakshmī says, that in Her supreme state She is undistinguishable from the "Windless Atmosphere" (Vasudeva), existing only as it were in the form of "darkness" and "emptiness" (that is of unmanifested formlessness). So the Mahānirvāna Tantra speaks of Her "dark formlessness". In the Kulachūdāmani Nigama Devī says (I. 16-24)—"I, though in the form of Prakriti, rest in consciousness-bliss" (Aham prakritirūpā chet chidānandaparayanā). Rāghava Bhatta in his commentary on the Shāradā Tilaka (Ch. I) says "She who is eternal existed in a subtle (that is, unmanifested) state, as consciousness, during the final dissolution" (Yā anādirūpā chaitanyādhyāsenā mahāpralaye sūkshmā sthitā). It would be simpler to say that She is then what She is (Svarūpa) namely Consciousness, but in creation that consciousness veils itself. These terms "formless", "subtle", "dark", "empty" all denote the same unmanifested state in which Shakti is in undistinguishable union with Shiva, the formless consciousness. The Pancharātra (Ahirbudhnya Samhita, Ch. IV), in manner similar to that of the other Āgamas, describes the supreme state of Shakti in the dissolution of the Universe as one in which manifested Shakti "returns to the condition of Brahman" (Brahmabhāvam brajate). "Owing to complete intensity of embrace" (Atisaṅkleshāt) the two all-pervading ones Nārāyana and His Shakti become as it were a single principle (Ekam tattvam iva). This return to the Brahman condition is said to take place in the same way as a conflagration, when there is no more combustible matter, returns to the latent condition of fire (Vahni-bhāva). There is the same fire in both cases but in one case there is the activity of combustion and in the other there is not. It follows from this that the Supreme Brahman is not a mere knowing without trace of objectivity. In It the Aham is the Self as Chit and the Idam is provided by Chidrūpinī-shakti. There is Ātmārāma or play of the Self with the Self in which the Self knows and enjoys the Self, not in the form of external objects, but as that aspect of consciousness whose projection all objects are. Shakti is always the object of the Self and one with it. For the object is always the Self, since there is nothing but the Self. But in the supreme experience the object is one in nature with Shiva being Chaitanya-rūpa; in the universe the object seems to the Jīva, the creation of and subject to Māyā, to be different from the Self as mind and matter.

The next point is the nature of creation or rather emanation (Ābhāsa) for the former term is associated with dualistic notions of an extra-Cosmic God, who produces a world which is as separate from Himself as is the pot from the potter. According to this doctrine there is an

Evolution of Consciousness or Chit-Shakti (associated with Māyā-Shakti) into certain forms. This is not to say that the Brahman is wholly transformed into its emanations, that is exhausted by them. The Brahman is infinite and can never, therefore, be wholly held in this sense in any form, or in the universe as a whole. It always transcends the universe. Therefore when Consciousness evolves, it nevertheless does not cease to be what it was, is, and will be. The Supreme Chit becomes as Shakti the universe but still remains supreme Chit. In the same way every stage of the emanation-process prior to the real evolution (Parināma of Prakriti) remains what it is, whilst giving birth to a new Evolution. In Parināma or Evolution as known to us on this plane, when one thing is evolved into another, it ceases to be what it was. Thus when milk is changed into curd, it ceases to be milk. The Evolution from Shiva-Shakti of the Pure Tattvas is not of this kind. It is an Ābhāsa or "shining forth", adopting the simile of the sun which shines without (it was supposed) change in, or diminution of, its light. This unaffectedness in spite of its being the material cause is called in the Pancharātra by the term Vīryya, a condition which, the Vaishnava Lakshmī Tantra says, is not found in the world "where milk quickly loses its nature when curds appear." It is a process in which one flame springs from another flame. Hence it is called "Flame to Flame". There is a second Flame but the first from which it comes is unexhausted and still there. The cause remains what it was and yet appears differently in the effect. God is never "emptied" as it is said wholly into the world. Brahman is ever changeless in one aspect; in another It changes, such change being as it were a mere point of stress in the infinite Ether of Chit. This Ābhāsa, therefore, is a form of Vivartta, distinguishable however from the Vivartta of Māyāvāda, because in the Āgama, whether

Vaishnava, or Shākta, the effect is regarded as real, whereas according to Shaṅkara, it is only empirically so. Hence the latter system is called Sat-kāranavāda or the doctrine of the reality of the original source or basis of things, and not also of the apparent effects of the cause. This Ābhāsa has been called Sadrisha Parināma (See Introduction to Principles of Tantra, Vol. II), a term borrowed from the Sāṅkhya but which is not altogether appropriate. In the latter Philosophy the term is used in connection with the state of the Gunas of Prakriti in dissolution when nothing is produced. Here on the contrary we are dealing with creation and an evolving Power-Consciousness. It is only appropriate to this extent that, as in Sadrisha Parināma there is no real evolution or objectivity, so also there is none in the evolution of the Tattvas until Māyā intervenes and Prakriti really evolves the objective universe.

This being the nature of the Supreme Shiva and of the evolution of consciousness, this doctrine assumes, with all others, a transcendent and a creative or immanent aspect of Brahman. The first is Nishkala Shiva; the second Sakala Shiva; or Nirguna, Saguna; Parama, Apara (in Shaṅkara's parlance); Paramātmā, Īshvara; and Paramabrahman, Shabdabrahman. From the second or changing aspect the universe is born. Birth means 'manifestation'. Manifestation to what? The answer is to consciousness. But there is nothing but Chit. Creation is then the evolution whereby the changeless Chit through the power of its Māyā-Shakti appears to Itself in the form of limited objects. All is Shiva whether as subject or object.

This evolution of consciousness is described in the scheme of the Thirty-six Tattvas.

Shaṅkara and Sāṅkhya speak of the 24 Tattvas from Prakriti to Prithivī. Both Shaivas and Shāktas speak of the Thirty-six Tattvas, showing, by the extra number of

Tattvas, how Purusha and Prakriti themselves originated. The northern or Advaita Shaiva Āgama and the Shākta Āgama are allied, though all Shaiva Scripture adopts the same Tattvas. In all the Āgamas whether Vaishnava, Shaiva, or Shākta, there are points of doctrine which are the same or similar. The Vaishnava Pancharātra, however, moves in a different sphere of thought. It speaks in lieu of the Ābhāsa here described of four Vyūha or forms of Nārāyana, *viz.*, Vāsudeva, Saṅkarshana, Pradyumna and Āniruddha. The Thirty-six Tattvas are the 24 from Prithivī to Prakriti together with (proceeding upwards) Purusha, Māyā and the five Kanchukas (Kalā, Kāla, Niyati, Vidyā, Rāga), Shuddhavidyā (or Sadvidyā), Shakti, Shiva. These are divided into three groups named Shiva Tattva, Vidyā Tattva, Ātma Tattva, and Shuddha, Shuddhāshuddha, Ashuddha Tattvas. The Shuddha or Pure Tattvas are all the Tattvas from *Shiva-Shakti* Tattvas to and including Sadvidya Tattva. The Pure—Impure or Mixed (Shuddhāshuddha) Tattvas are those between the first and third group which are the Impure Tattvas (Ashuddha Tattva) of the world of duality, namely, the 24 Tattvas from Prakriti to Prithivī. The other group of three is as follows: Shiva Tattva includes Shiva Tattva and Shakti Tattva, Vidyā Tattva includes all Tattvas from Sadāshiva to Sadvidyā, and Ātma Tattva includes all Tattvas from Māyā and the Kanchukas to Prithivī. The particular description here of the 36 Tattvas, held by both Shaivas and Shāktas, is taken from the northern Shaiva Kashmir philosophical school, itself based on the older Āgamas such as Mālinīvijaya Tantra and others.

It is common doctrine of Advaitavāda that the One is of dual aspect; the first static (Shiva) and the other kinetic (Shakti). This doctrine of aspects is a device whereby it is sought to reconcile the fact that there is changelessness and change. Philosophically it is an evasion of the problem and not a solution. The solution is to be found in revelation (Veda) and in direct Spiritual Experience (Samādhi). These states vary in different men and in different races and creeds. But in support of Advaitavāda, reliance may be placed on the fact that Samādhi or ecstacy, in all parts of the world and in all faiths, *tends* towards some kind of unity, more or less complete. All seek union with God. But the dispute is as to the nature of that union. Pure Advaitavāda is complete identity. The scheme now outlined shows how that unitary experience, without ceasing to be what it is, assumes limited forms.

The reader is referred to the Diagram.

Parāsamvit shown on top of the Diagram is Nishkala Shiva or the changeless Brahman aspect; and Shiva-Shakti below is the aspect of the supreme Brahman from which change comes and which appears as its products or changing forms. Both are Shiva-Shakti. When, however, Shiva is kinetic, He is called Shakti. Regarding the matter from the Shakti aspect both are Shakti. Neither ever exists without the other, though Shakti is in one aspect Chidrūpinī, and in the other in the form of the Universe (Vishvarūpinī). In themselves and throughout they are one. The divergence takes place in consciousness, after it has been subjected to the operation of Māyā, the effect of which is to polarize consciousness into an apparently separate "I" and "This". Parāsamvit is not accounted a Tattva, for It is beyond all Tattvas (Tattvātīta). Shiva Tattva and Shakti Tattva are counted separately, though Shakti Tattva is merely the negative aspect of Shiva Tattva. Shiva Tattva and Shakti Tattva are not produced. They thus are, even in dissolution. They are Saguna-Brahman; and Parāsamvit is the Nirguna-Brahman. The first evolved Tattva is Sadāshiva of Sadākhya Tattva of which the meaning is Sat ākhyā yatah, or

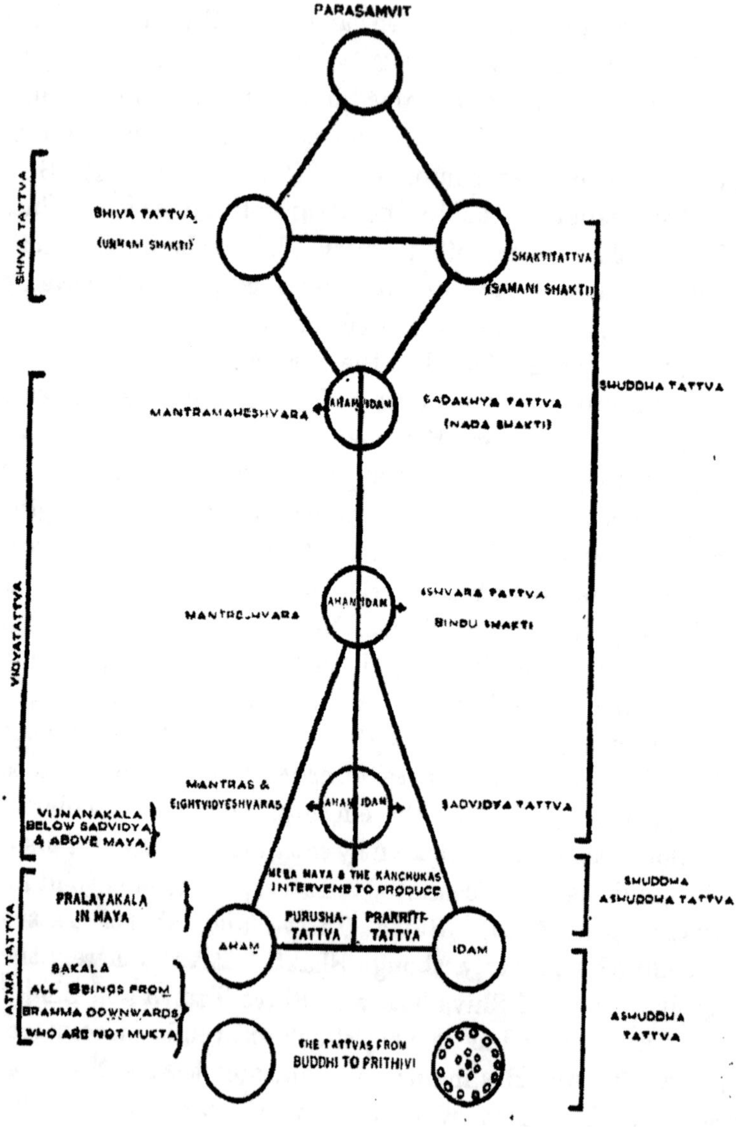
PARASAMVIT
SHIVA TATTVA
SHIVA TATTVA
(UNMANI SHAKTI)
SHAKTITATTVA
(SAMANI SHAKTI)
SHUDDHA TATTVA
MANTRAMAHESHVARA
AHAM IDAM
SADAKHYA TATTVA
(NADA SHAKTI)
VIDYATATTVA
MANTRESHVARA
AHAM IDAM
ISHVARA TATTVA
BINDU SHAKTI
MANTRAS & EIGHTVIDYESHVARAS
AHAM IDAM
SADVIDYA TATTVA
VIJNANAKALA BELOW SADVIDYA & ABOVE MAYA
MERA MAYA & THE KANCHUKAS INTERVENE TO PRODUCE
SHUDDHA ASHUDDHA TATTVA
PRALAYAKALA IN MAYA
PURUSHA-TATTVA
PRAKRITI-TATTVA
AHAM
IDAM
ATMA TATTVA
SAKALA
ALL BEINGS FROM BRAHMA DOWNWARDS WHO ARE NOT MUKTA
THE TATTVAS FROM BUDDHI TO PRITHIVI
ASHUDDHA TATTVA

that state in which there is the first notion of Being; for here is the first incipiency of the world-experience as the notion "I am this" which ultimately becomes a separate "I" and "This". In my "Garland of Letters" I have with more technical detail described the evolution of Jīva-consciousness. Here I will only shortly summarize the process.

As already stated, the Aham and Idam exist in an unitary state which is indescribable in Parāsamvit. Shakti Tattva is called negative because negation is the function of Shakti (Nishedha-vyāpāra-rūpā Shaktih). Negation of what? The answer is negation of consciousness. The universe is thus a product of negation. Where there is pure experience there is no manifested universe. Shakti negates the pure experience or consciousness to the extent that it appears to itself limited. Shakti disengages the unified elements (Aham and Idam) which are latent in the Supreme Experience as an undistinguishable unity. How? The answer is one of great subtlety.

Of the Shiva-Shakti Tattvas, Shiva represents the Prakāsha and Shakti the Vimarsha aspect, which contains potentially within it the seed of the Universe to be. The result is that the Prakāsha aspect is left standing alone. The Shiva Tattva is Prakāsha-mātra, that is, to use the imagery of our plane, an "I" without a "This". This is a state in which the unitary consciousness is broken up to this extent, that it is no longer a Perfect Experience in which the Aham and Idam exist in undistinguishable union, but there is one Supreme Aham Consciousness only, which is the root of all limited subjectivity. To this Aham or Shiva Tattva, Shakti gradually unveils Herself as the Idam or Vimarsha aspect of consciousness. The result is that from Shiva and Shakti (in which the latter takes the playful part) there is evolved the first produced consciousness called Sadākhya Tattva. There is then an

Aham and Idam aspect of experience. But that experience is not like the Jīva's, which arises at a later stage after the intervention of Māyā-Shakti. In the Jīvā consciousness (Jīvātmā) the object (Idam) is seen as something outside and different from itself. In Sadākhya Tattva and all the subsequent pure Tattvas, that is Īshvara Tattva and Shuddhavidyā Tattva, the "This" is experienced as part of the Self and not as separate from it. There is (as will appear from the Diagram) no outer and inner. The circle which represents the one Consciousness is divided into "I" and "This" which are yet parts of the same figure. The "This" is at first only by degree and hazily (Dhyāmala prāyam) presented to the Aham like a picture just forming itself (Unmīlitamātra-chitrākalpam). For this reason it is said that there is emphasis on the Aham which is indicated in the Diagram by the arrowhead. This is called the "Nimesha" or "closing of the eyes" of Shakti. It is so called because it is the last stage in dissolution before all effects are withdrawn into their first cause. Being the last stage in dissolution it is the first in creation. Then the Idam side becomes clear in the next evolved Īshvara Tattva in which the emphasis is therefore said to be on the "This" which the Aham subjectifies. This is the "Unmesha" or "opening of the eyes" state of Shakti; for this is the state of consciousness when it is first fully equipped to create and does so. The result again of this is the evolved consciousness called Shuddhavidyā Tattva in which the emphasis is equal on the "I" and "This". Consciousness is now in the state in which the two halves of experience are ready to be broken up and experienced separately. It is at this state that Māyā-Shakti intervenes and does so through its power and the Kanchukas which are forms of it. Māyā-Shakti is thus defined as the sense of difference

(Bhedabuddhi): that is the power by which things are seen as different from the Self in the dual manifested world. The Kanchukas which are evolved from, and are particular forms of, the operation of Māyā are limitations of the natural perfections of the Supreme Consciousness. These are Kāla which produces division (Parichchheda) in the partless and unlimited; Niyati which affects independence (Svatantratā); Rāga which produces interest in, and then attachment to, objects in that which wanted nothing (Pūrna); Vidyā which makes the Purusha a "little knower" in lieu of being all-knower (Sarvajnata) and Kalā which makes Purusha a "little doer", whereas the Supreme was in its Kartrittva or power action of almighty. The result of Māyā and its offshoots which are the Kanchukas is the production of the Purusha and Prakriti Tattvas. At this stage the Aham and Idam are completely severed. Each consciousness regards itself as a separate 'I' looking upon the "This" whether its own body or that of others as outside its consciousness. Each Purusha (and they are numberless) is mutually exclusive the one of the other. Prakriti is the collectivity of all Shaktis in contracted (Saṅkuchadrūpā) undifferentiated form. She is Feeling in the form of the undifferentiated mass of Buddhi and the rest and of the three Gunas in equilibrium. The Purusha or Self experiences Her as object. Then on the disturbance of the Gunas in Prakriti the latter evolves the Vikritis of mind and matter. The Purusha at this stage has experience of the multiple world of the twenty-four impure Tattvas.

Thus from the supreme "I" (Parāhantā) which is the creative Shiva-Shakti aspect of Parāsamvit which changelessly endures as Ṣachchhidānanda, Consciousness experiences Itself as object (Sadākhya, Īshvara, Sadvidyā Tattvas) and then through Māyā and the limitations or contractions which are the Kanchukas or Saṅkochas it loses the knowledge that it is itself its own object. It sees the separate "other"; and the one Consciousness becomes the limited experiencers which are the multiple selves and their objects of the dual universe. Shakti who in Herself (Svarūpa) is Feeling-Consciousness (Chidrūpinī) becomes more and more gross until physical energy assumes the form and becomes embedded in the "crust" of matter vitalized by Herself as the Life-Principle of all things. Throughout all forms it is the same Shakti who works and appears as Chit-Shakti and Māyā-Shakti, the Spirit and Matter aspect of the Power of the Self-Illumining Pure Super-Consciousness or Chit.

CHAPTER XV

MĀYĀ-SHAKTI

(THE PSYCHO-PHYSICAL ASPECT OF THE UNIVERSE)

SPIRIT, Mind and Matter are ultimately one, the two latter being the twin aspects of the Fundamental Substance or Brahman and Its Power or Shakti. Spirit is the substance of mind-matter, the Reality (in the sense of the lasting changelessness) out of which, by Its Power, all Appearance is fashioned not by the individual mind and senses but by the cosmic mind and senses of which they are but a part. What It creates It perceives. In the last chapter I dealt with the Spirit or Consciousness (Chit) aspect: in this I consider the mind-matter aspect in which Consciousness veils itself in apparent unconsciousness. These twin principles are called Purusha, Brahman, Shiva on the one hand: and Prakriti, Māyā, and Māyā-Shakti on the other by the Sāṅkhya, Māyāvāda Vedānta and Shaktivāda of the Shākta Āgama respectively. The latter Shāstra, however, alone treats them as aspects of the one Substance in the manner here described and thus most aptly in this respect accommodates itself to the doctrine of Western scientific monism. So, Professor Haeckel points out in conformity with Shākta Advaitavāda that Spirit and Matter are not two distinct entities but two forms or aspects of one single Entity or fundamental Substance. According to him, the One Entity with dual aspect is the sole Reality which presents itself to view as the infinitely varied and wondrous picture of the universe. Whatever be the case transcendentally in what the Buddhist Tantra aptly calls "The Void" (Shūnyatā. In Tibetan sTong-pa-nyid) which is not "nothing" as some have supposed, but That which is like nothing known to us; the ultimate formless (Arūpa) Reality as contrasted with appearance (sNang-va-dang) or form (Rūpa) of which the Prajnāpāramitā-hridayagarbha says only "neti neti" can be affirmed,—in this universe immaterial Spirit is just as unthinkable as spiritless matter. The two are inseparately combined in every atom which, itself and its forces, possess the elements of vitality, growth and intelligence in all their developments. In the four Ātmās which are contemplated in the Chitkunda in the Mūlādhāra Chakra, Ātmā prānarūpī represents the vital aspect, Jnānātmā the Intelligence aspect, and Antarātmā is that spark of the Paramātmā which inheres in all bodies, and which when spread (Vyāpta) appears as the Bhūta or five forms of sensible matter which go to the making of the gross body. These are all aspects of the one Paramātmā (Jnānārnava Tantra, Ch. XXI, Vv. 1—9).

The Vedānta recognizes four states of experience, Jāgrat, Svapna, Sushupti and Turīya. These, as my friend Professor Pramathanātha Mukhyopādhyāya has, in his radical clear-thinking way, pointed out, may be regarded from two standpoints. We may, with Shankara, from the standpoint of Siddhi alone, regard the last only, that is transcendental or pure experience (Nirvishesha-jnāna), as the real Fact or Experience: or we may, with the Shākta Āgama, looking at the matter from the standpoint of both Sādhanā (that is practical experience) and Siddhi (or transcendental experience), regard not only the supreme experience as alone real, but the whole of experience without any reservation whatever—the whole concrete Fact of Being and Becoming—and call it the Real. This is the view of the Shaiva-Shākta who says that the world is Shiva's Experience and Shiva's Experience can never be unreal. The question turns upon the definition of "Real". Shaṅkara's conception of that term is that, That to which it is applied must be absolutely changeless in all the "three times". It is That which absolutely continues through and underlies all the changes of experience; being that which is given in all the four states, Jāgrat and the rest. It is That which can never be contradicted (Vādhita) in all the three tenses of time and the four states of Experience. This is the Ether of Consciousness (Chidākāsha) and none of Its modes. Our ordinary experience, it is claimed, as well as Supreme non-polar Nirvikalpa Samādhi proves this unchanging aspect of the ultimate Substance, as the changeless principle of all our modes of changing experience, which according to this definition are unreal. Thus Shaṅkara's Real = Being = Sat-Chit-Ānanda: Unreal = Becoming = Vivartta = Jagat—Prapancha or universe. According to this view, there are three levels or planes of being (Sattā), namely transcendental (Pāramārthika), empirical (Vyāvahārika) and illusory (Prātibhāsika). The Real (Satya) is that which is given in all the three planes (Pāramārthika Satya): the empirical (Vyāvahārika Satya) is that which is given in the second and third planes but not in the first. It is worldly or dual experience, and not undual experience of Samādhi or Videha-Mukti which latter, however, underlies all states of experience, being the Ether of Consciousness Itself. The last (Prātibhāsika Satya) is given or obtains only in the last plane being only such reality as can be attributed to illusion such as "the rope-snake". A higher plane contradicts a lower: the third is contradicted by the second, the second by the first, and the first by nothing at all. Thus there is a process of gradual elimination from changing to changeless consciousness. Real change or Parināma is said by the Vedānta Paribhāshā to exist when the effect or phenomenon and its ground (Upādāna or material cause) belong to the same level or plane of existence; as in the case of clay and pot, milk and curd which both belong to the Vyāvahārika plane; milk being the Upādāna and curd the effect or change appertaining it (Parināmo hi upādāna-sama-sattaka-kāryyāpattih). When, however, the effect's level of existence is different from (Vishama) and therefore cannot be equalled to that of its material cause or Upādāna; when, for instance, one belongs to the Vyāvahārika experience and the other to the Prātibhāsika, there is Vivartta (Vivartto hi upādāna-vishama-sattaka-kāryyāpattih). Thus, in the case of the "rope-snake", the Sattā of the rope is Vyāvahārika, whilst that of the Rajju-sarpa is only Prātibhāsika. For the same reason, the rope, and the whole Jagat-prapancha (universe) for the matter of that, is a Vivartta in relation to the Supreme Experience of pure Chit. On its own plane or level of Sattā, every phenomenon may be a Parināma, but in relation to a higher level by which it becomes Vādhita, it is only a Vivartta.

The Shākta Āgama differs in its presentment as follows. The Fact or Concrete Experience presents two aspects—what Professor Mukhyopādhyāya has aptly called in his work the "Patent Wonder"—the Ether and the Stress—the quiescent background of Chit and the sprouting and evolving Shakti. Āgama takes this whole (Shiva-Shakti) embracing all the aspects as its real. If one aspect be taken apart from the others, we are landed in the unreal. Therefore, in the Shākta Āgama, all is real; whether the transcendent real of Shaṅkara (Turīya), or the empirical real of waking (Jāgrat), dreaming (Svapna) or dreamless sleep (Sushupti). If it is conceded that Real = Changelessness, then the last three states are not real. But this definition of Reality is not adopted. It is again conceded that the Supreme Substance (Paravastu) is alone real, in the sense of changeless, for the worlds come and go. But the Āgama says with the Sāṅkhya, that a thing is not unreal because it changes. The Substance has two aspects, in one of which It is changeless, and in the other of which It changes. It is the same Substance in both its Prākasha and Vimarsha aspects. Shaṅkara limits Reality to the Prākasha aspect alone. Āgama extends it to both Prākasha and Vimarsha; for these are aspects of the one. As explained later, this divergence of views turns upon the definition of Māyā given by Shaṅkara, and of Māyā-Shakti given by the Āgama. The Māyā of Shaṅkara is a mysterious Shakti of Īshvara, by which Vivartta is sought to be explained and which has two manifestations, *viz.*, Veiling (Āvarana) and moving, changing and projecting (Vikshepa) power. Īshvara is Brahman reflected in Māyā; a mystery which is separate, and yet not separate, from Brahman in Its Īshvara aspect. The Shākta Māyā-Shakti is an aspect of Shiva or Brahman Itself.

Starting from these premises we must assume a real nexus between the universe and its ultimate cause. The creation is real, and not Māyā in Shaṅkara's sense of Māyā, but is the operation of and is Shakti Herself. The cause being thus real, the effect or universe is real though it changes and passes away. Even when it is dissolved, it is merged in Shakti who is real; withdrawn into Her as the Sāṅkhyan tortoise or Prakriti withdraws its limbs (Vikriti) into itself. The universe either *is* as unmanifested Shakti, which is the perfect formless universe of Bliss, or *exists* as manifested Shakti, the limited and imperfect worlds of form. The assumption of such nexus necessarily involves that what is in the effect is in the cause potentially. Of course, the follower of Shaṅkara will say that if creation is the becoming patent or actual of what is latent or potential in Shiva, then Shiva is not really Nishkala. A truly Niranjana Brahman cannot admit potential differentiation within Itself (Svagatabheda). Again, potentiality is unmeaning in relation to the absolute and infinite Being, for it pertains to relation and finite existence. If it is suggested that Brahman passes from one condition in which Māyā lies as a seed in it, to another in which Māyā manifests Herself, we are involved in the doctrine of an Absolute in the making. It is illogical to affirm that whilst Brahman in one aspect does not change, It in another aspect, that is as Shakti, does truly change. All such objections have alogical foundation and it is for this reason that Shaṅkara says that all change (Srishti, Sthiti, Laya) are only apparent, being but a Kalpana or imagination.

But an answer is given to these objections. The Shākta will say that the one Brahman Shiva has two aspects in one of which, as Shakti, it changes and in the other of which, as Shiva, It does not. Reality is constituted of both these aspects. It is true that the doctrine of aspects does not solve the problem. Creation is ultimately inscrutable. It is, however, he urges, better to hold both the reality of the Brahman and the world leaving spiritual experience to synthesize them, than to neglect one at the cost of the others. For this, it is argued, is what Shaṅkara does. His solution is obtained at the cost of a denial of true reality to the world which all our worldly experience affirms; and this solution is supported by the illogical statement that Māyā is not real and is yet not unreal, not partly real and partly unreal. This also, it is said, flies in the face of the logical principle of contradiction. Both theories, therefore, it may be said in different ways, run counter to logic. All theories ultimately do. The matter is admittedly alogical that is beyond logic, for it is beyond the mind and its logical forms of thinking. Practically, therefore, it is said to be better to base our theory on our experience of the reality of the world, frankly leaving it to spiritual experience to solve a problem for which all logic, owing to the very constitution of the mind, fails. The ultimate proof of authority is Spiritual Experience either recorded in Veda or realized in Samādhi.

As I have already said in my chapter on the spirit-aspect of the One Substance, all occultism, whether of East or West, posits the principle that there is nothing in any one state or plane which is not in some way, actual or potential, in another state or plane. The Western Hermetic maxim, "as above so below", is stated in the Vishvasāra Tantra in the form, "what is here is there. What is not here is nowhere" (*Yad ihāsti tad anyatra yan nehāsti na tat kvachit*); and in the northern Shaiva Scripture in the form, "that which appears *without* only so appears *because* it exists *within*," "*Vartamānāvabhāsānām bhāvānām avabhāsanam antahsthitavatām eva ghatate bahirātmanā*". For these reasons man is rightly called a microcosm (Kshudrabrahmānda; *hominem quasi minorem quendam mundum*. Firm. Maternus Math. III init.). So Charaka says that the course of production, growth, decay and destruction of the universe and of man are the same. But these statements do not mean that what exists on one plane exists in that form or way on another plane. It is obvious that if it did, the planes would be the same and not different. It means that the same thing exists on one plane and on all other levels of being or planes, according either to the form of that plane, if it be what is called an intermediate causal body (Kāranāvantara-sharīra) or ultimately as mere formless potentiality. According to Shankara all such argument is itself Māyā. And it may be so to those who have realized true consciousness (Chitsvarūpa) which is beyond all causality. The Tantra Shāstra is, however, a practical and Sādhanā Shāstra. It takes the world to be real and then applies, so far as it may, to the question of its origin, the logic of the mind which forms a part of it. It says that it is true that there is a Supreme or Perfect Experience which is beyond all worlds (Shakti Vishvottīrṇā), but there is also a worldly or (relatively to the Supreme) imperfect (in the sense of limited) and partly sorrowful experience. Because the one exists, it does not follow that the other does not: though mere logic cannot construct an unassailable monism. It is the one Shiva who is Bliss itself, and who is in the form of the world (Vishvātmaka) which is Happiness-Unhappiness. Shiva is both changeless as Shiva and changeful as Shakti. How the One can be both is a mystery. To say, however, with Shaṅkara that it is Māyā, and in truth Brahman does not change, is not to explain, in an ultimate sense, the problem but to eliminate some other possible cause and to give to what remains a name. Māyā by itself does not explain the ultimate. What can? It is only a term which is given to the wondrous power of the Creatrix by which what seems impossible to us becomes possible to Her. This is recognized, as it must be, by Shaṅkara who says that Māyā is unexplainable (Anirvachanīyā) as of course it is. To "explain" the Creator, one would have to be the Creator Himself and then in such case there would be no need of any explanation. Looking, however, at the matter from our own practical standpoint, which is that which concerns us, we are drawn by the foregoing considerations to the conclusion that, what we call "matter", is, in some form, in the cause which, according to the doctrine here described, produces it. But matter as experienced by us is not there; for the Supreme is Spirit only. And yet in some sense it is there, or it would not be here at all. It is there as the Supreme Shakti which is Being-Consciousness-Bliss (Chitrūpinī, Ānandamayī) who contains within Herself the potentiality of all worlds to be projected by Her Shakti. It *is* there as unmanifested Consciousness Power (Chidrūpinī Shakti). It here *exists* as the mixed conscious-unconsciousness (in the sense of the limited consciousness) of the psychical and material universe. If the ultimate Reality be one, there is thus one Almighty Substance which is both Spirit (Shiva-Shakti Svarūpa) and force-mind-matter (Shiva-Shakti-Vishvātmaka). Spirit and Mind-Matter are thus in the end one.

This ultimate Supreme Substance (Paravastu) is Power or Shakti, which is, again, of dual aspect as Chit-Shakti which represents the spiritual, and Māyā-Shakti which represents the material and mental aspects. The two, however, exist in inseparable connection (Avinābhāva-sambandha); as inseparable to use a simile of the Shāstra as the winds of heaven from the Ether in which they blow. Shakti, who is in Herself (Svarūpa) Consciousness, appears as the Life-force, as subtle Mind, and as gross Matter. See volumes in my "World as Power" dealing in detail with Life (Prāna-Shakti), Mind (Mānasi-Shakti) and Matter (Bhūta-Shakti). As all is Shakti and as Shakti-svarūpa is Being-Consciousness-Bliss, there is, and can be, nothing absolutely unconscious. For Shakti-svarūpa is unchanging Being-Consciousness beyond all worlds (Chidrūpinī Vishvottīrnā), the unchanging principle of experience in such worlds; and appears as the limited psychical universe and as the apparently unconscious material forms which are the content of man's Experience (Vishvātmikā). The whole universe is Shakti under various forms. Therefore it is seen as commingled Spirit-Mind-Matter.

According to Shaiva-Shākta doctrine, Shiva and Shakti are one. Shiva represents the static aspect of the Supreme substance, and Shakti its kinetic aspect: the term being derived from the root "Shak" which denotes capacity of action or power. According to Shaṅkara, Brahman has two aspects, in one of which as Īshvara, it is associated with Māyā and seems to change, and in the other dissociated from Māyā (Parabrahman). In the Āgama, the one Shiva is both the changeless Parashiva and Parashakti and the really changing Shiva-Shakti or universe. As Shiva is one with Himself, He is never associated with anything but Himself. As, however, the Supreme, He is undisplayed (Shiva-Shakti Svarūpa) and, as Shiva-Shakti, He is manifest in the form of the universe of mind and matter (Vishvarūpa).

Before the manifestation of the universe there was Mahāsattā or Grand-being. Then also there was Shiva-Shakti, for there is no time when Shakti is not; though She is sometimes manifest and sometimes not. Power is Power both to Be and to Become. But then Shakti is not manifest and is in its own true nature (Svarūpa); that is, Being, Feeling-Consciousness-Bliss (Chinmayī, Ānandamayī). As Shiva is consciousness (Chit) and Bliss or Love (Ānanda), She is then simply Bliss and Love. Then when moved to create, the Great Power or *Megale Dunamis* of the Gnostics issues from the depths of Being and becomes Mind and Matter whilst remaining what She ever was: the Being (Sat) which is the foundation of manifested life and the Spirit which sustains and enlightens it. This primal Power (Ādyā Shakti), as object of worship, is the Great Mother (Magna-Mater) of all natural things (Natura Naturans) and nature itself (Natura Naturata). In herself (Svarūpa) She is not a person in man's sense of the term, but She is ever and incessantly *personalizing*; assuming the multiple masks (Persona) which are the varied forms of mind-matter.

As therefore manifest, She is all Personalities and as the collectivity thereof the Supreme Person (Parāhantā). But in Her own ground from which, clad in form, She emerges and personalizes, She is beyond all form, and therefore beyond all personality known to us. She works in and as all things; now greatly veiling Her consciousness-bliss in gross matter, now by gradual stages more fully revealing Herself in the forms of the one universal Life which She is.

Let us now first examine Her most gross manifestation, that is, sensible matter (Bhūta), then Her more subtle aspect as the Life-force and Mind, and lastly Her Supreme Shakti aspect as Consciousness. I here deal with the subject in a general way having treated of it in greater detail in the books just now cited ("World as Power" series).

The physical human body is composed of certain compounds of which the chief are water, gelatine, fat, phosphate of lime, albumen and fibrin, and, of these, water constitutes some two-thirds of the total weight. These compounds, again, are composed of simpler non-metallic elements of which the chief are oxygen (to the extent of about two-thirds), hydrogen, carbon, nitrogen, calcium and phosphorus. So about two-thirds of the body is water and this is H_2O. Substantially then our gross body is water. But when we get to these simpler elements, have we got to the root of the matter? No. It was formerly thought that matter was composed of certain elements beyond which it was not possible to go, and that these elements and their atoms were indestructible. These notions have been reversed by modern science. Though the alleged indestructibility of the elements and their atoms is still said by some to present the character of a "practical truth", well-known recent discoveries and experiments go to re-establish the ancient doctrine of a single primordial substance to which these various forms of matter may be reduced, with the resultant of the possible and hitherto derided transmutation of one element into another; since each is but one of the many plural manifestations of the same underlying unity. The so called elements are varied forms of this one substance which themselves combine to form the various compounds. The variety of our experience is due to permutation and combination of the atoms of the matter into which the primordial energy materializes. We thus find that owing to the variety of atomic combinations of H N O C there are differences in the compounds. It is curious to note in passing how apparently slight variations in the quantity and distribution of the atoms produce very varying substances. Thus gluten which is a nutrient food, and quinine and strychnine which are in varying degree poisons, are each compounds of C H N O. Strychnine, a powerful poison is $C_{21}H_{22}N_2O_2$ and quinine is $C_{20}H_{24}N_2O_2$. N and O are the same in both and there is a difference of one part only of C and 2 of H. But neither these compounds nor the so-called elements of which they are composed are permanent things. Scientific matter is now found to be only a relatively stable form of cosmic energy. All matter dissociates and passes into the energy of which it is a materialized form and again it issues from it.

Modern Western Science and Philosophy have thus removed many difficulties which were formerly thought to be objections to the ancient Indian doctrine on the subject here dealt with. In has, in the first place, dispelled the gross notions which were hitherto generally entertained as to the nature of "matter". According to the notions of quite recent science, "matter" was defined to be that which has mass, weight and inertia. It must be now admitted that the two latter qualities no longer stand the test of examination, since, putting aside our ignorance as to the nature of weight, this quality varies, if we conceive matter to be placed under conditions which admittedly affect it; and the belief in inertia is due to superficial observation, it being now generally conceded that the final elements of matter are in a state of spontaneous and perpetual motion. In fact, the most general phenomenon of the universe is vibration, to which the human body as all else is subject. Various vibrations affect differently each organ of sensation. When of certain quality and number, they denote to the skin the degree of external temperature; others incite the eye to see different colours; others again enable the ear to hear defined sounds. Moreover "inertia," which is alleged to be a distinguishing quality of "matter," is said to be the possession of electricity, which is considered not to be "material". What, then, is that to which we attribute "mass"? In the first place, it is now admitted that "matter," even with the addition of all possible forces, is insufficient to explain many phenomena, such as those of light; and it has, accordingly, come to be for some an article of scientific *faith* that there is a substance called "Ether": a medium which, filling the universe, transports by its vibrations the radiations of light, heat, electricity, and perhaps action from a distance, such as the attraction exercised between heavenly bodies. It is said, however, that this Ether is not "matter", but differs profoundly from it, and that it is only our infirmity of knowledge which obliges us, in our attempted descriptions of it, to borrow comparisons from "matter", in its ordinary physical sense, which alone is known by our senses. But if we assume the existence of Ether, we know that "material" bodies immersed in it can change their places therein. In fact, to use an Indian expression, the characteristic property of the vibrations of the Ākāsha Tattva is to make the space in which the other Tattvas and their derivatives exist. With "Matter" and Ether as their materials, Western purely "scientific" theories have sought to construct the world. The scientific atom which Du Bois Raymond described as an exceedingly useful fiction—"ausserst nutzliche fiction"—is no longer considered the ultimate indestructible element, but is held to be, in fact, a kind of miniature solar system, formed by a central group or nucleus charged with positive electricity, around which very much smaller elements, called electrons or corpuscles, charged with negative electricity, gravitate in closed orbits. These vibrate in the etheric medium in which they and the positively charged nucleus exist, constituting by their energy, and not by their mass, the unity of the atom. But what, again, is the constitution of this "nucleus" and the electrons revolving around it? There is no scientific certainty that any part of either is due to the presence of "matter". On the contrary, if a hypothetical corpuscle consisting solely of an electric charge without material mass is made the subject of mathematical analysis, the logical inference is that the electron is free of "matter", and is merely an electric charge moving in the Ether; and though the extent of our knowledge regarding the positive nucleus which constitutes the remainder of the atom is small, an eminent mathematician and physicist has expressed the opinion that, if there is no "matter" in the negative charges, the positive charges must also be free from it. Thus, in the words of the author upon whose lucid analysis I have drawn, (Houllevigue's "Evolution of Science") the atom has been *dematerialized*, if one may say so, and with it the molecules and the entire universe. "Matter" (in the scientific sense) *disappears*, and we and all that surround us are physically, according to these views, mere disturbed regions of the ether determined by moving electric charges—a logical if impressive conclusion, because it is by increasing their knowledge of "matter" that physicists have been led to doubt its reality. But the question, as he points out, does not remain there. For if the speculations of Helmholtz be adopted, there is nothing absurd in imaging that two possible directions of rotation of a vortex formed within, and consisting of, ether correspond to the positive and negative electric charges said to be attached to the final elements of matter. If that be so, then the trinity of matter, ether, and electricity, out of which science has hitherto attempted to construct the world, is reduced to a single element, the ether (which is not scientific "matter") in a state of motion, and which is the basis of the physical universe. The old duality of force and matter disappears, these being held to be differing forms of the same thing. Matter is a relatively stable form of energy into which, on disturbance of its equilibrium, it disappears; for all forms of matter dissociate. The ultimate basis is that energy called in Indian philosophy Prakriti, Māyā or Shakti.

Herbert Spencer, the Philosopher of Modern Science, carries the investigation farther, holding that the universe, whether physical or psychical, whether within or without us, is a play of Force, which, in the case of Matter, we experience as object, and that the notion that the ultimate realities are the supposed atoms of matter, to the properties and combinations of which the complex universe is due, is not true. Mind, Life and Matter are each varying aspects of the one cosmic process from the First Cause. Mind as such is as much a "material" organ as the brain and outer sense organs, though they are differing forms of force.

Both mind and matter derive from what Herbert Spencer calls the Primal Energy (Ādyā Shakti), and Hæckel the fundamental Spirit-Matter Substance. Professor Fitz Edward Hall described the Sāṅkhya philosophy as being "with all its folly and fanaticism little better than a chaotic impertinence". It has doubtless its weaknesses like all other systems. Wherein, however, consists its "fanaticism", I do not know. As for "impertinence", it is neither more nor less so than any other form of Western endeavour to solve the riddle of life. As regards its leading concept, "Prakriti", the Professor said that it was a notion for which the European languages were unable to supply a name; a failure, he added, which was "nowise to their discredit". The implication of this sarcastic statement is that it was not to the discredit of Western languages that they had no name for so foolish a notion. He wrote before the revolution of ideas in science to which I have referred, and with that marked antagonism to things Indian which has been and to some extent still is so common a feature of the more ordinary type of professional orientalist.

The notion of Prakriti is not absurd. The doctrine of a Primordial Substance was held by some of the greatest minds in the past and has support from the most modern developments of Science. Both now concur to reject what the great Sir William Jones called the "vulgar notion of material substance" (Opera I. 36). Many people were wont, as some still are, to laugh at the idea of Māyā. Was not matter solid, permanent and real enough? But according to science what are we (as physical beings) at base? The answer is, infinitely tenuous formless energy which materializes into relatively stable, yet essentially transitory, forms. According to the apt expression of the Shākta Shāstra, Shakti, as She creates, becomes Ghanībhūtā, that is, massive or thickened; just as milk becomes curd. The process by which the subtle becomes gradually more and more gross continues until it develops into what has been called the "crust" of solid matter (Pārthiva bhūta). This whilst it lasts is tangible enough. But it will not last for ever, and in some radio-active substances dissociates before our eyes. Where does it go, according to Shākta doctrine, but to that Mother-Power from whose womb it came; who exists as all forms, gross and subtle, and is the formless Consciousness Itself. The poet's inspiration led Shakespeare to say, "We are such stuff as dreams are made of." It is a wonderful saying from a Vedāntic standpoint, for centuries before him Advaitavāda had said, "Yes, dreams; for the Lord is Himself the Great World-dreamer slumbering in causal sleep as Īshvara, dreaming as Hiranyagarbha the universe experienced by Him as the Virāt or totality of all Jīvas, on waking. Scientific revision of the notion of "matter" helps the Vedāntic standpoint, by dispelling gross and vulgar notions upon the subject; by establishing its impermanence in its form as scientific matter; by positing a subtler physical substance which is not ponderable matter; by destroying the old duality of Matter and Force; and by these and other conclusions leading to the acceptance of one Primal Energy or Shakti which transforms itself into that relatively stable state which is perceived by the senses as gross "matter". As, however, science deals with matter only objectively, that is, from a dualistic standpoint, it does not (whatever hypotheses any particular scientist may maintain) resolve the essential problem which is stated in the word Māyā. That problem is, "How can the apparent duality be a real unity? How can we bridge the gulf between the object and the Self which perceives it? Into whatever tenuous energy the material world is resolved, we are still left in the region of duality of Spirit, Mind and Matter. The position is not advanced beyond that taken by Sāṅkhya. The answer to the problem stated is that Shakti which is the origin of, and is in, all things has the power to veil Itself so that whilst in truth it is only seeing itself as object, it does not, as the created Jīva, perceive this but takes things to be outside and different from the Self. For this reason Māyā is called, in the Shāstra, Bhedabuddhi or the sense of difference. This is the natural characteristic of man's experience.

Herbert Spencer, the Philosopher of Modern Science, carrying the investigation beyond physical matter, holds, as I have already said, that the universe, whether physical or psychical, whether as mind or matter, is a play of Force; Mind, Life and Matter being each varying aspects of the one cosmic process from the First Cause. This, again, is an Indian notion. For, the affirmation that "scientific matter" is an appearance produced by the play of Cosmic Force, and that mind is itself a product of the same play is what both Sāṅkhya and Māyāvāda Vedānta hold. Both these systems teach that mind, considered in itself, is, like matter, an unconscious thing, and that both it and matter ultimately issue from the same single Principle which the former calls Prakriti and the latter Māyā. Consciousness and Unconsciousness are in the universe inseparate, whatever be the degree of manifestation or veiling of Consciousness. For the purpose of analysis, Mind in itself—that is, considered hypothetically as dissociated from Consciousness, which, in fact, is never the case, (though Consciousness exists apart from the Mind)—is a force-process like the physical brain. Consciousness (Chit) is not to be identified with mind (Antahkarana) which is the organ of expression of mind. Consciousness is not a mere manifestation of material mind. Consciousness must not be identified with its *mental modes*; an identification which leads to the difficulties in which western metaphysics has so often found itself. It is the ultimate Reality in which all modes whether subjective or objective exist.

The assertion that mind is in itself unconscious may seem a strange statement to a Western reader who, if he does not identify mind and consciousness, at any rate, regards the latter as an attribute or function of mind. The point, however, is of such fundamental importance for the understanding of Indian doctrine that it may be further developed.

According to the Lokāyata School of Indian Materialism, mind was considered to be the result of the chemical combination of the four forms of material substance, earth, water, fire and air, in organic forms. According to the Pūrva-Mīmāṁsa and the Nyāya-Vaisheshika, the Self or Ātmā is in itself and that is by nature (Svabhāvatah), unconscious (Jada, Achidrūpa): for Ātmā is said to be unconscious (Achetana) in dreamless sleep (Sushupti); and consciousness arises as a produced thing, by association of the Ātmā with the mind, senses and body. The reader is referred to Pandit Chandra Kānta Tarkālaṅkāra's Bengali Lectures on Hindu Philosophy. At p. 105 he cites Prabhākāra Mīmāṁsakāchāryya, saying that Vaisheshika-Nyāya supports the view. *Sachetanashchittayogāt todyogena vinā jadah.* "Ātmā is Conscious by union with knowledge [Jnāna] which comes to it by association with mind and body. Without it, it is unconscious." Ātmā, according to this Darshana, is that in which (Āshraya) Jnāna inheres. Kumārila Bhatta says Ātmā is partly Prakāsha and Aprakāsha, (luminous and non-luminous) like a fire-fly. But this is denied, as Ātmā is Niraṁsha (partless). Knowledge thus arises from the association of mind (Manas) with Ātmā, the senses (Indriya) with Manas, and the senses with their objects, that is, worldly (Laukika) knowledge, which is the true—that is, non-illusive—apprehension of objects. Jnāna in the spiritual Vedāntic sense of Māyāvāda is Paramātmā, or pure Consciousness realized. The former Jnāna, in that it arises without effort on the presentation of the objects is not action (Kriyā), and differs from the forms of mental action (Mānasī Kriyā), such as will (Ichchhā), contemplation and the like. *Ātmā manasā saṁyujyate, mana indriyena, indriyam arthena, tato bhavati jnānam.* Both these theories are refuted by Sāṅkhya and Advaitavāda Vedānta (as interpreted by Shaṅkara, to which unless otherwise stated I refer) which affirm that the very nature of Ātmā is Consciousness (Chit), and all else, whether mind or matter, is unconscious, though the former appears not to be so. The Jīva mind is not itself conscious, but reflects consciousness, and therefore appears to be conscious. Consciousness as such is eternal and immutable; Mind is a creation and changeable. Consciousness as such is unconditional. In the mind of the Jīva, Consciousness appears to be conditioned by that Māyā-Shakti which produces mind, and of which Shakti, mind is a particular manifestation. Mind, however, is not the resultant of the operation of the Bhūta—that is, of gross natural forces or motions—but is, in Sāṅkhya and in Shākta monism, an evolution which is logically prior to them.

The mode of exposition in which Consciousness is treated as being in itself something apart from, though associated with, mind, is profound; because, while it recognizes the intermingling of Spirit and Matter in the embodied being (Jīva), it yet at the same time clearly distinguishes them. It thus avoids the imputation of change to Spirit (Ātmā). The latter is ever in Its own true nature immutable. Mind is ever changing, subject to sensations, forming ideas, making resolves, and so forth. Spirit in Itself is neither thus affected nor acts. Manifold change takes place, through motion and vibration, in the unconscious Prakriti and Māyā. Mind is one of the results of such motion, as matter is another. Each of them is a form of specific transformation of the one Principle whence unconsciousness, whether real or apparent, arises. That, however, mind *appears* to be conscious, the Māyāvāda Vedānta and Sāṅkhya admit. This is called Chidābhāsa—that is, the appearance of something as Chit (Consciousness) which is not really Chit. This appearance of Consciousness is due to the reflection of Chit upon it. A piece of polished steel which lies in the sunshine may appear to be self-luminous, when it is merely reflecting the sun, which is the source of the light it appears to give out. Chit as such is immutable and never evolves. What do evolve are the various forms of natural forces produced by Prakriti or Māyā. These two are, however, conceived as being in association in such a way that the result of such association is produced without Chit being really affected at all. The classical illustration of the mode and effect of such association is given in the Sāṅkhyan aphorism, "Just like the jewel and the flower"—*Kusuma-vachcha manih* (Sāṅkhya-Pravachana-Sutra, II, 35)—that is, when a scarlet hibiscus flower is placed in contiguity to a crystal, the latter appears to be red, though it still in fact retains its pure transparency, as is seen when the flower is removed. On the other hand, the flower as reflected in the crystal takes on a shining, transparent aspect which its opaque surface does not really possess. In the same way Consciousness appears to be conditioned by the force of unconsciousness in the Jīva, but is really not so. "Changeless Chit-Shakti, does not move towards anything, yet seems to do so" (Sāṅkhya-pravachana-Sūtra). And, on the other hand, Mind as one of such unconscious forces takes on the semblance of Consciousness, though this is borrowed from Chit and is not its own natural quality. This association of Unconscious Force with Consciousness has a two-fold result, both obscuring and revealing. It obscures, in so far as, and so long as it is in operation, it prevents the realization of pure Consciousness (Chit). When mind is absorbed pure Consciousness shines forth. In this sense, this Power or Māyā is spoken of as a Veil. In another sense, it reveals—that is, it manifests—the world, which does not exist except through the instrumentality of Māyā which the world is. Prakriti and Māyā produce both Mind and Matter; on the former of which Consciousness is reflected (Chidābhāsa). The human mind, then, appears to be conscious, but of its own nature and inherent quality is not so. The objective world of matter is, or appears to be, an unconscious reality. These alternatives are necessary, because, in Sāṅkhya, unconsciousness is a reality; in Vedānta, an appearance. In the Shākta Tantra, apparent unconsciousness is an aspect (Avidyā Shakti) of Conscious Shakti. Consciousness is according to Advaita Vedānta, the true existence of both, illumining the one, hidden in the other.

The internal instrument (Antahkarana) or Mind is one only, but is given different names—Buddhi, Ahaṅkāra, Manas—to denote the diversity of its functions. From the second of these issue the senses (Indriya) and their objects, the sensibles (Mahābhūta), or gross matter with the supersensibles (Tanmātra) as its intermediate cause. All these proceed from Prakriti and Māyā.

Therefore, according to these systems, Consciousness is Chit, and Mind or Antahkarana is a transformation of Prakriti and Māyā respectively. In itself, Mind is an unconscious specialized organ developed out of the Primordial Energy, Mūla-Prakriti or Māyā. It is thus, not in itself, consciousness but a special manifestation of conscious existence, borrowing its consciousness from the Chit which is reflected on it. Shākta doctrine states the same matter in a different form. Consciousness at rest is Chit-Svarūpa.

Consciousness in movement is Chit-Shakti associated with Māyā-Shakti. The Shiva-Shakti Svarūpa is consciousness (Chit, Chidrūpinī). There is no independent Prakriti as Sāṅkhya holds, nor an unconscious Māyā which is not Brahman and yet not separate from Brahman, as Shaṅkara teaches. What there is, is Māyā-Shakti; that is Consciousness (for Shakti is in itself such) veiling, as the Mother, Herself to herself as Her creation, the Jīva. There is no need then for Chidābhāsa. For mind is consciousness veiling itself in the forms or limitation of apparent unconsciousness.

This is an attractive exposition of the matter because in the universe consciousness and unconsciousness are mingled, and the abolition of unconscious Māyā satisfies the desire for unity. In all these cases, however, mind and matter represent either the real or apparent unconscious aspect of things. If man's consciousness is, or appears to be, limited, such limitation must be due to some principle without, or attached to, or inherent in consciousness; which in some sense or other must *ex hypothesi* be really, or apparently different from the consciousness, which it seems to affect or actually affects. In all these systems, mind and matter equally derive from a common *finitising* principle which actually or apparently limits the Infinite Consciousness. In all three, there is, beyond manifestion, Consciousness or Chit, which in manifestation appears as a parallelism of mind and matter; the substratum of which from a monistic standpoint is Chit.

Herbert Spencer, however, as many other Western Philosophers do, differs from the Vedānta in holding that the noumenon of these phenomena is not Consciousness, for the latter is by them considered to be by its very nature conditioned and concrete. This noumenon is therefore declared to be unknown and unknowable. But Force as such is blind, and can only act as it has been pre-determined. We discover consciousness in the universe. The cause must, therefore, it is argued, be Consciousness. It is but reasonable to hold that, if the first cause be of the nature of either Consciousness or Matter, and not of both, it must be of the nature of the former, and not of the latter. An unconscious object may well be conceived to modify Consciousness, but not to produce Consciousness out of its Self. According to Indian Realism, the Paramānus are the material (Upādāna) cause (Kārana), and Īshvara the instrumental (Nimitta) cause, for He makes them combine. According to Vedānta, Matter is really nothing but a determined modification of knowledge in the Īshvara Consciousness, itself unaffected by such determination. Īshvara is thus both the material and instrumental cause. A thing can only dissolve into its own cause. The agency (Kartritva) of Īshvara is in Māyāvāda attributed (Aupādhika) only.

The Vedānta, therefore, in its Shākta presentment says, that the Noumenon is knowable and known, for it is the inner Self, which is not an unconscious principle but Being-Consciousness, which, as above explained, is not conditioned or concrete, but is the absolute Self-identity. Nothing can be more intimately known than the Self. The objective side of knowledge is conditioned because of the nature of its organs which, whether mental or material, are conditioned. Sensation, perception, conception, intuition are but different modes in which the one Consciousness manifests itself, the differences being determined by the variety of condition and form of the different organs of knowledge through which consciousness manifests. There is thus a great difference between the Agnostic and the Vedāntist. The former, as for instance Herbert Spencer, says that the Absolute cannot be known because nothing can be predicated of it. Whereas the Vedāntin when he says that It cannot be known (in the ordinary sense) means that this is because It is knowledge itself. Our ordinary experience does not know a consciousness of pure being without difference. But, though it cannot be pictured, it may be apprehended. It cannot be thought because it is Pure Knowledge itself. It is that state which is realized only in Samādhi but is apprehended indirectly as the Unity which underlies and sustains all forms of changing finite experience.

What, lastly, is Life? The underlying substance is Being-in-itself. Life is a manifestation of such Being. If by Life we understand life in form, then the ultimate substance is not that; for it is formless. But in a supreme sense it is Life; for it is Eternal Life whence all life in form proceeds. It is not dead Being. If it were It could not produce Life. The Great Mother is Life; both the life of Her children and the Life of their lives. Nor does She produce what is without life or potency of life. What is in the cause is in the effect. Some Western Scientists have spoken of the "Origin of Life", and have sought to find it. It is a futile quest, for Life as such has no origin though life in form has. We cannot discover the beginnings of that which is essentially eternal. The question is vitiated by the false assumption that there is anything dead in the sense that it is wholly devoid of Life or potency of Life. There is no such thing. The whole world is a living manifestation of the source of all life which is Absolute Being. It is sometimes made a reproach against Hinduism that it knows not a "living God". What is meant I cannot say. For it is certain that it does not worship a "dead God", whatever such may be. Perhaps by "living" is meant "Personal". If so, the charge is again ill-founded. Īshvara and Īshvarī are Rulers in whom all personalities and personality itself are. But in their ground they are beyond all manifestation, that is limitation which personality, as we understand it, involves. Man, the animal and the plant alone, it is true, exhibit certain phenomena which are commonly called vital. What exhibits such phenomena, we have commonly called "living". But it does not follow that what does not exhibit the phenomena which belong to our definition of life is itself altogether "dead". We may have to revise our definition, as in fact we are commencing to do. Until recently it was commonly assumed that matter was of two kinds: inorganic or "dead", and organic or "living". The mineral was "dead", the vegetable, animal and man were endowed with "life". But these living forms are compounded of so-called "dead" matter. How, then, is it possible that there is life in the organic kingdom the parts of which are ultimately compounded of "dead" matter? This necessarily started the futile quest for the "origin of life". Life can only come from life: not from death. The greatest errors arise from the making of false partitions in nature which do not exist. We make these imaginary partitions and then vainly attempt to surmount them. There are no absolute partitions or gulfs. All is continuous, even if we cannot at present establish in each case the connection. That there should be such gulfs is unthinkable to any one who has even in small degree grasped the notion of the unity of things. There is a complete connected chain in the hierarchy of existence, from the lowest forms of apparently inert (but now held to be moving) matter, through the vegetable, animal, human worlds · and then through such Devatās as are super-human intelligences up to the Brahman. From the latter to a blade of grass (says the Shāstra) all are one.

Western scientific notions have, however, in recent years undergone a radical evolution as regards the underlying unity of substance, destructive of the hitherto accepted notions of the discontinuity of matter and its organization. The division of nature into the animal, vegetable and mineral kingdoms is still regarded as of practical use; but it is now recognized that no such clear line of demarcation exists between them as has hitherto been supposed in the West. Between each of nature's types there are said to be innumerable transitions. The notion of inert, "dead" matter, the result of superficial observation, has given way upon the revelation of the activities at work under this apparent inertia—forces which endow "brute substance" with many of the characteristics of living beings. It is no longer possible to dogmatically affirm where the inorganic kingdom ends and "life" begins. It must be rather asserted that many phenomena, hitherto considered characteristic of "life", belong to "inert matter", composed of molecules and atoms, as "animated matter" is of cells and micellœ. It has been found that so-called "inert matter", possesses an extraordinary power of organization, and is not only capable of apparently imitating the forms of "living" matter, but presents in a certain degree the same functions and properties.

Sentiency is a characteristic of all forms of Existence. Physiologists measure the sensibility of a being by the degree of excitement necessary to produce in it a reaction. Of this it has been said (Le Bon "Evolution of Matter," 250), "This sensibility of matter, so contrary to what popular observation seems to indicate, is becoming more and more familiar to physicists. This is why such an expression as the "life of matter", utterly meaningless twenty-five years ago has come into common use. The study of mere matter yields ever-increasing proofs that it has properties which were formerly deemed the exclusive appanage of living beings." Life exists throughout, but manifests in various ways. The arbitrary division which has been drawn between "dead" and "living" matter has no existence in fact, and speculations as to the origin of "life" are vitiated by the assumption that there is anything which exists without it, however much its presence may be veiled from us. Western science would thus appear to be moving to the conclusion that there is no "dead" matter, but that life exists everywhere, not merely in that in which, as in "organic matter," it is to us plainly and clearly expressed, but also in the ultimate "inorganic" atoms of which it is composed—atoms which, in fact, have their organizations as have the beings which they go to build—and that all, to the minutest particle, is vibrating with unending Energy (Tejas). (See Author's "World as Power", "Life".)

Manifested life is Prāna, a form of Kriyā Shakti in, and evolved from, the Linga Sharīra, itself born of Prakriti. Prāna or the vital principle has been well defined ("Hindu Realism", by J. C. Chatterji) to be, "the special relation of the Ātmā with a certain form of matter which, by this relation, the Ātmā *organizes* and builds up as a means of having experience." This special relation constitutes the individual Prāna in the individual body. Just as in the West, "life" is a term commonly used of organized body only, so also is the term Prāna used in the East. It is the technical name given to the phenomena, called "vital", exhibited by such bodies, the source of which is the Brahman Itself. The individual Prāna is limited to the particular body which it vitalizes and is a manifestation in all breathing creatures (Prānī), of the creative and sustaining activity of the Brahman. All beings exist so long as the Prāna is in the body. It is as the Kaushītakī Upanishad says, "the life duration of all". The cosmic all-pervading Prāna is the collectivity of all Prānas and is the Brahman as the source of the individual Prāna. On the physical plane, Prāna manifests as breath through inspiration, "Sa" or Shakti and expiration, "Ha" or Shiva. So the Niruttara Tantra (Chapter IV) says: "By Hangkāra it goes out and by Sakāra it comes in again. A Jīva always recites the Supreme Mantra Hangsa."

Hang-kārena bahir yāti sah-kārena vishet punah
Hangesti paramam mantram jīvo japati sarvadā.

Breathing is itself the Ajapā Mantra. Prāna is thus Shakti as the universally pervading source of life, organizing itself as matter into what we call living forms. When the Prāna goes, the organism which it holds together disintegrates. Nevertheless each of the atoms which remain has a life of its own, existing as such separately from the life of the organized body of which they formed a part; just as each of the cells of the living body has a life of its own. The gross outer body is heterogeneous (Parichchhinna) or made up of distinct or well-defined parts. But the Prānamaya Self which lies within the Annamaya Self is a homogeneous undivided whole (Sādhārana) permeating the whole physical body (Sarvapindavyāpin). It is not cut off into distinct regions (Asādhārana) as is the Pinda or microcosmic physical body. Unlike the latter it has no specialized organs each discharging a specific function.* It is a homogeneous unity (Sādhārana), present in every part of the body which it ensouls as its inner vital Self. Vāyu, as universal vital activity, on entry into each body, manifests itself in ten different ways. It is the one Prāna, though different names are given according to its functions, of which the five chief are Appropriation (Prāna), Rejection (Apāna), Assimilation (Samāna), Distribution

(Vyāna), and that vital function (Udāna) which is connected with self-expression in speech. Prāna in its general sense represents the involuntary reflex action of the organism ; just as the Indriyas are one aspect of its voluntary activity. Breathing is a manifestation of the Cosmic Rhythm to which the whole universe moves and according to which it appears and disappears. The life of Brahmā is the duration of the outgoing breath (Nishvāsa) of Kāla.

The Sāṅkhya rejecting the Lokāyata notion that Vāyu is a mere bio-mechanical force or mechanical motion resulting from such a Vāyu, holds, on the principle of the economy of categories, that life is a resultant of the various concurrent activities of other principles or forces in the organism. This, again, the Vedāntists deny, holding that it is a separate, independent principle and material form assumed through Māyā by the one Consciousness. In either case, it is an unconscious force, since, everything which is not the Ātmā or Purusha, is, according to Māyāvāda and Sāṅkhya, unconscious, or, in Western parlance, material (Jada).

If we apply Shākta principles, then Prāna is a name of the general Shakti displaying itself in the organization of matter and the vital phenomena which bodies, when organized, exhibit. Manifest Shakti is vitality, which is a limited concrete display in forms of Her own formless Being or Sat. All Shakti is Jnāna, Ichchhā, Kriyā, and in its form as Prakriti, the Gunas Sattva, Rajas, Tamas. She desires, impelled by Her nature (Ichchhā), to build up forms; sees how it should be done (Jnāna); and then does it (Kriyā). The most Tāmasic form of Kriyā is the apparently mechanical energy displayed in material bodies. But this is itself the product of Her Vitivity and not the cause of it. Ultimately then Prāna, like everything else, is consciousness which, as Shakti, limits Itself in form which it first creates and sustains; then builds up into other more elaborate forms and again sustains until their life-period is run. All creation and maintenance is a limiting power, with the appearance of unconsciousness, in so far as, and to the degree that, it confines the boundless Being-Consciousness-Bliss; yet that Power is nothing but Consciousness negating and limiting itself. The Great Mother (Shrī Mātā) limits Her infinite being in and as the universe and maintains it. In so far as the form and its life is a limited thing, it is apparently unconscious, for consciousness is thereby limited. At each moment there is creation, but we call the first appearance creation (Srishti), and its continuance, through the agency of Prāna, maintenance (Sthiti). But both that which is apparently limited and that whose operation has that effect is Being-Consciousness. Prāna Vāyu is the self-begotten but limited manifestation of the eternal Life. It is called Vāyu (Vā = to move) because it courses throughout the whole universe. Invisible in itself yet its operations are manifest. For it determines the birth, growth, and decay of all animated organisms and as such receives the homage of all created Being. For it is the Prānarūpī Ātmā, the Prāna Shakti.

For those by whom inorganic matter was considered to be "dead" or lifeless, it followed that it could have no Feeling-Consciousness, since the latter was deemed to be an attribute of life. Further, consciousness was denied because it was, and is indeed now, commonly assumed that every conscious experience pre-supposes a subject, conscious of being such, attending to an object. As Professor P. Mukhyopādhyāya ("Approaches to Truth") has well pointed out, consciousness was identified with intelligence or understanding—that is with directed consciousness; so that where no direction or form is discernible, Western thinkers have been apt to imagine that consciousness as such has also ceased. To their pragmatic eye consciousness is always particular having a particular direction and form.

According, however, to Indian views, there are three states of consciousness: (1) a supramental supreme consciousness dissociated from mind. This is the Paramātmā Chit which is the basis of all existence, whether organic or inorganic, and of thought; of which the Shruti says, "know that which does not think by the mind and by which the mind itself is thought." There are then two main manifested states of consciousness; (2) consciousness associated with mind in organic matter working through its vehicles of mind and matter; (3) consciousness associated with and almost entirely veiled by inorganic gross matter (Bhūta) only; such as the muffled consciousness, evidenced by its response to external stimuli, as shown in the experiments with which Sir Jagadish Bose's name is associated. Where are we to draw the lowest limit of sensation; and if a limit be assigned, why there? As Dr. Ernst Mach has pointed out (Analysis of Sensations, 243) the question is natural enough if we start from the commonly current physical conception. It is, of course, not asserted that inorganic matter is conscious to itself in the way that the higher organized life is. The response, however, which it makes to stimuli is evidence that consciousness is there, though it lies heavily veiled in and imprisoned by it. Inorganic matter displays it in the form of that seed or rudiment of sentiency which, enlarging into the simple pulses of feeling of the lowest degrees of organized life, at length emerges in the developed self-conscious sensations of human life. Owing to imperfect scientific knowledge, the first of these aspects was not in antiquity capable of physical proof in the same way or to the same extent, as Modern Science with its delicate instruments have made possible. Starting, however, from the revealed and intuitionally held truth that all was Brahman, the conclusion necessarily followed. All Bhūta is composed of the three Gunas or factors of Prakriti or the psycho-physical potentials. It is the Sattva or Principle of Presentation of Consciousness in gross matter (almost entirely suppressed by Tamas or the Principle of Veiling of Consciousness though it be) which manifests the phenomena of sensibility observed in matter. In short, nature, it has been well said, knows no sharp boundaries or yawning gulfs, though we may ignore the subtle connecting links between things. There is no break in continuity. Being and Consciousness are co-extensive. Consciousness is not limited to those centres in the Ether of consciousness which are called organized bodies. But just as life is differently expressed in the mineral and in man, so is Consciousness which many have been apt to think exists in the developed animal and even in man only.

Consciousness (Chit-Shakti) exists in all the hierarchy of Being, and is, in fact, Being. It is, however, in all bodies veiled by its power or Māyā-Shakti which is composed of the three Gunas. In inorganic matter, owing to the predominance of Tamas, Consciousness is so greatly veiled and the life force is so restrained that we get the appearance of insensibility, inertia and mere mechanical energy. In organized bodies, the action of Tamas is gradually lessened, so that the members of the universal hierarchy become more and more Sāttvik as they ascend in the scale of evolution. Consciousness itself does not change. It remains the same throughout. What does change is its wrappings, unconscious or apparently so, as they may alternatively be called. This wrapping is Māyā and Prakriti with their Gunas. The figure of "wrapping" is apt to illustrate the presentment of Sāṅkhya and Māyāvāda. From the Shākta aspect we may compare the process to one in which it being assumed that in one aspect there is an unchanging light, in another it is either turned up or turned down as the case may be. In gross matter the light is so turned down that it is not ordinarily perceptible and even delicate scientific experiment may give rise to contending assertions. When the veiling by Tamas is lessened in organic life, and the Jīva is thus less bound in matter, the same Consciousness (for there is no other) which previously manifested as, what seems to us, a mere mechanical reaction, manifests in its freer environment in that sensation which we associate with consciousness as popularly understood. Shakti who ever negates Herself as Māyā-Shakti, more and more reveals Herself as Chit-Shakti. There is thus a progressive *release* of Consciousness from the bonds of matter, until it attains complete freedom or liberation (Moksha) when the Ātmā is Itself (Ātma Svarūpī) or Pure Consciousness. At this point, the same Shakti, who had operated as Māyā, is Herself Consciousness (Chidrūpinī).

According to the Hindu books, plants have a sort of dormant Consciousness, and are capable of pleasure and pain. Chakrapāni says in the Bhānumatī that the Consciousness of plants is a kind of stupefied, darkened, or comatose Consciousness. Udayana also says that plants have a dormant Consciousness which is very dull. The differences between plant and animal life have always been regarded by the Hindus as being one not of kind, but of degree. And this principle may be applied throughout. Life and Consciousness is not a product of evolution. The latter merely manifests it. Manu speaks of plants as being creatures enveloped by darkness caused by past deeds having, however, an internal Consciousness and a capacity for pleasure and pain. And, in the Mahābhārata, Bhrigu says to Bharadhvāja that plants possess the various senses, for they are affected by heat, sounds, vision (whereby, for instance, the creeper pursues its path to the light), odours and the water which they taste. I may refer also to such stories as that of the Yāmalārjunavriksha of the Shrīmad Bhāgavata mentioned in Professor Brajendra Nath Seal's learned work on "The Positive Sciences of the Ancient Hindus", and Professor S. N. Das Gupta's scholarly paper on Parināma to which I am indebted for these instances.

Man is said to have passed through all lower states of Consciousness and is capable of reaching the highest through Yoga. The Jīva attains birth as man after having been, it is said, born 84 lakhs (84,00,000) of times as plants (Vrikshādi), aquatic animals (Jalayoni), insects and the like (Krimi), birds (Pakshi), beasts (Pashvādi), and monkeys (Bānara). He then is born 2 lakhs of times (2,00,000) in the inferior species of humanity, and then gradually attains a better and better birth until he is liberated from all the bonds of matter. The exact number of each kind of birth is in 20, 9, 11, 10, 30, and 4 lakhs, respectively—84 lakhs. As pointed out by Mahāmahopādhyāya Chandrakānta Tarkālaṅkāra Lectures on "Hindu Philosophy" (5th year, p. 227, Lecture VII), pre-appearance in monkey forms is not a Western theory only. The Consciousness which manifests in him is not altogether a new creation, but an unfolding of that which has ever existed in the elements of which he is composed, and in the Vegetable and Animal through which prior to his human birth he has passed. In him, however, matter is so re-arranged and organized as to permit of the fullest manifestation which has hitherto existed of the underlying Chit. Man's is the birth so "difficult of attainment" (Durlabha). This is an oft-repeated statement of Shāstra in order that he should avail himself of the opportunities which Evolution has brought him. If he does not, he falls back, and may do so without limit, into gross matter again, passing intermediately through the

Hells of suffering. Western writers in general describe such a descent as unscientific. How, they ask, can a man's Consciousness reside in an animal or plant? The correct answer (whatever be popular belief) is that it does not. When man sinks again into an animal he ceases to be a man. He does not continue to be both man and animal. His consciousness is an animal consciousness and not a human consciousness. It is a childish view which regards such a case as being the imprisonment of a man in an animal body. If he can go up he can also go down. The soul or subtle body is not a fixed but an evolving thing. Only Spirit (Chit) is eternal and unchanged. In man, the revealing constituent of Prakriti Shakti (Sattvaguna) commences to more fully develop, and his consciousness is fully aware of the objective world and his own Ego, and displays itself in all those functions of it which are called his faculties. We here reach the world of ideas, but these are a superstructure on consciousness and not its foundation or basis. Man's consciousness is still, however, veiled by Māyā-Shakti. With the greater predominance of Sattvaguna in man, consciousness becomes more and more divine, until he is altogether freed of the bonds of Māyā, and the Jīva Consciousness expands into the pure Brahman Consciousness. Thus life and Consciousness exist throughout. All is living. All is Consciousness. In the world of gross matter they seem to disappear, being almost suppressed by the veil of Māyā-Shakti's Tamoguna. As however ascent is made, they are less and less veiled, and True Consciousness is at length realized in Samādhi and Moksha. Chit-Shakti and Māyā-Shakti exist inseparable throughout the whole universe. There is therefore according to the principles of the Shākta Shāstra not a particle of matter which is without life and conciousness variously displayed or concealed though they be.

Manifest Māyā-Shakti is the universe in which Chit-Shakti is the changeless Spirit. Unmanifest Māyā-Shakti is Consciousness (Chidrūpinī). There are many persons who think that they have disposed of a doctrine when they have given it an opprobrious, or what they think to be an opprobrious, name. And so they dub all this "Animism", which the reader of Census Reports associates with primitive and savage tribes. There are some people who are frightened by names. It is not names but facts which should touch us. Certainly "Animism" is in some respects an incorrect and childlike way of putting the matter. It is, however, an imperfect presentment of a central truth which has been held by some of the profoundest thinkers in the world, even in an age which we are apt to think to be superior to all others. Primitive man in his simplicity made discovery of several such truths. And so it has been well said that the simple savage and the child who regard all existence as akin to their own, living and feeling like himself, have, notwithstanding their errors, more truly felt the pulse of being, than the civilized man of culture. How essentially stupid some of the latter can be needs no proof. For the process of civilization being one of abstraction, they are less removed from the concrete fact than he is. Hence their errors which seem the more contorted due to the mass of useless verbiage in which they are expressed. And yet, as extremes meet, so having passed through our present condition, we may regain the truths perceived by the simple, not only through formal worship but by that which consists of the pursuit of all knowledge and science, when once the husk of all material thinking is cast aside. For him who sees the Mother in all things, all scientific research is wonder and worship. So Gratry said that the *calculus* of Newton and Leibnitz was a supralogical procedure, and that geometric induction is essentially a *process of prayer*, by which he evidently meant an appeal from the finite mind to the Infinite, for light on finite concerns. The seeker looks upon not mere mechanical movements of so-called " dead " matter, but the wondrous play of Her Whose form all matter is. As She thus reveals Herself She induces in him a passionate exaltation and that sense of security which is only gained as approach is made to the Central Heart of things. For, as the Upanishad says, " He only fears who sees duality ". Some day may be, when one who unites in himself the scientific ardour of the West and the all-embracing religious feeling of India will create another and a modern Chandī, with its multiple salutations to the sovereign World-Mother (Namastasyai namo namah). Such an one, seeing the changing marvels of Her world-play, will exclaim with the Yoginīhridaya Tantra, " I salute Her the Samvid Kalā who shines in the form of Space, Time and all Objects therein."

Deshakālapadārthātma yad yad vastu yathā yathā,
Tattadrūpena yā bhāti tām shraye samvidam kalām.

This is, however, not mere Nature-worship as it is generally understood in the West, or the worship of Force as Keshub Chunder Sen took the Shākta doctrine to be. All things exist *in* the Supreme who in Itself infinitely transcends all finite forms. It is the worship of God as the Mother-Creatrix who manifests in the form of all things which are, as it were, but an atom of dust on the Feet of Her who is Infinite Being (Sat), Experience (Chit), Love (Ānanda) and Power (Shakti). As Philibert Commerson said : " La vie d'un naturaliste est, je L'ose dire, une adoration presque perpétuelle."

I have in my paper " Shakti and Māyā " (here reprinted from the Indian Philosophical Review, 1918, No. 2) contrasted the three different concepts of the Primal Energy as Prakriti, Māyā and Shakti of Sāṅkhya, Vedānta and the Āgama respectively. I will not, therefore, repeat myself but will only summarise conclusions here. In the first place, there are features common to all three concepts. Hitherto, greater pains have been taken to show the differences between the Darshanas than to co-ordinate them systematically, by regarding their points of agreement or as regard apparent disagreement, their view-point. It has been said that Truth cannot be found in such a country as India, in which, there are six systems of philosophy disputing with one another, and where, even in one system alone, there is a conflict between Dvaita, Vishishtādvaita and Advaita. One might suppose from such a criticism that all in Europe were of one mind, or that at least the Christian Community was agreed, instead of being split up, as it is, into hundreds of sects. An American humourist observed with truth that there was a good deal of human nature in man everywhere. Of course there is difference which, as the Radd-ul-Muhtar says, is also the gift of God. This is not to deny that Truth is only one. It is merely to recognize that whilst Truth is one, the nature and capacities of those who seek it, or claim to possess it, vary. To use a common metaphor, the same white light which passes through varicoloured glass takes on its various colours. All cannot apprehend the truth to the same extent or in the same way. Hence the sensible Indian doctrine of competency or Adhikāra. In the Christian Gospel it is also said, " Throw not your pearls before swine lest they trample upon them and then rend you." What can be given to any man is only what he can receive.

The Six Philosophies represent differing standards according to the manner and to the extent to which the one Truth may be apprehended. Each standard goes a step beyond the last, sharing, however, with it certain notions in common. As regards the present matter, all these systems start with the fact that there is Spirit and Mind-Matter,

Consciousness and Unconsciousness, apparent or real. Sāṅkhya, Vedānta and the Shākta Āgama called the first Purusha, Brahman, Shiva; and the second Prakriti, Māyā, Shakti respectively. All agree that it is from the association together of these two Principles that the universe arises and that such association is the universe. All, again, agree that one Principle, namely, the first, is infinite, formless consciousness, and the second is a *finitising* principle which makes forms. Thirdly, all regard this last as a veiling principle, that is, one which veils consciousness; and hold that it is eternal, all-pervading, existing now as seed (Mūlaprakriti, Avyakta) and now as fruit (Vikriti), composed of the Gunas Sattva, Rajas and Tamas (Principles of presentation of Consciousness, Action, and Veiling of Consciousness respectively); unperceivable except through its effects. In all, it is the Natural Principle the material cause of the material universe.

The word Prakriti has been said to be derived from the root "*Kri*", and the affix "*Ktin*", which is added to express Bhāva or the abstract idea, and sometimes the Karma or object of the action, corresponding with the Greek affix *Sis*. *Ktin* inflected in the nominative becomes *tis*. Prakriti, therefore, has been said to correspond with *Phusis* (Nature) of the Greeks. In all three systems, therefore, it is, as the "natural," contrasted with the "spiritual" aspect of things.

The first main point of difference is between Sāṅkhya, on the one hand, and the Advaita Vedānta, whether as interpreted by Shaṅkara or taught by the Shaiva-Shākta Tantra on the other. Classical Sāṅkhya is a dualistic system, whereas the other two are non-dualistic. The classical Sāṅkhya posits a plurality of Ātmans representing the formless consciousness, with one unconscious Prakriti which is formative activity. Prakriti is thus a real independent principle. Vedāntic monism does not altogether discard these two principles, but says that they cannot exist as two independent Realities. There is only one Brahman. The two categories of Sāṅkhya, Purusha and Prakriti are reduced to one Reality, the Brahman ; otherwise the Vākya, "All this is verily Brahman" (Sarvam khalvidam Brahma), is falsified.

But how is this effected? It is on this point that Māyāvāda of Shaṅkara and the Advaita of Shaiva-Shākta Āgama differ. Both systems agree that Brahman has two aspects in one of which It is transcendent and in another creative and immanent. According to Shaṅkara, Brahman is in one aspect Īshvara associated with, and in another one dissociated from Māyā which, in his system, occupies the place of the Sāṅkhyan Prakriti, to which it is (save as to reality and independence) similar. What is Māyā? It is not a real independent Principle like the Sāṅkhyan Prakriti. Then is it Brahman or not? According to Shaṅkara, it is an unthinkable, alogical, unexplainable (Anirvachanīya) mystery. It is an eternal falsity (Mithyā-bhūtā sanātanī), owing what false appearance of reality it possesses to the Brahman, with Which in one aspect it is associated. It is not real for there is only one such. It cannot, however, be said to be unreal for it is the cause of and is empirical experience. It is something which is neither real (Sat) nor unreal (Asat), nor partly real and partly unreal (Sadasat), and which though not forming part of Brahman, and therefore not Brahman, is yet, though not a second reality, inseparably associated and sheltering with .(Māyā brahmāshritā) Brahman in Its Īshvara aspect. Like the Sāṅkhyan Prakriti, Māyā (whatever it be) is in the nature of an unconscious principle. The universe appears by the reflection of consciousness (Purusha, Brahman) on unconsciousness (Prakriti, Māyā).

In this way the unconscious is made to appear conscious. This is Chidābhāsa.

Māyā is illusive and so is Shaṅkara's definition of it. Further, though Māyā is not a second reality, but a mysterious something of which neither reality nor unreality can be affirmed, the fact of positing it at all in this form gives to Shaṅkara's doctrine a tinge of dualism from which the Shākta doctrine is free. For, it is to be noted that notwithstanding that Māyā is a falsity, it is not, according to Shaṅkara, a mere negation or want of something (Abhāva), but a positive entity (Bhāvarūpam ajnānam), that is in the nature of a Power which veils (Āchchhādaka) consciousness, as Prakriti does in the case of Purusha. Shaṅkara's system, on the other hand, has this advantage from a monistic standpoint, that whilst he, like the Shākta, posits the doctrine of aspects saying that in one aspect the Brahman is associated with Māyā (Īshvara), and in another it is not (Parabrahman) ; yet in neither aspect does his Brahman change. Whereas, according to Shākta doctrine, Shiva does, in one aspect, that is as Shakti, change.

Whilst then Shaṅkara's teaching is consistent with the changelessness of Brahman, he is not so successful in establishing the saying, "All this is Brahman". The position is reversed as regards Shaiva-Shākta Darshana which puts forth its doctrine of Māyā-Shakti with greater simplicity. Shākta doctrine takes the saying, "All this is Brahman" (the realization of which, as the Mahānirvāna Tantra states, is the aim and end of Kulāchāra) in its literal sense. "This" is the universe. Then the universe is Brahman. But Brahman is Consciousness. Then the universe is really That. But in what way? Shaṅkara says that what we sense with our senses is Māyā, which is practically something, but in a real sense nothing; which yet appears to be something because it is associated with the Brahman which alone is Real. Its appearance of independent reality is thus borrowed and is in this sense said to be "illusory". When, therefore, we say, "All this is Brahman"—according to Shaṅkara, this means that what is at the back of that which we see is Brahman; the rest or appearance is Māyā. Again, according to Shaṅkara, man is spirit (Ātmā) vestured in the Māyik falsities of mind and matter. He, accordingly, can then only establish the unity of Īshvara and Jīva by eliminating from the first Māyā, and from the second Avidyā; when Brahman is left as a common denominator. The Shākta, however, eliminates nothing. For him, in the strictest sense, "All is Brahman". For him, man's spirit (Ātmā) is Shiva. His mind and body are Shakti. But Shiva and Shakti are one. Paramatmā is Shiva-Shakti in undistinguishable union. Jīvātmā is Shiva-Shakti in that state in which the Self is distinguished from the not-Self. Man, therefore, according to the Shākta Tantra, is not Spirit seemingly clothed by a non-Brahman falsity, but spirit covering Itself with its own power or Māyā-Shakti. All is Shakti whether as Chit-Shakti or Māyā-Shakti. When, therefore, the Shākta Tāntric says, "All this is Brahman", he means it literally. "This", here means Brahman as Shakti, as Māyā-Shakti, and Chit-Shakti.

Shiva as Parabrahman is Shiva-Shakti in that state when Shakti is not operating and in which She is Herself, that is, pure consciousness (Chidrūpiṇī). Shiva as Īshvara is Shiva-Shakti in that state in which Shiva, associated with Māyā-Shakti, is the source of movement and change; Shiva-Shakti as Jīva is the state produced by such action which is subject to Māyā, from which Īshvara, the Māyin is free. The creative Shakti is therefore changeless

Chit-Shakti and changing Māyā-Shakti. Yet the One Shakti must never be conceived as existing apart from, or without the other, for they are only twin aspects of the fundamental Substance (Paravastu). Vimarsha-Shakti (See Kāmakalāvilāsa, Vol. X, Tāntrik Texts, *Ed.* A. Avalon) as Māyā-Shakti produces the forms in which Spirit as Chit-Shakti inheres and which it illuminates (Prakāsha). But Māyā-Shakti is not unconscious. How can it be ; for it is Shakti and one with Chit-Shakti. All Shakti is and must be Consciousness. There is no unconscious Māyā which is not Brahman and yet not separate from Brahman. Brahman alone is and exists, whether as Chit or as manifestation of Māyā. All is Consciousness, as the so-called "New Thought" of the West also affirms.

But surely, it will be said, there is an unconscious element in things. How is this accounted for if there be no unconscious Māyā? It is conscious Shakti veiling Herself and so appearing as limited consciousness. In other words, whilst Shaṅkara says mind and matter are in themselves unconscious but appear to be conscious through Chidābhāsa ; the Shākta Āgama reverses the position, and says that they are in themselves, that is in their ground, conscious, for they are at base Chit ; but they yet appear to be unconscious, or more strictly limited consciousness, by the veiling power of Consciousness Itself as Māyā-Shakti. This being so, there is no need for Chidābhāsa which assumes, as it were, two things, the Brahman, and unconscious Māyā in which the former reflects itself. Though some of the Shāstras do speak of a reflection, Prativimba is between Shiva and Shakti. Brahman is Māyā-Shakti in that aspect in which it negates itself, for it is the function of Shakti to negate (Nishedhavyāpārarūpā shaktiḥ), as it is said by Yoga-Rāja or Yoga Muni (as he is also called) in his commentary on Abhinava Gupta's

Paramārthasāra. In the Shākta Tantras, it is a common saying of Shiva to Devī, "There is no difference between Me and Thee." Whilst Shaṅkara's Īshvara is associated with the unconscious Māyā, the Shaiva Shākta's Īshvara is never associated with anything but Himself, that is as Māyā-Shakti.

Whether this doctrine be accepted as the final solution of things or not, it is both great and powerful. It is great because the whole world is seen in glory according to the strictest monism as the manifestation of Him and Her. The mind is not distracted and kept from the realization of unity, by the notion of any unconscious Māyā which is not Brahman nor yet separate from It. Next, this doctrine accommodates itself to Western scientific monism, so far as the latter goes, adding to it however a religious and metaphysical basis; infusing it with the spirit of devotion. It is powerful because its standpoint is the 'here' and 'now', and not the transcendental *Siddhi* standpoint of which most men know nothing and cannot, outside Samādhi, realize. It assumes the reality of the world which to us is real. It allows the mind to work in its natural channel. It does not ask it to deny what goes against the grain of its constitution to deny. It is, again, powerful because we stand firmly planted on a basis which is real and natural to us. From the practical viewpoint, it does not ask man to eschew and flee from the world in the spirit of asceticism; a course repugnant to a large number of modern minds, not only because mere asceticism often involves what it thinks to be a futile self-denial; but because that mind is waking to the truth that all is one; that if so, to deny the world is in a sense to deny an aspect of That which is both Being and Becoming. It thinks also that whilst some natures are naturally ascetic, to attempt ascetic treatment in the case of most is to contort the natural being, and to intensify the very evils which asceticism seeks to avoid. Not one man in many thousands has true Vairāgya or detachment from the world. Most are thoroughly even glued to it. Again, there are many minds which are puzzled and confused by Māyāvāda; and which, therefore, falsely interpret it,—may be to their harm. These men, Māyāvāda, or rather their misunderstanding of it, weakens or destroys. Their grip on themselves and the world is in any case enfeebled. They become intellectual and moral derelicts who are neither on the path of power nor of renunciation, and who have neither the strength to follow worldly life, nor to truly abandon it. It is not necessary, however, to renounce when all is seen to be Her. And, when all is so seen, then the spiritual illumination which transfuses all thoughts and acts makes them noble and pure. It is impossible for a man, who in whatever sense truly sees God in all things, to err. If he does so, it is because his vision is not fully strong and pure; and to this extent scope is afforded to error. But given perfect spiritual eyesight then all "this" is pure. For, as the Greeks profoundly said, "panta kathara tois katharois", "To the pure all things are pure".

The Shākta doctrine is thus one which has not only grandeur but is greatly pragmatic and of excelling worth. It has always been to me a surprise that its value should not have been rightly appreciated. I can only suppose that its neglect is due to the fact that it is the doctrine of the Shākta Tantras. That fact has been enough to warrant its rejection, or at least a refusal to examine it. Like all practical doctrines, it is also intensely positive. There are none of those negations which weaken and which annoy those who, as the vital Western mind does, feel themselves to be strong and living in an atmosphere of might and power. For power is a glorious thing. What is wanted is only the sense that all Power is of God and is God, and that Bhāva or feeling which interprets all thoughts and acts and their objects in terms of the Divine, and which sees God in and as all things. Those who truly do so will exercise power not only without wrong, but with that compassion (Karunā) for all beings which is so beautiful a feature of the Buddha of northern and Tāntrik Buddhism. For in them Shakti Herself has descended. This is Shaktipāta, as it is technically called in the Tantra Shāstra ; the descent of Shakti which Western theology calls the grace of God. But grace is truly not some exterior thing, though we may pictorially think of it as 'streaming' from above below. Ātmā neither comes nor goes. To be in grace is that state in which man commences to realize himself as Shiva-Shakti. His power is, to use a Western phrase, "converted". It is turned from the husk of mere outwardness and of limited self-seeking, to that inner Reality which is the great Self Which, at base, he (in this doctrine) is.

The principles of Shākta doctrine which will vary according to race, are a regenerating doctrine, giving strength where there is weakness, and, where strength exists, directing it to right ends. "Shivo' ham", "I am Shiva", "Sā' ham", "I am She (the Devī)", the Tantras say. The Western may call It by some other name. Some call It this and some that, as the Veda says. "I am He", "I am She", "I am It", matters not to the Shākta so long as man identifies himself with the 'Oversoul', and thus harmonizes himself with its Being, with Dharmic actions (as it manifests in the world) and therefore necessarily with Its true ends. In its complete form the Shākta doctrine is monistic. But to those to whom monism makes no appeal, the Shākta will say that by adopting its spirit, so far as the forms of their belief and worship allow, they will experience a reflection of the joy and strength of those who truly live because they worship Her who is Eternal life—the Mother who is seated on the couch of Shivas (Mahāpreta), in the Isle of Gems (Manidvīpa), in the "Ocean of Nectar", which is all Being-Consciousness and Bliss.

This is the pearl which those who have churned the ocean of Tantra discover. That pearl is there in an Indian shell. There is a beautiful nacre on the inner shell which is the Mother of Pearl. Outside, the shell is naturally rough and coarse, and bears the accretions of weed and parasite and of things of all kind which exist, good or bad as we call them, in the ocean of existence (Samsāra). The Scripture leads man to remove these accretions, and to pass within through the crust, gross, though not on that account only, bad; for there is a gross (Sthūla) and subtle (Sūkshma) aspect of worship. Finally it leads man to seek to see the Mother of Pearl and lastly the Pearl which, enclosed therein, shines with the brilliant yet soft light which is that of the Moon-Chit (Chichchandra) Itself.

CHAPTER XVI

MATTER AND CONSCIOUSNESS[1]

THE subject of my lecture to-day is Consciousness or Chit, and Matter or Unconsciousness, that is, Achit; the unchanging formlessness and the changing forms. According to Shākta Advaitavāda, man is Consciousness-Unconsciousness or Chit-Achit; being Chit-Shakti as regards his Antarātmā, and the particularized Māyā-Shakti as to his material vehicles of mind and body. The reason that I have selected this subject, amongst the many others on which I might have addressed you, is that these two ideas are the key concepts of Indian Philosophy and religion. If they are fully understood both as to their definition and relations, then, all is understood so far as intellect can make such matters intelligible to us; if they are not understood then nothing is properly understood. Nor are they always understood even by those who profess to know and write on Indian Philosophy. Thus, the work on Vedānta, of an English Orientalist, now in its second edition, describes Chit as the condition of a stone or other inert substance. A more absurd error it is hard to imagine. Those who talk in this way have not learnt the elements

[1] Short Summary of Address delivered at the Dacca Sahitya Parishat, June 1916.

of their subject. It is true that you will find in the Shāstra, the state of the Yogī described as being like a log (Kāshtavat). But this does not mean that his Consciousness is that of a piece of wood: but that he no more perceives the external world than a log of wood does. He does not do so because he has the Samādhi consciousness that is Illumination and true Being itself.

I can to-night only scratch at the surface of a profound subject. To properly expound it would require a series of lectures, and to understand it in its depths, years of thinking thereon. I will look at the matter first from the scientific point of view; secondly, state what those concepts mean in themselves; and thirdly, show how they are related to one another in the Sāṅkhya and the Māyāvāda and Shaktivāda presentments of Vedānta doctrine. The Shaktivāda of which I deal to-night may be found in the Tantras. It has been supposed that the Āgamas arose at the close of the age of the Upanishads. They are Shāstras of the Upāsanā Kānda dealing with the worship of Saguna Īshvara. It has been conjectured that they arose partly because of the declining strength of the Vaidika Āchāra, and partly because of the increasing number of persons within the Hindu fold, who were not competent for the Vaidika Āchāra, and, for whom some spiritual discipline was necessary. One common feature distinguishes them; namely, their teaching is for all castes and all women. They express the liberal principle that whilst socially differences may exist, the path of religion is open to all, and that spiritual competency and not the external signs of caste determine the position of persons on that path. Īshvara in these Āgamas is worshipped in threefold forms as Vishnu, Shiva, Devī. Therefore, the Āgamas or Tantras are threefold, Vaishnava, Shaiva and Shākta, such as the Pancharātra Āgamas of the first group, the Shaiva Siddhānta (with its 28 Tantras), the

Nakulisha Pāshupata, and the Kashmirian Trika of the second group; and the alleged division into Kaula, Mishra, Sāmaya of the third group. I express no opinion on this last division. I merely refer to this matter in order to explain what I mean by the word Āgama. The Shaktivāda, however, which I contrast with Māyāvāda to-day, is taken from the Shākta Āgama. By Māyāvāda I mean Shaṅkara's exposition of Vedānta.

Now, with reference to the scientific aspect of the subject, I show you that in three main particulars, modern western physics and psychology support Indian philosophy whatever such support may be worth. Indeed, Mr. Lowes Dickinson, in an acute recent analysis of the state of ideas in India, China and Japan observes that the Indian form of religion and philosophy is that which most easily accommodates itself to modern western science. That does not prove it is true, until it is established that the conclusions of western science to which it does conform are true. But the fact is of great importance in countering those who have thought that eastern ideas were without rational foundation. It is of equal importance to those two classes who either believe in the ideas of India, or in the particular conclusions of science to which I refer. The three points on this head are firstly, that physicists, by increasing their knowledge of so-called "matter", have been led to doubt its reality, and have dematerialized the atom, and, with it, the entire universe which the various atoms compose. The trinity of matter, ether and electricity out of which science has hitherto attempted to construct the world, has been reduced to a single element—the ether (which is not scientific "matter") in a state of motion. According to Sāṅkhya, the objective world is composed of the Bhūtas which derive ultimately from Ākāsha. I do not say that scientific "ether" is Ākāsha, which is a concept belonging to a different train of thought. Moreover the sensible is derived from the supersensible Ākāsha Tanmātra, and is not therefore an ultimate. But it is important to note the agreement in this, that both in East and West, the various forms of gross matter derive from some single substance which is not "matter". Matter is *dematerialized*, and the way is made for the Indian concept of Māyā. There is a point at which the mind cannot any longer usefully work outward. Therefore, after the Tanmātra, the mind is turned within to discover their cause in that Egoism which, reaching forth to the world of enjoyment produces sensorium, senses, and objects of sensation. That the mind and senses are also material has the support of some forms of western philosophy, such as that of Herbert Spencer, for he holds that the Universe, whether physical or psychical, is a play of force which in the case of matter we experience as object. Mind as such is, he says, as much a "material" organ as the brain and outer sense-organs, though they are differing forms of Force. His affirmation that scientific "matter" is an appearance produced by the play of cosmic force, and that mind itself is a product of the same play, is what Sāṅkhya and Vedānta hold. The way again is opened for the concept, Māyā. Whilst, however, Spencer and the Agnostic School hold that the Reality behind these phenomena is unknowable, the Vedānta affirms that it is knowable and is Consciousness itself. This is the Self than which nothing can be more intimately known. Force is blind. We discover consciousness in the Universe. It is reasonable to suppose that if the first cause is of the nature of either Consciousness or Matter, and not of both, it must be of the nature of the former and not of the latter. Unconsciousness or object may be conceived to modify Consciousness, but not to produce Consciousness out of its unconscious Self. According to Indian ideas, Spirit which is the cause of the Universe is pure Consciousness. This is Nishkala Shiva: and, as the Creator, the great Mother or Devī. The existence of pure consciousness in the Indian sense has been decried by some thinkers in the West, where generally to its pragmatic eye, Consciousness is always particular having a particular direction and form. It assumes this particularity, however, through Māyā. We must distinguish between Consciousness as such and modes in consciousness. Consciousness is the unity behind all forms of consciousness, whether sensation, emotion, instinct, will or reason. The claim that Consciousness as such exists can only be verified by spiritual experience. All high mystic experiences, whether in East or West, have been experiences of unity in differing forms and degrees. Even, however, in normal life as well as in abnormal pathological states, we have occasional stretches of experience in which it becomes almost structureless. Secondly, the discovery of the subliminal Consciousness aids Shāstric doctrine, in so far as it shows that behind the surface consciousness of which we are ordinarily aware, there is yet another mysterious field in which all its operations grow. It is the Buddhi which here manifests. Well-established occult powers and phenomena now generally accepted such as telepathy, thought-reading, hypnotism and the like are only explainable on hypotheses which approach more nearly Eastern doctrine than any other theory which has in modern times prevailed in the West. Thirdly, as bearing on this subject, we have now the scientific recognition that from its *materia prima* all forms have evolved; that there is life or its potency in all things: and that there are no breaks in nature. There is the same matter and Consciousness throughout. There is unity of life. There is no such thing as "dead" matter. The well-known experiences of Dr. Jagadish Bose establish response to stimuli in inorganic matter. This response may be interpreted to indicate the existence of that Sattva Guna which Vedānta and Sāṅkhya affirm to exist in all things organic or inorganic. It is the play of Chit in this Sattva, so muffled in Tamas as not to be recognizable except by delicate scientific experiment, which appears as the so-called "mechanical" response. Consciousness is here veiled and imprisoned by Tamas. Inorganic matter displays it in the form of that seed or rudiment of sentiency which, enlarging into the simple pulses of feeling of the lowest degrees of organized life, at length emerges in the developed self-conscious sensations of human life. Consciousness is throughout the same. What varies is its wrappings. There is, thus, a progressive *release* of Consciousness from gross matter, through plants and animals to man. This evolution, Indian doctrine has taught in its 84 lakhs of previous births. According to the Hindu books, plants have a dormant consciousness. The Mahābhārata says that plants can see and thus they reach the light. Such power of vision would have been ridiculed not long ago, but, Professor Haberlandt, the well-known botanist, has established that plants possess an organ of vision in the shape of a convex lens on the upper surface of the leaf. The animal consciousness is greater, but seems to display itself almost entirely in the satisfaction of animal's wants. In man, we reach the world of ideas, but these are a superstructure on consciousness, and not its foundation or basis. It is in this modeless basis that the various modes of consciousness with which we are familiar in our waking and dreaming states arise.

The question then arises as to the relation of this principle of Form with Formlessness; the unconscious finite with infinite consciousness. It is noteworthy that in the Thomistic philosophy, Matter, like Prakriti, is the particularizing or *finitizing* principle. By their definition, however, they are opposed. How then can the two be one?

Sāṅkhya denies that they are one, and says they are two separate independent principles. This, Vedānta in its turn, denies for it says that there is in fact only one true Reality, though from the empirical, dualistic standpoint there seem to be two. The question then is asked, Is dualism, pluralism, or monism to be accepted? For the Vedāntist the answer of Shruti is that it is the last. But, apart from this, the question is, Does Shruti record a true experience, and is it the fact that spiritual experience is monistic or dualistic? The answer is, as we can see from history, that all high mystic experiences are experiences of unity in differing forms and degrees.

The question cannot be decided solely by discussion, but by our conclusion as to the conformity of the particular theory held with spiritual experience. But how can we reconcile the unity of pure consciousness with the plurality of unconscious forms which the world of experience gives us? Vedānta gives various intellectual interpretations, though experience alone can solve this question. Shaṅkara says there is only one Sadvastu, the Brahman. From a transcendental standpoint, It *is*, and nothing happens. There is, in the state of highest experience (Paramātma), no Īshvara, no creation, no world, no Jīva, no bondage, no liberation. But empirically he must and does admit the world or Māyā, which in its seed is the cosmic Saṅskāra, which is the cause of all these notions which from the highest state are rejected. But is it real or unreal? Shaṅkara says it is neither. It cannot be real, for then there would be two Reals. It is not unreal, for the world is an empirical fact—an experience of its kind, and it proceeds from the Power of Īshvara. In truth, it is unexplainable, and as Sāyana says, more wonderful than Chit itself.

But if it is neither Sat nor Asat, then as Māyā it is not the Brahman who is Sat. Does it then exist in Pralaya and if so how and where? How can unconsciousness exist in pure consciousness? Shaṅkara calls it eternal, and says that in Pralaya, Māyāsattā is Brahmasattā. At that time, Māyā, as the power of the ideating consciousness, and the world, its thought do not exist: and only the Brahman is. But if so how does the next universe arise on the assumption that there is Pralaya and that there is not with Him as Māyā the seed of the future universe? A Bīja of Māyā as Saṅskāra, even though Avyakta (not present to Consciousness), is yet by its terms different from consciousness. To all such questionings, Shaṅkara would say, they are themselves the product of the Māyā of the state in which they are put. This is true, but it is possible to put the matter in a simpler way against which there are not so many objections as may be laid against Māyāvāda.

It seems to me that Shaṅkara who combats Sāṅkhya is still much influenced by its notions, and as a result of his doctrine of Māyā he has laid himself open to the charge that his doctrine is not Shuddha Advaita. His notion of Māyā retains a trace of the Sāṅkhyan notion of separateness, though separateness is in fact denied. In Sāṅkhya, Māyā is the real Creatrix under the illumination of Purusha. We find similar notions in Shaṅkara, who compares Chit to the Ayaskāntamani, and denies all liberty of self-determination in the Brahman which, though itself unchanging, is the cause of change. Jnāna Kriyā is allowed only to Īshvara, a concept which is itself the product of Māyā. To some extent the distinctions made are perhaps a matter of words. To some extent particular notions of the Āgamas are more practical than those of Shaṅkara who was a transcendentalist.

The Āgama, giving the richest content to the Divine Consciousness, does not deny to it knowledge, but, in its supreme aspect, any dual knowledge; spiritual experience being likened by the Brihadāranyaka Upanishad to the union of man and wife in which duality exists as one and there is neither within nor without. It is this union which is the Divine Līlā of Shakti, Who is yet all the time one with Her Lord.

The Shākta exposition appears to be both simple and clear. I can only sketch it roughly—having no time for its detail. It is first the purest Advaitavāda. What then does it say? It starts with the Shruti, "Sarvam Khalvidam Brahma". Sarvam = world; Brahman = consciousness or Sachchidānanda; therefore this world is in itself Consciousness.

But we know we are not perfect consciousness. There is an apparent unconsciousness. How then is this explained? The unmanifested Brahman, before all the worlds, is Nirguna Shiva—the Blissful undual consciousness. This is the static aspect of Shiva. This manifests Shakti which is the kinetic aspect of Brahman. Shakti and Shaktimān are one; therefore, Shiva manifests as Shiva-Shakti, Who are one and the same. Therefore Shakti is consciousness.

But Shakti has two aspects (Mūrtti), *viz.*, Vidyā Shakti or Chit-Shakti, and Avidyā Shakti or Māyā-Shakti. Both as Shakti (which is the same as Shaktimān) are in themselves conscious. But the difference is that whilst Chit-Shakti is illuminating consciousness, Māyā is a Shakti which veils consciousness to itself, and by its wondrous power appears as unconscious. This Māyā-Shakti is Consciousness which by its power appears as unconsciousness. This Māyā-Shakti is Triguna Shakti, that is, Shakti composed of the three Gunas. This is Kāmakālā which is the Trigunātmakavibhūti. These Gunas are therefore at base nothing but Chit-Shakti. There is no necessity for the Māyāvādin's Chidābhāsa, that is, the reflection of conscious reality on unconscious unreality, as Māyāvāda says. All is real except, in the sense that some things endure and are therefore truly real: others pass and in that sense only are not real. All is Brahman. The Antarātmā in man is the enduring Chit-Shakti. His apparently unconscious vehicles of mind and body are Brahman as Māyā-Shakti, that is, consciousness appearing as unconsciousness by virtue of its inscrutable power. Īshvara is thus the name for Brahman as Shakti which is conjoined Chit-Shakti and Māyā-Shakti.

The Mother Devī is Īshvara considered in His feminine aspect (Īshvarī) as the Mother and Nourisher of the world. The Jīva or individual self is an Amsha or fragment of that great Shakti: the difference being that whilst Īshvara is Māyāvin or the controller of Māyā, Jīva is subject to Māyā. The World-thinker retains His Supreme undual Consciousness even in creation, but His thought, that is the forms created by His thinking are bound by His Māyā, that is the forms with which they identify themselves until by the power of the Vidyā Shakti in them they are liberated. All is truly Sat—or Brahman. In creation Shiva extends His power, and at Pralaya withdraws it into Himself. In creation, Māyā is in itself Consciousness which appears as unconsciousness. Before creation it is as consciousness.

Important practical results follow from the adoption of this view of looking at the world. The latter is the creation of Īshvara. The world is real; being unreal only in the sense that it is a shifting passing thing, whereas Ātma as the true Reality endures. Bondage is real, for Bondage is Avidyāshakti binding consciousness. Liberation is real for this is the grace of Vidyāshakti. Men are each Centres of Power, and if they would achieve success must, according to this Shāstra, realize themselves as such, knowing that it is Devaṭā which thinks and acts in, and as, them and that they are the Devatā. Their world enjoyment is His, and liberation is His peaceful nature. The Āgamas deal with the development of this Power which is not to be thought of as something without, but as within man's grasp through various forms of Shakti Sādhanā. Being in the world and working through the world, the world itself, in the words of the Kulārnava Tantra, *becomes the seat of liberation* (Mokshāyate Samsāra). The Vīra or heroic Sādhaka does not shun the world from fear of it. But he holds it in his grasp and wrests from it its secret. Realizing it at length as Consciousness the world of matter ceases to be an object of desire. Escaping from the unconscious drifting of a humanity which has not yet realized itself, He is the illumined master of himself, whether developing all his powers, or seeking liberation at his will.

[As M. Masson-Oursel so well puts it (Esquisse dune histoire de la philosophie indienne, p. 257) " Dans le tantrisme triomphent une conception immanentiste de l'intelligibilité, L'esprit s'assigne pour but, non de se laisser vivre mais de se créer une vie digne de lui, une existence omnisciente omnipotente, qu'il maitrisera parce qu'il en sera auteur " (by Sādhanā).]

CHAPTER XVII

SHAKTI AND MĀYĀ

In the Eighth Chapter of the unpublished Sammohana Tantra, it is said that Shaṅkara manifested on earth in the form of Shaṅkarāchāryya, in order to root out Buddhism from India. It compares his disciples and himself to the five Mahāpreta (who form the couch on which the Mother of the Worlds rests), and identifies his Maths with the Āmnāyas, namely, the Govardhana in Puri with Purvāmnāya (the Sampradāya being Bhogavāra), and so on with the rest. Whatever be the claims of Shaṅkara as destroyer of the great Buddhistic heresy, which owing to its subtlety was the most dangerous antagonist which the Vedānta has ever had, or his claims as expounder of Upanishad from the standpoint of Siddhi, his Māyāvāda finds no place in the Tantras of the Āgamas, for the doctrine and practice is given from the standpoint of Sādhanā. This is not to say that the doctrine is explicitly denied. It is not considered. It is true that in actual fact we often give accommodation to differing theories for which logic can find no living room, but it is obvious that in so far as man is a worshipper he must accept the world-standpoint, if he would not, like Kālīdāsa, cut from beneath himself the branch of the tree on which he sits. Next, it would be a mistake to overlook the possibility of the so-called "Tāntrik" tradition having been fed by ways of thought and practice which were not, in the strict sense of the term, part of the Vaidik cult, or in the line of its descent. The worship of the Great Mother, the Magna Mater of the Near East, the Ādyā Shakti of the Shākta Tantras, is in its essentials (as I have elsewhere pointed out) one of the oldest and most widespread religions of the world, and one which in India was possibly, in its origins, independent of the Brāhmanic religion as presented to us in the Vaidik Saṃhitas and Brāhmanas. If this be so, it was later on undoubtedly mingled with the Vedānta tradition, so that the Shākta faith of to-day is a particular presentation of the general Vedāntik teaching. This is historical speculation from an outside standpoint. As the Sarvollāsa of Sarvānandanātha points out, and as is well-known to all adherents of the Shākta Āgamas, Veda in its general sense includes these and other Shāstras in what is called the great Shatakoti Saṃhitā. Whatever be the origins of the doctrine (and this should not be altogether overlooked in any proper appreciation of it), I am here concerned with its philosophical aspect, as shown to us to-day in the teachings and practice of the Shāktas who are followers of the Āgama. This teaching occupies in some sense a middle place between the dualism of the Sāṅkhya, and Shaṅkara's ultra-monistic interpretation of Vedānta to which, unless otherwise stated, I refer. Both the Shaiva and Shākta schools accept the threefold aspect of the Supreme known as Prakāsha, Vimarsha, Prakāsha-Vimarsha; called in Tāntrik worship, "The Three Feet" (Charana-tritaya). Both adopt the Thirty-six Tattvas, Shiva, Shakti, Sadāshiva, Īshvara and Shuddhavidyā, preceding the Purusha-Prakriti Tattvas with which the Sāṅkhya commences. For whereas these are the ultimate Tattvas in that Philosophy, the Shaiva and Shākta schools claim to show how Purusha and Prakriti are themselves derived from higher Tattvas. These latter Tattvas are also dealt with from the Shabda side as Shakti, Nāda, Bindu and as Kalās which are the Kriyā of the various grades of Tattvas which are aspects of Shakti. The Shākta Tantras, such as the Saubhāgyaratnākara and other works, speak of ninety-four of such Kalās appropriate to Sadāshiva, Īshvara, Rudra, Vishnu, and Brahmā, "Sun," "Moon," and "Fire," (indicated in the form of the Ram Bīja with Chandrabindu transposed) of which fifty-one are Mātrikā Kalās, being the subtle aspects of the gross letters of the Sanskrit alphabet. This last is the Mīmāmsaka doctrine of Shabda adopted to the doctrine of Shakti. Common also to both Shākta and Shaiva Sampradāyas is the doctrine of the Shadadhvā. (See my "Garland of Letters".)

I am not however here concerned with these details, but with the general concept of Shakti which is their underlying basis. It is sufficient to say that Shākta doctrine is a form of Advaitavāda. In reply to the question what is "silent concealment" (Goptavyam), it is said: Ātmāhambhāva-bhāvanayā bhāvayitavyam ityarthah. Hitherto greater pains have been taken to show the differences between the Darshanas than, by regarding their points of agreement, to co-ordinate them systematically. So far as the subject of the present article is concerned, all three systems, Sāṅkhya, Māyāvāda, Shaktivāda, are in general agreement as to the nature of the infinite formless Consciousness, and posit therewith a finitizing principle called Prakriti, Māyā, and Shakti respectively. The main points on which Sāṅkhya (at any rate in what has been called its classical form) differs from Māyāvāda Vedanta are in its two doctrines of the plurality of Ātmans on the one hand, and the reality and independence of Prakriti on the other. When however we examine these two Sāṅkhya doctrines closely we find them to be mere accommodations to the infirmity of common thought. A Vedāntic conclusion is concealed within its dualistic presentment. For if each liberated (Mukta) Purusha is all-pervading (Vibhu), and if there is not the slightest difference between one and another, what is the actual or practical difference between such pluralism and the doctrine of Ātma? Again it is difficult for the ordinary mind to conceive that objects cease to exist when consciousness of objects ceases. The mind naturally conceives of their existing for others, although, according to the hypothesis, it has no right to conceive anything at all. But here again what do we find? In liberation Prakriti ceases to exist for the Mukta Purusha. In effect what is this but to say with Vedānta that Māyā is not a real independent category (Padārtha)?

A critic has taken exception to my statement that the classical Sāṅkhya conceals a Vedāntic solution behind its dualistic presentment. I was not then, of course, speaking from historical standpoint. Shiva in the Kulārnava Tantra says that the Six Philosophies are parts of His body, and he who severs them severs His body. They are each aspects of the Cosmic Mind as appearing in Humanity. The logical process which they manifest is one and continuous. The conclusions of each stage or standard can be shown to yield the material of that which follows. This is a logical necessity if it be assumed that the Vedānta is the truest and highest expression of that of which the lower dualistic and pluralistic stages are the approach.

In Sāṅkhya, the Purusha principle represents the formless consciousness, and Prakriti formative activity. Shaṅkara, defining Reality as that which exists as the same in all the three times, does not altogether discard these two principles, but says that they cannot exist as two independent Realities. He thus reduces the two categories of Sāṅkhya, the Purusha Consciousness and Prakriti

Unconsciousness to one Reality, the Brahman; otherwise the Vākya, "All is Brahman" (Sarvam khalvidam Brahma) is falsified. Brahman, however, in one aspect is dissociated from, and in another associated with Māyā, which in his system takes the place of the Sāṅkhyan Prakriti. But, whereas, Prakriti is an independent Reality, Māyā is something which is neither real (Sat) nor unreal (Asat) nor partly real and partly unreal (Sadasat), and which though not forming part of Brahman, and therefore not Brahman, is yet, though not a second reality, inseparably associated and sheltering with, Brahman (Māyā Brahmāshrita) in one of its aspects: owing what false appearance of reality it has, to the Brahman with which it is so associated. It is an Eternal Falsity (Mithyābhutā sanātanī), unthinkable, alogical, unexplainable (Anirvachanīya). In other points, the Vedāntic Māyā and Sāṅkhyan Prakriti agree. Though Māyā is not a second reality, but a mysterious something of which neither reality nor unreality can be affirmed, the fact of positing it at all gives to Shaṅkara's doctrine a tinge of dualism from which the Shākta theory is free. According to Sāṅkhya, Prakriti is real although it changes. This question of reality is one of definition. Both Mūlaprakriti and Māyā are eternal. The world, though a changing thing, has at least empirical reality in either view. Both are unconsciousness. Consciousness is reflected on or in unconsciousness: that is to state one view for, as is known, there is a difference of opinion. The light of Purusha-Consciousness (Chit) is thrown on the Prakriti-Unconsciousness (Achit) in the form of Buddhi. Vijnānabhikshu speaks of a mutual reflection. The Vedāntic Prativimbavādins say that Ātmā is reflected in Antahkarana, and the apparent likeness of the latter to Chit which is produced by such reflection is Chidābhāsa or Jīva. This question of Chidābhāsa is one of the main points of difference between Māyāvāda and Shaktivāda. Notwithstanding that Māyā is a falsity, it is not, according to Shaṅkara, a mere negation or want of something (Abhāva), but a positive entity (Bhāvarūpamajānam): that is, it is in the nature of a power which veils (Āchchhādaka) consciousness, as Prakriti does in the case of Purusha. The nature of the great "Unexplained" as it is in Itself, and whether we call it Prakriti or Māyā, is unknown. The Yoginīhridaya Tantra beautifully says that we speak of the Heart of Yoginī who is Knower of Herself (Yoginī svavid), because the heart is the place whence all things issue. "What man", it says, "knows the heart of a woman? Only Shiva knows the Heart of Yoginī." But from Shruti and its effects it is said to be one, all-pervading, eternal, existing now as seed and now as fruit, unconscious, composed of Gunas (Gunamayī); unperceivable except through its effects, evolving (Parināmī) these effects which are its products; that is the world, which however assumes in each system the character of the alleged cause; that is, in Sāṅkhya the effects are real: in Vedānta, neither real nor unreal. The forms psychic or physical arise in both cases as conscious-unconscious (Sadasat) effects, from the association of Consciousness (Purusha or Īshvara) with Unconsciousness (Prakriti or Māyā), *Mīyate anena iti Māyā.* Māyā is that by which forms are measured or limited. This too is the function of Prakriti. Māyā, as the collective name of eternal ignorance (Ajnāna), produces, as the Prapañchashakti, these forms, by first veiling (Avaranashakti) Consciousness in ignorance and then projecting these forms (Vikshepashakti) from the store of the cosmic Samskāras. But what is the Tamas Guna of the Sāṅkhyan Prakriti in effect but pure Avidyā? Sattva is the tendency to reflect consciousness and therefore to reduce unconsciousness. Rajas is the activity (Kriyā) which moves

Prakriti or Māyā to manifest in its Tāmasik and Sāttvik aspect. Avidyā means "na vidyate," "is not seen," and therefore is not experienced. Chit in association with Avidyā does not see Itself as such. The first experience of the Soul reawakening after dissolution to world experience is, "There is nothing", until the Samskāras arise from out this massive Ignorance. In short, Prakriti and Māyā are like the *materia prima* of the Thomistic philosophy, the *finitizing* principle; the activity which "measures out" (Mīyate), that is limits and *makes forms* in the *formless* (Chit). The devotee Kamalākānta lucidly and concisely calls Māyā, the form of the Formless (Shūnyasya ākāra iti Māyā).

In one respect, Māyāvāda is a more consistent presentation of Advaitavāda, than the Shākta doctrine to which we now proceed. For whilst Shaṅkara's system, like all others, posits the doctrine of aspects, saying that in one aspect the Brahman is associated with Māyā (Īshvara), and that in another it is not (Parabrahman); yet in neither aspect does his Brahman truly change. In Shākta doctrine, Shiva does in one aspect (Shakti) change. Brahman is changeless and yet changes. But as change is only experienced by Jīvātmā subject to Māyā, there is not perhaps substantial difference between such a statement, and that which affirms changelessness and only seeming change. In other respects, however, to which I now proceed, Shākta doctrine is a more monistic presentation of Advaitavāda. If one were asked its most essential characteristic, the reply should be, the absence of the concept of unconscious Māyā as taught by Shaṅkara. Shruti says, "All is Brahman." Brahman is Consciousness: and therefore all is consciousness. There is no second thing called Māyā which is not Brahman even though it be "not real", "not unreal"; a definition obviously given to avoid the imputation of having posited a second Real. To speak of Brahman, and

Māyā which is not Brahman is to speak of two categories, however much it may be sought to explain away the second by saying that it is "not real" and "not unreal"; a falsity which is yet eternal and so forth. Like a certain type of modern Western "New Thought", Shākta doctrine affirms, "all is consciousness", however much unconsciousness appears in it. The Kaulāchāryya Sadānanda says in his commentary on the 4th Mantra Īsha Upanishad (*Ed.* A. Avalon): "The changeless Brahman, which is consciousness appears in creation as Māyā which is Brahman, (Brahmamayī), consciousness (Chidrūpinī) holding in Herself unbeginning (Anādi) Karmik tendencies (Karmasamskāra) in the form of the three Gunas. Hence, She is Gunamayī, despite being Chinmayī. As there is no second principle these Gunas are Chit-Shakti." The Supreme Devī is thus Prakāshavimarshasāmarasyarūpinī, or the union of Prakāsha and Vimarsha.

According to Shaṅkara, man is Spirit (Ātmā) vestured in the Māyik 'falsities' of mind and matter. He, accordingly, can only establish the unity of Īshvara and Jīva by eliminating from the first Māyā, and from the second Avidyā; when Brahman is left as common denominator. The Shākta eliminates nothing. Man's spirit or Ātmā is Shiva, His mind and body are Shakti. Shakti and Shiva are one. The Jīvātmā is Shiva-Shakti. So is the Paramātmā. This latter exists as one: the former as the manifold. Man is then not a Spirit covered by a non-Brahman falsity, but Spirit covering Itself with Its own power or Shakti.

What then is Shakti, and how does it come about that there is some principle of unconsciousness in things, a fact which cannot be denied. Shakti comes from the root "*shak*", "to be able," "to have power". It may be applied to any form of activity. The power to see is visual Shakti, the power to burn is Shakti of fire, and so forth. These are all forms of activity which are ultimately reducible to the Primordial Shakti (Ādyā Shakti) whence every other form of Power proceeds. She is called Yoginī because of Her connection with all things as their origin. It is this Original Power which is known in worship as Devī or Mother of Many Names. Those who worship the Mother, worship nothing "illusory" or unconscious, but a Supreme Consciousness, whose body is all forms of consciousness-unconsciousness produced by Her as Shiva's power. Philosophically, the Mother or Daivashakti is the kinetic aspect of the Brahman. All three systems recognize that there is a static and kinetic aspect of things: Purusha, Brahman, Shiva on the one side, Prakriti, Māyā, Shakti on the other. This is the time-honoured attempt to reconcile the doctrine of a changeless Spirit, a changing Manifold, and the mysterious unity of the two. For Power (Shakti) and the possessor of the Power (Shaktimān) are one and the same. In the Tantras, Shiva constantly says to Devī, "There is no difference between Thee and Me." We say that the fire burns, but burning *is* fire. Fire is not one thing and burning another. In the supreme transcendental changeless state, Shiva and Shakti are one, for Shiva is never without Shakti. The connection is called Avinābhāvasambandha. Consciousness is never without its Power. Power is active Brahman or Consciousness. But, as there is then no activity, they exist in the supreme state as one Tattva (Ekam tattvam iva); Shiva as Chit, Shakti as Chidrūpinī. This is the state before the thrill of Nāda, the origin of all those currents of force which are the universe. According to Shankara, the Supreme Experience contains no trace or seed of objectivity whatever. In terms of speech, it is an abstract consciousness (Jnāna). According to the view here expressed, which has been profoundly elaborated by the Kashmir Shiva School, that which appears "without" only so appears because it, in some form or other, exists "within". So also the Shākta Vishvasāra Tantra says, "what is here is there, what is not here is nowhere." If therefore we know duality, it must be because the potentiality of it exists in that from which it arises. The Shaivashākta school thus assumes a real derivation of the universe and a causal nexus between Brahman and the world. According to Shaṅkara, this notion of creation is itself Māyā, and there is no need to find a cause for it. So it is held that the supreme experience (Āmarsha) is by the Self (Shiva) of Himself as Shakti, who as such is the Ideal or Perfect Universe; not in the sense of a perfected world of form, but that ultimate formless feeling (Bhāva) of Bliss (Ānanda) or Love which at root the whole world is. All is Love and by Love all is attained. The Shākta Tantras compare the state immediately prior to creation with that of a grain of gram (Chanaka) wherein the two seeds (Shiva and Shakti) are held as one under a single sheath. There is, as it were, a Maithuna in this unity of dual aspect, the thrill of which is Nāda, productive of the seed or Bindu from which the universe is born. When the sheath breaks and the seeds are pushed apart, the beginning of a dichotomy is established in the one consciousness, whereby, the "I", and the "This" (Idam or Universe) appear as separate. The specific Shiva aspect is, when viewed through Māyā, the Self, and the Shakti aspect the Not-Self. This is to the limited consciousness only. In truth the two Shiva and Shakti are ever one and the same, and never dissociated. Thus each of the Bindus of the Kāmakalā are Shiva-Shakti appearing as Purusha-Prakriti. At this point, Shakti assumes several forms, of which the two chief are Chit-Shakti or Chit as Shakti, and Māyā-Shakti or Māyā as Shakti. Māyā is not here a mysterious unconsciousness, a non-Brahman, non-real, non-unreal something. It is a form of Shakti, and Shakti is Shiva who is Consciousness which is real. Therefore Māyā Shakti is in itself (Svarūpa) Consciousness and Brahman. Being Brahman It is real. It is that aspect of conscious power which conceals Itself to Itself. "By veiling the own true form (Svarūpa = Consciousness), its Shaktis always arise", (Svarūpāvarane chāsya shaktayah satatotthitāh) as the Spandakārika says. This is a common principle in all doctrine relating to Shakti. Indeed, this theory of veiling, though expressed in another form, is common to Sāṅkhya and Vedānta. The difference lies in this that in Sāṅkhya it is a second, independent Principle which veils; in Māyāvāda Vedānta it is the non-Brahman Māyā (called a Shakti of Īshvara) which veils; and in Shākta Advaitavāda (for the Shāktas are nondualists) it is Consciousness which, without ceasing to be such, yet veils Itself. As already stated, the Monistic Shaivas and Shāktas hold certain doctrines in common such as the thirty-six Tattvas, and what are called Shadadhvā which also appear as part of the teaching of the other Shaiva Schools. In the thirty-six Tattva scheme, Māyā which is defined as "the sense of difference" (Bhedabuddhi), for it is that which makes the Self see things as different from the Self, is technically that Tattva which appears at the close of the pure creation, that is, after Shuddhavidyā. This Māyā reflects and limits in the Pashu or Jīva, the Ichchhā, Jnāna, Kriyā Shaktis of Īshvara. These again are the three Bindus which are "Moon", "Fire", and "Sun". (See Author's "Garland of Letters".) What are Jnāna and Kriyā (including Ichchhā its preliminary) on the part of the Pati (Lord) in all beings and things (Bhāveshu) which are His body: it is these two which, with Māyā as the third, are the Sattva, Rajas and Tamas Gunas of the Pashu. This veiling power explains how the undeniable element of unconsciousness which is seen in things exists. How, if all be consciousness, is that principle there? The answer is given in the luminous definition of Shakti; "*It is the function of Shakti to negate*" (Nishedhavyāpārarūpā shaktih), that is, to negate consciousness and make it appear to Itself as unconscious (Kārikā 4 of Yogarāja or Yogamuni's Commentary on Abhinava Gupta's Paramārthasāra). In truth the whole world is the Self whether as "I" (Aham) or "This" (Idam). The Self thus becomes its own object. It becomes object or form that it may enjoy dualistic experience. It yet remains what it was in its unitary blissful experience. This is the Eternal Play in which the Self hides and seeks itself. The formless cannot assume form unless formlessness is negated. Eternity is negated into finality; the all-pervading into the limited; the all-knowing into the "little knower"; the almighty into the "little doer", and so forth. It is only by negating Itself to Itself that the Self becomes its own object in the form of the universe.

It follows from the above that, to the Shākta worshipper, there is no unconscious Māyā in Shaṅkara's sense, and therefore there is no Chidābhāsa, in the sense of the reflection of consciousness on unconsciousness, giving the latter the appearance of consciousness which it does not truly possess. For all is Consciousness as Shakti. "Aham Strī", as the Advaitabhāvopanishad exclaims. In short, Shaṅkara says there is one Reality or Consciousness and a not-real not-unreal Unconsciousness. What is really unconscious appears to be conscious by the reflection of the light of Consciousness upon it. Shākta doctrine says consciousness appears to be unconscious, or more truly, to have an element of unconsciousness in it (for nothing even empirically is absolutely unconscious), owing to the veiling play of Consciousness Itself as Shakti.

As with so many other matters, these apparent differences are to some extent a matter of words. It is true that the Vedāntists speak of the conscious (Chetana) and unconscious (Achetana), but they, like the Shākta Advaitins, say that the thing in itself is Consciousness. When this is vividly displayed by reason of the reflection (Prativimbha) of consciousness in Tattva, (such as Buddhi), capable of displaying this reflection, then we can call that in which it is so displayed, conscious. Where, though consciousness is all-pervading, Chaitanya is not so displayed, there we speak of unconsciousness. Thus, gross matter (Bhūta) does not appear to reflect Chit, and so appears to us as unconscious. Though all things are at base consciousness, some appear as more, and some as less conscious. Shaṅkara explains this by saying that Chaitanya is associated with a non-conscious mystery or Māyā which veils consciousness, and Chaitanya gives to what is unconscious the appearance of consciousness through reflection. "Reflection" is a form of pictorial thinking. What is meant is that two principles are associated together without the nature (Svarūpa) of either being really affected, and yet producing that effect which is Jīva. Shākta doctrine says that all is consciousness, but this same consciousness assumes the appearance of changing degrees of unconsciousness, not through the operation of anything other than itself (Māyā), but by the operation of one of its own powers (Māyāshakti). It is not unconscious Māyā in Shaṅkara's sense which veils consciousness, but Consciousness as Shakti veils Itself, and, as so functioning, it is called Māyāshakti. It may be asked how can Consciousness become Unconsciousness and cease to be itself? The answer is that it does not. It never ceases to be Consciousness. It appears to itself, as Jīva, to be unconscious, and even then not wholly: for as recent scientific investigations have shown, even so-called "brute matter" exhibits the elements of that which, when evolved in man, is self-consciousness. If it be asked how consciousness can obscure itself partially or at all, the only answer is Achintyā Shakti, which Māyāvādins as all other Vedāntists admit. Of this, as of all ultimates, we must say with the Western Scholastics, "omnia exeunt in mysterium".

Prakriti is then, according to Sāṅkhya, a real independent category different from Purusha. This both Māyāvāda and Shaktivāda deny. Māyā is a not real, not-unreal Mystery dependent on, and associated with, and inhering in Brahman; but not Brahman or any part of Brahman. Māyā-Shakti is a power of, and, in its Svarūpa, not different from Shiva: is real, and is an aspect of Brahman itself. Whilst Brahman as Īshvara is associated with Māyā, Shiva is never associated with anything but Himself. But the function of all three is the same, namely to make forms in the formless. It is That by which the Īshvara or Collective Consciousness pictures the universe for the individual Jīva's experience. Shakti is threefold as Will (Ichchhā) Knowledge (Jnāna), and Action (Kriyā). All three are but differing aspects of the one Shakti. Consciousness and its power or action are at base the same. It is true that action is manifested in matter, that is apparent unconsciousness, but its root, as that of all else, is consciousness. Jnāna is self-proved and experienced (Svatah-siddha), whereas, Kriyā, being inherent in bodies, is perceived by others than by ourselves. The characteristic of action is the manifestation of all objects. These objects, again, characterized by consciousness-unconsciousness are in the nature of a shining forth (Ābhāsa) of Consciousness. (Here Ābhāsa is not used in its sense of Chidābhāsa, but as an intensive form of the term Bhāsa.) The power of activity and knowledge are only differing aspects of one and the same Consciousness. According to Shaṅkara, Brahman has no form of self-determination. Kriyā is a function of unconscious Māyā. When Īshvara is said to be a doer (Kartā), this is attributed (Aupādhika) to Him by ignorance only. It follows from the above that there are other material differences between Shākta doctrine and Māyāvāda, such as the nature of the Supreme Experience, the reality and mode of creation, the reality of the world, and so forth. The world, it is true, is not, as the Mahānirvāna Tantra says, absolute reality in the sense of unchanging being, for it comes and goes. It is nevertheless real, for it is the experience of Shiva, and Shiva's experience is not unreal. Thus again the evolution of the world as Ābhāsa, whilst resembling the Vivarta of Māyāvāda, differs from it in holding, as the Sāṅkhya does, that the effect is real and not unreal, as Shaṅkara contends. To treat of these and other matters would carry me beyond the scope of this essay which only deals, and that in a summary way, with the essential differences and similarities in the concepts Prakriti, Māyā and Shakti.

I may however conclude with a few general remarks. The doctrine of Shakti is a profound one, and I think likely to be attractive to Western minds when they have grasped it, just as they will appreciate the Tāntrik watchword, Kriya or action, its doctrine of progress with and through the world and not against it, which is involved in its liberation-enjoyment (Bhukti-mukti) theory and other matters. The philosophy is, in any case, not, as an American writer, in his ignorance, absurdly called it, "worthless," "religious Feminism run mad," and a "feminization of Vedānta for suffragette Monists". It is not a "feminization" of anything, but a distinctive, original and practical doctrine worthy of a careful study. The Western student will find much in it which is more acceptable to generally prevalent thought in Europe and America—than in the "illusion" doctrine (in itself an unsuitable term), and the ascetic practice of the Vedāntins of Shaṅkara's school. This is not to say that ways of reconciliation may not be found by those who go far enough. It would not be difficult to show ground for holding that ultimately the same intellectual results are attained by viewing the matter from the differing standpoints of Sādhanā and Siddhi.

The writer of an interesting article on the same subject in the Prabuddha Bhārata (August 1916) states that the Sannyāsī Totapurī, the Guru of Shrī Rāmakrishna, maintained that a (Māyāvādin) Vedāntist could not believe in Shakti, for if causality itself be unreal there is no need to admit any power to cause, and that it is Māyā to apply the principle of causation and to say that everything comes from Shakti. The Sannyāsī was converted to Shākta doctrine after all. For as the writer well says, it is not merely by intellectual denial, but by *living* beyond the "unreal", that the Real is found. He, however, goes on to say, "the Shaktivāda of Tantra is not an improvement on the Māyāvāda of Vedānta, (that is the doctrine of Shaṅkara) but only its symbolization through the chromatics of sentiment and concept." It is true that it is a form of Vedānta, for all which is truly Indian must be that. It is also a fact that the Āgama as a Shastra of worship is full of Symbolism. Intellectually, however, it is an original presentment of Vedānta, and from the practical point of view, it has some points of merit which Māyāvāda does not possess. Varieties of teaching may be different presentations of one truth leading to a similar end. But one set of "chromatics" may be more fruitful than another for the mass of men. It is in this that the strength of the Shākta doctrine and practice lies. Moreover (whether they be an improvement or not) there are differences between the two. Thus the followers of Shaṅkara do not, so far as I am aware, accept the thirty-six Tattvas. A question, however, which calls for enquiry is that of the relation of the Shākta and Shaiva (Advaita) Schools.

Māyāvāda is a doctrine which, whether true or not, is fitted only for advanced minds of great intellectuality, and for men of ascetic disposition, and of the highest moral development. This is implied in its theory of competency (Adhikāra) for Vedāntic teaching. When, as is generally the case, it is not understood, and in some cases when it is understood, but is otherwise not suitable, it is liable to be a weakening doctrine. The Shākta teaching to be found in the Tantras has also its profundities which are to be revealed only to the competent, and contains a practical doctrine for all classes of worshippers (Sādhaka). It has, in this form, for the mass of men, a strengthening pragmatic value which is beyond dispute. Whether, as some may have contended, it is the fruit of a truer spiritual experience I will not here discuss, for this would lead me into a polemic beyond the scope of my present purpose, which is an impartial statement of the respective teachings, on one particular point, given by the three philosophical systems here discussed.

CHAPTER XVIII

SHĀKTA ADVAITAVADA

I HAVE often been asked—in what consists the difference between Vedānta and 'Tantra'. This question is the product of substantial error, for it assumes that Tantra Shāstra is not based on Vedānta. I hope that, after many years of work, I have now made it clear that the Tantra Shāstra or Āgama (whatever be its ultimate origin as to which little is known by anybody) is now, and has been for centuries past, one of the recognized Scriptures of Hinduism, and every form of Hinduism is based on Veda and Vedānta. Another erroneous question, though less so, is—In what consists the difference between Advaita Vedānta and 'Tantra' Shāstra. But here again the question presupposes a misunderstanding of both Vedānta and Āgama. There are, as should be well known, several schools of Advaita Vedānta, such as Māyāvāda (with which too commonly the Advaita Vedānta is identified), such as the schools of the Northern Shaivāgama, and Shuddhādvaita of Vallabhāchāryya. In the same way, there are different schools of doctrine and worship in what are called the 'Tantras', and a grievous mistake is committed when the Tantra is made to mean the Shākta Tantra only, such as is prevalent in Bengal and which, according to some, is either the product of, or has been influenced by Buddhism. Some English-speaking Bengalis of a past day, too ready to say, "Aye aye", to the judgments of foreign critics, on their religion as on everything else, and in a hurry to dissociate themselves from their country's "superstitions", were the source of the notion which has had such currency amongst Europeans that, "Tantra" necessarily meant drinking wine and so forth.

A legitimate and accurate question is—In what consists the difference between, say, the Māyāvadin's Vedānta and that taught by the Shākta Sampradāya of Bengal. One obviously fundamental difference at once emerges. The Āgamas being essentially ritual or Sādhanā Shāstras are not immediately and practically concerned with the Yoga doctrine touching Paramārthika Sattā taught by Shaṅkarāchārya. A Sādhaka ever assumes the reality of the Universe, and is a practical dualist, whatever be the non-dual philosophical doctrines to which he may be intellectually attracted. He worships, that is assumes the being of some Other who is worshipped, that is a Real Lord who really creates, maintains, and really dissolves the Universe. He himself, the object of his worship and the means of worship are real, and his Advaita views are presented on this basis. It is on this presentment then that the next class of differences is to be found. What are they? The essence of them lies in this that the Sādhaka looks at the Brahman, through the world, whereas to the Māyāvādin Yogī, placing himself at the Brahman standpoint, there is neither creation nor world but the luminous Ātmā. The Clear Light of the Void, as the Mahāyānists call it, that alone *is*. Nevertheless, both the Advaita Sādhaka and the Advaita Yogī are one in holding that the Brahman alone is. *Sarvam Ḳhalvidam Brahma* is the great saying (Vākya) on which all Shākta Tantra Shāstra rests. The difference in interpretation then consists in the manner in which this Mahāvākya is to be explained. Does it really mean what it says, or does it mean that the saying applies only after elimination of Māyā and Avidyā. Here there is the necessary difference because, in the case of the Sādhaka, the Vākya must be explained on the basis of his presuppositions already given, whereas the Yogī who has passed the stage in which he became Siddha in Sādhanā surpasses, by auto-realization, all dualism. The vast mass of men are better warned off discussions on Paramārthika Sattā. Whether the concept be true or not, it only leads in their case to useless argument (Vichāra), and thus enfeebles them. Shākta doctrine, as its name implies, is a doctrine of power. It is true that Yoga is power, indeed the highest form of it (Yogabala). But it is a power only for those qualified (Adhikārī), and not for the mass. I am not therefore here adversely criticizing Māyāvāda. It is a pity that this country whose great glory it is to have preached *Abheda* in varying forms, and therefore tolerance, is to-day full of hateful *Bheda* of all kinds. I say "hateful", for *Bheda* is a natural thing, only hateful when accompanied by hate and intolerance. Profoundly it is said in Halhed's Gentoo laws that, "contrarieties of religion and diversity of belief are a demonstration of the power of the Supreme. Differences and varieties of created things are rays of the Glorious Essence, and types of His wonderful attributes whose complete power formed all creatures." There is also the saying attributed to the Apostle of God, Mahommad, in the Radd-ul-Muhtar and elsewhere—" difference of opinion is also the gift of God ". In these sayings speaks the high spirit of Asia. There may be political remedies for sectarian ill-feeling, but a medicine of more certain effect in this country is the teaching, " Rama Rahim ek hai ". Let us then not only objectively, but in all amity, examine the two great systems mentioned.

We all know what is normal world-experience in the Samsāra. Some through auto-realization have super-normal or "mystic" experience. This last is of varying kinds, and is had in all religions. The highest form of it, according to Māyāvāda, is Nirvāna Moksha, but there are many degrees short of this complete self-realization as the Whole (Pūrna). But the great majority of men are not concerned directly with such high matters, but with a realization of power in the world. World-experience is called ignorance, Ajnāna. This may confuse. It is ignorance only in this sense, that whilst we have normal experience, we are by that very fact ignoring, that is, not having super-normal experience. In super-normal experience again there is no finite world-experience. The Lord Himself cannot have man's experience except as and through man. *Avidyā* means *Na Vidyate*, that is, which is not seen or experienced. Some speak in foolish disparagement of the world which is our very close concern. As a link between Yoga and Bhoga, the Shākta teaches, *Yogo Bhogāyate.* I am now dealing with Māyāvāda. Whence does this ignorance in the individual or Avidyā come? The world is actually ignorant and man is part of it. This ignorance is the material cause of the world. This is not ignorance of the individual (Avidyā), for then there would be as many worlds as individuals; but the collective ignorance or Māyā. Avidyā exists to provide happiness or pain (Bhoga) for individuals, that is normal world-experience. Stated simply, ignorance in the sense of Māyā has no beginning or end, though worlds appear and go. What is this but to say that it is in the nature (Svabhāva) of the Real which manifests to do so, and the nature of its future manifestation proceeds upon lines indicated by the past collective Karma of the world.

Now, enjoyment and suffering cannot be denied, nor the existence of an element of unconsciousness in man. But the Paramātmā, as such, does not, it is said, suffer or enjoy, but is Pure Consciousness. What consciousness then does so? Shaṅkara, who is ever solicitous to preserve purity of the Supreme unchanging Self, says that it is not true consciousness, but a false image of it reflected in ignorance and which disappears when the latter is destroyed. This is in fact Sāṅkhyan Dualism in another form, and because of this Shaktivāda claims to have a purer Advaita doctrine. In Sāṅkhya the Purusha, and in Māyāvāda the Ātmā illumine Prakriti and Māyā respectively, but are never in fact bound by her. What is in bondage is the reflection of Purusha or Ātmā in Prakriti or Māyā. This is Chidābhāsa or the appearance of consciousness in a thing which is in fact not conscious; the appearance being due to the reflection of consciousness (Chit), or ignorance (Ajnāna), or unconsciousness (Achit). The false consciousness as Jīvātma suffers and enjoys. According to the Shākta view there is, as later explained, no Chidābhāsa.

Now, is this Ajnāna independent of Ātmā or not? Its independence, such as Sāṅkhya teaches, is denied. Ignorance then, whether collective or individual, must be traced to, and have its origin in, and rest on Consciousness as Ātmā. How this is so is unexplained, but the unreal which owes its existence in some inscrutable way to Reality is yet, it is said, in truth no part of it. It is Brahman then which is both the efficient and material cause of ignorance with its three Gunas, and of Chidābhāsa Brahma is the cause through its inscrutable power (Achintyāshaktitvāt) or Māyā-Shakti.

Now, is this Shakti real or unreal? According to the transcendent standpoint (Pāramārthika) of Māyāvāda it is unreal. The creative consciousness is a reflection on ignorance or Māyā. It is Brahman seen through the veil of Māyā. This is not a denial of Brahman, but of the fact that it creates. A true consciousness, it is said, can have no incentive to create. From the standpoint of the Supreme State nothing happens. Both the consciousness which as Īshvara creates, and as Jīva enjoys are Chidābhāsa, the only difference being that the first is not, and the second is under the influence of Māyā. Then it is asked, ignorance being unconscious and incapable of independent operation, true consciousness being inactive (Nishkriya), and Chidābhāsa being unreal, how is ignorance capable of hiding true consciousness and producing the world out of itself? To this the only reply is Svabhāva, that is, the very nature of ignorance makes it capable of producing apparently impossible effects. It is inscrutable (Anirvachanīya).

The Shākta then asks whether this Shakti is real or unreal, conscious or unconscious, Brahman or not Brahman? If it be a Shakti of Brahman it cannot be unreal, for there is no unreality in Brahman. It must be conscious for otherwise unconsciousness would be a factor in Brahman. It is Brahman then; for power (Shakti) and the possessor of power (Shaktimān) are one and the same.

Therefore, the Shākta Tantra Shāstra says that Shakti which, operating as Chit and Māyā, is Chit-Shakti and Māyā-Shakti, is real, conscious and Brahman itself (*Sarvam Khalvidam Brahma.*) It follows that Shakti which is Brahman in its aspect as Creator is, in fact, both the efficient and material cause of the world. If the first or cause is real, so is the second or world. If the first be the cause of unreality, then it is in itself unreal. But what is real is Brahman. Therefore, the world has a real cause which is not unreal unconsciousness or ignorance composed of three Gunas, but conscious Shakti and Brahman. It, therefore, does away with the necessity for Chidābhāsa; for, if real conscious Shakti is the cause of the world, then there is no need for unreal unconsciousness which

Māyāvāda is driven to posit to secure the absolute purity of the Brahman Consciousness.

From the standpoint of Māyāvāda, the objection to the exclusion of Chidābhāsa lies in the fact that, if the world is derived direct from conscious Shakti (as Shāktas hold), then the Supreme Consciousness is made both enjoyer and object of enjoyment. But it holds that Paramātma does not enjoy and has no need to do so; whilst the object of enjoyment is unconscious. Hence the trace of Sāṅkhyan dualism, the Ātmā exerting an influence over Māyā by virtue of its proximity only (Sannidhimātrena Upakārī). Pure Ātmā is not itself concerned. Māyā receives its influence. This is analagous to what is called in Chemistry catalytic action. The catalytic substance influences another by its mere presence, but remains itself apparently unchanged. Ātmā is in this sense an efficient but not instrumental or material cause of the world.

As Ātmā is only Sachchidānanda, the world, so long as it is considered to exist, must exist in Pure Consciousness (Ātmastha), though essentially it is different from it (Ātmā-vilakshana), and does not exist for its purpose. In Māyāvāda the world, from the transcendental standpoint, does not exist and Ātmā is not cognizant of it. Hence the question of the cause of Creation is bred of ignorance. So also is the idea of efficient cause, for it proceeds from a search for the cause of Creation which does not exist. Māyāvāda, from the standpoint of normal conventional experience (Vyavahārika Sattā), speaks of the Shakti of Ātmā as a cause of Creation, simply to provide the empirical world of the worldly man with a worldly interpretation of its worldly existence. From this point of view, Brahman is looked at through the world, which is the natural thing for all who are not liberated. From the other end or Brahman, there is no Creation nor world, and Ātmā alone is.

The Shākta may reply to this: Is not your Pāramārthika standpoint in fact empirical, arrived at by argument (Vichāra) with a limited intellect? If inscrutable power is a cause of the world, it is inscrutable because the intellect cannot grasp it, though it is known to be Ātmā. If the latter can show inscrutable power, how can you say that it is incapable of appearing as enjoyer and object of enjoyment? To deny this is to deny the unlimited character of inscrutable power. If it be objected that Ātmā cannot be object of enjoyment, because, the former is conscious and the latter unconscious, what proof is there that such an object is essentially unconscious? It may be that consciousness is not perceived in it, that is, the material world appears to be unconscious, and therefore unconsciousness comes in somewhere, otherwise it could not be perceived as unconscious. Thus, a school of European idealists hold the Universe to be a society of Spirits of all kinds and degrees, human, animal, and vegetable, and even inorganic objects. All are minds of various orders. Even the last are an order, though yet so low that they are in practice not apprehended as minds. The material world is merely the way in which these lower kinds of mind appear to our senses. The world of objects are (to use Berkely's word) "signs" of Spirit, and the way in which it communicates itself to us. Thus, to the Hindu, the Bhargah in the Sun is the Āditya Devatā, and the planets are intelligences. The physical sun is the body of the Sūrya Devatā. The whole Universe is an epiphany of Spirit. Matter is Chit as object to the mind, as mind is Chit as the Knower of such object. It is not, however, denied that there is an element of unconsciousness in the material world as it appears to us. But the Shākta says that Shakti has the power of hiding its consciousness, which is exercised to varying extent; thus, to a greater extent in the case of inorganic matter than in the case of the plant, and the less in the latter than in man, in whom consciousness is most manifest.

This power is Her Avidyā Murti, just as consciousness is her Vidyā Mūrti. Nothing then in the material world is absolutely unconscious, and nothing is perfectly conscious. The Vidyā Mūrti ever *is* because as consciousness it is the own nature or Svarūpa of Shakti. The Avidyā Mūrti which conceals consciousness appears in Creation and disappears in dissolution.

The Māyāvādin may however ask whether this Avidyā-shakti is conscious or unconscious. It cannot, he says, be the latter, for it is said to be Ātma which is conscious. How then can it conceal itself and appear as unconscious? For, nothing can be what it is not, and the nature of consciousness is to reveal and not to conceal. If, again, consciousness on account of its concealment, is incapable of knowing itself, it ceases to be consciousness. The reply is again that this also is empirical argument, based upon an imperfect idea of the nature of things. Every one knows that there is consciousness in him, but at the same time he recognizes that it is imperfect. The Māyāvādin seeks to explain this by saying that it is a false consciousness (Chidābhāsa), which is again explained by means of two opposites, namely, unconsciousness, which is an unreality to which Chidābhāsa adheres, and true consciousness or Ātmā, which, by virtue of its inscrutable power, acts as efficient cause in its production. This theory compels its adherents to ignore the world, the limited consciousness, and Shāstra itself in order that the perfection of Ātmā may be maintained, though at the same time, Shakti is admitted to be unlimited and inscrutable. The Shākta's answer on the other side is that there is in fact no false consciousness, and essentially speaking, no unconsciousness anywhere, though there appears to be some unconsciousness. In fact, Māyāvāda says that the unconscious appears to be conscious through the play of Ātmā on it, whilst the Shākta says that, really and at base, all is consciousness which appears to be unconsciousness in varying degrees. All consciousness, however imperfect, is real consciousness, its imperfection being due to its suppressing its own light to itself, and all apparent unconsciousness is due to this imperfection in the consciousness which sees it. Māyāvāda seeks to explain away the world, from which nevertheless, it derives the materials for its theory. But it is argued that it fails to do so. In its attempt to explain, it brings in a second principle namely unconsciousness, and even a third Chidābhāsa. Therefore, the theory of Shaktivāda which posits nothing but consciousness is (it is contended) a truer form of non-dualism. Yet we must note that the theories of both are made up with the imperfect light of man's knowledge. Something must then remain unexplained in all systems. The Māyāvāda does not explain the character of the Shakti of Ātmā as efficient cause of creation, and the Shākta does not explain the character of the Shakti of Ātmā which, in spite of being true consciousness, hides itself. But whilst the Shākta difficulty stands alone, the other theory brings, it is said, in its train a number of others. The Māyāvādin may also ask whether Avidyā Mūrti is permanent or transient. If the latter, it cannot be Atma which eternally is, whereas if it is, permanent liberation is impossible. It may be replied that this objection does not lie in the mouth of Māyāvāda which, in a transcendental sense, denies creation, world, bondage and liberation. The latter is a transition from bondage to freedom which presupposes the reality of the world and a connection between it and that which is beyond all worlds. This, Shaṅkara denies, and yet acknowledges a method of spiritual culture for liberation. The answer of course is that transcendentally Ātmā is ever free, and that such spiritual culture is required for the empirical (Vyavahārika) need of the empirical self or Chidābhāsa, for empirical liberation from an empirical world. But as all these conventional things are in an absolute sense "unreal", the Māyāvāda's instructions for spiritual culture have been likened to consolations given to soothe the grief of a sterile woman who has lost her son. [See J. N. Mazumdar's paper read before the Indian Research Society on the Philosophical, Religious and Social Significance of the Tantra Shāstra (July 31st, 1915), to which I am here indebted.]

Theoretically the answer may be sufficient, though this may not be allowed, but the method can in any case have full pragmatic value only in exceptional cases. Doubtless to the unliberated Māyāvādin Sādhaka the world is real, in the sense that it imposes its reality on him, whatever his theories may be. But it is plain that such a system does not (ordinarily at least) develop the same power as one in which doubt as to the reality of things does not exist. In order that instruction should work we must assume a real basis for them. Therefore, the Tantra Shāstra here spoken of, deals with true bondage in a true world, and aims at true liberation from it. It is Shakti who both binds and liberates, and Sādhanā of Her is the means of liberation. Nothing is unreal or false. Shakti is and Shakti creates and thus appears as the Universe. In positing an evolution (Parināma), the Shāstra follows Sāṅkhya, because, both systems consider the ultimate source of the world to be real, as unconscious Prakriti or conscious Shakti respectively. The Shākta takes literally the great saying, "All this (Universe) is Brahman"—every bit of it. Māyāvāda achieves its unity by saying that Jīvātma = Paramātma after elimination of Avidyā in the first and Māyā in the second. Ignorance is something neither real nor unreal. It is not real in comparison with the supreme unchanging Brahman. It is not unreal, for we experience it as real, and it is real for the length of the duration of such experience. Again, Shaktivāda assumes a real development (Parināma), with this proviso that the cause becomes effect, and yet remains what it was as cause. Māyāvāda says that there is transcendentally no real change but only the appearance of it; that is, the notion of Parināma is Māyā like all the rest.

The Tantra Shāstra deals with true bondage in a true world, and aims at true liberation from it. Ātmā binds itself by the Avidyā Mūrti of its Shakti, and liberates itself by its Vidyā Mūrti. Sādhanā is the means whereby bondage becomes liberation. Nothing is unreal or false. Ātmā by its Shakti causes the play in itself of a Shakti which is essentially nothing but itself but operates in a dual capacity, namely as Avidyā and Vidyā. Creation is thus an epiphany of the Ātmā, which appears and is withdrawn from and into itself like the limbs of a tortoise. The All-Pervading Ātmā manifests itself in many Jīvās; as the world which supplies the objects of their enjoyment; as the mind and senses for the attainment of the objects; as ignorance which binds; as knowledge which liberates when Ātmā ceases to present itself; as Avidya; and as Shāstra which provides the means for liberation. Shaktivāda affirms reality throughout, because, it is a practical Scripture for real men in a real world. Without such presupposition Sādhanā is not possible. When Sādhanā has achieved its object—Siddhi—as Auto-realization—no question of the real or unreal arises. In the Buddhacharita-kāvya it is said (cited in Hodgson "Nepal", 45) that Sākya being questioned on an abstruse point, is reported to have said,

"For myself I can tell you nothing on these matters. Meditate on Buddha and when you have obtained the supreme experience (Bodhijnāna) you will know the truth yourself." In these high realms we reach a point at which wisdom is silence.

After all man in the mass is concerned with worldly needs, and there is nothing to be ashamed of in this. One of the greatest doctrines in the Shākta Tantra is its Bhukti Mukti teaching, and it is not less great because it may have been abused. All systems are at the mercy of their followers. Instead of the ascetic method of the Māyāvādin suited for men of high spiritual development, whose *Ascesis* is not something laboured but an expression of their own true nature, the Kaula teaches liberation through enjoyment, that is the world. The path of enjoyment is a natural one. There is nothing bad in enjoyment itself if it be according to Dharma. It is only Adharma which is blamed. Liberation is thus had through the world (*Mokshāyate Samsāra*). In the natural order of development, power is developed in worldly things, but the power is controlled by a religious Sādhanā, which both prevents an excess of worldness, and moulds the mind and disposition (Bhāva) into a form which, at length and *naturally*, develops into that knowledge which produces dispassion (Vairāgya) for the world. The two paths lead to the same end. But this is itself too big a subject to be developed here. Sufficient be it to repeat what I have said elsewhere.

"The Vīra does not shun the world from fear of it. He holds it in his grasp and wrests from it its secret. Then escaping from the unconscious driftings of a humanity which has not yet realized itself, he is the illumined master of himself, whether developing all his powers or seeking liberation at his will."

As regards the state of dissolution (Pralaya) both systems are at one. In positing an evolution Tantra follows Sāṅkhya because both the two latter theories consider the ultimate source of the world to be real; real as unconscious Prakriti (Sāṅkhya); real as conscious Shakti (Shākta Tantra). In the Māyāvāda scheme, the source of the world is an unreal ignorance, and reveals itself first as Tanmātra which gradually assume the form of senses and mind in order to appear before Chidābhāsa as objects of enjoyment and suffering. The Tantra Shāstra again, subject to modifications in consonance with its doctrine, agrees with Nyāya-Vaisheshika in holding that the powers of consciousness which are Will (Ichchha), Knowledge (Jnāna) and Action (Kriyā) constitute the motive power in creation. These are the great Triangle of Energy (Kāmakalā) from which Shabda and Artha, the forces of the psychic and material worlds, arise.

CHAPTER XIX

CREATION AS EXPLAINED IN THE NON-DUALIST TANTRAS[1]

A PSYCHOLOGICAL analysis of our worldly experience ordinarily gives us both the feeling of persistence and change. This personal experience expresses a cosmic truth. An examination of any doctrine of creation similarly reveals two fundamental concepts, those of Being and Becoming, Changelessness and Change, the One and the Many. In Sanskrit they are called the Kūtastha and Bhāva or Bhāvana. The first is the Spirit or Purusha or Brahman and Ātman which is unlimited Being (Sat), Consciousness (Chit) and Bliss (Ānanda). According to Indian notions the Ātman as such *is* and never becomes. Its Power (Shakti) manifests as Nature, which is the subject of change. We may understand Nature in a two-fold sense: first, as the root principle or noumenal cause of the phenomenal world, that is, as the Principle of Becoming, and secondly, as such World. Nature in the former sense is Mūlaprakriti, which means that which exists as the root (Mūla) substance of things before (Pra) creation (Kriti), and which, in association with Chit, either truly or apparently creates,

---

[1] A paper read by the Author at the Silver Jubilee of the Chaitanya Library, Calcutta, held on the 18th January 1915, under the Presidency of H. E. The Governor of Bengal.

maintains and destroys the Universe. This Mūlaprakriti the Shāradā Tilaka calls Mūlabhūta Avyakta, and the Vedānta (of Shaṅkara to which alone I refer) Māyā.

Nature, in the second sense, that is the phenomenal world, which is a product of Mūlaprakriti is the compound of the evolutes from this root substance which are called Vikritis in the Sāṅkhya and Tantra, and name and form (Nāmarūpa) by the Vedāntins, who attribute them to ignorance (Avidyā). Mūlaprakriti as the material and instrumental cause of things is that potentiality of natural power (natura naturans) which manifests as the Universe (natura naturata).

Touching these two Principles, there are certain fundamental points of agreement in the three systems which I am examining—Sāṅkhya, Vedānta and the Advaitavāda of the Tantra. They are as follows. According to the first two systems, Brahman or Purusha as Sat, Chit and Ānanda is Eternal Conscious Being. It is changeless and has no activity (Kartrittva). It is not therefore in Itself a cause whether instrumental or material; though in so far as Its simple presence gives the appearance of consciousness to the activities of Prakriti, It may in such sense be designated an efficient cause. So, according to Sāṅkhya, Prakriti reflects Purusha, and in Vedānta, Avidyā of the three Gunas takes the reflection of Chidānanda. On the other hand, the substance or factors of Mūlaprakriti or Māyā are the three Gunas or the three characteristics of the principle of Nature, according to which it reveals (Sattva) or veils (Tamas) Consciousness (Chit) and the activity or energy (Rajas) which urges Sattva and Tamas to operation.

It also is Eternal, but is unconscious (Achit) Becoming. Though it is without consciousness (Chaitanya) it is essentially activity (Kartrittva) motion and change. It is a true cause instrumental and material of the World. But notwithstanding all the things to which Mūlaprakriti gives birth, Its substance is in no wise diminished by the production of the Vikritis or Tattvas: the Gunas which constitute it ever remaining the same. The source of all becoming is never exhausted, though the things which are therefrom produced appear and disappear.

Passing from the general points of agreement to those of difference, we note firstly, those between the Sāṅkhya and the Vedānta. The Sāṅkhya is commonly regarded as a dualistic system, which affirms that both Purusha and Prakriti are real, separate and independent Principles. The Vedānta, however, says that there cannot be two Principles which are both absolutely real. It does not, however, altogether discard the dual principles of the Sāṅkhya, but says that Mūlaprakriti which it calls Māyā, while real from one point of view, that is empirically, is not real from another and transcendental standpoint. It affirms therefore that the only Real (Sad-vastu) is the attributeless (Nirguna Brahman). All else is Māyā and its products. Whilst then the Sāṅkhyan Mūlaprakriti is an Eternal Reality, it is according to the transcendental method of Shaṅkara an eternal unreality (Mithyābhūtā Sanātanī). The empirical reality which is really false is due to the Avidyā which is inherent in the nature of the embodied spirit (Jīva). Māyā is Avastu or no real thing. It is Nistattva. As Avidyā is neither real nor unreal, so is its cause or Māyā. The kernel of the Vedāntik argument on this point is to be found in its interpretations of the Vaidik Mahāvākya, "That Thou art" (Tat tvam asi). Tat here is Īshvara, that is, Brahman with Māyā as His body or Upādhi. Tvam is the Jīva with Avidyā as its body. It is then shown that Jīva is only Brahman when Māyā is eliminated from Īshvara, and Avidyā from Jīva. Therefore, only as Brahman is the Tvam the Tat; therefore, neither Māyā nor Avidyā really exist (they are Avastu), for otherwise the equality of Jīva and Īshvara could not be affirmed. This conclusion that Māyā is Avastu has far-reaching consequences, both religious and philosophical, and so has the denial of it. It is on this question that there is a fundamental difference between Shaṅkara's Advaitavāda and that of the Shākta Tantra, which I am about to discuss.

Before, however, doing so I will first contrast the notions of creation in Sāṅkhya and Vedānta. It is common ground that creation is the appearance produced by the action of Mūlaprakriti or principle of Nature (Achit) existing in association with Chit. According to Sāṅkhya, in Mūlaprakriti or the potential condition of the Natural Principle, the Gunas are in a state of equality (Sāmyāvastha), that is, they are not affecting one another. But, as Mūlaprakriti is essentially movement, it is said that even when in this state of equality the Gunas are yet continually changing into themselves (Sarūpaparināma). This inherent subtle movement is the nature of the Guna itself, and exists without effecting any objective result. Owing to the ripening of Adrishta or Karma, creation takes place by the disturbance of this equality of the Gunas (Gunakshobha), which then commence to oscillate and act upon one another. It is this initial creative motion which is known in the Tantra as Cosmic Sound (Parāshabda). It is through the association of Purusha with Mūlaprakriti in cosmic vibration (Spandana) that creation takes place. The whole universe arises from varied forms of this grand initial motion. So, scientific "matter" is now currently held to be the varied appearance produced in our minds by vibration of, and in the single substance called ether. This new Western scientific doctrine of vibration is in India an ancient inheritance. "Hrīng, the Supreme Hangsa dwells in the brilliant heaven." The word "Hangsa" comes, it is said, from the word Hanti, which means Gati or Motion. Sāyana says that It is called Āditya, because It is in perpetual motion. But Indian teaching carries the application of this doctrine beyond the scientific ether which is a physical substance (Mahābhūta). There is vibration in the causal body that is of the Gunas of Mūlaprakriti as the result of Sadrishaparināma of Parāshabdasrishti; in the subtle body of mind (Antahkarana); and in the gross body, compounded of the Bhūtas which derive from the Tanmātras their immediate subtle source of origin. The Hiranyagarbha and Virāt Sound is called Madhyamā and Vaikharī. If this striking similarity between ancient Eastern wisdom and modern scientific research has not been recognized, it is due to the fact that the ordinary Western Orientalist and those who take their cue from him in this country, are prone to the somewhat contemptuous belief that, Indian notions are of "historical" interest only, and as such, a welcome addition possibly for some intellectual museum, but are otherwise without value or actuality. The vibrating Mūlaprakriti and its Gunas ever remain the same, though the predominance of now one, and now another of them, produces the various evolutes called Vikritis or Tattvas, which constitute the world of mind and matter. These Tattvas constitute the elements of the created world. They are the well-known Buddhi, Ahangkāra, Manas (constituting the Antahkarana), the ten Indriyas, five Tanmātras and five Mahābhūtas of "ether", "air," "fire", "water" and "earth," which of course must not be identified with the notions which the English terms connote. These Tattvas are names for the elements which we discover as a result of a psychological analysis of our worldly experience. That experience ordinarily gives us both the feeling of persistence and change. The former is due to the presence of the Ātmā or Chit-Shakti, which exists in us in association with Mūlaprakriti or Māyā-Shakti.

This is the Chaitanya in all bodies. Change is caused by Mūlaprakriti or Māyā-Shakti, and its elements may be divided into the subjective and objective Tattvas, or what we call mind and matter. Analysing, again, the former, we discover an individuality (Ahangkāra) sensing through the Indriyas, a world which forms the material of its percepts and concepts (Manas and Buddhi). The object of thought or "matter" are the varied compounds of the Vaikrita creation, which are made up of combinations of the gross elements (Mahābhūta), which themselves derive from the subtle elements or Tanmātra. Now, according to Sāṅkhya, all this is real, for all are Tattvas. Purusha and Prakriti are Tattvas, and so are the Vikritis of the latter.

According to the Vedānta also, creation takes place through the association of the Brahman, then known as the Lord or Īshvara (Māyopādhika-Chaitanyam Īshvarah), with Māyā. That is, Chit is associated with, though unaffected by Māyā which operates by reason of such association to produce the universe. The unchanging Sad-vastu is the Brahman. The ever-changing world is, when viewed by the spiritually wise (Jnānī), the form imposed by Avidyā on the Changeless Sat. It is true that it has the quality of being in accordance with the greatest principle of order, namely, that of causality. It is the Sat, however, which gives to the World the character of orderliness, because it is on and in association with that pure Chit or Sat that Māyā plays. It is true that behind all this unreal appearance there is the Real, the Brahman. But the phenomenal world has, from the alogical standpoint, no real substratum existing as its instrumental and material cause. The Brahman as such is no true cause, and Māyā is unreal (Avastu). The world has only the appearance of reality from the reflection which is cast by the real upon the unreal. Nor is Īshvara, the creative and ruling Lord, in a transcendental sense real.

For, as it is the Brahman in association with Māyā, which Shaṅkara calls Īshvara, the latter is nothing but the Brahman viewed through Māyā. It follows that the universe is the product of the association of the real and the unreal, and when world-experience ends in liberation (Mukti), the notion of Īshvara as its creator no longer exists. For His body is Māyā and this is Avastu. So long however as there is a world, that is, so long as one is subject to Māyā that is embodied, so long do we recognize the existence of Īshvara. The Lord truly exists for every Jīva so long as he is such. But on attainment of bodiless liberation (Videha Mukti), the Jīva becomes himself Sachchidānanda, and as such Īshvara does not exist for him, for Īshvara is but the Sat viewed through that Māyā of which the Sat is free. "The Brahman is true, the world is false. The Jīva is Brahman (Paramātmā) and nothing else."

The opponents of this system or Māyāvāda have charged it with being a covert form of Buddhistic nihilism (Māyāvādam asachchhāstram prachchhannam bauddham). It has, however, perhaps been more correctly said that Shrī Shaṅkara adjusted his philosophy to meet the Māyāvāda of the Buddhists, and so promulgated a new theory of Māyā without abandoning the faith or practice of his Shaiva-Shākta Dharma.

All systems obviously concede at least the empirical reality of the world. The question is, whether it has a greater reality than that, and if so, in what way? Sāṅkhya affirms its reality; Shaṅkara denies it in order to secure the complete unity of the Brahman. Each system has merits of its own. Sāṅkhya by its dualism is able to preserve in all its integrity the specific character of Chit as Niranjana. This result, on the other hand, is effected at the cost of that unity for which all minds have, in some form or other, a kind of metaphysical hunger. Shaṅkara by his Māyāvāda secures this unity, but this achievement is at the cost of a denial of the ultimate reality of the world, whether considered as the product (Vikriti) of Mūlaprakriti, or as Mūlaprakriti itself.

There is, however, another alternative, and that is the great Shākta doctrine of Duality in Unity. There is, this Shāstra says, a middle course in which the reality of the world is affirmed without compromising the truth of the unity of the Brahman, for which Shaṅkara by such lofty speculation contends. I here shortly state what is developed more fully later. The Shākta Advaitavāda recognizes the reality of Mūlaprakriti in the sense of Māyā-Shakti. Here in a qualified way it follows the Sāṅkhya. On the other hand, it differs from the Sāṅkhya in holding that Mūlaprakriti as Māyā-Shakti is not a principle separate from the Brahman, but exists in and as a principle of the one Brahman substance. The world, therefore, is the appearance of the Real. It is the Brahman as Power. The ground principle of such appearance or Māyā-Shakti is the Real as Ātmā and Power. There is thus a reality behind all appearances, a real substance behind the apparent transformations. Māyā-Shakti as such is both eternal and real, and so is Īshvara. The transformations are the changing forms of the Real. I pass now to the Advaitavāda of the Shākta Tantra.

The Shākta Tantra is not a formal system of philosophy (Darshana). It is, in the broadest sense, a generic term for the writings and various traditions which express the whole culture of a certain epoch in Indian History. The contents are therefore of an encyclopædic character, religion, ritual, domestic rites, law, medicine, magic, and so forth. It has thus great historical value, which appears to be the most fashionable form of recommendation for the Indian Scriptures now-a-days. The mere historian, I believe, derives encouragement from the fact that out of bad material may yet be made good history. I am not here concerned with this aspect of the matter. For my present purpose, the Shākta Tantra is part of the Upāsanā kānda of the three departments of Shruti, and is a system of physical, psychical and moral training (Sādhanā), worship and Yoga. It is thus essentially practical. This is what it claims to be. To its critics, it has appeared to be a system of immoral indiscipline. I am not here concerned with the charge but with the doctrine of creation to be found in the Shāstra. Underlying, however, all this practice, whatever be the worth or otherwise which is attributed to it, there is a philosophy which must be abstracted, as I have here done for the first time, with some difficulty, and on points with doubt, from the disquisitions on religion and the ritual and Yoga directions to be found in the various Tantras. The fundamental principles are as follows.

It is said that the equality (Sāmya) of the Gunas is Mūlaprakriti, which has activity (Kartrittva), but no consciousness (Chaitanya). Brahman is Sachchidānanda who has Chaitanya and no Kartrittva. But this is so only if we thus logically differentiate them. As a matter of fact, however, the two admittedly, ever and everywhere, co-exist and cannot, except for the purpose of formal analysis, be thought of without the other. The connection between the two is one of unseparateness (Avinābhāva Sambandha). Brahman does not exist without Prakriti-Shakti or Prakriti without the Brahman. Some call the Supreme Chaitanya with Prakriti, others Prakriti with Chaitanya. Some worship It as Shiva; others as Shakti. Both are one and the same. Shiva is the One viewed from Its Chit aspect. Shakti is the One viewed from Its Māyā aspect. They are the "male" and "female" aspects of the same Unity.

which is neither male nor female. Akula is Shiva. Kula is Shakti. The same Supreme is worshipped by Sādhanā of Brahman, as by Sādhanā of Ādyāshakti. The two cannot be separated, for Brahman without Prakriti is actionless, and Prakriti without Brahman is unconscious. There is Nishkala Shiva or the transcendent, attributeless (Nirguna) Brahman; and Sakala Shiva or the embodied, immanent Brahman with attributes (Saguna).

Kalā or Shakti corresponds with the Sāṅkhyan Mūlaprakriti or Sāmyāvasthā of the three Gunas and the Vedāntic Māyā. But Kalā which is Mūlaprakriti and Māyā eternally is, and therefore when we speak of Nishkala Shiva, it is not meant that there is then or at any time no Kalā, for Kalā ever is, but that Brahman is meant which is thought of as being without the working Prakriti (Prakriteranyah), Māyā-Shakti is then latent in it. As the Devī in the Kulachūdāmani says, "Aham Prakritirūpā chet Chidānandaparāyanā". Sakala Shiva is, on the other hand, Shiva considered as associated with Prakriti in operation and manifesting the world. In one case, Kalā is working or manifest, in the other it is not, but exists in a potential state. In the same way the two Shivas are one and the same. There is one Shiva who is Nirguna and Saguna. The Tāntrik Yoga treatise Shatchakranirūpana describes the Jīvātmā as the Paryyāya of, that is another name for, the Paramātmā; adding that the root of wisdom (Mūlavidyā) is a knowledge of their identity. When the Brahman manifests, It is called Shakti, which is the magnificent concept round which Tantra is built. The term comes from the root "Shak", which means "to be able". It is the power which is the Brahman and whereby the Brahman manifests Itself; for Shakti and possessor of Shakti (Shaktimān) are one and the same. As Shakti is Brahman it is also Nirgunā and Sagunā.

Īshvara is Chit Shakti, that is, Chit in association with the operating Prakriti as the efficient cause of the creation; and Māyā-Shakti which means Māyā as a Shakti that is in creative operation as the instrumental (Nimitta) and material (Upādāna) cause of the universe. This is the Shakti which produces Avidyā, just as Mahāmāyā or Īshvarī is the Great Liberatrix. These twin aspects of Shakti appear throughout creation. Thus in the body, the Chit or Brahman aspect is conscious Ātmā or Spirit, and the Māyā aspect is the Antahkarana and its derivatives or the unconscious (Jada) mind and body. When, however, we speak here of Shakti without any qualifications, what is meant is Chit-Shakti in association with Māyā-Shakti that is Īshvarī or Devī or Mahāmāyā, the Mother of all worlds. If we keep this in view, we shall not fall into the error of supposing that the Shāktas (whose religion is one of the oldest in the world; how old indeed is as yet little known) worship material force or gross matter. Īshvara or Ishvarī is not Achit, which, as pure Sattvaguna is only His or Her body. Māyā-Shakti in the sense of Mūlaprakriti is Chit. So also is Avidyā Shakti, though it appears to be Achit, for there is no Chidābhāsa.

In a certain class of Indian images, you will see the Lord, with a diminutive female figure on His lap. The makers and worshippers of those images thought of Shakti as being in the subordinate position which some persons consider a Hindu wife should occupy. This is however not the conception of Shākta Tantra, according to which, She is not a handmaid of the Lord, but the Lord Himself, being but the name for that aspect of His in which He is the Mother and Nourisher of the worlds. As Shiva is the transcendent, Shakti is the immanent aspect of the one Brahman who is Shiva-Shakti. Being Its aspect, It is not different from, but one with It. In the Kulachūdāmani Nigama, the

Bhairavī addressing Bhairava says, "Thou art the Guru of all, I entered into Thy body (as Shakti) and thereby Thou didst become the Lord (Prabhu). There is none but Myself Who is the Mother to create (Kāryyavibhāvinī). Therefore it is that when creation takes place Sonship is in Thee. Thou alone art the Father Who wills what I do (Kāryyavibhāvaka; that is, She is the vessel which receives the nectar which flows from Nityānanda). By the union of Shiva and Shakti creation comes (Shiva-Shakti-samāyogāt jāyate srishtikalpanā). As all in the universe is both Shiva and Shakti (Shivashaktimaya), therefore, Oh Maheshvara, Thou art in every place and I am in every place. Thou art in all and I am in all." The creative World thus sows Its seed in Its own womb.

Such being the nature of Shakti, the next question is whether Māyā as Shaṅkara affirms is Avastu. It is to be remembered that according to his empirical method it is taken as real, but transcendentally it is alleged to be an eternal unreality, because, the object of the latter method is to explain away the world altogether so as to secure the pure unity of the Brahman. The Shākta Tantra is however not concerned with any such purpose. It is an Upāsanā Shāstra in which the World and its Lord have reality. There cannot be Sādhanā in an unreal world by an unreal Sādhaka of an unreal Lord. The Shākta replies to Māyāvāda: If it be said that Māyā is in some unexplained way Avastu, yet it is admitted that there is something, however unreal it may be alleged to be, which is yet admittedly eternal and in association, whether manifest or unmanifest, with the Brahman. According to Shaṅkara, Māyā exists as the mere potentiality of some future World which shall arise on the ripening of Adrishta which Māyā is. But in the Mahānirvāna Tantra, Shiva says to Devī, "Thou art Thyself the Parā Prakriti of the Paramātmā"

(Ch. IV, v. 10). That is Māyā in the sense of Mūlaprakriti, which is admittedly eternal, is not Avastu, but is the Power of the Brahman one with which is Chit. In Nishkala Shiva, Shakti lies inactive. It manifests in and as creation, though Chit thus appearing through its Power is neither exhausted nor affected thereby. We thus find Īshvarī addressed in the Tantra both as Sachchidānandarūpinī and Trigunātmikā, referring to the two real principles which form part of the one Brahman substance. The philosophical difference between the two expositions appears to lie in this. Shaṅkara says that there are no distinctions in Brahman of either of the three kinds: svagata-bheda, that is, distinction of parts within one unit, svajātīya-bheda or distinction between units of one class, or vijātīya-bheda or distinction between units of different classes. Bhārati, however, the Commentator on the Mahānirvāna (Ch. II, v. 34) says that Advaita there mentioned means devoid of the last two classes of distinction. There is, therefore, for the purposes of Shākta Tantra, a svagata-bheda in the Brahman Itself namely, the two aspects according to which the Brahman is, on the one hand, Being, Chit and on the other, the principle of becoming which manifests as Nature or seeming Achit. In a mysterious way, however, there is a union of these two principles (Bhāvayoga), which thus exist without derogation from the partless unity of the Brahman which they are. In short, the Brahman may be conceived of as having twin aspects, in one of which, It is the cause of the changing world, and in the other of which It is the unchanging Soul of the World. Whilst the Brahman Svarūpa or Chit is Itself immutable, the Brahman is yet through its Power the cause of change, and is in one aspect the changeful world.

But what then is "real"; a term not always correctly understood. According to the Māyāvāda definition, the "real" is that which ever was, is and will be (Kālatraya-sattvāvān); in the words of the Christian liturgy, "as it was in the beginning, is now, and ever shall be world without end"; therefore that which changes, which was not, but is, and then ceases to be is according to this definition "unreal", however much from a practical point of view it may appear real to us. Now Māyāvāda calls Mūlaprakriti in the sense of Māyā the material cause of the world, no independent real (Avastu). The Shākta Tantra says that the Principle, whence all becoming comes, exists as a real substratum so to speak below the world of names and forms. This Māyā-Shakti is an eternal reality. What is "unreal" (according to the above definition), are these names and forms (Avidyā), that is, the changing worlds (asat-trilokī-sadbhāvam svarūpam Brahmanah smritam, Ch. III, v. 7, Mahānirvana Tantra). These are unreal however only in the sense that they are not permanent, but come and go. The body is called Sharīra, which comes from the root Shri—"to decay", for it is dissolving and being renewed at every moment until death. Again, however real it may seem to us, the world may be unreal in the sense that it is something other than what it seems to be. This thing which I now hold in my hands seems to me to be paper, which is white, smooth and so forth, yet we are told that it really is something different, namely, a number of extraordinarily rapid vibrations of etheric substance, producing the false appearance of scientific "matter". In the same way (as those who worship Yantras know), all nature is the appearance produced by various forms of motion in Prākritic substance. (*Sarvam Khalvidam Brahma.*) The real is the Brahman and its Power. The Brahman, whether in Its Chit or Māyā aspect, eternally and changelessly endures, but Avidyā breaks up its undivided unity into the changing manifold world of names and forms. It follows from the above that Brahman and Īshvara are two co-being aspects of the One ultimate Reality, as Power to Be and to Become. For as Shaṅkara points out (Comm. Shvetāshvatara Up. I. 2) Devātmashakti, the cause of the world, is not separate from the Paramātmā, as Sāṅkhya alleges its Pradhāna to be. And thus it is that Shiva in the Kulārnava Tantra (I. 110) says, "some desire dualism (Dvaitavāda), others monism (Advaitavāda). Such however know not My truth, which is beyond both monism and dualism (Dvaitādvaitavivarjita)." This saying may doubtless mean that to "the knower (Jnānī) the arguments of philosophical systems are of no account, as is indeed the case." It has also a more literal meaning as above explained. The Shāstra in fact makes high claims for itself. The Tantra, it has been said, takes into its arms as if they were its two children, both dualism and monism affording by its practical method (Sādhanā), and the spiritual knowledge generated thereby the means by which their antimonies are resolved and harmonized. Its purpose is to give liberation to the Jīva by a method according to which monistic truth is reached through the dualistic world; immersing its Sādhakas in the current of Divine Bliss, by changing duality into unity, and then evolving from the latter a dualistic play, thus proclaiming the wonderful glory of the Spouse of Paramashiva in the love embrace of Mind-Matter (Jada) and Consciousness (Chaitanya). It therefore says that those who have realized this, move, and yet remain unsoiled in the mud of worldly actions which lead others upon the downward path. It claims, therefore, that its practical method (Sādhanā) is more speedily fruitful than any other. Its practical method is an application of the general principles above described. In fact, one of its Āchāras which has led to abuse is an attempt to put into full practice the theory of Advaitavāda. Shaṅkara has in his transcendental method dealt with the subject as part of the Jnāna Kānda. Though the exponent of the Māyāvāda is esteemed to be a Mahāpurusha, this method is not in favour with the Tāntric Sādhaka who attributes much of the practical atheism which is to be found in this country, as elsewhere, to a misunderstanding of the transcendental doctrines of Māyāvāda. There is some truth in this charge, for, as has been well said, the vulgarization of Shaṅkara's "Higher Science" which is by its nature an esoteric doctrine destined for a small minority, must be reckoned a misfortune in so far as it has, in the language of the Gītā, induced many people to take to another's Dharma instead of to their own, which is the "Lower Science" of the great Vedāntin followed in all Shāstras of worship. Such a Shāstra must necessarily affirm God as a real object of worship. Dionysius, the Areopagite, the chief of the line of all Christian mystics said that we could only speak "apophatically" of the Supreme as It existed in Itself, that is, other than as It displays Itself to us. Of It nothing can be affirmed but that It is not this and not that. Here he followed the, "neti neti", of the Vedānta. Īshvarī is not less real than the things with which we are concerned every day. She is for the Indian Sādhaka the highest reality, and what may or may not be the state of Videha Mukti has for him, no practical concern. Those only who have attained it will know whether Shaṅkara is right or not; not that they will think about this or any other subject; but in the sense that when the Brahman is known all is known. A friend from whom I quote, writes that he had once occasion to learn to what ridiculous haughtiness, some of the modern "adepts" of Shrī Shaṅkara's school are apt to let themselves be carried away, when one of them spoke to him of the personal Īshvara as being a "pitiable creature". The truth is that such so-called "adepts" are no adepts at all, being without the attainment, and far from the spirit of Shaṅkara—whose devotion and powers made him seem to his followers to be an incarnation of Shiva Himself. Such a remark betrays a radical misunderstanding of the Vedānta. How many of those, who to-day discuss his Vedānta from a merely literary standpoint, have his, or indeed any faith? What some would do is to dismiss the faith and practice of Shaṅkara as idle superstition, and to adopt his philosophy. But what is the intrinsic value of a philosophy which emanates from a mind which is so ignorant as to be superstitious? Shaṅkara, however, has said that faith and Sādhanā are the preliminaries for competency (Adhikāra) for the Jnānakānda. He alone is competent (Adhikārī) who possesses all good moral and intellectual qualities, faith (Shraddhā), capacity for the highest contemplation (Samādhi), the Sāṅkhyan discrimination (Viveka), absence of all desire for anything in this world or the next, and an ardent longing for liberation. There are few indeed who can claim even imperfectly all such qualifications. But what of the rest? There is no Vaidik Karmakānda in operation in the present age, but there are other Shāstras of worship which is either Vaidik, Tāntrik or Paurānik. These provide for those who are still, as are most, on the path of desire. The Tantra affirms that nothing of worth can be achieved without Sādhanā. Mere speculation is without result. This principle is entirely sound whatever may be thought of the mode in which it is sought to be applied. Those to whom the questions here discussed are not mere matters for intellectual business or recreation will recall that Shaṅkara has said that liberation is attained not merely by the discussion of, and pondering upon revealed truth (Vichāra), for which few only are competent, but by the grace of God (Īshvara Anugraha), through the worship of the Mother and Father from whom all creation springs. Such worship produces knowledge. In the Kulachūdāmani, the Devī says: "Oh all-knowing One, if

Thou knowest Me then of what use are the Āmnāyas (revealed teachings) and Yājanam (ritual)? If Thou knowest Me not, then again, of what use are they?" But neither are, in another sense, without their uses for thereby the Sādhaka becomes qualified for some form of Urddhvāmnāya, in which there are no rites (Karma).

With this short exposition of the nature of Shaktitattva according to Shākta Tantra I pass to an equally brief account of its manifestation in the Universe. It is sufficient to deal with the main lines of the doctrine without going into their very great accompanying detail. I here follow, on the main theme, the account given in the celebrated Shāradā Tilaka a work written by Lakshmanāchāryya, the Guru of Abhinava Gupta, the great Kashmīrian Tāntrik, about the commencement of the eleventh century, and its Commentary by the learned Tāntrik Pandit Rāghava Bhatta which is dated 1454 A.D. This work has long been held to be of great authority in Bengal.

Why creation takes place cannot in an ultimate sense be explained. It is the play (Līlā) of the Mother. Could this be done the Brahman would be subject to the law of causality which governs the Universe but which its Cause necessarily transcends.

The Tantra, however, in common with other Indian Shāstras recognizes Adrishta Srishti, or the doctrine that the impulse to creation is proximately caused by the Adrishta or Karma of Jīvas. But Karma is eternal and itself requires explanation. Karma comes from Samskāra and Samskāra from Karma. The process of creation, maintenance and dissolution, according to this view, unceasingly recurs as an eternal rhythm of cosmic life and death which is the Mother's play (Līlā). And so it is said of Her in the Lalitā Sahasranāma that, "the series of universes appear and disappear with the opening and shutting of Her Eyes". The existence of Karma implies the will to cosmic life. We produce it as the result of such will. And when produced it becomes itself the cause of it.

In the aggregate of Karma which will at one period or another ripen, there is, at any particular time, some which are ripe and others which are not so. For the fruition of the former only creation takes place. When this seed ripens and the time therefore approaches for the creation of another universe, the Brahman manifests in Its Visva-rūpa aspect, so that the Jīva may enjoy or suffer therein the fruits of his Karma, and (unless liberation be attained) accumulate fresh Karma which will involve the creation of future worlds. When the unripened actions which are absorbed in Māyā become in course of time ripe, the Vritti of Māyā or Shakti in the form of desire for creation arises in Paramashiva, for the bestowal of the fruit of this Karma. This state of Māyā is variously called by Shruti, Īkshana, Kāma, Vichikīrshā.

It is when the Brahman "saw", "desired", or "thought" "May I be many", that there takes place what is known as Sadrishaparināma in which the Supreme Bindu appears. This, in its triple aspect, is known as Kāmakalā, a manifestation of Shakti whence in the manner hereafter described the Universe emanates. This Kāmakalā is the Mūla or root of all Mantra. Though creation takes place in order that Karma may be suffered and enjoyed, yet in the aggregate of Karma which will at one time or another ripen, there is at any particular period some which are ripe and others which are not so. For the fruition of the former only creation takes place. As creation will serve no purpose in the case of Karma which is not ripe, there is, after the exhaustion by fruition of the ripe Karma, a dissolution (Pralaya). Then the Universe is again merged in Māyā which thus abides until the ripening of the remaining actions. Karma, like everything else, re-enters the Brahman, and remains there in hidden potential state as it were a seed. When the seed ripens creation again takes place.

With Īkshana, or the manifestation of creative will, creation is really instantaneous. When the "Word" went forth, "Let there be light", there *was* light, for the ideation of Īshvara is creative. Our mind by its constitution is however led to think of creation as a gradual process. The Sāṅkhya starts with the oscillation of the Gunas (Gunakshobha) upon which the Vikritis immediately appear. But just as it explains its real Parināma in terms of successive emanations, so the Shākta Tantra describes a Sadrishaparināma in the body of Īshvara their cause. This development is not a real Parināma, but a resolution of like to like, that is, there is no actual change in the nature of the entity dealt with, the various stages of such Parināma being but names for the multiple aspects to us of the same unchanging Unity.

Shakti is one. It appears as various by its manifestations. In one aspect there is no Parināma, for Sachchidānanda is as such immutable. Before and after and in creation It remains what It was. There is therefore no Parināma in or of the Aksharabrahman as such. There is Parināma, however, in its Power aspect. The three Gunas do not change, each remaining what it is. They are the same in all forms but appear to the Jīva to exist in different combinations. The appearance of the Gunas in different proportions is due to Avidyā or Karma which is this apparent Gunakshobha. It is Samskāra which gives to the Sāmya Prakriti, existence as Vaishamya. What the Tantra describes as Sadrishaparināma is but an analysis of the different aspects of what is shortly called in other Shāstras,

Īkshana. This Sadrishaparināma is concerned with the evolution of what is named Parā Sound (Parashabdasrishti). This is Cosmic Sound; the causal vibration in the substance of Mūlaprakriti which gives birth to the Tattvas which are its Vikritis: such Cosmic Sound being that which is distinguished in thought from the Tattvas so produced.

The Shāradā says that from the Sakala Parameshvara who is Sachchidānanda issued Shakti that is, that power which is necessary for creation. God and His power are yet more than the creation which He manifests. Shakti is said to issue from that which is already Sakala or associated with Shakti, because as Rāghava Bhatta says, She who is eternal (Anādirūpa) was in a subtle state as Chaitanya during the great dissolution (Pralaya), (Yā Anādirūpā Chaitanyādhyāsena Mahāpralaye Sūkshmā Sthitā).

With however the disturbance of the Gunas, Prakriti became inclined (Uchchhūnā) to creation, and in this sense, is imagined to issue. Shakti, in other words, passes from a potential state to one of actuality. The Parameshvara is, he adds, described as Sachchidānanda in order to affirm that even when the Brahman is associated with Avidyā, its own true nature (Svarūpa) is not affected. According to the Shāradā, from this Shakti issues Nāda and from the latter Bindu (known as the Parabindu). The Shāradā thus enumerates seven aspects of Shakti. This it does, according to Rāghava Bhatta, so as to make up the seven component parts of the Omkāra. In some Shākta Tantras this first Nāda is omitted and there are thus only six aspects. The Shaiva Tantras mention five. Those which recognize Kalā as a Tattva identify Nāda with it. In some Tantras, Kalā is associated with Tamoguna, and is the Mahākāla who is both the child and spouse of Ādyāshakti; for creation comes from the Tāmasic aspect of Shakti. In the Shāradātilaka, Nāda and Bindu are one and the same Shakti, being the names of two of Her states which are considered to represent Her as being more prone to creation (Uchchhūnāvasthā). There are two states of Shaktibindu suitable for creation (Upayogyāvasthā). As there is no mass or Ghana in Nishkala Shiva, that Brahman represents the Aghanāvasthā. The Prapanchasāra Tantra says that She, who is in the first place Tattva (mere "thatness"), quickens under the influence of Chit which She reflects; then She longs to create (Vichikīrshu) and becomes massive (Ghanībhūtā) and appears as Bindu (Parabindu). Ghanībhūta means that which was not dense or Ghana but which has become so (Ghanāvasthā). It involves the notion of solidifying, coagulating, becoming massive. Thus milk is said to become Ghanībhūta when it condenses into cream or curd. This is the first gross condition (Sthūlāvasthā); the Brahman associated with Māyā in the form of Karma assumes that aspect in which It is regarded as the primal cause of the subtle and gross bodies. There then lies in it in a potential, undifferentiated mass (Ghana), the universe and beings about to be created. The Parabindu is thus a compact aspect of Shakti wherein action or Kriyā Shakti predominates. It is compared to a grain of gram (Chanaka) which under its outer sheath (Māyā) contains two seeds (Shivashakti) in close and undivided union. The Bindu is symbolized by a circle. The Shūnya or empty space within is the Brahmapada. The supreme Light is formless, but Bindu implies both the void and Guna, for, when Shiva becomes Bindurūpa He is with Guna. Rāghava says, "She alone can create. When the desire for appearance as all Her Tattvas seizes Her, She assumes the state of Bindu whose characteristic is action" (Kriyāshakti). This Bindu or Avyakta, as it is the sprouting root of the universe, is called the supreme Bindu (Parabindu), or causal or Kārana Bindu, to distinguish it from that aspect of Itself which is called Bindu (Kāryya), which appears as a state of Shakti after the differentiation of the Parabindu in Sadrishaparināma. The Parabindu is the Īshvara of the Vedānta with Māyā as His Upādhi. He is the Saguna Brahman, that is, the combined Chit-Shakti and Māyā-Shakti or Īshvara with undifferentiated Prakriti as His Avyaktasharīra. Some call Him Mahāvishnu and others the Brahmapurusha. Here is Paramashiva. "Some call the Hangsa, Devī. They are those who are filled with a passion for Her lotus feet." As Kālīcharana the Commentator of the Shatchakranirūpana says, it matters not what It is called. It is adored by all. It is this Bindu or state of supreme Shakti which is worshipped in secret by all Devas. In Nishkala Shiva, Prakriti exists in a hidden potential state. The Bindu Parashaktimaya (Shivashaktimaya) is the first movement of creative activity which is both the expression and result of the universal Karma or store of unfulfilled desire for cosmic life.

It is then said that the Parabindu "divides" or "differentiates". In the Satyaloka is the formless and lustrous One. She exists like a grain of gram (Chanaka) surrounding Herself with Māyā. When casting off (Utsrijya) the covering (Bandhana) of Māyā, She, intent on creation (Unmukhī), becomes twofold (Dvīdhā bhittvā), or according to the account here given threefold, and then on this differentiation in Shiva and Shakti (Shiva-Shaktivibhāgena) arises creative ideation (Srishtikalpanā). As so unfolding the Bindu is known as the Sound Brahman (Shabdabrahman). "On the differentiation of the Parabindu there arose unmanifested sound" (Bhidyamānāt parād bindoravyaktātmā ravo, 'bhavat). Shabda here of course does not mean physical sound, which is the Guna of the Kāryyākāsha or atomic Ākāsha. The latter is integrated and limited and evolved at a later stage in Vikriti Parināma from Tāmasika Ahangkāra. Shabdabrahman is the undifferentiated Chidākāsha or Spiritual Ether of philosophy, in association with its Kalā or Prakriti or the Sakala Shiva of religion. It is Chit-Shakti vehicled by undifferentiated Prakriti, from which is evolved Nādamātra ("Sound only" or the "Principle of Sound") which is unmanifest (Avyakta), from which again is displayed (Vyakta) the changing universe of names and forms. It is the Pranavarūpa Brahman or Om which is the cosmic causal principle and the manifested Shabdārtha. Avyakta Nāda or unmanifested Sound is the undifferentiated causal principle of Manifested Sound without any sign or characteristic manifestation such as letters and the like which mark its displayed product. Shabdabrahman is the all-pervading, impartite, unmanifested Nādabindu substance, the primary creative impulse in Parashiva which is the cause of the manifested Shabdārtha. This Bindu is called Para because It is the first and supreme Bindu. Although It is Shakti like the Shakti and Nāda which precede It, It is considered as Shakti on the point of creating the world, and as such It is from this Parabindu that Avyakta Sound is said to come.

Rāghava Bhatta ends the discussion of this matter by shortly saying that the Shabdabrahman is the Chaitanya in all creatures which as existing in breathing creatures (Prani) is known as the Shakti Kundalinī of the Mūlādhāra. The accuracy of this definition is contested by the Compiler of the Prānatoshinī, but if by Chaitanya we understand the Manifested Chit, that is, the latter displayed as and with Mūlaprakriti in Cosmic vibration (Spandana), then the apparently differing views are reconciled.

The Parabindu on such differentiation manifests under the threefold aspects of Bindu, Nāda, Bīja. This is the fully developed and kinetic aspect of Parashabda. The Bindu which thus becomes threefold is the Principle in which the germ of action sprouts to manifestation producing a state of compact intensive Shakti. The threefold aspect of Bindu, as Bindu (Kāryya), Nāda and Bīja are Shivamaya, Shivashaktimaya, Shaktimaya; Para, Sūkshma, Sthūla; Ichchhā, Jnāna, Kriyā; Tamas, Sattva, Rajas; Moon, Fire and Sun; and the Shaktis which are the cosmic bodies known as Īshvara, Hiranyagarbha, and Virāt. All three, Bindu, Bīja, Nāda are the different phases of Shakti in creation, being different aspects of Parabindu the Ghanāvasthā of Shakti. The order of the three Shaktis of will, action and knowledge differ in Īshvara and Jīva. Īshvara is all-knowing and therefore the order in Him is Ichchhā, Jnāna, Kriyā. In Jīva, it is Jnāna, Ichchhā, Kriyā. Ichchhā is said to be the capacity which conceives the idea of work or action; which brings the work before the mind and wills to do it. In this Bindu, Tamas is said to be predominant, for there is as yet no stir to action. Nāda is Jnāna Shakti, that is, the subjective direction of will by knowledge to the desired end. With it is associated Sattva. Bīja is Kriyā Shakti or the Shakti which arises from that effort or the action done. With it Rajoguna or the principle of activity is associated. Kriyā arises from the combination of Ichchhā and Jnāna. It is thus said, "Drawn by Ichchhā-shakti, illumined by Jnānashakti, Shakti the Lord appearing as Male creates (Kriyāshakti). From Bindu it is said arose Raudrī; from Nāda, Jyeshthā; and from Bīja, Vāmā. From these arose Rudra, Brahma, Vishnu." It is also said in the Goraksha Samhitā, "Ichchhā is Brāhmī, Kriyā is Vaishnavī and Jnāna is Gaurī. Wherever there are these three Shaktis there is the Supreme Light called Om." In the Sakala Parameshvara or Shabdabrahman in bodies (that is, Kundalinī Shakti), Bindu in which Tamas prevails is, Rāghava says, called Nirodhikā; Nāda in which Sattva prevails is called Ardhendhu, and Bīja the combination of the two

(Ichchhā and Jnāna) in which Rajas as Kriyā works is called Bindu. The three preceding states in Kundalinī are Shakti, Dhvani, and Nāda. Kundalinī is Chit-Shakti into which Sattva enters a state known as the Paramākāshāvasthā. When She into whom Sattva has entered is next pierced by Rajas, She is called Dhvani which is the Aksharāvasthā. When She is again pierced by Tamas, She is called Nāda. This is the Avyaktāvasthā, the Avyakta Nāda which is the Parabindu. The three Bindus which are aspects of Parabindu constitute the mysterious Kāmakalā triangle which with the Hārddhakalā forms the roseate body of the lovely limbed great *Devī* Tripurasundarī who is Shivakāmā and manifests the universe. She is the trinity of Divine energy of whom the Shrītattvārnava says: "Those glorious men who worship in that body in Sāmarasya are freed from the waves of poison in the untraversable sea of the Wandering (Samsāra)". The main principle which underlies the elaborate details here shortly summarised is this. The state in which Chit and Prakriti-Shākta are as one undivided whole, that is, in which Prakriti lies latent (Nishkala Shiva), is succeeded by one of differentiation, that is, manifestation of Māyā (Sakala Shiva). In such manifestation it displays several aspects. The totality of such aspects is the Māyā body of Īshvara in which are included the causal, subtle and gross bodies of the Jīva. These are, according to the Shāradā, seven aspects of the first or Parā state of Sound in Shabdasrishti which are the seven divisions of the Mantra Om, *viz.*: A, U, M, Nāda, Bindu, Shakti, Shānta. They constitute Parashabdasrishti in the Īshvara creation. They are Īshvara or Om and seven aspects of the cosmic causal body; the collectivity (Samashti) of the individual (Vyashti) causal, subtle and gross bodies of the Jīva.

Before passing to the manifested Word and Its meaning (Shabdārtha), it is necessary to note what is called

Arthasrishti in the Avikriti or Sadrishaparināma: that is the causal state of Sound called Parashabda; the other three states, *viz.*: Pashyantī, Madhyamā and Vaikharī manifesting only in gross bodies. As Parabindu is the causal body of Shabda, It is also the causal body of Artha which is inseparately associated with It as the combined Shabdārtha. As such, He is called Shambhu who is of the nature of both Bindu and Kalā and the associate of Kalā. From Him issued Sadāshiva, "the witness of the world," and from Him Īsha, and then Rudra, Vishnu and Brahmā. These six Shivas are various aspects of Chit as presiding over (the first) the subjective Tattvas and (the rest) the elemental world whose centres are the five lower Chakras. These Devatās when considered as belonging to the Avikriti Parināma are the Devatā aspect of apparently different states of causal sound by the process of resolution of like to like giving them the semblance of all pervasive creative energies. They are Sound powers in the aggregate (Samashti). As appearing in, that is, presiding over, bodies they are the ruling Lords of the individual (Vyeshti) evolutes from the primal cause of Shabda.

The completion of the causal Avikriti Parināma with its ensuing Cosmic vibration in the Gunas is followed by a real Parināma of the Vikritis from the substance of Mūlaprakriti. There then appears the manifested Shabdārtha or the individual bodies subtle or gross of the Jīva in which are the remaining three Bhāvas of Sound or Shaktis called Pashyantī, Madhyamā, Vaikharī. Shabda literally means sound, idea, word; and Artha its meaning; that is, the objective form which corresponds to the subjective conception formed and language spoken of it. The conception is due to Samskāra. Artha is the externalized thought. There is a psycho-physical parallelism in the Jīva. In Īshvara thought is truly creative. The two are inseparable, neither existing without the other. Shabdārtha has thus a composite meaning like the Greek word "Logos", which means both thought and word combined. By the manifested Shabdārtha is meant what the Vedāntins call Nāmarūpa, the world of names and form, but with this difference that according to the Tāntrik notions here discussed there is, underlying this world of names and forms, a real material cause that is Parashabda or Mūlaprakriti manifesting as the principle of evolution.

The Shāradā says that from the Unmanifested Root-Avyakta Being in Bindu form (Mūlabhūta Bindurūpa) or the Paravastu (Brahman), that is, from Mūlaprakriti in creative operation there is evolved the Sāṅkhyan Tattvas.

Transcendentally, creation of all things takes place simultaneously. But, from the standpoint of Jīva, there is a real development (Parināma) from the substance of Mūlabhūta Avyakta Bindurūpa (as the Shāradā calls Mūlaprakriti) of the Tattvas, Buddhi, Ahangkāra, Manas, the Indriyas, Tanmātras and Mahābhūtas in the order stated. The Tantra therefore adopts the Sāṅkhyan and not the Vedāntic order of emanation which starts with the Apanchikrita Tanmātra, the Tāmasik parts of which, on the one hand, develop by Panchīkarana into the Mahābhūta, and on the other, the Rājasik and Sāttvik parts of which are collectively and separately the source of the remaining Tattvas. In the Shākta Tantra, the Bhūtas derive directly and not by Panchīkarana from the Tanmātras. Panchīkarana exists in respect of the compounds derived from the Bhūtas. There is a further point of detail in the Tāntrik exposition to be noted. The Shākta Tantra, as the Purānas and Shaiva Shāstras do, speaks of a threefold aspect of Ahangkāra, according to the predominance therein of the respective Gunas. From the Vaikārika Ahangkāra issue the eleven Devatās who preside over Manas and the ten

Indriyas; from the Taijasa Ahangkāra is produced the Indriyas and Manas: and from the Bhūtādika Ahangkāra the Tanmātras. None of these differences in detail or order of emanation of the Tattvas has substantial importance. In one case start is made from the knowing principle (Buddhi), on the other from the subtle object of knowledge the Tanmātra.

The abovementioned creation is known as Īshvara Srishti. The Vishvasāra Tantra says that from the Earth come the herbs (Oshadhi), from the latter food, and from food seed (Retas). From the latter living beings are produced by the aid of sun and moon. Here what is called Jīva Srishti is indicated, a matter into which I have no time to enter here.

To sum up, upon this ripening of Karma and the urge therefrom to cosmic life, Nishkala Shiva becomes Sakala. Shakti manifests and the causal body of Īshvara is thought of as assuming seven causal aspects in Sadrishaparināma which are aspects of Shakti about to create. The Parabindu or state of Shakti thus developed is the causal body of both the manifested Shabda and Artha. The Parabindu is the source of all lines of development, whether of Shabda, or as Shambhu of Artha, or as the Mūlabhūta of the Manifested Shabdārtha. On the completed ideal development of this causal body manifesting as the triple Shaktis of will, knowledge and action, the Shabdārtha in the sense of the manifested world with its subtle and gross bodies appears in the order described.

From the above description, it will have been seen that the creation doctrine here described is compounded of various elements, some of which it shares with other Shāstras, and some of which are its own, the whole being set forth according to a method and terminology which is peculiar to itself. The theory which is a form of Advaitavāda has then some characteristics which are both Sāṅkhyan and Vedāntic. Thus it accepts a real Mūlaprakriti, not however as an independent principle in the Sāṅkhyan sense, but as a form of the Shakti of Shiva. By and out of Shiva-Shakti who are one, there is a real creation. In such creation there is a special Adrishta Shristi up to the transformation of Shakti as Parabindu. This is Īshvara Tattva of the thirty-six Tattvas, a scheme accepted by both Advaita Shaivas and Shāktas.

Then by the operation of Māyā-Shakti it is transformed into Purusha-Prakriti and from the latter are evolved the Tattvas of the Sāṅkhya. Lastly, there is Yaugika Srishti of the Nyāya Vaisheshika in that the world is held to be formed by a combination of the elements. It accepts, therefore, Adrishta Srishti from the appearance of Shakti, up to the complete formation of the Causal Body known in its subtle form as the Kāmakalā; thereafter Parināma Srishti of the Vikritis of the subtle and gross body produced from the causal body down to the Mahābhūtas; and finally Yaugika Srishti in so far as it is the Bhūtas which in varied combination go to make up the gross world.

There are (and the doctrine here discussed is an instance of it) common principles and mutual connections existing in and between the different Indian Shāstras, notwithstanding individual peculiarities of presentment due to natural variety of intellectual or temperamental standpoint or the purpose in view. Shiva in the Kulārnava says that all the Darshanas are parts of His body, and he who severs them severs His limbs. The meaning of this is that the six Darshanas are the Six Minds, and these, as all else, are parts of the Lord's Body.

Of these six minds, Nyāya and Vaisheshika teach Yaugika Srishti; Sāṅkhya and Patanjali teach Yaugika Srishti and Parināma Srishti; Māyāvāda Vedānta teaches Yaugika

Srishti, Parināmasrishti according to the empirical method and Vivartta according to the transcendental method. According to the Vivartta of Māyāvāda, there is no real change but only the appearance of it. According to Shāktavāda, Ultimate Reality does in one aspect really evolve but in another aspect is immutable. Māyāvāda effects its synthesis by its doctrine of grades of reality, and Shāktavāda by its doctrine of aspects of unity and duality, duality in unity and unity in duality. Ultimate Reality as the Whole is neither merely static nor merely active. It is both. The Natural and the Spiritual are one. In this sense the Shākta system claims to be the synthesis of all other doctrines.

CHAPTER XX

THE INDIAN MAGNA MATER[1]

Introductory

On the last occasion that I had the honour to address you, I dealt with the subject of the psychology of Hindu religious ritual from the particular standpoint of the religious community called Shāktas, or Worshippers of the Supreme Mother. To-day I speak of the Supreme Mother Herself as conceived and worshipped by them.

The worship of the Great Mother as the Grand Multiplier is one of the oldest in the world. As I have elsewhere said, when we throw our minds back upon the history of this worship, we discern even in the most remote and fading past the Figure, most ancient, of the mighty Mother of Nature. I suspect that in the beginning the Goddess everywhere antedated, or at least was predominant over, the God. It has been affirmed (Glotz: "Ægean Civilization," 243) that in all countries from the Euphrates to the Adriatic, the Chief Divinity was at first in woman form. Looking to the east of the Euphrates we see the Dusk Divinity of India, the Ādyā-Shaktí and Mahā-Shakti, or Supreme Power of many names—as Jagadambā, Mother of the World, which is the Play of Her

[1] From Vol. 2, No. 2, "Indian Arts and Letters" reporting a lecture given to the India Society, London, Nov. 18, 1926.

who is named Lalitā, Māyā, Mahātripurasundarī and Mahākundalinī, as Mahā-Vaishnavī, the Sapphire Devī who supports the World, as Mahākālī who dissolves it, as Guhyamahābhairavī, and all the rest.

This Supreme Mother is worshipped by Her devotees from the Himālayas, the "Abode of Snow", the northern home of Shiva, to Cape Comorin in the uttermost south—for the word Comorin is a corruption of Kumārī Devī or the Mother. Goddesses are spoken of in the Vedas as in the later Scriptures. Of these latter, the Shākta Tantras are the particular repository of Mother-worship.

To the Shākta, God is his Supreme Mother. In innumerable births he has had countless mothers and fathers, and he may in future have many, many more. The human, and indeed any, mother is sacred as the giver (under God) of life, but it is the Divine Mother of All (*Shrīmātā*), the "Treasure-House of Compassion", who alone is both the Giver of life in the world and of its joys, and who (as *Tārinī*) is the Saviouress from its miseries, and who again is, for all who unite with Her, the Life of all lives—that unalloyed bliss named Liberation. She is the Great Queen (*Mahārājnī*) of Heaven and of yet higher worlds, of Earth, and of the Underworlds. To Her both Devas, Devīs, and Men give worship. Her Feet are adored by even Brahmā, Vishnu, and Rudra.

The Shākta system, in its origin possibly Non-Vaidik, is in several respects an original presentment, both as regards doctrine and practice, of the great Vedāntic Theme concerning the One and the Many. As an organic and dynamic system it interprets all in terms of Power, from the atom of Matter, which is said by modern science to be a reservoir of tremendous energy, to the Almighty, which is the commonest name in all Religions for God. It is the cult of Power both as the Partial and as the Whole, as the worshipper may desire. God is here regarded under twin aspects: as Power-Holder or the "male" Shiva, and as Power or Shakti, the Divine Spouse and Mother.

The symbolism of the Shāktas' "Jewelled Tree of Tantra" is brilliant, and meets the demand of Nietzsche that the abstract should be made attractive to the senses. It is largely of the so-called "erotic" type which is to be found to some and varying degree in Hinduism as a whole.

The symbols employed are either geometric—that is, Yantric—or pictorial. A *Yantra* is a diagrammatic presentation of Divinity, as Mantra is its sound-expression. The former is the body of the latter. The higher worship is done with Yantra.

Pictorial symbolism is of higher and lower types. The former is popular, and the latter may be described by the French term *peuple*.

I will now describe a Yantra and the greatest of Yantras, namely the Shrīyantra, figured on the truth of the "Tāntrik Texts". We have no longer to deal with pictures of persons and their surroundings, but with lines, curves, circles, triangles, and the Point.

The great symbol of the Mother is the *Shrīyantra*, from the centre of which She arises like the solar orb at morn, but in a blaze of light excelling the brilliance of countless midday suns and the coolness of innumerable moons. The centre is the Point, or *Bindu*—that is, the Mother as Concentrated Power ready to create. Around Her is the Universe, together with its Divinities or Directing Intelligences. From the Point the World issues. Into it on dissolution it enters. The extended Universe then collapses into an unextended Point, which itself then subsides like a bubble on the surface of the Causal Waters, which are the Immense.

I. The Divine Mother

The Real as Shiva-Shakti may be regarded from three aspects—namely, as Universe, as God, and as Godhead. The Real is the World, but the Real is more than the World. The Real is God. The Real is God, but it is also more than what we understand by the word God. The Real is, as it were, beyond God as Godhead. This does not mean, as some have supposed, that God is a "fiction", but that the Real as it is in its own alogical being is not adequately described in terms of its relation to the world as God. I will deal, then, first with its aspect as Godhead, then as the Supreme Self, or Person, or God, and thirdly, with Shiva-Shakti as the manifest and limited Universe.

Pervading and transcending the Existent is the "Spiritual Ether", also called the "Immense" in which is the Measurable, which Immense is also called the "Fact" (*Sat*), in which are the Fact-Sections (*Kalā*), which Fact is also called the alogical Experience-Whole (*Pūrna*), in which are all Experience-Modes (*Vritti*) of the limited Selves.

The ultimate that is Irreducible Real is, in the system, not mere undetermined Being, but Power which is the source of all Determinations. This Power is both to Be, to self-conserve, and to resist change, as also to be the efficient cause of change, and as material cause to Become and suffer change. Relatively to the World, Immutable Being is as Divinity called Shiva the Power-Holder, and His Power is Shakti or the Mother Shiva, but in the supreme alogical state, Power to Be and Being-Power-Holder are merged in one another.

What is the nature of this Alogical Experience? In the Yoginīhridaya Tantra it is asked. "Who knows the heart of a woman? Only Shiva knows the heart of Yoginī" —that is, the Divine Mother so called, as being one with, that is in the form of, all that exists, and as being in Herself the One in which they are.

Since the Irreducible Real is the Whole, it cannot be conceived or described. It is neither Father nor Mother, for it is beyond Fatherhood and Motherhood and all other attributes. It is alogical.

Though it cannot be conceived or put into words, some concepts are held to be more appropriate to it than others. And thus it is approximately said to be infinite undetermined Being, mindless Experiencing, and Supreme Bliss unalloyed with pain and sorrow. As Being and Power are merged in this alogical state, Power, in its form as Power to Be (*Chidrūpinī*), is also Being-Consciousness and Bliss. Shiva-Shakti, the "two in one", are here the Nameless One.

The experience of this alogical state is not, however, that of an "I" (*Aham*) and "This" (*Idam*). The next or causal aspect of the Real is a Supreme Self. Its third and effectual aspect is the limited selves or Universe.

The physical Ether is a symbol of this alogical state, in which the twofold Shiva-Shakti are the One in the unitary state, which is called the "Ether of Consciousness" (*Chidākāsha*).

Physical Ether is the all-extending, homogeneous, relative *Plenum* in which the Universe of particulars exists. The "Spiritual Ether," or "Ether of Consciousness," is the undetermined, all-diffusive, though inextended, absolute *Plenum* (*Pūrna*), in which both these particulars and the physical Ether itself exists. Ether is the physical counterpart of Consciousness, just as the Notion of Space is its psychical counterpart. These are such counterparts because Consciousness becomes through its Power as material cause both Matter and Mind. Each is a manifested form of Spirit in Time and Space. The shoreless Ocean of Nectar or Deathlessness is another symbol of the alogical Whole.

We now pass to a consideration of the same Real in its aspect as related to the Universe, which is the appearance of the Immense as the Measurable or Form. The Real is here related to the Universe as its Cause, Maintainer, and Directing Consciousness. Form is *Māyā*, which, however, in this system (whatever be its meaning in *Māyāvāda*) does not mean "Illusion". All is power. All is real.

The alogical One is here of dual aspect as Shiva and Shakti. The two concepts of Being and Power are treated as two Persons. Shiva is the Power-Holder, who is Being-Consciousness-Bliss, and Shakti is Power and the Becoming. She, in the alogical state, is also Being-Consciousness-Bliss. Without ceasing to be in Herself what She ever was, is, and will be, She is now the Power of Shiva as efficient and material cause of the Universe and the Universe itself. Whilst Shiva represents the Consciousness aspect of the Real, She is its aspect as Mind, Life, and Matter. He is the Liberation (*Moksha*) aspect of the Real. She is in the form of the Universe or *Samsāra*. As Shiva-Shakti are in themselves one, so *Moksha* and *Samsāra* are at root one.

Shiva, in the Kulārnava Tantra, says that His doctrine is neither non-dualist nor dualist, but beyond both. We have here a non-dualistic system as regards its teaching concerning the Alogical Whole, in which Shiva-Shakti are fused in one. We have again a kind of Duo-Monotheism. It is Monotheistic because, Shiva and Shakti are two aspects of one and the same Reality. It is dual because, these two aspects are worshipped as two Persons, from whose union as Being and Power the Universe evolves.

The experience of this state, relative to the Alogical Whole, is a disruption of unitary alogical experience. I say "relative" because the Whole is always the Whole. Such disruption is the work of Power. She, as it were, disengages Herself as Power, from the embrace in which

Power-Holder and Power are fused in one, and then represents Herself to Him. On this representation, Consciousness-Power assumes certain postures (*Mudrā*) preparatory to the going forth as Universe, and then, when Power is fully concentrated, manifests as the World.

The term Consciousness, which is inadequate to describe the alogical state, is here approximately appropriate, for the experience of this state is that of an "I" and "This". But it is to be distinguished from man's Consciousness. For the experiencer as man is a limited (and not, as here, a Supreme Self) and the object is experienced as separate from, and outside, the Self (and not, as in the case of the Lord and Mother, as one with the experiencing Self). The experience of Shiva as the Supreme Self viewing the Universe is, "All this I am".

As contrasted with the alogical, all-diffusive, Spiritual Ether, the symbol of the second aspect of Shiva-Shakti, as the Supreme Self and Cause of the Universe is the metaphysical Point (*Bindu*) or Power as a Point. What, then, is the meaning of the latter term? In Being-Power about to evolve there is a stressing of Power which gathers itself together to expand again as Universe. When it has become concentrated and condensed (*Ghanībhūtā Shakti*) it is ready to evolve. *Bindu*, or the Point, is, therefore, Power in that Concentrated state in which it is ready and about to evolve the Universe. Though infinitely small, as the Absolute Little, when compared with the Absolute Great or Spiritual Ether, it is yet a source of infinite energy as (to borrow an example from modern science) the relatively Little or Atom, or other unit of matter, existing in the relatively Great or the physical Ether, is said to be a source of tremendous energy. Just as, again, the relative point or atom is as a fact in the relative Ether, so the Absolute Point is conceived to be in the Absolute Ether. I say "conceived", because, as both Spiritual Point and Spiritual Ether are each absolute, it is only figuratively that the one can be said to be "within" the other. The "Isle of Gems" (*Maṇidvīpa*) in the "Ocean of Nectar" (*Amritārnava*) is another symbol of this state.

There is a painting that exhibits both the Alogical Immense and the Point of Power or *Bindu* "in" it. The former is here symbolized by the shoreless "Ocean of Nectar" (*Amritārnava*)—that is, Immortality. This symbol of all-diffusive Consciousness is similar to that of the all-spreading Ether. In the blue, tranquil Waters of Eternal Life (*Amritārnava*) is set the Isle of Gems (*Manidvīpa*). This Island is the *Bindu* or metaphysical Point of Power. The Island is shown as a golden circular figure. The shores of the Island are made of powdered gems. It is forested with blooming and fragrant trees—Nipa, Mālati, Champaka, Pārijāta, and Kadamba. There, too, is the Kalpa tree laden with flower and fruit. In its leaves the black bees hum, and the Koel birds make love. Its four branches are the four Vedas. In the centre there is a house made of *Chintāmani* stone which grants all desires. In it is a jewelled *Mandapa* or awning. Under it and on a gemmed and golden throne there is the Mother Mahātripurasundarī as the Deity of the *Bindu*, which, as shown later, becomes the three *Bindus* or *Puras*. Hence Her name "Three Puras" or Tripurā. She is red, for red is the active colour, and She is here creative as *Vimarsha Shakti*, or, the "This" of the Supreme Experiencer, which through *Māyā* becomes the Universe. What man calls Matter is first experienced by mindless Consciousness as a "This", which is yet though the "Other" one with the Self. Then, by the operation of *Māyā*, the "This" is experienced by mind as separate and different from and outside the Self, as complete "otherness". She holds in Her four hands, bows and arrows, noose and goad, which are explained later. She sits on two inert male figures which lie on a six-sided throne. The upper figure is Shiva (*Sakala*), who is awake, because, he is associated with his Power as efficient and material cause. On His head is the crescent Digit of the Moon, called *Nāda*, the name for a state of stressing Power, His Shakti being now creative. He lies inert, for He is Immutable Being. He is white because he is Consciousness and Illumination (*Prakāsha*). Consciousness illuminates and makes manifest the forms evolved by its Power, which in its turn by supplying the form (as object unconscious) helps Shiva to display Himself as the Universe which is both Being and Becoming. Under him is another male figure, darker in colour, to represent colourlessness (*vivarna*), with closed eyes. This mysterious figure (*Nishkala Shiva*) is called *Shava* or the Corpse. It illustrates the doctrine that Shiva without his Power or Shakti can do and is, so far as the manifested is concerned, nothing. There is profundity in the doctrine of which this Corpse is a symbol. To those who have understood it a real insight is given into the Kaula Shākta system.

This representation of Shiva and Shakti as of the same size, but the former lying inert, is perhaps peculiar to the Kaula Shāktas, and is the antithesis of the well-known "Dancing Shiva".

I will here note some other symbolism, pictorial and geometric or Yantric.

Pictorially, Shakti is shown either as the equal of Her Spouse—that is, as an Androgyne figure in which the right half is male and the left female—or as two figures, male and female, of equal size. Inequality is indicated where the Shakti is smaller than the male Divinity. The meaning of this difference in dimension of the figures of Shakti lies in a difference of theological and philosophical concepts which may yet be reconciled. In the Shākta view, the Power-Holder and His Power as She is in Herself, that is, otherwise than as the manifested form, are one and equal. But He is recumbent. Alternatively, Shakti is the Mother as the Warrior Leader or Promachos with Shiva under Her feet. Where the figures are unequal it is meant to assert (a fact which is not denied) that Supreme Power as manifested is infinitely less than Power unmanifest. That Power is in no wise exhausted in the manifestation of the Worlds which are said to be as it were but dust on the feet of the Mother.

Passing to Yantric symbols, the Male Power-Holder Shiva is represented by a triangle standing on its base. A triangle is selected as being the only geometric figure which represents Trinity in Unity—the many Triads such as Willing, Knowing, and Acting in which the one Consciousness (*Chit*) displays itself. Power or the feminine principle or Shakti is necessarily represented by the same figure, for Power and Power-Holder are one. The Triangle, however, is shown reversed—that is standing on its apex. Students of ancient symbolism are aware of the physical significance of this symbol. To such reversal, however, philosophic meaning may also be given, since all is reversed when reflected in the Waters of *Māyā*.

Why, it may now be asked, does the Shākta lay stress on the Power or Mother aspect of Reality? Like all other Hindus, he believes in a Static Real as Immutable Being-Consciousness, which is the ground of and serves to maintain that which, in this system, is the Dynamic Real. He will point out, however, that the Mother is also in one of Her aspects of the same nature as Shiva, who is such Static Real. But it is She who does work. She alone also moves as material cause. He as Immutable Being does and can do nothing without Her as His Power. Hence the

Kaula Shākta symbolism shows Shiva as lying inert and to be, if deprived of His Power, but a corpse (*Shava*).

Even when associated with his Shakti as efficient cause, Shiva does not move. A not uncommon picture, counted obscene, is merely the pictorial symbol of the fact that Being, even when associated with its active Power, is Immutable. It is She as Power who takes the active and changeful part in generation, as also in conceiving, bearing, and giving birth to the World-Child. All this is the function of the divine, as it is of the human, mother. In such work the male is but a helper (*Sahakārī*) only. In other systems it is the Mother who is the Helper of Shiva. It is thus to the Mother that man owes the World of Form or Universe. Without Her as material cause, Being cannot display itself. It is but a corpse (*Shava*). Both Shiva and Shakti give that supreme beyond-world Joy which is Liberation (*Mukti, Paramānanda*). They are each Supreme Consciousness and Bliss. The Mother is *Ānandalaharī* or Wave of Bliss. To attain to that is to be liberated. But Shakti the Mother is alone the Giver of World-Joy (*Bhukti, Bhaumānanda*), since it is She who becomes the Universe. As such She is the Wave of Beauty (*Saundaryalaharī*). Further, it is through her Form as World that She, as also Shiva, are in their Formless Self attained. If, however, union is sought directly with Reality in its non-world aspect, it must necessarily be by renunciation. Liberation may, however, be attained by acceptance of, and through the World, the other aspect of the Real. In the Shākta method, it is not by denial of the World, but, by and through the World, when known as the Mother, that Liberation is attained. World enjoyment is made the means and instrument of Liberation (*Mokshāyate Samsāra*). The Shākta has both (*Bhukti, Mukti*). This essential unity of the World and Beyond World, and passage through and by means of the former to the latter is one of the most profound doctrines of the Shākta, and is none-the-less so because their application of these principles has been limited to man's gross physical functions, and such application has sometimes led to abuse. For these and other reasons primacy is given to the Mother, and it is said: "What care I for the Father if I but be on the lap of the Mother?"

I note here in connection with the primacy of the Mother-God that in the Mediterranean (Ægean) Civilization the Male God is said to have been of a standing inferior to the Mother, and present only to make plain Her character as the fruitful womb whence all that exists springs (Glotz, 243, *et seq.*).

Such, then, is the great Mother of India in Her aspect as She is in Herself as the alogical world-transcending Whole (*Pūrna*), and secondly, as She is as the Creatrix of the World. It remains now but to say a word of Her as She exists in the form of the universe.

The psycho-physical universe is *Māyā*. The devotee Kamalākānta lucidly defines *Māyā* as the Form (*Ākāra*) of the Void (*Shūnya*) or Formless (not Nothingness). Is it Real? It is real, because *Māyā*, considered as a Power, is Devī Shakti, and She is real. The effect of the transformation of that Power must also be real. Some make a contrast between Reality and Appearance. But why, it is asked (apart from persistence), should appearance be unreal, and that of which it is such appearance alone be real? Moreover, in a system such as this, in which Power transforms itself, no contrast between Reality and Appearance in the sense of unreality emerges. The distinction is between the Real as it is in its formless Self and the same Real as it appears in Form. Moreover, the World is experienced by the Lord and Mother, and their experience is never unreal. We are here on a healthy level above the miasma of Illusion.

The experience of man (to take him as the highest type of all other selves) is not the Experience-Whole. He knows the world as other than Himself, just because Power has made him man—that is, a limited Experiencer or centre in the Whole. That is *a* fact, and no Illusion or Deceit. When He realizes Himself as "All this I am" that is, as an "I" which knows all form as Itself—then Consciousness as man expands into the Experience-Whole which is *the* Fact (*Sat*).

Man is Shakti, or the Mother, in so far as he is Mind, Life in Form, and Matter. He is Shiva, in so far as his essence is Consciousness as It is in Itself, which is also the nature of the Mother in Her own alogical Self.

This union is achieved by rousing the sleeping Power in the lowest centre of solid matter and leading it upwards to the cerebrum as the centre of Consciousness.

I now pass to the second part of my paper, which deals with the cosmic evolution of Power—that is, the "going forth" of the Supreme Self upon its union with its Power in mañifestation. As the result of such evolution we have Shiva-Shakti as the limited selves. Shiva-Shakti are not terms limited to God only, but the forms into which Power evolves are also Shiva-Shakti. God as the Mother-Father is supreme Shiva-Shakti. The Limited Selves are Shiva-Shakti appearing as Form in Time and Space. The Measurable or World (*Samsāra*) and the Immense Experience-Whole (*Moksha*) are at root one. This is fundamental doctrine in the community to whose beliefs reference is now made.

II. Evolution

Shiva and Shakti as the Causal Head (Shiva-Shakti Tattvas) of the world-evolution are called Kāmeshvara and Kāmeshvari. Kāma is Desire. Here it is the Divine

Desire, or (to use a Western term) the *Libido*, which in the Veda is expressed as the wish of the One, "May I be many". So also the Veda says: "Desire first arose in it the primal germ." The form of this wish tells us what *Libido*, in its Indian sense, means. In its primary sense, it does not mean sensuous desire, but the will to, and affirmance of, "otherness" and differentiation, of which sensuous desire is a later and gross form in the evolutionary series. Procreation is the individual counterpart of Cosmic Creation.

Why were the worlds (for there are many) evolved? The answer given is because it is the nature (*Svabhāva*) of almighty formless Being-Power, whilst remaining what it *is*, to become Form—that is, to *exist*. The *Svabhāva*, or nature of Being-Power, is *Līlā*, or Play, a term which means free spontaneous activity. Hence Lalitā, or "Player", is a name of the Mother as She who Plays and whose Play is World-Play. She is both Joy (*Ānandā-mayī*) and Play (*Līlāmayī*). The action of man and of other selves is, in so far as they are the psycho-physical, determined by their *Karma*. The Mother's play is not idle or meaningless so far as man is concerned, for the world is the field on and means by which he attains all his worths, the greatest of which is Union with the Mother as She is in Herself as Highest Being. The Player is Power. How does it work?

The Whole (*Pūrna*), which means here, the Absolute Spiritual Whole, and not the relative Whole or psycho-physical universe, cannot as the Whole change. It is Immutable. Change can then take place only *in* It. This is the work of Power which becomes limited centres in the Whole, which centres, in relation to, and compared with, the Whole, are a contraction of it.

Power works by negation, contraction, and finitization. This subtle doctrine is explained profoundly and in detail in the scheme of the thirty-six Tattvas accepted by both non-dualists, Shaivas and Shāktas, and is also dealt with in the Mantra portion of their Scriptures. A Tattva is a Posture (*Mudrā*) of Power—that is, Reality-Power defined *in a particular way*, and, therefore the alogical aspect is that which is beyond all Tattvas (*Tattvātīta*). A *Tattva* is then a stage in the evolutionary process. *Mantra* is a most important subject in the Tantra Scriptures which treat of Sound and Movement, for the one implies the other. Sound as lettered speech is the vehicle of thought, and Mind is a vehicle of Consciousness for world-experience. The picture of Shiva riding a bull is a popular presentation of that fact. Bull in Sanskrit is "*Go*", and that word also means "sound". *Nāda* as inchoate stressing sound is shown in the form of a crescent-moon on His head. The cult of the Bull is an ancient one, and it may be that originally the animal had no significance as Sound, but subsequently, owing to the sameness of the Sanskrit term for Bull and Sound, the animal became a symbol for sound. Sometimes, however, a more lofty conception is degraded to a lower one. It is here noteworthy that the crescent-moon worn by Diana and used in the worship of other Goddesses is said to be the Ark or vessel of boat-like shape, symbol of fertility or the Container of the Germ of all life.

I can only in the most summary manner deal with the subject of the Evolution of Power, illustrating it by Yantric symbolism.

The Shiva and Shakti triangles are ever united. To represent the alogical state, we may place one triangle without reversal upon the other, thus making one triangular figure. This will give some idea of the state in which the two triangles as "I" and "This" are fused in one as Being-Consciousness-Bliss.

Here, however, we are concerned with the causal state which is the Supreme Self in Whose experience there is an

"I" and a "This", though the latter is experienced as the Self. There is, therefore, a double triangular figure; Shiva and Shakti are in union, but now not as the alogical Whole, but as the Supreme Self experiencing His object or Shakti as one with Himself. The marriage of the Divine couple, Kāmeshvara and Kāmeshvarī—that is, Being and Power to Become—is the archetype of all generative embraces.

To represent this aspect, the triangles are placed across one another, so as to produce a Hexagon, in which one triangle represents the "I", or Shiva, and the other the "This", or object, as Power and its transformations—that is, Shakti.

As the result of this union, Power assumes certain Postures (*Mudrā*) in its stressing to manifest as Universe. The first of such produced stresses is, from the *Tattva* aspect, Sadāshiva, and, from the Mantra aspect, inchoate sound or movement called *Nāda*. This state is shown by the Hexagon with a crescent-moon, the symbol of *Nāda*, in its centre. This *Nāda* is not manifested sound or movement, but an inchoate state of both.

In the next Mantric stage (corresponding to the Tattvas, Īshvara and Shuddhavidyā) the crescent-moon enlarges into the full moonlike *Bindu*. This also is stressing Power as inchoate sound and movement, but is now such Power ready to evolve into manifested sound and movement. The word *Bindu* also means seed, for it is the seed of the universe as the result of the union of its ultimate principles as Shiva and Shakti. The Point, or *Bindu*, is shown as a circle, so as to display its content and a line divides the Point, one half representing the "I", and the other, the "This" aspect of experience. They are shown in one circle to denote that the "This", or object, is not yet outside the self as non-self. The *Bindu* is compared in the Tantras to a grain of gram (*Chanaka*), which contains two seeds (*Aham* and *Idam*) so close to one another within their common sheath as to seem to be one seed.

At the stage when Consciousness lays equal emphasis on the "I" and "This" of experience, *Māyā-Shakti* and its derivative powers called sheaths (*Kanchuka*) and contractions (*Saṁkocha*) operate to disrupt the *Bindu*, which comes apart in two. Now the "I" and "This" are separated, the latter being experienced as *outside* the self or as non-self. The former becomes limited as "Little Knower" and "Little Doer". This is the work of *Māyā-Shakti*. Power again (as *Prakriti-Shakti*) evolves the psycho-physical organs of this limited Self, as Mind, Senses, and Body.

I have spoken of two *Bindus* standing for Shiva and Shakti. Their inter-relation and its product is another form of *Nāda*. These then make three *Bindus*, which are a grosser form of the *Kāmakalā*. The Divinity of the three *Bindus* is the Mother as Mahātripurasundarī, "the Beauteous One in whom are the three *Puras*," or *Bindus*.

The Mantra equivalent of the state in which the *Bindu* divides and becomes threefold is the first manifested sound, which is the Great Mantra *Om*. As the Supreme *Bindu* bursts there is a massive, homogeneous, vibratory movement, as it were a cosmic thrill (*sāmanya spandana*) in psycho-physical Substance the sound of which to man's gross ears is *Om*. The original sound of *Om* is that which was heard by the Absolute Ears of Him and Her who caused that movement. *Om* is the ground-sound and ground movement of Nature. The Mundakopanishad says that the Sun travels the universe chanting the mantra *Om*. From *Om* are derived all special (*vishesha spandana*) movements, sounds, and Mantras. It is itself threefold, since it is constituted by the union of the letters A, U, M. The Divinities of these three letters are Brahmā, Vishnu, Rudra, and their Shaktis. These, together with Sadāshiva and Īsha, are the Five Shivas to whom reference is made in the ritual, and who are pictured in the Shākta symbolism as the Five who are Dead (*Preta*).

Power, after involving itself in solid matter, technically called " Earth ", then rests in this last-named element.

The evolution of the *Tattvas* is not a temporal process. Time only comes in with sun and moon, on the completion of the evolution of the *Tattvas* as constituent elements of the universe. The *Tattvas* are given as the results of an analysis of experience, in which the *Prius* is logical not temporal. For these reasons a Causal Tattva does not cease to be what it is as Cause when it is transformed into its effect, which is not the case in the manifested world wherein, as the Lakshmī-Tantra says, "Milk when it becomes curd ceases to be milk." Reality does not cease to be the Alogical Whole because it is from the Causal aspect a Supreme Self. It does not cease to be the Cosmic Cause because it evolves as the Universe its effect. Nor in such evolution does any Tattva cease to be what it is as cause because it is transformed into its effect.

I am now in the position to explain the great *Yantra* or diagram which is used in the worship of the Mother and which is called the *Shrī Yantra*, a symbol of both the Universe and its Cause. (See Frontispiece).

I have not the time to describe it at length, but its meaning may be generally stated.

It is composed of two sets of Triangles. One set is composed of four male or Shiva triangles called *Shrīkanthas* denoting four aspects (*Tattva*) of evolved or limited Consciousness-Power, and the five female or Shakti triangles (*Shivayuvatīs*) denote the five vital functions, the five senses of knowledge, the five senses of action, and the five subtle and the five gross forms of matter. The place of the psychic element as Mind and the Psycho-physical Substance of both Mind and Matter, I will indicate later.

These two sets of triangles are superimposed to show the union of Shiva and Shakti. As so united they make the figure within the eight lotus petals in the full *Yantra.* Outside these eight lotuses there are sixteen other lotuses. There are then some lines, and a surround with four gates or doors, which surround is found in all *Yantras,* and is called *Bhūpura.* It serves the purpose of what in Magic is called a Fence.

This Yantra has nine *Chakras*, or compartments, formed by the intersection of the Triangles.

There is first a red central point or *Bindu,* the Chakra of Bliss. The central point or *Bindu* is Supreme Divinity —the Mother as the Grand Potential whence all the rest which this diagram signifies proceed. It is red, for that is the active colour, and thus the colour of *Vimarsha Shakti,* or Evolving Power.

The second Chakra is the white inverted Triangle, or "Chakra of All Accomplishment". In the corners of this white Triangle are the Divinities of the general Psycho-physical Substance and its first two evolutes as Cosmic Mind. Outside the Chakra is Kāma, the Divinity of Desire, with His Bow of Sugar-Cane, which is the Mind as director of the senses; with its Five Arrows, which are the five forms of subtle matter, which in their gross form are perceived by these senses; with his Noose, which is Attraction, and his Goad, which is Repulsion. Another version (taking the Bow and Arrow as one symbol) makes the three implements, the Powers of Will, Knowledge, and Action.

The third Chakra is eight red Triangles, and is called "Destroyer of all Disease," a term which means lack of that Wholeness (Apūrnam-manyatā) which is Spiritual Health.

The fourth Chakra is ten blue Triangles. The fifth is ten red Triangles. The sixth is fourteen blue Triangles. The seventh is eight red petals. The eighth is sixteen blue petals, and the ninth is the yellow surround. Each of these *Chakras* has its own name. In them there are a number of lesser Divinities presiding over forms of Mind, Life, and Body, and their special functions.

Those who hear the *Devas* spoken of as "Gods" are puzzled by their multitude. This is due to the ill-rendering of the terms *Devas* and *Devīs* as Gods and Goddesses. God is the Supreme Mother and Father, the "Two in One", who are alone the Supreme Self, and as such receive supreme worship. All forms—whether of *Devas*, or men, or other creatures—in so far as they are the psycho-physical form, subtle or gross, are manifestations of the Power of their Immanent Essence, which is Spirit or Infinite Consciousness. That Essence is in itself one and changeless, but as related to a particular psycho-physical form as its cause and Director of its functions it is its Presiding Consciousness. Mind and Matter are not, as such, self-guiding. They are evolved and directed by Consciousness. The presiding consciousness of the Form and its functions is its presiding *Devatā*. A *Deva* is thus the consciousness aspect of the psycho-physical form. So the *Deva* Agni is the one Consciousness in its aspect as the Lord of Fire. A *Devatā* may also mean an aspect of the Causal Consciousness itself. And so Mahātripurasundarī is the name given to the creative aspect of such Consciousness-Power, as Mahākālī is that aspect of the same Consciousness-Power which dissolves all worlds.

The object of the worship of the *Yantra* is to attain unity with the Mother of the Universe in Her forms as Mind, Life, and Matter and their *Devatās*, as preparatory to Yoga union with Her as She is in herself as Pure

Consciousness. The world is divinized in the consciousness of the Worshipper, or *Sādhaka*. The *Yantra* is thus transformed in his consciousness from a material object of lines and curves into a mental state of union with the Universe, its Divinities and Supreme Deity. This leads to autorealization as Mindless Consciousness. The *Shrī Yantra* is thus the Universe and its one Causal Power of various aspects. The worshipper, too, is a *Shrī Yantra*, and realizes himself as such.

III. Dissolution

I have dealt with the nature of Shiva-Shakti and the evolution of power as the Universe, and now will say a word as to the relative ending of the world on its withdrawal to reappear again, and as to the absolute ending for the individual who is liberated.

In Hindu belief, this Universe had a beginning, and will have an end. But it is only one of an infinite series in which there is no absolutely first Universe. These Universes come and go with the beating of the Pulse of Power now actively going forth, now returning to rest. For the World has its life period, which, reckoning up to the Great Dissolution, is the duration of an outgoing "Breath of Time". In due course another Universe will appear, and so on to all eternity. This series of Worlds of Birth, Death, and Reincarnation is called by the Hindus the *Samsāra*, and was named by the Greeks the Cycle of the Becoming (*kuklos tōn genesōn*). All selves which are withdrawn at the end of a world-period continue to reappear in the new worlds to be until they are liberated therefrom.

The picture now described depicts the Mother-Power which dissolves—that is, withdraws the World into Herself. This is another aspect of one and the same Mother. As such She is Mahākālī, dark blue like a rain cloud. *Nāda* is in Her head-dress. She is encircled by serpents, as is Shiva. She holds in Her hands, besides the Lotus and two weapons, a skull with blood in it. She wears a garland of human heads which are exoterically the heads of conquered Demons, but are esoterically the letters of the alphabet which, as well as the Universe of which they are the seed-*mantras*, are dissolved by Her. She stands on the white, inert Shiva, for it is not He but His power who withdraws the Universe to Herself. He lies on a funeral pyre, in the burning-ground, where jackals—favourite animals of Kālī—and carrion birds are gnawing and pecking at human flesh and bone. The Cremation ground is a symbol of cosmic dissolution.

In a similar picture, we see the Mother standing on two figures, the Shiva, and *Shava* previously explained. On the Corpse the hair has grown. The *Devas*, or "Gods", as they are commonly called, are shown making obeisance to Her on the left, for She is their Mother as well as being the Mother of men. There are some variations in the imagery. Thus Kālī, who is commonly represented naked—that is, free of her own *Māyā*—is shown clad in skins. Her function is commonly called Destruction, but as the Sanskrit saying goes, "the Deva does not Destroy". The Supreme Self withdraws the Universe into Itself. Nothing is destroyed. Things appear and disappear to reappear.

To pass beyond the Worlds of Birth and Death is to be Liberated. Human selves alone can attain liberation. Hence the supreme worth of human life. But few men understand and desire Liberation, which is the Experience-Whole. They have not reached the stage in which it is sought as the Supreme Worth. The majority are content to seek the Partial in the satisfaction of their individual interests. But as an unknown Sage cited by the Commentators on the Yoginīhridaya and Nityashodasika Tantras has profoundly said, "Identification of the Self with the Non-Whole or Partial (*Apūrnammanyatā*) is Disease and the sole source of every misery." Hence one of the Chakras of the *Shrī Yantra* which I have shown you is called "Destroyer of all Disease". Eternal Health is Wholeness, which is the Highest Worth as the Experience-Whole. The "Disease of the World" refers not to the World in itself, which is the Mother in form, but to that darkness of vision which does not see that it is Her. As Upanishad said, "He alone fears who sees Duality." This recognition of the unity of the World and the Mother has its degrees. That Whole is of varying kinds. It is thus physical or bodily health as the physical Whole which is sought in *Hathayoga*. Man, as he develops, lives more and more in that Current of Energy, which, having immersed itself in Mind and Matter for the purpose of World-Experience, returns to itself as the Perfect Experience, which is Transcendent Being-Power. With the transformation of man's nature his values become higher. At length he discerns that his Self is rooted in and is a flowering of Supreme Being-Power. His cramped experience, loosened of its limitations, expands into fulness. For, it must be ever remembered, that Consciousness as it is itself never evolves. It is the Immutable Essence, and Shakti the "Wave of Bliss" as they each are in themselves. Evolution is thus a gradual *release* from the limitations of Form created by Being-Power. Interest in the Partial and Relative Wholeness gives way to a striving towards the Mother as the Absolute Whole (*Pūrna*), which She is in Her own spaceless, and timeless, nature.

This complete Liberation is the Perfect Experience in which the Self, cramped in Mind and Body, overcomes its *māyik* bonds and expands into the Consciousness-Whole.

The practical question is therefore the conversion of Imperfect (*Apūrna*) into Perfect (*Pūrna*) Experience. This last is not the "standing aloof" (*Kaivalya*) "here" from some discarded universe "over there", upon the discovery that it is without reality and worth. For the World is the Mother in Form. It is one and the same Mother-Power which really appears as the psycho-physical universe, and which in itself is Perfect Consciousness. Liberation is, according to this system, the expansion of the empirical consciousness in and through and by means of the world into that Perfect Consciousness which is the Experience-Whole. This can only be by the grace of the Mother, for who otherwise can loosen the knot of *Māya* which She Herself has tied?

The state of Liberation can only be approximately described. Even those who have returned from ecstasy cannot find words for that which they have in fact experienced. "A full vessel," it is said, "makes no sound." It is not in this system an experience of mere empty "being", for this is an abstract concept of the intellect produced by the power of Consciousness. It is a concrete Experience-Whole of infinitely rich "content". The Mother is both the Whole and, as *Samvid Kalā*, is the Cause and archetype of all Partials (*Kalā*). She is Herself the Supreme Partial as She is also the Whole. So, She is the Supreme Word (*Paravāk*), Supreme Sound and Movement (*Parashabda Paranāda*), Supreme Space (*Paravyoma*), Supreme or Transcendental Time (*Parakāla*), the infinite "limit" of that which man knows on the rising of Sun and Moon. She is again the Life of all lives (*prāna-prānasya*). She thus contains within Herself in their "limit" all the realities and values of worldly life which is Her expression in Time and Space. But over and beyond this, She is also the alogical Experience-Whole. This experience neither supersedes nor is superseded by experience as the Supreme Self. This Alogical Experience is only approximately spoken of as Infinite Being, Consciousness and Joy which is the seamless (*akhanda*) Experience-Whole (*Pūrna*). Relative to the Supreme Self the Perfect Experiencer, She as His Power is the Perfect Universe. In the alogical transcendent state in which Shiva and Shakti are mingled as the One, She is the Massive Bliss (*Ānanda-ghana*) which is their union, of which it has been said: *Niratishaya premāspadatvam ānandatvam*, which may be translated: "Love in its limit or uttermost love is Joy". This is the love of the Self for its Power and for the Universe as which such Power manifests. She is called the Heart of the Supreme Lord (*Hridayam Parameshituh*), with whom the Shākta unites himself as he says *Sā'ham*—"She I am".

If we analyse this description we find that it can be summed up in the single Sanskrit term *Ānandaghana*, or Mass of Bliss. The essence of the Universe is, to the Shākta, nothing but that. Mystical states in all religions are experiences of joy. As I have elsewhere said, the creative and world-sustaining Mother, as seen in Shākta worship (*Hādimata*), is a Joyous Figure crowned with ruddy flashing gems, clad in red raiment (*Lauhityam etasya sarvasya vimarshah*, more effulgent than millions of red rising suns, with one hand granting all blessings (*varamudrā*), and with the other dispelling all fears (*abhayamudrā*). It is true that She seems fearful to the uninitiate in Her form as *Kālī*, but the worshippers of this Form (*Kādimata*) know Her as the Wielder of the Sword of Knowledge which, severing man from ignorance—that is, partial knowledge—gives him Perfect Experience. To such worshipper the burning ground—with its corpses, its apparitions, and haunting malignant spirits—is no terror. These forms, too, are Hers.

Hinduism has with deep insight seen that Fear is an essential mark of the animal, and of man in so far as he is an animal (*pashu*). The Shākta unites himself with this joyous and liberating Mother, saying *Sā'ham*—"She I am". As he realizes this he is the fearless Hero, or *Vīra*. For he who sees Duality, he alone fears. To see Duality means not merely to see otherness, but to see that other as alien non-self. The fearless win all worldly enterprises, and fearlessness is also the mark of the Illuminate Knower. Such an one is also in his degree independent of all outward power, and *Mrityunjaya*, or Master of Death. Such an one is not troubled for himself by the thought of Death. In the apt words of a French author ("L'Ame Paienne," 83), he no more fears than do the leaves of the trees, yellowing to their fall in the mists of autumn. An imperishable instinct tells him that if he, like the leaves, is about to fall, he is also the tree on which they will come out again, as also the Earth in which both grow, and yet again (as the Shākta would say) he is also, in his Body of Bliss, the Essence which as the Mother-Power sustains them all. As that Essence is imperishable, so in the deepest sense is its form as Nature. For whatever exists can never altogether cease to be. Either man's consciousness expands into that Lordliness which sees all as Itself, or he and all lower beings are withdrawn into the Womb of Power, in which they are conserved to reappear in that *Sphurana* or Blossoming which is the Springtide of some new World.

CHAPTER XXI

HINDU RITUAL[1]

I

It is well said that Ritual is the Art of Religion. As practised by the Hindus it is not rightly judged, because the religious and philosophical doctrines of which it is a practical expression and method are either unknown or misunderstood. If we add to incapacity, a temperament hostile to all Ritualism, the resultant criticism is "mummery," "idolatry," "gibberish," and so forth. It is true that Ritual is meaningless to those who do not know its meaning; just as a telegram sent in cypher is without sense to those who are ignorant of the code according to which it is written. It may, however, be admitted that in so far as, and to the extent that Ritual is carried out without understanding on the part of the worshipper, such criticisms may, to that extent, be justified. Despite shallow views, Ritual is a necessity for men as a whole. Those who profess to reject it in religion are yet found to adhere to it, in some form or other, in social and political life. The necessity of Ritual is shown by well-known historical reactions. Degeneracy leads to "Protestant" abolitions. The jejune worship of the "reformer" lacks appeal and power, and Ritual comes into its own again. This oscillation is well

[1] Reprinted from the "Theosophical Review".

marked in Europe in the history of Catholicism and Protestantism. It is displayed again in the East in Buddhism, which, starting as a revolt from an excessive Vaidik Ritual, adopted in the end the elaborate rites to be found in the Hindu and Buddhist Tantras. The Brahmanic position is the middle and stable way, acknowledging the value of both the "Protestant" and "Catholic" attitude. Its view is that all men need Ritual, but in varying degree and of various kinds, until they are *Siddha*, that is, until they have achieved the end which Ritual is designed to secure. When the end is gained there is no longer need for the means to it. Further, the need becomes less and less as approach is made to that end. The Ritual must be suitable to the spiritual attainments and disposition of the worshipper. For the simple and ignorant the Ritual is of a *Sthūla* or gross kind. The word *Sthūla* in Sanskrit does not necessarily imply any moral censure. It is here used as the opposite of *Sūkshmā* or subtle. Again, count is taken of human emotion and of its varieties. The dispositions or temperaments, or *Bhāva*, of worshippers vary. One worshipper may place himself before the Lord in the relation of a servant towards his Master, another in the relation of a friend, and yet another in the relation of a lover. In the same way, Yoga, in the sense of a system of self-control and self-fulfilment, varies. For those who are predominantly intellectual there is the Yoga of Knowledge (Jnāna); for those in whom emotion is strong there is the Yoga of Devotion (Bhakti); for such as belong to neither of these classes there is the great Yoga of Action (Karma). The end to which each mediately or directly works is the same. There is, in fact, no religion more Catholic than Hinduism. For this reason, those who dislike and fear it speak of its "rapacious maw". It has in fact, an enormous faculty of assimilation; for there is in it that which will satisfy all views and temperaments. In the West, we are too apt to quarrel with views and practices which we dislike. We will not, in such case, accept them, but that is not necessarily a reason why those who like them should not do so. Thus, to some, all Ritual is repellent, or some kinds of devotion, such as the use of erotic imagery. Let each take or reject what is suitable or unsuitable to him. Controversy is futile. Fitness or *Adhikāra* is a fundamental principle of Hinduism. Some may be fit for one doctrine and practice, and others not. The wisdom of the universal man with a world-mind converts many an absolute judgment into a relative one. For the judgment, "This is bad", he will substitute, "This is not good for me". In this way he will both save his own health and temper, and that of the other.

The term "Ritual", in its religious sense, is included in the Sanskrit term *Sādhanā*, though the latter word has a wider content. It is derived from the root *Sadh* = to exert or strive for, and includes any exertion or striving for anything. Thus a man who goes through a special training for an athletic match is doing *Sādhanā* with a view to win in that contest. The taking of lessons in a foreign language is *Sādhanā* with a view to attain proficiency in that language. Orientalists frequently translate the term by the English word "evocation". There is, of course, *Sādhanā*, to gain the fruits of magic. But this is only one form of *Sādhanā*. The form of which I write, and that to which reference is generally made, is that effort and striving in the form of self-training, discipline, and worship which has as its end a 'spiritual' and not merely physical or mental result—though such result necessarily involves a transformation of both mind and body. The end, then, is some form of Unity with God as the Universal Father, or Mother as the Shāktas say. The person who does *Sādhanā* is called *Sādhaka* or, if a woman, *Sādhikā*. The end sought by the process of *Sādhanā* is *Sādhya* or *Siddhi*. *Siddhi*, or accomplishment, means any successful result, and the man who attains it is, in respect of such attainment, called *Siddha*. The highest *Siddhi* is Unity with Brahman, the All-pervader, either by merger in or expansion into It, as some say, or, as others hold, by varying degrees of association with and proximity to the Lord. Dogmatic views on this or other points are necessarily, to some extent, reflected in the Ritual presented for their realization, but at the *Sādhanā* stage there is less divergence of practice than might be supposed, because whatever be the doctrine held, a worshipper must practically be a dualist. For worship includes both a worshipper and that which is worshipped. There are persons who, in popular language, "worship themselves," but this is not a spiritual exercise. Whatever God may be in Himself, Herself, or Itself, the worship is of a Supreme Person (Purnāham). The world sometimes distracts the Mind from this, its supreme object. Nevertheless there is another universal tendency towards it. This last tendency is proof of man's divine origin. Springing from such a source, he must needs return to it. The striving to realize God is part of man's nature. *Sādhanā* is such striving in the forms which experience has shown to be fruitful. In the Orphic Mysteries it was said: "I am the child of the earth and starry sky, but know that my origin is divine. I am devoured by and perish with thirst. Give me without delay the fresh water which flows from the 'Lake of Memory'." And again: "Pure, and issued from what is pure, I come towards Thee."

So again St. Augustine said that the Mind was not at rest until it found itself in God. Brahmanic doctrine also states the same and gives the reasons for it. A profound saying by an Indian sage runs: "Identification with the imperfect (Āpūrnammanyatā)—that is, want of *Wholeness*, is *Disease* and the source of every misery." Whole = Hale = Health. Every form of want of wholeness, be it physical, psychical or spiritual, is disease and inflicts unhappiness. God is the whole and complete (Pūrna), which is without parts or section (Akhanda). Man is the reverse of this. But having sprung from the Whole, he seeks self-completion either by becoming or reflecting the Whole. The greatest of illnesses is that which the Hindu Scriptures call the Disease of Existence itself, in so far as such finite existence involves a hindrance to the realization of perfect infinite Being. For these reasons one of the *Chakras* or compartments of the great *Shrī Yantra* (See Frontispiece), is called *Rogahara Chakra*, that is, the "Disease-destroying *Chakra*". What is meant by the saying is that man's identification of the self with its particular form, that is with imperfection, is Disease, just as the knowledge that he is one with the whole is Health lasting. To gain this it is necessary that man should worship his Lord in one or other of the many ways in which his fellows have done so. For that purpose he may invent a ritual. But the more effective forms for the mass are those which tradition accredits. Amongst the greatest of ritual systems is that of the Hindus. Hinduism (to use a popular term) cannot be understood without a knowledge of it.

But, it may be said, there are many Rituals. Which are to be adopted, and how can we know that they will give result? The answer is that the Ritual for any particular individual is that for which he is fit (*Adhikārī*). The proof of its efficacy is given by experience. The Āyurveda, or the Veda which teaches the rules to secure a long life (Āyuh) says that that only is a medicine which cures the disease and which, at the same time, gives rise to no other.

To those who put the question, the answer of the Teacher is—"Try". If the seeker will not try he cannot complain that he has no success. The Teacher has himself or herself (for according to the Tantras a woman may be a Guru) been through the training, and warrants success to those who will faithfully adopt the means he has himself adopted.

What, then, are the basic principles of *Sādhanā*, and how does it work? To understand this we must have correct ideas of what the Hindus understand by the terms Spirit, Mind, and Body. I have in my volumes on "Mind" and "Matter" explained these two terms and will now very shortly summarize what is there said, so far as it touches the main principles governing the subject of this paper.

II

The ultimate object of the ritual—that is, the realization of God—is effected by the transformation of the worshipper into likeness with the worshipped. Let us assume that the Sādhaka is doctrinally an adherent of the Advaita Vedānta which is called Monism, but which is more accurately translated "Not two," or non-dual, because, whilst it can be affirmed that the ultimate Reality is not two, still as it is beyond number and all other predicates, it cannot be affirmed to be one. Let us, then, investigate some of the general principles on which the Ritual expressing this doctrine works.

Man is said to be Spirit—to use an English term—with two vehicles of Mind and Body. Spirit, or Brahman as it is in Itself (Svarūpa), according to the Vedānta is, relative to us, pure infinite Being, Consciousness, Bliss (*Sat*, *Chit*, *Ānanda*). That is Spirit viewed from our side and in relation to us. What Spirit is Itself only Spirit in Itself can say. This is only known in the experience of the perfect (*Siddha*) Yogī, who has completely transformed himself through the elimination of those elements of Mind and Body which constitute a finite individuality. "To *know* Brahman is *to be* Brahman." God, or the Lord (Īshvara) is pure, infinite Spirit, in its aspect relative to the world as its Creator, Maintainer, and Ruler. Man is, according to this school, that self-same Spirit or Consciousness which, in one aspect is immutable, and in another is finitized by Mind and Matter. Consciousness and Mind are, then, two different and, indeed, opposite things. Mind is not Consciousness, but is (considered in itself) an *Unconscious* force. Consciousness is infinite. Mind is a product of a finitizing principle or power inherent in Consciousness itself, which appears to limit consciousness. Mind *per se* is thus an unconscious force limiting Consciousness. This statement may seem strange in the West, but is coming to be acknowledged to some extent there, where it is now recognized that there is such a thing as unconscious mind. Vedānta says that mind in itself is always an unconscious force. The mind appears to be conscious, not because it is so in itself, but because it is associated with and is the vehicle of Spirit which alone is Consciousness in Itself. The function of Mind, on the contrary, is to cut up into sections sectionless Consciousness. Let us suppose that Consciousness is represented by an unbroken light thrown on a blank screen. This unbroken light imperfectly represents—(for images fail us in one respect or another)—Consciousness. Let us suppose, then, another metal screen cut up unto patterns, imposed on the former, and thus letting the light through in parts and in various shapes, and shutting it out in others. This last opaque screen represents Mind. Consciousness is self-revealing. Mind occludes it in varying ways, and is a subtle form of the power (Shakti) possessed by Spirit to appear in finite form. Matter or Body is another but grosser form of the same Power. And because Mind or Body have a common origin, the one as subject can know the other as object. Cognition is then recognition. The same Power which has the capacity to so veil itself can unveil itself. The first step towards such unveiling is taken by Sādhanā in its form as self-purification, both as regards body and mind, self-discipline and worship in its various ritual forms. At a high point of advance this Sādhanā enters what is generally known as Yoga.

How then does Sādhanā work? It must be remembered that there is no such thing as mind or soul without some form of body, be it gross or subtle. The individual mind has always a body. It is only Spirit which is Mind-less, and therefore wholly bodiless. Mind and Body are each as real as the other. When there is subject or mind there is always object or matter. The proper discipline purifies and controls both. A pure body helps to the attainment of a pure mind, because they are each aspects of one Power—Substance. Whenever, then, there is mind, it has some object or content. It is never without content. That object may be good or bad. The first design of the Ritual, then, is to secure that the mind shall always have a good object. The best of all objects is its Lord. What, then, is the result o meditation on the Lord?

What is the process of knowing? When the mind knows an object, that process consists in the projection from the Mind of a Mind-Ray, which goes out to the object, takes its form, and returns and models the mind itself into the form of the object. Thus, if attention is completely given, that is without any distraction, to an image or Deity, a jar or any other object, the mind so long as it holds that object is completely transformed into the shape of that object. Thus, with complete concentration on the Lord, the mind is shaped into the image of Him, with all His qualities. That image is formulated by what is called the Dhyāna. The Ritual gives the Dhyāna of each of the forms of God or Spirit.

Let it be assumed, then, that the mind is thus transformed; it is then necessary to keep it so. The mind is so unsteady, agile and variable that it has been compared both with mercury and the restless monkey. If this variability displayed itself in the choice of good thoughts only, it would not so much matter. But there are others which are not good. Moreover, both intensity and durability of transformation are desired. The endeavour then is to attain complete power of concentration and for periods of increasing length. The effect of this is to establish in the mind a tendency in the direction desired. All have experience of the psychological truth that the longer and more firmly an object is held in the mind, the less is the tendency towards distraction from it. A tendency is called *Sangskāra*. Such tendency may be physical or psychical. Thus, the tendency of an India-rubber band when stretched to return to its original condition before such stretching, is a physical *sangskāra* of India-rubber. In the same way, there are psychical *sangskāras*. Thus, a man of miserly disposition is influenced by some sufficient impulse to be, on a particular occasion, generous, but when that or other sufficient impulse lacks, his miserly disposition or *sangskāra* asserts itself. On the other hand, but little is required to call out generosity in a naturally charitable man, for the good tendency is there. *Sādhanā* confirms good and eradicates bad *sangskāras*. As tendencies are produced by past action, intellectual or bodily, present and future good actions will secure that good *sangskāras* are kept and others eliminated. Man is both born with *sangskāras* and acquires others. No Hindu holds that the mind at birth is *tabula rasa*. On the contrary, it is compounded of all the *sangskāras* or tendencies which result from the actions of the previous lives of the individual in question. These are added to, varied, reversed or confirmed by actions taken in the present life. Many of such *Sangskāras* are bad, and steps must be taken to substitute for them others. All are aware that bad acts and thoughts, if repeated, result in the establishment of a bad habit, that is a bad *Sangskāra* realized. The object of *Sādhanā* is, then, firstly to substitute good objects for the mind in lieu of bad objects, and to overcome the tendency towards distraction and to revert to what is bad. This means the stabilizing of character in a good mould.

How is this to be effected? The *Sādhanā* must avoid all distractions by keeping the mind occupied with what is good. We accordingly find the repetitions which may be, but by no means necessarily are, "vain". A common instance of this is *Japa*, or repetition of mantra. This is done by count on a rosary (*Mālā*) or with the thumb on the twelve phalanges of the fingers. There are also forms of repetition in varying ways. Thoughts are intensified and confirmed by appropriate bodily gestures *Mudrā*. Again, real processes are imagined. Thus, in *Nyāsa*, the worshipper with appropriate bodily actions places different parts of the body of the Divinity on the corresponding parts of his own body. Thus the *Sādhaka* imagines that he has acquired a new divine body. Again, in the more subtle rite called *Bhūtashuddhi*, the worshipper imagines that each of the component elements of the body is absorbed in the next higher element until all are merged in the Supreme Power of whom man, as a compound of such elements, is a limited manifestation. Whilst this is merely imagined in Sādhanā, it objectively and actually takes place in Kundalinī Yoga. The mind is thus constantly occupied in one form or another with, and thus shaped into, that which is divine and becomes itself, by being kept in such shape, at length permanently divine. For, as the Chchhāndogya Upanishad says: "What a man thinks that he becomes." So also the Gandharva Tantra says: "By meditating on anything as oneself, man becomes that." Thinking always on the Lord, man is transformed, within limits, into an image of Him. The preparatory work of Sādhanā is completed in Yoga.

I will next shortly note some of the principal forms of ritual employed in worship, *viz.*, image and emblem, *Yantra, Pūja, Mantrā, Mudrā, Nyāsa, Bhūtashuddhi.* These are in constant use, either daily or on special occasions. The ritual of the Sacraments, or *Sangskāras,* are performed once, *viz.*, on the date of that sacrament, such as naming ceremony, marriage and so forth.

III

The third Chapter (here summarized and explained) of the Sanskrit work called "*Wave of Bliss*, for worshippers of the Mother-Power (Shakti)", deals with the necessity for the use of images and other forms as representations of the formless All-Pervader (Brahman). The latter is, in Its own true nature, bodiless (asharīri) and pure Consciousness, or in Western language, Spirit. But Brahman, through Its power (shakti), assumes all the forms of the Universe, just as it is said an actor (natavat) assumes various roles. Thus Brahman has two aspects: the subtile, in which It its own unmanifested Self; and the gross, in which It appears as the manifested universe. Or, if we reserve the word "subtile" for what, though it is not pure Spirit, is yet finer than gross matter—that is, Mind, we may say that the Ultimate Reality has three aspects: (*a*) Supreme or transcendent, that is pure formless Spirit; (*b*) subtile, or the same Spirit as manifested in mind; (*c*) gross, or the same spirit as manifested in Matter. It is clear that one cannot meditate on that which is wholly formless as is the supreme Brahman, which is without body.

In meditation (Dhyāna) there is duality, namely, the subject who meditates and the object of such meditation, though, in fact, the two are (according to the Advaita or non-dualism of the Shāktas), both differing aspects of the one Brahman through Its Power. As the mind cannot remain steady on what is formless (amūrta), therefore, a form (mūrti) is necessary. Form is gross or subtile. Form is necessary both in Sādhanā and *Yoga*—in the latter for acquiring accomplishment in Trātaka-Yoga, that is, steady gaze which leads to one-pointedness (Ekāgrata), and this latter to Samādhi or ecstasy. The grossest form is that which is shown in the round, with hands, feet, and so forth—that is, the image. Nothing is here left to the imagination. The particulars of the image, that is, how it should be shaped, its colour, posture, and so forth, is given in what are called the meditations or *Dhyānas*, and the dimensions may be found in the Silpa Shāstras. These describe the form, attitude, the position of the hands and legs, the articles such as weapons and the like carried, the vehicle or Vāhana—and the attendant Divinities (*Āvarana Devatā*). Less gross forms are pictures or representations in the flat, emblems such as the Shālagrama stone sacred to Vishnu, the Linga or sign of Shiva, and the inverted triangle which is the emblem of the Mother. Thus a Linga set in the Yoni or triangle represents the union of Shiva and Shakti, of God and His Power, or in philosophical language, the union of the static and kinetic aspects of the one Ultimate Reality. A still more subtile form is the *Yantra*, which literally means "instrument," *viz.*, the instrument by which worship is done. It is as shown on the flat, a diagram which varies with each of the *Devatās* or Divinities, and has been called "the body of *Mantra*". Whilst gross (sthūla) meditation takes place on the gross image, emblem or Yantra, subtile (sūkshma) meditation has as its object the Mantra. The Mantra and the Devatā are one. A *Mantra* is *Devatā* in that form, that is as sound. Hearing is considered the finest of the senses. What is called Supreme Meditation is nothing but ecstasy, or—Consciousness, freed of both its subtile and gross vehicles, and, therefore, limitations.

As the Brahman is only directly known in the ecstasy of Yoga, It is imagined with form, or, as some translate this passage, It assumes form for the sake of the worshippers (*upāsakānām kāryyārtham*). These forms are male or female, such as, in the first class, Brahmā, Vishnu, Siva and others, and in the second Tripurasundarī, Lakshmī, Kālī and others. The worship of a Eunuch (napungsaka) form does not bear fruit. What shall be the selected or patron Divinity depends on the competency (adhikāra) of the worshipper, that is, what is suitable or fit for him given his character and attainments. The Yāmala says: "Men see Him in various ways, each according to his own inclinations." But an advaitist worshipper should at the same time remember that each is an aspect of one and the same Deity.

Varāha Purāna says: "What Durgā is, that is Vishnu, and that also is Shiva. The wise know that they are not different from one another. The fool, who in his partiality thinks otherwise, goes to the Raurava Hell." There is, however, from the nature of the case, some distinction in the case of the worship of those on the path of enjoyment, who should worship according to the mode in which they have been initiated. But the renouncer should discard in every way all notions of difference. The *Wave of Bliss*, citing Samaya Tantra, says: "By the worship of some Deva, liberation is with difficulty attained, and by the worship of others enjoyment is to be had, but in the case of the worshipper of the Mother, both enjoyment and liberation lie in the hollow of his hands." But, unless prayed to, the Mother or Devī does not give fruit, and naturally so. For the Devī is moved to action through the prayers of the worshipper. Essentially the worshipper is the Devī Herself, and unless She in Her form as the worshipper is moved, She in Her aspect as the Supreme Lord—" Our Lady "—does not move.

By " worshipper " is meant one who is proficient in *Karma* and *Bhakti* Yoga. The *Jnānayogi's* effort is directed towards the attainment of the formless Brahman. Worship implies duality, and so does *Mantra-yoga* of which worship is a part. From the *Bīja-mantra* or seed mantra the Devatā arises and this Devatā is the Brahman. In the Kūrma Purāna it is said: " Those who think themselves to be different from the Supreme Lord will never see Him. All their labour is in vain." Therefore, the Shrīkrama says: " Meditate upon yourself as the Supreme Mother—the primordial Power—by your mind, word, and body." All three take part in the ritual. The mind, which must from its nature have an object, is given a good object, that is, the image of its Lord. It holds to that. The worshipper utters the ritual words and with his body performs the ritual acts, such as the gestures (Mudrā), the giving of offerings, and so forth. And the reason is, as the Gandharva Tantra says: " By meditating on anything as oneself, man becomes that." The mind assumes the form of its object—that is, by good thoughts man is transformed into what is good. So the worshipper is enjoined constantly to think: " I am the *Devī* and none other." By meditating on Vishnu, man becomes Vishnu. By meditating on *Devī*, man becomes *Devī*. He is freed from bodily ills and is liberated, for he attains spiritual knowledge. Such knowledge, in the Advaita sense (though there are also other schools) means " to be ",

To know Brahman is *to be* Brahman. Brahman in Itself is not an object, and is not known as such. Brahman is known by being Brahman, which man attains through ritual forms, and Yoga processes, of which worship is a necessary preliminary.

IV

In the preceding paragraphs, I have, in very general outline, dealt with the meaning of *Sādhanā* as ritual worship, both as to its object and the principles on which it is based. I have given at the same time some examples. I propose here to pass a few remarks on certain other particular forms of ritual. I have already referred to image worship upon which, however, I will add a word.

Western peoples speak of the image worshipped as being an "idol", just as some so-called "reformed" Hindus influenced by Western views call it a "doll". The Hindu term is *Pratīka* and *Pratimā* indicating that which is *placed before* one as the immediate and apparent object of worship, *representative* of the Invisible Supreme. The mind cannot seize pure Spirit any more than (to use the simile of an Indian author) a pair of tongs can seize the air. The mind must, however, necessarily have before it some definite object, and one of such objects is the image or emblem. At the same time, the Hindu image is something more than a mere aid to devotion such as is the case in general as regards images in the Catholic ritual. For, by the "life-giving" (*prāna-pratishtha*) ceremony the life of the Devatā or Divinity is invoked into the image. Deity is all-pervading and therefore cannot come or go. The image, like everything else, is already an appearance of Deity immanent in it, in the particular form or mould of earth, stone, metal, wood or whatever other the substance may be. Therefore, "invocation" (*Āvāhanā*) and "dismissal" (*Visarjana*) in the

Ritual by which the Deity is invoked "to be present" and bid "to depart" mean this—that the immanence of Deity in the object of worship is recognized, kept present before, and ultimately released from the mind of the worshipper. In fact, the Deity is there, ritual or no ritual. By the ritual the Deity is not only there in fact, but is so for the consciousness of the worshipper whose mind is transformed into a Divine mould. The Deity does not move, but the mind of the wórshipper does so. It is the particular modification, a *Vritti* of the mind which comes and goes. Personally, I believe that "Idolatry" in its strictest literal sense is not to be found anywhere. The most ignorant individuals belonging to a primitive humanity are aware that they are, in one sense, in the presence of "stocks and stones", and that the worshipful character of the image is not because it is such stock and stone, for, in that case all stock and stone is worshipful, but for other reasons. It has been noted already that the ritual is graded in this matter, as in others, into gross and subtle. The subtle form is that in which the least is left to the imagination, namely, an image in the round. Less so, in the order given, is the picture on the flat; the emblem which has no external likeness to Divinity (such as the *Linga* and *Shālagrama* stone), and then the *Yantra* or diagram of worship. This *Yantra* is made up of different combinations of lines and curves, and is described as the body of the Mantra. Besides these external objects, there are mental representations of them and of other things. Thus actual flowers may be offered physically, or mental "flowers" may be offered by the mind, or the "flowers" of the virtues may be laid before the *Devatā*.

How often the word *Mantra* is used, and yet how few can say correctly what the term means? It is only possible here to lay down a few general lines of explanation of a subject with which I have endeavoured to deal in my recent work, *The Garland of Letters;* for Garland or Rosary are names given to the alphabet or Sanskrit letters, which are each a manifestation of the Mother of the Universe.

The Universe is movement, of various kinds, of the ultimate substance. This movement is sensed in five ways. Whatever is heard is the sound made by some particular form of movement, and the hearing by mind and ear is again a form of movement. If there be no movement there is nothing to hear. When a letter is uttered in our hearing there is a particular movement which can be represented as a form for the eye, which form again involves colour, for what is perfectly colourless is formless, and, therefore, invisible. The letters are temporarily manifested by the action of the vocal organs and the circumambient air, but are in themselves, that is, as attitudes of Power, eternal. As Postures of Power they are eternal, though as manifestations they appear with each universe and disappear with it. They are, like all else, a form of appearance of the *Magna Mater*, the one great Mother-Power, and are particular world-aspects of Her. The sound which is heard, and the mind and ear which hear it, are each such appearances. Each thing has a double aspect—one as a produced thing, or effect; the other as the particular Causal Power which produces or more accurately manifests as that thing. That power again, relative to any of its particular productions, is an aspect of the general Mother-Power, and is, as such, a Devatā. Thus, the sun is a glorious epiphany of the Brahman, or All-Pervader which, in its character as the power inherent in that particular manifestation, is the Sun-Lord or *Sūrya-Devatā*. *Devatā* in its supreme (*para*) sense is the Lord of All, manifesting as the All. The Sun Devatā is the same Lord in the character of a particular power of the All-Powerful manifesting in this form of the Sun. Whilst, therefore, in a sense, Mantra is the Sound-aspect of all that is, each Devatā has His or Her own *Mantra*, and it is to such mantras that the Scripture refers. The Mantra does not merely stand for or symbolize the *Devatā*. Still less is it a mere conventional label for the *Devatā*. It *is* the *Devatā*. The *Devatā* and Mantra are therefore one.

In each mantra, however, there are two Shaktis or powers. The *Devatā* who is the mantra is called the indicating power (*Vāchaka Shakti*). The *Devatā* who is indicated (*Vāchya Shakti*) is the Ultimate Reality, or Supreme Brahman. The former leads to the latter. As each worshipper has his own Patron Deity or Ishtadevatā, so each worshipper is initiated in and practises a particular mantra. The Patron Deity is a particular aspect of the One Supreme Reality which cannot be directly worshipped, but which is worshipped indirectly as an aspect of that Reality in a world of duality. What Mantra a worshipper should practise is determined by the Guru who initiates. He should settle what it shall be by reference to the physical, psychical and spiritual characteristics of the worshipper. This is the theory, but in practice a state of things often exists which has led to the criticism that *Mantra* is "jabber". Thus (to take but one example), I, though not a Hindu, was once asked by a Brahmin lady, through a pundit known to both of us, to tell her the meaning of her mantra, and this though she had passed fifty, she had never been told, nor could she find out even from the pundit. She was led to ask me and thus to reveal her mantra which should be kept secret, because she had heard that I had a manuscript *Bīja Kosha*, or Dictionary, which gave the meanings of mantras. This incident is significant of the present state things. Initiation has often and perhaps in most cases now-a-days little reality, being merely a "whispering in the ear". A true and high initiation is one in which not merely instruction is given, but there is also an actual transference of power by teacher to disciple which enables the disciple both to understand, and then transforms him by infusing him with the powers of his Guru.

Mantra-sādhanā consists of the union of the *Sādhanā shakti* or the power of the individual worshipper and the *Mantra shakti* or the power of the mantra itself. The worshipper exerts his own individual power to achieve through the mantra, and as he does this, the power of the mantra, which is as far greater than his own as the *Devatā* is greater than he, aids his effort. On the theory this must be so, because as the worshipper more and more realizes the *Devatā* in mantra form, and identifies himself with the *Devatā*, he gains divine powers which supplement his human power as a worshipper. There are some *Mantras* which may be called prayers, such as the great Gāyatrī Mantra which prays for illumination of the understanding. A mantra, however, is not to be identified with prayer, which may be said in any form and in any language that the worshipper chooses. Prayer may be, of course, a great power, but it is nevertheless the power of the particular worshipper only whatever that may be.

Worship (*Pūjā*) is done with meditation, recital of mantras, obeisance, manual gestures, the making of offerings and the like. The gestures (*Mudrā*) are part of a system which employs both body and mind, and makes the former express and emphasize the intentions of the latter. Similarly, an orator gives expression to his thought and emphasizes it by gesture. Thus, in the *Matsya Mudrā*, the hands are put into the form of a fish to indicate that the worshipper is offering to the Deity not merely the little quantity of water which is used in the worship, but that his intention is to offer all the oceans with the fish and other marine animals therein. This is part of what has been called "mummery". Well—it is "acting"; but it is not necessarily more foolish than touching one's hat as a sign of respect. The charge of mummery as against all religions is largely due to the fact that there are many people who will pass judgments on matters which they do not understand. Ignorant and half-educated persons everywhere people the world with fools because they are themselves such.

Āsana, or posture belongs to Yoga, except that the general posture for worship is *Padmāsana,* and worship is part of Mantra Yoga.

Japa is "recital" of Mantra. There is no exact English equivalent for it, for "recital" signifies ordinary utterance, whereas *Japa* is of three kinds, namely: (*a*) that in which the *Mantra* is audibly uttered; (*b*) where the lips are moved, but no sound is heard; and (*c*) mental or by the mind only. The count is done on a rosary (*mālā*) or on the phalanges of the fingers.

One of the great Mantras is the physical act of breathing. As this is done of itself so many times a day, now through the right, and then through the left nostril automatically, it is called the *Ajapa Mantra*—that is, the mantra which is said without *Japa* or willed effort on man's part. The mantra which is thus automatically said is *Hangsah.* Breath goes out with *Hang*, and comes in with *Sah.* When outbreathing and inbreathing takes place, the throat and mouth are said to be in the position in which they are when pronouncing the letters H and S respectively. In other words, outbreathing is the same form of movement which is heard as the letter H.

An important rite much referred to in the Tantras is *Nyāsa,* which means the "placing" of the hands of the worshipper on different parts of his body, imagining at the same time that thereby the corresponding parts of the body of his *Ishtadevatā* are being there placed. It terminates with a movement, "spreading" the Divinity all over the body. "How absurd," someone may say, "You cannot spread Divinity like jam on bread." Quite so; but the Hindu knows well that the word Brahman means the All-spreading Immense and cannot therefore be spread. But what may be and is spread is the mind—often circumscribed enough—of the worshipper, who by this thought and act is taught to remember and realize that he is pervaded by Divinity, and to affirm this by his bodily gesture. The ritual is full of affirmations. Affirm again, affirm, and still affirm. This injunction one might expect from a system which regards man and all that exists as limited forms of unlimited Power (*Shakti*). Affirm in every way is a principle of the ritual, a principle which ought to be as easily understood as a child's repetition in order to learn a lesson. A man who truly thinks himself to be becoming divine becomes, in fact, in varying degrees, so.

It is not possible in an account such as this to note more than a few of the leading rituals, and I conclude therefore with the very important *Bhūtashuddhi.* This term does not mean, as an English orientalist thought, "the driving away of demons" but purification of the Elements (*Bhūta*) of which the body is composed. There are five of these with centres or *Chakras* in the spinal column. The grossest is at the base of the spine which is the seat of the power called Kundalinī. In Yoga, this power is roused, and led up through the column, when it absorbs as it goes, each of the centres and the elements, and then the psychic centre, finally merging with Spirit or Pure Consciousness in the upper brain which is the "seat" of the latter. In Yoga this actually takes place, but very few are Yogis: and not all Yogis possess this power. Therefore, in the case of ritual worship this ascent, purification of the body, and merging of Matter and Mind in Consciousness takes place in imagination only. The "man of sin" is burnt in mental fire, and a new body is created, refreshed with the nectar of divine joy arising from the union of the "Divine pair" (Shiva and Shakti) or Consciousness and its Power. This is done in the imagination of the worshipper, and not without result since as the Chohhāndogya Upanishad says: "What a man thinks that he becomes." So also the Gandharva Tantra says: "By thinking of That, one becomes That."

In Kundalinī Yoga or Laya Yoga, there is effected a progressive absorption of all limited and discrete forms of experience, that is fact-sections into the Primary Continuum which is Shiva and Shakti united together. Therefore, it is a merging or more properly expansion of the finite into the infinite, of the part into the whole, of the thinkable and measurable into the unthinkable and immeasurable. When we worship this progress is imagined. There is in time a transformation of Mind and Body into a condition which renders them fit for the spiritual experience, which is the *Samādhi* of Yoga or the *ecstasis* or "standing out" of Spirit from its limiting vehicles. Consciousness is then the *Pūrna* or Whole.

CHAPTER XXII

VEDĀNTA AND TANTRA SHĀSTRA[1]

WHEN your representative asked me to speak this evening, he suggested to me as my subject, that Shāstra which is a practical application of the Vedāntic teaching. Mere talk about Vedānta is nothing but a high form of amusement. If more than this is to be achieved, definite Sādhanā is necessary. In the grand opening chapter of the Kulārnava Tantra it is said: "In this world are countless masses of beings suffering all manner of pain. Old age is waiting like a tigress. Life ebbs away as it were water from out of a broken pot. Disease kills like enemies. Prosperity is but a dream; youth is like a flower. Life is seen and is gone like lightning. The body is but a bubble of water. How then can one know this and yet remain content? The Jīvātmā passes through lakhs of existence, yet only as man can he obtain the truth. It is with great difficulty that one is born as man. Therefore, he is a self-killer who, having obtained such excellent birth does not know what is for his good. Some there be who having drunk the wine of delusion are lost in worldly pursuits, reck not the flight of time and are moved not at the sight of suffering. There are others who have tumbled in the deep well of the Six Philosophies—idle disputants tossed on the bewildering ocean of the Vedas and Shāstras. They

[1] Speech at the Meeting held in Calcutta on the Anniversary of Swami Vivekananda on 28th January 1917.

study day and night and learn words. Some again, overpowered by conceit, talk of *Unmani* though not in any way realizing it. Mere words and talk cannot dispel the delusion of the wandering. Darkness is not dispelled by the mention of the word 'lamp'. What then is there to do? The Shāstras are many, life is short and there are a million obstacles. Therefore should their essence be mastered just as the Hangsa separates the milk from the water with which it has been mixed."

It then says that knowledge alone can gain liberation. But, what is this knowledge, and how may it be got? Knowledge in the Shāstric sense is actual immediate experience (Sākshātkāra), not the mere reading about it in books, however divine, and however useful as a preliminary such study may be.

How then to gain it? The answer is, by Sādhanā —a term which comes from the root "to exert". It is necessary to exert oneself according to certain disciplines which the various religions of the world provide for their adherents. Much shallow talk takes place on the subject of ritual. It is quite true that some overlook the fact that it is merely a means to an end. But it is a necessary means all the same. This end cannot be achieved by merely sitting in Padmāsana and attempting to meditate on the Nirguna Brahman. One may as well try to seize the air with a pair of tongs. How then may the Vedāntic truth be realized? The Indian Shāstra purports to give the means for the Indian body and mind. What Shāstra? Not the Karma-kānda of the Vedas, because with the exception of a few hardly surviving rites, such as Homa, it has passed away. The actual discipline you will find in the Tantras of the Āgamas.

I prefer the use of this term to that of "the Tantra", now so common, but which has risen from a misconception and leads to others. Tantra means injunction (Vidhi) or regulation (Niyama) or treatise, *i.e.*, simply Shāstra. Thus Shaṅkara calls the Sāṅkhya "Tantra". One cannot speak of "the Tantra" any more than one can speak of "the treatise". We do not speak of the Purāna, the Samhita, but of the Purānas and Samhītas. Why then speak of "the Tantra"? One can speak of the Tantras or Tantra Shāstra. The fact is that there is an Āgama of several schools, Shaiva, Shākta and Vaishnava. Shiva and Shakti are one. The Shaiva (in the narrower sense) predominantly worships the right side of the Ardhanarīshvara Mūrti, the Shākta worships the left (Vāma or Shakti) side; the place of woman being on the left. The Vaishnava Āgama is the famous Pancharātra, though there are Tantras not of this school in which Vishnu is the Ishtadevatā. All Āgamas of whatever group share certain common ideas, outlook and practice. There are also certain differences. Thus, the Northern Shaivāgama which is called Trika and not "the Tantra" is, as is also the Shākta Tantra, Advaita. The Southern Shaiva school which is called Shaiva Siddhānta and not "the Tantra", as also the Vaishnava Āgama or Pancharātra (and not "the Tantra") are Vishishtādvaita. There is some variance in ritual also as follows from variance in the Ishtadevatā worshipped. Thus, as you all know, it is only in some forms of worship that there is animal sacrifice, and in one division, again, of worshippers, there are rites which have led to those abuses which have gained for "the Tantra" its ill fame. A person who eats meat can never, it is said, attain Siddhi in the Shiva Mantra according to Dakshinopāsana. Each one of these schools has its own Tantras of which there were at one time probably thousands. The Shaiva Siddhānta speaks of 28 chief Tantras or Āgamas with many Upatantras. In Bengal mention is made of 64. There are numerous Tantras of the Northern

Shaiva school of which the Mālinīvijaya and Svachchhanda Tantras are leading examples. The original connection between the Shaiva schools of North and South is shown by the fact that there are some books which are common to both, such as the Mātanga and Mrigendra Tantras. The Pancharātra is composed of many Tantras, such as Lakshmī and Padma Tantras and other works called Samhītas. In the Commentary to the Brahma Samhīta which has been called the "essence of Vaishnavism", you will find Jīva Goswami constantly referring to Gautamīya Tantra. How then has it come about that there is the ignorant notion that (to use the words of an English work on Tibetan Buddhism) "Tantras is restricted to the necromantic books of the later Shivaic or Shakti mysticism"? I can only explain this by the fact that those who so speak had no knowledge of the Tantras as a whole, and were possibly to some extent misled by the Bengali use of the term "the Tantra", to denote the Shākta Tantras current in Bengal. Naturally, the Bengalis spoke of their Tantras as "Tantra", but it does not follow that this expression truly represents the fact. I might develop this point at great length but cannot do so here. I wish merely to correct a common notion.

Well, it is in these Tantras or the Āgamas that you will find the ritual and Sādhanā which governs the orthodox life of the day, as also in some of the Purānas which contain much Tāntrik ritual.

I am not concerned to discuss the merits or the reverse of these various forms of Sādhanā. But the Āgama teaches an important lesson the value of which all must admit, namely: mere talk about Religion and its truths will achieve nothing spiritual. There must be action (Kriyā). Definite means must be adopted if the truth is to be realized. The Vedānta is not spoken of as a mere speculation as some Western Orientalists describe it to be. It claims to be based on experience. The Āgamas say that if you follow their direction you will gain Siddhi. As a Tibetan Buddhist once explained to me, the Tantras were regarded by his people rather as a scientific discovery than as a revelation; that is, something discovered by the self rather than imparted from without. They claim to be the revealed means by which the Tattva or other matters may be discovered. But the point is, whether you follow these directions or not, you must follow some. For this reason every ancient faith has its ritual. It is only in modern times that persons with but little understanding of the subject have thought ritual to be unnecessary. Their condemnation of it is based on the undoubted abuses of mechanical and unintelligent devotion. But because a thing is abused it does not follow that it is itself bad.

The Āgama is, as a friend of mine well put it, a practical philosophy, adding what the intellectual world wants most to-day is this sort of philosophy—a philosophy which not merely *argues* but *experiments*. He rightly points out that the latest tendency in modern Western philosophy is to rest upon intuition, as it was formerly the tendency to glorify dialectics. But, as to the latter "Tarkapratishthānāt," intuition, however, has to be led into higher and higher possibilities by means of Sādhanā, which is merely the gradual unfolding of the Spirit's vast latent magazine of power, enjoyment, and vision which every one possesses in himself. All that exists is *here*. There is no need to throw one's eyes into the heavens for it. The Vishvasāra Tantra says, "What is here is there: what is not here is nowhere." As I have said, I am not here concerned with the truth or expediency of any particular religion or method (a question which each must decide for himself), but to point out that the principle is fully sound, namely, that Religion is and is based on spiritual experience, and if you wish to gain such experience it is not enough to talk about or have a vague wish for it, but you must adopt some definite means well calculated to produce it. The claim of the Āgama is that it provides such means and is thus a practical application of the teaching of the Vedānta. The watchword of every Tāntrik is Kriyā—to be up and doing. You will find in the useful compilation called Yatidharmanirnaya that even Dandins of Shaṅkara's school follow a Tāntrik ritual suited to their state. In fact all must act who have not achieved.

This leads me to say a word on the Svāmi in whose honour we meet to-day. He was always up and doing. The qualities I most admire in him are his activity, manliness and courage. There are still Indians (though fortunately not so numerous as there were when I first came to India 30 years ago) who seem to be ashamed of and would apologize for their life, customs, race, art, philosophy and religion and so forth. The Svāmi was not of this sort. He was, on the contrary, amongst the first to affirm his Hindu faith and to issue a bold challenge to all who attacked it. This was the attitude of a man. It is also a manly attitude to boldly reject this faith if after fully studying and understanding it you find that the doctrines it preaches do not commend themselves to your reason. For we must, at all cost, have intellectual, as well as every other form of honesty. But this is another thing from the shame-faced apology of which I speak and which is neither one thing nor another. The Svāmi spoke up and acted. And for this all must honour him who, whatever be their own religious beliefs, value sincerity, truth and courage which are the badge of every nobility. And so I offer these few words to his memory which we all here, either by our speech or presence, honour to-day.

CHAPTER XXIII

THE PSYCHOLOGY OF HINDU RELIGIOUS RITUAL[1]

THE word "religious" in the title of this lecture has been inserted in order to exclude magical ritual, with which I do not deal, though I have a word or two to say on the subject.

As regards the word "Hindu", it must be remembered that there is considerable variety of doctrine and ritual, for there are a number of communities of Indian worshippers. Though, perhaps, too much stress is generally laid on these differences, and sufficient notice is not taken of fundamental points of agreement, yet there are differences, and if we are to be exact, we must not forget that fact. It is not, of course, possible, during the hour or so at my disposal, to treat of all these differences. I have, therefore, selected the ritual of one of these communities called Shāktas. These worshippers are so called because they worship the great Mother-Power or Mahāshakti. Their doctrine and practice is of importance, because, (as an Italian author has recently observed,) of its accentuation of Will and Power. He describes it as "a magnificent ensemble of metaphysic, magic and devotion raised on grandiose foundations." And so, whether it be acceptable or not, I think it is. The title, therefore, is, in this matter,

[1] Lecture delivered before the India Society on June 24, 1925, Chairman: Sir Francis Younghusband.

not exact. Some of what is here said is of common application and some is peculiar to the Shāktas.

Now as to the word "Ritual". Ritual is the Art both of Religion and Magic. Magic, however, is more completely identified with ritual than is religion; for magic is ritual, using the latter term to include both mental and bodily activity; whereas religion, in the wide sense of Dharma, is not merely ritual-worship, but covers morality also. And so, it is finely said: "The doing of good to others is the highest Dharma." In this sense of the term Dharma, we are not concerned with ritual. Ritual has been the subject of age-long dispute. Whilst there are some who favour it, others are fanatically opposed to it. In this matter, India, as usual, shows her great reconciling wisdom. She holds (I speak of those who follow the old ways) that ritual is a necessity for the mass of men. To this extent she adopts what I may call the "Catholic" attitude. She makes, however, concession on the other hand to the "Protestant" view, in holding that, as a man becomes more and more spiritual, he is less and less dependent on externals, and therefore on ritual, which may be practically dispensed with in the case of the highest.

Then as to the word "Psychology". In order to understand the ritual, one must know the psychology of the people whose it is; and in order to know and to understand their psychology, we must know their metaphysic. There are some who claim to dispense with metaphysic, but the Indian people have been, throughout their history, pre-eminently thinkers. The three greatest metaphysical peoples have been, in the past, the Greeks and the Indians, both Brahmanist and Buddhist, and, in modern times, the Germans. The Greek, Sanskrit, and German languages are pre-eminently fitted for metaphysical use. We must then deal with metaphysic when treating of Hindu ritual,

I do not propose, however, here to enter upon the subject more than is absolutely necessary to understand the matter in hand.

Now, when we look around us, we see everywhere Power, or Shakti. The world is called Jagat, which means "the moving thing", because, anticipating modern doctrine, the Ancient Hindus held that everything was in a state of ceaseless activity, which was not the Brahman in Itself (Svarūpa). Such movement is either due to the inherent power of mind and matter, or to a cause which, though immanent in the universe, yet is not wholly manifested by, but transcends it. This latter alternative represents the Indian view. Power (Shakti) connotes a Power-holder (Shaktimān). Power as universe is called Samsāra. The state of power, as it is in itself, that is, the state of Power-holder, is (to use one of the better-known terms, though there are others) Nirvāna.

What, then, is the nature of experience in the Samsāra? The latter is the world of form, and Dharma is the Law of Form. Form necessarily implies duality and limitation. Therefore, experience in Samsāra is an experience of form by form. It is limited, dualistic experience. It is limited or Apūrna (not the whole or complete), relative to the state of Nirvāna, which is the whole (Pūrna) or complete or Perfect Experience. Therefore, whilst the latter is a state of all-knowingness and all-mightiness, man is a contraction (Saṅkocha), and is a "little-knower" and "little-doer". The Power-holder is called Shiva-shakti—that is, the supreme Shiva-shakti, for the universe, being but the manifestation of the transcendent Shiva-shakti, is also itself Shiva-shakti. The names Shiva and Shakti are the twin aspects of one and the same Reality. Shiva denotes the masculine, unchanging aspect of Divinity, while Shakti denotes its changing feminine aspect. These two are

Hamsah, Ham being Shiva and male, and Sah being Shakti and female. It is this Hamsah, or legendary "Bird", which is said, in the poem called "Wave of Bliss," "to swim in the waters of the mind of the great". The unmanifest Shiva-shakti aspect is unknown, except in the Samādhi or ecstasy of Yoga. But the Shakti aspect, as manifested in the universe, is near to the Shākta worshipper. He can see Her and touch Her, for it is She who appears as the universe, and so it is said: "What care I for the Father, if I but be on the lap of the Mother?" This is the Great Mother, the *Magna Mater* of the Mediterranean civilization, and the Mahādevī of India—that August Image whose vast body is the universe, whose breasts are Sun and Moon. It was to Her that the "mad", wine-drinking Sadhu Bhāma referred, when he said to a man I knew who had lost his mother: "Earthly mothers and those who suck their breasts are mortal; but deathless are those who have fed at the breast of the Mother of the Universe". It is She who personalizes in the form of all the beings in the universe; and it is She again who, as the essence of such personalizing, is the Supreme Personality (Parāhanta), who in manifestation is "God in Action". Why, it may be asked, is God thought of as Mother? This question may be countered by another—"Why is God called Father?" God is sexless. Divinity is spoken of as Mother because It "conceives, bears, gives birth to, and nourishes the Universe". In generation man is said to be a helper only. The learned may call this mother-notion, "infantilism" and "anthropomorphism". But the Shākta will not be afraid, and will reply that it is not he who has arbitrarily invented this image of the Mother, but that is the form in which She has herself presented Herself to his mind. The great Shākta poet, Rāmaprasāda, says: "By feeling (Bhāva) is She known. How then can Abhāva (that is, lack of feeling) find her?" In any case he may recall the lines of the Indian poet: "If I understand, and you understand, O my mind, what matters it whether any other understand or not?"

Viewing the matter more drily and metaphysically, we have then to deal with two states. Firstly, the limited experience of Samsāra the *Becoming*, and the Perfect Experience or transcendent *Being*, which is Nirvāna. This last state is not for the Shākta mere abstract Being. This is a fiction of the ratiocinating intellect. It is a massive, rich, and concrete experience, a state which—being powerful to produce from out itself the Universe—must therefore hold the seed or essence of it within itself. It is a mistake on this view to suppose that those who attain to it will lose anything of worth by so doing.

The first point which is therefore established is that there are these two states. Both are so established by experience—the first by the ordinary experience man has of this world, and the second by supernormal spiritual experience. For the Hindu holds that the Supreme State is proved not by speculation or argument (which may yet render its support), but by actual spiritual experience.

The second point to remember is that *these two states are one.* We must not think of "creation" in the sense, in which there is an infinite break between man and God, and, therefore, man cannot become God. Man, in this system of Vedānta, is, though a contraction of Power, nevertheless, in essence, the self-same Power which is God. There is unity (Abheda) as Essence, and difference (Bheda) as Manifestation. Similarly, Islamic philosophy distinguishes between independent *Zat*, or essence, and dependent and derivative Attribute, or *Sifat*. Essence is one, Manifestation is different. The two are thus neither identical nor separate. There is that which the Hindus call Abheda-Bheda.

The third point then is that Man, being such Power, he can by his effort, and the grace of his patron Deity, enhance it even to the extent that he becomes one with Divinity. And so it is said that "by the worship of Vishnu, man becomes Vishnu". To know a being or thing is, according to non-dual Vedānta, to *be* that thing. To know God, then, is to *be* God. Man can then pass from limited experience, or Samsāra, to Perfect Experience, or Nirvāna. This "towering tenet," to use Brian Hodgson's phrase ("Nepal"), that finite mind may be raised to infinite consciousness, is also held by Buddhism.

The practical question then is: How is this experience of oneness with Divinity, its powers and attributes, obtained? The answer is that this is the work of Sādhanā and Yoga.

The term Sādhanā comes from the root Sādh, which means to exert, to strive to attain a particular result or Siddhi, as it is called. The person making the effort is called Sādhaka, and if he obtains the result desired, or Siddhi, he is called Siddha. Etymologically Sādhanā may refer to any effort. Thus a person who takes lessons in French or in riding, with a view to learn that language or to become a horseman, is doing Sādhanā for those purposes respectively. If French or riding is learnt, then Siddhi is obtained, and the man who attains it is Siddha, or proficient in French and riding respectively. But technically Sādhanā refers either to Ritual Worship or Ritual Magic. A Sādhaka is always a dualist, whatever his theoretical doctrine may be, because worship implies both worshipped and worshipper. The highest aim of religious worship is attainment of the Abode or Heaven of the Divinity worshipped. This Heaven is not Nirvāna. The latter is a formless state, whereas Heaven is a pleasurable abode of forms—a state intermediate between Death and Rebirth.

According to the ordinary view, Ritual Worship is a preparation for Yoga. When a man is Siddha in Sādhanā he becomes qualified for Yoga, and when he is Siddha in Yoga he attains Perfect Experience. Yoga is thus the process whereby man is raised from Limited to Perfect experience. The Sādhanā with which I am now concerned is religious Sādhanā, a spiritual effort to achieve a moral and spiritual aim, though it may also seek material blessings from the Divinity worshipped.

Magic is the development of supernormal power, either by extension of natural faculty or by control over other beings and forces of nature. I use the word "supernormal" and not "supernatural" because all power is natural. Thus one man may see to a certain extent with his eyes. Another man with more powerful eyes will see better. A man with a telescope will see further than either of these two. For the telescope is a scientific extension of the natural faculty of sight. Over and beyond this is the "magical" extension of power called clairvoyance. The last power is natural but not normal. Magic (of which there has been abuse) has yet been indiscriminately condemned. Whether an act is good or bad depends upon the intention and the surrounding circumstances, and this same rule applies whether the act is normal or magical. Thus a man may in defence of his life use physical means for self-protection, even to the causing of the death of his adversary. Killing in such a case does not become bad because the means employed are not normal but "magical". On the other hand, Black Magic, or Abhichāra, is the doing of harm to another without lawful excuse. This the Scripture (Shāstra) condemns as a great sin. As the "Kulārnava Tantra" says (XII. 63), *Ātmavat sarvabhutebhyo hitam kuryyāt Kuleshvari*"—that is, a man should not injure, but should do good to others as if they were his own self.

In the Tantra Shāstras are to be found magical rituals. Some classes of works, such as the "Dāmaras," are largely occupied with this subject. It is a mistake, however, to suppose that because a practice is described in the Scripture, it is counselled by it. A book on legal medicine may state the substances by and manner in which a man may be poisoned. It describes the process which, if carried out, produces a particular result, but it does not on that account counsel killing. As regards the magical rites themselves, the view that they are mere childish superstition is not an understanding one. The objective ritual stimulates, is a support of, and serves the Mind-Rays, which, the Hindus would say, are not less but more powerful than the physical forms we call X-rays and the like. It has long been known in India, as it is becoming known in the West, that the mind is not merely a passive mirror of objects, but is a great and active Power. As I have already said, however, I do not propose to deal with this subject, and now return to that of religious worship.

Religious ritual is either formal (Karma, such as the Hōma rite, or is devotional (Upāsanā), according as the act done belongs to the Karma or Upāsanā Kāndas, which together with the Jnāna Kānda, constitute the three-fold division of Veda. The distinction between Karma and Upāsanā is this. In ritual Karma the result is produced by performance of the rite, such as Hōma, independently of the effort of the Sādhaka, provided there be strict ritual accuracy; whereas, the fruit of Upāsanā, or psychological worship, depends on the personal devotion of the worshipper, and without it the act is of no avail. Upāsanā, or devotional worship, is again either gross (Sthūla) or subtle (Sūkshma), according to the degree of competency or advancement of the Sādhaka or person who does Sādhanā. We must not understand by the word "gross" anything bad. It is merely used in contra-distinction to the word "subtle". Thus, a worshipper who is doing his Sādhanā before an exterior image is performing gross worship, whereas he who worships a mentally conceived image is doing subtle worship. A man who offers real flowers is doing a part of gross worship. Subtle worship in such a case would be the offering of flowers of the mind.

I will now shortly examine the Vedāntic theory of Mind, which must be known if the ritual is to be understood. There is no Mind without Matter or Matter without Mind, except in dreamless sleep, when the latter is wholly withdrawn. The Mind has always an object. In a literal sense, there is no vacuous mind. It is not aware, of course, of all objects, but only of those to which it pays attention. Nextly, Mind is not Consciousness (Chit) which is immaterial. Mind, on the contrary, is a quasi-material principle of Unconsciousness, which, on one view, appears to be conscious by reason of the association of Consciousness with it. According to the Shākta view, Mind is an unconscious quasi-material force, being the power of Consciousness to limit itself, and to the extent of such limitation, to appear as unconscious. How then does Mind operate? A Mind-Ray goes forth to the object, which in its turn *shapes* the mental substance into the form of the object. Thus, when a man thinks of an image of Divinity intently and without distraction, his mental substance takes the form of the image. The object which is perceived leaves an impress on the mind, and this impress, if repeated, sets up a tendency or Samskāra. Thus a man who repeatedly thinks good thoughts has a tendency towards the thinking of such thoughts, and by continued good thought character is moulded and transformed. As the Chhandogya Upanishad says: "As a man thinks that he becomes." Similarly, the Gandharva Tantra says: "By meditating on anything as the self, one becomes that thing." A man can thus shape his mind for good or bad.

The mind affects the body. As it is said in the West, "the soul is form and doth the body make." Every thought has a corresponding change in the material substance of the brain.

Well, then, as the mind must have an object which again shapes the mind, the ritual selects a good object, namely, the Divinity of worship with all good attributes.

The Sādhaka meditates on and worships that. Continued thought, repetition, the engagement of the body in the mental action co-operate to produce a lasting and good tendency in the mental substance. Sincere and continued effort effects the transformation of the worshipper into a likeness with the Divinity worshipped. For as he who is always thinking bad thoughts becomes bad, so he who thinks divine thoughts becomes himself divine. The transformation which is commenced in Sādhanā is completed in Yoga, when the difference between worshipper and worshipped ceases in that unitary consciousness which is ecstasy or Samādhi, or transcendent perfect experience.

Let us now examine some illustrations of the psychological principles stated.

Divinity as it is in Itself cannot (as an Indian writer has said) be seized by the mind any more than air can be grasped by a pair of tongs. It is necessary, therefore, to have something placed *before* one as a *representative* of something else, which is what the Sanskrit terms, Pratīka and Pratimā, for the object worshipped, mean. This may be an external object or a mental one. As regards the former, there are varying degrees of grossness and subtlety. The grossest is that in which there is no call upon imagination—that is, the Image of three dimensions. Less so is the painting on the flat; then comes the emblem, which may be quite unlike the Devata or Divinity, of which it is an emblem, such as the Shālagrāma stone in the worship of Vishnu, and, lastly, the Yantra, which is the diagrammatic body of a Mantra.

Worship is outer—that is, of an outer object with physical acts such as bodily prostrations, offering of real flowers, and so on: or it may be partly or wholly mental, as in the latter case, where both the form of the Divinity is imagined (according to the meditational form or Dhyāna given in the Scriptures) as also the offerings.

The forms of worship vary according to the capacity of the worshipper. In the simplest form, the worshipper draws upon the daily life, and treats the Divinity whom he invokes as he would a guest, welcoming It after its journey, offering water for the dusty feet and the mouth, presenting It with flowers, lights, clothes, and so on. These ingredients of worship are called Upāchāra. In the psycho-physiological rites of some Shāktas; the abuse of which has brought them ill-fame, the Upāchārā are the functions of the body. In image-worship, the mind is shaped into the form of the object perceived. But the perception of a material image is not enough. The worshipper must see Divinity before him. This he invokes into the image by what is called the welcoming (Āvāhana) and Life-giving (Prānapratishthā) ceremonies, just as, at the conclusion of the worship, he bids the Deity depart (Visarjana). Uncomprehending minds have asked: "How can God be made to come and go?" The answer is that He does not. What come and go are the modifications, or vrittis, of and in the mind of the Sādhaka or worshipper. To invoke the Deity means, then, a direction not to the Deity, but by the worshipper to himself to understand that the Deity is there. Deity which is omnipresent is in the Image as elsewhere, whatever the Sādhaka may do or not do. The Sādhaka informs his own mind with the notion that the Deity is present. He is then conscious of the presence of and meditates on Divinity and its attributes, and if he be undistracted, his mind and its thought are thereby divinely shaped. Before the Divinity so present, both objectively and to the mind of the Sādhaka, worship is done. It is clear that the more this worship is sincerely continued, the greater both in degree and persistence is the transformation effected. The body is made to take its part either by appropriate gestures, called Mudrā, or other acts such as prostrations, offerings, libations, and so forth. By constant worship the mind and disposition become good, for good thoughts repeated make a man good. Ritual produces by degrees transformation, at first temporary, later lasting. "Bidding the Divinity depart" means that the mind of the Sādhaka has ceased to worship the Image. It is not that the Deity is made to retire at the behest of his worshipper. A true Sādhaka has Divinity ever in his thoughts, whether he is doing formal worship or not. "Invitation" and "Bidding Depart" are done for the purposes of the worship of the Image only. Personally, I doubt whether idolatry exists anywhere in the sense that a worshipper believes a material image as such to be God. But, in any case, Indian image-worship requires for its understanding and practice some knowledge of Vedānta.

Transformation of consciousness-feeling by ritual may be illustrated by a short examination of some other of its forms.

Gesture of the hands, or Mudrā, is a common part of the ritual. There is necessarily movement of the hands and body in any worship which requires external action, but I here speak of the specially designed gestures. For instance, I am now making the Fish gesture, or Matsya Mudrā. The hands represent a fish and its fins. The making of this gesture indicates that the worshipper is offering not only the small quantity of water which is contained in the ritual vessel, but that (such is his devotion) his intention is to give to the Deity all the oceans with the fish and other marine animals therein. The Sādhaka might, of course, form this intention without gesture, but experience shows that gesture emphasizes and intensifies thought, as in the case of public speaking. The body is made to move with the thought. I refer here to ritual gestures. The term Mudrā is also employed to denote bodily postures assumed in Hathayoga as a health-giving gymnastic.

Āsana, or seat, has more importance in Yoga than in Sādhanā. The principle as regards Āsana is to secure a comfortable seat, because that is favourable to meditation and worship generally. If one is not comfortable there is distraction and worry. Both Mudrā and Āsana are, therefore, ancillary to worship as Pūjā, the principle of which has been described.

Japa is recital of Mantra, the count being done either on a rosary or the phalanges of the fingers. What is a Mantra? A Mantra is Divinity. It is Divine Power, or Daivi Shakti, manifesting in a sound body. The Shāstra says that those go to Hell who think that an image is a mere stone, that Mantras are merely letters, and that a Guru is a mere man, and not a manifestation and representative of the Lord as Supreme Teacher, Illuminator, and Director. The chief Mantra is *Om*. This represents to human ears the sound of the first general movement of Divine Power towards the manifestation of the Universe. All other Mantras are particular movements and sounds (for the two co-exist) derived from *Om*. Here the Sādhaka strives to realize his unity with the Mantra, or Divinity, and to the extent that he does so, the Mantra Power

(Mantra-Shakti) supplements his worship-power (Sādhanā Shakti). This rite is also an illustration of the principle that repetition makes perfect, for the repetition is done (it may be) thousands of times.

Japa is of three kinds—gross, subtle, and supreme. In the first, the Mantra is audibly repeated, the objective body-aspect or sound predominating; in the second, there is no audible sound, the lips and other organs forming themselves into the position which, together with contact with the air, produce the sound of the letters; in the third, the Japa is mental—that is, there is emphasis on the Divine, or subjective aspect. This is a means for the ritual realization—that is, by mind—of the unity of human power and Divine Power.

Nyāsa is an important rite. The word means "placing" —that is, of the hands of the Sādhaka on different parts of his body, at the same time, saying the appropriate Mantras, and imagining that by his action the corresponding parts of the body of the Deity are placed there. The rite terminates with a movement of the hands, "spreading" the Divinity all over the body. It is not supposed that the Divinity can be spread like butter on bread. The Supreme Mother-Power is the Brahman, or All-Pervading Immense. What is all-spreading cannot be moved or spread. What can, however, be "spread" is the thought of the worshipper, who, with appropriate bodily gesture, imagines that the Deity pervades his body, which is renewed and divinized. By imagining the body of the Deity to be his body, he purifies himself, and affirms his unity with the Devatā.

An essential element in all rites is Bhūtashuddhi, which means the purification of the elements of which the body is composed. Man is physical and psychical. The physical body is constituted of five modes of motion of material substance, which have each, it is said, centres in the spinal column, at points which in the body correspond to the position of various plexuses. These centres extend from the base of the spine to the throat. Between the eyebrows is the sixth or psychical centre, or mind. At the top of the brain, or cerebrum, is the place of consciousness; not that Consciousness in itself—that is, as distinct from Mind—can have a centre or be localized in any way; for, it is immaterial and all-pervading. But, at this point, it is the least veiled by mind and matter, and is, therefore, most manifest. This place is the abode of transcendent Shiva-Shakti as Power-holder. In the lowest centre (Mūlādhāra), which is at the base of the spine, there sleeps the Immanent Cosmic Power in bodies called Kundalinī Shakti. Here She is ordinarily at rest. She is so, so long as man enjoys limited world-experience. She is then roused. "*Jāgrahi Janani*" ("Arise, O Mother!",) calls out the Sādhaka poet, Rāmaprasāda, "How long wilt thou sleep in the Mūlādhāra?" When so roused, She is led up through the spinal column, absorbing all the physical and psychical centres, and unites with Shiva as consciousness in the cerebrum, which is known as the "thousand-petalled lotus". The body is then drenched with and renewed by the nectar which is the result of their union and is immortal life. This is the ecstasy which is the marriage of the Inner Divine Man and Woman. Metaphysically speaking, for the duration of such union, there is a substitution of the Supreme Experience for World-Experience.

This is the real process in Yoga. But in ritual (for all are not Yogīs) it is imagined only. In imagination, the "man of sin" (Pāpapurusha) is burnt in mental fire, Kundalinī absorbs the centres, unites with Shiva, and then, redescending, recreates the centres, bathing them in nectar. By the mental representation of this process, the mind and body are purified, and the former is made to realize the unity of man and the Supreme Power, whose limited form he is, and the manner whereby the Universe is involved into and evolved from Shiva-Shakti.

All these, and other rituals keep the mind of the Sâdhaka occupied with the thought of the Supreme Power and of his essential unity with It, with the result that he becomes more and more that which he thinks upon. His Bhâva, or disposition, becomes purified and divinized so far as that can be in the world. At length practice makes perfect in Sâdhanâ, and on the arising in such purified and illuminated mind, of knowledge and detachment from the world, there is competency for Yoga. When in turn practice in Yoga makes perfect, all limitations on experience are shed, and Nirvâna is attained.

Ordinarily it is said that enjoyment (Bhoga) only enchains and Yoga only liberates. Enjoyment (Bhoga) does not only mean that which is bad (Adharma). Bad enjoyment certainly enchains and also leads to Hell. Good—that is, lawful—enjoyment also enchains, even though Heaven is its fruit. Moreover, Bhoga means both enjoyment and suffering. But, according to the Bengal Shâkta worshippers, Enjoyment (which must necessarily be lawful) and Yoga may be one. According to this method (see Masson-Oursel, " Esquisse d'une Histoire de la Philosophie Indienne "), the body is not of necessity an obstacle to liberation. For, there is no antinomy, except such as we ourselves fancy, between Nature and Spirit, and therefore there is nothing wrong or low in natural function. Nature is the instrument for the realization of the aims of the Spirit. Yoga controls but does not frustrate enjoyment, which may be itself Yoga in so far as it pacifies the mind and makes man one with his inner self,

The spontaneity of life is under no suspicion. Supreme power is immanent in body and mind, and these are also forms of its expression. And so, in the psycho-physiological rites of these Shāktas, to which I have referred, the body and its functions are sought to be made a means of, as they may otherwise be an obstacle to, liberation. The Vīra, or heroic man, is powerful for mastery on all the plains and to pass beyond them. He does not shun the world from fear of it, but holds it in his grasp and learns its secret. He can do so because the world does not exist in isolation from some transcendent Divinity exterior to Nature, but is itself the Divine Power inseparate from the Divine Essence. He knows that he is himself as body and mind such power, and as Spirit or Self such essence. When he has learned this, he escapes both from the servile subjection to circumstance, and the ignorant driftings of a humanity which has not yet realized itself. Most are still not men but candidates for Humanity. But he is the illumined master of himself, whether he is developing all his powers in this world, or liberating himself therefrom at his will.

I conclude by citing a verse from a Hymn in the great "Mahākāla Samhitā," by a Sādhaka who had surpassed the stage of formal external ritual, and was of a highly advanced devotional type. I first read the verse and then give a commentary thereon which is my own.

"I torture not my body by austerity."

(For the body is the Divine Mother. Why then torture it? The Hymnist is speaking of those who, like himself, have realized that the body is a manifestion of the Divine Essence. He does not say that no one is to practise austerities. These may be necessary for those who have not realized that the body is divine, and who, on the contrary, look upon it as a material obstacle which must be strictly controlled. It is a common mistake of Western critics to take that which is meant for the particular case as applying to all.)

"I make no pilgrimages."

(For the sacred places in their esoteric sense are in the body of the worshipper. Why should he who knows this travel? Those, however, who do not know this may profitably travel to the exterior sacred places such as Benares, Puri, Brindaban.)

"I waste not my time in reading the Vedas."

(This does not mean that no one is to read the Vedas. He has already done so, but the Kulārnava Tantra says: "Extract the essence of the Scriptures, and then cast away the rest, as chaff is separated from the grain." When the essence has been extracted, what need is there of further reading and study? Moreover, the Veda recalls the spiritual experiences of others. What each man wants is that experience for himself, and this is not to be had by reading and speculation, but by practice, as worship or Yoga.)

But, says the author of the Hymn, addressing the Divine Mother:

"I take refuge at thy Sacred Feet."

(For this is both the highest Sādhanā and the fruit of it.)

In conclusion, I will say a word upon the Tantra Shāstra to which I have referred. The four chief Scriptures of the Hindus are Veda, Smriti, Purāna and Āgama. There are four Ages, and to each of these Ages is assigned its own peculiar Scripture. For the present Age the governing Scripture is the Āgama. The Āgama or "traditions," is made up of several schools such as Vaishnava, Shaiva and Shākta. It is a mistake to suppose that Āgama is a name given only to the Southern Scriptures, and that Tantra is the name of the Scriptures of the Bengal

School of Shāktas. The Scripture of all these communities is the Āgama, and the Āgama is constituted of Scriptures called Tantra and also by other names. To these Tantras titles are given just as they are given to chapters in a book, such as the Lakshmī Tantra of the Vaishnava Pancharātra, Mālinīvijaya Tantra of the Kashmir Shaiva Āgama, and the Kulārnava Tantra of the Bengal Shākta Āgama. These four Scriptures do not supersede or contradict one another, but are said to be various expressions of the one truth presented in diverse forms, suited to the inhabitants of the different Ages. As a Pandit very learned in the Āgama told me, all the Scriptures constitute one great "Many-millioned Collection" (Shatakoti Samhita). Only portions of the Vaidik Ritual have survived to-day. The bulk of the ritual which to-day governs all the old schools of Hindu worshippers is to be found in the Āgamas and their Tantras. And in this lies one reason for their importance.

CHAPTER XXIV

SHAKTI AS MANTRA

(Mantramayi Shakti)

This is in every way both a most important, as well as a most difficult, subject in the Tantra Shāstra; so difficult that it is not understood, and on this account has been ridiculed. Mantra, in the words of a distinguished Indian, has been called "meaningless jabber". When we find Indians thus talking of their Shāstra, it is not surprising that Europeans should take it to be of no account. They naturally, though erroneously, suppose that the Indian always understands his own beliefs, and if he says they are absurd it is taken that they are so. Even, however, amongst Indians, who have not lost themselves through an English Education, the Science of Mantra is largely unknown. There are not many students of the Mīmāmsā now-a-days. The English-educated have in this, as in other matters, generally taken the cue from their Western Gurus, and passed upon Mantravidyā a borrowed condemnation. There are those among them (particularly in this part of India), those who have in the past thought little of their old culture, and have been only too willing to sell their old lamps for new ones. Because they are new they will not always be found to give better light. Let us hope this will change, as indeed it will. Before the Indian condemns his cultural inheritance let him at least first study and understand it. It is true that Mantra is meaningless—*to those who do not know its meaning*: but to those who do, it is not "Jabber"; though of course like everything else it may become, and indeed has become, the subject of ignorance and superstitious use. A telegram written in code in a merchant's office will seem the merest gibberish to those who do not know that code. Those who do may spell thereout a transaction bringing lakhs of "real" Rupees for those who have sent it. Mantra-vidyā, whether it be true or not, is a profoundly conceived science, and, as interpreted by the Shākta Āgama, is a practical application of Vedāntic doctrine.

The textual source of Mantras is to be found in the Vedas (see in particular the Mantra portion of the Atharva-veda so associated with the Tantra Shāstra), the Purānas and Tantras. The latter Scripture is essentially the Mantra-Shāstra. In fact it is so called generally by Sādhakas and not Tantra Shāstra. And so it is said of all the Shāstras, symbolized as a body, that Tantra Shāstra which consists of Mantra is the Paramātmā, the Vedas are the Jīvātmā, Darshana or systems of philosophy are the senses, Purānas are the body and the Smritis are the limbs. Tantra Shāstra is thus the Shakti of Consciousness consisting of Mantra. For, as the Vishvasāra Tantra (Ch. 2) says, the Para-brahman in Its form as the Sound Brahman (Shabda-Brahman or Saguna-Brahman), whose substance is all Mantra, exists in the body of the Jīvātmā. Kundalinī Shakti is a form of the Shabda-Brahman in individual bodies (Shāradā-Tilaka, Ch. 1). It is from this Shabda-Brahman that the whole universe proceeds in the form of sound (Shabda) and the objects (Artha) which sound or words denote. And this is the meaning of the statement that the Devī and the Universe are composed of letters, that is, the signs for the sounds which denote all that is.

At any point in the flow of phenomena, we can enter the stream, and realize therein the changeless Real. The latter is everywhere and in all things, and is hidden in, and manifested by, sound as by all else. Any form (and all which is not the Formless is that) can be pierced by the mind, and union may be had therein with the Devatā who is at its core. It matters not what that form may be. And why? What I have said concerning Shakti gives the answer. All is Shakti. All is Consciousness. We desire to think and speak. This is Ichchhā Shakti. We make an effort towards realization. This is Kriyā Shakti. We think and know. This is Jnāna Shakti. Through Prānavāyu, another form of Shakti, we speak; and the word we utter is Shakti Mantramayī. For what is a letter (Varna) which is made into syllable (Pada) and sentences (Vākya)? It may be heard in speech, thus affecting the sense of hearing. It may be seen as a form in writing. It may be tactually sensed by the blind through the perforated dots of Braille type. The same thing thus affecting the various senses. But what is the thing which does so? The senses are Shakti, and so is the objective form which evokes the sensation. Both are in themselves Shakti as Chit Shakti and Māyā Shakti, and the Svarūpa of these is Chit or Feeling-Consciousness. When, therefore, a Mantra is realized; when there is what is called in the Shāstra Mantra-Chaitanya, what happens is the union of the consciousness of the Sādhaka with that Consciousness which manifests in the form of the Mantra. It is this union which makes the Mantra "work".

The subject is of such importance in the Tantras that their other name is Mantra Shāstra. But what is a Mantra? Commonly Orientalists and others describe Mantra as "Prayer," "Formulæ of worship," "Mystic syllables" and so forth. These are but the superficialities of those who do not know their subject. Wherever we find the word "Mystic", we may be on our guard; for it is a word which covers much ignorance. Thus Mantra is said to be a "mystic" word; Yantra a "mystic" diagram, and Mudrā a "mystic" gesture. But have these definitions taught us anything? No, nothing. Those who framed these definitions knew nothing of their subject. And yet, whilst I am aware of no work in any European language which shows a knowledge of what Mantra is or of its science (Mantra-vidya), there is nevertheless perhaps no subject which has been so ridiculed; a not unusual attitude of ignorance. There is a widely diffused lower mind which says, "what I do not understand is absurd". But this science, whether well-founded or not, is not that. Those who so think might expect Mantras which are prayers and the meaning of which they understand; for with prayer the whole world is familiar. But such appreciation itself displays a lack of understanding. For there is nothing necessarily holy or prayerful alone in Mantras as some think. Some combinations of letters constitute prayers and are called Mantras, as for instance the most celebrated Gāyatri Mantra.

A Mantra is not the same thing as prayer or self-dedication (Ātma-nivedana). Prayer is conveyed in the words the Sādhaka chooses. Any set of words or letters is not a Mantra. Only that Mantra in which the Devatā has revealed His or Her particular aspects can reveal that aspect, and is therefore the Mantra of that one of His or Her particular aspects. The relations of the letters (Varna), whether vowel or consonant, Nāda and Bindu, in a Mantra indicate the appearance of Devatā in different forms. Certain Vibhūti or aspects of the Devatā are inherent in certain Varna, but perfect Shakti does not appear in any but a whole Mantra. All letters are forms of the Shabda-Brahman, but only particular combinations of letters are a particular form, just as the name of a particular being is made up of certain letters and not of any indiscriminately.

The whole universe is Shakti and is pervaded by Shakti. Nāda, Bindu, Varna are all forms of Shakti and combinations of these, and these combinations only are the Shabda corresponding to the Artha or forms of any particular Devatā. The gross lettered sound is, as explained later, the manifestation of sound in a more subtle form, and this again is the production of causal "sound" in its supreme (Para) form. Mantras are manifestations of Kulakundalinī (see Chapter on the same) which is a name for the Shabda-Brahman or Saguna-Brahman in individual bodies. Produced Shabda is an aspect of the Jīva's vital Shakti. Kundalī is the Shakti who gives life to the Jīva. She it is who in the Mūlādhāra Chakra (or basal bodily centre) is the cause of the sweet, indistinct and murmuring Dhvani which is compared to the humming of a black bee. Thence Shabda originates and, being first Parā, gradually manifests upwards as Pashyantī, Madhyamā, Vaikharī (see *post.*) Just as in outer space, waves of sound are produced by movements of air (Vāyu), so in the space within the Jīva's body, waves of sound are said to be produced according to the movements of the vital air (Prāna-vāyu) and the process of in and out breathing. As the Svarūpa of Kundalī, in whom are all sounds, is Paramātmā, so the substance of all Mantra, Her manifestation, is Consciousness (Chit) manifesting as letters and words. In fact the letters of the Alphabet which are called Akshara are nothing but the Yantra of the Akshara or Imperishable Brahman. This is however only realized by the Sādhaka, when his Shakti generated by Sādhanā is united with Mantra-Shakti. Kundalinī, who is extremely subtle, manifests in gross (Sthūla) form in differing aspects as different Devatās. It is this gross form which is the Presiding Deity (Adhishthātrī Devatā) of a Mantra, though it is the subtle (Sūkshma) form at which all Sādhakas aim. Mantra and Devatā are thus one and particular forms of Brahman as Shiva-Shakti. Therefore the Shāstra says that they go to Hell who think that the Image (or "Idol" as it is commonly called) is but a stone and the Mantra merely letters of the alphabet. It is therefore also ignorance of Shāstric principle which supposes that Mantra is merely the name for the words in which one expresses what one has to say to the Divinity. If it were, the Sādhaka might choose his own language without recourse to the eternal and determined sounds of Shāstra. (See generally as to the above the Chapter on Mantra-tattva in second volume of "Principles of Tantra," Ed. A. Avalon.) The particular Mantra of a Devatā is that Devatā. A Mantra, on the contrary, consists of certain letters arranged in definite sequence of sounds of which the letters are the representative signs. To produce the designed effect, the Mantra must be intoned in the proper way, according to both sound (Varna) and rhythm (Svara). For these reasons, a Mantra when translated ceases to be such, and becomes a mere word or sentence.

By Mantra, the sought-for (Sādhya) Devatā appears, and by Siddhi therein is had vision of the three worlds. As the Mantra is in fact Devatā, by practice thereof this is known. Not merely do the rhythmical vibrations of its sounds regulate the unsteady vibrations of the sheaths of the worshipper, but therefrom the image of the Devatā appears. As the Brihad-Gandharva Tantra says (Ch. V):

Shrinu devi pravakshyāmi bījānām deva-rūpatām
Mantrochchāranamātrena deva-rūpam prajāyate.

Mantrasiddhi is the ability to make a Mantra efficacious and to gather its fruit in which case the Sādhaka is Mantrasiddha. As the Prānatoshinī (619) says, "Whatever the Sādhaka desires that he surely obtains." Whilst therefore prayer may end in merely physical sound, Mantra is ever, when rightly said, a potent compelling force, a word of power effective both to produce material gain and accomplish worldly desires, as also to promote the fourth aim of sentient being (Chaturvarga), Advaitic knowledge, and liberation. And thus it is said that Siddhi (success) is the certain result of Japa or recitation of Mantra.

Some Mantras constitute also what the European would call "prayers", as for instance the celebrated Gāyatrī. But neither this nor any other Mantra is simply a prayer. The Gāyatrī runs *Om* (The thought is directed to the *three-fold Energy of the One* as represented by the three letters of which *Om* is composed, namely, A or Brahmā, the Shakti which creates; U or Vishnu, the Shakti which maintains; and M or Rudra, the Shakti which "destroys," that is, withdraws the world): Nāda and Bindu, *Earth, Middle region, Heaven* (of which as the transmigrating worlds of Samsāra, God, as *Om*, as also in the form of the Sun, is the Creator). *Let us contemplate upon the Adorable Spirit of the Divine Creator who is in the form of the Sun* (Āditya-Devatā). *May He direct our minds, towards attainment of the four-fold aims* (Dharma, Artha, Kāma, Moksha) *of all sentient being. Om.* This great Mantra bears a meaning on its face, though the Commentaries explain and amplify it. The Self of all which exists in the three regions appears in the form of the Sun-god with His body of fire. The Brahman is the cause of all, and as the visible Devatā is the Eye of the World and the Maker of the day who vivifies, ripens and reveals all beings and things. The Sun-god is to the sun what the Spirit (Ātmā) is to the body. He is the Supreme in the form of the great Luminary. His body is the Light of the world, and He Himself is the Light of the lives of all beings. He is everywhere. He is in the outer ether as the sun, and in the inner ethereal region of the heart. He is the Wondrous Light which is the smokeless Fire. He it is who is in constant play with creation (Srishti), maintenance (Sthiti) and "destruction" (Pralaya); and by His radiance pleases both eye and mind. Let us adore Him that we may escape the misery of birth and death. May He ever direct our minds (Buddhivritti) upon the path of the world (Trivarga) and liberation (Moksha). Only the twice-born castes and men may utter this Gāyatrī. To the Shūdra, whether man or woman, and to women of all castes, it is forbidden. But the Tantra Shāstra has not the exclusiveness of the Vaidik system. Thus the Mahānirvāna provides (IV. 109-111) a Brahmagāyatrī for all: "May we know the Supreme Lord. Let us contemplate the Supreme Essence. And may the Brahman direct us." All will readily understand such Mantras as the Gāyatrī, though some comment, which is thought amusing, has been made on the "meaningless" *Om*. I have already stated what it means, namely, (shortly speaking) the Energy (Nāda) in Sadākhya Tattva which, springing from Shiva-Shakti Tattva, "solidifies" itself (Ghanībhūta) as the creative Power of the Lord (Bindu or Īshvara Tattva) manifesting in the Trinity or Creative Energies. (For further details see my "Garland of Letters".) "Om" then stands for the most general aspect of That as the Source of all. As it is recited, the idea arises in the mind corresponding with the sound which has been said to be the expression on the gross plane of that subtle "sound" which accompanied the first creative vibration. When rightly uttered this great syllable has an awe-inspiring effect. As I heard this Mantra chanted by some hundred Buddhist monks (one after the other) in a northern monastery it seemed to be the distant murmuring roll of some vast cosmic ocean. "Om" is the most prominent example of a "meaningless" Mantra, that is, one which does not bear its meaning on its face, and of what is called a seed or Bīja Mantra, because they are the very quintessence of Mantra, and the seed (Bīja) of the fruit which is Siddhi (spiritual achievement). These are properly monosyllabic. *Om* is a Vaidik Bīja, but it is the source of all the other Tāntrik Bījas which represent particular Devatā aspects of that which is presented as a whole in *Om*. As a Mantra-Shāstra, the Tantras have greatly elaborated the Bījas, and thus incurred the charge of "gibberish," for such the Bījas sound to those who do not know what they mean. Though a Mantra such as a Bīja-mantra may not convey its meaning on its face, the initiate knows that its meaning is the own form (Svarūpa) of the particular Devatā whose Mantra it is, and that the essence of the Bīja is that which makes letters sound, and exists in all which we say or hear. Every Mantra is thus a particular sound form (Rūpa) of the Brahman. There are a very large number of these short unetymological vocables or Bījas such as Hrīm,, Shrīm, Krīm, Hūm, Hum, Phat called by various names. Thus the first is called the Māyā Bīja, the second Lakshmī Bīja, the third Kālī Bīja, the fourth Kūrcha Bīja, the fifth Varma Bīja, the sixth Astra Bīja. Ram is Agni Bīja, Em is Yoni Bīja, Klīm is Kāma Bīja, Shrīm is Badhū Bīja, Aim Sarasvati Bīja and so forth. Each Devatā has His or Her Bīja. Thus Hrīm is the Māyā Bīja, Krīm the Kālī Bīja. The Bīja is used in the worship of the Devatā whose Mantra it is. All these Bījas mentioned are in common use. There are a large number of others, some of which are formed with the first letters of the name of the Devatā for whom they stand, such as for Gam (Ganesha), Dūm for Durgā.

Let us then shortly see by examples what the meaning of such a Bīja is. (For a fuller account see my "Garland of Letters".) In the first place, the reader will observe the common ending "m" which represents the Sanskrit breathings known as Nāda and Bindu or Chandrabindu. These have the same meaning in all. They are the Shaktis of that name appearing in the table of the 36 Tattvas given *ante.* They are states of Divine Power immediately preceding the manifestation of the objective universe. The other letters denote subsequent developments of Shakti, and various aspects of the manifested Devatā mentioned below. There are sometimes variant interpretations given. Take the great Bhubaneshvari or Māyā Bīja, Hrīm. I have given one interpretation in my Studies above cited. From the Tāntrik compendium the Prānatoshinī quoting the Baradā Tantra we get the following: Hrīm = H + R + Ī + M. H = Shiva. R = Shakti Prakriti. Ī = Mahāmāyā. "M" is as above explained, but is here stated in the form that Nāda is the Progenitrix of the Universe, and Bindu which is Brahman as Īshvara and Īshvarī (Īshvaratattva) is described for the Sādhaka as the "Dispeller of Sorrow". The meaning therefore of this Bīja Mantra which is used in the worship of Mahāmāyā or Bhubaneshvarī is, that that Devī in Her Turīya or transcendent state is Nāda and Bindu, and is the causal body manifesting as Shiva-Shakti in the form of the manifested universe. The same idea is expressed in varying form but with the same substance by the Devīgītā (Ch. IV) which says that H = gross body, R = subtle body, Ī = causal body and M = the Turīya or transcendent fourth state. In other words, the Sādhaka worshipping the Devī with Hrīm, by that Bīja calls to mind the transcendent Shakti who is the causal body of the subtle and gross bodies of all existing things. Shrīm (see Baradā Tantra) is used in the worship of Lakshmī Devī. Sh = Mahalakshmī, R = Wealth (Dhanārtham) which as well as Ī = (satisfaction or Tushtyartham) She gives. Krīm is used in the worship of Kālī. K = Kālī (Shakti worshipped for relief from the world and its sorrows). R = Brahma (Shiva with whom She is ever associated). Ī = Mahāmāyā (Her aspect in which She overcomes for the Sādhaka the Māyā in which as Creatrix She has involved him). "Aim" is used in the worship of Sarasvatī and is Vāgbhava Bīja. Dūm is used in the worship of Durgā. D = Durgā. U = protection. Nādā = Her aspect as Mother of the Universe, and Bindu is its Lord. The Sādhaka asks Durgā as Mother-Lord to protect him, and looks on Her in her protecting aspect as upholder of the universe (Jagaddhātrī). In "Strīm," S = saving from difficulty. T = deliverer. R = (here) liberation (Muktyartho repha ukto'tra). I = Mahāmāyā. Bindu = Dispeller of grief. Nāda = Mother of the Universe. She as the Lord is the dispeller of Māyā and the sorrows it produces, the Saviour and deliverer from all difficulties by grant of liberation. I have dealt elsewhere ("Serpent Power") with Hum and Hūm the former of which is called Varma (armour) Bīja and the latter Kūrcha, H denoting Shiva and "ū", His Bhairava or formidable aspect (see generally Vol. I, Tāntrik Texts. Tantrābhidhāna). He is an armour to the Sādhaka by His destruction of evil. Phat is the weapon or guarding Mantra used with Hum, just as Svāhā (the Shakti of Fire), is used with Vashat, in making offerings. The primary Mantra of a Devatā is called Mūla-Mantra. Mantras are solar (Saura) and masculine, and lunar (Saumya) and feminine, as also neuter. If it be asked why things of mind are given sex, the answer is for the sake of the requirements of the worshipper. The masculine and neuter forms are called specifically Mantra and the feminine Vidyā, though the first term may be used for both. Neuter Mantras end with Namah. Hum, Phat are masculine terminations, and "Tham" or Svāhā, feminine (see Shāradātilaka II. Nāradapancharātra VII, Prayogasāra, Prānatoshinī 70).

The Nityā Tantra gives various names to Mantra according to the number of the syllables such as Pinda, Kartarī, Bīja, Mantra, Mālā. Commonly however the term Bīja is applied to monosyllabic Mantras,

The word "Mantra" comes from the root "*man*" to think. "*Man*" is the first syllable of *manana* or thinking. It is also the root of the word "Man" who alone of all creation is properly a Thinker. "*Tra*" comes from the root "trā," for the effect of a Mantra when used with that end, is to save him who utters and realizes it. *Tra* is the first syllable of *Trāna* or liberation from the Samsāra. By combination of *man* and *tra*, that is called Mantra which, from the religious stand-point, calls forth (Āmantrana) the four aims (Chaturvarga) of sentient being as happiness in the world and eternal bliss in Liberation. Mantra is thus Thought-movement vehicled by, and expressed in, speech. Its Svarūpa is, like all else, consciousness (Chit) which is the Shabda-Brahman. A Mantra is not merely sound or letters. This is a form in which Shakti manifests Herself. The mere utterance of a Mantra without knowing its meaning, without realization of the consciousness which Mantra manifests is a mere movement of the lips and nothing else. We are then in the outer husk of consciousness; just as we are when we identify ourselves with any other form of gross matter which is, as it were, the "crust" (as a friend of mine has aptly called it) of those subtler forces which emerge from the Yoni or Cause of all, who is, in Herself Consciousness (Chidrūpinī). When the Sādhaka knows the meaning of the Mantra he makes an advance. But this is not enough. He must, through his consciousness, realize that Consciousness which appears in the form of the Mantra, and thus attain Mantra-Chaitanya. At this point, thought is vitalized by contact with the centre of all thinking. At this point again thought becomes truly vital and creative. Then an effect is created by the realization thus induced.

The creative power of thought is now receiving increasing acceptance in the West, which is in some cases taking over, and in others, discovering anew, for itself, what was thought by the ancients in India. Because they have discovered it anew they call it "New Thought"; but its fundamental principle is as old as the Upanishads which said, "what you think that you become". All recognize this principle in the limited form that a man who thinks good becomes good, and he who is ever harbouring bad thoughts becomes bad. But the Indian and "New Thought" doctrine is more profound than this. In Vedāntic India, thought has been ever held creative. The world is a creation of the thought (Chit Shakti associated with Māyā Shakti) of the Lord (Īshvara and Īshvarī). Her and His thought is the aggregate, with almighty powers of all thought. But each man is Shiva and can attain His powers to the degree of his ability to consciously realize himself as such. Thought now works in man's small magic just as it first worked in the grand magical display of the World-Creator. Each man is in various degrees a creator. Thought is as real as any form of gross matter. Indeed it is more real in the sense that the world is itself a projection of the World-thought, which again is nothing but the aggregate in the form of the Samskāras or impressions of past experience, which give rise to the world. The universe exists for each Jīva because he consciously or unconsciously wills it. It exists for the totality of beings because of the totality of Samskāras which are held in the Great Womb of the manifesting Chit Itself. There is theoretically nothing that man cannot accomplish, for he is at base the Accomplisher of all. But, in practice, he can only accomplish to the degree that he identifies himself with the Supreme Consciousness and Its forces, which underlie, are at work in, and manifest as, the universe. This the basal doctrine of all magic, of all powers (Siddhi) including the greatest Siddhi which is Liberation itself. He who knows Brahman, becomes

Brahman to the extent of his "knowing". Thought-reading, thought-transference, hypnotic suggestion, magical projections (Mokshana) and shields (Grahana) are becoming known and practised in the West, not always with good results. For this reason some doctrines and practices are kept concealed. Projection (Mokshana) the occultist will understand. But Grahana, I may here explain, is not so much a "fence" in the Western sense, to which use a Kavacha is put, but the knowledge of how to "catch" a Mantra thus projected. A stone thrown at one may be warded off or caught and, if the person so wishes, thrown back at him who threw it. So may a Mantra. It is not necessary, however, to do so. Those who are sheltered by their own pure strength, automatically throw back all evil influences, which, coming back to the ill-wisher, harm or destroy him. Those familiar with the Western presentment of similar matters will more readily understand than others who, like the Orientalist and Missionary, as a rule know nothing of occultism and regard it as superstition. For this reason their presentment of Indian teaching is so often ignorant and absurd. The occultist, however, will understand the Indian doctrine which regards thought like mind, of which it is the operation, as a Power or Shakti; something therefore, very real and creative by which man can accomplish things for himself and others. Kind thoughts, without a word, will do good to all who surround us, and may travel round the world to distant friends. So we may suffer from the ill-wishes of those who surround us, even if such wishes do not materialize into deeds. Telepathy is the transference of thought from a distance without the use of the ordinary sense organs So, in initiation, the thought of a true Guru may pass to his disciple all his powers. Mantra is thus a Shakti (Mantra Shakti) which lends itself impartially to any use. Man can identify himself with any of nature's forces and for any end. Thus, to deal with the physical effects of Mantra, it may be used to injure, kill or do good; by Mantra again a kind of union with the physical Shakti is, by some, said to be effected. So the Vishnu-Purāna speaks of generation by will power, as some Westerners believe will be the case when man passes beyond the domination of his gross sheath and its physical instruments. Children will then again be "mind-born". By Mantra, the Homa fire may, it is said, be lit. By Mantra, again, in the Tāntrik initiation called Vedha-dīkshā there is, it is said, such a transference of power from the Guru to his disciple that the latter swoons under the impulse of the thought-power which pierces him. But Mantra is also that by which man identifies himself with That which is the Ground of all. In short, Mantra is a power (Shakti) in the form of idea clothed with sound. What, however, is not yet understood in the West is the particular Thought-science which is Mantravidyā, or its basis. Much of the "New Thought" lacks this philosophical basis which is supplied by Mantravidyā, resting itself on the Vedāntik doctrine. Mantravidyā is thus that form of Sādhanā by which union is had with the Mother Shakti in the Mantra form (Mantramayī), in Her Sthūla and Sūkshma aspects respectively. The Sādhaka passes from the first to the second. This Sādhanā works through the letters, as other forms of Sādhanā work through form in the shape of the Yantra, Ghata or Pratimā. All such Sādhanā belongs to Shāktopāya Yoga as distinguished from the introspective meditative processes of Shāmbhavopāya which seeks more directly the realization of Shakti, which is the end common to both. The Tāntrik doctrine as regards Shabda is that of the Mīmāmsā with this exception that it is modified to meet its main doctrine of Shakti.

In order to understand what a Mantra is, we must know its cosmic history. The mouth speaks a word. What is it and whence has it come? As regards the evolution of consciousness as the world, I refer my reader to the Chapters on 'Chit-Shakti and Māyā-Shakti' dealing with the 36 Tattvas. Ultimately, there is Consciousness which in its aspect as the great "I" sees the object as part of itself, and then as other than itself, and thus has experience of the universe. This is achieved through Shakti who, in the words of the Kāmakalāvilāsa, is the pure mirror in which Shiva experiences Himself (Shivarūpa-vimarsha-nirmalā-darshah). Neither Shiva nor Shakti alone suffices for creation. Shivarūpa here = Svarūpa. Aham ityevamākāram, that is, the form (or experience) which consists in the notion of "I". Shakti is the pure mirror for the manifestation of Shiva's experience as "I" (Aham). Aham ityevam rūpam jnānam tasya prakāshane nirmalādarshah: as the commentator Natanānanda (V-2) says. The notion is, of course, similar to that of the reflection of Purusha on Prakriti as Sattvamayī Buddhi and of Brahman on Māyā. From the Mantra aspect starting from Shakti (Shakti-Tattva) associated with Shiva (Shiva-Tattva), there was produced Nāda, and from Nādā, came Bindu which, to distinguish it from other Bindus, is known as the causal, supreme or Great Bindu (Kārana, Para, Mahābindu). This is very clearly set forth in the Shāradā Tilaka, a Tāntrik work by an author of the Kashmirian School which was formerly of great authority among the Bengal Shāktas. I have dealt with this subject in detail in my "Garland of Letters". Here I only summarize conclusions.

Shabda literally means and is usually translated "sound", the word coming from the root *Shabd* "to sound". It must not, however, be wholly identified with sound in the sense of that which is heard by the ear, or sound as effect of cosmic stress. Sound in this sense is the effect produced through excitation of the ear and brain, by vibrations of the atmosphere between certain limits. Sound so understood exists only with the sense organs of hearing. And even then it may be perceived by some and not by others, due to keenness or otherwise of natural hearing. Further the best ears will miss what the microphone gives. Considering Shabda from its primary or causal aspect, independent of the effect which it may or may not produce on the sense organs, it is vibration (Spandana) of any kind or motion, which is not merely physical motion, which may become sound for human ears, given the existence of ear and brain and the fulfilment of other physical conditions. Thus, Shabda is the possibility of sound, and may not be actual sound for this individual or that. There is thus Shabda wherever there is motion or vibration of any kind. It is now said that the electrons revolve in a sphere of positive electrification at an enormous rate of motion. If the arrangement be stable, we have an atom of matter. If some of the electrons are pitched off from the atomic system, what is called radio-activity is observed. Both these rotating and shooting electrons are forms of vibration as Shabda, though it is no sound for mortal ears. To a Divine Ear all such movements would constitute the "music of the spheres". Were the human ear subtle enough, a living tree would present itself to it in the form of a particular sound which is the natural word for that tree. It is said of ether (Ākāsha) that its Guna or quality is sound (Shabda); that is, ether is the possibility of Spandana or vibration of any kind. It is that state of the primordial "material" substance (Prakriti) which makes motion or vibration of any kind possible (Shabdaguna ākāshah). The Brahman Svarūpa or Chit is motionless. It is also known as Chidākāsha. But this Ākāsha is not created. Chidākāsha is the Brahman in which stress of any kind manifests itself, a condition from which the whole creation proceeds. This Chidākāsha is known as the Shabda-Brahman through its Māyāshakti, which is the cause of all vibrations manifesting themselves as sound to the ear, as touch to the tactile sense, as colour and form to the eye, as taste to the tongue and as odour to the nose. All mental functioning again is a form of vibration (Spandana). Thought is a vibration of mental substance just as the expression of thought in the form of the spoken word is a vibration affecting the ear. All Spandana presupposes heterogeneity (Vaishamya). Movement of any kind implies inequality of tensions. Electric current flows between two points because there is a difference of potential between them. Fluid flows from one point to another because there is difference of pressure. Heat travels because there is difference of temperature. In creation (Srishti) this condition of heterogeneity appears and renders motion possible. Ākāsha is the possibility of Spandana of any kind. Hence its precedence in the order of creation. Ākāsha means Brahman with Māyā, which Māyāshakti or (to use the words of Professor P. N. Mukhyopādhyāya) Stress is rendered actual from a previous state of possibility of stress which is the Shakti's natural condition of equilibrium (Prakriti = Sāmyāvasthā). In dissolution, the Mayā-shakti of Brahman (according to the periodic law which is a fundamental postulate of Indian cosmogony) returns to homogeneity when in consequence Ākāsha disappears. This disappearance means that Shakti is equilibrated, and that therefore there is no further possibility of motion of any kind. As the Tantras say, the Divine Mother becomes one with Paramashiva.

The Shāradā says—From the Sakala Parameshvara who is Sachchidānanda issued Shakti; from Shakti came Nāda; and from Nāda issued Bindu.

Sachchidānandavibhavāt sakalāt parameshvarāt
Āsīchchhaktistato nādo nādād bindusamudbhavah.

Here the Sakala Parameshvara is Shiva Tattva. Shakti is Shakti Tattva wherein are Samanī, Vyāpinī, and Anjanī Shaktis. Nâda is the first produced source of Mantra, and the subtlest form of Shabda of which Mantra is a manifestation. Nāda is threefold, as Mahānāda or Nādānta and Nirodhinī representing the first moving forth of the Shabda-Brahman as Nāda, the filling up of the whole universe with Nādānta and the specific tendency towards the next state of unmanifested Shabda respectively. Nāda in its three forms is in the Sadākhya Tattva. Nāda becoming slightly operative towards the "speakable" (Vāchya), [the former operation being in regard to the thinkable (Mantavya)] is called Arddhachandra which develops into Bindu. Both of these are in Īshvara Tattva. This Mahābindu is threefold as the Kāmakalā. The undifferentiated Shabda-Brahman or Brahman as the immediate cause of the manifested Shabda and Artha is an unity of consciousness (Chaitanya) which then expresses itself in three-fold function as the three Shaktis, Ichchhā, Jnāna, Kriyā; the three Gunas, Sattva, Rajas, Tamas; the three Bindus (Kāryya) which are Sun, Moon and Fire; the three Devatas, Rudra, Vishnu, Brahmā and so forth. These are the product of the union of Prakāsha and Vimarsha Shakti. This Triangle of Divine Desire is the Kāmakalā, or Creative Will and its first subtle manifestation, the cause of the Universe which is personified as the Great Devī Tripurasundarī, the Kāmeshvara and Kāmeshvarī, the object of worship in the Āgamas. Kāmakalāvilāsa, as explained in the work of that name, is the manifestation of the union of Shiva and Shakti, the great "I" (Aham) which develops through the inherent power of its thought-activity (Vimarsha-Shakti) into the universe, unknowing as Jīva its true nature and the secret of its growth through Avidyā Shakti. Here then there appears the duality of subject and object; of mind and matter, of the word (Shabda) and its meaning (Artha). The one is not the cause of the other, but each is inseparable from, and concomitant with, the other as a bifurcation of the undifferentiated unity of Shabda-Brahman whence they proceed. The one cosmic movement produces at the same time the mind and the object which it cognizes; names (Nāma) and language (Shabda) on the one hand; and forms (Rūpa) or object (Artha) on the other. These are all parts of one co-ordinated contemporaneous movement, and, therefore, each aspect of the process is related the one to the other. The genesis of Shabda is only one aspect of the creative process, namely, that in which the Brahman is regarded as the Author of Shabda and Artha into which the undifferentiated Shabda-Brahman divides Itself. Shakti is Shabda-Brahman ready to create both Shabda and Artha on the differentiation of the Parabindu into the Kāmakalā, which is the root (Mūla) of all Mantras. Shabda-Brahman is Supreme "Speech" (Parā-Vāk) or Supreme Shabda (Para-Shabda). From this fourth state of Shabda, there are three others—Pashyantī, Madhyamā and Vaikharī, which are the Shabda aspect of the stages whereby the seed of formless consciousness explicates into the multitudinous concrete ideas (expressed in language of the mental world) the counterpart of the objective universe. But for the last three states of sound the body is required and, therefore, they only exist in the Jīva. In the latter, the Shabda-Brahman is in the form of Kundalinī Shakti in the Mūlādhāra Chakra. In Kundalinī is Parashabda. This develops into the "Mātrikās" or "Little Mothers" which are the subtle forms of the gross manifested letters (Varna). The letters make up syllables (Pada) and syllables make sentences (Vākya), of which elements the Mantra is composed. Para Shabda in the body develops in Pashyantī Shabda or Shakti of general movement (Sāmānya Spanda) located in the tract from the Mūlādhāra to the Manipūra associated with Manas. It then in the tract upwards to the Anāhata becomes Madhyamā or Hiranyagarbha sound with particularized movement (Vishesha Spanda) associated with Buddhi-Tattva. Vāyu proceeding upwards to the throat expresses itself in spoken speech which is Vaikharī or Virāt Shabda. Now it is that the Mantra issues from the mouth and is heard by the ear. Because the one cosmic movement produces the ideating mind and its accompanying Shabda and the objects cognized or Artha, the creative force of the universe is identified with the Mātrikās and Varnas, and Devī is said to be in the forms of the letters from A to Ha, which are the gross expressions of the forces called Mātrikā; which again are not different from, but are the same forces that evolve into the universe of mind and matter. These Varnas are, for the same reason, associated with certain vital and physiological centres which are produced by the same power that gives birth to the letters. It is by virtue of these centres and their controlled area in the body that all the phenomena of human psychosis run on, and keep man in bondage. The creative force is the union of Shiva and Shakti, and each of the letters (Varna) produced therefrom and thereby are part and parcel of that Force, and are, therefore, Shiva and Shakti in those particular forms. For this reason, the Tantra Shāstra says that Devatā and Mantra composed of letters, are one. In short, Mantras are made of letters (Varna). Letters are Mātrikā. Mātrikā is Shakti and Shakti is Shiva. Through Shakti (one with Shiva) Nāda-Shakti, Bindu-Shakti, the Shabda-Brahman or Para Shabda, arise the Mātrikā, Varna, Pada, Vākya of the lettered Mantra or manifested Shabda.

But what is Shabda or "Sound"? Here the Shākta Tantra Shāstra follows the Mīmāmsā doctrine of Shabda, with such modifications as are necessary to adapt it to its doctrine of Shakti. Sound (Shabda) which is quality (Guna) of ether (Ākāsha) and is sensed by hearing is twofold, namely, lettered (Varnātmaka Shabda) and unlettered or Dhvani (Dhvanyātmaka Shabda). The latter is caused by the striking of two things together, and is apparently meaningless. Shabda, on the contrary, which is Anāhata (a term applied to the Heart-Lotus) is that Brahman sound which is not caused by the striking of two things together. Lettered sound is composed of sentences (Vākya), words (Pada) and letters (Varna). Such sound has a meaning. Shabda manifesting as speech is said to be eternal. This the Naiyāyikas deny saying that it is transitory. A word is uttered and it is gone. This opinion the Mīmāmsā denies saying that the perception of lettered sound must be distinguished from lettered sound itself. Perception is due to Dhvani caused by the striking of the air in contact with the vocal organs, namely, the throat, palate and tongue and so forth. Before there is Dhvani there must be the striking of one thing against another. It is not the mere striking which is the lettered Shabda. This manifests it. The lettered sound is produced by the formation of the vocal organs in contact with air; which formation is in response to the mental movement or idea which by the will thus seeks outward expression in audible sound. It is this perception which is transitory, for the Dhvani which manifests ideas in language is such. But lettered sound as it is in itself, that is, as the Consciousness manifesting Idea expressed in speech is eternal. It was not produced at the moment it was perceived. It was only manifested by the Dhvani. It existed before, as it exists after, such manifestation, just as a jar in a dark room which is revealed by a flash of lightning is not then produced, nor does it cease to exist on its ceasing to be perceived through the disappearance of its manifester, the lightning. The air in contact with the voice organs reveals sound in the form of the letters of the alphabet, and their combinations in words and sentences. The letters are produced for hearing by the person desiring to speak, and become audible to the ear of others through the operation of unlettered sound or Dhvani. The latter being a manifester only, lettered Shabda is something other than its manifester.

Before describing the nature of Shabda in its different form of development, it is necessary to understand the Indian psychology of perception. At each moment, the Jīva is subject to innumerable influences which from all quarters of the Universe pour upon him. Only those reach his Consciousness which attract his attention and are thus selected by his Manas. The latter attends to one or other of these sense-impressions and conveys it to the Buddhi. When an object (Artha) is presented to the mind, and perceived, the latter is formed into the shape of the object perceived. This is called a mental Vritti (modification) which it is the object of Yoga to suppress. The mind as a Vritti is thus a representation of the outer subject. But, in so far as it is such representation, the mind is as much an object as the outer one. The latter, that is, the physical object, is called the gross object (Sthūla artha), and the former or mental impression is called the subtle object (Sūkshma artha). But, besides the object, there is the mind which perceives it. It follows that the mind has two aspects, in one of which it is the perceiver, and in the other the perceived in the form of the mental formation (Vritti), which in creation precedes its outer projection, and after the creation follows as the impression produced in the mind by the sensing of a gross physical object. The mental impression and the physical object exactly correspond, for the physical object is in fact but a projection of the cosmic imagination, though it has the same reality as the mind has; no more and no less. The mind is thus both cognizer (Grāhaka) and cognized (Grāhya), revealer (Prakāshaka) and revealed (Prakāshya), denoter (Vāchaka) and denoted (Vāchya). When the mind perceives an object, it is transformed into the shape of that object. So the mind which thinks of the Divinity which it worships (Ishtadevatā) is, at length, through continued devotion, transformed into the likeness of that Devatā. By allowing the Devatā thus to occupy the mind for long, it becomes as pure as the Devatā. This is a fundamental principle of Tāntrik Sādhanā or religious practice. The object perceived is called Artha, a term which comes from the root "Ri", which means to get, to know, to enjoy. Artha is that which is known and which, therefore, is an object of enjoyment. The mind as Artha, that is in the form of the mental impression, is an exact reflection of the outer object or gross Artha. As the outer object is Artha, so is the interior subtle mental form which corresponds to it. That aspect of the mind which cognizes is called Shabda or Nāma (name), and that aspect in which it is its own object or cognized is called Artha or Rūpa (form). The outer physical object, of which the latter is in the individual an impression, is also Artha or Rūpa, and spoken speech is the outer Shabda. The mind is thus, from the Mantra aspect, Shabda and Artha, terms corresponding to the Vedāntic Nāma and Rūpa or concepts and concepts objectified. The Māyāvāda Vedānta says that the whole creation is Nāma and Rūpa. Mind as Shabda is the Power (Shakti) the function of which is to distinguish and identify (Bhedasamsargavritti-Shakti).

Just as the body is causal, subtle and gross, so is Shabda, of which there are four states (Bhāva) called Parā,

Pashyantī, Madhyamā and Vaikharī. Parā sound is that which exists on the differentiation of the Mahābindu before actual manifestation. This is motionless, causal Shabda in Kundalinī, in the Mūlādhāra centre of the body. That aspect of it in which it commences to move with a general, that is, non-particularized, motion (Sāmānya Spanda) is Pashyantī whose place is from the Mūlādhāra to the Manipūra Chakra, the next centre. It is here associated with Manas. These represent the motionless and first moving Īshvara aspect or Shabda. Madhyamā Shabda is associated with Buddhi. It is Hiranyagarbha sound (Hiranyagarbharūpa) extending from Pashyantī to the heart. Both Madhyamā sound which is the inner "naming" by the cognitive aspect of mental movement, as also its Artha or subtle (Sūkshma) object (Artha) belong to the mental or subtle body (Sūkshma or Linga Sharīra). Perception is dependent on distinguishing and identification. In the perception of an object that part of the mind which identifies and distinguishes and thus "names" or the cognizing part is, from the Shabda aspect, subtle Shabda: and that part of it which takes the shape of, and thus constitutes, the object (a shape which corresponds with the outer thing) is subtle Artha. The perception of an object is thus consequent on the simultaneous functioning of the mind in its two-fold aspect as Shabda and Artha, which are in indissoluble relation with one another as cognizer (Grāhaka) and cognized (Grāhya). Both belong to the subtle body. In creation Madhyamā sound first appeared. At that movement there was no outer Artha. Then the Cosmic Mind projected this inner Madhyamā Artha into the world of sensual experience and named it in spoken speech (Vaikharī Shabda). The last or Vaikharī Shabda is uttered speech, developed in the throat, issuing from the mouth. This is Virāt Shabda. Vaikharī Shabda is therefore language or gross lettered sound. Its corresponding Artha is the physical or gross object which language denotes. This belongs to the gross body (Sthūla Sharīra). Madhyamā Shabda is mental movement or ideation in its cognitive aspect, and Madhyamā Artha is the mental impression of the gross object. The inner thought-movement in its aspect as Shabdārtha, and considered both in its knowing aspect (Shabda) and as the subtle known object (Artha) belongs to the subtle body (Sūkshma Sharīra). The cause of these two is the first general movement towards particular ideation (Pashyantī) from the motionless cause Para Shabda or Supreme Speech. Two forms of inner or hidden speech, causal, subtle, accompanying mind movement thus precede and lead up to spoken language. The inner forms of ideating movement constitute the subtle, and the uttered sound the gross aspect of Mantra which is the manifested Shabda-Brahman.

The gross Shabda called Vaikharī or uttered speech, and the gross Artha or the physical object denoted by that speech are the projection of the subtle Shabda and Artha, through the initial activity of the Shabda-Brahman into the world of gross sensual perception. Therefore, in the gross physical world, Shabda means language, that is, sentences, words and letters which are the expression of ideas and are Mantra. In the subtle or mental world, Madhyamā sound is the Shabda aspect of the mind which "names" in its aspect as cognizer, and Artha, is the same mind in its aspect as the mental object of its cognition. It is defined to be the outer in the form of the mind. It is thus similar to the state of dreams (Svapna), as Parashabda is the causal dreamless (Sushupti), and Vaikharī the waking (Jāgrat) state. Mental Artha is a Samsāra, an impression left on the subtle body by previous experience, which is recalled when the Jīva reawakes to world experience, and recollects the experience temporarily lost in the cosmic dreamless state (Sushupti) which is destruction (Pralaya). What is it which arouses this Samskāra? As an effect (Kriyā) it must have a cause (Kārana). This Kārana is the Shabda or Name (Nāma) subtle or gross corresponding to that particular Artha. When the word "Ghata" is uttered, this evokes in the mind the image of an object, namely, a jar; just as the presentation of that object does. In the Hiranyagarbha state, Shabda as Samskāra worked to evoke mental images. The whole world is thus Shabda and Artha, that is Name and Form (Nāma, Rūpa). These two are inseparably associated. There is no Shabda without Artha or Artha without Shabda. The Greek word "Logos" also means thought and word combined. There is thus a double line of creation, Shabda and Artha; ideas and language together with their objects. Speech as that which is heard, or the outer manifestation of Shabda, stands for the Shabda creation. The Artha creation are the inner and outer objects seen by the mental or physical vision. From the cosmic creative standpoint, the mind comes first, and from it is evolved the physical world according to the ripened Samskāras which led to the existence of the particular existing universe. Therefore, the mental Artha precedes the physical Artha which is an evolution in gross matter of the former. This mental state corresponds to that of dreams (Svapna), when man lives in the mental world only. After creation which is the waking (Jāgrat) state, there is for the individual an already existing parallelism of names and objects.

Uttered speech is a manifestation of the inner naming or thought. This thought-movement is similar in men of all races. When an Englishman or an Indian thinks of an object, the image is to both the same, whether evoked by the object itself or by the utterance of its name. For this reason possibly if thought-reading be accepted, a thought-reader whose cerebral centre is *en rapport* with that of another, may read the hidden "speech", that is thought, of one whose spoken speech he cannot understand. Thus, whilst the thought-movement is similar in all men, the expression of it as Vaikharī Shabda differs. According to tradition there was once an universal language. According to the Biblical account, this was so before the confusion of tongues at the Tower of Babel. Similarly there is, (a friend tells me though he has forgotten to send me the reference), in the Rigveda, a mysterious passage which speaks of the "Three Fathers and three Mothers", by whose action like that of the Elohim "all-comprehending speech" was made into that which was not so. Nor is this unlikely, when we consider that difference in gross speech is due to difference of races evolved in the course of time. If the instruments by which, and conditions under which thought is revealed in speech, were the same for all men then there would be but one language. But now this is not so. Racial characteristics and physical conditions, such as the nature of the vocal organs, climate, inherited impressions and so forth differ. So also does language. But for each particular man speaking any particular language, the uttered name of any object is the gross expression of his inner thought-movement. It evokes the idea and the idea is consciousness as mental operation. That operation can be so intensified as to be itself creative. This is Mantra-Chaitanya.

It is said in the Tantra Shāstras that the fifty letters of the alphabet are in the six bodily Chakras called Mūlādhāra, Svādhishthāna, Manipūra, Anāhata, Vishuddha and Ājnā. These 50 letters multiplied by 20 are in the thousand-petalled Lotus or Sahasrāra.

From the above account, it will be understood that, when it is said that the "Letters" are in the six bodily

Chakras, it is not to be supposed that it is intended to absurdly affirm that the letters as written shapes, or as the uttered sounds which are heard by the ear are there. The letters in this sense, that is, as gross things, are manifested only in speech and writing. This much is clear. But the precise significance of this statement is a matter of some difficulty. There is in fact no subject which presents more difficulties than Mantravidyā, whether considered generally or in relation to the particular matters in hand. I do not pretend to have elucidated all its difficulties.

What proceeds from the body is in it in subtle or causal form. Why, however, it may be asked are particular letters assigned to particular Chakras. I have heard several explanations given which do not, in my opinion, bear the test of examination.

If the arrangement be not artificial for the purpose of Sādhanā, the simplest explanation is that which follows: From the Brahman are produced the five Bhūtas, Ether, Air, Fire, Water, Earth, in the order stated; and from them issued the six Chakras from Ājnā to Mūlādhāra. The letters are (with the exception next stated) placed in the Chakras in their alphabetical order; that is, the vowels as being the first letters or Shaktis of the consonants (which cannot be pronounced without them) are placed in Vishuddha Chakra: the first consonants Ka to Tha in Anāhata and so forth until the Mūlādhāra wherein are set the last four letters from Va to Sa. Thus in Ājnā there are Ha and Ksha as being Brahmabījas. In the next or Vishuddha Chakra are the 16 vowels which originated first. Therefore, they are placed in Vishuddha the ethereal Chakra; ether also having originated first. The same principle applies to the other letters in the Chakras, namely, Ka to Tha (12 letters and petals) in Anāhata; Ḍa to Pha (10) in Maṇipūra; Ba to La (6) in Svādhiṣhṭhāna; and Va to Sa (4) in Mūlādhāra. The connection between particular letters and the Chakras in which they are placed is further said to be due to the fact that in uttering any particular letter, the Chakra in which it is placed and its surroundings are brought into play. The sounds of the Sanskrit alphabet are classified according to the organs used in their articulation, and are guttural (Kantha), palatals (Tālu), cerebrals (Mūrddhā), dentals (Danta) and labials (Oshtha). When so articulated, each letter, it is said, "touches" the Chakra in which it is, and in which on this account it has been placed. In uttering them certain Chakras are affected; that is, brought into play. This, it is alleged, will be found to be so, if the letter is carefully pronounced and attention is paid to the accompanying bodily movement. Thus, in uttering Ha, the head (Ājnā) is touched, and in uttering the deep-seated Va, the basal Chakra or Mūlādhāra. In making the first sound the forehead is felt to be affected, and in making the last the lower part of the body around the root-lotus. This is the theory put forth as accounting for the position of the letters in the Chakras.

A Mantra is, like everything else, Shakti. But the mere utterance of a Mantra without more is a mere movement of the lips. The Mantra must be awakened (Prabuddha) just like any other Shakti if effect is to be had thereform. This is the union of sound and idea through a knowledge of the Mantra and its meaning. The recitation of a Mantra without knowing its meaning is practically fruitless. I say "practically" because devotion, even though it be ignorant, is never wholly void of fruit. But a knowledge of the meaning is not enough; for it is possible by reading a book or receiving oral instructions to get to know the meaning of a Mantra, without anything further following. Each Mantra is the embodiment of a particular form of Consciousness or Shakti. This is the Mantra-Shakti. Consciousness or Shakti also exists in the form of the Sādhaka. The object then is to unite these two, when thought is not only in the outer husk, but is vitalized by will, knowledge, and action through its conscious centre in union with that of the Mantra. The latter is Devatā or a particular manifestation of Shakti: and the Sādhaka who identifies himself therewith, identifies himself with that Shakti. According to Yoga when the mind is concentrated on any object it is unified with it. When man is so identified with a Varna or Tattva, then the power of objects to bind ceases, and he becomes the controller. Thus, in Kundalinī-Yoga, the static bodily Shakti pierces the Chakras, to meet Shiva-Shakti in the Sahasrāra. As the Sādhaka is, through the power of the rising Shakti, identified with each of the Centres, Tattvas and Mātrikā Shaktis they cease to bind, until passing through all he attains Samādhi. As the Varnas are Siva-Shakti, concentration on them draws the mind towards, and then unifies it with, the Devatā which is one with the Mantra. The Devatā of the Mantra is only the creative Shakti assuming that particular form. As already stated, Devatā may be realized in any object, not merely in Mantras, Yantras, Ghatas, Pratimās or other ritual objects of worship. The same power which manifests to the ear in the Mantra is represented in the lines and curves of the Yantra which, the Kaulavalī Tantra says, is the body of the Devatā:

Yantram mantramayam proktam mantrātmā devataiva hi
Dehātmanor yathā bhedo yantra-devatayostathā.

The Yantra is thus the graphic symbol of the Shakti, indicated by the Mantra with which identification takes place. The Pratimā or image is a grosser visual form of the Devatā. But the Mantras are particular forms of Divine Shakti, the realization of which is efficacious to produce particular results. As in Kundalinī-Yoga, so also here the identification of the Sādhaka with different Mantras gives rise to various Vibhūtis or powers: for each grouping of the letters represents a new combination of the Mātrikā Shaktis. It is the eternal Shakti who is the life of the Mantra. Therefore, Siddhi in Mantra Sādhanā is the union of the Sādhaka's Shakti with the Mantra Shakti; the identification of the Sādhaka with the Mantra is the identification of the knower (Vedaka), knowing (Vidyā) and known (Vedya) or the Sādhaka, Mantra and Devatā. Then the Mantra works. The mind must feed, and is always feeding, on something. It seizes the Mantra and works its way to its heart. When there, it is the Chitta or mind of the Sādhaka unified with the Shakti of the Mantra which works. Then subject and object, in its Mantra form, meet as one. By meditation the Sādhaka gains unity with the Devatā behind, as it were, the Mantra and Whose form the Mantra is. The union of the Sādhaka of the Mantra and the Devatā of the Mantra is the result of the effort to realize permanently the incipient desire for such union. The will towards Divinity is a dynamic force which pierces everything and finds there Divinity itself. It is because Westerners and some Westernized Hindus do not understand the principles of Mantra; principles which lie at the centre of Indian religious theory and practice, that they see nothing in it where they do not regard it as gross superstition. It must be admitted that Mantra Sādhanā is often done ignorantly. Faith is placed in externals and the inner meaning is often lost. But even such ignorant worship is better than none at all. "It is better to bow to Nārāyana with one's shoes on than never to bow at all." Much also is said of "vain repetitions". What Christ condemned was not repetition but "vain" repetition. That man is a poor psychologist who does not know the effect of repetition, when done with faith and devotion. It is a fact that the inner kingdom yields to violence and can be taken by assault. Indeed, it yields to nothing but the strong will of the Sādhaka, for it is that will in its purest and fullest strength. By practice with the Mantra, the Devatā is invoked. This means that the mind itself is Devatā when unified with Devatā. This is attained through repetition of the Mantra (Japa).

Japa is compared to the action of a man shaking a sleeper to wake him up. The Sādhaka's own consciousness is awakened. The two lips are Shiva and Shakti. The movement in utterance is the "coition" (Maithuna) of the two. Shabda which issues therefrom is in the nature of Bindu. The Devatā then appearing is, as it were, the son of the Sādhaka. It is not the supreme Devatā who appears (for It is actionless), but in all cases an emanation produced by the Sādhaka's worship for his benefit only. In the case of worshippers of the Shiva-Mantra, a Boy-Shiva (Bāla-Shiva) appears who is then made strong by the nurture which the Sādhaka gives him. The occultist will understand all such symbolism to mean that the Devatā is a form of the Consciousness which becomes the Boy-Shiva, and which, when strengthened is the full-grown Divine Power Itself. All Mantras are forms of consciousness (Vijnānarūpa), and when the Mantra is fully practised it enlivens the Samskāra, and the Artha appears to the mind. Mantras used in worship are thus a form of the Samskāras of Jīvas; the Artha of which manifests to the consciousness which is pure. The essence of all this is—concentrate and vitalize thought and will power, that is Shakti.

The Mantra method is Shāktopāya Yoga working with concepts and form, whilst Shāmbhavopāya Yoga has been well said to be a more direct attempt at intuition of Shakti, apart from all passing concepts, which, as they cannot show the Reality, only serve to hide it the more from one's view and thus maintain bondage. These Yoga methods are but examples of the universal principle of Sādhanā, that the Sādhaka should first work with and through form, and then, so far as may be, by a meditation which dispenses with it.

It has been pointed out to me by Professor Surendra Nath Das Gupta that this Varna-Sādhanā, so important a content of the Tantra Shāstra, is not altogether its creation, but, as I have often in other matters observed, a development of ancient Vaidik teaching. For it was, he says, first attempted in the Āranyaka Epoch upon the Pratīkopāsanā on which the Tāntrik Sādhanā is, he suggests, based; though, of course, that Shāstra has elaborated the notion into a highly complicated system which is so peculiar a feature of its religious discipline. There is thus a synthesis of this Pratīkopāsanā with Yoga method, resting as all else upon a Vedāntic basis.

CHAPTER XXV

VARNAMĀLĀ

(The Garland of Letters)

The world has never altogether been without the Wisdom, nor its Teachers. The degree and manner in which it has been imparted have, however, necessarily varied according to the capacities of men to receive it. So also have the symbols by which it has been conveyed. These symbols further have varying significance according to the spiritual advancement of the worshipper. This question of degree and variety of presentation have led to the superficial view that the difference in beliefs negatives existence of any commonly established Truth. But if the matter be regarded more deeply, it will be seen that whilst there is one essential Wisdom, its revelation has been more or less complete according to symbols evolved by, and, therefore, fitting to, particular racial temperaments and characters. Symbols are naturally misunderstood by those to whom the beliefs they typify are unfamiliar, and who differ in temperament from those who have evolved them. To the ordinary Western mind the symbols of Hinduism are often repulsive and absurd. It must not, however, be forgotten that some of the Symbols of Western Faiths have the same effect on the Hindu. From the picture of the "Slain Lamb," and other symbols in terms of blood and death, he naturally shrinks in disgust. The same effect, on the other hand, is not seldom produced in the Western at the sight of the terrible forms in which India has embodied Her vision of the undoubted Terrors which exist in and around us. All is not smiling in this world. Even amongst persons of the same race and indeed of the same faith we may observe such differences. Before the Catholic Cultus of the "Sacred Heart" had overcome the opposition which it at first encountered, and for a considerable time after, its imagery was regarded with aversion by some who spoke of it in terms which would be to-day counted as shocking irreverence. These differences are likely to exist so long as men vary in mental attitude and temperament, and until they reach the stage in which, having discovered the essential truths, they become indifferent to the mode in which they are presented. We must also in such matters distinguish between what a symbol may have meant and what it now means. Until quite recent times, the English peasant folk and others danced around the flower-wreathed Maypole. That the pole originally (like other similar forms) represented the great Linga admits of as little doubt as that these folk, who in recent ages danced around it, were ignorant of that fact. The Bishop's mitre is said to be the head of a fish worn by ancient near-eastern hierophants. But what of that? It has other associations now.

Let us illustrate these general remarks by a short study of one portion of the Kālī symbolism which affects so many, who are not Hindus, with disgust or horror. Kālī is the Deity in that aspect in which It withdraws all things which It had created, into Itself. Kālī is so called because She devours Kāla (Time) and then resumes Her own dark formlessness. The scene is laid in the cremation ground (Shmashāna), amidst white sun-dried bones and fragments of flesh, gnawed and pecked at by carrion beasts and birds.

Here the "heroic" (Vīra) worshipper (Sādhaka) performs at dead of night his awe-inspiring rituals. Kālī is set in such a scene, for She is that aspect of the great Power which withdraws all things into Herself at, and by, the dissolution of the universe. He alone worships without fear, who has abandoned all worldly desires, and seeks union with Her as the One Blissful and Perfect Experience. On the burning ground all worldly desires are burnt away. She is naked, and dark like a threatening rain-cloud. She is dark, for She who is Herself beyond mind and speech, reduces all things into that worldly, "nothingness," which, as the Void (Shūnya) of all which we now know, is at the same time the All (Pūrna) which is Peace. She is naked, being clothed in space alone (Digambarī), because the great Power is unlimited; further, She is in Herself beyond Māyā (Māyātītā); that power of Hers which creates all universes. She stands upon the white corpse-like (Shavarūpa) body of Shiva. He is white, because he is the illuminating transcendental aspect of consciousness. He is inert, because he is the changeless aspect of the Supreme and She the apparently changing aspect of the same. In truth, She and He are one and the same, being twin aspects of the One who is changelessness in, and exists as, change. Much might be said in explanation of these and other symbols such as Her loosened hair, the lolling tongue, the thin stream of blood which trickles from the corners of the mouth, the position of Her feet, the apron of dead men's hands around Her waist, Her implements and so forth. (See *Hymn to Kālī* by Arthur Avalon. Vol. 9, Tantrik Texts.) Here I take only the garland of freshly-severed heads which hangs low from Her neck.

Some have conjectured that Kālī was originally the Goddess of the dark-skinned inhabitants of the Vindhya Hills taken over by the Brāhmanas into their worship. One of them has thought that She was a deified Princess of these folk, who fought against the white in-coming Āryans. He pointed to the significant fact that the severed heads are those of white men. The Western may say that Kālī was an objectification of the Indian mind, making a Divinity of the Power of Death. An Eastern may reply that She is the Sañketa (symbol) which is the effect of the impress of a Spiritual Power on the Indian mind. I do not pause to consider these matters here.

The question before us is, what does this imagery mean now, and what has it meant for centuries past to the initiate in Her symbolism? An exoteric explanation describes this Garland as made up of the heads of Demons, which She, as a power of righteousness, has conquered. According to an inner explanation, given in the Indian Tantra Shāstra, this string of heads is the Garland of Letters (Varnamālā), that is, the fifty, and as some count it, fifty-one letters, of the Sanskrit Alphabet. The same interpretation is given in the Buddhist Demchog Tantra in respect of the garland worn by the great Heruka. These letters represent the universe of names and forms (Nāmarūpa), that is, Speech (Shabda) and its meaning or object (Artha). She the Devourer of all "slaughters" (that is, withdraws), both into Her undivided Consciousness at the Great dissolution of the Universe which they are. She wears the Letters which, She as the Creatrix bore. She wears the Letters which, She as the Dissolving Power takes to Herself again. A very profound doctrine is connected with these Letters which space prevents me from fully entering into here. This has been set out in greater detail in the "Serpent Power" (Kundalinī) which projects Consciousness, in Its true nature blissful and beyond all dualism, into the World of good and evil. The movements of Her projection are indicated by the Letters subtle and gross which exist on the Petals of the inner bodily centres or Lotuses.

Very shortly stated, Shabda which literally means Sound—here lettered sound—is in its causal state (Parashabda) known as "Supreme Speech" (Parā Vāk). This is the Shabda-Brahman or Logos; that aspect of Reality or Consciousness (Chit) in which it is the immediate cause of creation; that is of the dichotomy in Consciousness which is "I" and "This," subject and object, mind and matter. This condition of causal Shabda is the Cosmic Dreamless State (Sushupti). This Logos, awakening from its causal sleep, "sees," that is, creatively ideates the universe, and is then known as Pashyantī Shabda. As Consciousness "sees" or ideates, forms arise in the Creative Mind, which are themselves impressions (Samskāra) carried over from previous worlds, which ceased to exist as such when the Universe entered the state of causal dreamless sleep on the previous dissolution. These re-arise as the formless Consciousness awakes to enjoy once again sensual life in the world of forms.

The Cosmic Mind is at first itself both cognizing subject (Grāhaka) and cognized object (Grāhya); for it has not yet projected its thought into the plane of Matter; the mind as subject cognizer is Shabda, and the mind as the object cognized, that is, the mind in the form of object, is subtle Artha. This Shabda called Madhyamā Shabda is an "Inner Naming" or "Hidden Speech". At this stage, that which answers to the spoken letters (Varna) are the "Little Mothers" or Mātrikā, the subtle forms of gross speech. There is at this stage a differentiation of Consciousness into subject and object, but the latter is now within and forms part of the Self. This is the state of Cosmic Dreaming (Svapna). This "Hidden Speech" is understandable of all men if they can get in mental *rapport* one with the other. So a thought-reader can, it is said, read the thoughts of a man whose spoken speech he cannot understand. The Cosmic Mind then projects these mental images on to the material plane, and they there become materialized as gross physical objects (Sthūla artha) which make impressions from without on the mind of the created consciousness. This is the cosmic waking state (Jāgrat). At this last stage, the thought-movement expresses itself through the vocal organs in contact with the air as uttered speech (Vaikharī Shabda) made up of letters, syllables and sentences. The physical unlettered sound which manifests Shabda is called Dhvani. The lettered sound is manifested Shabda or Name (Nāma), and the physical objects denoted by speech are the gross Artha or form (Rūpa).

This manifested speech varies in men, for their individual and racial characteristics and the conditions, such as country and climate in which they live, differ. There is a tradition that there was once an universal speech before the building of the Tower of Babel, signifying the confusion of tongues. As previously stated, a friend has drawn my attention to a passage in the Rig-Veda which he interprets in a similar sense. For, it says, that the Three Fathers and the Three Mothers, like the Elohim, made (in the interest of creation) all-comprehending speech into that which was not so.

Of these letters and names and their meaning or objects, that is, concepts and concepts objectified, the whole Universe is composed. When Kālī withdraws the world, that is, the names and forms which the letters signify, the dualism in consciousness, which is creation, vanishes. There is neither "I" (Aham) nor "This" (Idam) but the one non-dual Perfect Experience which Kālī in Her own true nature (Svarūpa) is. In this way Her garland is understood.

"Surely," I hear it said, "not by all. Does every Hindu worshipper think such profundities when he sees the figure of Mother Kālī?" Of course not, no more than, (say) an ordinary Italian peasant knows of, or can understand, the subtleties of either the catholic mystics or doctors of theology. When, however, the Western man undertakes to depict and explain Indian symbolism, he should, in the interest both of knowledge and fairness, understand what it means both to the high as well as to the humble worshipper.

CHAPTER XXVI

SHĀKTA SĀDHANĀ

(The Ordinary Ritual)

SĀDHANĀ is that which produces Siddhi or the result sought, be it material or spiritual advancement. It is the means or practice by which the desired end may be attained and consists in the training and exercise of the body and psychic faculties, upon the gradual perfection of which Siddhi follows. The nature or degree of spiritual Siddhi depends upon the progress made towards the realization of the Ātmā whose veiling vesture the body is. The means employed are numerous and elaborate, such as worship (Pūjā) exterior or mental, Shāstric learning, austerities (Tapas), Japa or recitation of Mantra, Hymns, meditation, and so forth. The Sādhanā is necessarily of a nature and character appropriate to the end sought. Thus Sādhanā for spiritual knowledge (Brahmajnāna) which consists of external control (Dama) over the ten senses (Indriya), internal control (Shama) over the mind (Buddhi, Ahankāra, Manas), discrimination between the transitory and eternal, renunciation of both the world and heaven (Svarga), differs from the lower Sādhanā of the ordinary householder, and both are obviously of a kind different from that prescribed and followed by the practitioners of malevolent magic (Abhichāra). Sādhakas again vary in their physical, mental and moral qualities and are thus divided into four classes,

Mridu, Madhya, Adhimātraka, and the highest Adhimātrama who is qualified (Adhikārī) for all forms of Yoga. In a similar way, the Shākta Kaulas are divided into the Prākrita or common Kaula following Vīrāchāra with the Pancha-tattvas described in the following Chapter; the middling (Madhyama) Kaula who (may be) follows the same or other Sādhanā but who is of a higher type, and the highest Kaula (Kaulikottama) who, having surpassed all ritualism, meditates upon the Universal Self. These are more particularly described in the next Chapter.

Until a Sādhaka is Siddha all Sādhanā is or should be undertaken with the authority and under the direction of a Guru or Spiritual Teacher and Director. There is in reality but one Guru and that is the Lord (Īshvara) Himself. He is the Supreme Guru as also is Devī His Power one with Himself. But he acts through man and human means. The ordinary human Guru is but the manifestation on earth of the Ādi-nātha Mahākāla and Mahākālī the Supreme Guru abiding in Kailāsa. As the Yoginī Tantra (Ch. 1) says *Guroh sthānam hi kailāsam.* He it is who is in, and speaks with the voice of, the Earthly Guru. So, to turn to an analogy in the West, it is Christ who speaks in the voice of the Pontifex Maximus when declaring faith and morals, and in the voice of the priest who confers upon the penitent absolution for his sins. It is not the man who speaks in either case but God through him. It is the Guru who initiates and helps, and the relationship between him and the disciple (Shishya) continues until the attainment of spiritual Siddhi. It is only from him that Sādhanā and Yoga are learnt and not (as it is commonly said) from a thousand Shāstras. As the Shatkarmadīpikā says, mere book-knowledge is useless.

Pustake likhitā vidyā yena sundari japyate
Siddhir na jāyate tasya kalpakoti-shatair api.

(O Beauteous one! he who does Japa of a Vidyā (=Mantra) learnt from a book can never attain Siddhi even if he persists for countless millions of years.)

Manu therefore says, "of him who gives natural birth, and of him who gives knowledge of the Veda, the giver of sacred knowledge is the more venerable father." The Tantra Shāstras also are full of the greatness of the Guru. He is not to be thought of as a mere man. There is no difference between Guru, Mantra and Deva. Guru is father, mother and Brahman. Guru, it is said, can save from the wrath of Shiva, but in no way can one be saved from the wrath of the Guru. Attached to this greatness there is, however, responsibility; for the sins of the disciple may recoil upon him. The Tantra Shāstras deal with the high qualities which are demanded of a Guru and the good qualities which are to be looked for in an intending disciple (see for instance Tantrasāra, Ch. I). Before initiation, the Guru examines and tests the intending disciple for a specified period. The latter's moral qualifications are purity of soul (Suddhātmā), control of the senses (Jitendriya), the following of the Purushārtha or aims of all sentient being (Purushārthaparāyana). Amongst others, those who are lewd (Kāmuka), adulterous (Para-dārātura), addicted to sin, ignorant, slothful and devoid of religion should be rejected (see Matsyasūkta Tantra, XIII, Prānatoshinī 108, Mahārudrayāmala, I. XV, II. ii, Kulārnava Tantra, Ch. XIII). The good Sādhaka who is entitled to the knowledge of all Shāstra is he who is pure-minded, self-controlled, ever engaged in doing good to all beings, free from false notions of dualism attached to the speaking of, taking shelter with and ever living in the consciousness of, the Supreme Brahman (Gandharva Tantra, Ch. ii).

All orthodox Hindus of all divisions of worshippers submit themselves to the direction of a Guru. The latter initiates. The Vaidik initiation into the twice-born classes is by the Upanayana. This is for the first three castes only, *viz.*, Brāhmana (priesthood and teaching), Kshatriya (warrior), Vaishya (merchant). All are (it is said) by birth, Shūdra (Janmanā jāyate Shudrah) and by sacrament (that is, the Upanayana ceremony) twice-born. By study of the Vedas one is a Vipra. And he who has knowledge of the Brahman is a Brāhmana (Brahma jānāti brāhmanah). From this well-known verse it will be seen how few there really are who are entitled to the noble name of Brāhmana. The Tāntrik Mantra-initiation is a different ceremony and is for all castes. Initiation (Dīkshā) is the giving of Mantra by the Guru. The latter should first establish the life of the Guru in his own body; that is the vital power (Prānashakti) of the Supreme Guru in the thousand-petalled lotus (Sahasrāra). He then transmits it to the disciple. As an image is the instrument (Yantra) in which Divinity (Devatva) inheres, so also is the body of the Guru. The candidate is prepared for initiation, fasts and lives chastely. Initiation (which follows) gives spiritual knowledge and destroys sin. As one lamp is lit at the flame of another, so the divine Shakti consisting of Mantra is communicated from the Guru's body to that of the Shishya. I need not be always repeating that this is the theory and ideal, which to-day is generally remote from the fact. The Supreme Guru speaks with the voice of the earthly Guru at the time of giving Mantra. As the Yoginī Tantra (Ch. I) says:

Mantra-pradāna-kāle hi mānushe Naganandini
Adhishthānam bhavet tatra Mahākālasya Shankari
Ato na gurutā devi mānushe nātra samshayah.

(At the time the Mantra is communicated, there is in man (*i.e.*, Guru) the Presence of Mahākāla. There is no doubt that man is not the Guru.) Guru is the root (Mūla) of initiation (Dīkshā). Dīkshā is the root of Mantra. Mantra is the root of Devatā, and Devatā is the root of Siddhi. The Mundamālā Tantra says that Mantra is born of Guru, and Devatā of Mantra, so that the Guru is in the position of Father's Father to the Ishtadevatā. Without initiation, Japa (recitation) of the Mantra, Pūjā, and other ritual acts are useless. The Mantra chosen for the candidate must be suitable (Anukūla). Whether a Mantra is Svakula or Akula to the person about to be initiated is ascertained by the Kulākulachakra, the zodiacal circle called Rāshichakra and other Chakras which may be found in the Tantrasāra. Initiation by a woman is efficacious; that by the mother is eightfold so (*ib.*). For, according to the Tantra Shāstra, a woman with the necessary qualifications, may be a Guru and give initiation. The Kulagurus are four in number, each of them being the Guru of the preceding ones. There are also three lines of Gurus (see Mahānirvāna, Ed. A. Avalon, p 111, n. 10; p. 120, n. 3).

So long as the Shakti communicated by a Guru to his disciple is not fully developed, the relation of Teacher and Director and Disciple exists. A man is Shishya so long as he is Sādhaka. When, however, Siddhi is attained, Guru and Shishya, as also all other dualisms, and relations, disappear. Besides the preliminary initiation, there are a number of other initiations or consecrations (Abhisheka) which mark greater and greater degrees of advance from Shāktābhisheka when entrance is made on the path of Shākta Sādhanā to Pūrnadīkshābhisheka and Mahāpūrnadīkshābhisheka also called Virajā-grahanābhisheka. On the attainment of perfection in the last grade the Sādhaka performs his own funeral rite (Shrāddha), makes Pūrnāhuti with his sacred thread and crown lock. The relation of Guru and Shishya now ceases. From this point he ascends by himself until he realizes the great saying So'ham "He I am", Sā'ham "She I am". Now he is Jīvan-mukta and Paramahamsa.

The word Sādhanā comes from the root *Sādh*, to exert or strive, and Sādhanā is therefore striving, practice, discipline and worship in order to obtain success or Siddhi, which may be of any of the kinds, worldly or spiritual, desired, but which, on the religious side of the Shāstras, means spiritual advancement with its fruit of happiness in this world and in Heaven and at length Liberation (Moksha). He who practises Sādhanā is (if a man) called Sādhaka or (if a woman) Sādhikā. But men vary in capacity, temperament, knowledge and general advancement, and therefore the means (for Sādhanā also means instrument) by which they are to be led to Siddhi must vary. Methods which are suitable for highly advanced men will fail as regards the ignorant and undeveloped for they cannot understand them. What suits the latter has been long out-passed by the former. At least that is the Hindu view. It is called Adhikāra or competency. Thus some few men are competent (Adhikārī) to study Vedānta and to follow high mental rituals and Yoga processes. Others are not. Some are grown-up children and must be dealt with as such. As all men, and indeed all beings, are, as to their psychical and physical bodies, made of the primordial substance Prakriti-shakti (Prakrityātmaka), as Prakriti is Herself the three Gunas, Sattva, Rajas and Tamas, and as all things and beings are composed of these three Gunas in varying proportions, it follows that men are divisible into three general classes, namely, those in which the Sattva, Rajas, and Tamas Gunas, predominate respectively. There are, of course, degrees in each of these three classes. Amongst Sāttvika men, in whom Sattva predominates, some are more and some less Sāttvika than others and so on with the rest. These three classes of temperament (Bhāva) are known in the Shākta Tantras as the Divine (Divyabhāva), Heroic (Vīrabhāva) and Animal (Pashubhāva) temperaments respectively. Bhāva is defined as a property or quality (Dharma) of the Manas or mind (Prānatoshinī, 570). The Divyabhāva is that in which Sattva-guna predominates only, because it is to be noted that none of the Gunas are, or ever can be, absent. Prakriti cannot be partitioned. Prakriti *is* the three Gunas. Sattva is essentially the spiritual Guna, for it is that which manifests Spirit or Pure Consciousness (Chit). A Sāttvika man is thus a spiritual man. His is a calm, pure, equable, refined, wise, spiritual temperament, free of materiality and of passion, or he possesses these qualities imperfectly, and to the degree that he possesses them he is Sāttvik. Pashubhāva is, on the other hand, the temperament of the man in whom Tamas guna prevails and produces such dark characteristics as ignorance, error, apathy, sloth and so forth. He is called a Pashu or animal because Tamas predominates in the merely animal nature as compared with the disposition of spiritually-minded men. He is also Pashu because he is bound by the bonds (Pāsha). The term Pāsha comes from the root *Pash* to bind. The Kulārnava enumerates eight bonds, namely, pity (Dayā, of the type which Taoists call "inferior benevolence" as opposed to the divine compassion or Karunā) ignorance and delusion (Moha), fear (Bhaya), shame (Lajjā), disgust (Ghrinā), family (Kula), habit and observance (Shīla), and caste (Varna). Other larger enumerations are given. The Pashu is the man caught by the world, in ignorance and bondage. Bhāskararāya, on the Sūtra "have no converse with a Pashu", says that a Pashu is Bahirmukha or outward looking, seeing the outside only of things and not inner realities. The injunction, he says, only applies to converse as regards things spiritual.

The Shaiva Shāstra speaks of three classes of Pashu, namely, Sakala bound by the three Pāshas, Anu, Bheda, Karma, that is, limited knowledge, the seeing of the one Self as many by the operation of Māyā, and action and its product. These are the three impurities (Mala) called Ānavamala, Māyāmala, and Kārmamala. The Sakala Jīva or Pashu is bound by all three, the Pralayākala by the first and last, and the Vijnānākala by the first only. (See as to these the diagram of the 36 Tattvas.) He who is wholly freed of the remaining impurity of Anu is Shiva Himself. Here however Pashu is used in a different sense, that is, as denoting the creature as constrasted with the Lord (Pati). In this sense, Pashu is a name for all men. In the Shākta use of the term, though all men are certainly Pashu, as compared with the Lord, yet as between themselves one may be Pashu (in the narrower sense above stated) and the other not. Some men are more Pashu than others. It is a mistake to suppose that the Pashu is necessarily a bad man. He may be and often is a good one. He is certainly better than a bad Vīra who is really no Vīra at all. He is, however, not, according to this Shāstra, an enlightened man in the sense that the Vīra or Divya is, and he is generally marked by various degrees of ignorance and material-mindedness. It is the mark of a bad Pashu to be given over to gross acts of sin. Between these two comes the Hero or Vīra of whose temperament (Vīrabhāva) so much is heard in the Shākta Shāstras. In him there is prevalent the strongly active Rajas Guna. Rajas is always active either to incite Tamas or Sattva. In the former case the result is a Pashu, in the latter case either a Vīra or Divya. Where Sattva approaches perfection of development there is the Divyabhāva. Sattva is here firmly established in calm and in high degree. But, until such time, and whilst man who has largely liberated himself through knowledge of the influence of Tamas, is active to promote Sattva, he is a Vīra. Being heroic, he is permitted to meet his enemy Tamas face to face, counter-attacking where the lower developed man flees away. It has been pointed out by Dr. Garbe (Philosophy of Ancient India, 481), as before him by Baur, that the analogous Gnostic classification of men as material, psychical, and spiritual also corresponds (as does this) to the three Gunas of the Sāṅkhya Darshana.

Even in its limited Shākta sense, there are degrees of Pashu, one man being more so than another. The Pāshas are the creations of Māya Shakti. The Devī therefore is pictured as bearing them. But as She is in Her form as Māyā and Avidyā Shakti the cause of bondage, so as Vidyā Shakti She breaks the bonds (Pashupāsha-Vimochinī) (see v. 78, Lalitāsahasranāma), and is thus the Liberatrix of the Pashu from his bondage.

Nityā Tantra says that the Bhāva of the Divya is the best, the Vīra the next best, and Pashu the lowest. In fact, the state of the last is the starting point in Sādhanā, that of the first the goal, and that of the Vīra is the stage of one who having ceased to be a Pashu is on the way to the attainment of the goal. From being a Pashu, a man rises in this or some other birth to be a Vīra and Divyabhāva or Devatābhāva is awakened through Vīrabhāva. The Pichchhilā Tantra says (X, see also Utpatti Tantra, LXIV) that the difference between the Vīra and the Divya lies in the Uddhatamānasa, that is, passionateness or activity by which the former is characterized, and which is due to the great effort of Rajas to procure for the Sādhaka a Sāttvik state. Just as there are degrees in the Pashu state, so there are classes of Vīras, some being higher than others.

The Divya Sādhaka also is of higher or lower kinds. The lowest is only a degree higher than the best type of Vīra. The highest completely realize the Deva-nature wherein Sattva exists in a state lasting stability. Amongst this class are the Tattvajnānī and Yogī. The latter are emancipated from all ritual. The lower Divya class may apparently take part in the ritual of the Vīra. The object and end of all Sādhanā, whether of Pashu or Vīra or Divya, is to develop Sattvaguna. The Tantras give descriptions of each of these three classes. The chief general distinction, which is constantly repeated, between the pure Pashu (for there are also Vibhāva-pashus) and the Vīra, is that the former does not, and the latter does, follow the Panchatattva ritual, in the form prescribed for Vīrāchāra and described in the next Chapter. Other portions of the description are characteristics of the Tāmasik character of the Pashu. So Kubjikā Tantra (VII) after describing this class of man to be the lowest, points out various forms of their ignorance. So it says that he talks ill of other classes of believers. That is, he is sectarian-minded and decries other forms of worship than his own, a characteristic of the Pashu the world over. He distinguishes one Deva from another as if they were really different and not merely the plural manifestations of the One. So, the worshipper of Rāma may abuse the worshipper of Krishna, and both decry the worship of Shiva or Devī. As the Veda says, the One is called by various names. Owing to his ignorance "he is always bathing", that is, he is always thinking about external and ceremonial purity. This, though good in its way, is nothing compared with internal purity of mind. He has ignorant or wrong ideas, or want of faith, concerning (Shākta) Tantra Shāstra, Sacrifices, Guru, Images, and Mantra, the last of which he thinks to be mere letters only and not Devatā (see Prānatoshinī, 547, *et seq.*, Pichchhilā, X). He follows the Vaidik rule relating to Maithuna on the fifth day when the wife is Ritusnātā (*Ritu-kālam vinā devi ramanam parivarjayet*). Some of the descriptions of the Pashu seem to refer to the lowest class. Generally, however, one may say that from the standpoint of a Vīrāchārī, all those who follow Vedāchāra, Vaishnavāchāra and Shaivāchāra are Pashus. The Kubjikā Tantra (VII) gives a description of the Divya. Its eulogies would seem to imply that in all matters which it mentions, the Pashu is lacking. But this, as regards some matters, is Stuti (praise) only. Thus he has a strong faith in Veda, Shāstra, Deva and Guru, and ever speaks the truth which, as also other good qualities, must be allowed to the Pashu. He avoids all cruelty and other bad action and regards alike both friend and foe. He avoids the company of the irreligious who decry the Devatā. All Devas he regards as beneficial, worshipping all without drawing distinctions. Thus, for instance, whilst an orthodox upcountry Hindu of the Pashu kind who is a worshipper of Rāma cannot even bear to hear the name of Krishna, though both Rāma and Krishna are each Avatāra of the same Vishnu, the Divya would equally reverence both knowing each to be an aspect of the one Great Shakti Mother of Devas and Men. This is one of the first qualities of the high Shākta worshipper. As a worshipper of Shakti he bows down at the feet of women regarding them as his Guru (*Strīnām pādatalam drishtvā guruvad bhāvayet sadā*). He offers everything to the supreme Devī regarding the whole universe as pervaded by Strī (Shakti, not "woman") and as Devatā. Shiva is (he knows) in all men. The whole universe (Brahmānda) is pervaded by Shiva Shakti.

The description cited also deals with his ritual, saying that he does daily ablutions, Sandhyā, wears clean cloth, the Tripundra mark in ashes or red sandal, and ornaments of Rudrāksha beads. He does Japa (recitation of Mantras external and mental) and worship (Archanā). He worships the Pitris and Devas and performs all the daily rites. He gives daily charity. He meditates upon his Guru daily, and does worship thrice daily and, as a Bhairava, worships Parameshvarī with Divyabhāva. He worships Devī at night (Vaidik worship being by day), and after food (ordinary Vaidik worship being done before taking food). He makes obeisance to the Kaula Shakti (Kulastrī) versed in Tantra and Mantra, whoever She be and whether youthful or old. He bows to the Kula-trees (Kulavriksha). He ever strives for the attainment and maintenance of Devatābhāva and is himself of the nature of a Devatā.

Portions of this description appear to refer to the ritual and not Avadhūta Divya, and to this extent are applicable to the high Vīra also. The Mahānirvāna (I. 56) describes the Divya as all but a Deva, ever pure of heart, to whom all opposites are alike (Dvandvātīta) such as pain and pleasure, heat and cold, who is free from attachment to worldly things, the same to all creatures and forgiving. The text I have published, therefore, says that there is no Divyabhāva in the Kaliyuga nor Pashubhāva; for the Pashu (or his wife) must, with his own hand, collect leaves, flowers and fruit, and cook his food, which regulations and others are impossible or difficult in the Kali age. As a follower of Smriti, he should not "see the face of a Shūdra at worship, or even think of a woman" (referring to the Panchatattva ritual). The Shyāmārchana (cited in Haratattvadīdhiti, 348) speaks to the same effect. On the other hand, there is authority for the proposition that in the Kaliyuga there is only Pashubhāva. Thus, the Prānatoshinī (510-517) cites a passage purporting to come from the Mahānirvāna which is in direct opposition to the above:

Divya-vīra-mayo bhāvah kalau nāsti kadāchana
Kevalampashu-bhāvena mantra-siddhir bhaven nrinām.

(In the Kali age there is no Divya or Vīrabhāva. It is only by the Pashu-bhāva that men may attain Mantra-siddhi.)

I have discussed this latter question in greater detail in the introduction to the sixth volume of the series of "Tāntrik Texts".

Dealing with the former passage from the Mahānirvāna, the Commentator explains it as meaning "that the conditions and characters of the Kaliyuga are not such as to be productive of Pashubhāva, or to allow of its Āchāra (in the sense of the strict Vaidik ritual). No one, he says, can now-a-days fully perform the Vedāchāra, Vaishnavāchāra, and Shaivāchāra rites without which the Vaidik and Paurānic Yajna and Mantra are fruitless. No one now goes through the Brahmacharya Āshrama or adopts, after the fiftieth year, Vānaprastha. Those whom the Vaidik rites do not control cannot expect the fruit of their observances. On the contrary, men have taken to drink, associate with the low and are fallen, as are also those who associate with them. There can, therefore, be no pure Pashu. (That is apparently whilst there may be a natural Pashu disposition the Vaidik rites appropriate to this Bhāva cannot be carried out.) Under these circumstances, the duties prescribed by the Vedas which are appropriate for the Pashu being incapable of performance, Shiva, for the liberation of men of the Kali age, has proclaimed the Āgama. Now there is no other way."

We are, perhaps, therefore, correct in saying that it comes to this: In a bad age, such as the Kali, Divya men are (to say the least) very scarce, though common-sense and experience must, I suppose, allow for exceptions. Whilst the Pashu natural disposition exists, the Vaidik ritual which he should follow cannot be done. It is in fact largely obsolete. The Vaidik Pashu or man who followed the

Vaidik rituals in their entirety is non-existent. He must follow the Āgamic rituals which, as a fact, the bulk of men do. The Āgama must now govern the Pashu, Vīra and would-be Divya alike.

As I have frequently explained, there are various communities of the followers of Tantra or Āgama according to the several divisions of the worshippers of the five Devatās (Panchopāsaka). Of the five classes, the most important are Vaishnava, Shaiva and Shākta. I do not, however, hesitate to repeat a statement of a fact of which those who speak of "The Tantra" ignore.

The main elements of Sādhanā are common to all such communities following the Āgamas; such as Pūjā (inner and outer), Pratimā or other emblems (Linga, Shālagrama), Upachāra, Sandhyā, Yajna, Vrata, Tapas, Mandala, Yantra, Mantra, Japa, Purashcharana, Nyāsa, Bhūtashuddhi, Mudra, Dhyāna, Samskāra and so forth. Even the Vāmāchāra ritual which some wrongly think to be peculiar to the Shāktas, is or was followed (I am told) by members of other Sampradāyas including Jainas and Bauddhas. Both, in so far as they follow this ritual, are reckoned amongst Kaulas though, as being non-Vaidik, of a lower class.

A main point to be here remembered, and one which establishes both the historical and practical importance of the Āgamas is this: That whilst some Vaidik rites still exist, the bulk of the ritual of to-day is Āgamic, that is, what is popularly called Tāntrik. The Purānas are replete with Tāntrik rituals.

Notwithstanding a general community of ritual forms. there are some variances which are due to two causes; firstly, to difference in the Devatā worship, and secondly, to difference of philosophical basis according as it is Advaita, Vishishtādvaita, or Dvaita. The presentment of fundamental ideas is sometimes in different terms. Thus the

Vaishnava Pancharātra Āgama describes the creative process in terms of the Vyūhas, and the Shaiva-Shākta Āgamas explain it as the Ābhāsa of the thirty-six Tattvas. I here deal with only one form, namely, Shākta Sādhanā in which the Ishtadevatā is Shakti in Her many forms.

I will here shortly describe some of the ritual forms above-mentioned, premising that so cursory an account does not do justice to the beauty and profundity of many of them.

There are four different forms of worship corresponding to four different states and dispositions (Bhāva) of the Sādhaka himself. The realization that the Supreme Spirit (Paramātmā) and the individual spirit (Jīvātmā) are one, that everything is Brahman, and that nothing but the Brahman has lasting being is the highest state or Brahmabhāva. Constant meditation with Yoga-processes upon the Devatā in the heart is the lower form (Dhyānabhāva). Lower still is that Bhāva of which Japa (recitations of Mantra) and Hymns of praise (Stava) are the expression; and lowest of all is external worship (Bāhyapūja).

Pūjābhāva is that which arises out of the dualistic notions of worshipper and worshipped, the servant and the Lord, a dualism which necessarily exists in greater or less degree until Monistic experience (Advaita-bhāva) is attained. He who realizes the Advaitatattva knows that all is Brahman. For him there is neither worshipper nor worshipped, neither Yoga, nor Pūjā nor Dhāranā, Dhyāna, Stava, Japa, Vrata or other ritual or process of Sādhanā. For, he is Siddha in its fullest sense, that is, he has attained Siddhi which is the aim of Sādhanā. As the Mahānirvāna says, "for him who has faith in and knowledge of the root, of what use are the branches and leaves?" Brāhmanism thus sagely resolves the Western dispute as to the necessity or advisability of ritual. It affirms it for those who have not attained the end of all ritual. It lessens and refines ritual as spiritual progress is made upwards; it dispenses with it altogether when there is no longer need for it. But, until a man is a real "Knower", some Sādhanā is necessary if he would become one. The nature of Sādhanā, again, differs according to the temperaments (Bhāva) above described, and also with reference to the capacities and spiritual advancement of each in his own Bhāva. What may be suitable for the unlettered peasant may not be so for those more intellectually and spiritually advanced. It is, however, a fine general principle of Tāntrik worship that capacity, and not social distinction such as caste, determines competency for any particular worship. This is not so as regards the Vaidik ritual proper. One might have supposed that credit would have been given to the Tantra Shāstra for this. But credit is given for nothing. Those who dilate on Vaidik exclusiveness have nothing to say as regards the absence of it in the Āgama. The Shūdra is precluded from the performance of Vaidik rites, the reading of the Vedas, and the recital of Vaidik Mantras. His worship is practically limited to that of his Ishtadevatā, the Vāna-linga-pūjā with Tāntrik and Paurānik mantra and such Vrata as consist in penance and charity. In other cases, the Vrata is performed through a Brāhmana. The Tantra Shāstra makes no caste distinction as regards worship, in the sense that though it may not challenge the exclusive right of the twice-born to Vaidik rites, it provides other and similar rites for the Shūdra. Thus there is both a Vaidik and Tāntrik Gāyatrī and Sandhyā, and there are rites available for worshippers of all castes. All may read the Tantras which contain their form of worship, and carry them out and recite the Tāntrik Mantras. All castes, even the lowest Chandāla may, if otherwise fit, receive the Tāntrik initiation and be a member of a Chakra or circle of worship. In the Chakra all the members partake of food and drink together, and are then deemed to be greater than Brāhmanas, though upon the break-up of the Chakra the ordinary caste and social relations are re-established. It is necessary to distinguish between social differences and competency (Adhikāra) for worship. Adhikāra, so fundamental a principle of Brāhmanism, means that all are not equally entitled to the same teaching and ritual. They are entitled to that of which they are capable, irrespective (according to the Āgama) of such social distinctions as caste. All are competent for Tāntrik worship, for, in the words of the Gautamīya which is a Vaishnava Tantra (Cap. I), the Tantra Shāstra is for all castes and all women.

Sarva-varnādhikārash cha nārīnām yogya eva cha.

Though according to Vaidik usage, the wife was co-operator (Sahadharminī) in the household rites, now-a-days, so far as I can gather, they are not accounted much in such matters, though it is said that the wife may, with the consent of her husband, fast, take vows, perform Homa, Vrata and the like. According to the Tantra Shāstra, a woman may not only receive Mantra, but may, as Guru, initiate and give it (see Rudrayāmala II. ii, and XV). She is worshipped both as wife of Guru and as Guru herself (see *ib.* I. i. Mātrikābheda Tantra (c. vii), Annadākalpa Tantra cited in Prānatoshinī, p. 68, and as regards the former Yoginī Tantra cap. i. *Gurupatni Maheshāni gurur eva*). The Devī is Herself the Guru of all Shāstras and woman, as indeed all females Her embodiments, are in a peculiar sense, Her representatives. For this reason all women are worshipful, and no harm should be ever done them, nor should any female animal be sacrificed.

Pūjā is the common term for ritual worship, of which there are numerous synonyms in the Sanskrit language such as Archanā, Vandanā, Saparyyā, Arhanā, Namasyā, Archā, Bhajanā, though some of these stress certain aspects of it. Pūjā as also Vrata which are Kāmya, that is, done to gain a particular end, are preceded by the Sankalpa, that is, a statement of the resolve to worship, as also of the particular object (if any) with which it is done. It runs in the form, "I——of Gotra——and so forth (identifying the individual) am about to perform this Pūjā (or Vrata) with the object——." Thereby the attention and will of the Sādhaka are focussed and braced up for the matter in hand. Here, as elsewhere, the ritual which follows is designed both by its complexity and variety (which prevents the tiring of the mind) to keep the attention always fixed, to prevent it from straying and to emphasize both attention and will by continued acts and mental workings.

The object of the worship is the Ishtadevatā, that is, the particular form of the Deity whom the Sādhaka worships, such as Devī in the case of a Shākta, Shiva in the case of the Shaiva (in eight forms in the case of Ashtamūrti-pūjā as to which see Todala Tantra, cap. V) and Vishnu as such or in His forms as Rāma and Krishna in the case of the Vaishnava Sādhaka.

An object is used in the outer Pūjā (Bāhyapūjā) such as an image (Pratimā), a picture, and emblem such as a jar (Kalasa), Shālagrāma (in the case of Vishnu worship), Linga and Yoni or Gaurīpatta (in the case of the worship) of Shiva (with Devī), or a geometrical design called Yantra. In the case of outer worship the first is the lowest form and the last the highest. It is not all who are capable of worshipping with a Yantra. It is obvious that simpler mind must be satisfied with images which delineate the form of the Devatā completely and in material form. The advanced contemplate Devatā in the lines and curves of a Yantra.

In external worship, the Sādhaka should first worship inwardly the mental image of the Devatā which the outer objects assist to produce, and then by the life-giving (Prāna-pratishthā) ceremony he should infuse the image with life by the communication to it of the light, consciousness, and energy (Tejas) of the Brahman within him to the image without, from which there then bursts the lustre of Her whose substance is Consciousness Itself (Chaitanyamayī). In every place She exists as Shakti, whether in stone or metal as elsewhere, but in matter is veiled and seemingly inert. Chaitanya (Consciousness) is aroused by the worshipper through the Prānapratishthā Mantra. An object exists for a Sādhaka only in so far as his mind perceives it. For and in him its essence as Consciousness is realized.

This is a fitting place to say a word on the subject of the alleged "Idolatry" of the Hindus. We are all aware that a similar charge has been made against Christians of the Catholic Church, and those who are conversant with this controversy will be better equipped both with knowledge and caution against the making of general and indiscriminate charges.

It may be well doubted whether the world contains an idolater in the sense in which that term is used by persons who speak of "the heathen worship of sticks and stones". According to the traveller A. B. Ellis ("The Tshi speaking peoples of the Gold Coast of West Africa"), even "negroes of the Gold Coast are always conscious that their offerings and worship are not paid to the inanimate object itself but to the indwelling God, and every native with whom I have conversed on the subject has laughed at the possibility of its being supposed that he would worship or offer sacrifice to some such object as a stone." Nevertheless a missionary or some traveller might tell him that he did. An absurd attitude on the part of the superior Western is that in which the latter not merely tells the coloured races what they should believe, but what notwithstanding denial, they *in fact* believe and *ought* to hold according to the tenets of the latter's religion.

The charge of idolatry is kept up, notwithstanding the explanations given of their beliefs by those against whom it is made. In fact, the conviction that Eastern races are inferior is responsible for this. If we disregard such beliefs, then, anything may be idolatrous. Thus, to those who disbelieve in the "Real Presence", the Catholic worshipper of the Host is an idolater worshipping the material substance, bread. But, to the worshipper who believes that it is the Body of the Lord under the form of bread, such worship can never be idolatrous. Similarly as regards the Hindu worship of images. They are not to be held to worship clay or stone because others disbelieve in the efficacy of the Prānapratishthā ceremony. When impartially considered, there is nothing necessarily superstitious or ignorant in this rite. Nor is this the case with the doctrine of the Real Presence which is interpreted in various ways. Whether either rite has the alleged effect attributed to it is another question. All matter is, according to Shākta doctrine, a manifestation of Shakti, that is, the Mother Herself in material guise. She is present in and as everything which exists. The ordinary man does not so view things. He sees merely gross unconscious matter. If, with such an outlook, he were fool enough to worship what was inferior to himself, he would be an idolater. But the very act of worship implies that the object is superior and conscious. To the truly enlightened Shākta everything is an object of worship, for all is a manifestation of God who is therein worshipped. But that way of looking at things must be attained. The untutored mind must be aided to see that this is so. This is effected by the Prānapratishthā rite by which "life is established" in the image of gross matter. The Hindu then believes that the Pratimā or image is a representation and the dwelling place of Deity. What difference, it may be asked, does this really make? How can a man's belief alter the objective fact? The answer is, it does not. God is not manifested by the image merely because the worshipper believes Him to be there. He is there in fact already. All that the Prānapratishthā rite does is to enliven the consciousness of the worshipper into a realization of His presence. And if He be both in fact, and to the belief of the worshipper, present, then the Image is a proper object of worship. It is the subjective state of the worshipper's mind which determines whether an act is idolatrous or not. The Prānapratishthā rite is thus a mode by which the Sādhaka is given a true object of worship and is enabled to affirm a belief in the divine omnipresence with respect to that particular object of his devotion. The ordinary notion that it is mere matter is cast aside, and the divine notion that Divinity is manifested in all that is, is held and affirmed. "Why not then" (some missionary has said) "worship my boot?" There are contemptible people who do so in the European sense of that phrase. But, nevertheless, there is no reason, according to Shākta teaching, why even his boot should not be worshipped by one who regards it and all else as a manifestation of the One who is in every object which constitutes the Many. Thus this Monistic belief is affirmed in the worship by some Shāktas of that which to the gross and ordinary mind is merely an object of lust. To such minds, this is a revolting and obscene worship. To those for whom such object of worship is obscene, such worship is and must be obscene. But what of the mind which is so purified that it sees the Divine presence in that which, to the mass of men, is an incitement to and object of lust? A man who, without desire, can *truly* so worship must be a very high Sādhaka indeed. The Shākta Tantra affirms the Greek saying that to the pure all things are pure. In this belief and with, as the Jnānārnava Tantra says, the object of teaching men that this is so, we find the ritual use of substances ordinarily accounted impure. The real objection to the general adoption or even knowledge of such rites lies, from the Monistic standpoint, in the fact that the vast bulk of humanity are either of impure or weak mind, and that the worship of an object which is capable of exciting lust will produce it, not to mention the hypocrites who, under cover of such a worship, would seek to gratify their desires. In the Paradise Legend, just as amongst some primitive tribes, man and woman go naked. It was and is after they have fallen that nakedness is observed by minds no longer innocent. Rightly, therefore, from their standpoint, the bulk of men condemn such worship. Because, whatever may be its theoretical justification under conditions which rarely occur, pragmatically and for the bulk of men they are full of danger. Those who go to meet temptation should remember the risk. I have read that it is recorded of Robert d'Arbrissel, the saintly founder of the community of Fonte d'Evrault that he was wont on occasions to sleep with his nuns, to mortify his flesh and as a mode of strengthening his will against its demands. He did not touch them, but his exceptional success in preserving his chastity would be no ground for the ordinary man undertaking so dangerous an experiment. In short, in order to be completely just, we must, in individual cases, consider intention and good faith. But, practically and for the mass, the counsel and duty to avoid the occasion of sin is, according to Shāstrik principles themselves, enjoined. As a matter of fact, such worship has been confined to so limited a class that it would not have been necessary to deal with the subject were it not connected with Shākta worship, the matter in hand. To revert again to the "missionary's boot": whilst all things may be the object of worship, choice is naturally made of those objects which, by reason of their effect on the mind, are more fitted for it. An image or one of the usual emblems is more likely to raise in the mind of the worshipper the thought of a Devatā than a boot, and therefore, even apart from scriptural authority, it would not be chosen. But, it has been again objected, if the Brahman is in and appears equally in all things, how do we find some affirming that one image is more worthy of worship than another. Similarly, in Catholic countries, we find worshippers who prefer certain churches, shrines, places of pilgrimage and representations of Christ, His Mother and the Saints. Such preferences are not statements of absolute worth but of personal inclinations in the worshipper due to his belief in their special efficacy for him. Psychologically all this means that a particular mind finds that it works best in the direction desired by means of particular instruments. The image of Kālī provokes in general only disgust in an European mind. But to the race-consciousness which has evolved that image of Deity, it is the cause and object of fervent devotion. In every case, those means must be sought and applied which will produce a practical and good result for the individual consciousness in question. It must be admitted, however, that image worship like everything else is capable of abuse; that is a wrong and (for want of a better term) an idolatrous tendency may manifest. This is due to ignorance. Thus the aunt of a Catholic school-boy friend of mine had a statue of St. Anthony of Padua. If the saint did not answer her prayers, she used to give the image a beating, and then shut it up in a cupboard with its "face to the wall" by way of punishment. I could cite numbers of instances of this ignorant state of mind taken from the past and present history of Europe.

It is quite erroneous to suppose that such absurdities are confined to India, Africa or other coloured countries. Nevertheless, we must, in each case, distinguish between the true scriptural teaching and the acts and notions of which they are an abuse.

The materials used or things done in Pūjā are called Upachārā. The common number of these is sixteen, but there are more and less (see "Principles of Tantra," vol. ii). The sixteen which include some of the lesser number and are included in the greater are: (1) Āsana (seating of the image), (2) Svāgata (welcoming of the Devatā), (3) Pādya (water for washing the feet), (4) Arghya (offerings which may be general or Sāmānya and special or Vishesha) made in the vessel, (5) (6) Āchamana (water for sipping and cleansing the lips—offered twice), (7) Madhuparka (honey, ghee, milk and curd), (8) Snāna (water for bathing), (9) Vasana (cloth for garment), (10) Ābharana (jewels), (11) Gandha (Perfume), (12) Pushpa (flowers), (13) Dhūpa (incense), (14) Dīpa (lights), (15) Naivedya (food), and (16) Vandana or Namaskriyā (prayer).

Why should such things be chosen? The Westerner who has heard of lights, flower and incense in Christian worship may yet ask the reason of the rest. The answer is simple. Honour is paid to the Devatā in the way honour is paid to friends and those men who are worthy of veneration. So the Sādhaka gives that same honour to the Devatā, a course that the least advanced mind can understand. When the guest arrives he is bidden to take a seat, he is welcomed and asked how he has journeyed. Water is given to him to wash his dusty feet and his mouth. Food and other things are given him, and so on. These are done in honour of men, and the Deity is honoured in the same way.

Some particular articles vary with the Pūjā. Thus, Tulasī leaf is issued in the Vishnu-pūjā; bael leaf (Bilva) in the Shiva-pūjā, and to the Devī is offered the scarlet hibiscus (Jabā). The Mantras said and other ritual details may vary according to the Devatā worshipped. The seat (Āsana) of the worshipper is purified as also the Upachāra. Salutation is made to the Shakti of support (Ādhāra-shakti) the Power sustaining all. Obstructive Spirits are driven away (Bhūtāpasarpana) and the ten quarters are fenced from their attack by striking the earth three times with the left foot, uttering the weapon-mantra (Astrabīja) "Phat", and by snapping the fingers round the head. Other rituals also enter into the worship besides the offering of Upachāra such as Prānāyāma or Breath control, Bhūtashuddhi or purification of the element of the body, Japa of Mantra, Nyāsa (v. *post*), meditation (Dhyāna) and obeisance (Pranāma).

Besides the outer and material Pūjā, there is a higher inner (Antarpūja) and mental (Mānasapūjā). Here there is no offering of material things to an image or emblem, but the ingredients (Upachāra) of worship are imagined only. Thus the Sādhaka, in lieu of material flowers offered with the hands, lays at the feet of the Devatā the flower of good action. In the secret Rājasik Pūjā of the Vāmāchārī, the Upachāra are the five Tattvas (Panchatattva), wine, meat and so forth described in the next Chapter. Just as flowers and incense and so forth are offered in the general public ritual, so in this special secret ritual, dealt with in the next Chapter, the functions of eating, drinking and sexual union are offered to the Devatā.

A marked feature of the Tantra Shāstras is the use of the Yantra in worship. This then takes the place of the image or emblem, when the Sādhaka has arrived at the stage when he is qualified to worship with Yantra. Yantra, in its most general sense, means simply instrument or that by which anything is accomplished. In worship, it is that by which the mind is fixed on its object. The Yantra, in lieu of the image or emblem holds the attention, and is both the object of worship, and the means by which it is carried out. It is said to be so called because it subdues (Niyantrana) lust, anger and the other sufferings of Jīva, and the sufferings caused thereby. (Tantra-tattva, 519. Sādhārana Upāsanā-tattva.) The Yantra is a diagram drawn or painted on paper, or other substances, engraved on metal, cut on crystal or stone. The magical treatises mention extraordinary Yantras drawn on leopard's and donkey's skin, human bones and so forth. The Yantras vary in design according to the Devatā whose Yantra it is and in whose worship it is used. The difference between a Mandala (which is also a figure, marked generally on the ground) is that whilst a Mandala may be used in the case of any Devatā, a Yantra is appropriate to a specific Devatā only. As different Mantras are different Devatās, and differing Mantras are used in the worship of each of the Devatās, so variously formed Yantras are peculiar to each Devatā and are used in its worship. The Yantras are therefore of various designs, according to the object of worship. The cover of "Tāntrik Texts" shows the great Shri Yantra. In the metal or stone Yantras no figures of Devatās are shown, though these together with the appropriate Mantras commonly appear in Yantras drawn or painted on paper, such as the Devatā of worship, Āvarana Shaktis and so forth. All Yantras have a common edging called Bhūpura, a quadrangular figure with four "doors" which encloses and separates the Yantra from the outside world. A Yantra in my possession shows serpents crawling outside the Bhūpura. The Kaulāvalīya Tantra says that the distinction between Yantra and Devatā is that between the body and the self. Mantra is Devatā and Yantra is Mantra, in that it is the body of the Devatā who is Mantra.

Yantram mantra-mayam proktam mantrātmā devataiva hi
Dehātmanor yathā bhedo yantradevatayos tathā.

As in the case of the image, certain preliminaries precede the worship of Yantra. The worshipper first meditates upon the Devatā and then arouses Him or Her in himself. He then communicates the Divine Presence thus aroused to the Yantra. When the Devatā has by the appropriate Mantra been invoked into the Yantra, the vital airs (Prāna) of the Devatā are infused therein by the Prānapratishthā ceremony, Mantra and Mudrā (see for ritual Mahānirvanā VI. 63 *et seq.*) The Devatā is thereby installed in the Yantra which is no longer mere gross matter veiling the Spirit which has been always there, but instinct with its aroused presence which the Sādhaka first welcomes and then worships.

In Tāntrik worship, the body as well as the mind has to do its part, the former being made to follow the latter. This is of course seen in all ritual, where there is bowing, genuflection and so forth. As all else, gesture is here much elaborated. Thus, certain postures (Āsana) are assumed in worship and Yoga. There is obeisance (Pranāma), sometimes with eight parts of the body (Ashtāngapranāma), and circumambulation (Pradakshina) of the image. In Nyāsa the hands are made to touch various parts of the body and so forth. A notable instance of this practice are the Mudrās which are largely used in the Tāntrik ritual. Mudrā in this sense is ritual manual gesture. The term Mudrā has three meanings. In worship (Upāsanā) it means these gestures. In Yoga it means postures in which not only the hands but the whole body takes part. And, in the secret worship with the Panchatattva, Mudrā means various kinds of parched cereals which are taken with the wine and other ingredients (Upachāra) of that particular worship.

The term Mudrā is derived from the root "to please" (Mud). The Tantrarāja says that in its Upāsanā form, Mudrā is so called because it gives pleasure to the Devatās. These Mudrās are very numerous. It has been said that there are 108 of which 55 are in common use (Shabdakalpadruma *Sub, Voc* Mudrā and see Nirvāna Tantra, Chap. XI). Possibly there are more. 108 is a favourite number. The Mudrā of Upāsanā is the outward bodily expression of inner resolve which it at the same time intensifies. We all know how in speaking we emphasize and illustrate our thought by gesture. So in welcoming (Āvāhana) the Devatā, an appropriate gesture is made. When veiling anything, the hands assume that position (Avagunthana Mudrā). Thus again in making offering (Arghya) a gesture is made which represents a fish (Matsya Mudrā), by placing the right hand on the back of the left and extending the two thumbs finlike on each side of the hands. This is done as the expression of the wish and intention that the vessel which contains water may be regarded as an ocean with fish and all other aquatic animals. The Sādhaka says to the Devatā of his worship, "this is but a small offering of water in fact, but so far as my desire to honour you is concerned, regard it is as if I were offering you an ocean." The Yoni in the form of an inverted triangle represents the Devī. By the Yonī Mudrā the fingers form a triangle as a manifestation of the inner desire that the Devī should come and place Herself before the worshipper, for the Yoni is Her Pītha or Yantra. Some of the Mudrā of Hathayoga which are in the nature both of a health-giving gymnastic and special positions required in Yoga-practice are described in A. Avalon's "The Serpent Power". The Gheranda Samhitā, a Tāntrik Yoga work, says (III. 4. 8. 10) that knowledge of the Yoga Mudrās grant all Siddhi, and that their performance produces physical benefits, such as stability, firmness, and cure of disease.

Bhūtashuddhi, an important Tāntrik rite, means purification of five "elements" of which the body is composed, and not "removal of evil demons," as Professor Monier-Williams' Dictionary has it. Though one of the meanings of Bhūta is Ghost or Spirit, it is never safe to give such literal translations without knowledge, or absurd mistakes are likely to be made. The Mantramahodadhi (Taranga I) speaks of it as a rite which is preliminary to the worship of a Deva.

Devārchā-yogyatā-prāptyai bhūta-shuddhim samācharet.

(For the attainment of competency to worship, the elements of which the body is composed, should be purified.) The material human body is a compound of the five Bhūtas of "earth", "water", "fire", "air", and "ether". These terms have not their usual English meaning but denote the five forms in which Prakriti the Divine Power as *materia prima* manifests Herself. These have each a centre of operation in the five Chakras or Padmas (Centres or Lotuses) which exist in the spinal column of the human body (see A. Avalon's "Serpent Power" where this matter is fully described). In the lowest of these centres (Mūlādhāra), the Great Devī Kundalinī, a form of the Saguna Brahman, resides. She is ordinarily sleeping there. In Kundalinī-yoga, She is aroused and brought up through the five centres, absorbing, as She passes through each, the Bhūta of that centre, the subtle Tanmātra from which it derives and the connected organ of sense (Indriya). Having absorbed all these, She is led to the sixth or mind centre (Ājnā) between the eyebrows where the last Bhūta or ether is absorbed in mind, and the latter in the Subtle Prakriti. The last in the form of Kundalī Shakti then unites with Shiva in the upper brain called the thousand-petalled lotus (Sahasrāra). In Yoga this involution actually takes place with the result that ecstasy (Samādhi) is attained. But very few are successful Yogīs. Therefore, Bhūtashuddhi in the case of the ordinary worshipper is an imaginary process only. The Sādhaka imagines Kundalī, that She is roused, that one element is absorbed into the other and so on, until all is absorbed in Brahman. The Yoga process will be found described in "The Serpent Power", and Ch. V. 93 *et seq.* of the Mahānirvāna gives an account of the ritual process. The Sādhaka having dissolved all in Brahman, a process which instils into his mind the unity of all, then thinks of the "black man of sin" in his body. The body is then purified. By breathing and Mantra it is first dried and then burnt with all its sinful inclinations. It is then mentally bathed with the nectar of the water-mantra from head to feet. The Sādhaka then thinks that in lieu of his old sinful body a new Deva body has come into being. He who with faith and sincerity believes that he is regenerated is in fact so. To each who truly believes that his body is a Deva body it becomes a Deva body. The Deva body thus brought into being is strengthened by the Earth-mantra and divine gaze (Divya-drishti). Saying, with Bījās, the Mantra "He I am" (So'ham) the Sādhaka by Jīvanyāsa infuses his body with the life of the Devī, the Mother of all.

Nyāsa is a very important and powerful Tāntrik rite. The word comes from the root, "to place", and means the placing of the tips of the fingers and palm of the right hand on various parts of the body, accompanied by Mantra. There are four general divisions of Nyāsa, *viz.*, inner (Antar), outer (Bahir), according to the creative (Srishti) and dissolving (Samhāra) order (Krama). Nyāsa is of many kinds such as Jīva-nyāsa, Mātrikā or Lipi-nyāsa, Rishi-nyāsa, Shadanganyāsa on the body (Hridayādi-shadanga-nyāsa) and with the hands (Angushthādi-shadanga-nyāsa), Pīthanyāsa and so on. The Kulārnava (IV. 20) mentions six kinds. Each of these might come under one or the other of the four general heads.

Before indicating the principle of this rite, let us briefly see what it is. After the Sādhaka has by Bhūta-shuddhi dissolved the sinful body and made a new Deva body, he, by Jīva-nyāsa infuses into it the life of the Devī. Placing his hand on his heart he says, "He I am" thereby identifying himself with Shiva-Shakti. He then emphasizes it by going over the parts of the body in detail with the Mantra Ām and the rest thus: saying the Mantra and what he is doing, and touching the body on the particular part with his fingers, he recites: "Ām (and the rest) the vital force (Prāna) of the blessed Kālikā (in this instance) are here. Ām (and the rest) the life of the Blessed Kālikā is here; Ām (and the rest) all the senses of the Blessed Kālikā are here; Ām (and the rest) may the speech, mind, sight, hearing, sense of smell of the Blessed Kālikā coming here ever abide here in peace and happiness. Svāhā." By this, the body is thought to become like that of Devatā (Devatāmaya). Mātrikā are the fifty letters of the Sanskrit alphabet, for as from a mother comes birth, so from the Brahman who, as the creator of "sound" is called "Shabdabrahman", the universe proceeds. The Mantra-bodies of the Devatā are composed of the Mātrikā or letters. The Sādhaka first sets the letters mentally (Antar-mātrikā-nyāsa) in their several places in the six inner centres (Chakra), and then externally by physical action (Bāhya-mātrikā-nyāsa). The letters of the alphabet form the different parts of the body of the Devatā which is thus built up in the Sādhaka himself. He places his hand on different parts of his body, uttering distinctly at the same time the appropriate Mātrikā for that part. The mental disposition in the Chakra is that given in the "Serpent-Power" by A. Avalon, each letter being repeated thus, Om Ham Namah (obeisance), Om

Ksham Namah and so on with the rest. The external disposition is as follows: The vowels are placed on the forehead, face, right and left eye, right and left ear, right and left nostril, right and left cheek, upper and lower lip, upper and lower teeth, head and hollow of the mouth. The consonants, Ka to Va are placed on the base of the right arm and the elbow, wrist base and tips of fingers, left arm, and right and left leg, right and left side, back navel, belly, heart, right and left shoulder, and space between the shoulders (Kakuda). Then, from the heart to the right palm, Sha; from the heart to the left palm, Sha (second); from the heart to the right foot, Sa; from the heart to the left foot, Ha; and lastly from the heart to the belly and the heart to the mouth, Ksha. This Mātrikā-nyāsa is of several kinds.

One form of Rishi-nyāsa is as follows: " In the head, salutation to Brahma and the Brahmarshis; in the mouth, salutation to Gāyatrī and other forms of Verse; in the heart, salutation to the primordial Devatā Kālī; in the hidden part (Guhya), salutation to the Bīja Krīm, in the two feet, salutation to Hrīm; in all the body, salutation to Shrīm and Kālikā. In Shadanga-nyāsa on the body, certain letters are placed with the salutation Namah, and with the Mantras Svāhā, Vashat, Vaushat, Hrīm, Phat on the heart, head, crown-lock (Shikhā), eyes, the front and back of the palm. In Kara-nyāsa, the Mantras are assigned to the thumbs, index fingers, middle fingers, fourth fingers, little fingers, and the front and back of the palm. From the above examples the meaning of Nyāsa is seen. By associating the Divine with every part of the body and with the whole of it, the mind and body are sought to be made divine to the consciousness of the Sādhaka. They are that already, but the mind is made to so regard them. What if it does the English reader may ask? How can the regarding a thing as divine make it so? In one sense it does not, for mind and body are as Shakti divine, whether this be known or not. But this must be known to the Sādhaka or they are not divine *for him*. His mind is trained to look upon them as divine manifestations of the one Supreme Essence which at base he and they are. According to Hindu views, primary importance is attached to mental states, for as the Divine Thought made the World, man makes his character therein by what he thinks. If he is always thinking on material things and has desires therefor, he becomes himself material and is given over to lust and other passions. If, on the contrary, he has always his mind on God, and associates everything with the thought of Him, his mind becomes pure and divine. As the Upanishad says, "What a man thinks that he becomes." Thought is everything moulding our bodily features, moral and intellectual character and disposition, leading to and appearing in our actions. Much superficial criticism is levelled at this or other ritual, its variety, complexity, its lengthy character and so forth. If it is performed mechanically and without attention, doubtless it is mere waste of time. But if it is done with will, attention, faith and devotion, it must necessarily achieve the result intended. The reiteration of the same idea under varying forms brings home with emphasis to the consciousness of the Sādhaka the doctrine his Scripture teaches him, *viz.*, that his essence is Spirit and his mind and body are its manifestation. All is divine. All is Consciousness. The object of this and all the other ritual is to make that statement a real experience for the Sādhaka. For the attainment of that state in which the Sādhaka feels that the nature (Bhāva) of the Devatā has come upon him, Nyāsa is a great auxiliary. It is as it were the wearing of Divine jewels in different parts of the body. The Bījas of the Devatās (which are Devatās) are the jewels which the Sādhaka places on the different parts of his body. By the particular Nyāsa he places his Abhīshtadevatā in such parts, and by Vyāpaka-Nyāsa he spreads its presence throughout himself. He becomes thus permeated by the Divine and its manifestations, thus merging or mingling himself in or with the Divine Self or Lord. Nyāsa, Āsana and other ritual are necessary for the production of the desired state of mind and its purification (Chittashuddhi). The whole aim and end of ritual is Chittashuddhi. Transformation of thought is transformation of being, for particular existence is a projection of thought, and thought is a projection from the Consciousness which is the Root of all.

This is the essential principle and rational basis of this, as of all, Tāntrik Sādhanā. Nyāsa also has certain physical effects, for these are dependent on the state of mind. The pure restful state of meditation is reflected in the body of the worshipper. The actions of Nyāsa are said to stimulate the nerve centres and to effect the proper distribution of the Shaktis of the human frame according to their dispositions and relations, preventing discord and distraction during worship, which itself holds steady the state thus induced.

In the Chapters on Mantramayī Shakti and Varnamālā, as also in my "Garland of Letters", I have dealt with the nature of Mantra and of its Sādhanā. An account will also be found of the subject in the Mantratattva Chapter of the second volume of "Principles of Tantra". Mantra is Devatā and by Sādhanā therewith the sought-for (Sādhya) Devatā is attained, that is, becomes present to the consciousness of the Sādhaka or Mantrin. Though the purpose of Worship (Pūjā), Reading (Pātha), Hymn (Stava) Sacrifice (Homa), Meditation (Dhyāna), and that of the

Dīkshā-mantra obtained on initiation are the same, yet the latter is said to be far more powerful, and this for the reason that in the first the Sādhaka's Sādhanā-shakti only operates whilst in the case of Mantra that Sādhanā-shakti works in conjunction with Mantra-shakti which has the revelation and force of fire, than which nothing is more powerful. The special Mantra which is received at initiation (Dīkshā) is the Bīja or Seed-Mantra sown in the field of the Sādhaka's heart, and the Tāntrik Sandhya, Nyāsa, Pūjā, and the like are the stem and branches upon which hymns of praise (Stuti) and prayer and homage (Vandana) are the leaves and flower, and the Kavacha consisting of Mantra, the fruit. (See Chapter on Mantratattva, vol. ii, "Principles of Tantra," Ed. A. Avalon.)

The utterance of a Mantra without knowledge of its meaning or of the Mantra-sādhanā is a mere movement of the lips and nothing more. The Mantra sleeps. This is not infrequently the case in the present degeneracy of Hindu religion. For example, a Brāhman lady confided to me her Dīkshā-mantra and asked me for its meaning, as she understood that I had a Bīja-kosha or Lexicon which gave the meaning of the letters. Her Guru had not told her of its meaning, and enquiries elsewhere amongst Brāhmanas were fruitless. She had been repeating the Mantra for years, and time had brought the wisdom that it could not do her much good to repeat what was without meaning to her. Japa is the utterance of Mantra as described later. Mantra-sādhanā is elaborate. There are various processes preliminary to and involved in its right utterance which again consists of Mantra. There are the sacraments or purifications (Samskāra) of the Mantra (Tantrasāra, p. 90). There are "birth" and "death" defilements of a Mantra (*ib.*, 75, *et seq.*) which have to be cleansed,

This and, of course, much else mean that the mind of the Mantrin has to be prepared and cleansed for the realization of the Devatā. There are a number of defects (Dosha) which have to be avoided or cured. There is purification of the mouth which utters the Mantra (Mukha-shodhana) [see as to this and the following Shāradā Tilaka (Chap. x)], purification of the tongue (Jihvā-shodhana) and of the Mantra (Ashaucha-bhanga), Mantra processes called Kullūka, Nirvāna, Setu (see Shāradā Tilaka *loc cit* Tantrasāra, and Purashcharanabodhinī, p. 48) which vary with the Devatā of worship, awakening of Mantra (Nidrābhanga) its vitalizing through consciousness (Mantrachaitanya), pondering on the meaning of the Mantra and of the Mātrikās constituting the body of the Devatā (Mantrārtha bhāvanā). There are Dīpanī, Yoni-mudrā (see Purohita-darpanam) with meditation on the Yoni-rūpa-bhagavatī with the Yonibīja (Eng.) and so forth.

In ascertaining what Mantra may be given to any particular individual, certain Chakra calculations are made, according to which Mantras are divided into those which are friendly, serving supporting or destroying (Siddha, Sādhya, Susiddha, Ari). All this ritual has as its object the establishment of that pure state of mind and feeling which are necessary for success (Mantra-siddhi). At length the Mantrin through his Chit-shakti awakening and vitalzing the Mantra which in truth is one with his own consciousness (in that form) pierces through all its centres and contemplates the Spotless One (Kubjikā Tantra V). The Shakti of the Mantra is called the Vāchikā Shakti or the means by which the Vāchyā Shakti or ultimate object is attained. The Mantra lives by the energy of the former. The Saguna-Shakti in the form of the Mantra is awakened by Sādhanā and worshipped and She it is who opens the portals whereby the Vāchyā-Shakti is reached. Thus the

Mother in the Saguna form is the Presiding Deity (Adhisthātrī Devatā) of the Gāyatrī Mantra. As the Nirguna (formless) One, She is its Vāchyā Shakti. Both are in truth one and the same. But the Sādhaka, by the laws of his nature and its three Gunas, must first meditate on the gross Sthūla) form before he can realize the subtle (Sūkshma) form which is his liberator. So far from being merely superstition, the Mantra-sādhanā is, in large part, based on profound notions of the nature of Consciousness and the psychology of its workings. The Sādhaka's mind and disposition are purified, the Devatā is put before him in Mantra form and by his own power of devotion (Sādhanā Shakti) and that latent in the Mantra itself (Mantra-shakti) and expressed in his mind on realization therein, such mind is first identified with the gross, and then with the subtle form which is his own transformed consciousness and its powers.

Japa is defined as *Vidhānena mantrochchāranam*, that is (for default of other more suitable words), the utterance or recitation of Mantra according to certain rules. Japa may however be of a nature which is not defined by the word, recitation. It is of three kinds (Jnānārnava Tantra, XX) namely, Vāchika Japa, Upāṁshu Japa Mānasa Japa. The first is the lowest and the last the highest form. Vāchika is verbal Japa in which the Mantra is distinctly and audibly recited (Spashta-vāchā). Upāṁshu Japa is less gross and therefore superior to this. Here the Mantra is not uttered (Avyakta) but there is a movement of the lips and tongue (Sphuradvaktra) but no articulate sound is heard. In the highest form or mental utterance (Mānasa-japa) there is neither articulate sound nor movement. Japa takes place in the mind only by meditation on the letters (Chintanākshararūpavān). Certain conditions are prescribed as those under which Japa should be done, relating to physical cleanliness, the dressing of the hair, garments worn, the seated posture (Āsana), the avoidance of certain states of mind and actions, and the nature of the recitation. Japa is done a specified number of times, in lakhs by great Sādhakas. If the mind is really centred and not distracted throughout these long and repeated exercises the result must be successful. Repetition is in all things the usual process by which a certain thing is fixed in the mind. It is not considered foolish for one who has to learn a lesson to repeat it himself over and over again until it is got by heart. The same principle applies to Sādhanā. If the "Hail Mary" is said again and again in the Catholic rosary, and if the Mantra is similarly said in the Indian Japa, neither proceeding is foolish, provided that both be done with attention and devotion. The injunction against "vain repetition" was not against repetition but that of a vain character. Counting is done either with a Mālā or rosary (Mālā-japa or with the thumb of the right hand upon the joints of the fingers of that hand according to a method varying according to the Mantra (Kara-japa).

Purashcharana is a form of Sādhanā in which, with other ritual, Japa of Mantra, done a large number of times, forms the chief part. A short account of the rite is given in the Purashcharana-bodhinī by Harakumāra Tagore (1895). (See also Tantrasāra 71 and the Purashcharyārnava of the King of Nepal.) The ritual deals with preparation for the Sādhanā as regards chastity, food, worship, measurements of the Mandapa or Pandal and of the altar, the time and place of performance and other matters. The Sādhaka must lead a chaste life (Brahmacharyya) during the period prescribed. He must eat the pure food called Havishyānnam or boiled milk (Kshīra), fruits, Indian vegetables, and avoid all other food which has the effects of stimulating the passions. He must bathe, do Japa of the Sāvitrī

Mantra, entertain Brāhmanas and so forth. Panchagavya is eaten, that is, the five products of the cow, namely, milk, curd, ghee, urine, and dung, the two last (except in the case of the rigorously pious) in smaller quantity. Before the Pūjā there is worship of Ganesha and Kshetrapāla and the Sun, Moon, and Devas are invoked. Then follows the Sankalpa. The Ghata or Kalasa (jar) is placed in which the Devatā is invoked. A Mandala or figure of a particular design is marked on the ground and on it the jar is placed. Then the five or nine gems are placed in the jar which is painted red and covered with leaves. The ritual then prescribes for the tying of the crown lock (Shikhā), the posture (Āsana) of the Sādhaka, Japa, Nyāsa, and the Mantra ritual. There is meditation as directed, Mantra-chaitanya and Japa of the Mantra the number of times for which vow has been made.

The daily life of the religious Hindu was in former times replete with worship. I refer those who are interested in the matter to the little work, "The Daily Practices of the Hindus" by Srīsha Chandra Vasu, the Sandhyāvandana of all Vedic Shākhās by B. V. Kamesvara Aiyyar, the Kriyākāndavāridhi and Purohita-darpanam. The positions and Mudrās are illustrated in Mrs. S. C. Belnos' "Sandhyā or daily prayer of the Brahmin" published in 1831. It is not here possible to do more than indicate the general outlines of the rites followed.

As the Sādhaka awakes he makes salutation to the Guru of all and recites the appropriate Mantras and confessing his inherent human frailty ("I know Dharma and yet would not do it. I know Adharma and yet would not renounce it,")—the Hindu form of the common experience "Video meliora", he prays that he may do right and offers all the actions of the day to God. Upon touching the ground on leaving his bed he salutes the Earth, the manifestation of the All-Good. He then bathes to the accompaniment of Mantra and makes oblation to the Devas, Rishis or Seers and the Pitris who issued from Sandhyā, Brahmā the Pitāmaha of humanity, and then does rite.

This is the Vaidik form which differs according to Veda and Shākhā for the twice-born and there is a Tāntrikī Sandhyā for others. It is performed thrice a day at morn, at noon, and evening. The Sandhyā consists generally speaking, of Āchamana (sipping of water), Mārjjana-snāna (sprinkling of the whole body), Prānāyāma (Breath-control), Aghamarshana (expulsion of sin), prayer to the Sun and then (the canon of the Sandhyā) Japa of the Gāyatrī-mantra. Rishi-nyāsa and Shadanga-nyāsa (v. *ante*), and meditation of the Devī Gāyatrī, in the morning as Brahmanī (Shakti of Creation), at midday as Vaishnavī (Shakti of maintenance), and in evening as Rudrānī (Shakti which "destroys" in the sense of withdrawing creation). The Sandhyā with the Aupāsana fire-rite and Panchayajna are the three main daily rites, the last being offerings to the Devas, to the Pitris, to animals and birds (after the Vaishvadeva rite), to men (as by entertainment of guests) and the study of Vaidik texts. By these five Yajnas, the worshipper daily places himself in right relations with all being, affirming such relation between Devas, Pitris, Spirits, men, the organic creation and himself.

The word "Yajna" comes from the root *Yaj* (to worship) and is commonly translated "sacrifice", though it includes other rituals than what an English reader might understand by that term. Thus, Manu speaks of four kinds of Yajna as Deva, Bhauta (where ingredients are used), Nir-yajna and Pitriyajna. Sometimes the term is used in connection with any kind of ceremonial rite, and so one hears of Japa-yajna (recitation of Mantra), Dhyāna-yajna (meditation) and so on. The Panchatattva ritual with wine and the rest is accounted a Yajna. Yajnas are also classified according to the dispositions and intentions of the worshipper into Sāttvika, Rājasika and Tāmasika Yajna. A common form of Yajna is the Deva-yajna Homa rite in which offerings of ghee are made (in the Kunda or firepit) to the Deva of Fire who is the carrier of oblations to the Devas. Homa is an ancient Vaidik rite incorporated with others in the General Tāntrik ritual. It is of several kinds, and is performed either daily, or on special occasions, such as the sacred thread ceremony, marriage and so forth. Besides the daily (Nitya) ceremonies such as Sandhyā there are occasional rites (Naimittika) and the purificatory sacraments (Samskāra) performed only once.

The ordinary ten Samkāras (see Mahānirvāna Tantra, Ch. IX) are Vaidik rites done to aid and purify the individual in the important events of his life, namely, the Garbhādhāna sanctifying conception prior to the actual placing of the seed in the womb, the Puṁsavana and Sīmantonnyana or actual conception and during pregnancy. It has been suggested that the first Samskāra is performed with reference to the impulse to development from the " fertilization of the ovum to the critical period : the second with reference to the same impulse from the last period to that of the viability stage of the fœtus ", and the third refers to the period in which there is viability to the full term (see Appendix on Samskāras. Pranavavāda, I. 194). Then follows the Samskāra on birth (Jāta-karma), the naming ceremony (Nāma-karana), the taking of the child outdoors for the first time to see the sun (Nishkramana), the child's first eating of rice (Annaprāsana), his tonsure (Chūdākarana), and the investiture in the case of the twice-born with the sacred thread (Upanayana) when the child is reborn into spiritual life. This initiation must be distinguished from the Tāntrik initiation (Mantra-dikshā) when the Bīja-mantra is given by the Guru. Lastly there is marriage (Udvāha). These Samskāras, which are all described in the ninth Chapter of the Mahānirvāna Tantra, are performed at certain stages in the human body with a view to effect results beneficial to the human organism through the superphysical and subjective methods of ancient East science.

Vrata is a part of Naimittika—occasional ritual or Karma. Commonly translated as vows, they are voluntary devotions performed at specified times in honour of particular Devatās (such as Krishna's birthday), or at any time (such as the Sāvitrīvrata). Each Vrata has its peculiarities, but there are certain features common to all, such as chastity, fasting, bathing, taking of pure food only and no flesh or fish. The great Vrata for a Shākta is the Durgā-pūjā in honour of the Devī as Durgā.

The fasting which is done in these or other cases is called Tapas, a term wich includes all forms of ascetic austerity and zealous Sādhanā such as the sitting between five fires (Panchāgni-tapah) and the like. Tapas has however a still wider meaning and is then of three kinds, namely, bodily (Shārīraka), by speech (Vāchika) and by mind (Mānasa), a common division both of Indian and Buddhist Tantra. The first includes external worship, reverence, support of the Guru, Brāhmanas and the wise (Prājna), bodily cleanliness, continence, simplicity of life and avoidance of hurt to any being (Ahimsā). The second form includes truth, good, gentle and affectionate speech and study of the Vedas. The third or mental Tapas includes self-restraint, purity of disposition, tranquillity and silence. Each of these classes has three sub-divisions, for Tapas may be Sāttvika, Rājasika, or Tāmasika according as it is done with faith, and without regard to its fruit; or for its fruit; or is done through pride and to gain honour or respect or power; or lastly which is done ignorantly or with a view to injure and destroy others such as Abhichāra or the Sādhanā of the Tāntrik Shatkarma (other than Shānti), that is, fascination or Vashīkarana, paralyzing or Stambhana, creating enmity or Vidveshana, driving away or Uchchātana, and killing or Marana when performed for a malevolent purpose. Karma ritual is called Kāmya when it is done to gain some particular end such as health, prosperity and the like. The highest worship is called Nishkāma-karma, that is, it is done not to secure any material benefit but for worship's sake only.

Though it is not part of ordinary ritual, this is the only place where I can conveniently mention a peculiar Sādhanā, prevalent, so far as I am aware, mainly if not wholly amongst Tāntrikas of a Shākṭa type which is called Nīlasādhanā or Black Sādhanā. This is of very limited application being practised by some Vīra Sādhakas in the cremation ground. There are terrifying things in these rituals and therefore only the fearless practise them. The Vīra trains himself to be indifferent and above all fear. A leading rite is that called Shava Sādhanā which is done with the means of a human corpse. I have explained elsewhere (see "Serpent Power") why a corpse is chosen. The corpse is laid with its face to the ground. The Sādhaka sits on the back of the body of the dead man on which he draws a Yantra and then worships. If the rite is successful it is said that the head of the corpse turns round and asks the Sādhaka what is the boon he craves, be it liberation or some material benefit. It is believed that the Devī speaks through the mouth of the corpse which is thus the material medium by which She manifests Her presence. In another rite, the corpse is used as a seat (Shavāsana). There are sittings also (Āsana) on skulls

(Mundāsana) and the funeral pyre (Chitāsana). However repellent or suspect these rites may appear to be to a Western, it is nevertheless the fact that they have been and are practised by genuine Sādhakas of fame such as in the past the famed Mahārāja of Nattore and others. The interior cremation ground is within the body that being the place where the passions are burnt away in the fire of knowledge.

The Ādyā Shakti or Supreme Power of the Shāktas is, in the words of the Trishatī, concisely described as Ekānanda-chidākritih. Eka = Mukya, Ānanda = Sukham, Chit = Chaitanyam or Prakāsha = Jnānam; and Ākritih = Svarūpa. She is thus Sachchidānanda-brahmarūpā. Therefore, the worship of Her is direct worship of the Highest. This worship is based on Advaitavāda. Therefore, for all Advaitins, its Sādhanā is the highest. The Shākta Tantra is thus a Sādhanā Shāstra of Advaitavāda. This will explain why it is dear to, and so highly considered by Advaitins. It is claimed to be the one and only stepping stone which leads directly to Kaivalya or Nirvānamukti; other forms of worship procuring for their followers (from the Saura to the Shaiva) various ascending forms of Gauna mukti. Others of course may claim this priority. Every sect considers itself to be the best and is in fact the best for those who, with intelligence, adopt it. Were it not so its members would presumably not belong to it but would choose some other. No true Shākta, however, will wrangle with others over this. He will be content with his faith of which the Nigamakalpataru says, that as among castes the Brāhmanas are foremost, so amongst Sādhakas are the Shāktas. For, as Niruttara Tantra says, there is no Nirvāna without knowledge of Shakti (*Shaktijnānam vinā devi nirvānam naiva jāyate*). Amongst the Shāktas, the foremost are said to be the worshippers of the Kālī Mantra.

The Adimahāvidya is Kālikā. Other forms are Mūrttibheda of Brahmarūpinī Kālikā. Kālīkula is followed by Jnānis of Divya and Vīra Bhāvas; and Shrīkula by Karmin Sādhakas. According to Niruttara, Kālīkula includes Kālī, Tārā, Raktakālī, Bhuvanā, Mardinī, Triputā, Tvaritā, Pratyangirāvidyā, Durgā; and Shrīkula includes Sundarī, Bhairavī, Bālā, Bagalā, Kamalā, Dhūmāvatī, Mātangī, Svapnavatīvidyā, Madhumatī Mahāvidyā. Of these forms Kālikā is the highest or Ādyamūrti as being Shuddhasattvagunapradhānā, Nirvikāra, Nirgunabrahmasvarūpaprakāshikā, and, as the Kāmadhenu Tantra says, directly Kaivalyadāyinī. Tārā is Sattvagunātmikā, Tattvavidyādāyinī, for by Tattvajnāna one attains Kaivalya. Shodashī, Bhuvaneshvarī Chhinnamastā are Rajahpradhānā Sattvagunātmikā, the givers of Gaunamukti and Svarga. Dhūmāvatī, Kamalā, Bagalā, Mātangī are Tamahpradhānā whose action is invoked in the magical Shatkarma.

The most essential point to remember as giving the key to all which follows is that Shāktadharma is Monism (Advaitavāda). Gandharva Tantra says, "Having as enjoined saluted the Guru and thought 'So'ham', the wise Sādhaka, the performer of the rite should meditate upon the unity of Jīva and Brahman."

Gurūn natvā vidhānena so'ham iti purodhasah
Aikyam sambhāvayet dhimān jīvasya brahmano'pi cha.

Kālī Tantra says: "Having thus meditated, the Sādhaka should worship Devī with the notion, 'So'ham'."

Evam dhyātvā tato devīm so'hamātmānam archayet.

Kubjikā Tantra says: "A Sādhaka should meditate upon himself as one and the same with Her" (*Tayā sahitamātmānam ekībhūtam vichintayet*). The same teaching is to be found throughout the Shāstra: Nīla Tantra directing the Sādhaka to think of himself as one with Tārinī;

Gandharva Tantra telling him to meditate on the self as one with Tripurā not different from Paramātma; and Kālīkulasarvasva as one with Kālikā and so forth. For as the Kulārnava Tantra says: "The body is the temple of God. Jīva is Sadāshiva. Let him give up his ignorance as the offering which is thrown away (Nirmālya) and worship with the thought and feeling, 'I am He'."

Deho devālayah proktah jīvo devah Sadāshivah
Tyajed ajnānanirmālyam so'ham bhāvena pūjayet.

This Advaitavāda is naturally expressed in the ritual. The Samhitā and Brāhmanas of the four Vedas are (as contrasted with the Upanishads) Traigunyavishaya. There is therefore much in the Vaidik Karmakānda which is contrary to Brahmajnāna. The same remarks apply to the ordinary Pashu ritual of the day. There are differences of touchable and untouchable, food, caste, and sex. How can a man directly qualify for Brahmajnāna who even in worship is always harping on distinctions of caste and sex and the life? He who distinguishes does not know. Of such distinctions the higher Tāntrik worship of the Shākta type knows nothing. As the Yoginī Tantra says, the Shāstra is for all castes and for women as well as men. Tantra Shāstra is Upāsanā Kānda, and in this Shākta Upāsanā the Karma and Jnāna Kāndas are mingled (Mishra). That is, Karma is the ritual expression of the teaching of Jnāna Kānda and is calculated to lead to it. There is nothing in it which contradicts Brahmajnāna. This fact, therefore, renders it more conducive to the attainment of such spiritual experience. Such higher ritual serves to reveal Jnāna in the mind of the Pashu. So it is rightly said that a Kulajnānī even if he be a Chandāla, is better than a Brāhmana. It is on these old Tāntrik principles that the Indian religion of to-day can alone, if at all, maintain itself. They have no concern, however, with social life and what is called "social reform". For all secular purposes the Tantras recognize caste, but in spiritual matters spiritual qualifications alone prevail. There are many such sound and high principles in the Tantra Shāstra for which it would receive credit, if it could only obtain a fair and unprejudiced consideration. But there are none so blind as those who will not see. And so we find that the "pure and high" ritual of the Veda is set in contrast with the supposed "low and impure" notions of the Tantras. On the contrary, a Tāntrik Pandit once said to me: "The Vaidik Karmakānda is as useful for ordinary men as is a washerman for dirty clothes. It helps to remove their impurities. But the Tantra Shāstra is like a glorious tree which gives jewelled fruit."

Sādhanā, as I have said, is defined as that which leads to Siddhi. Sādhanā comes from the root "Sādh"—to exert to strive. For what? That depends on the Sādhanā and its object. Sādhanā is any means to any end and not necessarily religious worship, ritual and discipline. He who does Hathayoga, for physical health and strength, who accomplishes a magical Prayoga, who practises to gain an "eightfold memory" and so forth are each doing Sādhanā to gain a particular result (Siddhi), namely, health and strength, a definite magical result, increased power of recollection and so forth. A Siddhi again is any power gained as the result of practice. Thus, the Siddhi of Vetāla Agni Sādhanā is control over the fire-element. But the Sādhanā which is of most account and that of which I here speak, is religious worship and discipline to attain true spiritual experience. What is thus sought and gained may be either Heaven (Svarga), secondary liberation (Gaunamukti) or full Nirvāna. It is the latter which in the highest sense is Siddhi, and striving for that end is the chief and highest form of Sādhanā. The latter term includes not merely ritual worship in the sense of adoration or prayer, but every form of spiritual discipline such as sacraments (Samskāra), austerities (Tapas), the reading of Scripture (Svādhyāya) meditation (Dhyāna) and so forth. Yoga is a still higher form of Sādhanā; for the term Yoga means strictly not the result but the means whereby Siddhi in the form of Samādhi may be had. Ordinarily, however, Sādhanā is used to express all spiritual disciplines based on the notion of worshipper and worshipped; referring thus to Upāsanā not Yoga. The latter passes beyond these and all other dualisms to Monistic experience (Samādhi). The first leads up to the second by purifying the mind (Chittashuddhi), character and disposition (Bhāva) so as to render it capable of Jnāna or Laya Yoga; or becomes itself Parabhakti which, as the Devībhagavata says, is not different from Jnāna.

The great Siddhi is thus Moksha; and Moksha is Paramātmā, that is, the Svarūpa of Ātmā. But the Sādhaka is Jīvātmā, that is, Ātmā associated with Avidyā of which Moksha or Paramātmā is free. Avidyā manifests as mind and body, the subtle and gross vehicles of spirit. Man is thus therefore Spirit (Ātmasvarūpa), which is Sachchidānanda, Mind (Antahkarana) and body (Sthūla-sharīra). The two latter are forms of Shakti, that is, projections of the Creative Consciousness through and as its Māyā. The essential operation of Māyā and of the Kanchukas is to seemingly *contract* consciousness. As the Yoginīhridaya Tantra says, the going forth (Prasara) of Consciousness (Samvit) is in fact a contraction (Samkocha as Mātri, Māna, Meya or known, knowing, being known). Consciousness is thus finitized into a limited self which and other selves regard one another as mutually exclusive. The One Self becomes its own object as the many forms of the universe. It conceives itself as separate from them. Oblivious in separateness of its essential nature it regards all other persons and things as different from itself. It acts for the benefit of its limited self. It is in fact selfish in the primary sense of the term; and this selfishness is the root of all its desires, of all its sins. The more mere worldly desires are fostered, the greater is the bondage of man to the mental and material planes. Excessively selfish desires display themselves as the sins of lust, greed, anger, envy and so forth. These bind more firmly than regulated desire and moreover lead to Hell (Naraka). The most general and ultimate object of Sādhanā is therefore to cast off from the Self this veil of Avidyā and to attain that Perfect experience which is Ātmasvarūpa or Moksha. But to know Brahman is to *be* Brahman. *Brahma veda brahmaiva bhavati* as Shruti says. In essence man is Brahman. But owing to Avidyā it is necessary to do something in order that this ever existent fact may be realized. That action (Kriyā) is the work of Sādhanā in its endeavour to clear away the veiling of Avidyā which is ignorance. In the sense that Avidyā is being removed man may be said by Sādhanā to become Brahman: that is, he realizes himself as what he truly is and was. Sādhanā, therefore, by the grace of Devī or "descent of Shakti" (Shaktipāta) "converts" (to use an English term) the Sādhaka, that is, turns him away from separatist worldly enjoyment to seek his own true self as the pure Spiritual Experience. This transformation is the work and aim of Sādhanā. But this experience is not to be had in its completest sense at once and at a bound. It is, as Patanjali says, very rare. Indeed those who truly desire it are very few. Brahman is mindless (Amanah); for mind is a fetter on true consciousness. This mindlessness (Nirālambapurī) is sought through the means of Yoga. But no would-be

Yogī can attain this state unless his mind is already pure; that is, not only free from gross sin, but already possessing some freedom from the bondage of worldly desires, cultivated and trained, and desirous of liberation (Mumukshu). The aim, therefore, of preliminary Sādhanā is to secure that purification of mind (Chittashuddhi) which is alone the basis on which Yoga works. The first object then is to restrain the natural appetites, to control the senses, and all that excessive selfishness beyond the bounds of Dharma which is sin (Pāpa). Dharma prescribes these bounds because unrestricted selfish enjoyment leads man downward from the path of his true evolution. Man is, as regards part of his nature, an animal, and has, according to the Shāstra, passed through all animal forms in his 84 lakhs of previous births. But he has also a higher nature and if he conforms to the path laid out for him will progress by degrees to the state of that Spirit whose limited form he now is. If he strays from that path he falls back, and continued descent may bring him again to the state of apparently unconscious matter through many intervening Hells in this and other worlds. For this reason, the Shāstra repeats that he is a "self-killer" who, having with difficulty attained to manhood, neglects the opportunities of further progress which they give him (Kulārnava Tantra I). Therefore, he must avoid sin which leads to a fall. How can the impure realize the Pure? How can the mere seeker of sensual enjoyment desire formless liberating Bliss? How can he recognize his unity with all if he is bound in selfishness which is the root of all sin? How can he realize the Brahman who thinks himself to be the separate enjoyer of worldly objects and is bound by all sensualities? In various forms this is the teaching of all religions. It would be hardly necessary to elaborate what is so plain were it not apparently supposed that the Tantra Shāstra is a strange exception to these universally recognized principles. "I thought", said a recent English correspondent of mine, "that the Tantra was a wholly bad lot belonging to the left hand path." This is not so: common though the notion be. The Shāstra teaches that the Sādhaka must slay his "Six Enemies" which are the six cardinal sins and all others allied with them. Whether all the *means* enjoined are good, expedient, and fitting for the purpose is a different matter. This is a distinction which none of its critics ever make; but which accuracy and justice require they should make if they condemn the method. It is one thing to say that a particular method prescribed for a good end is bad, dangerous, or having regard to the present position of the generality of men, unadvisable; and a totally different thing to say that the *end* which is sought is itself bad. The Tantra, like all Shāstras, seeks the Paramārtha and nothing else. Whether all the forms of search are good (and against the bulk of them no moral objection can be raised) is another question. Let it be for argument supposed that one or other of the means prescribed is not good but evil. Is it accurate or just to condemn not only the particular Shāstra in which they occur (as the discipline of a particular class of Sādhakas only), but also the whole of the Āgamas of all classes of worshippers under the misleading designation "The Tantra"?

I am here speaking from the point of view of one who is not a Hindu. Those, however, who are Hindus must logically either deny that the Tantra Shāstra is the Word of Shiva or accept all which that Word says. For if a Tantra prescribes what is wrong this vitiates the authority, in all matters, of the Tantra in which wrong is ordained. It may be that other matters dealt with should be accepted, but this is so not because of any authority in the particular

Tantra, but because they have the countenance elsewhere of a true authoritative scripture. From this logical position no escape is possible.

Let us for the moment turn to the celebrated Hymn to Kālī (of, as those who read it might call, the extremist, that is Vīra Shākta worship) entitled the Karpūrādi Stotra (Tāntrik Texts, Vol. IX), which like most (probably all) of its kind has both a material (Sthūla) and subtle (Sūkshma) meaning. In the 19th verse it is said that the Devī delights to receive in sacrifice the flesh, with bones and hair, of goat, buffalo, cat, sheep, camel and of man. In its literal sense this passage may be taken as an instance of the man-sacrifice of which we find traces throughout the world (and in some of the Tantras) in past stages of man's evolution. Human sacrifices permitted by other Semites were forbidden by the Mosaic Code, although there is an obvious allusion to such a custom in the account of the contemplated sacrifice of Isaac by Abraham (Gen. xxii). The Israelites, however, offered bloody sacrifices the savour of which God (Yahweh) is represented as enjoying, they being necessary in His honour and to avert His wrath (Gen. viii. 21; Lev. i. 9. 13, 17; Judges vi. 17, xiii. 15; Gen. viii. 20-21; 1 Sam, xxvi. 19). Nothing is more common in all religions (and Christianity as by some understood provides many examples) than to materially understand spiritual truths. For such is the understanding of material of Sthūladarshin (grossly seeing) men. But, even in the past, those who were spiritual referred all sacrifice to the self; an inner sacrifice which all must make who would attain to that Spririt which we may call Kālī, God, Allah, or what we will. But what is the Svarūpa-vyākhyā or true meaning of this apparently revolting verse? The meaning is that inner or mental worship (Antaryāga) is done to Her who is black (Asitā) because She is the boundless (Sitā = Baddhā)

Consciousness (Chidrūpā) whose true nature is eternal liberation (Nityamukta-Svabhāvā). And just as in outer worship material offerings (Upachāra) are made, so the Sādhaka sacrifices to Her his lust (the Goat-Kāma), his anger (the Buffalo-Krodha), his greed (the Cat-Lobha), his stupidity of illusion (the Sheep-Moha), his envy (the Camel-Mātsaryya) and his pride and infatuation with worldly things (the Man-Mada). All will readily recognize in these animals and man the qualities (Guna) here attributed to them. It is to such as so sacrifice to whom is given Siddhi in the form of the five kinds of Mukti.

Competency for Tantra (Tantrashāstrādhikāra) is described in the second Chapter of the Gandharva Tantra as follows: The aspirant must be intelligent (Daksha), with senses controlled (Jitendriya), abstaining from injury to all beings (Sarvahimsā-vinirmukta), ever doing good to all (Sarvaprāni-hite rata), pure (Shuchi), a believer in Veda (Āstika), a non-dualist (Dvaitahīna), whose faith and refuge is in Brahman (Brahmanishtha, Brahmavādī, Brāhma, Brahmaparāyana). "Such an one", it adds, "is competent for this Scripture *otherwise he is no Sādhaka*" (*So'smin shastre' dhikāri tad anyatra na sādhakah*). It will be allowed by all that these are strange qualifications for a follower of "a bad scripture of the left hand path." Those who are on such a path are not supposed to be seekers of the Brahman, nor solicitous for the good of all being. Rather the reverse. The Kulārnava Tantra (which I may observe deals with the ill-famed Panchatattva ritual) gives in the thirteenth Chapter a long list of qualifications necessary in the case of a Tāntrik disciple (Shishya). Amongst these, it rejects the slave of food and sexual pleasure (Jihvopasthapara); the lustful (Kāmuka), shameless (Nirlajja), the greedy and voracious eater, the sinner in general who does not follow Dharma and Āchāra, who is ignorant, who has no desire for spiritual knowledge, who is a hypocrite, with Brahman on his lips but not in his heart, and who is without devotion (Bhakti). Such qualifications are inconsistent with its alleged intention to encourage sensuality unless we assume that all such talk in all the Shāstras throughout all time is mere hypocrisy.

It is not however sufficient for the Sādhaka to turn from sin and the occasions of it. It is necessary to present the mind with a pure object and to busy it in pure actions. This not only excludes other objects and actions but trains the mind in such a way towards goodness and illumination that it at length no longer desires wrongful enjoyment; or lawful Pashu enjoyment or even enjoyment infused with a spiritual Bhāva, and thus finally attains desirelessness (Nishkāmabhāva). The mind dominated *by* matter, then regulated *in* matter, consciously releases itself to first work *through* matter, then *against* matter; then rising *above* matter it, at length, enters the Supreme State in which all the antithesis of Matter and Spirit have gone.

What then are the means by which spiritual Siddhi is attained? Some are possibly common to all religions; some are certainly common to more than one religion, such as objective ritual worship (Bāhyapūjā), inner or mental worship (Mānasa-Pūjā or Antarpūjā) of the Ishtadevatā, prayer (Prārthanā), sacraments (Samskāra), self-discipline for the control of the will and natural appetites (Tapas), meditation (Dhyāna) and so forth. There is, for instance, as I have elsewhere pointed out, a remarkable similarity between the Tāntrik ritual of the Āgamas and Christian ritual in its Catholic form. It has been suggested that Catholicism is really a legacy of the ancient civilization, an adaptation of the old religions (allied in many respects with Shākta worship) of the Mediterranean races; deriving much of its strength from its non-Christian elements. I will not observe on this except to say that you do not dispose of the merits of any ritual by showing (if it be the fact) that it is extremely old and non-Christian. Christianity is one of the great religions, but even its adherents, unless ignorant, will not claim for it the monopoly of all that is good.

To deal in detail with Tāntrik Sādhaka would take more than a volume. I have shortly summarized some important rituals. I will now shortly indicate some of the general psychological principles on which it is based and which is understood, will give the key to an understanding of the extraordinary complexity and variety of the actual ritual details. I will also illustrate the application of these principles in some of the more common forms of worship.

It is recognized in the first place that mind and body mutually react upon one another. There must therefore be a physical Sādhanā as the groundwork of the mental Sādhanā to follow. India has for ages recognized what is now becoming generally admitted, namely, that not only health but clarity of mind, character, disposition, and morals are affected by the nourishment, exercise, and general treatment of the body. Thus, from the moral aspect, one of the arguments against the use of meat and strong drink is the encouragement they give to animal passions. Why then it may be asked do these form a part of some forms of Shākta Sādhanā? I answer this later. It is however a Hindu trait to insist on purity of food and person. Tāntrik Hathayoga deals in full with the question of bodily cleanliness, food, sexual continence, and physical exercise. But there are injunctions, though less strict, for the ordinary householder to whom wine and other intoxicating drinks and the eating of beef (thought by some to be a material foundation of the British Empire, but now recognized by several medical authorities to be the source of physical ills) and some other foods, as also all gluttony, as regards permitted food, are forbidden. Periodical fasts are enjoined; as also, during certain religious exercises, the eating of the pure food called Havishyānnam made of fruit, vegetable and rice. The sexual life has also its regulations. In short, it is said, let the body be well treated and kept pure in order to keep the mind sane and pure and a good and not rebellious instrument for mental Sādhanā. In the Tantras will be found instances of several necessary bodily perfections in the Sādhaka. Thus he should not be deformed, with defective limbs, wanting in, or having excess of any limb, weak of limb, crippled, blind, deaf, dirty, diseased, with unnatural movements, paralysed, slothful in action (Kulārnava, XIII).

Let us now pass to the mind. For the understanding of Hindu ritual it is necessary to understand both Hindu philosophy and Hindu psychology. This point, so far as I am aware, has never been observed. Certainly Indian ritual has never been dealt with on this basis. It has generally been considered sufficient to class it as "Mummery" and then to pass on to something supposed to be more worthy of consideration. It is necessary to remember that (outside successful Yoga) the mind (at any rate in its normal state) is never for one moment unoccupied. At every moment of time, worldly objects are seeking to influence it. Only those actually do so, to which the mind, in its faculty as Manas, gives attention. In one of the Tāntrik Texts (Shatchakranirūpana), the Manas is aptly spoken of as a doorkeeper who lets some enter and keeps others outside. For this reason it is called Sankalpavikalpātmaka: that is, it selects (Saṁkalpa) some things which the senses (Indriya) present to it and rejects (Vikalpa) others. If the Manas attends to the sensation demanding entrance it is admitted and passed on to the Buddhi and not otherwise. So the Brihadāranyaka Upanishad says, "My Manas was elsewhere and therefore I did not hear." This is a secret for the endurance of pain which not only the martyrs and the witches knew, but some others who have suffered lesser pains. When the sensation is passed on to the Buddhi, as also when the latter acts upon the material of remembered percepts, there is formed in the Buddhi a Vritti. The latter is a modification of the Mind into the form of the perceived object. Unless a man is a Siddhayogī, it is not possible to avoid the formation of mental Vrittis. The object, therefore, of Sādhanā is firstly to take the attention away from undesirable objects and then to place a desirable object in their stead. For the mind must feed on something. The object is the Ishtadevatā. When a Sādhaka fully, sincerely and deeply contemplates and worships his Ishtadevatā, his mind is formed into a Vritti in the form of the Devatā. As the latter is all purity, the mind, which contemplates it, is during, and to the depth of such contemplation pure. By prolonged and repeated worship the mind becomes naturally pure and of itself tends to reject all impure notions. What to others is a source of impurity is pure. To the pure, as the Hellenes said, all things are pure. Things are not impure. It is the impure mind which makes them so. He learns to see that everything and act are manifestations of the Divine. He who realizes Consciousness in all objects no longer has desire therefor. In this way a good disposition or Bhāva, as it is called, is attained which ripens into that which is divine or Devatābhāva. This is the principle on which all Sādhanā, as well as what is called specifically Mantrayoga, is based. It is profoundly said in the Kulārnava Tantra that a man must rise by means of the same things which are the cause of his fall. If you fall on the ground you must raise yourself by it. The mind is thus controlled by means of its own object (Vishaya); that is, the world of name and form (Nāmarūpa). The unregulated mind is distracted by Nāmarūpa. But the same Nāmarūpa may be used as the first means of escape therefrom. A particular form therefore of Nāmarūpa productive of pure Bhāva is therefore given as the object of meditation. This is called Sthūla or Saguna Dhyāna of the five Devatās. Material media are used as the first steps whereby the Formless One is, through Yoga, attained, such as Images (Pratimā), emblems (Linga, Shālagrāma), pictures (Chitra), mural markings (Bhittirekhā), Jar (Ghata), Mandalas and Yantras. To these worship (Pūjā) is done with other rites such as Japa, Nyāsa and so forth, and gestures (Mudrā). Siddhi in this is the Samādhi called Mahābhāva.

The second principle to be noted is that the object or mind's content, as also the service (Sevā) of it, may be either gross (Sthūla) or subtle (Sūkshma). This distinction pervades all the rituals and rightly so. Men are not all at the same degree of intellectual and spiritual advancement. For the simple-minded there are simple material and mental images. Progressively considered, the objects used to fix in the mind the thought of the Devatā are images in human or semi-human form, similar pictures, non-human forms or emblems (such as Linga and Gaurīpatta, Shālagrāma, the Jar or Ghata, Mandalas) and lastly Yantras. The image is not merely used for instruction (*ut pictura pro scriptura haberetur*), or to incite in the mind a mental picture, but after the Prānapratishthā rite is itself worshipped. So also amongst Christians, where however this rite is unknown, "eikones acheiropoietoi" (what are called in Sanskrit Svayambhu emblems) and wonder-working images have been directly venerated. Superficial persons doubtless think themselves profound when they ask how the Devatā can be invoked (Āvāhana). To them also the dismissal (Visarjana) savours of childish impudence and absurdity. How (I have read) can God be told to come and go? A Christian who sings the Hymn, "Veni creator Spiritus", is indeed ignorant if he fancies that at his request the Holy Ghost comes to him flying through the skies. As Shaṁkara says, Spirit (Ātmā) never comes and never goes. That which in fact moves is the mind of the Sādhaka in which, if pure, Spirit manifests Itself. That Spirit is in all places, and when the Sādhaka's mind fully realizes its presence in the Image, the latter as the manifestation of that Spirit is a fitting object of worship. Some knowledge of Vedānta is needful for the understanding and performance of image-worship. Yantra worship is however higher and is fitter for those who have reached a more advanced stage in Sādhanā. The term, as I have said, literally means an instrument; that by which anything is accomplished. In Upāsanā it is that instrument by which the mind is fixed upon the Devatā of worship. It is, as drawn, a diagram consisting of lines, angles and curves, varying with the Devatā worshipped as also, to some extent, according as it is a Pūjā or Dhārana Yantra, the whole being included in a common Bhūpura. A Yantra is three-dimensional, though it is very generally represented by a drawing on the flat. The Yantra and each part of it, as representing certain Shaktis, has a significance which is known to the instructed Sādhaka. On the great Shrī Yantra with its Baindava and other Chakras there is an entire literature. It is neglected now-a-days. Those who have fully understood it are masters in Tantra Shāstras. The subject is shortly dealt with in the Introduction to the Tantrarāja (Vol. VIII, p. xii, Tāntrik Texts, Ed. A. Avalon). Not only is the object of worship subtle or gross, but so also is the ritual with which it is worshipped. For the simple Indian worship avails itself of the ordinary incidents of daily life understood by even the most ignorant. And so we see the tending of the idol, waking it, bathing it, giving it food, putting it to sleep and so forth. In ordinary worship there is the offer of flowers, light, incense and the like Upachāra. In the subtle inner or mental worship (Antarpūjā) these are but symbols. Thus the Jnāneshvara Samhitā cited in the Mantrayoga-rahasyanirnaya speaks of the offering of "flowers of feeling" (Bhāvapushpa) to the Divinity—namely, the virtue of selflessness (Anahaṁkāra), desirelessness (Arāga), guilelessness (Adambha), freedom from malice and envy (Advesha, Amātsaryya) and infatuation and delusion (Amada and Amoha), and control over the feelings and mind (Akshobhaka, Amanaka). He who can truly make such offerings to Devī is a high Sādhaka indeed. The Shāstra makes wonderful provision for all types. It recognizes that there must be a definite object to which the mind must turn; chooses that object with a view to the capacities of the Sādhaka; and similarly regulates the ensuing worship. Much ignorant talk takes place as to the supposed worship of the Formless. Worship implies an object of worship and every object has some form. But that form and the ritual vary to meet the needs of differing capacities and temperaments; commencing with the more or less anthropomorphic image (or Doll; Puttalī, as those who dislike such worship call it) with its material service reproducing the ways of daily life, passing through pictures, emblems, Yantras, and mental worship to adoration of the Point of Light (Jyotirbindu) in which at length, consciousness being merged, all worship ceases.

The Shaktirahasya summarises the stages of progress in a short verse, thus: "By images, ceremonies, mind, identification, and knowing the Self, a mortal attains Liberation (Kaivalya)."

In the same way, meditation is either gross (Sthūla) or subtle (Sūkshma). The forms of the Mother of the Universe are threefold. There is first the Supreme (Para) form of which the Vishnuyāmala says "None know". There is next Her subtle form which consists of Mantra. But as the mind cannot settle itself upon that which is formless, She appears also in physical form as celebrated in the Devīstotras of the Purānas and Tantras.

The third principle to be noticed is the part which the body is made to take in the ritual. Necessarily there is action in any case to carry out the ritual, but this is so prescribed as to emphasize the mental operation (Mānasīkriyā), and in addition certain symbolic gestures (Mudrā) are prescribed. The body is made to take its part in the ritual, the mental processes being thus emphasized and intensified. This is based on a well-known natural tendency. When we speak with conviction and intensity of feeling, we naturally adopt appropriate movements of the body and gestures of the hands. We thus speak with the whole body.

Take for example Nyāsa which like Yantra is peculiar to the Tantras. The object of the Sādhaka is to identify himself with the Devatā he contemplates and thus to attain Devatābhāva for which it is, in its many forms, a most powerful means. Regarding the body of the Devatā as composed of Bīja Mantras, he not merely imagines that his own body is so composed but he actually places (Nyāsa means placing) these Bījas with the tip of his fingers on the various parts of his own body. The Abhīshta Devatā is thus in imagination (expressed by outward acts) placed in each of the parts and members of the Sādhaka's body, and then with the motion of his arms he, by Vyāpaka Nyāsa, as it were, spreads the presence of the Devatā all over his body. He thus feels himself permeated in every part by the presence of Devatā and identified with the Divine Self in that its form. How, it may be asked, can the Devatā be spread as it were butter on bread? These are crude questionings and because critics of the ritual do not get beyond this crude state of mind, this ritual is not understood. Devatā is not spread. God is everywhere and He is not to be placed by man's fingers anywhere. What is done is to produce in man's mind the notion that he is so spread. Again with certain ritual acts Mudrā is made. This Mudrā expresses by the hands the thought of the worshipper of which it is sometimes a kind of manual shorthand.

A further important point for consideration is that the mental Vritti is not only strengthened by accompanying physical action, but by a prolonged repetition of either or both. There may be a literal repetition of either or both, of which a prominent example is Japa of Mantra with which I have dealt in the Chapters on Shakti as Mantra and on the Varnamālā; or the object of contemplation may be severed into parts, as where meditation is done not simply on the Devatā as a whole, but on each of the parts of His body and then on the whole; or a particular result, such as the dissolution of the Tattvas in Bhūtashuddhi, may be analysed into the component parts of a process commencing with the first movement and ending with the last. Repetition of a word and idea fixes it in the mind, and if the same essential thought can be presented in varied forms the effect is more powerful and at the same time less calculated to tire. "Vain repetition" is itself in the mouths of many a vain criticism when not a platitude. If it is in fact vain it is vain. But it need not be so. In the current gross way of looking at things it is asked, "Will the Deity yield (like a modern politician) to repeated clamour?" The answer is the Devatā is not so affected. What is in fact affected is the mind of the Sādhaka himself which, being thus purified by insistent effort, becomes a fit medium for the manifestation of a divine consciousness (Devatābhāva). In short fact Indian ritual cannot be understood unless the Vedāntik *principles* of which they are a particular practical *application* are understood. Even when in devotion, complete understanding and feeling are not attained, the intention to gain both will achieve success by quickening worshipper's interest and strengthening the forces of the will.

A word now as to Symbolism which exists in all religions in varying degrees. The Tantra Shāstra is extraordinarily full of it in all its kinds—form, colour, language, number, action. The subject is a highly interesting but very lengthy one. I can only make two remarks with regard to it here. Red is a favourite colour in the Shākta Tantras. As pointed out in the Bhāvanopanishad (Sūtra 28) an Upanishad of the Kādimata and Bhāskararāya's commentary thereon, Redness denotes Rāga and Vimarsha Shakti. (See Introduction to Tantrarāja, Vol. VIII, Tāntrik Texts, Ed. by A. Avalon and Vol. XI, Tāntrik Texts.) There is a good deal of what is called erotic symbolism in some of the Tantras. This is apt to shock many English people, who are by no means all so moral in fact as some might think this sensitivity suggests. "The Hindus are very natural as regards sexual matters." An English clergyman remarks (E. F. Elwin "India and the Indians", p. 70) "A leading Indian Christian said to me 'there is no reserve among us in the sense that you English people have it. There is nothing which our children do not know.'" It should be added, says this author, "that the knowledge of evil (why I may ask is it always evil?) does not as a matter of course produce evil." The mind of the ancients was a natural one and they called a spade a spade and not an horticultural instrument, and were not shocked thereby. For instance, coupled *Yab-Yum* figures were not thought impure. Another point has been observed upon by the Italian author Guido Gozzano, namely, that the European has lost the power of "worshipping through the flesh" which existed in antique pagan times. (Verso la cuna del Mondo). Fear of erotic symbols is rather indicative in the generality of cases of a tendency to weakness and want of self-control. The great Edward Carpenter speaks of the "impure hush" in these matters. A person whose mind is naturally bent towards sensual thoughts but who desires to control them has no doubt a fear, which one readily understands, of anything which may provoke such thoughts. But such a man is, in this respect, lower than him who looks upon natural things in a natural way without fear of injury to himself; and greatly lower than him to whom all is a manifestation of the One Consciousness, and who realizes this in those things which are the cause of all to the imperfectly self-governed Pashu. Nothing is in itself impure. It is the mind which makes it so. It is however absolutely right that persons who feel that they have not sufficient self-control should, until they gain it, avoid what they think may do them injury. Apart from symbolism there are statements in some Shāstras or so-called Shāstras which are, in the ordinary modern sense, obscene. Some years ago a man wrote to me that he had come across in the Tantras "obscenities the very reading of which was demoralizing". The very fact that these portions of the Scripture had such an effect on him is a sufficient reason that he and others similary situated should not read them. The Tantra Shāstra recognizes this principle by certain injunctions into which I cannot enter here. The Kulārnava expressly says that the Chapter on the Wine ritual is not to be read (*Na pathed āsavollāsam*); that is, by the unqualified.

Again it is not necessary to admit either that every Text which calls Itself a Tantra is a genuine one or if so that it was the product of a high class Sādhaka. What is authoritative is that which is generally admitted to be so. Even if the Scripture be one of general acceptance, there is another matter to be remembered. As pointed out in Karpūrādistotra (Vol. IX, Tāntrik Texts, p. 11, where instances are given), an apparently "obscene" statement may disguise something which is not so. Why it may be asked? An intending disciple may be questioned as to such passages. If he is a gross-minded or stupid man his answers will show it. Those who are not fit for the reception of the doctrine may be kept off on hearing or reading such statements which may be of such a character that anyone but a fool would know that they were not to be taken literally. It may be that the passages which my correspondent read were of this character.

As regards erotic symbolism, however, (for to this I now limit myself) it is not peculiar to the Tantras. It is as old as the hills and may be found in other Scriptures. It is a matter of embarrassment to the class I have mentioned that the Bible is not free from it. Milton, after referring to Solomon's wedded leisures says, "In the Song of Songs which is generally believed, even in the jolliest expressions, to figure the spousals of the Church with Christ, sings of a thousand raptures between those two lovely ones far on the hither side of carnal enjoyment." If we would picture the cosmic processes we must take the materials therefor from our own life. It is not always necessary to go to the erotic life. But man has generally done so for reason I need not discuss here; and his selections must sometimes be admitted to be very apt. It has however been said that "throughout Shākta symbolism and pseudo-philosophising, there lies at the basis of the whole system, the conception of sexual relationship as the ultimate explanation of the universe." Reading these words as they stand, they are nonsense. What is true is that some Shākta Tantras convey philosophic and scientific truths by the media of erotic imagery; which is another matter. But so also does Upanishad. The charge of pseudo-philosophy is ill-founded, unless the Advaita-vedānta is such. The Shākta Tantra simply presents the Vedāntik teachings in a symbolical ritualistic form for the worshipper to whom it also prescribes the means whereby they may be realized in fact. Those who think otherwise have not mastered the alphabet of the subject.

I will conclude with a reply to a possible objection to what I have above written. It may be said that some of the rituals to which I have alluded are not merely the property of the Tantra Shāstras, and that they are not entitled to any credit for them. It is a fact that some (many have become extinct) Vaidik rituals such as the ten Samskāras, Sandhyā, Homa and so forth are imbedded in and have been adopted by the Āgamas. These and other rituals are to be found also in the Purānas. In any case, the Āgama is what it is, whether its elements are original or derived. If the rites adopted are creditable then praise must be given for the adoption of that which is good. If they are not, blame equally attaches to the original as to the copy. What however the Āgamas have adopted has been shaped so as to be suitable for all, that is, for others than those for whom the original rituals were intended. Further many of the rituals here described seem to have been introduced by and to be peculiar to the Āgamas. Possibly some of these may have been developed from other forms or seeds of form in the Vaidik ritual. The whole subject of Indian ritual and its origins is still awaiting enquiry. Personally I am disposed to favour the view that the Āgamas have made a contribution which is both original and considerable. To me also the contribution seems to have greater conformity with Vedāntik doctrine, which is applied by the ritual in a psychological manner which is profound. On an "historical" view of the matter this seems necessarily to be so. For, according to that view, the early Vaidik ritual either antedated or was contemporaneous with the promulgation of the Vedāntik doctrine to be found in the Upanishads, for the general acceptance of which considerable time was necessary. It could not therefore (if at all) embody that doctrine in the same way or to the same degree as a Ritual developed at a time when that doctrine had been widely disseminated, generally accepted and at least to a greater degree systematized. Ritual is only a practical expression of doctrine, and the Āgamas, according to a generally accepted view, did not come into being earlier than a date later than the first and chief Upanishads, and perhaps at the close of what is generally called the Aupanishadik age. No "historical" argument, however, is yet entirely trustworthy, as the material upon which it is to be based has not been sufficiently explored. For myself I am content to deal with present-day facts. According to the Indian view, all Shāstras are various parts of one whole and that Part which as a present-day fact contains the bulk of the ritual, now or recently in practice, consists of the Tantras of the various schools of Āgama. As an Indian author and follower of the Shaivāgama has said—the Temple ritual throughout India is governed by the Āgamas. And this must be so, if it be the fact as alleged, that Temples, Images, and other matters were unknown to the original Vaidik Āryas. If the Āgamas have adopted some of the ritual of the latter, those in their turn in course of time took to themselves the practices of those outside the body of men for whom the Vaidik Karmakānda was originally designed. Vedānta in its various forms has now for centuries constituted the religious notions of India, and the Āgamas in their differing schools are its practical expression in worship and ritual affording the means whereby Vedāntik doctrine is realized,

CHAPTER XXVII

THE PANCHATATTVA

(The Secret Ritual)

The notoriety of the Shākta Panchatattva ritual with wine and woman has thrown into the shade not only the practical topics with which I have dealt, but every other, including the valuable philosophical presentment of Vedānta contained in the Shākta Tantra. Notwithstanding, and indeed because of, the off-hand and (in certain respects) ignorant condemnation which this ritual has received, the interests of both scholarship and fairness (which by the way should be identical) require that we should first ascertain the facts, think clearly and fearlessly, and then determine without prejudice. From both the Shāstrik and historical point of view the subject is of such importance that it is not possible for me to here deal with it otherwise than in a very general way. It is necessary, however, in a paper on Upāsanā, to at least touch upon the matter because as against everything one says about the Tantras, there is raised the express or implied query "That may be all very well. But what about the infamous Panchamakāra?" Anything said in favour of the Shāstra is thus discounted in advance.

We must first disentangle the general *principles* involved from their particular *application*. The principle may be sound and yet the application may not be so. We may, for instance, approve striving for Vedāntik detachment (Audāsīnya), whilst at the same time we may reject the

Aghora's application of it in eating human carrion. Next, let us see *what in fact is the ritual* application of these principles. Then let us judge the *intention* with which the ritual was prescribed. A principle may be good and the intention may be good, but its application may be intrinsically bad, or at least dangerous, and therefore inexpedient as leading to abuse. In life it is a mistake to altogether neglect the pragmatical aspect of any theory. Logic and life do not always go hand in hand. Lastly, let us see whether the *application* is good or bad or inexpedient; or whether it is partially one or the other.

In the first place it is necessary to clear the air of some common misconceptions. It is commonly thought that all the practitioners of the Panchatattva ritual with wine, woman, and so forth are immoral men, professing to follow a Scripture which does not accept the ordinary rules of morality as regards food, drink and woman which enjoin that men should curb their sensual desires. Rather is it thought that it teaches that men should yield to them and thus "enjoy" themselves. This view turns at least this portion of the Shākta Tantra into a scripture of libertinism, thinly veiling itself in pseudo-religious forms. Its followers are supposed to be in the condition of a sensual man who finds his wishes thwarted by the rules of morality of his fellows around him and who, asking himself how he can infringe those rules under colour of some supposed authority, gives to the fulfilment of desire a "religious" sanction. In the words of an English writer, the bent towards religion of some sort is so strong in India that some of its people even "sin religiously". They are, on this view, hypocrites putting themselves to a deal of unnecessary trouble, for men can and do in India, as elsewhere, gratify their desires without religious rituals, and if wishful to establish a theory of enjoyment justifying their conduct, they can, as some have also done in India as elsewhere, advocate an "epicurean" materialism for that purpose. For the true sensualist who wishes to get at the object of his desire, these long Tāntrik rituals would be obstructive and wearisome. Whatever may be thought of the ritual in question, these notions of it are wrong. The charge, however, if unrefuted, constitutes a blot on this country's civilization, which has been allowed to remain because some who know better are either afraid to acknowledge that they follow these rites, or if they do not, that it may be supposed that they do so. This blot, in so far as it is not justified by actual fact, I propose in the present Chapter to remove.

The word Shāstra or Scriptures comes from the root *Shās*, to control, because its object is to control the conduct of men otherwise prone to evil. Whether its *methods* be mistaken or not, the Shākta Scripture is a Shāstra. Morality or Dharma is preached by all Shāstra whether of East or West. That morality (Dharma) is in its essentials the same in all the great Scriptures. For what purpose is conduct controlled? The Indian answer is—in order that man may make for himself a good Karma which spells happiness in this and the next world (Paraloka), and that then he may at length free himself of all Karma and attain Liberation (Moksha). Bad Karma leads to suffering here and in the Hells of the after-life. This is taught in the Shākta, as in other Shāstras, which seek to train the Sādhaka to attain Liberation. In a work of the present scope, I have not the space to cite authority in support of all these elementary propositions. There is, however, an abundance of Texts in support of them. Consult, for instance, the grand opening Chapter of the Kulārnava Tantra, which points out the frailty of Man, the passing nature of this world and of all it gives to Man, and his duty to avail himself of that Manhood which is so difficult of attainment so that he does not fall but rises and advances to Liberation. I cite the Kulārnava not merely because it is reputed to be a great Tantra and authority readily accessible, but because it teaches in full the practice of the rituals under consideration. But what is Liberation? It is the state of Brahman the Pure. How can the Pure be attained by counselling the practice of what the author of the Shāstra thought to be impure. Every Tantra counsels the following of Dharma or morality. The same Tantra (above cited) in its Chapter dealing with the necessary qualifications of a disciple points out that he must be of good character and in particular must not be lewd (Kāmuka) and given over to drink, gluttony and woman. If he is so, he is not competent for this particular ritual and must be trained by other disciplines (Pashvāchāra).

I here and hereafter deal with these particular infractions of morality because they alone in this matter concern us in our attempt to understand a ritual which is supposed to be an instance of the commission of these very sins.

The Mahānirvāna Tantra, which is of special interest because it is an attempt to provide a general code including law (in its European sense) for the followers of its cult, makes provision, amongst other matters, for general decency and so forth, for the state-punishment (unknown to English legislation) of men who go with prostitutes (XI. 43) as also with unmarried girls (*ib.*, 29-34), with women of prohibited degree (*ib.*), with the wives of others (*ib.*, 35-41), or who merely look with an eye of lust upon them (*ib.*, 47), stating (*ib.*, 46) "A man should consider as wife only that woman who has been married to him according to Brāhma (the common) or Shaiva form. All other women are the wives of others." It deplores (I-37) the evil customs of the present age (Kaliyuga) with its irreligion, lust, adultery, gluttony and addiction to strong drinks. How strangely hypocritical are these laments in a Shāstra which is supposed to consciously promote the very tendencies it deplores. It has been said that the Mahānirvāna is a worthy exception in an unworthy class. It is true that this Tantra evidences what may be called a reforming tendency on account of abuses which had occurred and thus puts restrictions on the ordinary householder as regards particular portions of the ritual, a fact which made a Pandit, of whom I was told, say that in comparison with the Mahānīla Tantra it was "a woman's Shāstra". Nevertheless on the general matters here dealt with it is not an exception. Possibly those who so speak had only read the Mahānirvāna which is the sole Tantra which has been translated in English. Certainly nothing that they say indicates any real acquaintance with any other. There are in fact other fine and more philosophical Tantras, and all the great authoritative Scriptures are at one, so far as I am aware, on the general question of morality and the search for Liberation with which I here deal. How, as I have said, could it, on commonly accepted principles, be otherwise? Whether the Sādhanā they teach is good and effective for the end sought is another matter, and still more so is the question whether it has been productive in fact of abuse.

What then are the general Indian rules touching drinking, eating, and sexual intercourse? In ancient Vaidik times intoxicating liquor was taken in the form of Soma. Such drink was found, however, in the course of time to be productive of great evils, and was thrice cursed by Brahmā, Shukrāchārya and Krishna. It was then prohibited with the result that India has been the most temperate among the great peoples of the world, Manu having declared that though the drinking of wine was a natural tendency, abstention therefrom was productive of great fruit. The Ushanah Samhitā says "Wine should not be drunk, given or taken" (*Madyam apeyam adeyam agrāhyam*). The drinking of wine is one of the great sins (Mahāpātaka) involving expiation (Prāyashchitta), and otherwise leading the sinner to that great Hell in which the slayer of a Brāhmana is confined (Vishnu Purāna, II. c. vi). In ancient Vaidik times, meat was eaten by the fair-coloured auburn-haired Aryans, including even beef, as is done by their fellow-Aryans of the West. But in process of time the slaughter of cattle for food was absolutely prohibited and certain meats such as that of the domesticated fowl and pig were held to be impure. As regards the eating of flesh and fish to-day, I believe the higher castes (outside Bengal) who submit to the orthodox Smārta discipline take neither. Nor do high and strict Brāhmanas in that province. But the bulk of the people there, both men and women, eat fish, and men consume the flesh of male goats previously offered to the Deity. Grain of all kinds is a common diet. I speak, of course, of orthodox Hindus. Some who have adopted Western civilization have taken over with it the eating of beef, the whisky peg and champagne, the curses of Brahmā, Shukra, Krishna, and the Hell of their Shāstras being nothing to them.

As regards Durgā Devī the absurd statement has been made ("Empire of India" by Sir Bampfylde Fuller, 161) that "to extremists among Her votaries any sexual restraint is a denial of Her authority." Yet it is common ground to all Shāstras that sexual intercourse (Maithuna) by a man with a woman who is not lawful to him is a sin. The Vaidik Dharma is strict on this point. It forbids not merely actual Maithuna but what is called Ashtānga (eightfold) Maithuna, namely, Smaranam (thinking upon it), Kīrttanam (talking of it), Keli (play with women), Prekshanam (making eyes at women), Guhyabhāshanam (talk in private with women), Saṁkalpa (wish or resolve for sexual union), Adhyavasāya (determination towards it), Kriyānishpatti (actual accomplishment of the sexual act). In short, the Pashu or follower of the ordinary ritual (and except for ritual purposes those who are not Pashu) should, in the words of the Shâktakramīya (cited by Mahāmahopādhyāya Krishnanātha Nyāyapanchānana Bhattāchāryya in his Commentary to v. 15 of the Karpūrādistotra, Tāntrik Texts, Vol. IX), avoid Maithuna, conversation on the subject and assemblies of women.

Maithunam tatkathālāpam tadgoshthīm parivarjayet

Even in marriage certain rules are to be observed such as that which prescribes intercourse on the fifth day after the termination of the period (*Ritukālam vinā devi ramanam parivarjayet*) which is said by the Nityā Tantra to be a characteristic of the Pashu. Polygamy is permissible to all Hindus.

The Divinity in woman, which the Shākta Tantra in particular proclaims, is also recognized in the ordinary Vaidik teaching. The wife is a House-Goddess (Grihadevatā) united to her husband by the sacrament (Saṁskāra) of marriage and is not to be regarded merely as an object of enjoyment. Further, Vaidik Dharma (now neglected) prescribes that the householder should ever worship with his wife as necessary partner therein, *Sastrīko dharmamācharet* (see also Matsyasūkta Tantra, XXXI). According to the sublime notions of Shruti the union of man and wife is a veritable sacrificial rite—a sacrifice in fire (Homa) wherein she is both hearth (Kunda) and flame—and he who knows this as Homa attains Liberation (see Mantra 13 of Homaprakarana of Brihadāranyaka Upanishad and Edward Carpenter's remarks on what is called the "obscenity" of this Upanishad). Similarly, the Tāntrik Mantra for Maithuna runs (see Prānatoshinī and Tantrasāra 698), "Om, Into the Fire which is Spirit (Ātmā) brightened by (the pouring thereon) of the ghee of merit and demerit, I by the path of Sushumnā (the central 'nerve') ever sacrifice (do Homa of) the functions of the senses using the mind as the ladle. Svāhā." (In the Homa rite the performer pours ghee into the fire which causes it to shoot up and flame. The ghee is poured in with a ladle. This being internal Homa the mind is the ladle which makes the offering of ghee).

Om

Dharmādharma-havirdīpte ātmāgnau manasā sruchā
Sushumnāvartmanā nityam akshavrittīr juhomyaham:
Svāhā.

Here sexual union takes on the grandeur of a great rite (Yajna) compared with which the ordinary mere animal copulation to ease desire, whether done grossly, shamefacedly, or with flippant gallantry is base. It is because this high conception of the function is not known that a "grossness" is charged against the association of sexual function with religion which does not belong to it. Grossness is properly attributable to those who mate like dumb animals, or coarsely and vulgarly, not to such as realize in this function the cosmic activity of the active Brahman or Shiva-Shakti with which they then, as always, unify themselves.

It has been already explained that Sādhakas have been divided into three classes—Pashu, Vīra and Divya, and for each the Shāstra prescribes a suitable Sādhanā, Tāmasik, Rājasik and Sāttvik accordingly. As later stated, the Panchatattva ritual in its full literal sense is not for the Pashu, and (judging upon principle) the Divya, unless of the lower ritual order, should be beyond it. In its fullest and literal sense it is for the Vīra and is therefore called Rājasik Sādhanā or Upāsanā. It is to be noted however that Pashu,

Vīra and Divya are the three primary classes (Mukhya-sādhaka). Besides these there are secondary divisions (Gaunasādhaka). Thus in addition to the primary or Svabhāva Pashu there is the Vibhāva Pashu who is a step towards Vīrāchāra. Vīras again have been said to be of three kinds, Svabhāva Vīra, Vibhāva Vīra, and Mantrasiddha Vīra. It is to this Rājasik Pūjā that the Hymn to Chhinnamastā from the Devīrahasyakhanda of the Rudrayāmala refers when the Vīra therein says,

Alipishitapurandhrī-bhogapūjāparo'ham
Bahuvidhakulamārgārambha-sambhāvito'ham
Pashujanavimukho'ham Bhairavīm āshrito'ham
Gurucharanarato'ham Bhairavo'ham Shivo'ham

(" I follow the worship wherein there is enjoyment of wine, flesh and wife as also other different forms of Kula worship. In Bhairavī (the Goddess) I seek my refuge. To the feet of Guru I am devoted. Bhairava am I. Shiva am I.")

To the ordinary English reader the association of eating, drinking and sexual union with worship will probably be incongruous, if not downright repulsive. " Surely," he might say, " such things are far apart from prayer to God. We go and do them, it is true, because they are a necessity of our animal nature, but prayer or worship have nothing to do with such coarseness. We may pray before or after (as in Grace) on taking food, but the physical acts between are not prayer. Such notions are based partly on that dualism which keeps separate and apart God and His creature, and partly on certain false and depreciatory notions concerning matter and material functions. According to Indian Monism such worship is not only understandable but (I am not speaking of any particular form of it) the only religious attitude consistent with its principles.

Man is, in his essence or spirit, divine and one with the universal Spirit. His mind and body and all their functions are divine, for they are not merely a manifestation of the Power (Shakti) of God but that Power itself. To say that matter is in itself low or evil is to calumniate that Power. Nothing in natural function is low or impure to the mind which recognizes it as Shakti and the working of Shakti. It is the ignorant and, in a true sense, vulgar mind which regards any natural function as low or coarse. The action in this case is seen in the light of the inner vulgarity of mind. It has been suggested that in its proper application the Maithuna Karma is only an application to sexual function of the principles of Yoga (Masson-Oursel Historie de la Philosophie Indienne, pp. 231-233). Once the reality of the world as grounded in the Absolute is established, the body seems to be less an obstacle to freedom, for it is a form of that self-same Absolute. The creative function being natural is not in itself culpable. There is no real antinomy between Spirit and Nature which is an instrument for the realization of the Spirit. The method borrows, it is said (*ib.*), that of Yoga not to frustrate, but to regulate enjoyment. Conversely enjoyment produces Yoga by the union of body and spirit. In the psycho-physiological rites of these Shāktas enjoyment is not an obstacle to Yoga but may also be a means to it. This, he says, is an important conception which recalls the discovery of the Mahāyāna that Samsāra and Nirvāna are one. For here are made one, Yoga which liberates and Bhoga which enchains (*ib.*). It will then be readily understood that according to this doctrine only those are competent for this Yoga who are truly free, or on the way to freedom, of all dualism.

External worship demands certain acts and instruments, such as bodily attitude, speech, and materials with which the rite is done, such as flowers, incense, lights, water and other offerings. These materials and instruments are called Upachāra. Ordinarily there are sixteen of these, but they may be more or less. There is nothing absolute in either the quality, quantity or nature of the offerings. Ordinarily such things are offered as might be given to guests or friends or others whom the worshipper loves, such as seat (Āsana), welcome (Svāgata), water to wash the feet (Pādya), food (Naivedya), cloths (Vasana), jewels (Ābharana), with other things such as lights, incense and flowers. In inner or mental worship (Mānasapūjā) these are not things material, but of the mind of the worshipper. Pleasing things are selected as offering to the Devatā because the worshipper wishing to please Devatā offers what he thinks to be pleasant and would be glad himself to receive. But a man who recognized the divinity (and therefore value) of all things might offer any. With such a disposition a piece of mud or a stone would be as good an offering as any other. There are some things the ordinary man looks upon as "unclean" and, as long as he does so, to offer such a thing would be an offence. But, if to his "equal eye" these things are not so, they might be given. Thus the Vīra-sādhanā of the Shākta Tantra makes ritual use of what will appear to most to be impure and repulsive substances. This (as the Jnānārnava Tantra says) is done to accustom the worshipper not to see impurity in them but to regard them as all else, as manifestation of Divinity. He is taught that there is nothing impure in itself in natural functions though they be made, by misuse or abuse, the instruments of impurity. Here again impurity consists not in the act *per se* but in the way and in the intention with which it is done. To a Vīra all things, acts, and functions, done with right intention, may be instruments of worship. For, a Vīra is one who seeks to overcome Tamas by Sattva. Therefore, the natural functions of eating, drinking and sexual union may be used as Upachāra of worship. This does not mean that a man may do what he likes as regards these things and pass them off as worship. They must be rightly done, otherwise, a man would be offering his sin to Devatā. The *principle* of all this is entirely sound. The only question which exists is as regards the *application* to which the ritual in question puts it. Worship and prayer are not merely the going aside at a particular time or place to utter set formulæ or to perform particular ritual acts. The whole of life, in all its rightful particulars, without any single exception, may be an act of worship if man but makes it so. Who can rightly deny this? Of course, as long as a man regards any function as impure or matter of shame, his mental disposition is such that he cannot worship therewith. To do so would distract and perturb him. But both to the natural-minded and illuminate man this is possible. The principle here dealt with is not entirely peculiar to this school. Those Hindus who are not Monists, [and whatever be their philosophical theories, no worshippers in practice are so, for worship connotes the dualism of worshipped (Upāsya) and worshipper (Upāsaka), of the means or instrument (Sādhana) and that to be attained thereby (Sādhya)], yet make offering of their acts to Devatā. By thus offering all their daily speech, each word they say becomes, in the words of Shāstra, Mantra. Nor, if we examine it, is the principle alien to Christianity, for the Christian may, in opening his day, offer all his acts therein to God. What he thereafter does is worship. The difference in these cases and that of the Vīra principle lies (at any rate in practice) in this, that the latter is more thorough in its application, no act or function being excluded, and in worship, the Shākta being a Monist is taught to regard the offering not as given to someone other than his own essential Self, but to That. He is thus, according to the theory of this practice, led to divinise his functions, and by their constant association with the thought of Brahman his mind is, it is said, purified and led away from all carnal desires. If these functions are set apart as something common or impure, victory is not easily won. There is still some part of his life into which Brahman does not enter and which remains the source of distraction. By associating them with religion, it is the religious feeling which works first *through* and then *supersedes* them. He thus gradually attains Divyabhāva and the state of the Devatā he has worshipped. For it is common Indian principle that the end of worship is to assimilate oneself to its object or Devatā. Thus it is said in the Agni Purāna that by worship of Rudra one become Rudra, by worship of Vishnu one becomes Vishnu, and by worship of Shakti one becomes Shakti. This is so because the mind mentally transforms itself into the likeness of that on which it is set. By thinking always, on the other hand, on sensual objects one becomes sensual. Even before worship, one should strive to attain the true attitude of worship, and so the Gandharva Tantra says, "He who is not Deva (Adeva) should not worship Deva. The Deva alone should worship Deva." The Vīra or strictly the Sādhaka qualified to enter Vīrāchāra—since the true Vīra is its finished product—commences Sādhanā with this Rājasik Upāsanā with the Panchatattva as Upachāra which are employed for the transformation of the sensual tendencies they connote. I have heard the view expressed that this part of the Shāstra was really promulgated for Shūdras. Shiva knowing the animal propensities of their common life must lead them to take flesh and wine, prescribed these rites with a view to lessen the evil and to gradually wean them from enjoyment by promulgating conditions under which alone such enjoyment could be had, and in associating it with religion. "It is better to bow to Nārāyana with one's shoes on than never to bow at all." A man with a taste for drink will only increase his thirst by animal satisfaction (Pashupāna). But if when he drinks he can be made to regard the liquid as a divine manifestation and have thought of God, gradually such thoughts will overcome and oust his sensual desires. On the same principle children are given powders in jam, though this method is not confined to actual children only. Those who so argue contend that a Brāhmana should, on no account, take wine, and Texts are cited which are said to support this view. I have dealt with this matter in the Introduction to the sixth volume of "Tāntrik Texts". It is sufficient to say here that the reply given is that such Texts refer to the unauthorized consumption of wine as by uninitiated (Anabhishikta) Brāhmanas. In the same place I have discussed the question whether wine can be taken at all by any one in this Kali age. For, according to some authorities, there is only Pashubhāva in the Kaliyuga. If this be correct then all wine-drinking, whether ritual or otherwise, is prohibited.

For the worship of Shakti, the Panchatattva are declared to be essential. Without the Panchatattva in one form or another Shaktipūjā cannot be performed (Mahānirvāna, V. 23-24). The reason of this is that those who worship Shakti, worship Divinity as Creatrix and in the form of the universe. If She appears as and in natural function, She must be worshipped therewith, otherwise, as the Tantra cited says, worship is fruitless. The Mother of the Universe must be worshipped with these five elements, namely, wine, meat, fish, grain, and woman, or their substitutes. By their use the universe (Jagad-brahmānda) itself is used as the article of worship (Upachāra). The

Mahānirvāna (VII. 103-111) says that wine which gives joy and dispels the sorrows of men is Fire; flesh which nourishes and increases the strength of mind and body is Air; fish which increases generative power is Water, cereals grown on earth and which are the basis of life are Earth, and sexual union, which is the root of the world and the origin of all creation, is Ether. They thus signify the Power (Shakti) which produces all fiery elements, all terrestrial and aquatic life, all vegetable life, and the will, knowledge and action of the Supreme Prakriti productive of that great bliss which accompanies the process of creation. (See also Haratattvadīdhiti XV, Kāmākhya Tantra, Nigamatattvasāra IV). The Kailāsa Tantra (Pūrvākhyā, Ch. XC) identifies this Pentad (Panchatattva) with the five vital airs (Prānādi) and the five Mahāpreta which support the couch of Tripurasundarī.

With these preliminaries, and postponing for the moment further comment, we may proceed to an examination in greater detail of the five (Pancha) elements (Tattva), namely, Wine (Madya), Meat (Māmsa), Fish (Matsya), Parched Cereal (Mudrā), and Sexual Union (Maithuna) which stand for drinking, eating and propagation. Because they all commence with the letter M, they are vulgarly called Pancha-ma-kāra (or five M's).

These Panchatattva, Kuladravya or Kulatattva as they are called, have more esoteric names. Thus the last is known as "the fifth". Woman is called Shakti or Prakriti. A Tāntrik commonly calls his wife his Shakti or Bhairavī. Woman is also called Latā or "creeper", because woman clings to and depends on man as the creeper does to the tree. Hence the ritual in which woman is enjoyed is called Latāsādhana. Wine is called "causal water" (Kāranavāri) or Tīrtha water (Tīrthavāri).

But the Panchatattva have not always their literal meaning. The meaning differs according as they refer to the Tāmasik (Pashvāchāra), Rājasik (Vīrāchāra) or Sāttvik (Divyāchāra) Sādhanās respectively. "Wine" is only wine and Maithuna is only sexual union in the ritual of the Vīra. To the Pashu, the Vīra ritual (Vīrāchāra) is prohibited as unsuitable to his state, and the Divya, unless of the lower ritual kind, is beyond such things. The result is that the Panchatattva have each three meanings. Thus "wine" may be wine (Vīra ritual), or it may be cocoanut water (Pashu ritual) or it may mean the intoxicating knowledge of the Supreme attained by Yoga, according as it is used in connection with the Vīra, the Pashu, or the Divya respectively. The Panchatattva are thus threefold, namely, real (Pratyakshatattva) where "wine" means wine, substitutional (Anukalpatattva) where wine means cocoanut water or some other liquid, and symbolical or divine (Divyatattva) where it is a symbol to denote the joy of Yoga-knowledge. The Pashu worships with the substitutional Tattvas mentioned later and never takes wine, the Vīra worships with wine, and the Divya's "wine" is spiritual knowledge. There are further modifications of these general rules in the case of the intermediate Bhāvas. Thus the author next cited says that whilst the Svabhāva Vīra is a drinker of wine, the Vibhāva Vīra worships internally with the five mental Tattvas and externally with substitutes. The Mantrasiddhavīra is free to do as he pleases in this matter, subject to the general Shāstrik rules. In an essay by Pandit Jayachandra Siddhāntabhūshana, answering certain charges made against the Tantra Shāstra, he, after stating that neither the Vibhāva Vīra nor Vibhāva Pashu need worship with real wine, says that in modern Bengal this kind of worship is greatly prevalent. Such Tāntriks do not take wine but otherwise worship according to the rule of Tantra Shāstra. It is, as he says, an erroneous but common notion that a "Tāntrika" necessarily means a drinker of wine. Some Sādhakas again, in lieu of the material Maithuna, imagine the union of Shiva and Shakti in the upper brain centre known as the Sahasrāra.

The Divya Panchatattva for those of a truly Sāttvika or spiritual temperament (Divyabhāva) have been described as follows: "Wine" (Madya) according to Kaula Tantra (see p. 85 of Panchattva-vichāra by Nīlamani Mukhyopādhyāya) is not any liquid, but that intoxicating knowledge acquired by Yoga of the Parabrahman which renders the worshipper senseless as regards the external world. "Meat" (Māmsa) is not any fleshly thing, but the act whereby the Sādhaka consigns all his acts to Me (Mām), that is, the Lord, "Fish" (Matsya) is that Sāttvik knowledge by which through the sense of "Mineness" (a play upon the word Matsya) the worshipper sympathizes with the pleasure and pain of all beings. Mudrā is the act of relinquishing all association with evil which results in bondage. Coition (Maithuna) is the union of the Shakti Kundalinī, the "Inner woman" and World-force in the lowest centre (Mūlādhāra Chakra) of the Sādhaka's body with the Supreme Shiva in the highest centre (Sahasrāra) in the upper Brain (see Essay on Kundalinī Shakti *post*). This, the Yoginī Tantra (Ch. VI) says, is the best of all unions for those who are Yati, that is, who have controlled their passions.

Sahasrāropari bindau kundalyā melanam Shīve
Maithunam paramaṁ dravyam yatīnām parikīrtitam.

According to the Āgamasāra, 'wine' is the Somadhārā or lunar ambrosia which drops from the Sahasrāra. "Meat" (Māmsa) is the tongue (Mā) of which its part (Amsha) is speech. The Sādhaka in eating it controls his speech. "Fish" (Matsya) are those two (Vāyu or currents) which are constantly moving, in the two "rivers" (that is, Yoga "nerves" or Nādīs) called Idā and Pingalā, that is, the sympathetics on each side of the spinal column. He who controls his breath by Prāṇāyāma, "eats" then by Kumbhaka or retention of breath. Mudrā is the awakening of knowledge in the pericarp of the great Sahasrāra Lotus (the upper brain) where the Ātmā resplendent as ten million suns and deliciously cool as ten million moons is united with the Devī Kundalinī, the World-force and Consciousness in individual bodies, after Her ascent thereto from the Mūlādhāra in Yoga. The esoteric meaning of coition or Maithuna is thus stated in the Āgama. The ruddy hued Ra is in the Kunda (ordinarily the seed-mantra Ram is in Manipūra but perhaps here the Kunda in the Mūlādhāra is meant). The letter Ma [white like the autumnal moon, Sattvaguna, Kaivalyarūpa-prakritirūpī (Ch. 2, Kāmadhenu Tantra)] is in the Mahāyoni (not I may observe the genitals but the lightning-like triangle or Yoni in the Sahasrāra or upper brain) in the form of Bindu (a Ghanībhūta or "condensed" form of Shakti and transformation of Nāda-shakti). When M (Makāra) seated on the Hamsa (the "bird" which is the pair Shiva-Shakti as Jīva) in the form of A (A-kāra) unites with R (Ra-kāra) then Brahman knowledge (Brahmajnāna) which is the source of supreme bliss is gained by the Sādhaka who is then called Ātmārāma (Enjoyer with the Self), for his enjoyment is in the Ātmā in the Sahasrāra. (For this reason too the word Rāma, which also means sexual enjoyment, is equivalent to the liberator-Brahman, Ra + a + ma.) The union of Shiva and Shakti is described (Tantrasāra, 702) as true Yoga (*Shivashaktisamāyogo yoga eva na samshayah*) from which, as the Yāmala says, arises that Joy which is known as the Supreme Bliss (*ib.*, 703) (*Samyogāj jāyate saukhyam paramānandalakshanam*).

This is the union on the purely Sāttvik plane which corresponds in the Rājasik plane to the union of Shiva and Shakti in the persons of their worshippers. It will have been observed that here in this Divya or Sāttvik Sādhanā

"Wine", "Woman" and so forth are really names for Yogik operations.

The substitutional Tattvas of Pashvāchāra also do not answer to their names, being other substances which are taken as substitutes of wine, meat, fish (see Kulachūdāmani; Bhairavayāmala, Ch. I). These have been variously described and sometimes as follows: In lieu of wine the Pashu should, if a Brāhmana, take milk, if a Kshatriya ghee, if a Vaishya honey, and if a Shūdra a liquor made from rice. Cocoanut water in a bell-metal utensil is also taken as a substitute. Salt, ginger, sesamum, wheat beans (Māshakalāi) and garlic are some of the substitutes for meat; the white brinjal vegetable, red radish, masur (a kind of gram), red sesamum and Pāniphala (an aquatic plant) take the place of fish. Paddy, rice, wheat and grain generally are Mudrā both in Tāmasik (Pashvāchāra) and Rājasik (Vīrāchāra) Sādhanās. In lieu of Maithuna there may be an offering of flowers with the hands formed into the gesture called Kachchhapa-mudrā, the union of the Karavīra flower (representative of the Liṁga) with the Aprājitā (Clitoria) flower which is shaped as and represents the female Yoni and other substitutes, or there may be union with the Sādhaka's wife. On this and some other matters here dealt with there is variant practice.

The Kaulikārchanadīpikā speaks of what is called the Ādyatattvas. Ādyamadya or wine is hemp (Vijayā), Ādyashuddhi or meat is ginger (Ādraka), Ādyamīna or fish is citron (Jambīra), Ādyamudrā is Dhānyaja that is, made from paddy and Ādyashakti is the worshipper's own wife. Quoting from the Tantrāntara it says that worship without these Ādya forms is fruitless. Even the strictest total abstainer and vegetarian will not object to "wine" in the shape of hot milk or cocoanut water, or to ginger or other substitutes for meat. Nor is there any offence in regarding sexual union between the Sādhaka and his wife not as a mere animal function but as a sacrificial rite (Yajna).

At this point we may pass to the literal Tattvas. Wine here is not merely grape-wine but that which is made from various substances such as molasses (Gaudī), rice (Paishtī) or the Madhūka flower (Mādhvī) which are said by the Mahānirvāna Tantra (Ch. VI) to be the best. There are others such as wine made from the juice of the Palmyra and date tree, and aniseed (Maureya wine). Meat is of three kinds, that is, animals of the water, earth, and sky. But no female animal must be slain. Superior kinds of fish are Shāla, Pāthīna, and Rohita. Mudrā which every Orientalist whom I have read calls "ritual gesture" or the like is nothing of the kind here, though that is a meaning of the term Mudrā in another connection. They cannot have gone far into the subject, for it is elementary knowledge that in the Panchatattva, Mudrā means parched cereal of various kinds and is defined in Yoginī Tantra (Ch. VI) as:

Bhrishtadhānyādikam yadyad charvanīyam prachakshate
Sā mudrā kathitā Devi sarveshām Naganandini.

(Oh Daughter of the Mountain, fried paddy and the like—in fact all such (cereals) as are chewed—are called Mudrā.)

The Mahānirvāna (Ch. VI) says that the most excellent is that made from Shāli rice or from barley or wheat and which has been fried in clarified butter. Meat, fish, Mudrā offered to the Devatā along with wine is technically called Shuddhi. The Mahānirvāna says that the drinking of wine without Shuddhi is like the swallowing of poison and the Sādhanā is fruitless. It is not difficult to see why. For, wine taken without food has greater effect and produces greater injury. Moreover, another check on indiscriminate drinking is placed, for wine cannot be taken unless Shuddhi is obtained, prepared, and eaten with the necessary rites. Woman, or Shakti, as She is properly called, since She is purified and consecrated for the rite and represents the Devī, is of three kinds, namely, Svīyā or Svakīyā (one's own wife), Parakīyā the wife of another or some other woman, and Sādhāranī or one who is common. This aspect of the subject I deal with later. Here I will only say that, where sexual union is permitted at all, the ordinary Shakti is the Sādhaka's Brāhmī wife. It is only under certain conditions that there can be any other Shakti. Shaktis are also of two kinds, namely, those who are enjoyed (Bhogyā) and those who are worshipped only (Pūjyā). A Sādhaka who yields to desire for the latter commits the sin of incest with his own mother.

Here again, according to Shākta notions, one must not think of these substances as mere gross matter in the form of wine, meat and so forth, nor on woman as mere woman; nor upon the rite as a mere common meal. The usual daily rites must be performed in the morning, midday and evening (Mahānirvāna, V. 25). These are elaborate (*ib.*) and take up a large part of the day. Bhūtashuddhi is accomplished, at which time the Sādhaka thinks that a Deva body has arisen as his own. Various Nyāsas are done. Mental worship is performed of the Devī, the Ādyā Kālikā, who is thought of as being in red raiment seated on a red lotus. Her body dark like a rain-cloud, Her forehead gleaming with the light of the crescent moon. Japa of Mantra is then done and outer worship follows. A further elaborate ritual succeeds.

I pause here to ask the reader to conceive the nature of the mind and disposition of the Sādhaka who has sincerely performed these rites. Is it likely to be lustful or gluttonous? The curse is removed from the wine and the Sādhaka meditates upon the union of Deva and Devī in it. Wine is to be considered as Devatā. After the consecration of the wine, the meat, fish and grain are purified and are made like unto nectar. The Shakti is sprinkled with Mantra and made the Sādhaka's own. She is the Devī Herself in the form of woman. The wine is charged with Mantras ending with the realization (Mahānirvāna Tantra, VI. 42) when Homa is done, that offering is made of the excellent nectar of "This-ness" (Idantā) held in the cup of "I-ness" (Ahantā) into the Fire which is the Supreme I-ness (Parāhantā).

Ahantāpātra-bharitam idantāparamāmritam
Parāhantāmaye vahnau homasvīkāralākshanam.

Here the distinction is drawn between the "I" (Aham) and the "This". The former is either the Supreme "I" (Parāhantā or Shiva) or the individual "I" (Jīva) vehicled by the "This" or Vimarsha-Shakti. The Sādhaka is the cup or vessel which is the individual Ego. "This-ness" is offered to the Supreme. Drinking is an offering to that Fire which is the transcendent Self "whence all individual selves (Jīva) proceed". Wine is then Tārā Dravamayī, that is, the Saviouress Herself in the form of liquid matter (Mahānirvāna, XI. 105-107). None of the Tattvas can be offered unless first purified and consecrated, otherwise the Sādhaka goes to Hell. With further ritual the first four Tattvas are consumed, the wine being poured as an oblation into the mouth of Kundali, after meditation upon Her as Consciousness (Chit) spread from Her seat, the Mūlādhāra to the tip of the tongue. The whole ritual is of great interest, and I hope to give a fuller exposition of it on some future day.

Worship with the Panchatattva generally takes place in a Chakra or circle composed of men and women, Sādhakas and Sādhikās, Bhairavas and Bhairavīs sitting in a circle, the Shakti being on the Sādhaka's Left. Hence it is called Chakrapūjā. A Lord of the Chakra (Chakreshvara) presides sitting with his Shakti in the centre. During the Chakra, there is no distinction of caste, but Pashus of any caste are excluded. There are various kinds of Chakra—productive, it is said, of differing fruits for the participator therein. As amongst Tāntrik Sādhakas we come across the high, the low, and mere pretenders, so the Chakras vary in their characteristics from say the Tattva-chakra for the Brahma-kaulas, and the Bhairavī-chakra (as described in Mahānirvāna, VIII. 153) in which, in lieu of wine, the householder takes milk, sugar and honey (Madhura-traya), and in lieu of sexual union does meditation upon the Lotus Feet of the Divine Mother with Mantra, to Chakras the ritual of which will not be approved such as Chūdāchakra, Ānandabhuvana-yoga and others referred to later. Just as there are some inferior "Tāntrik" writings, so we find rituals of a lower type of men whose notions or practices were neither adopted by high Sādhakas in the past nor will, if they survive, be approved for practice to-day. What is wanted is a discrimination which avoids both unjust general condemnations and, with equal ignorance, unqualified commendations which do harm. I refer, in my Essay on "Shakti and Shākta", to a modern Chakra. I heard a short time ago of a Guru, influenced by an English education, whose strictness went so far that the women did not form part of the Chakra but sat in another room. This was of course absurd.

The two main objections to the Rājasik Pūjā are from both the Hindu and European standpoint the alleged infraction of sexual morality, and from the former standpoint, the use of wine. By "Hindu" I mean those who are not Shāktas. I will deal with the latter point first. The Vīra Shākta admits the Smārta rule against the drinking of wine. He, however, says that drinking is of two kinds, namely, extra-ritual drinking for the satisfaction of sensual appetite, and the ritual drinking of previously purified and consecrated wine. The former is called Pashupāna or "animal drinking," and Vrithāpāna or "useless drinking": for, being no part of worship, it is forbidden, does no good, but on the contrary injury, and leads to Hell. The Western's drinking (even a moderate "whisky and soda") is Pashupāna. The Vīrāchārī, like every other Hindu, condemns this and regards it as a great sin. But drinking for the purpose of worship is held to stand on a different ground. Just as the ancient Vaidiks drank Soma as part of the Sacrifice (Yajna), so does the Vīra drink wine as part of his ritual. Just as the killing of animals for the purpose of sacrifice is accounted no "killing", so that it does not infringe against the rule against injury (Ahimsā), so also drinking as part of worship is said not to be the drinking which the Smritis forbid. For this reason it is contended that the Tāntrik secret worship (Rahasya-pūjā) is not opposed to Veda. The wine is no longer the gross injurious material substance, but has been purified and spiritualized, so that the true Sādhaka looks upon it as the liquid form of the Saviour, Devī (Tārā Dravamayī). The joy it produces is but a faint welling up of the Bliss (Ānanda), which in its essence it is. Wine, moreover, is then taken under certain restrictions and conditions which should, if adhered to, prevent the abuse which follows on merely sensual drinking (Pashupāna). The true Sādhaka does not perform the ritual for the purpose of drinking wine, (though possibly in these degenerate days many do) but drinks wine in order that he may perform the ritual. Thus, to take an analogous case, a Christian abstainer might receive wine in the Eucharist believing it to be the blood of his Lord. He would not partake of the sacrament in order that he might have the opportunity of drinking wine, but he would drink wine because that is the way by which he might take the Eucharist, of which wine together with bread (Mudrā) is an element. I may here mention in this connection that not only are drops of wine sometimes sprinkled on the Prasāda (sacred food) at Durgā-pūjā and thus consumed by persons who are not Vīrāchārīs, but (though this is not generally known and will perhaps not be admitted) on the Prasāda which all consume at the Vaishnava shrine of Jagannātha at Puri.

This question about the consumption of wine will not appear to the average European a serious affair, though it is so to the non-Shākta Hindu. So strong is the general feeling against it that when Babu Keshab Chandra Sen, in one of his imitations of Christian doctrine and ritual, started an Eucharist of his own, the elements were rice and water. It is, however, a matter of common reproach against these Tāntriks that some at least drink to excess. That may be so. From what I have heard but little credit attaches to the common run of this class of Tāntriks to-day. Apart from the general degeneracy which has affected all forms of Hindu religion, it is to be remembered that in ancient times nothing was done except under the authority of the Guru. He alone could say whether his disciple was competent for any particular ritual. It was not open to any one to enter upon it and do as he pleased. Nevertheless, we must clearly distinguish between the commands of the Shāstra itself and abuses of its provisions by pretended Sādhakas. It is obvious that excessive drinking prevents the attainment of success and is a fall. As the Mahānirvāna (VI. 195-197; see also VIII. 171) with good sense says, "How is it possible for a sinner who becomes a fool through drink to say "I worship Adyā Kālikā'." William James says ("Varieties of Religious Experience", 387) "The sway of alcohol over mankind is unquestionably due to its power to stimulate the mystical faculties of human nature, usually crushed to earth by the cold fact and dry criticisms of the sober hour. It unites. It is in fact the greatest exciter of the "Yes" function in man. It brings him from the chill periphery of things to the radiant core." In its effect it is one bit of the mystic consciousness. Wine, as is well-known, also manifests and emphasizes the true disposition of a man ("In vino veritas."). (As to wine, drugs and 'anæsthetic revelation' as to the clue to the meaning of life see R. Thouless, "Introduction to Psychology of Religion," 61.) When the worshipper is of a previously pure and devout disposition, the moderate use of wine heightens his feelings of devotion. But if it is drunk in excess there can be no devotion at all, but only sin. This same Tantra therefore, whilst doing away with wine in the case of one class of Chakra, and limiting the consumption in any case for householders, says that excessive drinking prevents success coming to Kaula worshippers, who may not drink to such an extent that the mind is affected (literally "goes round"). "To drink beyond this", it says, "is bestial."

Yāvan na chālayed drishtir yāvan na chālayen manah
Tāvat pānam prakurvvīta pashu-pānam atah param.

Yet the fact that the Mahānirvāna thought it necessary to give this injunction is significant of some abuse. Similar counsel may be found however elsewhere; as in the Shyāmarahasya which says that excessive drinking leads to Hell. Thus also the great Tantrarāja (Kādimata) says (Ch. VIII) (Tāntrik Texts, Vol. VIII).

Na kadāchit pivet siddho devyarghyam aniveditam
Pānancha tāvat kurvīta yāvatā syān manolayah
Tatah karoti chet sadyah pātakī bhavati dhruvam
Devatāgurusevānyat pivannāsavam āshayā
Pātakī rājadandyash chāvidyopāsaka eva cha.

(The Siddha should never drink the Arghya (wine) meant for the Devī, unless the same has been first offered (to Her). Drinking, again, should only be continued so long as the mind is absorbed (in the Devī). He who does so thereafter is verily a sinner. He who drinks wine through mere sensual desire and not for the purpose of worship of Devatā and Guru is a worshipper of Ignorance (Avidyā) and a sinner punishable by the King.)

It must be admitted, however, that there are to be found words and passages which, if they are to be taken literally, would indicate that wine was not always taken in moderation. (See Āsavollāsa in Kulārnava. The Ullāsas, however, are stated to be stages of initiation.) In reading any Hindu Scripture, however, one must allow for exaggeration which is called "Stuti". Thus if there is much meat and wine we may read of "mountains of flesh" and "oceans of wine". Such statements were not made to be taken literally. Some descriptions again may refer to Kaulāvadhūtas who, like other "great" men in other matters, appear to have more liberty than ordinary folk. Some things may not be "the word of Shiva" at all. It is open to any one to sit down and write a "Tantra," "Stotra" or what not. The Ānanda Stotra, for example, reads in parts like a libertine's drinking song. Though it has been attributed both to the Kulachūdāmani and Kulārnava, a learned Tāntrik Pandit, to whom I am much indebted and to whom I showed it, laughed and said, "How can this be the word of Shiva. It is not Shiva Shāstra. If it is not the writing of some fallen Upāsaka (worshipper), it is the work of Āchāryyas trying to tempt disciples to themselves." Though a man of Tāntrik learning of a kind rarely met with to-day, and a practitioner of the Chakrapūjā, he told me that he had never heard of this Stotra until it was sung at a Chakra in Benares. On asking another

Pandit there about it, he was told not to trouble himself over "what these kind of people did". Even when the words *Shiva uvācha* (Shiva said) appear in a work, it does not follow that it has any authority. Though all the world condemns, as does the Shāstra itself, excessive drinking, yet it cannot be said that, according to views generally accepted by the mass of men in the world to-day, the drinking of alcohol is a sin. General morality may yet account it such in some future day.

I pass then to the other matter, namely, sexual union. The ordinary rule, as the Kaulīkārchana-Dīpikā says (I refer to the exception later), is that worship should be done with the worshipper's own wife, called the Ādyā Shakti. This is the general Tāntrik rule. Possibly because the exception to it led to abuse, the Mahānirvāna (VIII. 173), after pointing out that men in the Kali age are weak of mind and distracted by lust, and so do not recognize woman (Shakti) to be the image of Deity, prescribes for such as these (in the Bhairavī Chakra) meditation on the Feet of the Divine Mother in lieu of Maithuna, or where the worship is with the Shakti (Bhogyā) in Bhairavī and Tattva Chakra the worshipper should be wedded to his Shakti according to Shaiva rites. It adds (*ib.*, 129) that "the Vīra, who without marriage worships by enjoyment a Shakti, is without doubt guilty of the sin of going with another woman." Elsewhere (VI. 14) it points out that when the evil age (Kaliyuga) is at its strength, the wife alone should be the fifth Tattva for "this is void of all defect" (Sarva-dosha-vivarjita). The Sammohana Tantra (Ch. 2) also says that the Kali age is dominated by lust (Kāma) and it is then most difficult to subjugate the senses and that by reason of the prevalence of ignorance (Avidyā) the female Yoni is used for worship. That is, by reason of the material nature of man a material form is used to depict the supreme

Yoni or Cause of all. The commentator on the Mahānirvāna Tantra, Pandit Jaganmohana Tarkālankāra (see Bhakta Ed. 345) says, however, that this rule is not of universal application. Shiva (he says) in this Tantra prohibited Sādhanā with the fifth Tattva with other Shaktis in the case of men of ordinary weak intellect ruled by lust; but for those who have by Sādhanā conquered their passions and attained the state of a true Siddha Vīra, there is no prohibition as to the mode of Latāsādhanā. With this I deal later, but meanwhile I may observe that because there is a Shakti in the Chakra it does not follow that there is sexual intercourse, which, when it occurs in the worship of householders, ordinarily takes place outside the Chakra. Shaktis are of two kinds—those who are enjoyed (Bhogyā Shakti) and those who are worshipped only (Pūjyā) as earthly representatives of the Supreme Mother of all. Those who yield to desire, even in thought, as regards the latter commit the sin of incest with their mother. Similarly, there is a widespread practice amongst all Shāktas of worship of Virgins (Kumārīpūjā)—a very beautiful ceremony. So also in Brahmarājayoga there is worship of virgins only.

It is plain that up to this point there is (apart from the objection of other Hindus to wine) nothing to be said against the morality of the Sādhanā prescribed, though some may take exception to the association of natural function of any kind, however legitimate, with what they regard as worship. This is not a question of morality and I have dealt with it. The reader will also remember that the ritual already described applies to the general mass of worshippers, and that to which I am passing is the ritual of the comparatively few, and so-called advanced Sādhakas. The charge of immorality against all Shāktas, whether following this ritual or not, fails, and people need not run away in fear on hearing that a man is a "Tāntrik". He may not be a Shākta Tāntrik at all, and if he is a Shākta, he may have done nothing to which the world at large will take moral exception.

I now pass to another class of cases. Generally speaking, we may distinguish not only between Dakshināchāra and Vāmāchāra in which the full rites with wine and Shakti are performed, but also between a Vāma and Dakshina division of the latter Āchāra itself. It is on the former side that there is worship with a woman (Parakīyā Shakti) other than the Sādhaka's own wife (Svakīyā Shakti). But under what circumstances? It is necessary (as Professor de la Vallée Poussin, the Catholic Belgian Sanskritist, says (Adhikarma-pradīpa, 141) of the Buddhist Tantra) to remember the *conditions* under which these Tāntrik rituals are, according to the Shāstra, admissible, when judging of their morality, otherwise, he says condemnation becomes excessive ("*Je crois d'ailleurs qu'on a exageré la charactére d'immoralite des actes liturgiques de Maithuna faute d'avoir fixé les diverses conditions dans lesquelles ils, doivent etre pratiqués.*" See also Masson-Oursel Esquisse dune Histoire de la Philosophie Indienne 1923, p. 230, who says that Western people often see obscenity where there is only symbolism.) As I have said, the ordinary rule is that the wife or Ādyā Shakti should be co-performer (Sahadharminī) in the rite. An exception, however, exists where the Sādhaka has no wife or she is incompetent (Anadhikārinī). There seems to be a notion that the Shāstra directs union with some other person than the Sādhakā's wife. This is not so. A direction to go after other women as such would be counsel to commit fornication or adultery. What the Shāstra says is—that if the Sādhaka has no wife, or she is incompetent (Anadhikārinī) then only may the Ṣādhaka take some other Shakti. Next, this is for the purpose of ritual worship only. Just as any extra-ritual drinking is sin, so also outside worship any Maithuna, otherwise than with the wife, is sin. The Tattvas of each kind can only be offered after purification (Shodhana) and during worship according to the rules, restrictions, and conditions of the Tāntrik ritual. (See Tantrasāra, 698, citing Bhāvachūdāmani, Uttara-Kulāmrita. In Ch. IV, Brihannīla Tantra it is said *Paradārān na gachchheran gachchhech cha prāpayed yadi*, but that is for purposes of worship). Outside worship the mind is not even to think of the subject, as is said concerning the Shakti in the Uttara Tantra.

Pūjākālam vinā nānyam purusham manasā sprishet
Pūjā-kāle cha Deveshi veshyeva paritoshayet.

What then is the meaning of this "competency" the non-existence of which relaxes the ordinary rule? The principle on which worship is done with another Shakti is stated in the Guhyakālīkhanda of the Mahākāla Samhitā as follows:

Yādrishah sādhakah proktah sādhikā 'pi cha tādrishī
Tatah siddhim avāpnoti nānyathā varsha-kotibhih.

("As is the competency of the Sādhaka so must be that of the Sādhikā. In this way only is success attained and not otherwise even in ten million years.") That is both the man and the woman must be on the same level and plane of development. Thus, in the performance of the great Shodhānyāsa, the Shakti must be possessed of the same powers and competency as the Sādhaka. In other words, a Sahadharminī must have the same competency as the Sādhaka with whom she performs the rite. Next, it is not for any man at his own undisciplined will to embark on a practice of this kind. He can only do so if adjudged competent by his Guru. A person of an ignorant, irreligious, and lewd disposition is, properly, incompetent. Then, it is commonly thought, that because another Shakti is permitted, unlimited promiscuity is allowed. This is of course not so. It must be admitted that the Shākta Tantra at least pretends to be a religious Scripture, and could not as such directly promote immorality in this way. For, under no pretence can morality, or Sādhanā for spiritual advancement, be served by directions for, or tacit permissions of, uncontrolled promiscuous sexual intercourse. There may, of course, have been hypocrites wandering around the country and its women who sought to cover their lasciviousness with the cloak of a pretended religion. But this is not Sādhanā but conscious sin. The fruit of Sādhanā is lost by license and the growth of sensuality. The proper rule, I am told, is that the relationship with such a Shakti should be of a permanent character; it being indeed held that a Shakti who is abandoned by the Sādhaka takes away with her the latter's merit (Punya). The position of such a Shakti may be described as a wife "in religion" for the Sādhaka, one who being of his competency (Adhikāra) works with him as Sahadharminī, in the performance of the rituals of their common cult. In all cases, the Shakti must be first made lawful according to the rules of the cult by the performance of the Shaiva sacrament (Shaiva-samskāra). From a third party view it may, of course, be said that the necessity for all this is not seen. I am not here concerned with that, but state the rules of the cult as I find it. It is desirable, in the interests both of the history of religion and of justice to the cult described, to state these facts accurately. For, it is sound theology, that good faith is inconsistent with sin. We cannot call a man immoral who is acting according to his lights and in good faith. Amongst a polygamous people such as were the Jews and as are the Hindus, it would be absurd to call a man immoral, who in good faith practised that polygamy which was allowable by the usage which governed him. Other Hindus might or might not acknowledge the status of a Shaiva wife. But a Shaiva who was bound to a woman in that form would not be an immoral man. Immorality, in the sense in which an individual is made responsible for his actions, exists where what is believed to be wrong is consciously followed. And so whilst a Tāntrik acting in good faith and according to his Shāstra is not in this sense immoral, other Tāntriks who misused the ritual for their libidinous purposes would be so. So, of course, would also be those who to-day, without belief in the Tantra Shāstra, and to satisfy their passions, practised such rituals as run counter to prevalent social morality. Though the genuine Tāntrik might be excused, they would not escape the charge. When, however, we are judging a religion by the standard of another, which claims to be higher, the lower religion may be considered immoral. The distinction is commonly overlooked which exists between the question whether an individual is immoral and whether the teaching and practice which he follows is so. We may, with logical consistency, answer the first in the negative and the second in the affirmative. Nevertheless, we must mention the existence of some practices which seem difficult to explain and justify, even on the general principles upon which Tāntrik Sādhanā proceeds. Peculiar liberties have been allowed to the Siddha Vīras who are said to have taken part in them. Possibly they are non-existent to-day. A Siddha Vīra, I may incidentally explain, is a Vīra who has become accomplished (Siddha) by doing the rite called Purashcharana of his Mantra the number of times multiplied by one lakh (100,000) that the Mantra contains letters. A Pandit friend tells me that the Siddhamālarahasya describes a rite (Chūdāchakra) in which fifty Siddha Vīras go with fifty Shaktis, each man getting his companion by lot by selecting one out of a heap of the Shakti's jackets (Chūdā). His Shakti is the woman to whom the jacket belongs. In the Snehachakra (Love Chakra), the Siddha Vīras pair with the Shaktis according as they have a liking for them. Ānandabhuvana-yoga is another unknown rite performed with not less than three and not more than one hundred and eight Shaktis who surround the Vīra. He unites with one Shakti (Bhogyā shakti) and touches the rest. In the Urnā Chakra (Urnā = spider's web) the Vīras sit in pairs tied to one another with cloths. A clue to the meaning of these rites may perhaps be found in the fact that they are said to have been performed at the instance, and at the cost, of third parties for the attainment of some worldly success. Thus the first was done, I am told, by the Rājās to gain success in battle. If this be so they belong rather to the side of magic than of religion, and are in any case no part of the ordinary Sādhanā to attain the true Siddhi which is spiritual advancement. It may also be that just as in the ordinary ritual Brāhmanas are fed and receive gifts, these Chakras were, in part at least, held with the same purpose by the class of people who had them performed. It is also to be noted (I report what I am told) that the body of the Shakti in the Chakra is the Yantra. By the union of Vīra and Shakti, who is a form (Ākāra) of the Devī, direct union is had with the latter who being pleased grants all that is desired of Her. There is thus what is technically called Pratyaksha of Devatā whereas in Kumārī-pūjā and in Shavasādhanā the Devī speaks through the mouth of the virgin or the corpse respectively. The Siddha Vīras communicate with Shiva and Shakti in Avadhūtaloka.

This question of differing views and practice was noted long ago by the author of the Dabistan (Vol. 2, pp. 154, 164. Ed. 1843) who says that on a learned Shākta being shown a statement, apparently counselling immorality, in a book abused it, saying that the Text was contrary to custom and that no such thing was to be found in the ancient books. The Muslim author of the Dabistan says that there is another class of Shāktas, quite different from those previously alluded to by him, who drink no wine and never have intercourse with the wife of another.

I, the more readily here and elsewhere state what is unfavourable to this Shāstra, as my object is not to "idealise" it (a process to which my strong bent towards the clear and accurate statement of facts is averse) but to describe the practice as I find it to be; on which statement a just judgment may be founded. After all men have been and are of all kinds high and low, ignorant and wise, bad and good, and just as in the Āgamas there are differing schools, so it is probable that in the Shākta practices themselves there are the same differences.

Lastly, the doctrine that the illuminate knower of Brahman (Brahmajnānī) is above both good (Dharma) and evil (Adharma) should be noted. Such an one is a Svechchhāchārī whose way is Svechchhāchāra or "do as you will". Similar doctrines and practice in Europe are there called Antinomianism. The doctrine is not peculiar to the Tantras. It is to be found in the Upanishads, and is in fact a very commonly held doctrine in India. Here again, as so stated and as understood outside India, it has the appearance of being worse than it really is. If Monistic views are accepted, then theoretically we must admit that Brahman is beyond good and evil, for these are terms of relativity applicable to beings in this world only. Good has no meaning except in relation to evil and *vice versa*. Brahman is beyond all dualities, and a Jnānī who has become Brahman (Jīvanmukta) is also logically so. It is, however, equally obvious that if a man has complete Brāhman-consciousness he will not, otherwise than unconsciously, do an act which if done consciously would be wrong. He is *ex hypothesi* beyond lust, gluttony and all other passions. A theoretical statement of fact that a Brahmajnānī is beyond good and evil is not a statement that he may will to do, and is permitted to do, evil. Statements as regards the position of a Jīvanmukta are mere praise or Stuti. In Svechchhāchāra there is theoretical freedom, but it is not consciously availed of to do what is known to be wrong without fall and pollution. Svechchhāchārinī is a name of the Devī, for She does what She pleases since She is the Lord of all. But of others the Shaktisanggama Tantra (Part IV) says—

Yadyapyasti trikālajnastrailokyākarshana-kshamah
Tathā 'pi laukikāchāram manasāpi na langhayet.

("Though a man be a knower of the Three Times, past, present, and future, and though he be a Controller of the three worlds, even then he should not transgress the rules of conduct for men in the world, were it only in his mind.")

What these rules of conduct are the Shāstra provides. Those who wrote this and similar counsels to be found in the Tantra Shāstras may have prescribed methods of Sādhanā which will not be approved, but they were not immoral-minded men. Nor, whatever be the actual results of their working (and some have been evil) was their Scripture devised with the intention of sanctioning or promoting what they believed to be immoral. They promoted or countenanced some dangerous practices under certain limitations which they thought to be safeguards. They have led to abuse as might have been thought to be probable.

Let us now distil from the mass of material to which I have only cursorily referred, those principles underlying the practice which are of worth from the standpoint of Indian Monism of which the practice is a remarkable illustration.

The three chief physical appetites of man are eating and drinking whereby his body is sustained, and sexual intercourse whereby it is propagated. Considered in themselves they are natural and harmless. Manu puts this very clearly when he says, "There is no wrong (Dosha) in the eating of meat and drinking of wine, nor in sexual intercourse, for these are natural inclinations of men. But abstention therefrom is productive of great fruit." Here I may interpose and say that the Tāntrik method is not a forced abstention but a regulated use with the right Bhāva, that is, Advaitabhāva or monistic feeling. When this is perfected, natural desires drop away (except so far as their fulfilment is absolutely necessary for physical existence) as things which are otherwise of no account. How is this done? By transforming Pashubhāva into Vīrabhāva. The latter is the feeling, disposition, and character of a Vīra.

All things spring from and are at base Ānanda or Bliss whether it is perceived or not. The latter, therefore, exists in two forms; as Mukti which is Ānandasvarūpa or transcendent, unlimited, one, and as Bhukti or limited worldly bliss. Tāntrik Sādhanā claims to give both, because the one of dual aspect is both. The Vīra thus knows that Jīvātmā and Paramātmā are one; that it is the One Shiva who appears in the form of the multitude of men and who acts, suffers, and enjoys through them. The Shivasvarūpa is Bliss itself (Paramānanda). The Bliss of enjoyment (Bhogānanda) is one and the same Bliss manifesting itself through the limiting forms of mind and matter. Who is it who then enjoys and what Bliss is thus manifested? It is Shiva in the forms of the Universe (Vishvarūpa) who enjoys, and the manifested bliss is a limited form of that Supreme Bliss which in His ultimate nature He is. In his physical functions the Vīra identifies himself with the collectivity of all functions which constitute the universal life. He is then consciously Shiva in the form of his own and all other lives. As Shiva exists both in His Svarūpa and as the world (Vishvarūpa), so union may, and should, be had with Him in both aspects. These are known as Sūkshma and Sthūla Sāmarasya respectively. The Sādhaka is taught not to think that we are one with the Divine in Liberation only, but here and now, in every act we do. For in truth all such is Shakti. It is Shiva who as Shakti is acting in and through the Sādhaka. So though, according to the Vaidik injunctions, there is no eating or drinking before worship, it is said in the Shākta Tantra that he who worships Kālikā when hungry and thirsty angers Her. Those who worship a God who is other than their own Essential Self may think to please Him by such acts, but to the Shākta, Shiva and Jīva are one and the same. Why then should one give pain to Jīva? It was, I think, Professor Royce who said, borrowing (though probably unconsciously) an essential Tāntrik idea, that God suffers and enjoys *in* and *as* and *through* man. This is so. Though the Brahmasvarūpa is nothing but the perfect, actionless Bliss, yet it is also the one Brahman who as Jīva suffers and enjoys; for there is none other. When this is realized in every natural function, then, each exercise thereof ceases to be a mere animal act and becomes a religious rite—a Yajna. Every function is a part of the Divine Action (Shakti) in Nature. Thus, when taking drink in the form of wine the Vīra knows it to be Tārā Dravamayī, that is, "the Saviour Herself in liquid form". How (it is said) can he who truly sees in it the Saviour Mother receive from it harm? Meditating on Kundalinī as pervading his body to the tip of his tongue, thinking himself to be Light which is also the Light of the wine he takes, he says, "I am She", (Sā 'ham) "I am Brahman", "I Myself offer offering (Ahuti) to the Self, Svāhā." When, therefore, the Vīra eats, drinks or has sexual intercourse he does so not with the thought of himself as a separate individual satisfying his own peculiar limited wants; an animal filching as it were from nature the enjoyment he has, but thinking of himself in such enjoyment as Shiva, saying "Shivo'ham," "Bhairavo'ham". Right sexual union may, if associated with meditation and ritual, be the means of spiritual advance; though persons who take a vulgar and animal view of this function will not readily understand it. The function is thereby ennobled and receives a new significance. The dualistic notions entertained, by both some Easterns and Westerns, that the "dignity" of worship is necessarily offended by association with natural function is erroneous. As Tertullian says, the Eucharist was established at a meal. (As to sacramental meals and "Feeding on the Gods", see Dr. Angus' "The Mystery Religions and Christianity", p. 127.) Desire is often an enemy but it may be made an ally. A right method does not exclude the body, for it is Devatā. It is a phase of Spirit and belongs to, and is an expression of, the Power of the Self. The Universe was created by and with Bliss. That same Bliss manifests, though faintly, in the bodies of men and women in union. At such time the ignorant Pashu is intent on the satisfaction of his passion only, but Kulasādhakas then meditate on the Yogānanda Mūrti of Shiva-Shakti and do Japa of their Ishtamantra thus making them, in the words of the Kālīkulasarvasva, like sinless Shuka. If the union be legitimate what, I may ask, is wrong in this? On the contrary the physical function is ennobled and divinised. An act which is legitimate does not become illegitimate because it is made a part of worship (Upāsanā). This is Vīrabhāva. An English writer has aptly spoken of "the profound pagan instinct to glorify the generative impulse with religious ritual" (Times Lit. Sup., 11-6-1922). The Shākta is a developed and typical case.

The notions of the Pashu are in varying degrees the reverse of all this. If of the lowest type, he only knows himself as a separate entity who enjoys. Some more sophisticated, yet in truth ignorant, enjoy and are ashamed; and thus think it unseemly to implicate God in the supposed coarseness of His handiwork as physical function. Some again, who are higher, regard these functions as an acceptable gift of God to them as lowly creatures who enjoy and are separate from Him. The Vaidikas took enjoyment to be the fruit of the sacrifice and the gift of the Devas. Others who are yet higher offer all that they do to the One Lord. This dualistic worship is embodied in the command of the Gītā, "*Tat madarpanam kurushva.*" "Do all this as an offering to Me." What is "all"? Does it mean all or some particular things only? But the highest Sādhanā from the Monistic standpoint, and which in its Advaitabhāva differs from all others, is that of the Shākta Tantra which proclaims that the Sādhaka *is* Shiva and that it is Shiva who in the form of the Sādhaka enjoys.

So much for the principle involved to which, whether it be accepted or not, cannot be truly denied nobility and grandeur.

The application of this principle is of greatly less interest and importance. To certain of such ritual applications may be assigned the charges commonly made against this Shāstra, though without accurate knowledge and discrimination. It was the practice of an age the character of which was not that of our own. The particular shape which the ritual has taken is due, I think, to historical causes. Though the history of the Āgamas is still obscure, it is possible that this Panchatattva-Karma is in substance a continuation, in altered form, of the old Vaidik usage in which eating and drinking were a part of the sacrifice (Yajna), though any extra-ritual drinking called "useless" (Vrithāpāna) or Pashu drinking (Pashupāna) in which the Western (mostly a hostile critic of the Tantra Shāstra) so largely indulges, is a great sin. The influence, however, of the original

Buddhism and Jainism were against the consumption of meat and wine; an influence which perhaps continued to operate on post-Buddhistic Hinduism up to the present day, except among certain followers of the Āgamas who claimed to represent the earlier traditions and usages. I say "certain," because (as I have mentioned) for the Pashu there are substitutes for wine and meat and so forth; and for the Divya the Tattvas are not material things but Yoga processes. I have shown the similarities between the Vaidik and Tāntrik ritual in my paper on "Shakti and Shākta" to which I refer. If this suggestion of mine be correct, whilst the importance and prevalence of the ancient ritual will diminish with the passage of time and the changes in religion which it effects, the principle will always retain its inherent value for the followers of the Advaita Vedānta. It is capable of application according to the modern spirit without recourse to Chakras and their ritual details in the ordinary daily life of the householder within the bounds of his Dharmashāstra.

Nevertheless the ritual has existed and still exists, though at the present day often in a form free from the objections which are raised against certain ancient liberties of practice which led to abuse. It is necessary, therefore, both for the purpose of accuracy and of a just criticism of its present adherents, to consider the *intention* with which the ritual was prescribed and the *mode* in which that intention was given effect to. It is not the fact, as commonly alleged, that the intention of the Shāstra was to promote and foster any form of sensual indulgence. If it was, then, the Tantras would not be a Shāstra at all whatever else they might contain. Shāstra, as I have previously said, comes from the root "Shās" to control; that is, Shāstra exists to control men within the bounds set by Dharma. The intention of this ritual, when rightly understood, is, on the contrary, to regulate natural appetite, to curb it, to lift it from the trough of mere animality; and by associating it with religious worship, to effect a passage from the state of desire of the ignorant Pashu to the completed Divyabhāva in which there is desirelessness. It is another instance of the general principle to which I have referred that man must be led from the gross to the subtle. A Sādhaka once well explained the matter to me thus: Let us suppose, he said, that man's body is a vessel filled with oil which is the passions. If you simply empty it and do nothing more, fresh oil will take its place issuing from the Source of Desire which you have left undestroyed. If, however, into the vessel there is dropped by slow degrees the Water of Knowledge (Jnāna), it will, as being heavier than oil, descend to the bottom of the vessel and will then expel an equal quantity of oil. In this way all the oil of passion is gradually expelled and no more can re-enter, for the water of Jnāna will then have wholly taken its place. Here again the general principle of the method is good. As the Latins said, "If you attempt to expel nature with a pitchfork it will come back again." You must infuse something else as a medicament against the ills which follow the natural tendency of desire to exceed the limits which Dharma sets.

The Tāntrik Pandit Jaganmohana Tarkālankāra in his valuable notes appended to the commentary on the Mahānirvāna Tantra of Hariharānanda Bhāratī, the Guru of the celebrated "Reformer" Rājā Ram Mohan Roy (Ed. of K. G. Bhakta, 1888), says, "Let us consider what most contributes to the fall of a man, making him forget his duty, sink into sin and die an early death. First among these are wine and women, fish, meat, Mudrā and accessories. By these things men have lost their manhood. Shiva then desires to employ these very poisons in order to eradicate the poison in the human system. Poison is the antidote for poison.

This is the right treatment for those who long for drink or lust for women. The physician must, however, be an experienced one. If there be a mistake as to the application the patient is likely to die. Shiva has said that the way of Kulāchāra is as difficult as it is to walk on the edge of a sword or to hold a wild tiger. There is a secret argument in favour of the Panchatattva, and those Tattvas so understood should be followed by all. None, however, but the initiate can grasp this argument, and therefore Shiva has directed that it should not be revealed before anybody and everybody. An initiate when he sees a woman will worship her as his own mother and Goddess (Ishtadevatā) and bow before her. The Vishnu Purāna says that by feeding your desires you cannot satisfy them. It is like pouring ghee on fire. Though this is true, an experienced spiritual teacher (Guru) will know how, by the application of this poisonous medicine, to kill the poison of the world (Samsāra). Shiva has, however, prohibited the indiscriminate publication of this. The object of Tāntrik worship is Brahmasāyujya or union with Brahman. If that is not attained nothing is attained. And with men's propensities as they are, this can only be attained through the special treatment prescribed by the Tantras. If this is not followed, then the sensual propensities are not eradicated and the work is, for the desired end of Tantra, as useless as harmful magic (Abhichāra) which, worked by such a man, leads only to the injury of himself and others." The passage cited refers to the necessity for the spiritual direction of the Guru. To the want of such is accredited the abuse of the system. When the patient (Shishya) and the disease are working together, there is poor hope for the former: but when the patient, the disease and the physician are on one, and that the wrong side, then nothing can save him from a descent in that downward path which it is the object of Sādhanā to prevent.

All Hindu schools seek the suppressions of mere animal worldly desire. What is peculiar to the Kaulas is the particular method employed for the transformation of desire. The Kulārnava Tantra says that man must be taught to rise by the means of those very things which are the cause of his fall. "As one falls on the ground, one must lift oneself by aid of the ground." So also the Buddhist Subhāsita Sangraha says that a thorn is used to pick out a thorn. Properly applied the method is a sound one. Man falls through the natural functions of drinking, eating, and sexual intercourse. If these are done with the feeling (Bhāva) and under the conditions prescribed, then they become (it is taught) the instruments of his uplift to a point at which such ritual is no longer necessary and is surpassed.

In the first edition of the work, I spoke of Antinomian Doctrine and Practice, and of some Shākta theories and rituals which have been supposed to be instances of it. This word, however, requires explanation, or it may (I have since thought) lead to error in the present connection. There is always danger in applying Western terms to facts of Eastern life. Antinomianism is the name for heretical theories and practices which have arisen in Christian Europe. In short, the term, as generally understood, has a meaning in reference to Christianity, namely, contrary or opposed to Law, which here is the Judaic law as adopted and modified by that religion. The Antinomian, for varying reasons, considered himself not bound by the ordinary laws of conduct. It is not always possible to state with certainty whether any particular sect or person alleged to be Antinomian was in fact such, for one of the commonest charges made against sects by their opponents is that of immorality. We are rightly warned against placing implicit reliance on the accounts of adversaries. Thus charges of nocturnal orgies were made against the early Christians, and by the latter against those whom they regarded as heretical dissidents, such as Manichæans, Montanists, Priscillianists and others, and against most of the mediæval sects such as the Cathari, Waldenses and Fracticelli. Nor can we be always certain as to the nature of the theories held by persons said to be Antinomian, for in a large number of cases we have only the accounts of orthodox opponents. Similarly, hitherto every account of the Shâkta Tantra was given by persons both ignorant of, and hostile to it. In some cases it would seem (I speak of the West) that Matter was held in contempt as the evil product of the Demiurge. In others Antinomian doctrine and practice was based on "Pantheism". The latter in the West has always had as one of its tendencies a leaning towards, or adoption of Antinomianism. Mystics in their identification with God supposed that upon their conscious union with Him they were exempt from the rules governing ordinary men. The law was spiritualized into the one precept of the Love of God which ripened into a conscious union with Him, one with man's essence. This was deemed to be a sinless state. Thus Amalric of Bena (d. 1204) is reputed to have said that to those constituted in love no sin is imputed (*Dixerat etiam quod in charitate constitutis nullum peccatum imputabatur*). His followers are alleged to have maintained that harlotry and other carnal vices are not sinful for the spiritual man, because the spirit in him, which is God, is not affected by the flesh and cannot sin, and because the man who is nothing cannot sin so long as the Spirit which is God is in him. In other words, sin is a term relative to man who may be virtuous or sinful. But in that state beyond duty, which is identification with the Divine Essence, which at root man is, there is no question of sin. The body at no time sins. It is the state of mind which constitutes sin, and that state is only possible for a mind with a human and not divine consciousness. Johann

Hartmann is reputed to have said that he had become completely one with God; that a man free in spirit is impeccable and can do whatever he will, or in Indian parlance he is Svechchhāchārī. (See Dollinger's Beiträge zur Sektengeschichte des Mittelalter's ii. 384.) This type of Antinomianism is said to have been widespread during the later middle ages and was perpetuated in some of the parties of the so-called Reformation. Other notions leading to similar results were based on Quietistic and Calvinistic tenets in which the human will was so subordinated to the Divine will as to lose its freedom. Thus Gomar (A.D. 1641) maintained that "sins take place, God procuring and Himself willing that they take place". God was thus made the author of sin. It has been alleged that the Jesuit casuists were "constructively antinomian" because of their doctrines of philosophical sin, direction of attention, mental reservation, and probabilism. But this is not so, whatever may be thought of such doctrines. For here there was no question of opposition to the law of morality, but theories touching the question "in what that law consisted" and whether any particular act was in fact a violation of it. They did not teach that the law could in any case be violated, but dealt with the question whether any particular act was such a violation. Antinomianism of several kinds and based on varying grounds has been charged against the Manichæans, the Gnostics generally, Cainites, Carpocrates, Epiphanes, Messalians (with their promiscuous sleeping together of men and women), Adamites, Bogomiles, followers of Amalric of Bena, Brethren of the Free Spirit, Beghards, Fratricelli, Johann Hartmann ("a man free in spirit is impeccable"); the pantheistic "Libertines" and "Familists" and Ranters of the Sixteenth and Seventeenth Centuries ("Nothing is sin but what a man thinks to be so"; "God sees no sin in him who knows himself to be in a state of grace"; see Gataker's Antinomianism Discovered and Refuted', A.D. 1632 and see Rufus Jones' "Studies in Mystical Religion", Ch. XIX), the Alumbrados or Spanish Illuminate (Prabuddha) Mystics of the Sixteenth Century; Magdalena de Cruce d'Aguilar and others (Mendes y Pelayo—"Historia de los Heterodoxos Espanoles") whose teachings according to Malvasia (Catalogus onmium haeresium et conciliorum) contained the following proposition, "A perfect man cannot sin; even an act which outwardly regarded must be looked upon as vicious cannot contaminate the soul which lives in mystical union with God." "The Holy and Sinless Baptists" held that the elect could not sin, an antinomian doctrine which has often appeared in the history of theological-ethical speculation to the effect that the believer might do what he liked, since if he sinned, it affected the body only, with which his soul had no more to do than with any of the other things of this world (Belfort Bax Anabaptists 35). The Free Brothers held that for the rebaptized, sin was impossible as no bodily act could affect the soul of the believer. Women did not sin who went with Brethren because there was a spiritual bond between them (*ib.*, 38). Kessler alleges that the Votaries practised sensuality on the plea that their souls were dead to the flesh and that all the flesh did was by the will of God (*ib.*, 62). The Alumbrada Francisca Garcia is alleged to have said that her sexual excesses were in obedience to the voice of God and that "carnal indulgence was embracing God" (Lea's Inquisition in Spain, III. 62). Similar doctrines are alleged of the French Illuminés called Guerinets of the Seventeenth Century; the German "Theosophers" of Schonherr: Eva Von Buttler: the Muckers of the Eighteenth Century; some modern Russian sects (Tsakni "La Russie Sectaire") and others. Whilst it is to be remembered that in these and other cases we must receive with caution the accounts given by opponents, there is no doubt that Antinomianism, Svechchhāchāra and the like is a well-known phenomenon in religious history often associated with so-called "Pantheistic" doctrines. The Antinomian doctrines of the Italian nuns, Spighi and Buonamici, recorded by Bishop Scipio de Ricci "*L'uomo e nato libero y nessuno lo puo legare nello spirito :*" "man is born free and none can chain his free Spirit" are here dealt with in more detail, for the writer Edward Sellon ("Annotations on the writings of the Hindus)" thought that he had found in the last cited case an instance of "Tāntrik doctrine" in the convents of Italy in the Eighteenth Century. I will give some reasons, which refute his view, the more particularly because they are contained in a very rare work, namely, the first edition of De Potter's "Vie de Scipion de Ricci Eveque de Pistoie et Prato", published at Brussels in 1825, and largely withdrawn at the instance of the Papal Court. The second edition is, I believe, much expurgated. Receiving report of abuses in the Dominican convent of St. Catherine de Prato, the Bishop of Pistoia and Prato made an inquisition into the conduct of the nuns, and in particular as to the teaching and practice of their leaders, the Sister Buonamici, formerly Prioress and afterwards novice-mistress, and the Sister Spighi, assistant novice-mistress. De Potter's work contains the original interrogatories, in Italian (I. 381) in the writing of 'Abbe Laurent Palli', Vicar-Episcopal at Prato, taken in 1781 and kept in the archives of the Ricci family. The Teaching of the two Sisters I summarise as follows: "God" (I. 413, 418) "is a first principle (*Primo principio*) who is a collectivity (in Sanskrit *Samashti*) of all men and things (*un cemplesso di tutti le cose anzi di tutto il genere umano*). The univesal Master or God is Nature (*ci e il maestro, ohe e Iddio ceve la natura*). As God is the totality of the universe and is nothing but Nature we all participate in the Divine Essence (*Questo Dio non e altro che la Natura. Noi medesimi per questa ragione participiamo in qualche maniera dell'esser divino*). Man's soul is a mortal thing consisting of Memory, Intelligence and Will. It dies with the body disappearing as might a mist. Man is free and therefore none can enchain his free spirit (I. 428). The only Heaven and Hell which exists is the Heaven and Hell in this world. There is none other. After death there is neither pleasure nor suffering. The Spirit, being free, it is the intention which renders an act bad. It is sufficient (I. 460) to elevate the spirit to God and then no action, whatever it be, is sin (*Essendo il nostro spirito libro, l'intenzione e quello que rende cattiva l'azione. Basta dunque colla mente elevarsi a Dio perche qualsivoglia azione non sia peccato*). There is no sin. Certain (impure) acts are not sin provided that the spirit is always elevated to God. Love of God and one's neighbour is the whole of the commandments. Man (I. 458) who unites with God by means of woman satisfies both commandments. So also does he who, lifting his spirit to God, has enjoyment with a person of the same sex or alone (*Usciamo con alcuno d'equal sesso o da se soli*). To be united with God is to be united as man and woman. The eternal life (I. 418) of the soul and Paradise in this world is the transubstantiation (or it may be transfusion) which takes place when man is united with woman (*Depone.credere questa vita eterna dell'anima essere la transustanziazione (forse transfusione) nell'unirsi che fa l'uomo con la donna*). Marie Clodesinde Spighi having stated that Paradise consisted in the fruition in this world of the Enjoyment of God (*la fruizione di Dio*) was asked "How is this attained?" Her reply was, by that act by which one unites oneself with God. "How again", she was questioned, "is this union effected?" To which the answer was "by co-operation of man and woman in which I recognize God Himself." I. 428. (*Mediante l'uomo nel quale ci riconosco Iddio.*) Everything was permissible because man was free, though sots might obey the law enjoined for the general governance of the world. Man, she said, (I. 420) can be saved in all religions (*In tutti le religione ci passiamo salvare*). In doing that which we erroneously call impure is real purity ordained by God, without which man cannot arrive at a knowledge of Him who is the truth (*e esercitando erroneamente quello che diciamo impurita era la vera purita : quella Iddio ci comanda e virole noi pratichiamo, e senza della quale non vi e maniera di trovare Iddio, che e verita*). "Where did you get all this doctrine ?" The sister said "I gathered it from my natural inclinations" (*L'ho ricevato dall inclinazione della natura*).

Whilst it will not be necessary to tell the most ignorant Indian that the above doctrines are not Christian teaching, it is necessary (as Sellon's remark shows) to inform the English reader that this pantheistic libertinism is not "Tānṭrik". This imperfect charge is due to the author's knowledge of the principles of Kaulo Sādhanā. I will not describe all the obscene and perverse acts which these "Religious" practised. It is sufficient that the reader should throw his eye back a few lines and see that their teaching justified sodomy, lesbianism and masturbation, sins as abhorrent to the Tantra Shāstra as any other. Owing, however, to ignorance or prejudice, everything is called "Tāntrik" into which woman enters and in which sexual union takes on a religious or so-called religious character or complexion. The Shāstra, on the contrary, teaches that there is a God who transcends Nature, that Dharma or morality governs all men, that there is sin and that the acts here referred to are impurities leading to Hell; for there is (it says) both suffering and enjoyment not only in this but in an after-life. It was apparently enough for Edward Sellon to adjudge the theories and practices to be Tāntrik, that these women preached the doctrine of intention and of sexual union with the feeling or Bhāva (to use a Sanskrit term) that man and woman were parts of the one Divine essence. A little knowledge is a dangerous thing, and this is an instance of it. These corrupt theories are merely the "religious" and "philosophical" basis for a life of unrestrained libertinism which the Tantra Shāstra condemns as emphatically as any other Scripture. The object of the Tāntrik ritual is to forward the morality of the senses by converting mere animal functions into acts of worship. The Scripture says in effect, "Just as you offer flowers, incense and so forth to the Devatā, in the Rājasik worship let these physical functions take their place, remembering that it is Shiva who is working in and through you." The doctrine of the Brethren of the Free Spirit (Delacroix "Le Mysticisme speculatif en Allemagne au quatorzième siecle) so far as it was probably really held, has, in points, resemblance to some of the Tāntrik and indeed Aupanishadic teachings, for they both hold in common certain general principles to which I will refer (see also Preger's "Geshichte der Deutschen Mystik im Mittelalter"). Other doctrines and practices with which they have been charged are wholly hostile to the Shākta Darshana and Sādhanā. Amalric of Bena, a disciple of Scotus Erigena, held that God is all, both creature and creator, and the Essence of all which is. The soul which attains to Him by contemplation becomes God Himself. It was charged against him that man could act in the manner of God's action, and do what he pleased without falling into sin. The doctrine that the Brahmajnānī is above good and evil is so generally misunderstood that it is probable that, whatever may have been the case with some of his disciples, the charges made against the master himself on this point are false. It has been well said that one is prompt to accuse of immorality any one who places himself beyond traditional morality. As regards the Brethren of the Free Spirit also, this alleged doctrine comes to us from the mouths of their adversaries. They are said to have held that there were two religions, one for the ignorant (Mūdha), the other for the illuminate (Prabuddha), the first being the traditional religion of the letter and ritual observance, and the other of freedom and spirituality. The soul is of the same substance as God (identity of Jīvātmā and Paramātmā). When this is realized man is deified. Then he is (as Brahmajnānī) above all law (Dharma). The ordinary rules of morality bind only those who do not see beyond them, and who do not realize in themselves that Power which is superior to all these laws. United with God (*Anima deo unita*) man enjoys a blessed freedom. He sees the inanity of prayers, of fasts, of all those supplications which can do nothing to change the order of nature. He is one with the Spirit of all. Free of the law he follows his own will (Svechchhāchārī). What the vulgar call "sin", he can commit without soiling himself. There is a distinction between the act which is called sinful and sin. Nothing is sin but what the doer takes to be such. The body does not sin. It is the intention with which an act is done which constitutes sin. "The angel would not have fallen if what he did had been done with a good intention" (*Quod angelus non cecidisset si bona intentione fecissit quod fecit*). Man becomes God in all the powers of his being including the ultimate elements of his body. Therefore, wisdom lies not in renunciation, but in enjoyment and the satisfaction of his desires. The tormenting and insatiable passion for woman is a form of the creative spontaneous principle. The worth of instinct renders noble the acts of the flesh, and he who is united in spirit with God can with impunity fulfil the sensual desires of the body (*item quod unitus deo audacter possit explere libidinamcarnis*). There is no more sin in sexual union without marriage than within it and so forth. With the historian of this sect and with our knowledge of the degree to which pantheistic doctrines are misunderstood, we may reasonably doubt whether these accusations of their enemies represent in all particulars their true teaching. It seems, however, to have been held by those who have dealt with this question that the pantheistic doctrine of the Brethren led to conclusions contrary to the common morality. It is also highly probable that some at least of the excesses condemned were the work of false brethren, who finding in the doctrine a convenient excuse for, and an encouragement of their licentiousness, sheltered themselves behind its alleged authority. As this remark of Dr. Delacroix suggests, one must judge a doctrine (and we may instance that of the Shāktas) by what its sincere adherents hold and do, and not by the practices of impostors who always hie to sects which seem to hold theories offering opportunities for libertinism. One may here recall Milton who says with insight "That sort of men who follow Antinomianism and other fanatic dreams be such most commonly as are by nature gifted to religion, of life also *not* debauched and that their opinions having full swing do end in satisfaction of the flesh."

Whilst there is a similarity on some points between Kaula teaching and some of the Western pantheistic theories above alluded to, in others the two are manifestly and diametrically opposed. There are some who talk as if intellectual and moral aberrations were peculiar to India. No country is without them, but the West, owing to its chaos of thought and morals, has exhibited the worst. With the exception of the atheistic Chārvākas and Lokāyatas no sect in India has taught the pursuit of sensual enjoyment for its own sake, or justified the commission of any and every (even unnatural) sin. To do so would be to run counter to ideas which are those of the whole intellectual and moral Cosmos of India. These ideas include those of a Law (Dharma) inherent in the nature of all being; of sin as its infraction, and of the punishment of sin as bad Karma in this and the next world (Paraloka). It is believed and taught that the end of man is lasting happiness, but that this is not to be had by the satisfaction of worldly desires. Indeed the Kaula teaches that Liberation (Moksha) cannot be had so long as a man has any worldly desires whether good or bad. Whilst, however, there is an eternal Dharma (Sanātana Dharma), one and the same for all, there are also particular forms of Dharma governing particular bodies of men. It is thus a general rule that a man should not unlawfully satisfy his sexual desires. But the conditions under which he may lawfully do so have varied in every form and degree in times and places. In this sense, as the Sarvollāsa says, marriage is a conventional (Pāribhāshika) thing. The convention which is binding on the individual must yet be followed, that being his Dharma. Sin again, it is taught, consists in intention, not in a physical act divorced therefrom. Were this otherwise, then it is said that the child which, when issuing from the mother's body, touches her Yoni would be guilty of the heinous offence called Guru-talpaga. The doctrine of a single act with differing intentions is illustrated by the Tāntrik maxim, "A wife is kissed with one feeling, a daughter's face with another" (*Bhāvena chumbitā kāntā bhāvena duhitānanam*). In the words of the Sarvollāsa, a man who goes with a woman, in the belief that by commission of such act he will go to Hell, will of a surety go thither. On the other hand it may be said that if an act is really lawful but is done in the belief that it is unlawful and with the deliberate intention of doing what is unlawful, there is subjective sin. The intention of the Shāstra is not to unlawfully satisfy carnal desire in the way of eating and drinking and so forth, but that man should unite with Shiva-Shakti in worldly enjoyment (Bhaumānanda) as a step towards the supreme enjoyment (Paramānanda) of Liberation. In so doing he must follow the Dharma prescribed by Shiva. It is true that there are different observances for the illuminate, for those whose power (Shakti) is awake (Prabuddha) and for the rest. But the Sādhanā of these last is as necessary as the first and a stepping stone to it. The Kaula doctrine and practice may, from a Western standpoint, only be called Antinomian, in the sense that it holds, in common with the Upanishads, that the Brahmajnānī is above both good (Dharma) and evil (Adharma), and in the sense that some of these practices are contrary to what the general body of Hindu worshippers consider to be lawful. Thus Shākta Darshana is said by some to be Avaidika. It is, however, best to leave to the West its own labels and to state the case of the East in its own terms.

After all, when everything unfavourable has been said, the abuses of some Tāntriks are not to be compared either in nature or extent with those of the West with its widespread sordid prostitution, its drunkenness and gluttony, its sexual perversities and its so-called pathological but truly demoniacal enormities. To take a specific example— Is the drinking of wine, by a limited number of Vāmāchārī Tāntriks in the whole of this country to be compared with (say) the consumption of whisky in the single city of Calcutta? Is this whisky drinking less worthy of condemnation because it is Pashupāna or done for the satisfaction of sensual appetite alone? The dualistic notion that the "dignity" of religion is impaired by association with natural function is erroneous.

The well-known English writer, Sir Conan Doyle, doubtless referring to these and other wrongs, has expressed the opinion that during the then last quarter of a century we Westerns have been living in what (with some few ameliorating features) is the wickedest epoch in the world's history. However this may be, if our own great sins were here known, the abuses, real and alleged, of Tāntriks would be seen in better proportion. Moreover an effective reply would be to hand against those who are always harping on Devadāsīs and other sensualities (supposed or real) of, or, connected with, Indian worship. India's general present record for temperance and sexual control is better than that of the West. It is no doubt a just observation that abuses committed under the supposed sanction of religion are worse than wrongs done with the sense that they are wrong. That there have been hypocrites covering the satisfaction of their appetites with the cloak of religion is likely. But all Sādhakas are not hypocrites, and all cases do not show abuse. I cannot, therefore, help thinking that this constant insistence on one particular feature of the Shāstra, together with ignorance both of the particular rites, and neglect and ignorance of all else in the Āgama Scripture is simply part of the general polemic carried on in some quarters against the Indian religion. The Tantra Shāstra is doubtless thought to be a very useful heavy gun and is therefore constantly fired in the attack. There may be some who will not readily believe that the weapon is not as formidable as was thought. All this is not to say that there have not been abuses, or that some forms of rite will not be considered repugnant, and in fact open to objection founded on the interests of society at large. All this again is not to say that I counsel the acceptance of any theories or practice, not justified by the evolved morality of the day. According to the Shāstra itself, some of these methods, even if carried out as directed, have their dangers. This is obvious in the actions of a lower class of men, whose conduct has made the Scripture notorious. The ordinary man will then ask: "Why then court danger when there is enough of it in ordinary life?" I may here recall an observation of the Emperor Akbar which, though not made with regard to the matter in hand, is yet well in point. He said, "I have never known of a man who was lost on a straight road."

It is necessary for me to so guard myself because those who cannot judge with detachment are prone to think that others who deal fairly and dispassionately with any doctrine or practice are necessarily its adherents and the counsellors of it to others.

My own view is this.—Probably on the whole it would be, in general, better if men took neither Alcohol in the form of Spirits or Meat, particularly the latter, which is the source of much disease. Though it is said that killing for sacrifice is no "killing", it can hardly be denied that total abstention from slaughter of animals constitutes a more complete conformity with Ahimsā or doctrine of non-injury to any being. Moreover, at a certain stage meat-eating is repugnant. A feeling of this kind is growing in the West, where even the Meat-eater, impelled by disgust and a rising regard for decency, hides away the slaughter houses producing the meat which he openly displays at his table. In the same way, sexual errors are common to-day. Whatever licence any person may allow himself in this matter, few if any will claim it for others and foster their vices. Nor was this the intention of the Shāstra. It is well-known, however, that much of what passes for religious sentiment is connected with sex instinct even if religious life is not a mere "irradiation of the reproductive instinct" (see "Religion and Sex", Cohen).

I understand the basis on which these Tāntrik practices rest. Thus what seems repellent is sought to be justified on the ground that the Sādhaka should be above all likes and dislikes, and should see Brahman in all things. But the Western critic will say that we must judge practice from the practical standpoint. It was this consideration which was at the back of the statement of Professor de la Vallee Poussine (Boudhism. Etudes et Materiaux) that there is in this country what Taine called a 'reasoning madness' which makes the Hindu stick at no conclusion however strange, willingly accepting even the absurd. *(Il y regne des l' origine ce que Taine appelle la folie raisonante. Les Hindous vont volontiers jusquā l'absurde)*. This may be too strongly put; but the saying contains this truth that the Indian temperament is an absolutist one. But such a temperament, if it has its fascinating grandeur, also carries with it the defects of its qualities; namely, dangers from which those, who make a compromise between life and reason, are free. The answer again is, that some of the doctrines and practices here described were never meant for the general body of men.

After all, as I have elsewhere said, the question of this particular ritual practice is largely of historical interest only. Such practice to-day is, under the influences of the time, being transformed, where it is not altogether disappearing, with other ritual customs of a past age. Apart from my desire to clear away, so far as is rightly possible, charges which have lain heavily on this country, I am only interested here to show firstly that the practice is not a modern invention but seems to be a continuation in another form of ancient Vaidik usage; secondly that it claims, like the rest of the ritual with which I have dealt, to be an application of the Advaitavāda of the Upanishads; and lastly that (putting aside things generally repugnant and extremist practices which have led to abuse) a great principle is involved which may find legitimate and ennobling application in all daily acts of physical function within the bounds of man's ordinary Dharma. Those who so practise this principle may become the true Vīra who has been said to be not the man of great physical or sexual strength, the great fighter, eater, drinker, or the like, but

Jitendriyah satyavādī nityānushthāna-tatparah
Kāmādi-validānashcha sa vīra iti gīyate.

"He is a Hero who has controlled his senses, and is a speaker of truth; who is ever engaged in worship and has sacrificed lust and all other passions."

The attainment of these qualities is the aim, whatever is said of some of the means, of all such Tāntrik Sādhanā.

CHAPTER XXVIII

MATAM RUTRA

(The Right and Wrong Interpretation)

In connection with the doctrine and Sādhanā just described it is apposite to cite the following legend from Tibet, which shows how, according to its Sādhakas, it may be either rightly or wrongly interpreted, and how, in the latter case, it leads to terrible evils and their punishment.

Guru Padma-sambhava, the so-called founder of "Lamaism," had five women disciples who compiled several accounts of the teachings of their Master and hid them in various places for the benefit of future believers. One of these disciples—Khandro Yeshe Tsogyal—was a Tibetan lady who is said to have possessed such a wonderful power of memory that if she was told a thing only once she remembered it for ever. She gathered what she had heard from her Guru into a book called the Padma Thangyig Serteng or Golden Rosary of the history of her Guru who was entitled the Lotus-born (Padma-sambhava). The book was hidden away and was subsequently, under inspiration, revealed some five hundred years ago by a Terton.

The first Chapter of the Work deals with Sukhavatī the realm of Buddha Amitābha. In the second the Buddha emanates a ray which is incarnated for the welfare of the Universe. In Chapter III it is said that there have been a Buddha and a Guru working together in various worlds and at various times, the former preaching the Sūtras and the latter the Tantras. The fourth Chapter speaks of the Mantras and the five Dhyānī Buddhas (as to which see Shrī-chakra-sambhara Tantra in Tāntrik Texts, edited by Arthur Avalon), and in the fifth we find the subject of the present Chapter, an account of the origin of the Vajrayāna Faith. The present Chapter is based on a translation, which I asked Kazi Dawasamdup to prepare for me, of portions of the Thangyig Serteng. I have further had, and here acknowledge, the assistance of the very learned Lama Ugyen Tanzin, in the elucidation of the inner meaning of the legend. I cannot go fully into this but give certain indications which will enable the competent to work out much of the rest for themselves from the terrible symbolism in which evil for evil's sake is here expressed.

The story is that of the rise and fall of the Self. The disciple "Transcendent Faith" who became the Bodhisattva Vajrapāni illustrates the former; the case of "Black Salvation" who incarnated as a Demoniac Rutra displays the latter. He was no ordinary man, for at the time of his initiation he had already attained eight out of the thirteen stages (Bhūmikā) on the way to perfect Buddhahood. His powers were correspondingly great. But the higher the rise the greater the fall if it comes. Through misunderstanding and misapplying, as so many others have done, the Tāntrik doctrine, he "fell back" into Hell. Extraordinary men who were teachers of recondite doctrines such as those of Thubka, who was himself "hard to overcome", seem not to have failed to warn lesser brethren against their dangers. It is commonly said in Tibet of the so-called "heroic" modes of extremist Yoga, that they waft the disciple with the utmost speed either to the heights of Nirvāna or to the depths of Hell. For the aspirant is compared to a snake which is made to go up a hollow Bamboo. It must ascend and escape at the top, at the peril otherwise of falling down. Notwithstanding these warnings many of the vulgar, the vicious, the misunderstanding, and the fools who play with fire have gone to Hells far more terrible than those which await human frailties in pursuance of the common life of men whose progress if slow is sure. "Black Salvation", though an advanced disciple, misinterpreted his teacher's doctrine and consciously identifying himself with the world-evil fell into Hell. In time he rose therefrom and incarnating at first in gross material forms, he at length manifested as a great Rutra, the embodiment of all wickedness. The Tibetan Rutra here spoken of and the Indian Rudra seem to be etymologically the same but their meaning is different. Both are fierce and terrible Spirits; but a Rutra as here depicted is essentially evil, and neither the Lord of any sensual celestial paradise, nor the Cosmic Shakti which loosens forms. A Rutra is rather what in some secret circles is called (though in ungrammatical Sanskrit) an Adhātmā, or a soul upon the lower and destructive path. The general destructive energy (Saṃhāra-Shakti), however, uses for its purpose the disintegranting propensities of these forms. The evil which appears as Rutra is the expression of various kinds of Egoism. Thus Matam Rutra is Egoism as attached to the gross physical body. Again, all sentient worldly being gives expression to its feelings, saying "I am happy, unhappy, and so forth." All this is here embodied in the speech of the Rutra and is called Akar Rutra. Khatram Rutra is Egoism of the mind, as when it is said of any object "this is mine". "Black Salvation" became a Rutra of such terrific power that to save him and the world the Buddhas intervened. There are four methods by which they and the Bodhisattvas subdue and save sentient being, namely, the Peaceful, the Grand or Attractive, the Fascinating which renders powerless (Vashīkaranam), and the stern method of downright Force. All forms of Egoism must be destroyed in order that the pure "That Which Is" or formless Consciousness may be attained. "Black Salvation" incarnated as the Pride of Egoism in its most terrible form. And, in order to subdue him, the last two methods had to be employed. He was, through the Glorious One, redeemed by the suffering which attends all sin and became the "Dark Defender of the Faith", which by his egoistic apostasy he had abjured, to be later the Buddha known as the "Lord of Ashes" in that world which is called "the immediately self-produced". How this came about the legend describes.

The fifth Chapter of the Golden Rosary says that Guru Padma-Vajradhara was reborn as Bhikshu Thubkazhonnu, which means the "youth who is hard to overcome". He was a Tāntrik who preached an abstruse doctrine which is condensed in the following verse:

"He who has attained the 'That Which Is'
Or uncreated In-itself-ness
Is unaffected even by the 'four things'
Just as the cloud which floats in the sky
Adheres not thereto.
This is the way of Supreme Yoga.
Than this in all the three worlds
There is not a higher wisdom."

This Guru had two disciples, Kuntri and his servant Pramadeva. To the latter was given, on initiation, the name "Transcendent Faith", and to the former "Black Salvation". This last name was a prophetic prediction that he would be saved, not through peaceful or agreeable means but through the just wrath of the Jinas. The real meaning of the verse as understood and practised by Pramadeva and as declared to be right by the Guru was as follows; "The pure Consciousness (Dagpa-ye-shes) is the foundation (Gshi-hdsin) of the limited consciousness (Rnam-shes) and is in Scripture "That which is," the real uncreated "In-Itself-ness". This being unaffected or unruffled is the path of Tantra. Passions (Klesha) are like clouds wandering in the wide spaces of the sky. (These clouds are distinct from, and do not touch the back-ground of space against which they appear.) So passions do not touch but disappear from the Void (Shūnyatā). Whilst ascending upwards the three-fold accomplishment (Activity, non-activity, absolute repose) must be persevered in; and this is the meaning of our Teacher Thubka's doctrine."

The latter, however, was misunderstood by "Black Salvation" (Tharpa Nagpo) who took it to mean that he was to make no effort to save himself by the gaining of merit, but that he was to indulge in the four acts of sinful enjoyment, by the eye, nose, tongue and organ of generation. On this account he fell out with his brother in the faith Pramadeva, and later with his Guru, both of whom he caused to be persecuted and banished the country. Continuing in a career of reckless and sin-hardened life, he died unrepentant after a score of years passed in various diabolical practices. He fell into Hell and continued there for countless ages. At the close of the time of Buddha Dīpankara (Marmedzad or "Light maker") he was reborn several times as huge sea monsters. At length, just before the time of the last Buddha Shākya Muni, he was born as the son of a woman of loose morals in a country called Lankāpurī of the Rākshasas. This woman used to consort with three Spirits—a Deva in the morning, a Fire Genius at noon, and a Daitya in the evening. "Black Salvation" was reborn in the eighth month as the offspring of these three Spirits. The child was a terrible monster, black of colour, with three heads, each of which had three eyes, six hands, four feet and two wings. He was horrible to look at, and immediately at his birth all the auspicious signs of the country disappeared, and the eighteen inauspicious signs were seen. Malignant epidemics attacked the whole region of Lankāpurī. Some died, others only suffered, but all were in misery. Lamentation, famine and sorrow beset the land. There were disease, bloodshed, mildew, hailstorms, droughts, floods and all other kinds of calamities. Even dreams were frightful, and ominous signs portending a great catastrophe oppressed all. Evil spirits roamed the land. So great were the evils that it seemed as if the good merits of everyone had been exhausted all at once.

The mother who had given birth to this monster died nine days after its birth. The people of the country decreed that this monstrous infant should be bound to the mother's corpse and left in the cemetery. The infant was then tied to his mother's breast. The mother was borne away in a stretcher to the cemetery, and the stretcher was left at the foot of a poisonous tree which had a boar's den at its root, a poisonous snake coiled round the middle of its trunk, and a bird of prey sitting in its uppermost branches. (These animals are the emblems of lust, anger and greed respectively which "kindle the fire of individuality".) At this place there was a huge sepulchre built by the Rākshasas where they used to leave their dead at the foot of the tree. Elephants and tigers came there to die; serpents infested it, and witch-like spirits called Dākinīs and Ghouls brought human bodies there. After the bearers of the corpse had left, the infant sustained his life by sucking the breasts of his mother's corpse. These yielded only a thin, yellowish, watery fluid for seven days. Next he sucked the blood and lived a week; then he gnawed at the breast and lived the third week; then he ate the entrails and lived for a week. Then he ate the outer flesh and lived for the fifth week. Lastly he crunched the bones, sucked the marrow, licked the humours and brains and lived a week. He thus in six weeks developed full physical maturity. Having exhausted his stock of food he moved about; and his motion shook the cemetery building to pieces. He observed the Ghouls and Dākinīs feasting on human corpses which he took as his food and human blood as his drink, filling the skulls with it. His clothing was dried human skins as also the hides of dead elephants, the flesh of which he also ate. He ate also the flesh of tigers and wrapped his loins in their furs. He used serpents as bracelets, anklets, armlets and as necklaces and garlands. His lips were thick with frozen fat, and his body was covered with ashes from the burning ground. He wore a garland of dead skulls on one string; freshly severed heads on another; and decomposing heads on a third. These were worn crosswise as a triple garland. Each cheek was adorned with a spot of blood. His three great heads ever wrathful, of three different colours, were fierce and horrible to look at. The middle head was dark blue and those to the right and left were white and red respectively. His body and limbs which were of gigantic size and proportions were ashy grey. His skin was coarse and his hair as stiff as hog's bristles. His mouth wide agape showed fangs. His terrible eyes were fixed in a stare. Half of the dark brown hair on his head stood erect, bound with four kinds of snakes. The nails of his fingers and toes were like the talons of a great bird of prey, which seized hold of everything within reach, whether animals or human corpses which he crushed and swallowed. He bore a trident and other weapons in his right hands, and with his left he filled the emptied skulls with blood which he drank with great relish. He was a monster of ugliness who delighted in every kind of impious act. His unnatural food produced a strange lustre on his face, which shone with a dull though great and terrible light. His breath was so poisonous that those touched by it were attacked with various diseases. For his nostrils breathed forth disease. His eyes, ears and arms produced the 404 different ills. Thus, the diseases paralysis, epilepsy bubonic swellings, urinary ills, skin diseases, aches, rheumatism, gout, colic, cholera, leprosy, cancer, small-pox, dropsy and various other sores and boils appeared in this world at that time. (For evil thoughts and acts make the vital spirit sick and thence springs gross disease.)

The name of this great Demon was Matam Rutra. He was the fruit of the Karma of the great wickedness of his former life as Tharpa Nagpo. At that time, in each of the 24 Pilgrimages, there was a powerful destructive Bhairava Spirit. These Devas, Gandharvas, Rākshasas, Asuras and Nāgas were proud, malignant and mighty Spirits, despotic masters of men, with great magical powers of illusion and transformation. These Spirits used to wander over these countries dressed in the eight sepulchral raiments, wearing the six kinds of bone ornaments, and armed with various weapons, accompanied by their female consorts, and revelled in all kinds of obscene orgies. Their chief occupation consisted in depriving all sentient beings of their lives. After consultation, all these Spirits elected Matam Rutra as their Chief. Thus all these non-human beings became his slaves. In the midst of his horrible retinue he continued to devour human beings alive until the race became almost destroyed and the cities emptied. He was thus the most terrible scourge that the earth had ever seen. All who died in those days fell into Hell. But, as for Matam Rutra himself, his pride knew no bounds: he thought there was no one greater than himself and would roar out:

"Who is there greater and mightier than I? If there be any Lord who would excel me, Him too will I subjugate."

42

As there was no one to gainsay him, the world was oppressed by heavy gloom. At that time, however, Kālī proclaimed,

"In the country of Lankā, the land of Rākshasas,
In a portion of the city called Koka-Thangmaling,
On the peak of Malaya, the abode of Thunder,
There dwells the Lord of Lankā, King of Rākshasas.
He is a disciple of the light-giving Buddha.
His fame far excels thine.
He is unconquerable in fight by any foe.
He sleeps secure and doth awake in peace."

Hearing this, the pride and ambition of the Demon became aflame. His body emitted flames great enough to have consumed all worlds at the great Kalpa dissolution. His voice resounded in a deep thundering roar like that of a thousand clasp of thunder heard together. With sparks of fire flying from his mouth he summoned a huge force. He filled the very heavens with them, and moving with the speed of a meteor he invaded the Rākshasa's capital of Koka-Thangmaling. Encamping, Matam Rutra proclaimed his name proudly, at which the entire country of Lankā trembled and was shaken terribly as though by an earthquake. The Rākshasas, both male and female, became terrified. The King of the Rākshasas sent spies to find out the cause of these happenings. They went and saw the terrible force, and being terrified at the sight reported the fearful news to their king. He sat in Samādhi for a while, and divined the following: According to the Sūtra of King Gunadhara it was said, "One who has vexed his Guru's heart, and broken his friend and brother's heart: the haughty son, being released from the three Hells, will take rebirth here, and he will surely conquer the Lord of Lankā. In the end, he will be conquered by many Sugatas (the blissful ones, or Buddhas). And this event will give birth to the Anuttara-Vajrayāna Faith." The Buddha Marmedzad having revealed the event, he wished to see whether this was the Matam Rutra Demon referred to in the prophesy. So he collected a force of Rākshasas and went forth to fight a battle with the Demon force. Matam Rutra was very angry and said:

> "I am the Great Invincible One, who is without a peer,
> I am the Īshvara Mahādeva.
> The four great Kings of the four quarters are my vassals,
> The eight different tribes of Spirits are my slaves,
> I am the Lord of the whole World.
> Who is going to withstand and confront me?
> Rutra, Matra, Marutra."

With this battle cry he overcame the forces of the Rākshasas. Then the King of the Rākshasas and all his forces submitted to the King of the Demons, saying "I repent me of my attempt to withstand you, in the hope of upholding the Faith of the Buddhas, and to spread it far and wide. I now submit to you and become your loyal subject. I will not rebel against you." When he had thus overcome the Rākshasas, he assumed the title of Matamka, the Chief of all the Rākshasas. His pride increased, and he proclaimed, "Who is there greater than I?"

Then, Kālī again cleverly excited his ambition and pride by saying, "The Chief of the armies of the Asuras (Lhamin that is "not Devas"), named Mahākaru, is mightier than you." Thereupon he invaded the realms of the Asuras, with his demon force, and all the Asuras becoming affected with various terrible maladies were powerless to resist him. The Rutra caught hold of the Asura King by the leg and whirling him thrice round his head flung him into the Jambudvīpa where he fell in a place called the Ge-ne-gyad, meaning the place of eight merits. Then those of the Asuras who had not been killed, the eight planets (Grahas) and the twenty-eight constellations (Nakshatras) and their hosts sought refuge in every direction, but failing to obtain safety anywhere, they returned and surrendered themselves to the Demon Matam Rutra. Then the Asuras guided the Rutra and his forces to a Palace named the Globular Palace like a skull where they established their Capital. In the centre of this Palace, the Rutra hoisted his banner of Victory. They arranged their dreadful weapons by the side of the entrance, and the place was surrounded by numerous followers with magical powers. Having thus shewn his own great magical powers, he took up the King of Mountains, Meru, upon the tip of his finger and whirling it round his head, he proclaimed these boastful words, " Rutra, Matra, Marutra, who is there in this universe greater than myself? In all the three Lokas, there is none greater than I. And if there be any, him also will I subdue." To these boastful words Kālī answered,

" In the thirty-third Deva-Loka and in the happy celestial regions of the Tushita Heavens,
Sitting amidst the golden assembly of disciples,
Is the Holy Saviour of all beings, Regent of the Devas (Dampa-Togkar)
Having been anointed, He is venerated and praised by all the Deva Kings.
He summons all the Devas to his assembly by sounding the various instruments of heavenly music
Accompanied by a celestial Chorus.
He is greater than yourself."

On her so saying, the Archdemon blazed forth into a fury of pride and wrath, and set forth to conquer the Tushita

Heavens. The Bodhisattva (Dampa-Togkar) was sitting enthroned on a throne of precious metals, in the midst of thousands of Devatās, both male and female, and was preaching Dharma to them. The Archdemon seized Dampa-Togkar from his throne, and threw him down into this world-system. All the Devas and Devīs there gathered exclaimed, "Alas, what a fate, O, the sinful wretch!" seven times over. Thereupon the Rutra fiercely said:

"Put on two cloths, and sit down on your seats, every one of you!
How can I be conquered by you? I am the mighty destroyer and subjugator of all.

(The expression "Put on two cloths" was said by way of contempt for the priestly robes which consist of three pieces, being a wrapper above, and one below and one over both. Dampa-Togkar is the Bodhisattva who is coming as Buddha to teach in the human world. He descends from the Tushita Heavens where he reigns as Regent.)

When the celestial Regent of the Tushita Heavens (Dampa-Togkar) was about to pass away from there, he uttered this prophesy to his disciples, who were around him:

"Listen unto me, Ye my disciples:

This apostate disciple, Tharpa-Nagpo (Black Salvation),
Who does not believe in the Buddha's Doctrine,
He is destined to pervert the Devas and Asuras,
And to bend them to his yoke.
He hates the perfect Buddha, and he will work much evil in this world-system.
There are two, who can deprive him of his terrible power;
They are Thubka-Zhonnu and Dad-Phags (Pramadeva, Arya Shrāddha called Transcendent Faith)

They will be able to make him taste the fruits of his evil deeds in this very life.
He will not be subdued by peaceful, nor by any generous means.
He will only be conquered by the methods of Fascination and Sternness.

(The various means of redemption have been previously explained. Thubka and his good disciple "Transcendent Faith" who had then become Buddha Vajra-Sattva, and Bodhisattva Vajrapāni were selected for this purpose. They assumed the forms of the Devatās with the Horse's head (Hayagrīva) and the Sow's head (Vajra-Vārāhī).

"Who, of the Noble Sangha, will doubt this,
That Hayagrīva and Vajra-Vārāhī will give him their bodies.

(When it is said "These will give him their bodies" this means, as hereafter described, entering the Rutra's body, assuming his shape and destroying his Rutra life and nature. They give him their divine bodies so that they may destroy his demoniac body.)

"And who will not trust in the Wisdom of the Jinas, to conquer him by the upward-piercing method,
From this (demon) will come the Precious-nectar, which will be of use in acquiring Virtue.
From this (demon) will originate the changing of poison into elixir.

(There are various Tāntrik methods suited to various natures. "The upward-piercing" (Khatar-yar-phig) is that of Vajrayāna. This is the method which goes upward and upward, that is straight upward without delay and without going to right or left. To change poison into nectar or elixir is a well-known principle of these schools.

"This Demon will have to be ground down and destroyed
to the last atom, in one body.

(It is said "in one body" because, ordinarily, several lives are necessary; but in this case and by this method Liberation is achieved in a single life-time and in one body. Not one atom of the Rutra body is left, for Egoism is wholly destroyed.)

"The Divine Horse-headed Deity (Vajra-Hayagrīva),
is he who will dispel this threatening misfortune,
Dad-phags, (Pramadeva who was given on initiation
the name "Transcendent faith") is at present
Vajrapāni (Bodhisattva).
And Thubka-Zhonnu is, at present, the Buddha
Vajrasattva.
The divine prophesies of the Jinas are to be interpreted thus:
'They will exterminate their opponents
For myself I go to take birth in Māyā-Devī's womb.
I will practise Samādhi at the root of the Bodhi-Tree.
I will not hold those beliefs in doubt.
For it has been said that the Buddha's Faith will
triumph over this,
And will remain long in the Jambudvīpa.
By means of the mysterious practice of Emancipating
by means of Communion.'

(The practice here referred to is the method called Jordol (sByor sGrol) which has both exoteric and esoteric meanings, such as in the case of the latter the communion of the Divine Male and Female whose union destroys to its uttermost root egoistic attachment; the communion with Shūnyatā whose innermost significance is the non-dual Consciousness (gṄyismed-yeshes) which dispels ignorance and cuts at the root of all Sāmsāric life by the destruction of all the Rutra forms. "Female" here is Shūnyatā and not a woman. When a learned Lama is asked why the terms of sex are used they say it is to symbolise Thabs (Upāya) and Shes-rabs (Prajnā) which it is not possible to further explain here. (See Vol. XIII, XIV of Tāntrik Texts, Ed. A. Avalon.)

> "The Matam Rutra, which is clinging to the body as 'I' will be dispelled,
> All forms of worldly happiness and pain, the Egoism of Speech (Akar Rutra),
> Will be destroyed.
> The saying 'this is mine' of anything,
> The mental 'I' (or Khatram-Rutra) is freed.
> The true nature and distinguishing attributes of a Rutra,
> Which is manifest outwardly, exists inwardly, and lies hidden secretly,
> In short all the fifty-eight Rutras, with their hosts, will be destroyed completely.

(I have already dealt with the meaning of the term, Rutra. Here the Egoisms of body, feelings, mind are referred to. The Glorious One will eradicate the physical and all other Rutras, the monster of the self in all its forms, gross, subtle and causal.)

> "The world though deprived of happiness will rejoice again.
> The world will be filled with the Precious Dharma of the Tri-Ratna.
> The Righteous Faith has not declined, nor has it passed away."

(Thus did the Regent of the Tushita Heavens prophesy the advent of the Tāntrik method for the complete destruction and the elimination of the demon of "Egotism" from the nature of the devotees on the path by means of Jordol.)

After uttering these prophecies he passed away and took re-birth in the womb of Queen Māyā Devī. Then the Archdemon, having subjugated all the Devas of the thirty-third and the Tushita Heavens, appointed the two Demons Māra and Devadatta, his two chief officers, to suppress Indra and Brahmā. The Archdemon himself took up his abode in the Malaya Mountain, in the place called the Human skull-like Mansion. He used to feed upon Devas and human beings, both males and females. Drums, bells, cymbals and every kind of stringed and other musical instruments were played to him in a perpetual concert with songs and dances. Every kind of enjoyment which the Devas used to enjoy, he enjoyed perpetually. (8th Chapter ends.)

The 9th Chapter deals with the defeat and destruction of the Archdemon Matam Rutra by the Buddhas of the ten directions:

Then there assembled together Dharmakāya Buddha Samantabhadra (Chosku Kuntu Zangpo) and his attendants from the Wogmin (Akanishta) Heavens, from other Heavens, Sambhoga-kāya Vajra-dhara with his attendants; and Vajrapāni Nirmānakāya with his attendants. In short, from the various heavens of the ten directions came the different Buddhas and Bodhisattvas. All held a consultation together and came to this resolution:

"Unless the power of the Buddhas be exerted to subjugate the Rutra, the Faith of the Buddhas will cease to spread and will degenerate. That body which has committed such violent outrages on every other being, must be made to suffer the agonies of being hurt by weapons, wielded by avengers. If he is not made to feel the consequences of his deeds, the Jinas who have proclaimed the Truth will be falsified. He is not to be destroyed but to be subdued." Having thus agreed, all the Buddhas began to seek with their omniscient eyes, him who was destined to conquer this Rutra. They saw that Thubka-Zhonnu who had attained the state of Buddha Vajra-sattva and Dadphags who had become Vajra-pāni were to subdue him, and that the time was also ripe. So both of them came with their respective retinue and were blessed and endowed with Power by all the Buddhas, who gave these instructions. "Do ye assume the forms and sexes of Chenrezi and Dolma (Avalokita and Tārā) and do ye subdue the Enemy by assuming the shapes of the Deities having the Horse-mane and the Sow's head (Haya-grīva and Vajra-Vārāhī).

(The latter is commonly known in English translations as the "Diamond Sow". Vajra is the Sanskrit equivalent of the word Dorje in Tibetan. The latter has many meanings; Indra's thunderbolt, the Lamas' sceptre, diamond and so forth: and is in fact used of anything of a high and mystical character which is lasting, indestructible, powerful and irresistible. Thus the high priest presiding at Tāntrik Rites is called Dorje Lopon. In fact, diamond is so called because of the hard character of this gem. In the Indian Tāntrik worship, Vajra occurs as in Vajrapushpa (Vajra-flower), Vajra-bhūmi (Vajra-ground), and so forth, but these are not "diamond" flowers or earth. An extremely interesting enquiry is here opened which is beyond the scope of this Chapter, for the term Vajra, which is again the appellation of this particular school (Vajrayāna), and is of great significance in the history of that power-side of religion which is dealt with in the Shākta Tantra. See Introduction to Shrī-Chakra-Sambhara, edited by Arthur Avalon, Vol. VII of Tāntrik Texts. Here, without further attempt at explanation, I keep the term Vajra adding only that Harinisa is not, as has been thought, Vajra-Vārāhī (Dorje-phagmo) Herself but the Bīja Mantras (Ha, ri, ni, sa) of Her four attendant Dākinīs.)

Vajra-Sattva and Vajrapāni, Buddha and Bodhisattva of the Vajrayāna faith transformed themselves into the forms of Haya-grīva and Vajra-Vārāhī, and assumed the costumes of Herukas. (The Herukas are a class of Vajrayāna Devatās, of half terrible features, represented as partly nude with an upper garment of human skin and tiger skin round the loins. They have a skull head-dress, carry bone rosaries, a staff and Damaru like Shiva. The Herukas are described in the Tibetan books as being beautiful, heroic, awe-inspiring, stern and majestic.) Blazing in the nine kinds of physical magnificence and splendour, they proceeded to the Malaya Mountain,—the abode of the Rutra. On the four sides of the Mountain were four gates. Each gate was guarded by a Demoness, bearing respectively aMare's, Sow's, Lion's and a Dog's head. These the Glorious One conquered, and united therewith in a spirit of nonattachment. From their union were born the following female issue: (1) The White Horse-faced, (2) The Black Sow-faced, (3) The Red Lion-faced, (4) and the Green Dog-faced daughters. Proceeding still further He met another cordon of sentries, who too were females, bearing the heads of (1) Lioness, (2) Tigress, (3) Fox, (4) Wolf, (5) Vulture, (6) Kanka, (?) (7) Raven, and (8) Owl. With these Demonesses too, the Glorious One united in a spirit of non-attachment, and blessed the act. Of this union were born female offspring, each of whom took after the mother in outward shape or Matter, and after the father in Mind. Thus were the eight Demi-goddesses born: *viz.*, the Lion-headed, Tiger-headed and so forth. Being divine in mind, they possess prescience and wisdom, although from their mother they retained their shape and features, which are those of brutes.

Then again proceeding further inward, He came upon the daughters of the Rutras and of Rākshasas, named respectively, Nyobyed-ma or "She who maddens," Tagbyed-ma "She who frightens," Dri-medma "The unsullied," Kempama "She who dries one up," Phorthogma "She who bears the Cup" and Zhyongthogma the "bowl bearer".

The Glorious One united with these in the same manner, and from them, were born the eight Mātrikās of the eight Sthānas (sacred places), known as Gaurīmā and so forth. These, too, possessed divine wisdom from their father and terrific features and shapes from their mothers.

(There are 24 Sthānas which are places of pilgrimage and eight great cemeteries making 32 in all. In each of these cemeteries there is a powerful Goddess also called Mamo, that is, Mātrikā. These terrible Goddesses are, according to the Zhi-Khro, Gaurīmā, Tsaurīmā, Chāndālī, Vetālī, Ghasmarī, Shonamā, Pramo, Puskasī. These are in colour white, yellow, yellowish white, black, dark green, dark blue, red, reddish yellow, and are situated in the East, South, N.W., North, S.W., N.E., West, S.E., "nerve-leafs of the conch-shell mansion" (brain) respectively. These are the eight great Mātrikās of the eight great Cemeteries, to whom prayer is made, that when forms are changed and entrance is made on the intermediate plane (Bardo. See as to this Dr. Evans-Wentz, "Tibetan Book of the Dead"), they may place the spirit on the clear light path of Radiance (Hodsal).

(These various accomplements denote the union of Divine Mind with gross matter. In working with matter the Divine mind is always detached. Work is possible even for the liberated consciousness when free from attachment, that is, desire (Kāma), which is bondage. The Divine Mind unites with terrible forms of gross matter that these may be instruments; in this case instruments whereby the gross Egoism of the Rutra is to be subdued.)

Then going right into the innermost abode, he found that the Rutra had gone out in search of food, which consisted of human flesh and of Devas. Adopting the disguise of the Rutra, the Glorious One went in to the Consort of the Rutra, the Rākshasī-Queen Krodheshvarī (Lady of wrath) in the same spirit as before, and blessed the act. By Krodheshvarī, He had male issue, Bhagavān Vajra-Heruka, with three faces and six hands, terrific to behold. Then the Glorious One, Hayagrīva, and his divine Consort, Vajra-Vārāhī, each expressed their triumph by neighing and grunting thrice. Upon hearing these sounds the Rutra was struck with mortal fear, and coming to the spot, he said:

" What sayest Thou, little son of Hayagrīva and Vajra-Vārāhī.
All the world of Devas and Asuras
Proclaim my virtues and sing my praises.
I cannot be conquered. Rest yourselves in peace,
Regard me with humility, and bow down to me.
Even the Regent of the Devas,
of the odd garment (priestly dress),
Failed to conquer me in days of yore."

Saying this he raised his hands, and came to lay them on the young one's head. Thereupon, Hayagrīva at once entered the body of the Rutra by the secret path (Guhya) from below and piercing him right through from below upwards, He showed His Horse's Head, on the top of the head of the Rutra. The oily fat of the Rutra's body made the Horse's head look green. The mane, being dyed with blood, became red, and the eye-brows, having been splashed with the bile of the Demon, became yellow. The forehead, being splashed with the brains, became white. Thus the Glorious One, having assumed the shape and dresses of the Rutra, took on a terrible majesty.

At the same time, Vajra-Vārāhī, His Consort, also entered the body of the Rutra's Consort Krodheshvarī, in the same manner piercing and impaling her. She forced Her own Sow's head right up through the crown of the Demoness' head, until it towered above it. The Sow's head had assumed a black colour, from having been steeped in the fat of the Rākshasī. Then the two Divine Beings embraced each other, and begot an offspring, a Divine Being, a male of the Terrific Order, a Krodhabhairava. Having done this, Hayagrīva neighed shrilly six times, and Vajra-Vārāhī grunted deeply five times. Then the hosts of the Buddhas and the Bodhisattvas assembled there as thickly as birds of prey settling down on carrion. They filled all space. They were of the peaceful, the wrathful, the half-peaceful and the half-wrathful orders, in inconceivably large numbers. They began to surround the Rutra-Tharpa-Nagpo, who, being unable to bear the pain of being stretched asunder, cried in agony:

"Oh, I am defeated! The Horse and the Sow have defeated the Rutra.
The Buddhas have defeated the Demons.
Religion has conquered Ir-religion,
The Sangha has defeated the Tīrthikas.
Indra has defeated the Asuras,
The Asuras have defeated the Moon
The Garuda has defeated the Ocean
Fire defeats fuel, Wind scatters the Clouds
Diamond (Vajra) pierces metals
Oh! it was I who said that last night's dream portended evil.
Oh! slay me quick, if you are going to slay me."

As he said this, his bowels were involuntarily loosened, and from the excreta which, being thus purified, fell into the Ocean, there at once arose a precious sandal tree, which was a wish-granting tree. This tree struck its root in the nether world of the Serpent-spirits, spread its foliage in the Asura-lokas, and bore its fruits in the Deva-lokas. And the fruits were named Amrita (the essence and elixir of life).

Then the two Chief Actor and Actress, Hayagrīva and Vajra-Vārāhī acted the joyful plays called the 'Plays of Happy Cause,' 'Happy Path', and 'Happy Result', in the nine glorious measures. (That is, plays in which the actors are happy being the male and female Divinities, in this case Hayagrīva and Vajra-Vārāhī. They are the cause; their play being exoterically "Dalliance" (Līlā), and their result the dispelling of Egoism which is Illumination.)

Just as a victor in a battle, who has slain his enemy, wins the armour and the accoutrements of his slain opponent, and puts them on as a sign of triumph, so also, the Glorious One having conquered the Rutra, assumed the eight accoutrements of the foe, including the wings, and the other adornments which made him look so bright and magnificent. These the Glorious One blessed and consecrated to the use of the Divine Deities. Having done all this, both Hayagrīva and Vajra-Vārāhī returned to the Realm of pure Spiritual Being (Dharmadhātu). Thus it comes about that those costumes, assumed by the Rutra, came to be adopted as the attire of the Deities. Their having three heads, the eight sepulchral ornaments, and the eight glorious costumes and wings, had origin in this event.

Then Pal Chag-na-dorje (Shrī Vajrapāni) multiplied himself into countless Avatāras, and these again multiplied themselves into myriads of Avatāras, all of the terrible and wrathful type. The Rutra too showed supernatural powers, for he transformed himself into a nine-headed Monster, having eighteen hands, as huge as the Mount Meru. Should it be doubted, how this sinful being could still possess such supernatural powers, one must know that he was a Bodhisattva of the eighth degree (One who has attained eight Bhūmikās or stages of advance out of thirteen) who had fallen back. Hence was it, that even the Buddhas found it difficult to subdue him, not to count the world of Devas and men. Then Vajrapāni manifested still greater divine powers of every imaginable description, and all the Buddhas and Bodhisattvas fixed their abodes on the greatly enlarged and distended body of the Rutra. The latter being unable to bear the agony of this pressure, roared with pain,

"Come quick to the rescue, O my followers, who inhabit the ten directions
To the right and left of the Skull-like Mansion
And those who live in the gardens and the orchards.
Yakshas, Rākshasas, and Pretas millions in number, advance to the rescue at once.
O ye followers and adherents of the Rutra, who dwell in the twenty-four places, and countries
Numbering millions and tens of million, who have sworn allegiance to me
And promised to serve me faithfully, and ye from the illimitable spaces in every direction
Fill the heavens and the earth with your innumerable hosts
And all in one body strike (at the foe) with the weapons in your hands, sounding the battle cry
Om-rulu-rulu."

Though he uttered these commands, there was none to obey him. Everyone surrendered to Bhagavān Vajra-Heruka. Thus all the subordinates of the Rutra, the thirty-two Dākinīs, the seven Mātrikās, and the four "Sisters," Sringbzhi), the eight Furies (Barmas or flaming ones), the eight Genii (spirits or attendants on the Devatās) and the sixty-four Messengers all came over to the Heruka and the Divine offspring (the Krodha-Bhairava) took upon himself the duty of serving the food of the Deities.

(This is the Deity usually invoked when any purification and religious contrition has to be performed or done. By this it is seen that his undertaking to serve the food of the Deities means purifying and absolving the sins of the Rutra.)

Vajrapāni, producing ten divine beings of the terrific type (Krodhabhairava), gave a Phurpa (triangular-shaped dagger) to each of them, and commanded them to go and destroy the Rutra and his party. Thereupon Hayagrīva came again, and neighed three times; upon hearing which sound, the entire host of the Rutra were seized with a panic and all were subdued. Then "Black Salvation" (Tharpa-Nagpo) and his followers were rendered powerless and helpless: humbled and quite submissive. So they surrendered their own homes, personal ornaments, and lives, and uttered these words of entreaty:

"Obeisance to Thee, O, Thou field of the Buddhas' influence,
Obeisance to Thee, O, Thou who dost cause Karma to bear fruit.
I and all of us having sown previous evil Karma
Are now reaping the fruits thereof, which all indeed may see.
Our future depends on what we have done now;
Karma follows us, as inexorably as the shadow does the body.
Everyone must taste the fruit of what each has himself done.
Even should one repent, and be sorry for his deeds
There is no help for him as Karma cannot be avoided.

So we who are destined by Karma to drink the bitter cup to the very dregs,
We do therefore offer up our bodies to serve as the cushion of Thy footstool.
Pray accept them as such."

Having said so, they laid themselves prostrate, and from this originates the symbolism of every Deity having a Rutra underneath his feet. Then the vassal Chiefs of the Rutra submitted their prayers:

"We have no claim to sit in the middle,
Be pleased to place us at the extermities of the Mandalas.
We have no right to demand of the best of the banquets.
We pray to be favoured with the leavings, and the dregs of food and drink.
Henceforth, we are Your subjects, and will never disobey Your commands.
We will obey You in whatever You are pleased to command.
As a loving mother is attracted towards her son,
So shall we, too, be surely drawn near those who remind us of this oath of allegiance."

Thus did they take the oath of allegiance. Then the Holder of the Mysteries, the Glorious One—Vajrapāni, pierced the heart of the prostrate Rutra with the Phurpa dagger and absolved him. All his Kārmik sins and his Passions (Klesha) were thus immediately absolved. Then power was conferred on him, and vows were laid on him, and the water of Faith was poured on him. His body, speech and mind were blessed and consecrated towards Divine Service, and the Dorje of Faith was laid on the head, throat and heart. Thenceforward he was empowered to be the Guardian of the Faith, and named the Good dark One, and his secret name conferred at the Initiation was Mahākāla. Thus was he included in the assembly of the Vajrayāna Deities. Finally, it was revealed to him that he would become a Buddha, by the name of Thalwai-Wangpo (the Lord of Ashes) in the World called Kod-pa-lhundrup (that is "self-produced" or "made-all-at-once"). Then the Rutra's dead body was thrown on this Jambu-dvīpa, where it fell on its back. The head fell on Sinhala (Ceylon), the right arm and hand upon the Thogar (?) country and the left hand on Le (Ladak country). The right leg fell on Nepal, and the left on Kashmir. The entrails fell over Zahor. The heart fell on Urgyen (Cabul), and the Linga on Magadha. These form the eight chief countries. Thus the eight Mātrikās of the eight Sthānas, headed by Gaurīmā and others: the eight natural Stūpas headed by Potala; the eight occult powers, which fascinate; the eight guardians (female), who enchant; the eight great trees, the eight great realm-protectors (Shing-kyong), the eight lakes, the eight great Nāga spirits, the eight clouds, and the eight great Dikpālas (Chyogs-kyong or Protectors of the Directions) as well as the eight great cemeteries originated.

With the end of the sixth Chapter of the Golden Rosary is concluded the account of the Vajrayāna Devatās who appeared to aid in the conquest of human Egoism which had manifested itself in terrible form in the person of the great Rutra. As all but the fully pure have in them Rutra elements, they are enjoined in Vajrayāna to follow the methods of expurgation there revealed.

CHAPTER XXIX

KUNDALINĪ SHAKTI

(YOGA)

THE word 'Yoga' comes from the root "*yuj*" which means "to join" and, in its spiritual sense, it is that process by which the human spirit is brought into near and conscious communion with, or is merged in, the Divine Spirit, according as the nature of the human spirit is held to be separate from (Dvaita, Vishishtādvaita) or one with (Advaita) the Divine Spirit. As, according to Shākta doctrine, with which alone we are concerned, the latter proposition is affirmed, Yoga is that process by which the identity of the two (Jīvātmā and Paramātmā),—which identity ever in fact exists,—is realized by the Yogī or practitioner of Yoga. It is so realized because the Spirit has then pierced through the veil of Māyā which as mind and matter obscures this knowledge from itself. The means by which this is achieved is the Yoga process which liberates from Māyā. So the Gheranda Samhitā, a Hathayoga treatise of the Tāntrik school, says (Chap. 5): "There is no bond equal in strength to Māyā, and no power greater to destroy that bond than Yoga." From an Advaita or Monistic standpoint, Yoga in the sense of a final union is inapplicable, for union implies a dualism of the Divine and Human spirit. In such case, it denotes the process rather than the result. When the two are regarded as distinct, Yoga may apply to both. A person who practises Yoga is called a "Yogī". According to Indian notions all are not competent (Adhikārī) to attempt Yoga; only a very few are. One must, in this or in other lives, have first gone through Karma or ritual, and Upāsanā or devotional, worship and obtained the fruit thereof, namely, a pure mind (Chittashuddhi). This Sanskrit term does not merely mean a mind free from sexual impurity, as an English reader might suppose. The attainment of this and other good qualities is the A B C of Sādhanā. A person may have a pure mind in this sense and yet be wholly incapable of Yoga. Chittashuddhi consists not merely in moral purity of every kind, but in knowledge, detachment, capacity for pure intellectual functioning, attention, meditation and so forth. When, by Karma and Upāsanā, the mind is brought to this point and when, in the case of Vedāntik Yoga, there is dispassion and detachment from the world and its desires, then the Yoga path is open for the realization of Tattvajnāna, that is ultimate Truth. Very few persons indeed are competent for Yoga in its higher forms. The majority should seek their advancement along the path of ritual and devotion.

There are four main forms of Yoga, according to a common computation, namely, Mantrayoga, Hathayoga, Layayoga, and Rājayoga, the general characteristics of which have been described in "The Serpent Power". It is only necessary here to note that Kundalī-yoga is Layayoga. The Eighth Chapter of the Sammohana Tantra, however, speaks of five kinds, namely, Jnāna, Rāja, Laya, Hatha, and Mantra, and mentions as five aspects of the spiritual life, Dharma, Kriyā, Bhāva, Jnāna, and Yoga; Mantrayoga being said to be of two kinds, according as it is pursued along the path of Kriyā or Bhāva. Many forms of Yoga are in fact mentioned in the Books. There are seven Sādhanās of Yoga, namely, Shatkarma, Āsana, Mudrā, Pratyāhāra, Prānāyāma, Dhyāna, and Samādhi, which are cleansing of the body, seat, postures for gymnastic and Yoga purposes, the abstraction of the senses from their objects, breath control (the celebrated Prānāyāma), meditation, and ecstasy, which is of two kinds, imperfect (Savikalpa) in which dualism is not wholly overcome, and perfect (Nirvikalpa) which is complete Monistic experience—"Aham Brahmāsmi", "I am the Brahman"—a knowledge in the sense of realization which, it is to be observed, does not produce Liberation (Moksha) but *is* Liberation itself. The Samādhi of Laya-yoga is said to be Savikalpasamādhi, and that of complete Rāja-yoga is said to be Nirvikalpasamādhi. The first four processes are physical and the last three mental and supramental (see Gheranda Samhitā Upadesha, I). By these seven processes respectively certain qualities are gained, namely, purity (Shodhana), firmness and strength (Dridhatā), fortitude (Sthiratā), steadiness (Dhairya), lightness (Lāghava), realization (Pratyaksha), and detachment leading to Liberation (Nirliptattva).

What is known as the eight-limbed Yoga (Ashtānga-yoga) contains five of the above Sādhanās (Āsana, Prānāyāma, Pratyāhāra, Dhyāna, and Samādhi) and three others, namely, Yama or self-control by way of chastity, temperance, avoidance of harm (Ahimsā) and other virtues, Niyama or religious observances, charity and so forth, with Devotion to the Lord (Īshvara-pranidhāna), and Dhāranā, the fixing of the internal organ on its subject as directed in the Yoga practice. For further details, I refer the reader to my introduction to the work entitled "The Serpent Power". Here I will only deal shortly with Laya-yoga or the arousing of Kundalinī Shakti, a subject of the highest importance in the Tantra Shāstra, and without some knowledge of which much of its ritual will not be understood. I cannot here enter into all the details which demand a lengthy exposition, and which I have given in the Introduction to the two Sanskrit works called Shatchakranirūpana, and Pādukāpanchaka translated in the volume, "The Serpent Power" which deals with Kundalinī Shakti and the piercing by Her of the six bodily centres or Chakras. The general principle and meaning of this Yoga has never yet been published, and the present Chapter is devoted to a short summary of these two points only.

All the world (I speak, of course, of those interested in such subjects) is beginning to speak of Kundalinī Shakti, "cette fameuse Kundalinī" as a French friend of mine calls Her. There is considerable talk about the Chakras and the Serpent Power but lack of understanding as to what they mean. This, as usual, is sought to be covered by an air of mystery, mystical mists, and sometimes the attitude; "I should much like to tell you if only I were allowed to give it out." A silly Indian boast of which I lately read is, "I have the key and I keep it." Those who really have the key to anything are superior men, above boasting. "Mysticism," which is often confused thinking, is also a fertile soil of humbug. I do not, of course, speak of true Mysticism. Like all other matters in this Indian Shāstra the basis of this Yoga is essentially rational. Its thought, like that of the ancients generally, whether of East or West, has in general the form and brilliance of a cut gem. It is this quality which makes it so dear to some of those who have had to wade through the slush of much modern thought and literature. No attempt has hitherto been made to explain the general principles which underlie it. This form of Yoga is an application of the general principles relating to Shakti with which I have already dealt. The subject has both a theoretical and practical aspect. The latter is concerned with the teaching of the method in such a way that the aspirant may give effect to it. This cannot be learnt from books but only from the Guru who has himself successfully practised this Yoga. Apart from difficulties, inherent in written explanations, it cannot be practically learnt from books, because the carrying out of the method is affected by the nature and capacity of the Sādhaka and what takes place during his Sādhanā. Further, though some general features of the method have been explained to me, I have had no practical experience myself of this Power. I am not speaking as a Yogī in this method, which I am not; but as one who has read and studied the Shāstra on this matter, and has had the further advantage of some oral explanations which have enabled me to better understand it. I have dealt with this practical side, so far as it is possible to me, in my work on "The Serpent Power". Even so far as the matter can be dealt with in writing, I cannot, within the limits of such a paper as this, deal with it in any way fully. A detailed description of the Chakras and their significance cannot be attempted here. I refer the reader to the work entitled "The Serpent Power". What I wish to do is to treat the subject on the broadest lines possible and to explain the fundamental principles which underlie this Yoga method. It is because these are not understood that there is much confused thinking and misty, if not mystical, talk upon the subject. How many persons, for instance, can correctly answer the question, "What is Kundalinī Shakti?" One may be told that it is a Power or Shakti; that it is coiled like a serpent in the Mūlādhāra; and that it is wakened and goes up through the Chakras to the Sahasrāra. But what Shakti is it? Why, again, is it coiled like a serpent? What is the meaning of this? What is the nature of the Power? Why is it in the Mūlādhāra? What is the meaning of "awakening" the power? Why if awakened should it go up? What are the Chakras? It is easy to say that they are regions or lotuses. What are they in themselves? Why have each of the lotuses a different number of petals? What is a petal? What and why are the "Letters" on them? What is the effect of going to the Sahasrāra: and how does that effect come about? These and other similar questions require an answer before this form of Yoga can be understood. I have said something as to the Letters in the chapters on Shakti as Mantra and Varnamālā. With these and with other general questions, rather than with the details of the six Chakras, set forth in "The Serpent Power" I will here deal.

In the first place, it is necessary to remember the fundamental principle of the Tantra Shāstra to which I have already referred, *viz.*, that man is a microcosm (Kshudrabrahmānda). Whatever exists in the outer universe exists in him. All the Tattvas and the worlds are within him and so are the supreme Shiva-Shakti.

The body may be divided into two main parts, namely, the head and trunk on one hand, and the legs on the other. In man, the centre of the body is between these two, at the base of the spine where the legs begin. Supporting the trunk and throughout the whole body there is the spinal cord. This is the axis of the body, just as Mount Meru is the axis of the earth. Hence man's spine is called Merudanda, the Meru or axis-staff. The legs and feet are gross matter which show less signs of consciousness than the trunk with its spinal white and grey matter; which trunk itself is greatly subordinate in this respect to the head containing the organ of mind, or physical brain, with its white and grey matter. The position of the white and grey matter in the head and spinal column respectively are reversed. The body and legs below the centre are the seven lower or nether worlds upheld by the sustaining Shaktis of the universe. From the centre upwards, consciousness more freely manifests through the spinal and cerebral centres. Here there are the seven upper regions or Lokas, a term which Satyānanda in his commentary on Īsha Upanishad says, means "what are seen" (Lokyante), that is, experienced and are hence the fruits of Karma in the form of particular re-birth. These regions, namely, Bhūh, Bhuvah, Svah, Tapah, Jana, Mahah, and Satya Lokas correspond with the six centres; five in the trunk, the sixth in the lower cerebral centre; and the seventh in the upper Brain or Satyaloka, the abode of the supreme Shiva-Shakti.

The six centres are the Mūlādhāra or root-support situated at the base of the spinal column in a position midway in the perinæum between the root of the genitals and the anus. Above it, in the region of the genitals, abdomen, heart, chest or throat and in the forehead between the two eyes (Bhrūmadhye) are the Svādhishthāna, Manipūra, Anāhata, Vishuddha and Ājnā Chakras or lotuses (Padma) respectively. These are the chief centres, though the books speak of others such as the Lalanā and Manas and Soma Chakras. In fact, in the Advaita Mārtanda, a modern Sanskrit book by the late Guru of the Mahārājā of Kashmir, some fifty Chakras and Ādhāras are mentioned: though the six stated are the chief upon which all accounts agree. And so it is said, "How can there be any Siddhi for him who knows not the six Chakras, the sixteen Ādhāras, the five Ethers and the three Lingas in his own body?" The seventh region beyond the Chakras is the upper brain, the highest centre of manifestation of Consciousness in the body and therefore the abode of the supreme Shiva-Shakti. When "abode" is said, it is not meant, of course, that the Supreme is there placed in the sense of our "placing", namely, it is there and not elsewhere. The Supreme is never localized whilst its manifestations are. It is everywhere both within and without the body, but it is said to be in the Sahasrāra, because it is there that the Supreme Shiva-Shakti is realized. And this must be so, because consciousness is realized by entering in and passing through the highest manifestation of mind, the Sattvamayī Buddhi, above and beyond which is Chit and Chidrūpinī Shakti themselves. From their Shiva-Shakti Tattva aspect are evolved Mind in its form as Buddhi, Ahamkāra, Manas and associated senses (Indriyas) the centre of which is in and above the Ājnā Chakra and below the Sahasrāra. From Ahamkāra proceed the Tanmātras or generals of the sense-particulars which evolve the five forms of sensible matter (Bhūta), namely, Ākāsha ("Ether"), Vāyu ("Air"), Agni ("Fire"), Apas ("Water"), and Prithivī ("Earth"). The English translation given of these terms do not imply that the Bhūtas are the same as the English elements of air, fire, water, earth. The terms indicate varying degrees of matter from the ethereal to the solid. Thus Prithivī or earth is any matter in the Prithivī state; that is, which may be sensed by the Indriya of smell. Mind and matter pervade the whole body. But there are centres therein in which they are predominant. Thus Ājnā is a centre of mind, and the five lower Chakras are centres of the five Bhūtas; Vishuddha of Ākāsha, Anāhata of Vāyu, Manipūra of Agni, Svādhishthāna of Apas, and Mūlādhāra of Prithivī.

In short, man as a microcosm is the all-pervading Spirit (which most purely manifests in the Sahasrāra) vehicled by Shakti in the form of Mind and Matter the centres of which are the sixth and following five Chakras respectively.

The six Chakras have been indentified with the following plexuses commencing from the lowest, the Mūlādhāra: The Sacrococcygeal plexus, the Sacral plexus, the Solar plexus (which forms the great junction of the right and left sympathetic chains Idā and Pingalā) with the cerebro-spinal axis. Connected with this is the Lumbar plexus. Then follows the Cardiac plexus (Anāhata), Laryngeal plexus, and lastly the Ājnā or cerebellum with its two lobes, and above this the Manas Chakra or sensorium with its six lobes, the Soma-chakra or middle Cerebrum, and lastly the Sahasrāra or upper Cerebrum. To some extent these localizations are yet tentative. This statement may involve an erroneous view of what the Chakras really are, and is likely to produce wrong notions concerning them in others. The six Chakras themselves are vital centres within the spinal column in the white and grey matter there. They may, however, and probably do, influence and govern the gross tract outside the spine in the bodily region lateral to, and co-extensive with, the section of the spinal column in which a particular centre is situated. The Chakras are centres of Shakti as vital force. In other words, they are centres of Prānashakti manifested by Prānavāyu in the living body, the presiding Devatās of which are names for the Universal Consciousness as It manifests in the form of those centres. The Chakras are not perceptible to the gross senses, whatever may be a Yogi's powers to observe what is beyond the senses (Atīndriya). Even if they were perceptible in the living body which they help to organize, they disappear with the disintegration of organism at death.

In an article on "The Physical Errors of Hinduism", (Calcutta Review, XI, 436-440) it was said: "It would indeed excite the surprise of our readers to hear that the Hindus, who would not even touch a dead body, much less dissect it (which is incorrect), should possess any anatomical knowledge at all . . . It is the Tantras that furnish us with some extraordinary pieces of information concerning the human body. . . . But of all the Hindu Shāstras extant, the Tantras lie in the greatest obscurity. . . . The Tāntrik theory, on which the well-known Yoga called 'Shatchakrabheda' is founded, supposes the existence of six main internal organs, called Chakras or Padmas, all bearing a special resemblance to that famous flower, the lotus. These are placed one above the other, and connected by three imaginary chains, the emblems of the Ganges, the Yamunā, and the Sarasvatī. . . Such is the obstinacy with which the Hindus adhere to these erroneous notions, that, even when we show them by actual dissection the non-existence of the imaginary Chakras in the human body, they will rather have recourse to excuses revolting to common-sense than acknowledge the evidence of their own eyes. They say, with a shamelessness unparalleled, that these Padmas exist as long as a man lives, but disappear the moment he dies." This alleged "Shamelessness" reminds me of the story of a doctor who told my father "that he had performed many postmortems and had never yet discovered a soul."

The petals of the lotuses vary being 4, 6, 10, 12, 16, 2 respectively; commencing from the Mūlādhāra and ending with Ājnā. There are 50 in all, as are the letters of the alphabet which are in the petals; that is, the Mātrikās are associated with the Tattvas since both are products of the same creative Cosmic Process manifesting either as physiological or psychological function. It is noteworthy that the number of the petals is that of the letters leaving out either Ksha or the Second La, and that these 50 multiplied by 20 are in the 1000 petals of the Sahasrāra, a number which is probably only indicative of multitude and magnitude.

But why, it may be asked, do the petals vary in number? Why, for instance, are there 4 in the Mūlādhāra and 6 in the Svādhishthāna? The answer given is that the number of petals in any Chakra is determined by the number and position of the Nādis or Yoga "nerves" around that Chakra. Thus, four Nādīs surrounding and passing through the vital movements of the Mūlādhāra Chakra give it the appearance of a lotus of four petals. The petals are thus configurations made by the position of Nādīs at any particular centre. These Nādīs are not those which are known to the Vaidya of Medical Shāstras. The latter are gross physical nerves. But the former here spoken of are called Yoga-Nādīs and are subtle channels (Vivara) along which the Pranik currents flow. The term Nādī comes from the root "Nad" which means motion. The body is filled with an uncountable number of Nādīs. If they were revealed to the eye the body would present the appearance of a highly complicated chart of ocean currents. Superficially the water seems one and the same. But examination shows that it is moving with varying degrees of force in all directions. All these lotuses exist in the spinal column.

An Indian physician and Sanskritist has, in the Guy's Hospital Gazette, expressed the opinion that better anatomy is given in the Tantras than in the purely medical works of the Hindus. I have attempted elsewhere to co-relate present and ancient anatomy and physiology. I can, however, only mention here some salient points, first pointing out that the Shivasvarodaya Shāstra gives prominence to nerve centres and nerve currents (Vāyu) and their control, such teaching being for the purpose of worship (Upāsanā) and Yoga. The aims and object of the two Shāstras are not the same.

The Merudanda is the vertebral column. Western Anatomy divides it into five regions; and it is to be noted in corroboration of the theory here exposed that these correspond with the regions in which the five Chakras are situate. The central spinal system comprises the brain or encephalon contained within the skull (in which are the

Lalanā, Ājnā, Manas, Soma Chakras and the Sahasrāra); as also the spinal cord extending from the upper border of the Atlas below the cerebellum and descending to the second lumbar vertebra where it tapers to a point called the *filum terminale.* Within the spine is the cord, a compound of grey and white brain matter, in which are the five lower Chakras. It is noteworthy that the *filum terminale* was formerly thought to be mere fibrous cord, an unsuitable vehicle, one might think, for the Mūlādhāra Chakra and Kundalī Shakti. Recent microscopic investigations have, however, disclosed the existence of highly sensitive grey matter in the *filum terminale* which represents the position of the Mūlādhāra. According to Western science, the spinal cord is not merely a conductor between the periphery and the centres of sensation and volition, but is also an independent centre or group of centres. The Sushumnā is a Nādī in the centre of the spinal column. Its base is called the Brahmadvāra or Gate of Brahman. As regards the physiological relations of the Chakras all that can be said with any degree of certainty is that the four above the Mūlādhāra have relation to the genito-excretory, digestive, cardiac and respiratory functions, and that the two upper centres, the Ājnā (with associated Chakras) and the Sahasrāra denote various forms of its cerebral activity ending in the respose of Pure Consciousness therein gained through Yoga. The Nādīs on each side called Idā and Pingalā are the left and right sympathetic cords crossing the central column from one side to the other, making at the Ājnā with the Sushumnā a three-fold knot called Trivenī; which is to be the spot in the Medulla where the sympathetic cords join together and whence they take their origin—these Nādīs together with the two-lobed Ājnā and the Sushumnā forming the figure of the *Caduceus* of the God Mercury which is said by some to represent them,

How then does this Yoga compare with others?

It will now be asked what are the general principles which underlie the Yoga practice above described. How is it that the rousing of Kundalinī Shakti and her Union with Shiva effect the state of ecstatic union (Samādhi) and spiritual experience which is alleged. The reader who has understood the general principles recorded in the previous essays should, if he has not already divined it, readily appreciate the answer here given.

In the first place, there are two main lines of Yoga, namely, Dhyāna or Bhāvanā Yoga and Kundalī Yoga, the subject of this work; and there is a marked difference between the two. The first class of Yoga is that in which ecstasy (Samādhi) is attained by intellective processes (Kriyā-jnāna) of meditation and the like, with the aid, it may be, of auxiliary processes of Mantra or Hatha Yoga (other than the rousing of Kundalinī Shakti) and by detachment from the world; the second stands apart as that portion of Hatha Yoga in which, though intellective processes are not neglected, the creative and sustaining Shakti of the whole body is actually and truly united with the Lord Consciousness. The yogī makes Her introduce him to Her Lord, and enjoys the bliss of union through Her. Though it is he who arouses Her, it is She who gives Jnāna, for She is Herself *that*. The Dhyānayogī gains what acquaintance with the supreme state his own meditative powers can give him and knows not the enjoyment of union with Shiva in and through his fundamental Body-Power. The two forms of Yoga differ both as to method and result. The Hathayogī regards his Yoga and its fruit as the highest. The Jnānayogī may think similarly of his own. Kundalinī is so renowned that many seek to know Her. Having studied the theory of this Yoga, I have been often asked "Whether one can get on without it." The answer is, "It depends upon what you are looking for." If you want to rouse Kundalinī Shakti to enjoy the bliss of union of Shiva and Shakti through Her and to gain the accompanying Powers (Siddhi), it is obvious that this end can only, if at all, be achieved by the Yoga here described. But if Liberation is sought without desire for union through Kundalī then such Yoga is not necessary; for Liberation may be obtained by pure Jnānayoga through detachment, the exercise, and then the stilling of the mind, without any reference to the central Bodily-Power at all. Instead of setting out in and from the world to unite with Shiva, the Jnānayogī, to attain this result, detaches himself from the world. The one is the path of enjoyment and the other of asceticism. Samādhi may also be obtained on the path of devotion (Bhakti) as on that of knowledge. Indeed, the highest devotion (Parabhakti) is not different from knowledge. Both are realization. But, whilst Liberation (Mukti) is attainable by either method, there are other marked differences between the two. A Dhyānayogī should not neglect his body knowing that as he is both mind and matter each reacts, the one upon the other. Neglect or mere mortification of the body is more apt to produce disordered imagination than a true spiritual experience. He is not concerned, however, with the body in the sense that the Hathayogī is. It is possible to be a successful Dhyānayogī and yet to be weak in body and health, sick, and short-lived. His body and not he himself determines when he shall die. He cannot die at will. When he is in Samādhi, Kundalī Shakti is still sleeping in the Mūlādhāra and none of the physical symptoms and psychical bliss, or powers (Siddhi) described as accompanying Her rousing are observed in his case. The Ecstasis which he calls "Liberation while yet living" (Jīvanmukti) is not a state like that of real Liberation. He may be still subject to a suffering body from which he escapes only at death, when, if at all, he is liberated. His ecstasy is in the nature of a meditation which passes into the Void (Bhāvanāsamādhi) effected through negation of all thought-form (Chitta-vritti) and detachment from the world; a comparatively negative process in which the positive act of raising the central power of the body takes no part. By his effort the mind, which is a product of Kundalinī as Prakriti Shakti, together with its worldly desires is stilled so that the veil produced by mental functioning is removed from Consciousness. In Layayoga, Kundalinī Herself, when roused by the Yogī (for such rousing is his act and part), *achieves for him* this illumination.

But why, it may be asked, should one trouble over the body and its Central Power, the more particularly as there are unusual risks and difficulties involved? The answer has been already given—alleged completeness and certainty of realization through the agency of the Power which is knowledge itself (Jnānarūpā Shakti), an intermediate acquisition of Powers (Siddhi), and intermediate and final enjoyment. This answer may, however, be usefully developed as a fundamental principle of the Shākta Tantra.

The Shākta Tantra claims to give both Enjoyment (Bhukti) in the world and Liberation (Mukti) from all worlds. This claim is based on a profoundly true principle, given Advaitavāda as a basis. If the ultimate reality is the One which exists in two aspects of quiescent enjoyment of the Self, in liberation from all form and active enjoyment of objects, that is, as pure spirit and spirit in matter, then a complete union with Reality demands such unity in both of Its aspects. It must be known both "here" (Iha) and "there" (Amutra). When rightly apprehended and practised, there is truth in the doctrine which teaches that man should make the best of both worlds. There is no real incompatibility between the two, provided action is taken in conformity with the universal law of manifestation. It is held to be false teaching that happiness hereafter can only be had by absence of enjoyment now, or in deliberately sought-for suffering and mortification. It is the one Shiva who is the Supreme Blissful Experience and who appears in the form of man with a life of mingled pleasure and pain. Both happiness here and the bliss of Liberation here and hereafter may be attained, if the identity of these Shivas be realized in every human act. This will be achieved by making every human function, without exception, a religious act of sacrifice and worship (Yajna). In the ancient Vaidik ritual, enjoyment by way of food and drink was preceded and accompanied by ceremonial sacrifice and ritual. Such enjoyment was the fruit of the sacrifice and the gift of the Devas. At a higher stage in the life of a Sādhaka, it is offered to the One from whom all gifts come and of whom the Devatās are inferior limited forms. But this offering also involves a dualism from which the highest Monistic (Advaita) Sādhanā of the Shākta Tantra is free. Here the individual life and the world-life are known as one. And so the Tāntrik Sādhaka, when eating or drinking or fulfilling any other of the natural functions of the body does so, saying and believing, Shivo'ham, "I am Shiva", Bhairavo'ham, "I am Bhairava", "Sā'ham", "I am She". It is not merely the separate individual who thus acts and enjoys. It is Shiva who does so *in* and *through* him. Such an one recognizes, as has been well said, that his life and the play of all its activities are not a thing apart, to be held and pursued egotistically for its and his own separate sake, as though enjoyment was something to be filched from life by his own unaided strength and with a sense of separatedness; but his life and all its activities are conceived as part of the Divine action in nature—Shakti manifesting and operating in the form of man. He realizes in the pulsing beat of his heart the rhythm which throbs through and is the sign of the Universal Life. To neglect or to deny the needs of the body, to think of it as something not divine, is to neglect and deny the greater life of which it is a part; and to falsify the great doctrine of the unity of all and of the ultimate identity of Matter and Spirit. Governed by such a concept, even the lowliest physical needs take on a cosmic significance. The body is Shakti. Its needs are Shakti's needs; when man enjoys, it is Shakti who enjoys through him. In all he sees and does, it is the Mother who looks and acts. His eyes and hands are Hers. The whole body and all its functions are Her manifestation. To fully realize Her as such is to perfect this particular manifestation of Hers which is himself. Man when seeking to be the master of himself, seeks so on all the planes to be physical, mental and spiritual; nor can they be severed, for they are all related, being but differing aspects of the one all-pervading Consciousness. Who is the more divine; he who neglects and spurns the body or mind that he may attain some fancied spiritual superiority, or he who rightly cherishes both as forms of the one Spirit which they clothe? Realization is more speedily and truly attained by discerning Spirit in and as all being and its activities, than by fleeing from and casting these aside as being either unspiritual or illusory and impediments in the path. If not rightly conceived, they *may* be impediments and the cause of fall; otherwise they become instruments of attainment; and what others are there to hand? And so the Kulārnava Tantra says, "By what men fall by that they rise." When acts are done in the right feeling and frame of mind (Bhāva), those acts give enjoyment (Bhukti), and the repeated and prolonged Bhāva produces at length that divine experience (Tattvajnāna) which is Liberation. When the Mother is seen *in* all things, She is at length realized as She who is *beyond* them all.

These general principles have their more frequent application in the life of the world before entrance on the path of Yoga proper. The Yoga here described is, however, also an application of these same principles, in so far as it is claimed that thereby both Bhukti and Mukti are attained. Ordinarily, it is said, that where there is Yoga there is no Bhoga (enjoyment); but in Kaula teaching, Yoga is Bhoga, and Bhoga is Yoga, and the world itself becomes the seat of Liberation (*Yogo bhogāyate, mokshāyate samsārah*).

By the lower processes of Hathayoga it is sought to attain a perfect physical body which will also be a wholly fit instrument by which the mind may function. A perfect mind, again, approaches, and in Samādhi passes into, Pure Consciousness itself. The Hathayogī thus seeks a body which shall be as strong as steel, healthy, free from suffering and therefore long-lived. Master of the body he is, master of both life and death. His lustrous form enjoys the vitality of youth. He lives as long as he has the will to live and enjoy in the world of forms. His death is the "death at will" (*Ichchhā-mrityu*); when making the great and wonderfully expressive gesture of dissolution (Samhāra-mudrā) he grandly departs. But, it may be said, the Hatha-yogīs do get sick and die. In the first place, the full discipline is one of difficulty and risk, and can only be pursued under the guidance of a skilled Guru. As the Goraksha Samhitā says, unaided and unsuccessful practice may lead not only to disease but death. He who seeks to conquer the Lord of Death incurs the risk, on failure, of a more speedy conquest by Him. All who attempt this Yoga do not of course succeed or meet with the same measure of success. Those who fail not only incur the infirmities of ordinary men, but also others brought on by practices which have been ill pursued or for which they are not fit. Those again who do succeed, do so in varying degree. One may prolong his life to the sacred age of 84, others to 100, others yet further. In theory at least those who are perfected (Siddha) go from this plane when they will. All have not the same capacity or opportunity, through want of will, bodily strength, or circumstance. All may not be willing or able to follow the strict rules necessary for success. Nor does modern life offer in general the opportunities for so complete a physical culture. All men may not desire such a life or may think the attainment of it not worth the trouble involved. Some may wish to be rid of their body and that as speedily as possible. It is therefore said that it is easier to gain Liberation than Deathlessness. The former may be had by unselfishness, detachment from the world, moral and mental discipline. But to conquer death is harder than this, for these qualities and acts will not alone avail. He who does so conquer holds life in the hollow of one hand, and if he be a successful (Siddha) Yogī, Liberation in the other. He has Enjoyment and Liberation. He is the Emperor who is Master of the World and the Possessor of the Bliss which is beyond all worlds. Therefore it is claimed by the Hathayogī that every Sādhanā is inferior to Hathayoga.

The Hathayogī who works for Liberation does so through the Yoga Sādhanā here described which gives both Enjoyment and Liberation. At every centre to which he rouses Kundalinī he experiences a special form of bliss (Ānanda) and gains special powers (Siddhi). Carrying Her to the Shiva of his cerebral centre he enjoys the Supreme Bliss which in its nature is that of Liberation, and which when established in permanence is Liberation itself on the loosening of Spirit and Body. She who "shines like a chain of lights", a lightning flash—in the centre of his body is the "Inner Woman" to whom reference was made when it was said, "What need have I of any outer woman?

I have an Inner Woman within myself." The Vīra (Heroic) Sādhaka, knowing himself as the embodiment of Shiva (Shivo'ham), unites with woman as the embodiment of Shakti on the physical plane. The Divya (Divine) Sādhaka or Yogī unites within himself his own Principles, female and male, which are the "Heart of the Lord" (Hridayam Parameshituh) or Shakti and Her Lord Consciousness or Shiva. It is their union which is the mystic coition (Maithuna) of the Tantras. There are two forms of union (Sāmarasya), namely, the first which is the gross (Sthūla), or the union of the physical embodiments of the Supreme Consciousness; and the second which is the subtle (Sūkshma), or the union of the quiescent and active principles in Consciousness itself. It is the latter which is Liberation.

Lastly, what, in a philosophical sense, is the nature of the process here described? Shortly stated, Energy (Shakti) polarises itself into two forms, namely, static or potential (Kundalinī) and dynamic (the working forces of the body as Prāna). Behind all activity there is a static background. This static centre in the human body is the central Serpent Power in the Mūlādhāra (Root-support). It is the Power which is the static support (Ādhāra) of the whole body and all its moving Prānik forces. This Centre (Kendra) of Power is a gross form of Chit or Consciousness; that is, in itself (Svarūpa), it is Consciousness; and by appearance it is a Power which, as the highest form of Force, is a manifestation of it. Just as there is a distinction (though identical at base) between the supreme quiescent Consciousness and Its active Power (Shakti): so when Consciousness manifests as Energy (Shakti), it possesses the twin aspects of potential and kinetic Energy. There can be no partition in fact of Reality. To the perfect eye of the Siddha the process of Becoming is an ascription (Adhyāsa). To the imperfect eye of the Sādhaka, that is, the aspirant for Siddhi (perfected accomplishment), to the spirit which is still toiling through the lower planes and variously identifying itself with them, Becoming is tending to appear and appearance is real. The Shākta Tantra is a rendering of Vedāntik Truth from this practical point of view, and represents the world-process as a polarization in Consciousness itself. This polarity as it exists in, and as, the body is destroyed by Yoga which disturbs the equilibrium of bodily consciousness, which consciousness is the result of the maintenance of these two poles. In the human body the potential pole of Energy which is the Supreme Power is stirred to action, on which the moving forces (dynamic Shakti) supported by it are drawn thereto, and the whole dynamism thus engendered moves upward to unite with the quiescent Consciousness in the Highest Lotus.

There is a polarization of Shakti into two forms—static and dynamic. In a correspondence I had with Professor Pramatha Nātha Mukhyopādhyāya, on this subject, he very well developed this point and brought forward some suitable illustrations of it, of which I am glad to avail myself of. He pointed out that, in the first place, in the mind or experience this polarization or polarity is patent to reflection: namely, the polarity between pure Chit and the Stress which is involved in it. This Stress or Shakti develops the mind through an infinity of forms and changes, themselves involved in the pure unbounded Ether of Consciousness, the Chidākāsha. This analysis exhibits the primordial Shakti in the same two polar forms as before, static and dynamic. Here the polarity is most fundamental and approaches absoluteness, though of course, it is to be remembered that there is no absolute rest except in pure Chit. Cosmic energy is in an equilibrium which is relative and not absolute.

Passing from mind, let us take matter. The atom of modern science has, as I have already pointed out, ceased to be an atom in the sense of an indivisible unit of matter. According to the electron theory, the so-called atom is a miniature universe resembling our solar system. At the centre of this atomic system we have a charge of positive electricity round which a cloud of negative charges called Electrons revolve. The positive and negative charges hold each other in check so that the atom is in a condition of equilibrated energy and does not ordinarily break up, though it may do so on the dissociation which is the characteristic of all matter, but which is so clearly manifest in radio-activity of radium. We have thus here again a positive charge at rest at the centre, and negative charges in motion round about the centre. What is thus said about the atom applies to the whole cosmic system and universe. In the world-system, the planets revolve round the Sun, and that system itself is probably (taken as a whole) a moving mass around some other relatively static centre, until we arrive at the Brahma-bindu which is the point of Absolute Rest, round which all forms revolve and by which all are maintained. He has aptly suggested other illustrations of the same process. Thus, in the tissues of the living body, the operative energy is polarized into two forms of energy—anabolic and katabolic, the one tending to change and the other to conserve the tissues; the actual condition of the tissues being simply the resultant of these two co-existent or concurrent activities. In the case, again, of the impregnated ovum, Shakti is already presented in its two polar aspects, namely, the ovum (possibly the static) and the spermatazoon, the dynamic. The germ cell does not cease to be such. It splits into two, one half, the somatic cell gradually developing itself into the body of the animal, the other half remaining encased within the body practically unchanged and as the germ-plasm is transmitted in the process of reproduction to the offspring.

In short, Shakti, when manifesting, divides itself into two polar aspects—static and dynamic—which implies that you cannot have it in a dynamic form without at the same time having it in a static form, much like the poles of a magnet. In any given sphere of activity of force, we must have, according to the cosmic principle, a static background —Shakti *at rest* or "coiled" as the Tantras say. This scientific truth is illustrated in the figure of the Tāntrik Kālī. The Divine Mother moves as the Kinetic Shakti on the breast of Sadāshiva who is the static background of pure Chit which is actionless (Nishkriya); the Gunamayī Mother being all activity.

The Cosmic Shakti is the collectivity (Samashti) in relation to which the Kundalī in particular bodies is the Vyashti (individual) Shakti. The body is, as I have stated, a microcosm (Kshudrabrahmānda). In the living body there is, therefore, the same polarization of which I have spoken. From the Mahākundalī the universe has sprung. In Her supreme form She is at rest, coiled round and one (as Chidrūpinī) with the Shivabindu. She is then at rest. She next uncoils Herself to manifest. Here the three coils of which the Tantras speak are the three Gunas, and the three and a half coils to which the Kubjikā Tantra alludes are Prakriti and its three Gunas together with the Vikritis. Her 50 coils are the letters of the alphabet. As She goes on uncoiling, the Tattvas and the Mātrikās, the Mothers of the Varnas, issue from Her. She is thus moving, and continues even after creation to move in the Tattvas so created. For as they are born of movement, they continue to move. The whole world (Jagat) as the Sanskrit term implies, is moving. She thus continues creatively active until She has evolved Prithivī, the last of the Tattvas. First She creates mind and then matter. This latter becomes more and more dense. It has been suggested that the

Mahābhūtas are the Densities of modern science: Air density associated with the maximum velocity of gravity; Fire density associated with the velocity of light; Water or fluid density associated with molecular velocity and the equatorial velocity of the Earth's rotation; and Earth density, that of basalt associated with the Newtonian velocity of sound. However this be, it is plain that the Bhūtas represent an increasing density of matter until it reaches its three-dimensional solid form. When Shakti has created this last or Prithivī Tattva, what is there further for Her to do? Nothing. She therefore, then again *rests.* She is again coiled, which means that She is at rest. "At rest", again, means that She assumes a static form. Shakti, however, is never exhausted, that is, emptied into any of its forms. Therefore, Kundalī Shakti at this point is, as it were, the Shakti *left over* (though yet a plenum) after the Prithivī, the last of the Bhūtas has been created. We have thus Mahākundalī at rest as Chidrūpinī Shakti in the Sahasrāra, the point of absolute rest; and then the body in which the relative static centre is Kundalī at rest, and round this centre the whole of the bodily forces move. They are Shakti, and so is Kundalī Shakti. The difference between the two is that they are Shakti in specific differentiated forms *in movement*; and Kundalī Shakti is undifferentiated, residual Shakti *at rest,* that is, coiled. She is coiled in the Mūlādhāra, which means fundamental support, and which is at the same time the seat of the Prithivī or last solid Tattva and of the residual Shakti or Kundalinī. The body may, therefore, be compared to a magnet with two poles. The Mūlādhāra, in so far as it is the seat of Kundalī Shakti, a comparatively gross form of Chit (being Chit-Shakti and Māyā-Shakti) is the static pole in relation to the rest of the body which is dynamic. The "working" that is the body necessarily presupposes and finds such a static support; hence the name Mūlādhāra. In one sense the static Shakti at the Mūlādhāra is necessarily co-existent with the creating and evolving Shakti of the body; because the dynamic aspect or pole can never be without its static counterpart. In another sense, it is the residual Shakti left over after such operation.

What, then, happens in the accomplishment of this Yoga? This static Shakti is affected by Prānāyāma and other Yogik processes and becomes dynamic. Thus, when completely dynamic, that is, when Kundalī unites with Shiva in the Sahasrāra, the polarization of the body gives way. The two poles are united in one and there is the state of consciousness called Samādhi. The polarization, of course, takes place in consciousness. The body actually continues to exist as an object of observation to others. It continues its organic life. But man's consciousness of his body and all other objects is withdrawn because the mind has ceased, so far as his consciousness is concerned, the function, having been withdrawn into its ground which is consciousness.

How is the body sustained? In the first place, though Kundalī Shakti is the static centre of the whole body as a complete conscious organism, yet each of the parts of the body and their constituent cells have their own static centres which uphold such parts or cells. Next, the theory of the Tāntriks themselves is that Kundalī ascends, and that the body, as a complete organism, is maintained by the "nectar" which flows from the union of Shiva and Shakti in the Sahasrāra. This nectar is an ejection of power generated by their union. My friend, however, whom I have cited, is of opinion (and for this grounds may be urged) that the potential Kundalī Shakti becomes only partly and not wholly converted into kinetic Shakti; and yet since Shakti—even as given in the Mūla centre—is an infinitude, it is not depleted; the potential store always remaining unexhausted. In this case, the dynamic equivalent is a partial conversion of one mode of energy into another. If, however, the coiled power at the Mūla became absolutely uncoiled, there would result the dissolution of the three bodies, gross, subtle and causal, and consequently Videha-Mukti,—because the static background in relation to a particular form of existence would, according to this hypothesis, have wholly given way. He would explain the fact that the body becomes cold as a corpse as the Shakti leaves it, as being due, not to the depletion or privation of the static power at the Mūlādhāra, but to the concentration or convergence of the dynamic power ordinarily diffused over the whole body, so that the dynamic equivalent which is set up against the static background of Kundalī Shakti is only the diffused five-fold Prāna gathered home—withdrawn from the other tissues of the body and concentrated along the axis. Thus, ordinarily, the dynamic equivalent is the Prāna diffused over all the tissues: in Yoga, it is converged along the axis, the static equivalent of Kundalī Shakti enduring in both cases. Some part of the already available dynamic Prana is made to act at the base of the axis in a suitable manner, by which means the basal centre or Mūlādhāra becomes, as it were, over-saturated and re-acts on the whole diffused dynamic power (or Prāna) of the body by withdrawing it from the tissues and converging it along the line of the axis. In this way the diffused dynamic equivalent becomes the converged dynamic equivalent along the axis. What, according to this view, ascends, is not the whole Shakti but an eject like condensed lightning, which at length reaches the Parama-Shivasthāna. There the Central Power which upholds the individual world-consciousness is merged in the Supreme Consciousness. The limited consciousness, transcending the passing concepts of worldly life, directly intuits the unchanging Reality which underlies the whole phenomenal flow. When Kundalī Shakti *sleeps* in the Mūlādhāra, man is *awake* to the world; when she *awakes* to unite, and does unite, with the supreme static Consciousness which is Shiva, then consciousness is *asleep* to the world and is one with the Light of all things.

Putting aside detail, the main principle appears to be that, when "wakened", Kundalī Shakti either Herself (or as my friend suggests in Her eject) ceases to be a static Power which sustains the world-consciousness, the content of which is held only so long as She "sleeps": and when once set in movement is drawn to that other static centre in the Thousand-petalled Lotus (Sahasrāra) which is Herself in union with the Shiva-consciousness or the consciousness of ecstasy beyond the world of forms. When Kundalī "sleeps" man is awake to this world. When She "awakes" he sleeps, that is loses all consciousness of the world and enters his causal body. In Yoga he passes beyond to formless Consciousness.

I have only to add, without further discussion of the point, that practitioners of this Yoga claim that it is higher than any other and that the Samādhi (ecstasy) attained thereby is more perfect. The reason which they allege is this. In Dhyānayoga, ecstasy takes place through detachment from the world, and mental concentration leading to vacuity of mental operation (Vritti) or the uprising of pure Consciousness unhindered by the limitations of the mind. The degree to which this unveiling of consciousness is effected depends upon the meditative powers (Jnānashakti) of the Sādhaka and the extent of his detachment from the world. On the other hand, Kundalī who is all Shakti and who is therefore Jnānashakti Herself produces, when awakened by the Yogī, full Jnāna for him. Secondly, in the Samādhi of Dhyānayoga there is no rousing and union of

Kundalī Shakti with the accompanying bliss and acquisition of special Powers (Siddhi). Further, in Kundalī Yoga there is not merely a Samādhi through meditation, but through the central power of the Jīva a power which carries with it the forces of both body and mind. The union in that sense is claimed to be more complete than that enacted through mental methods only. Though in both cases bodily consciousness is lost, in Kundalinī-yoga not only the mind, but the body, in so far as it is represented by its central power (or may be its eject) is actually united with Shiva. This union produces an enjoyment (Bhukti) which the Dhyānayogī does not possess. Whilst both the Divya Yogī and the Vīra Sādhaka have enjoyment (Bhukti), that of the former is said to be infinitely more intense, being an experience of Bliss Itself. The enjoyment of the Vīra Sādhaka is but a reflection of it on the physical plane, a welling up of the true Bliss through the deadening coverings and trammels of matter. Again, whilst it is said that both have Liberation (Mukti), this word is used in Vīra Sādhanā in a figurative sense only, indicating a bliss which is the nearest approach on the physical plane to that of Mukti, and a Bhāva or feeling of momentary union of Shiva and Shakti which ripens in the higher Yoga Sādhanā into the literal liberation of the Yogī. He has both Enjoyment (Bhukti) and Liberation (Mukti) in the fullest and literal sense. Hence its claim to be the Emperor of all Yogas.

However this may be, I leave the subject at this point, with the hope that others will continue the enquiry I have here initiated. It and other matters in the Tantra Shāstra seem to me (whatever be their inherent value) worthy of an investigation which they have not yet received.[1]

---

[1] See "Mysterious Kundali", by Dr. Rele (Taraporevala, Bombay), and "The Chakras," by Dr. C. Leadbeater (Theosophical Publishing House, Madras).

CHAPTER XXX

THE ĀGAMAS AND THE FUTURE

[The following is a reprint of a very understanding article in the *Modern Review* (February 1918), by Dr. James H. Cousins, reviewing the works on Tantra Shāstra then published by Arthur Avalon which have been considerably added to during later years.]

INDIA is at present experiencing the interesting sensation of a national revival; and, like all other such happenings, a *national* revival is no more confined to nationality or nationalism than a religious revival is confined to religion. Such phenomena in the course of human history have revealed themselves in retrospect as incursions of energy from the hidden sources of life, to which the circumstances of the time have given an adventitious bent; and it is not always even certain that the physical location of such movements was their true home. This reminds me that Mr. G. K. Chesterton has remarked in his book on "The Victorian Age in English Literature," with his usual inconsequential profundity, that, "towards the end of the eighteenth century, the most important event in English history happened in France." That is to say, the upheaval in human consciousness and emotion called the French Revolution was far from being exclusively French in the scene of its operation or its results. It revolved the world over: it moved in Wordsworth and Byron and Shelley, and in the latter is carrying its influence, in democratic thought expressed with the force of compelling imagination, right into the coming times.

It will be the same with the Indian National Revival. The extent to which it means a revival, or perhaps a revolution, for instance, in *European* drama and poetry is a matter with regard to which positive prophecy may be safely indulged in by anyone who has come into contact with the stage and literature of the last twenty years in Great Britain and Ireland, and who has also touched not merely the outer side of the work of Rabindranath Tagore to which publishers and book-sellers have an eye, but the vital force that Yeats felt and communicated when he murmured the songs of "Gitānjali" through the streets of Dublin and along the country lanes of Normandy.

But, even within its own territory, the Indian National Revival cannot be restricted to the political interpretation of nationality. One listens instinctively for reverberations in the arts, in science, in religion, and one is not disappointed. The Calcutta painters and the researches of Bose come readily to the mind. Religion, however, is not so obvious; and yet I am inclined to think that a series of stout books, and some slender ones, all bound in bright red covers, which have been growing in number on my bookshelf during the last four or five years, will be found in future to be not isolated literary phenomena, interesting translations for the Sanskrit scholar, but an integral and perhaps vitally important constituent of the revival. I refer to the series of translations of works on the Tantra Shāstra or Āgama, with introductions and commentaries, by Arthur Avalon. [Principles of Tantra, 2 vols.; Tantra of the Great Liberation; Hymns to the Goddess; Wave of Bliss; Greatness of Shiva. Tāntrik Texts, 6 vols. (containing Tantrābhidhāna, Shatchakranirūpana, Prapanchasāra in Kulachūdāmani, Kulārnava, and Kālīvilāsa); Studies in Mantra Shāstra and various Essays.] The number of their cursory readers is probably small, the number of their students smaller still;

but I think these books will rank among the precious things of the first quarter of the twentieth century, in much the same way as "The Secret Doctrine" of Madame Blavatsky and "The Perfect Way" of Dr. Anna Kingsford ranked in the last quarter of the nineteenth.

My purpose in writing this note on the first translations of this venerable scripture into a European language is not to enter into exposition or criticism, but to express a few general thoughts of a Western mind which have arisen during a sympathetic reading of the translations and the discovery of their affinity with and satisfaction of a need, which is showing itself outside India, for a restatement of religious and philosophical principles that will be at once wider in their contact with the actual constitution of humanity, and more explicit in contrast with the current sentimentality and vagueness of Western doctrine and mawkish practice.

My first contact with the Tāntrik teaching was through a footnote in "The Voice of the Silence" in which Madame Blavatsky referred to several sects of "sorcerers" as being "all Tāntrikas". The assumption that, since the sorcerers were all Tāntrikas, all Tāntrikas were therefore sorcerers, is not necessarily involved in the footnote as I now read it with greater knowledge and experience. In any case, even if Madame Blavatsky adopted a hostile attitude to the Tantra, as she adopted a hostile attitude to spiritualism, we have the example of her great successor, Mrs. Besant, who has bridged the gulf between Theosophy and Spiritualism—or perhaps more accurately, between Theosophists and Spiritualists in their mutual search for the realization of the inner worlds of faculty and experience; an example which encourages those who, in the increasing light of modern research to which the translations under consideration are a notable contribution, are impelled to seek for the great unities underlying all diversities of religious thought and experience, even though they may, like myself, have found their own path towards the centre along another radius of the vast circle of manifestation.

Apart altogether from the question of Vāmāchāra, antinomianism or abuses of Shākta Tāntrik ritual within the bounds of the general morality (which ritual, after all, is only concerned with one portion of a vast Scripture governing not only the Vāmāchāris, Shākta or otherwise, but other communities), the fact that some of the root principles and ideas as well as practices of Hinduism, ancient and modern, are contained in the Tāntrik Scriptures makes it incumbent on those who wish to understand fully the significance and development of religion to rid themselves of pre-conceptions and to study these books, in which the translator endeavours to substitute an accurate statement of the facts for the "general statements by way of condemnation" which have been the only kind of literature on the Tantras heretofore in the English language. "The abuses of the commoner people," he complains, "as time went on developed such proportions as to ultimately obscure all other matters in the Tantra, thus depriving them of that attention which is their due." Unfortunately, it is just such developments that the purposely critical eye lights upon. It abuses Islam for the banalities of Mohurram festivities, ignoring the fact that tiger-dancing and sword feats have no more bearing on the teachings of Koran than "Blind man's buff" at a Christmas party has on the Sermon on the Mount. The translator undertakes to show that behind the alleged "black magic and sensual rites", there exists within the Tantra, "a high philosophical doctrine and the means whereby its truth may be realized through development," and the student who is worthy of the name can hardly escape the conclusion that the translator has succeeded in his great and memorable work. Indeed, the success achieved on the purely expository side is all the time enhanced by the challenging phenomenon of a decried and abused Eastern scripture being championed with missionary ardour (albeit in the most judicial manner) by a writer whose name takes him outside India in race (though the suggestion of France in one magazine might be modified in front of Burne Jones' unfinished picture of *Arthur* in *Avalon*), and who expresses the most ancient and profound truths in the most excellent of modern English. Mr. Kipling may try to put a big "barrage" between East and West on the surface of the earth, but apparently under the surface there may be passages and channels beyond his ken. Reincarnation may be a useful key.

The press criticisms in the West which followed the first publication of the translations offered an excellent example of that process of finding in a thing that which we are capable of finding, which is referred to in a non-Tāntrik scripture as "the savour of life unto life or of death unto death." Such journals as had been in touch with recent Western movements in the direction of cultivating the esoteric sense, not merely in mythological and theological matters, but in all relations of life—seeing layer upon layer of significance and analogy in the simplest of acts—welcomed the work on the strength of the percentage of wisdom which it disclosed, and notwithstanding a frankly observed percentage of matter which is unfamiliar, and therefore repugnant, to the Western mind.

But, there were other journals of the "literary" and "oriental" order, to which the surface value of a thing makes most appeal, which fixed their critical eyes on certain phases of the Tantra Shāstra. They found a spot on the sun, ignored the shining surface, and proceeded to prophesy worse than the plagues of Egypt, as a sequel to the publication of books on the Tantra.

To value this kind of criticism for what it is worth, one has only to imagine the effect of a first reading of certain portions of the Old Testament, on a simple follower of some gentle and peace-loving faith. If he was as verbally clever as he was forgetful, or perhaps ignorant, of human psychology, he would probably spend himself in a piece of parallel "smartness" to that of the "Athenæum" thus: "It appears that this Psalm of David is the first to be translated into English. Unfortunately the programme of similar enterprises projected by the translator deprives us of the hope that it might also prove the last."

The objection of the "Athenæum" reviewer, to the publication of the Tantra Shāstra is that, in it, "we find the lofty conceptions of earlier and purer beliefs often almost entirely obscured by brainless hocus-pocus and debasing and sensual rites." We may pass by the suggestion of hocus-pocus with a reference to the illuminating circumstance that a man of the eminence of Edward Carpenter (in his recently published Autobiographical Notes) can see nothing but literary hocus-pocus in the prose of George Meredith. The calling up of the ghosts of the dead, or the evocation of unseen powers by *mantra*, may be hocus-pocus in the East: when it is done by the witch of Endor in the Hebrew scriptures it is quite another matter!

The objection of the non-Christian reader to certain of the Psalms of David and to certain incidents in his history, would probably be grounded on the blood-thirstiness of the poet, his claims to the monopoly of a Divine Power which seems more savage than divine, and a sensuality that had no qualms (until afterwards when found out) in stooping to conspiracy and lying, not to mention murder by proxy. This is not, of course, all that is to be said on the subject, but it is the parallel to the "Athenæum" attitude to the Tantra. The "Athenæum" would assert that the iniquities of the Psalmist were part of his human nature and the circumstances of his time, and did not invalidate the truth of Christian teaching, precisely as an apologist of the Tantras might claim that past abuses in the application of some general principles of the Shākta Shāstra do not touch their truth.

This attitude of exclusiveness on both sides is one of the inevitable things in human nature, and one of the most interesting of psychological problems. It is also the greatest bar to the unification of religion, and can only be undermined by scientific and rational advance, or overleaped by intuition which comes from spiritual experience. I remember well a quaint and much respected figure in Dublin university life, some twenty years ago, a Professor of Oriental Languages or something of the kind, whose name now eludes me. Indeed, my only memory of his personality is of a brown skin and a foreign head-dress. But I remember the impact which a reply of his to some teasing undergraduates made on me. They twitted him of heathen ignorance in worshipping a God with three heads. He smiled and said it was almost as bad as worshipping a God with three *persons*, a sly dig at their Trinitarianism which they did not anticipate, and which helped at least one searcher after truth a stage nearer his desire. It is easy for the Westerner to condemn the "heathen practice" of slaughtering goats in the Temple of Kālī, and it is equally easy for the Westerner to excuse the slaughtering, not for religious sacrifice but for appetite, of vast numbers of cattle and sheep; which is funny and very sad.

It is somewhere round this point that the twin globes of heterodoxy ("your 'doxy") and orthodoxy ("my 'doxy") revolve. There *are* reprehensible practices connected with

Tāntrik observance; but honesty compels the recognition of the fact that every practice supposed to be encouraged by the Tantras with a view to the attainment of occult powers or spiritual illumination is duplicated outside Tāntrik observance, and with no other motive than self-gratification.

The difference in position seems to be this; Christianity (which is the nominal religion of the critics of Tantra in the West, and must therefore mainly be referred to) narrows itself to a counsel of perfection in conduct, and hence, since the true observers of Christ's injunctions ("Recompense no man evil for evil"—illustrated by the Great War!) are in an obvious "microscopic minority," reduces the participants in salvation to a small and choice company, Christianity, as ordinarily interpreted, puts an impassable gulf between the ideal and human nature. The Āgama, on the contrary, throws its circumference around the whole circle of human activity, and by linking every phase of conduct with religion, endeavours to lift conduct from stage to stage, not, as in non-Tāntrik observance, by focussing attention on the act itself, which only intensifies it, but by gradually raising consciousness which will, in due time, influence conduct. It includes worship with flesh-foods, intoxicants and sex, because it recognizes that these are inherent in certain stage of human development, and because it believes that they are more certain to be transcended through being associated with the religious idea, than through being left alone, or in an antagonistic relationship to religion. I am quite aware that this statement of the matter will shock any of my Western friends who happen to read these lines: it shocks the Nonconformist lobe of my own brain which had a quarter of a century of careful development. But I cannot ignore the phallic element involved in every Christian marriage ceremony, and I cannot forget the fragments of slaughtered and cooked animals that are on every wedding-breakfast table. It all depends on mental adjustments, and what the great educationist, Herbart, calls the "apperception masses" that spring into relationship in response to impacts from without. The Mahādevī herself anticipated the degrading tendency of human nature in the *Kali Yuga*, when she said to Shiva: "I fear, O Lord! that even that which thou hast ordained for the good of men will, through them, turn out for evil." But it would be as foolish to attribute the debasement of the observance to the Tantra as a whole, as it would be to blame the gigantic slaughter and gluttony of Christmas on the teachings of Jesus Christ. He Himself commanded his followers to do all things in His Name: Tantra takes the *all* to its fullest extent.

We must not, however, allow ourselves to be lured into the very mistake which we are condemning, that is, the fixing of attention on that which is, in reality, only a fractional part of Tāntrik teaching and practice even in its Shākta form. It is enough to expose the falsity of the current attitude of criticism, and to point out that the Tantra, recognizing the spiritual gradations of human evolution, not only takes cognizance of the "debasing and sensual" aspects of human nature, and tries to elevate them through religion, but puts its severest condemnation on those who participate in the lower rites when in consciousness they belong to the higher levels of evolution.

It is this recognition of psychic distinctions that marks the Tantra as a scripture that will appeal more and more to the future. Science has passed inwards from the physical to the psychical, and it will draw religion with it in due time, and leave those systems outside that have not a psychological basis to their faith and practice. In this respect, the Āgamas present a contrast to Christianity; not that the kernel of Christianity does not come from the same hidden Tree as all the other great Religions, but the overgrowths have, in the case of Christian faith and practice, obscured the implicit psychology of the system by sentimentality. The Tantra Shāstra, in this respect, also presents a contrast to that other venerable presentation of the relationship of Humanity to Divinity and the Universe, the Vedānta, not, however, in ultimates, but in method. "The Tantra," as the editor says, "harmonises Vedāntic monism and dualism. Its purpose is to give liberation to the *jiva* by a method through which monistic truth is reached through the dualistic world." That is to say, it accepts the principle of the One Absolute as the source and goal of evolution, but it focusses its attention on a point nearer human power, and substitutes for philosophical dissertation, practice based on knowledge of, and relation with the relative world, though with the Absolute as aim. It says to the spiritual athlete, "Your aim of a development so harmonious that it will appear to be as one, is excellent, but you will not secure it by discussion or meditation merely: you must realize the actuality (if not the philosophical *reality*) of biceps and triceps, and descend to pushing against walls and moving yourself up and down on a piece of common iron stretched between two ordinary wooden supports." It says, "Faith is good, but it is unwise to defer practice until faith is secure. Get to work, and faith will follow, and be more than mere faith;"—an injunction which is not far removed from the Christian commandment to the disciple to live the life and he shall know of the doctrine.

There is a further distinction which has to be marked. Simple religion, such as Christianity, removes God from His creation, and removes Him also from full contact with a complete humanity by speaking of Him as single-sexed, and so vitiating the whole superstructure of commentary and custom. Simple philosophy, on the other hand, reduces everything to abstraction. The Tāntrik teacher, however, declares: "It is as impossible to hold the firmament between a pair of tongs as it is to worship an attributeless Brahman by a mind with attributes." Tantra replaces the attributeless as an object of contemplation, by *Shakti* (the Creative Energy in all its forms, personified as feminine) as an object of worship, and holds that the subtler aspects of Shakti can only be reached through Her physical and mantra forms.

Thus, the Tantra Shāstra unites the religious and philosophic functions of human nature, by presenting a system which is in line with modern psychology in its recognition of human divergencies on the level and in the vertical, and which at the same time gives to human and extra-human powers the warmth and appeal of personality. It is as monotheistic as Christianity or Islam, notwithstanding the weird kind of propagandist arithmetic that taught me in my ignorant youth that Hindus worshipped a thousand "gods" (but always spelt with a small *g*) when in simple reality, the thousand gods (as far as Tantra Shāstra is concerned) are but names for aspects and operations of the Mahādeva as recognition of the "Divine immanence", which is slowly but certainly finding its way into the advanced religions of the West.

But the monotheism of the Shākta Tantra (that is, its unification of the fundamental duality of Shiva-Pārvati on the thither side of manifestation) is unassailable. This Shāstra is never guilty of the inconsistency of attributing to the One Absolute actions and qualities which can only properly belong to degrees of relativity. Thus it escapes the maze of contradiction in which orthodox Christian exegesis has lost itself (like Daedalus and Icarus in the labyrinth of their own building) by claiming its God as the One and

Only, and then degrading that lofty conception to participation in prejudices and actions belonging purely to the relative planes of the universe. The Āgama also escapes the coldness and impersonality of philosophical abstraction which is only endurable by the few who are able to breathe in "the chill air that enfolds the wise". Pure philosophy has never countenanced the personal element in devotion; otherwise it would not have been philosophy but religion. Long ago Cæsar said that those who followed philosophy did not worship the gods. So much the worse for philosophy as a moving influence in human advancement; it remains the intellectual interest of the learned few, when it might have been the inspirer and uplifter of the unlearned but intelligent many. The need of the future, nay, of the present, as I have pointed out in my book, "The Bases of Theosophy"—is a restatement of truth in a form and through a method that will make religion philosophical and philosophy religious; and it appears to me that the Tantra Shāstra, being based on an experimental and demonstrable psychology, and vivified by the breath of personal devotion, and made practical by application in daily life, is bound to exert an ever-increasing influence on humanity as it rises towards the needs which the Shāstra supplies, including a ritual, with regard to which the editor, in a moment of refreshing belligerency, says: "Doubtless, to the newer 'protestant' spirit, whether issuing from Europe, Arabia or elsewhere, all ritual is liable to be regarded as 'mummery,' except, possibly, the particular and perhaps jejune variety which it calls its own . . . for even the most desiccated Protestantism has not been able altogether to dispense with it."

It is declared that the Tantra Shāstra was given as the scripture suitable to the Kali Yuga. The degeneracy of humanity in the present age was not considered to be capable of being influenced through speculation and meditation alone; but rather through discipline and mantrik practices that would vibrate through the material incrustations of the ages, and shake consciousness into activity. "The word is a mere display of letters," says the author, referring to mere philosophical discussion, "whilst mantra is a mass of radiant energy. Sayings give advice to men of the world, whilst mantras awaken superhuman Shakti."

Yet, while it may be quite true that a people gets just the government which it deserves, it is certain that an age does not get the regenerating influence that it needs in the same measure as the need. That which would assuredly be its salvation is always in advance. In earlier and less sophisticated times, the disease and its remedy may have existed and been applied side by side; but, to-day, we have an extraordinary monster (compounded of cheap literature and cheaper education) called Enlightened Public Opinion, or sometimes The Man in the Street, that interposes itself between principles of reform and their execution, and labels as "premature" the age's most urgent need. That has been the experience of reform in the West, particularly during the last six or seven years in which it has become obvious to a few clear-seeing minds that the general vulgarization and materialization of life which was setting in all over the world (not excluding India) was the direct outcome of a predominantly masculine attitude and organization in affairs, including religion. Hence the struggle which developed not only in Great Britain and Ireland, but in America, Russia and elsewhere, with faint echoes in India as yet, for the active participation of the feminine element in all departments of life; with all that hangs upon that element not merely in the matter of sex difference, but in the qualities of conservation (which is not conservatism as many erroneously think), intuition, devotion, sacrifice, which must become active complements of the masculine qualities of aggression, reason, question, acquisitiveness, if a balanced human organization and character are to be achieved.

That struggle not only challenged the male exclusiveness of politics, in its personnel and its interests and methods, but invaded the very pulpits of Christendom. So acutely, indeed, did some women feel the lack of the presentation of the feminine side of life in the ordinary churches, that they banded themselves into a church run by women, but with a pulpit freely open to both sexes, and a liturgy and attitude that was exclusively human.

This innovation was, I am convinced, the deepest indicator of the source of the lopsided order of things; that is, a purely masculine concept of Divinity, and a consequent purely masculine religious organization with its sequel, a purely masculine social machine. The consciousness of that defect is growing in Europe, aided by the last great example of the logical end of unrelieved masculine aggression, the European War. The full inclusion of the feminine element in public life will be the great fight of the immediate future, together with the uprising of a complete democracy (displacing the pseudo-democracies of to-day) based on the equal rights and duties of men and women in the human household of the State.

These circumstances, and the manner in which they are capable of being met by the Tantra Shăstra, give another ground for the belief that some of the fundamental principles of this ancient scripture will become one of the religious influences in modern life, not necessarily directly, in the sense of superseding Christianity in the West, but certainly in an interaction through which the Shăkta Shăstra will help as an irritant, so to speak, in the great oyster of Western, and perhaps Eastern, religion, to produce the Mother-pearl of a complete and true religious exegesis and practice.

All things are possible to a scripture whose supreme personifications, Shiva and Pārvati, give and receive instruction mutually, the feminine side being of equal importance with the masculine. On the knees of the Mother, as the author puts it, "all quarrels about duality and non-duality are settled. When the Mother seats herself in the heart, then everything, be it stained or stainless, becomes but an ornament for Her lotus feet." "She lives in the bodies of all living creatures wherein She is present in the form of energy, even in such lifeless things as rocks and stones. There is no place in the world where Mahāmāya is not." Here we have an anticipation of modern scientific thought as to the universal permeation of energy; but the Tāntrik idea of energy is of a Consciousness, and therefore of a Power related to personality, and so, capable not merely of scientific study but of worship, though the worship is always (to the higher Tāntrika) with the realization of the passing nature (Māya) of all limitation by contrast with the Supreme Reality.

With such an ideal as the Divine Father and Mother, equal in all respects in manifestation, and One beyond manifestation; and with all the implications of influence on conduct and organization inherent in such a belief; one is moved to pray for the purification of practice where such purification is needed, so that the Shāstra may without obstruction fulfil the prophecy of its future; for it is no less a spiritual than it is a physical truth, that it is only when masculine and feminine are in equal co-operation, though through dissimilar functions, that there is the possibility and promise of a future.

CHAPTER XXXI

CONCLUSIONS

BRAHMANISM or Hinduism, as in its later development the former has been called, is not merely a religion. It is a Socio-Economic System, the foundation of which is the Law of Caste and Stages of Life.[1] That System has its culture of which several forms of Religion, resting on a certain common basis, are but a part. Dealing, however, with Brahmanism in its religious aspect, we may say that it, together with Jainism and Buddhism, are the three chief religions of India, as opposed to those of the Semitic origin. All three religious systems share in common certain fundamental concepts which are denoted by the Sanskrit terms *Karma, Samsāra* and *Moksha.* These concepts constitute a common denominator of Indian Belief as next stated.

The Universe is in constant activity.[2] Nothing which is Psycho-physical is at rest. Karma is Action. The Psycho-physical as such is determined by Karma or action, and, therefore, man's present condition is determined by

---

[1] Varnāshrama Dharma. For this reason it was commonly thought that an individual non-Hindu cannot become a Hindu because there is no place for him in the caste system. The Patna H. C. have, however, recently held that Hindu Law recognizes conversion to Hinduism and conversion makes the person converted a Hindu in every sense, *e.g.*, for marriage. (Thompson or Maharaja of Tikari).

[2] A Sanskrit term for world is *Jagat* or that which moves, since the Universe is in constant motion.

past Karma, either his own, or that of collectivities of men of which he is a member, or with which he is in relation, as also by the action of natural causes. In the same way, present Karma determines the future Karma. The doctrine of Karma is thus the affirmance of the Law of Causality operating not only in this but in an infinity of Universes. As you sow so shall you reap. The present Universe is not the first and last only. It is true that this particular Universe has a beginning and an end called dissolution,[1] for nothing composite is eternal; but it is only one of a series which has neither beginning nor end. There has been, is now, and ever will be an Universe.

Mental action as desire for worldly enjoyment, even though such enjoyment be lawful, keeps man in the Worlds of repeated Birth and Death, or (to use the English term) of Reincarnation. These worlds the Greeks called the Cycle of Becoming,[2] and Hindus the *Samsāra*, a term which literally means the unending 'moving on' or wandering, that is, being born and dying repeatedly.[3] These worlds comprise not only Earth but Heaven and Hell, in which are reaped the fruits of man's actions on Earth. Heaven and Hell are states of enjoyment and suffering which exist here on earth as well as in the after-death state as the result of man's good and bad actions returning. When man dies there is no resurrection of the gross body. That is resolved into its subtle elements, and the specific relation between man and a particular gross body comes to an end. But there is always some body until bodiless liberation[4] is achieved. On death man in his subtle body enjoys the state

[1] Pralaya— The Mīmāmsā doctrine as to this is exceptional.

[2] Kuklos Tôn Geneseôn.

[3] Punarutpatti.

[4] Videha Mukti.

called Heaven or suffers in that called Hell. Neither is eternal, but each a part of the Cycle of the Becoming. When, then, man has had Heavenly enjoyment or suffered the pains of Hell in his subtle body, in the after-death state, according to his merits or demerits, he is 'reincarnated' in a gross body on Earth. He continues thus to be 'reincarnated' until he has found and desires the way out from the Cycle, that is, until he ceases to desire world-existence. His desire is then not only for release from the sufferings and limited happiness of the Cycle but also (according to Vedānta) for the attainment of the Supreme Worth[1] which is Supreme Bliss. There is, in short, a change of values and states. Man, as Nietzsche said, is something to be transcended. He cannot transcend his present state so long as he is attached to and desires to remain in it. This liberation from the Cycle is called *Moksha* or *Mukti*. For all Three Systems are at one in holding that, notwithstanding the Law of Causality, man is free to liberate himself from the Cycle. Causality governs the Psycho-physical. Spirit as such is Freedom from the Psycho-physical. All three Systems assume a State of Liberation.

Whether the Universe as a play of force is the work of a Personal God is a question which Philosophers have disputed both in the East and the West. One set of Buddhists[2] professed belief in Deity as the Lord. Another[3] affirmed Svabhāva which means the proper vigour of Nature and what is called creation is truly spontaneity resulting from powers inherent in the Psycho-physical substance eternally.[4]

---

[1] Paramārtha.

[2] The Aishvarika School.

[3] Svabhāvikas. The first term means belief in a Lord and the second is derived from Svabhāva or own nature.

[4] As Brian Hodgson has pointed out (Nepal 23).

Māyāvāda Vedānta reconciles to a great extent these two views by its doctrine that the personal Brahman or the Lord is the self-less absolute Brahman as conceived by the Psycho-physical experiencer, though the latter as the Absolute exclusive of all relations is not the former. In Shākta doctrine Brahman is the Lord or Creator and Director of the Universe but in its own nature is more than that.

Whether there is or is not a Personal God or Lord[1] (as held by some systems), belief in such a Lord is no essential portion of the Common Doctrine. Both Jainism and Buddhism are atheistic in the sense of being Lordless,[2] though the latter system, in some forms of the later Northern schools, takes on a theistic colour. In fact, the notion of a Personal God is no essential part even of Brahmanism itself. For, putting aside downright atheists in the Western sense, such as the Indian Chārvakas and Lokāyatas who denied God, Soul, immortality and future life, it is to be observed that some schools[3] posit no such Lord whilst others[4] do.

Two other concepts of first rate importance are *Dharma* and its correlative *Adharma*. These two terms, in the Brahmanic sense, mean right activity and its opposite. They are therefore connected with Karma of which they are two species. The term Dharma comes from the root *Dhri* which means to uphold and maintain, for right activity does that. All three systems posit right[5] and wrong[6] activity and their results as well-being and suffering respectively. Dharma is thus the Law of Being as Form. Morality is part of man's nature. It may therefore be said that the substance

[1] Īshvara. [2] Nirīshvara.

[3] Mīmāmsā and Nirīshvarasānkhya.

[4] Seshvara Sānkhya or Yoga School and the Nyāya-Vaisheshika and Vedānta.

[5] Punya. [6] Papa.

of the Brahmanic concept is held by all. *Dharma* as a technical term is not here included amongst the common concepts, because, its sense varies in Buddhism in which it has its own peculiar meaning, whilst in Jainism the word means something wholly different from what it does in any other system.[1]

Each of the common concepts must be interpreted in the case of any particular Indian faith in terms of its own peculiar tenets as regards these concepts and other matters such as the Reality[2] and Dissolution[3] of the Universe, Karma[4] and Liberation. Thus, the latter is defined differently in Buddhism, Jainism and in the various Brahmanical schools. According to all systems, Liberation is described as the release from the bondage of Birth and Death, Limitation and Suffering. In some systems[5] it is not positively said to be Joy,[6] but is described as a pure painless state of That which, in association with mind and matter, manifests as the empirical self. The Jainas regard it as a state of happiness. Some Buddhist descriptions are to the same effect, but in general Buddhism deprecates the discussion of so inconceivable a state. The Vedānta, on the other hand, positively describes it to be unalloyed and unending Joy so that the nature of such Joy, whether as arising through the identification of the individual self with the Supreme Self or in association therewith, is variously affirmed by

---

[1] In Jainism the word means a principle of motion (Dharma) as its opposite (Adharma) is the principle of rest.

[2] Brahmanism and Jainism are opposed to Buddhistic subjectivism.

[3] The views of the Mīmāmsā on Dissolution are peculiar to it.

[4] Thus, Jainism speaks in its own peculiar way of the term 'matter'.

[5] Mīmāmsā, Sānkhya-Yoga, and Nyāya-Vaisheshika.

[6] Ānanda.

the non-dualist, qualified non-dualist and dualist Brahmanic Schools.

Brahmanism adds to these concepts of the Cycle, (Samsāra), right and wrong action (Dharma, Adharma), Causality (Karma), and Liberation (Moksha), that of the Ātman.

All recognized Brahmanic systems affirm the Ātman, though they differ on the question of its nature [1] as also whether it is one [2] or many.[3] It is on this question whether there is or is not an Ātman that the Brahmanic [4] and Buddhistic Schools are in dispute. The point in issue as formulated from the standpoint of Vedānta may be shortly stated to be as follows:

Every one admits the existence of a psycho-physical Flux either as the Individual or the Universe of his experience. Indeed, one of the Sanskrit names of the world is *Jagat*, which means "the moving thing". For the Universe is in constant activity. At every moment there is molar or molecular change. As an object of sensible perception the Universe is transitory; though some things endure longer or shorter than others. The question is, then, whether, besides psycho-physical transience, there is a spiritual enduring Essence of the Universe and of man, which manifests in the latter as the empirical self whereby knows itself as permanent amidst all its changeful experiences. The Buddhists are reputed to have held that there is nothing but the flow. Man is only a continually changing psycho-physical complex without a static centre, a series of

---

[1] In Nyāya-Vaisheshika it is the Seat of Consciousness, and in Sānkhya and Advaita Vedānta it is Consciousness.

[2] As in Vedānta.

[3] As the Ātmans and Purushas of Nyāya-Vaisheshika and Sānkhya-Yoga respectively.

[4] The Jainas also combated the Buddhistic doctrine of Anātmā.

momentary mental and bodily states, necessarily generated one from the other in continuous transformation. In this Flux there is no principle of permanence on which "as on a thread"[1] the worlds as beads are strung. Man may have the notion that he is a Self, but this does not, it is said, prove that there is an Ātman as 'substratum' of such empirical self. To this Vedānta asks—If so, who is it that is born and dies and re-incarnates? It then answers its question by saying that the embodied self[2] is born and dies, but that the Ātman as such is not a Self and is neither born nor does it die. Birth and Death are attributed to it when it appears in connection with psycho-physical bodies. It is the embodied Ātman which is born and dies. The Ātman as it is in its own bodiless nature is unborn and eternal.

Change and changelessness are terms of logical, that is, dualistic thinking, and have no meaning except in relation to one another. All activity implies a static condition relative to which it is active. There can be no Universe except by the combination of the active and non-active. Without activity the Universe does not become. Without some principle of stability it cannot exist even for a moment as an object of the senses. The alogical Ātman as such eternally endures. The Universe as the Psycho-physical is the product of the Ātman as Power. As such product it is transient. It presents, however, the appearance of relative or limited stability because of the immanence of the Ātman. The Ātman manifests as the relatively stable and empirical self, and That which manifests as such self is also the Brahman as essence of the Universe which is the object of such self. For Ātman and Brahman are one and the same.

[1] Sutrātmā. [2] Jīvātmā.

According to the second standard, Ātman is the seat of consciousness. In the Vedānta, however, Ātman is consciousness itself. Whatever may have been its origin, as to which nothing is of a certainty known (Mother Goddess Worship is as old as the world), Shākta doctrine is now a form of Vedānta which may be called Shakti-vāda or Shākta Vedānta.

Kulārnava Tantra speaks of that "Monism of which Shiva speaks" (Advaitantu Shivenoktam, I. 108). See also Mahānirvāna Tantra, Chapter II, 33-34, III, 33-35, 50-64; Prapanchasāra Tantra, II, XIX, XXIX; Advaitabhāvopanishad. For the identity of Jīvātmā and Paramātmā in liberation (Mukti), which the Vedāntasāra defines to be Jīvabrāhmanoh aikyam, see Mahānirvāna Tantra, VIII, 264, 265; V, 105). See also Prapanchasāra Tantra, II, where Hrīm is identified with Kundalī and Hamsah, and then with "So'ham". See also *ib.*, Chapter XXIV: "That which is subtle I am" (Yah Sukshmah So'ham); and Jnānārnava Tantra, XXI, 10. As to Brahmāsmi, see Kulārnava Tantra, IX, 32, and *ib.*, 41: So'ham bhāvena pujayet. The Shākta disciple (Sādhaka) should not be a dualist (Mahārudrayāmala, I Khanda, Chapter 15; II Khanda, Chapter 2). Similarly, the Gandharva Tantra, Chapter 2, says that he must be devoid of dualism (Dvaitahīna) (see Prānatoshinī, 108). In fact, that particular form of worship which has earned the Kaula Tantras their ill name is a practical application of Advaitavāda. Kaulāchāra is said to properly follow a full knowledge of Vedāntik doctrine. As the Shatchakranirūpana (see "Serpent Power") says, the Jīvātmā or embodied spirit is the same as the Paramātmā or Supreme Spirit, and knowledge of this is the root of all wisdom (Mūlavidyā).

Shākta Vedānta teaches its doctrine from the practical standpoint which Māyāvāda calls Vyavahārika. It lays stress on the concept of Power. Ātman is not mere Being only. Even in the dissolution of the world Being is Power, though Power or Shakti is then consciousness as such (Chidrupinī). Ātman manifests as the universe by and out of its power. Ātman and Power are never separated, and so it is said that "there is no Shiva without Shakti or Shakti without Shiva". Shiva without Power is but a "corpse". Both Shiva and Shakti are of the same nature since they are both Being-Consciousness-Bliss. But Power manifests as the Becoming or Psycho-physical universe. Power is both Power to Be, to self-conserve, and resist change, as well as Power to Become the universe and as material cause the universe itself. Power to Be is the static aspect of Shiva-Shakti. Power to Become is the changeful aspect of Shiva-Shakti.

In Māyāvāda the world is said to be produced by the Power of the Lord—or Īshvara. But whilst Īshvara is Brahman or Godhead as conceived by the Psycho-physical experiencer, Brahman, on the other hand, is not Īshvara. The former is beyond (in the sense of, exclusive of) all relations with the universe, and so, though wrongly, some people call Īshvara "Unreal" and the universe created by Him an 'illusion'. According to Shaktivāda, not only is Īshvara Brahman, but Brahman is Īshvara, and no question of the reality of either Īshvara or the world arises. We may, however, say at once that Godhead is real, God is real and the universe is real. The use of the term 'illusion' only tends to mislead even in Māyāvāda. According to the concise definition of Kamalakanta, a celebrated Sādhaka, Māyā is the 'Form of the Formless' (*Shūnyasya ākara iti Māyā*). The world is the Divine Mother in form. As She is in Herself She is formless.

Discussion on the subject of the reality of the World is often vain and tedious, because, the word 'Real' has several meanings, and that in which it is used is not stated.

The terms "Absolute" and "Transcendental" should also be clearly defined. The distinction between Māyā-vāda and *Shakti-vāda* hinges on these definitions.

Both "Absolute" and "Transcendental" mean "beyond relation". But the term "beyond" may be used in two senses: (*a*) exceeding or wider than relation; (*b*) having no relation at all. The first does not deny or exclude relation, but says that the Absolute, though involving all relations within Itself, is not their sum-total; is not exhausted by them; has Being transcending them. The latter denies every trace of relation to the Absolute; and says that the Absolute must have no intrinsic or extrinsic relation; that relation, therefore, has no place in the Being of the Absolute.

Shakti-vāda adopts the first view, Māyā-vāda the second. From the first point of view, the Absolute is relationless Being *as well as* Manifestation as an infinity of relations. This is the true and complete Alogical-Whole. Inasmuch as the Absolute exceeds all relation and thought, we cannot say that It is the Cause; that It is the Root of Creation; and so forth; but inasmuch also as It does involve relation and thought, we can say that It is the First Cause; that there has been a real creation, and so forth.

The Māyā-vāda view by negating all relation from the reality of Brahman negates from its transcendent standpoint the reality of causation, creation and so forth.

"Beyond" may, therefore, mean (1) "exceeding", "fuller than", "not exhausted by", or (2) excluding, negating, expunging.

In *Shakti-vāda*, the Supreme Reality is fuller than any definition (limitation) which may be proposed. It is even beyond duality and non-duality. It is thus the Experience-Whole, the Alogical. The Māyā-vāda Pure Brahman *is* an aspect of It: but It is not the Whole (*Pūrna*).

The expression "wider than relation" may be thus illustrated: I am related in one way to my wife; in another way to my children; in yet another way to my brothers, friends, and so on. I am not fully expressed by any one of these relations, nor even by their aggregate; for, as a member of an infinite Stress-system, I bear an infinity of relations. Pragmatically, most of these are ignored, and it is thought that I am expressed by a certain set of relations which distinguish me from another person who has his own "set". But Brahman as Absolute can have no such "Set". It is expressed, but not fully expressed, even by the infinite set of relations which the cosmos is, because relations, finite or infinite, imply a logical, and therefore segmenting and defining thought; but Brahman as Absolute = Experience-Whole = the Alogical.

Since Brahman = Experience-Whole = *Chit* as Power-to-Be-and-Become, it is nothing like the unknown and unknowable Being ("Thing-in-Itself") of Western Sceptics and Agnostics.

In all Indian Systems, the world is real, in the sense that it has objective existence for, and is not a projection of, the individual mind. In all such Systems, Mind and Matter co-exist, and this is so even in that form of *Ekajīva-vāda* which holds that *Brahman* by Its own veiling and limiting Power makes one Primary Self of Itself, and that all other selves are but reflexes of the Primary Self, having as reflexes no existence apart from that of the Primary one. The world of matter is not a projection of an individual mind, but its reality is co-ordinate with that of the individual mind, both bing derived from the Self-veiling and Self-limiting operation of *Brahman* appearing as the One

Jiva or Primary Self. *Brahman*, in appearing as Primary Self, also appears as its (logical) Correlate or Pole—the Not-Self; and this Not-Self is the Root-Matter on which the Primary Self is reflected as multiple selves and their varied relations. Matter, in this fundamental sense, is not therefore the product of the first or primary individual (Self); it is with Self the co-effect (logically speaking) of a common fundamental activity which is the veiling and limiting action of the Supreme Being.

The version commonly given of Ekajīva-vāda—namely, that the one Primary Self is Me, and that You, He and the rest, and the world of objects are the projection of Me—is loose and unpsychological. In the first place, Me cannot be there (logically conceiving) without its Correlate or Pole—the Not-Me; so that, by the very act by which Me is evolved from Brahman, its Correlate is also evolved, and this Correlate is Root-Matter. In the second place, projection, reflexion, and so forth presuppose not only the projecting or reflecting Being (that which projects or reflects), but also something on which the projection or reflection is cast. Projection out of nothing and projection into nothing will give us only nothing.

Where then there is Matter there is Mind. Where there is no Matter there is no Mind. One is meaningless without the other. Each is every whit as real as the other. But there is no Indian system which is Realist in the sense that it holds that Matter exists when there is no Mind to perceive it. Such a state is inconceivable. He who alleges it, himself supplies the perceiving Mind. In the First Standard,[1] Mind[2] and the so-called "atoms"[3] of Matter are

[1] Nyāya-Vaisheshika.

[2] Manas.

[3] Paramānu.

separate, distinct and independent Reals.[1] Matter does not derive from Mind nor the latter from the former. In the Second Standard,[2] both Matter and Mind are equally real, but derive from a common source the Psycho-physical Potential[3] which as such is neither. 'Psychic' here means Mind as distinct from Consciousness in the sense of Chit. This Psycho-physical Potential is a Real[4] independent of Consciousness which is the other Real. In the Third Standard as non-dual Vedānta the position is the same, except that the Psycho-physical Potential is not an independent Real but is the power of the One Supreme Real as God. The world is then Real in the sense that it has true objective Reality for the individual Experiencers for the duration of their experience of it. No one denies this.

The next question is the problem of Monism. If ultimate Reality be One, how can it be the cause of and become the Universe. It is said that Reality is of dual aspect, namely, as it is in relation to the World as Īshvara, the Lord or God, and as it is in itself beyond such relation which we may call Brahman. According to Māyāvāda, Īshvara is Brahman, for Īshvara is Brahman as seen through the Veil of Māyā, that is, by the Psycho-physical Experiencer. But Brahman is not Īshvara because Brahman is the absolute alogical Real, that is, Reality, not as conceived by Mind but as it is in itself beyond all relation. The notion of God as the Supreme Self is the highest concept imposed on the alogical which, as it is in itself, is not a Self either supreme or limited. The Absolute as such is not a cause. There is, transcendentally speaking, no

[1] Dravya.

[2] Sānkhya-Yoga.

[3] Prakriti.

[4] In Sānkhya one: in Shaiva Darshana many.

creation, no Universe. The Absolute is and nothing happens. It is only pragmatically a Cause. There is from this aspect no nexus between Brahman and the World. In the logical order there is. What then is the Universe? It is in this connection that it is said by some to be an "illusion", which is an inapt term. For to whom is it an "illusion"? Not to the Psycho-physical Experiencer to whom it is admittedly real. Nor is it an illusion for the Experience-Whole. It is only by the importation of the logical notion of a Self to whom an object is real or unreal that we can speak of illusion. But there is in this state of Liberation no Self.[1] More correctly we say that the World is Māyā. But what is Māyā in Māyāvāda? It is not real, for it is neither Brahman nor an independent Real. Nor is it unreal for in the logical order it is real. It is neither Brahman nor different from it as an independent reality. It is unexplainable.[2] For this reason one of the scholastics of this System calls it the doctrine of the Inscrutable.

In the doctrine of Power (Shaktivāda), Māyā is the Divine Mother Power or Mahāmāya. The two aspects of Reality as Brahman and Īshvara are accepted. The Lord is real, but that which we call 'Lord' is more than Lord, for the Real is not adequately defined in terms only of its relations to the Universe. In this sense it is alogical, that is, "beyond Mind and Speech". As the one ultimate Reality is both Īshvara and Brahman, in one aspect it is the Cause, and in the other it is not. But it is one and the same Reality which is both as Shiva-Shakti. As these are real so are their appearance, the Universe. For the Universe is Shiva-Shakti. It is their appearance. When we

[1] As the Buddhists said, in Nirvāna even the knowledge that the phenomena have ceased to appear and are therefore unreal is not found. See Das Gupta: *Indian Philosophy*, p. 142.

[2] Anirvachanīya.

say it is their appearance we imply that there has been a real becoming issuing from them as Power. Reality has two aspects. First as it is in itself, and secondly as it exists as Universe. At base the *Samsāra* or worlds of Birth and Death and *Moksha* or Liberation are One. For Shiva-Shakti are both the Experience-Whole and the Part which exists therein as the Universe. Reality is a concrete unity in duality and duality in unity. In practice the One is realized in and as the Many and the Many as the One. So in the Shākta Wine ritual the worshipper conceives himself to be Shiva-Shakti as the Divine Mother. It is She who as and in the person of the worshipper, Her manifestation, consumes the wine which is again Herself, the Saviouress in liquid form.[1] It is not only he who as a separate Self does so. This principle is applied to all Man's functionings and is of cardinal importance from a Monistic standpoint notwithstanding its well-known abuse in fact.

Real is again used in the sense of eminence. The Real is that which is for itself and has a reason for its being in itself. The Real as God is the perfect and changeless and the "Good".[2] The Universe is dependent on the *Ens Realissimum,* for it proceeds from it and is imperfect as limited and changeful and in a sense it is that which does not endure and in this sense is called 'unreal'. Though, however, the Universe comes and goes it does so eternally. The Supreme Cause is eternally creative. The Real is then both infinite Changeless Being as also unbeginning and unending process as the Becoming. In this system the Real both is and becomes. It yet becomes without derogation from its own changelessness, as it were a Fountain of Life which pours itself forth incessantly from an infinite

[1] Tārā Dravamayī.

[2] The meaning of Shiva.

and inexhaustible source. Both the infinite and finite are real.

Real is again used in the sense of interest and value and of the 'worth while'. In this sense, the worshipper prays to be led from Unreality to Reality, but this does not mean that the world is unreal, but that it is not the supreme worth for him.

In whatever sense, then, the term Real is used the Universe is that. All is real for as Upanishad says, "All this Universe is verily Brahman".[1] The Scriptural Text says "All". It does not say "This" but not "That". The whole is an alogical concrete Reality which is Unity in Duality and Duality in Unity. The doctrine does not lose hold of either the One or the Many, and for this reason the Lord Shiva says in the Kulārnava Tantra, "There are some who seek dualism and some non-dualism, but my doctrine is beyond both." That is, it takes account of and reconciles both Dualism and Non-Dualism.

Reality is no mere abstraction of the intellect making jettison of all that is concrete and varied. It is the Experience-Whole whose object is Itself as such Whole. It is also Partial Experience within that Whole. This union of Whole and Part is alogical, not unknowable, for their unity is a fact of actual experience just as we have the unity of Power to Be and Power to Become, of the Conscious and Unconscious, of Mind and Body, of freedom and determination, and other dualities of Man's experiencing.

---

[1] Sarvam Khalvidam Bṛahma,